POPSTROLOGY

THE ART AND SCIENCE OF READING THE POP STARS

POPSTROLOGY

IAN VAN TUYL

AND OWEN GROVER

BLOOMSBURY

Published by Bloomsbury Publishing, New York and London
Distributed to the trade by Holtzbrinck Publishers

All papers used by Bloomsbury Publishing are natural, recyclable products made from wood grown in well-managed forests. The manufacturing processes conform to the environmental regulations of the country of origin.

Van Tuyl, Ian.
    Popstrology : the art and science of reading the pop stars / by Ian Van Tuyl.
        p. cm.
     ISBN 1–58234–422–1 (pb)
     1. Popular music—Psychological aspects. 2. Music, Influence of. 3. Self-perception.
I. Title.

ML3838.V24 2004
781.64—dc22
2004014032

Designed by Elizabeth Van Itallie
Constellation art by Kandy Littrell

First U.S. edition 2004

10 9 8 7 6 5 4 3 2 1

Typeset by Palimpsest Book Production Limited, Polmont, Stirlingshire
Printed in the United States of America by
The Maple-Vail Book Manufacturing Group, York, Pennsylvania

Contents

INTRODUCTION

Some people go through life like they've got all the answers, but I never did. Like a lot of people, I spent my childhood growing and nurturing a wide range of neuroses and insecurities, and I entered adulthood lacking both a plan and a guiding philosophy. At times I wished that religion had been a bigger part of my upbringing, but even if it had been, I think I still would have been troubled by questions that fell outside the spiritual realm. What was I meant to do with my life? How was I to find true love and know that I'd found it when I did? I was raised near the epicenter of the New Age movement, so I did not lack for exposure to belief systems that might have provided me with some answers, but I was also raised by an electrical engineer, and the hyper-rational frame of mind this instilled in me always trumped my desire to believe in any of those systems.

And then one day I came upon a piece of information that changed my life. I discovered that on the day I was born—January 24, 1967—the #1 song in America was *I'm A Believer*, by the Monkees. On an intellectual level, I wasn't exactly sure what to make of this fact, but I knew in my gut that there was something deeply, even disturbingly *right* about it. It wasn't just that I could look at Michael Nesmith and Mickey Dolenz and see in them little pieces of myself, and it wasn't just that I shared a birthday with Neil Diamond, the man who wrote *I'm A Believer*. It was that so much of what defined me—my strengths, my weaknesses, my struggles—made perfect sense when viewed against the backdrop of the enterprise that launched the wholly artificial, yet clearly irresistible Monkees. I began to ponder the implications of being born at a moment when America threw its embrace around a made-for-television rip-off of the most important group in pop-music history, and suddenly the pieces started falling into place.

Why was I so obsessed with originality? Why did I have trouble taking many important things seriously? And why did my occasional moments of originality yield things that many people would never consider taking seriously? My head was spinning and my hands were shaking as I realized that the answer to these nagging questions lay in my response to the powerful sonic and psychic vibrations that penetrated my soft little skull at the moment I entered the world. I wasn't just born to the sound of the Monkees—I *was* a Monkee, and with that realization, a sense of peace and comfort settled over me that I'd never experienced before. Of *course* I was a Monkee. I'd spent a large part of my adolescence trying to act as if I were a Beatle or a Rolling Stone, but the fact is that I was born at a moment when America was throwing its record-buying dollars and its collective psychic energies behind an entity that was those groups' antithesis, and it was high time I learned to live with it.

The process by which my personal moment of clarity led to the fully realized science of popstrology is somewhat murky even to me. Was it a matter of seconds, or was it a matter of months before I realized that I had tripped upon something much bigger than myself? All I can say for certain is that the science of the pop stars seemed to emerge fully formed once I began to look at the world through a popstrological lens. The dawn of Elvis Presley as the Big Bang that opened the popstrological era, and the twilight of Richard Marx as the quiet whimper that closed it thirty-three and a third years later, the 450 stars in the popstrological firmament, and the forty-five constellations into which they fall—these structures were revealed to me in what seemed like a mere instant, and their interpretive power was undeniable. Learning that Courtney Love was born under the influence of the #1 song *I Get Around* nearly convinced me I'd discovered something real, and learning that Kurt Cobain was born under the #1 song *Kind Of A Drag* sealed it.

It wasn't just myself that I could understand better through the science of popstrology, I realized—it was my friends, my loved ones, and everyone around me. Where once I saw each of them as an utterly unique bundle of gifts, contradictions, and idiosyncrasies, I now saw them as quintessential Double Beatles, blameless Carly Simons, and stubbornly oppositional Breads. And most gratifying of all, I found that when I began to introduce others to their popstrological identities, they made leaps of insight I'd never have been capable of making myself, and so popstrology began to spread, and its methodology began to take shape.

Popstrology is a powerful and flexible science, and where its adherents take it in the years ahead is anyone's guess. This book represents a mere scratch at the surface of popstrology's potential, and if its insights are someday replaced by those of an entirely new school of popstrological thought, so be it. The important thing is simply that we acknowledge the power of the pop stars to shape our mortal lives, and that we open ourselves to the lessons the pop stars have to teach us.

Ian Van Tuyl
May 2004

Frequently Asked Questions

What is popstrology?

Popstrology is the science of the pop stars—a revolutionary method for gaining self-knowledge by examining the alignment of the pop music charts on the date of your birth.

What does pop music have to do with self-knowledge?

Few of us would deny that the pop songs of our childhood played a profound role in shaping our views on life and love, but many fail to realize that this process was already at work when they first entered a world that was fairly humming with radio waves and other, deeper vibrations in the pop universe. Who was the dominant pop star in the year that you were born? Which star and which song ruled the charts at the very moment of your birth? The science of popstrology reveals how the answers to these questions are far from mere trivia, teaching us to read the pop stars carefully for critical insights into our personalities, our career potential, and our personal relationships.

What exactly can popstrology teach me?

Popstrology can be a powerful tool for revealing the source of any number of conditions. Perhaps the roots of your chronic restlessness lie in the fact that you are an ABBA born in the Year of Debby Boone. Or perhaps the key to finally overcoming your crippling sexual inhibition is to acknowledge that you are a Pat Boone born in the Year of Elvis Presley. These and thousands of other possible lessons are to be found in the pop stars, and even popstrological novices can easily learn the tools necessary to reveal them.

Does popstrology work for everyone?

In the broadest sense, yes, but strictly speaking this introduction to popstrology applies only to the tens of millions of humans born in the United States and Canada within the span of the popstrological era, which began with Elvis Presley's first #1 single on April 21, 1956, and ended thirty-three and a third years later with Richard Marx's *Right Here Waiting*, on August 26, 1989.

Great, so what's my sign?

Let's look at a couple of examples. If you were born between January 12 and January 18, 1975, you were born under the influence of the #1 song *Mandy*, but in a year that was generally dominated by Elton John. In the language of popstrology, you are therefore said to be "a Barry Manilow born in the Year of Elton John." Someone born between April 6 and April 19 of that same year, on the other hand, was born under the influence of *Philadelphia Freedom*, and is therefore an Elton John born in the Year of Elton John—colloquially, "a Double Elton." So you see that there are three primary points of data in your popstrological profile: your **Birth Year** (or, more accurately, the Dominant Star of your Birth Year), your **Birthsong** (the song that was #1 on the pop charts at the moment you were born), and your **Birthstar** (the pop star who performed your Birthsong). Popstrologically speaking, these are the three essential forces that created you, warts and all, and each bears close examination.

What about relationships—can popstrology tell me why mine are so screwed up?

Well, popstrology can certainly help. Perhaps your problem is that your Birthstar belongs to a constellation of pop stars associated with a fear of commitment, such as the constellation *Shape-Shifter*. Perhaps you are an Olivia Newton-John who just keeps falling for Rod Stewarts. Or maybe you have certain feelings that can go along with being a Double George Michael. The answer to your relationship issues could be straightforward and obvious, or it might be revealed only through a deeper popstrological analysis.

What if my Birthsong is really, really uncool?

First of all, it is a central tenet of popstrological thought that there are no bad pop songs—there are only songs whose deeper meanings are, shall we say, less groovy to contemplate than others. The fact of the matter is that we don't get to choose many of the things that affect our lives profoundly. Did you choose your parents? Are they "cool"? One of the greatest mistakes you could make on your road to popstrological elightenment would be to take undue pleasure or pain in the "coolness" or "lameness" of your Birthsong or Birthstar. After all, if everyone born under a cool pop song were cool themselves, there would be a hell of a lot more cool people in the world, wouldn't there? Popstrology acknowledges that we all have within us the potential to be great and the potential to stink, but the process of unlocking your positive potential requires suspending your knee-jerk aesthetic judgments and opening your ears and your mind to the valuable lessons embedded in the musical forces that shaped you.

What if I've never even heard of my Birthstar or Birthsong?

Then you've probably never even met a little thing called your true self. If the songs and stars who affected you most are total mysteries to you, it might take a little extra work to learn the lessons that popstrology has to teach you. The first step is to run, not walk, to the nearest record store or Web site to get your hands on the necessary raw material.

So does this mean that my horoscope is pure bullsh*t?

No, no, no. No more than it means that the lessons of numerology, the *I Ching* and the Magic 8 Ball are. It is considered a breach of professional ethics for any practicing popstrologist to urge you to reject an alternative belief system like astrology upon your embrace of popstrology. It is yours and yours alone to decide in the end whether it feels as meaningful to call yourself a Pisces born in the Year of the Goat as it does to call yourself a Beatle born in the Year of the Monkees.

The Popstrological Manifesto

Long before you ever bought a record or chose a favorite radio station, the incredible power of pop music had already begun to shape you. In fact, pop music placed an indelible imprint upon you at the very moment of your birth, when you entered a world filled not only with sound and radio waves, but also with the invisible vibrations of human longing. Did Elvis Presley and the Beatles become what they became purely on the strength of their own talent and ambition? No, they became the most powerful stars in pop music history because mortal record buyers and radio listeners allowed them to. And did mortal audiences choose Elvis and the Beatles merely because they sounded so good? No, they were chosen because they represented something their mortal fans needed—something that went beyond mere music.

Perhaps it strikes you as obvious to say that giants like Elvis and the Beatles, or the Rolling Stones and Madonna, arose in very specific historical contexts and responded to very specific sociological and psychosexual needs. That's good, because if it does, you should have little difficulty making the jump to viewing stars like the Partridge Family and Barry Manilow in the same light. They were democratically elected rulers of the pop universe, after all, just as surely as Elvis and the Beatles were, and they achieved that status the same way any star powerful enough to earn a #1 record does: by touching something deep within the American soul. Perhaps those who let them touch that place feel less than good about it in retrospect, but it hardly matters. The fact is that on more than one occasion, the music and the magnetism of Barry Manilow formed a powerful feedback loop with the American public's psychic need for what he had to offer, and strong popstrological vibrations were generated in the process. Exploring the impact of those vibrations on the innocent children born under the influence of a #1 song like *Mandy* or *I Write The Songs* is what the science of popstrology is all about.

But what can popstrology say of the vibrations generated by stars of lesser stature than Barry Manilow and Elvis Presley? Did Bobby Vee, for instance, or Little Eva attain the highest reaches of the pop universe because they spoke to some unspoken longing on the part of the American public? Perhaps not, but Bobby Vee rose only because Buddy Holly's plane crashed, and Little Eva only because she babysat the children of the young couple who wrote *The Loco-Motion*. The karmic significance of these stars' stories and of their shared connection to Carole King is inescapable, and it forms the basis of their respective legacies to those born under their popstrological influence.

In the thirty-three and a third years of the popstrological era, precisely 450 unique stars achieved the pinnacle of pop music success by earning a #1 record. Most did it only once, and many held their position for just one short week, but each and every one of them is worthy of close attention, for each of them put its distinctive stamp on tens of thousands of newborn boys and girls at least. The power of the pop stars is impossible to deny, even if you are at first inclined to deny the power of popstrology. But popstrology is a science that anyone with a creative mind-set and a working knowledge of our shared pop-musical past can practice. It is a science that welcomes new practitioners and new insights, and as such, it is a science whose potential is limited only by our own ability to apply it. Like other, more established methods for examining your spirit and your soul, pop-

strology requires of its believers a certain leap but perhaps the leap is not so great. After can believe that there are powers hidden in and planets of the physical universe, is it unreasonable to suggest that even greater powers lie hidden in a galaxy of stars we all can name? Popstrology does not seek to overturn any established systems of belief, but popstrology is unafraid of stating its case. Which force do *you* think was more likely to have penetrated your essence and shaped your destiny if you were born in the final week of January 1964: the quiet orbital shufflings of Mars and Jupiter, or the explosive rise of a star called the Beatles?

Building Your Popstrological Profile

Achieving true popstrological self-awareness is a lifelong process, but getting started is easy. A handful of elements make up your individual popstrological profile, and they are easy to determine in a few simple steps.

➤ **STEP 1:** Look up and learn about your **Birth Year** (pages 17–85).

➤ **STEP 2:** Determine your **Birthstar** and **Birthsong** (on your Birth Year page).

➤ **STEP 3:** Look up and learn about your **Birthstar** (pages 86–331).

➤ **STEP 4:** Determine the popstrological **constellations** with which your Birthstar is aligned (on your Birthstar page).

➤ **STEP 5:** Look up and read about your ruling **constellations** (pages 333–379).

Repeat as necessary, supplementing the interpretations offered herein with the insights gained through your own research and reflection.

We will turn our attention to appreciating the full meaning of your popstrological profile later, but for now, let's imagine for the purposes of illustration that you were born on July 24, 1970, and walk through the straightforward process of building your profile from there.

STEP 1: Look up and learn about your Birth Year
Beginning on page 17 of this book, you will find a year-by-year guide to the entire popstrological era—the thirty-three and a third years from the dawn of Elvis Presley (4/21/56) to the twilight of Richard Marx (8/26/89). You will use these pages to determine the Dominant Star and Opposing Star in the year of your birth, to learn of their impact on your entire micro-generation, and to determine the central elements of your individual popstrological profile: your Birthstar and Birthsong.

For our example birthdate, we turn to the overview of 1970 on page 46 and learn that you were born in the Year of the Jackson 5—a year in which Simon and Garfunkel were the Opposing Star to the Jackson 5's Dominant Star, and in which the Guess Who were the popstrological Wildcard. After reading about the implications of these facts, we move on to our next step.

STEP 2: Determine your Birthstar and Birthsong
At the end of every Birth Year overview, you will find a table listing every star and every song that reached the top of the pop charts in that year. In the left-hand column of this table, you will find spans of dates of varying length—some a single week, others many weeks in a row. Find the span of dates into which your birthdate falls, and next to it you will find the name of your Birthstar and Birthsong, along with the number of the page on which you will find your Birthstar profile.

For our example birthdate, we look at the table of songs and stars for the year 1970, and in the middle of that table we find the following entries:

July 24, 1970, falls within the span of dates marked "Jul 19–Aug 15," so now we know the central elements of your popstrological profile: you are a Carpenter born in the Year of the Jackson 5, and your Birthsong is *Close To You*. After taking a moment to assimilate this piece of information, we turn to page 116 as directed and continue with our next step.

STEP 3: Look up and learn about your Birthstar
The largest section of this book is devoted to detailed Birthstar profiles—one for each of the 450 stars in the popstrological firmament. We will focus our attention on the full interpretative meaning of your Birthstar in a moment, but for now let's look at the basic elements that make up each profile: the "official" popstrological reading of your Birthstar, and the Starchart indicating your Birthstar's Critical Aspects.

Our example birthdate has led us to page 116 and the profile of the glorious and tragic Carpenters. In our official reading, we learn of the primary popstrological forces associated with the Carpenters and of the role those forces might play in your life if you were born under their direct influence. On our Starchart, we see a graphical representation of your Birthstar's Critical Aspects, indicating that the Carpenters made an impact that was both Massive and Lasting, that they were contextually quite Fresh and somewhat Sexy, and that their vibe was overwhelmingly Whitebread. A star and Starchart this fascinating could occupy hours of discussion and contemplation, but for now let's move on to our next important step.

STEP 4: Determine the popstrological constellations with which your Birthstar is aligned
As part of each Birthstar profile, you will find an entry

WHAT'S YOUR SIGN?

1970 BIRTHDATES	BIRTHSTAR / BIRTHSONG	PAGE
Jul 5 - Jul 18	Three Dog Night / Mama Told Me (Not To Come)	307
Jul 19 - Aug 15	The Carpenters / Close To You	116
Aug 16 - Aug 22	Bread / Make It With You	111
Aug 23 - Sep 12	Edwin Starr / War	293
Sep 13 - Oct 3	Diana Ross / Ain't No Mountain High Enough	273

indicating the popstrological constellation or constellations to which each Birthstar belongs. Each constellation represents a group of stars with some important shared attribute—a style, a place of origin, a path that was followed to popstrological greatness. Multiple affiliations are possible for any given star because certain stars hold multiple important attributes in common with their fellow stars.

Looking at our example, we see that since your Birthstar is the Carpenters, you fall under the influence of three different constellations: the constellation *Gene Pool*, the constellation *Lite & White*, and the constellation *Tragic Demise*. This gives us three separate avenues of inquiry to pursue in our next and final step in building your popstrological profile.

STEP 5: Look up and read about your ruling constellations

There are forty-five constellations in the popstrological firmament, and all but nine of the 450 stars that rose within the popstrological era found a home within at least one of them. A great deal can be learned about a given star by looking at its popstrological connectedness (or lack thereof), but the primary impact is on relationship dynamics. The attributes that bind your Birthstar to other stars in the popstrological firmament are very likely to color the way in which you form relationships—romantic or platonic—with your fellow humans, and the final section of this book is devoted to exploring those attributes and their impact. Beginning on page 333, you will find a detailed description and complete roster for each of the forty-five constellations in the popstrological firmament, and also for the non-constellation *Neither/Nor*, the home of those nine unaffiliated stars.

For our example of the Carpenters, we turn to pages 344, 353, and 377, respectively, for introductions to the constellations *Gene Pool*, *Lite & White*, and *Tragic Demise*. After reading about these constellations and discovering the many connections you have as a child of the Carpenters to stars ranging from the Everly Brothers and the Jackson 5 to Barry Manilow and Milli Vanilli, you have completed the task of building your popstrological profile. The task of understanding its meaning, however, and of interpreting its lessons, warnings, and exhortations, has just begun. It is to that process that we will now turn our attention.

Interpreting Your Popstrological Profile

If you've already built your popstrological profile, then you've worked your way through a great deal of interpretive material already, but the interpretations offered in this book are merely a starting point. If true popstrological self-awareness is your goal, you'll need to understand the underlying framework of popstrological thought and commit yourself to a lifelong process of evaluation and reevaluation. But don't be intimidated. The methodology of popstrological inquiry isn't difficult to master, and it is the rare individual who cannot quickly begin to find his own answers in the pop stars if he approaches the task patiently, creatively, and with an open mind.

The Meaning of Your Birth Year

Unless you were born in 1974, the year of your birth was popstrologically dominated by a single star, and this Dominant Star set a tone for the entire microgeneration born in the same calendar year. Everyone born in 1977, for instance, carries within himself a little piece of Debby Boone, even if he was born under the direct influence of Stevie Wonder. By the same token, everyone born in 1977 carries within himself a little piece of Stevie Wonder, for he was that year's Opposing Star—the star whose popstrological vibrations ran most strongly against those of Debby Boone. A third layer of meaning is added to every year but 1956 and 1974 by the presence of a popstrological Wildcard—the star who either generated the strangest vibrations in a given year or who, more often, simply represented something entirely unrelated to the tension between the year's Dominant and Opposing Stars. For the children of 1977, this Wildcard is Meco, the long-Forgotten discofier of the *Star Wars Title Theme*.

At the microgenerational level, the effects of the interplay among the Dominant, Opposing, and Wildcard Stars of a given year are readily apparent. One will find certain subtle yet unmistakable differences, for instance, between the popstrological classes of 1966 and 1967—years in which the Beatles and the Monkees swapped positions as Dominant and Opposing Stars. At the individual level, trace influences of each of these influential stars are likely to turn up, but the most important effect stems from your Birthstar's place in the overall scheme of your Birth Year's popstrological dynamics. What is the difference between being a Monkee born in the Year of the Beatles and a Monkee born in the Year of the Monkees? It's the difference between being a square peg in a round hole and a square peg in a square hole. What is the relationship of *your* Birthstar to the Dominant Star in the year of your birth? Are they one and the same? Are they of the same genre and the same general vibe, or are they as different as different can be? At the very least, the answers to these questions are likely to shed new light on your place in the social hierarchy of your immediate peer group.

Your Birthstar and You

Your Birth Year is an important starting point, but far and away the greatest and most direct popstrological influence in your life flows from your Birthstar— the star who ruled the pop universe at the precise moment of your birth. The relationship you have to your Birthstar, however, is probably anything but simple. This is especially true if you were born under the influence of a star like the Beatles or Elvis Presley, for it is highly unlikely that your life could directly reflect either of those stars' Massive and multilayered influence. But it is also true if you were born under the influence of a relatively Minor star like the Singing Nun or C. W. McCall, for just because a star is Minor does not mean that a star is one-dimensional. Ultimately, though, it is not just the complexity of your Birthstar that makes your relationship to it so complicated—it's the complexity of *you*, too.

The power of the pop stars is great, but it is not so great as to be able to wipe away all of the other aspects of your makeup and dictate your destiny. Two children raised by the same parents are capable of growing up to be polar opposites, and two children born under the same Birthstar are, too. But two wildly different people with the same biological or popstrological parents often turn out that way in response to the same set of influences. Consciously or not, we chose to fulfill certain expectations placed on us in childhood and to oppose others with all our might, and the same thing was true in our popstrological development. For every fully realized Monkee

out there, there is also a fully oppositional Monkee— an individual who has become what he's become precisely because he has defined himself in opposition to every aspect of his Birthstar's popstrological influence. But far more common is the individual who falls somewhere in between the extremes of popstrological compliance and popstrological opposition. Indeed, most of us will find as we ponder the significance of our Birthstars that we have struggled against as many of their influences as we have embraced.

Reading Your Starchart

The primary essence of your Birthstar is very likely to reside in some entirely unique attribute, but there are certain measures of popstrological influence that can be applied consistently to each and every Birthstar. These measures yield values known as Critical Aspects, and they are traditionally represented on a circular **Starchart** made up of five axes created by five central dichotomies: Massive vs. Minor, Lasting vs. Forgotten, Fresh vs. Familiar, Sexy vs. Not Sexy, and Whitebread vs. Soul.

With very few exceptions, every star in the popstrological firmament can be mapped somewhere along each of these axes, but do not make the mistake of assuming that your Birthstar's Fresh Soulfulness or Forgotten Whitebreadiness translates simply and directly into the same qualities in yourself. Instead, think of each value represented on your Starchart as a wind blowing in one direction or the other, with the distance from center representing the intensity of that wind. If after reading about the meaning of these Critical Aspects you were to draw an honest

Starchart of *yourself*, you might learn a great deal, for the values that contradicted your Birthstar's would surely represent those areas of life in which you have exercised your free will most strongly, and the values that matched or exceeded your Birthstar's would represent the areas in which you have been the most passive.

Massive vs. Minor

This aspect reflects your Birthstar's relative impact on the universe of pop, and not just in terms of chart performance. Stars that shine brightly and intensely are not the only kind that have a Massive impact, after all. Stars like the Beatles and the Supremes are extraordinarily Massive, naturally, but nearly as Massive is a star like Carole King, who had a profound influence on the pop universe despite earning just a single #1 hit as a performer. Olivia Newton-John and Lionel Richie? Very Massive. Connie Francis and Blondie? Massive, but less so. Tommy Roe and the Starland Vocal Band? Quite Minor. Maureen McGovern and Jimmy Soul? Fabulous in their own ways, but popstrologically as Minor as Minor can get.

What does this Critical Aspect mean for you?
This Critical Aspect is very strongly associated with career issues, and specifically with the scale of your career ambitions. Those who were born under the influence of truly Massive stars are unlikely to dream on a small scale, and those who were born under Minor stars are somewhat likely to set low expectations for themselves. It is important to realize, though, that your Birthstar's Massive/Minor aspect says nothing of your ability to live out your dreams, however great or modest they may be. Indeed, it is only in combination with the second Critical Aspect that your likelihood of actually fulfilling your career ambitions can be calculated.

Lasting vs. Forgotten

This aspect marks the dichotomy between those stars whose personas remain a powerful part of our popular consciousness and those whose names, faces, and songs have faded into obscurity. It goes without saying that popstrologically Massive stars like Elvis Presley and the Rolling Stones have also proven to be Lasting while popstrologically Minor stars like Alan O'Day and Mr. Acker Bilk have been Forgotten. But

you probably can't put a face or a song to the names of stars like Bobby Lewis or Zager and Evans, either, for they have been decidedly Forgotten despite having been rather Massive during one brief moment in popstrological time.

What does this Critical Aspect mean for you?
This Critical Aspect, too, is associated with matters of career, but specifically with career achievement rather than career ambition. Taken on its own, your Birthstar's Lasting/Forgotten aspect has relatively little interpretive value, but in combination with your Birthstar's Massive/Minor aspect, its power is very great indeed. Is your Birthstar much more Massive than Lasting? If so, this does not augur well for your ability to achieve the career goals you set for yourself. If the situation is reversed, on the other hand, you might live out your dreams but be haunted by the feeling that they were a bit too modest. And if your Birthstar's Massive/Minor and Lasting/Forgotten aspects are in perfect harmony, congratulations. You are blessed with the popstrological potential to achieve real career satisfaction.

Fresh vs. Familiar

This aspect relates directly to the musical output of a given star, which was either Fresh or Familiar to the ears of the listening audience at the time of that star's first appearance. The Freshest stars ever to rise in the popstrological firmament can be found in the constellation *Fresh Breeze*, and their music sounds as Fresh today as it did in their respective heydays. But popstrological Freshness is measured *contextually*, so you should not be surprised to find certain stars whose music you regard as rather stale—the Carpenters, say—ranking instead as rather Fresh on the basis of how they sounded during their original heyday. Nor is a relatively Fresh sound always an entirely new sound. When the New Vaudeville Band topped the charts with *Winchester Cathedral*, their sound was rather Fresh indeed to the ears of 1966, though it would have been regarded as extremely Familiar by the standards of 1926.

What does this Critical Aspect mean for you?
Your Birthstar's Fresh/Familiar aspect is strongly associated with your feelings about conformity and originality. But with so many other social forces also affecting those feelings, this element of your

popstrological profile is easily overwhelmed. It is safe to say, though, that those whose Birthstars rank as extremely Fresh will at least *regard* themselves as non-conformists even if there is little evidence to support that self-image. Those whose Birthstars fall toward the other extreme along the Fresh/Familiar axis, on the other hand, may actually be more capable than anyone of achieving true originality if they reach a point at which their overwhelming natural tendency toward conformity becomes too stifling for them to bear.

Sexy vs. Not Sexy

Sexy may be a difficult word to define, but you know it when you see it, and you can see a great deal of it in the stars of the popstrological firmament, many of whom depended on sex appeal to fuel their popstrological rise. But unlike our current era, in which eye-popping sex appeal is a sine qua non for any aspiring pop star, the popstrological era was relatively friendly to stars of the Not Sexy variety. In fact, one can find in the popstrological firmament any number of stars like Roy Orbison and Barry Manilow, whose *lack* of sex appeal was a source of strength because it forced them to develop other powers of allure more fully. It is important to point out, though, that popstrological Sexiness does not flow merely from attractiveness. The objectively lovely Debby Boone, for example, is Not Sexy at all in popstrological terms, while the ragged-looking Janis Joplin was rather Sexy indeed.

What does this Critical Aspect mean for you?
If your Birthstar is extremely Sexy, you may want to believe that the same can naturally be said of you, but popstrology is never so straightforward, and you probably know yourself better than this anyway. No, a high score for your Birthstar on the Sexy/Not Sexy aspect cannot make you sexy, but it can make you into someone who places great importance on sexiness. In this respect, of course, you would simply be going with the flow of modern times. The best examples of this Critical Aspect's power are probably to be found among those whose Birthstars are resoundingly Not Sexy, for they may be the only ones among us who needn't be reminded that substance will generally triumph over style, at least for us mortals.

Whitebread vs. Soul

One of the biggest misconceptions among newcomers to popstrology concerns this dichotomy, which many mistakenly read as "white artist vs. black artist." It certainly is fair to imagine the Whitebread/Soul axis as a spectrum defined by the extremes of, say, Air Supply on the one hand and Barry White on the other, but it would be a mistake to assume that its essence relates to skin color. By virtue of the style of music they produced, the majority of black artists in the popstrological firmament do, in fact, fall on the Soul side of the midpoint along this axis, but many are surpassed in popstrological Soulfulness by white stars like Carole King and Charlie Rich. And it should come as no surprise to learn that the reverse is also true—that even many white stars with strong Whitebread tendencies are surpassed in Whitebreadiness by the likes of Lionel Richie and even Stevie Wonder in his incarnation as half of a popstrological ***Power Couple*** with Paul McCartney.

What does this Critical Aspect mean for you?
There's nothing wrong with white bread, if a bland, non-nutritive sandwich platform is what you're looking for, and there's nothing wrong with popstrological Whitebread if you're looking for the musical equivalent of the same. The vast majority of stars in the popstrological firmament fall slightly to the Whitebread side, not very far from the center of the Whitebread/Soul axis, reflecting rather appropriately the tastes of American pop audiences between 1956 and 1989. There are outliers, however, and the children of these stars are the most likely to be affected by their Birthstars' Whitebread/Soul aspect. Is your Birthstar as popstrologically Soulful as Sam Cooke or Aretha Franklin? If so, your connection and commitment to deep emotional truths is probably much greater than average. If, on the other hand, your Birthstar is as popstrologically Whitebread as John Denver or Anne Murray, your natural tendency is to avoid or repress those truths in the interest of keeping things light. Most of our Birthstars fall somewhere in the middle, so most of us will be in touch with the deep stuff only occasionally, and will choose very carefully when and where we allow ourselves to express anything approaching raw and vulnerable passion.

Reading Your Birthsong

Your Birthsong adds layers to your popstrological profile that might confirm, complement, or even counteract the primary influence of your Birth Year and Birthstar, but the most important thing about your Birthsong is that it contains critical messages uniquely capable of guiding you on your path through life—messages that you alone are capable of deciphering. Think of your Birthsong as a kind of sacred text filled with lessons, warnings, and exhortations, and be prepared for the fact that those lessons, warnings, and exhortations may sometimes be more unsettling than they are empowering. Popstrologists are often asked to interpret the Birthsongs of those they counsel, but generally they prefer to leave that task up to the individual, for the meaning of a given song can and should be different to any two individuals born under its influence. Occasionally they oblige, however, and for the purposes of illustration, let us now look at several examples of how a trained popstrologist might read your Birthsong. For the purposes of illustration, let's use the three #1 songs of the Carpenters, the Birthstar we explored earlier when walking through the steps involved in building your popstrological profile.

➤ *Close To You* (Jul 19–Aug 16, 1970)
Tell most people that the angels got together on the day of their birth to create a stardust-eyed dream-come-true, and they'd just laugh, but you might not. The **ability to light up a room** and **inspire devoted followings** may be yours for the taking, if that's the path you choose, but never forget that your Birthsong puts you at risk of **debilitating narcissism**. Your mixed blessing is that **others will be drawn to you regardless of the effort you put into attracting them**. So make the most of it if you like, but the time will come when you'll wish you'd **focused more attention on your substantive qualities than on your appearance**.

➤ *Top Of The World* (Nov 25–Dec 8, 1973)
The **capacity to feel** and the **willingness to express your feelings** are incredibly valuable traits to possess, especially in the context of romantic relationships. The **capacity to become emotionally unhinged**, however, and to lose all sense of proportion at the first tinglings of infatuation—that's just plain unhealthy. Cue up your Birthsong next time love begins to pull at your strings and carefully gauge

your reactions. Does your stomach churn at the cloying cuteness of it all? Perhaps you need to suspend your cynicism for once and give in to your soft side. Or do you instead find yourself beginning to drift on a sea of warm touchy-feelies? Step back and beware: if love is a drug, you may be at risk of becoming an addict.

➤ *Please Mr. Postman* (Jan 19–25, 1975)
There are times in life when **patience is a virtue**, when waiting just a little bit longer is the very best course of action. But there are also times when we **fritter away valuable time** waiting for the answer that never comes. The perky spin your Birthsong puts on a tale of marathon mailbox-watching with uncertain results serves, perhaps, as a valuable object lesson in either case. Will your patience be rewarded? Or will your steadfastness prove to be in vain? It may be impossible to tell, but one lesson to draw may be this: if a simple letter would really make you feel better, the best bet may be to **seize the initiative** and mail it to yourself.

Exploring Your Constellations

The modern pop universe was brought into being suddenly and dramatically with the rise of Elvis Presley, and in the very first moments following this Big Bang, signs of structure were already visible. No sooner had Elvis risen than a group of stars emerged to oppose his influence and defend the status quo. They were the stars of the constellation *Old Guard*, the first of the constellations in the young pop universe to make its meaning clear. In the years that followed, dozens of other coalitions of stars would begin to take shape, some with popstrological agendas as clear as that of the *Old Guard*, but others simply organized around shared pedigrees or aesthetic attributes. By the end of the 1959, nearly half of the forty-five constellations in the popstrological firmament had begun to take shape, jockeying for position and competing to gain new members. By the mid-1960s, it was difficult—though not impossible—for any new star to rise into the highest reaches of the pop universe without being claimed by one constellation or another. By 1980, forty-four constellations had staked their claims on a particular region in popstrological space, and the forty-fifth to do so—the constellation

Reaganrock—was so powerful as to put an end to the process of constellation formation for good.

Constellations reflect the relationships among the stars of the popstrological firmament, and as such, they have a great deal to say about the way you relate to your fellow humans. For instance, the specific shared attribute that defines each constellation is a powerful predictor of the issues those born under its influence bring into their relationships. Children of the constellation *Invisible Hand* are well known for putting the needs of others ahead of their own, while children of the constellation *Spin-Off* tend to keep their priorities focused on themselves. Children of the constellation *Shape-Shifter* often have difficulty with commitment, whereas children of the constellation *Folkie* can't seem to commit themselves quickly enough, and can't seem to stop proclaiming their commitment once they give it.

Your Birthstar's constellation alignment can also be used to understand the strengths and weaknesses of your existing relationships, and to determine your compatibility with potential new friends, colleagues, and lovers. With so many potential combinations of constellations possible, it would be impractical for popstrologists to develop a complete guide to favorable and unfavorable matches, but as with every aspect of popstrology, you can probably work out for yourself the meaning of the constellation combinations that apply in your own relationships if you give it a try. Do you share an alignment with the constellation *Reaganrock* with someone special in your life? If so, the only conflict in your relationship may be fighting over who gets to compromise himself or herself more. Are you a child of the constellation *Fresh Breeze* who has attracted the attention of someone born under the constellation *Old Guard*? Tread carefully, for while they may allow themselves the occasional flirtation with the fresh and new, their commitment to the status quo may eventually come to the fore.

A Word in Closing

We are who we are for any number of reasons, not all of them related to the forces at work in the pop universe at the moment of your birth. The goal of popstrology is to open a new window onto the sometimes mysterious inner workings of our hearts and our minds—a window through which the bright light of the pop stars might be made to shine upon areas of our experience inadequately illuminated by sciences like psychology and astrology. But only you can decide how wide to open that window, and only you can truly understand and appreciate all that the act of opening it reveals. Indeed, of the many things that popstrology can do for you, perhaps the most important is empowering you to apply it for yourself. There is no voodoo to it—no advanced degrees or psychic gifts required to begin applying it in your own life. Once armed with a basic understanding of popstrological methodology, anyone with a passion for pop music and a desire to understand their place in the world can begin practicing the science of the pop stars, whether as a guiding life-philosophy or as just one more implement in an extensive self-help tool kit.

BIRTH YEARS

The First Year of Elvis Presley

Picture yourself in a boat on a river, or on a pond, let's say, abutting the eighteenth hole and clubhouse of some middle-American country club where a dance party is under way on a balmy spring evening in April of 1956. A group of well-fed white people is standing on the veranda smoking Chesterfields, drinking gin, and talking about television.

"Say, Bill, did you catch Uncle Miltie Tuesday night?" one of them asks, knowing full well that Bill and every other TV-owning human watches *The Milton Berle Show* religiously. "What did you make of that Presley character?"

"Oh, don't get me started on *him*," chimes in Bill's wife. "Do you know that I had to threaten to ground our Trish last week before I could get her to stop playing that 'Blue Shoes' song and give little Billy a chance to listen to his 'Tennessee' Ernie Ford record?"

"Good for Trish!" says Bill. "I was beginning to get as sick of *Sixteen Tons* as I was of that Pat Boone song she wouldn't stop playing last month!"

The assembled middle-aged adults share a laugh over their children's charming and harmless obsession with pop music, but then one of them ventures:

"Gosh, I don't know. I'm not sure I really want my kids listening to this Elvis fellow. He seems, well, *different* from Pat Boone."

"I think you can relax," says Bill. "He's just a singer. And anyway, they'll outgrow him—they always do."

As you float away from this little scene, you will probably shake your head and smile, because you already know what lies ahead. Within a week or two, the pent-up yearnings of an entire

generation of young Americans will coalesce around the young **Elvis Presley**, and when that psychic energy comes into contact with his otherworldly talent and charisma, the result will be explosive. The result, in fact, will be the Big Bang that brings the modern pop universe into existence.

Heartbreak Hotel was the song that started it all on April 21, 1956, and as April turned into May, and May into June, *Heartbreak Hotel* was still sitting at the top of the pop charts, and the world was beginning to catch on to what was happening. Elvis made a second, unrestrained appearance on *Milton Berle* on June 3, and in its aftermath, the Catholic weekly *America* published a piece called "Beware of Elvis Presley." The deepest, darkest fears of various other reactionary elements were also awakened: sexual degeneracy, race mixing—these were the logical extensions of what Elvis Presley stood for in some people's eyes. Soon, though, these people would get a brief respite from the unspeakable horror of Elvis.

Their respite would come in the form of an old-fashioned girl-singer named **Gogi Grant**, whose *Wayward Wind* succeeded *Heartbreak Hotel* at the top of the pop charts on June 16. Though popstrologically Minor and long Forgotten, Gogi Grant occupies a place of profound and fundamental significance to all of us, for she introduced the first note of conflict into the modern pop universe—the first clear indication that the stars of the popstrological firmament might not constitute a mutual admiration society.

No, the king of rock and roll would not rule unopposed in the first, partial year of the popstrological era, and neither would rock and roll itself. In fact,

THE DOMINANT STAR
Elvis Presley
• #1 Hits this year: 4
• Weeks at #1 this year: 25
• #1 Hits in Career: 17
• Weeks at #1 in Career: 79

THE OPPOSING STAR
Guy Mitchell
• #1 Hits this year: 2
• Weeks at #1 this year: 7
• #1 Hits in Career: 3
• Weeks at #1 in Career: 8

WILDCARD
None

no star and no sound would ever rule unopposed again, and it all began with Gogi Grant. By year's end, she would be joined by two more members of the pop status quo—**Guy Mitchell** and **the Platters**—in the constellation *Old Guard*. And though the *Old Guard* would recede from significance long before the thirty-three and a third years of the popstrological era were up, it would first threaten to change the very course of that era by engaging Elvis Presley and his fellow rock and roll revolutionaries in a bloody battle for dominance in the universe of pop.

The forces of the status quo failed, of course, in their effort to stop Elvis Presley, and Elvis went on to achieve a level of pop greatness we may never see again. But you were born at a moment when the outcome of the struggle between Elvis and the enemies of change was still in doubt, and this fact is of great significance to you and to the other members of the first Elvis Presley generation.

Change versus fear of change. That was the only issue at play in the primitive pop universe into which you were born, and it's very likely to have been the central issue in your life, too.

WHAT'S YOUR SIGN?

1956 BIRTHDATES	BIRTHSTAR / BIRTHSONG	PAGE
Apr 21 - Jun 15	Elvis Presley / Heartbreak Hotel	255
Jun 16 - Jul 27	Gogi Grant / The Wayward Wind	174
Jul 28 - Aug 3	Elvis Presley / I Want You, I Need You, I Love You	255
Aug 4 - Aug 17	The Platters / My Prayer	253
Aug 18 - Nov 2	Elvis Presley / Don't Be Cruel • Hound Dog	255
Nov 3 - Dec 7	Elvis Presley / Love Me Tender	255
Dec 8 - Dec 31	Guy Mitchell / Singing The Blues	234

The Second Year of Elvis Presley

The farther we look back in time, the easier it is for us to let our knowledge of all that's happened since hamper our effort to understand the past. But we must remember that things aren't always what they seem to be in hindsight, as the year of your birth—the Second Year of Elvis Presley—clearly illustrates. For while time and television have conspired to reduce 1957 in memory to a year in which rock and roll swept all cobwebs of the past aside, the truth in popstrological terms is markedly different, though no less dramatic.

Elvis Presley in the year of your birth was Elvis Presley as most of us like to remember him, in his full aesthetic glory and at the height of his considerable musical powers. There were no cardigans or sequined jumpsuits for Elvis in 1957, no *Pocketful of Rainbows* or *In The Ghetto*. This was the year of *All Shook Up* and *Jailhouse Rock*—records that affirmed Elvis's continuing allegiance to the constellation **Fresh Breeze** in his first full year on the popstrological throne. With a growing army led by **Buddy Holly** and **the Everly Brothers** lining up behind him, the future looked bright for rock and roll and its glorious young king, but as they say, uneasy lies the head that wears the crown.

Without question, the presence of the resplendent Elvis Presley as the Dominant Star of 1957 marked those born in just the second year of the popstrological era with his unmistakable stamp. The **potential to start revolutions** may not be theirs, but the **potential to bring about change of a more modest sort** is. Whether they can do even this without bringing the full and vengeful weight of the status

THE DOMINANT STAR
Elvis Presley
- #1 Hits this year: 4
- Weeks at #1 this year: 25
- #1 Hits in Career: 17
- Weeks at #1 in Career: 79

THE OPPOSING STAR
Pat Boone
- #1 Hits this year: 2
- Weeks at #1 this year: 7
- #1 Hits in Career: 3
- Weeks at #1 in Career: 8

WILDCARD
Sam Cooke
- #1 Hits this year: 1
- Weeks at #1 this year: 2
- #1 Hits in Career: 1
- Weeks at #1 in Career: 2

quo down upon themselves, though, is another question altogether.

With the benefit of hindsight, it seems a historical inevitability that rock and roll would emerge as the sole viable force in the modern pop universe. But history is never inevitable, and if you could transport yourself back to the year of your birth, you would see just how strong the enemies of rock and roll really were. You would see how history might well have gone down another path entirely.

The enemies of Elvis were led by the Opposing Star of 1957, a star who was not to be taken lightly. He was **Pat Boone**, the tight-*ss white man who blocked Little Richard from entering the popstrological firmament by covering *Tutti-Frutti*, and he was far from alone in his commitment to oppose the growing threat of rock and roll. Pat Boone was the unquestioned leader of the constellation **Old Guard**, a well-organized cadre of stars whose future career prospects had been called into question suddenly and dramatically with the rise of Elvis Presley. Far from willing to go down without a fight, the forces of the **Old Guard** engaged the forces of youth head-on in 1957.

The **Old Guard** led off the year with the spooky crooner **Guy Mitchell**, but the brand-new constellation **Teen Idol** rose immediately to counterattack with **Tab Hunter**. The army of Elvis launched youthful, sex-hungry **Buddy Knox**, but the defenders of the status quo countered with the mighty **Perry Como**. From that point forward, it was like watching a young Cassius Clay standing toe to toe and trading blows with a tired but still-dangerous Sonny Liston. Elvis Presley?

Pat Boone. Elvis again? Debbie Reynolds. *Teen Idol* Paul Anka? Debbie Reynolds again.

Yes, there was **Sam Cooke**, the year's Wildcard star, offering a third way out of this lily-white battle, but he offered Elvis little respite. The problem, from Elvis's perspective, wasn't just the existence of an enemy, but his enemy's ability to win popular support. Don't think for a minute that it was only grown-ups buying the records of the *Old Guard*. No, America's teens were as susceptible to moments of doubt and to the siren

song of Perry Como as anyone, and they were as responsible as anyone for leaving Elvis limping as the second year of his popstrological reign came to an end.

And if there is a lesson in that fact for the children of 1957, perhaps it is never to take progress for granted. **The enemies of change do not wear buttons** that say, "I Hate Change." They are everywhere, they are indistinguishable from the rest of us, and **if we are truly honest about it, they often are us**.

WHAT'S YOUR SIGN?

1957 BIRTHDATES	BIRTHSTAR / BIRTHSONG	PAGE
Jan 1 - Feb 8	Guy Mitchell / Singing The Blues	234
Feb 9 - Mar 1	Elvis Presley / Too Much	255
Mar 2 - Mar 29	Tab Hunter / Young Love	187
Mar 30 - Apr 5	Buddy Knox / Party Doll	201
Apr 6 - Apr 12	Perry Como / Round And Round	129
Apr 13 - Jun 2	Elvis Presley / Ali Shook Up	255
Jun 3 - Jul 7	Pat Boone / Love Letters In The Sand	108
Jul 8 - Aug 25	Elvis Presley / (Let Me Be Your) Teddy Bear	255
Aug 26 - Sep 8	Debbie Reynolds / Tammy	262
Sep 9 - Sep 15	Paul Anka / Diana	93
Sep 16 - Sep 22	Debbie Reynolds / Tammy	262
Sep 23 - Sep 29	Buddy Holly and the Crickets / That'll Be The Day	182
Sep 30 - Oct 13	Jimmie Rodgers / Honeycomb	268
Oct 14 - Oct 20	The Everly Brothers / Wake Up Little Susie	156
Oct 21 - Dec 1	Elvis Presley / Jailhouse Rock	255
Dec 2 - Dec 8	Sam Cooke / You Send Me	130
Dec 9 - Dec 15	Elvis Presley / Jailhouse Rock	255
Dec 16 - Dec 22	Sam Cooke / You Send Me	130
Dec 23 - Dec 31	Pat Boone / April Love	108

The Third Year of Elvis Presley

The science of popstrology seeks to reveal the meaning and impact of collective human longing as expressed in the figures we elevate to the highest reaches of our pop universe. And if the longings on which popstrology casts its light are sometimes disappointing or embarrassing to contemplate, then so be it, for if disappointment and embarrassment are not among the most fundamental driving forces in our lives, then what is?

From the nonjudgmental viewpoint of popstrologists, the year of your birth is, of course, neither disappointing nor embarrassing but simply fascinating. It is only from the viewpoint of staunch rock and roll fans that the popstrological scene in 1958 can be viewed in such a negative light. Theirs is a point of view that regards the **Elvis Presley** of *Hound Dog* (1956) as a vastly better Elvis than, say, the Elvis Presley of *Rock-A-Hula Baby* (1960). And if you share this point of view, then there is every reason to point your gaze toward 1958 in searching for the cause of Elvis's decline.

With the constellation *Old Guard* soundly defeated in the popstrological battle of 1957, one might have expected the glorious young king of rock and roll to tighten his grip on power in 1958, but of Elvis's four years as the pop universe's Dominant Star, the year of your birth was clearly his weakest. Exhausted from his epic battle with the constellation *Old Guard* in 1957, Elvis could surely have benefited from the support of strong popstrological lieutenants in 1958. Yet in what would prove to be a pivotal year, the teenage **Ricky Nelson** and the soon-to-be *Shape-Shifter*

Conway Twitty were the only new stars to rally to the king's side by playing something even approaching his thrilling brand of rock and roll. Still, with only the moderate wing of the constellation *Old Guard* showing overt signs of life via **the Platters** and **Tommy Edwards**, it would seem that Elvis faced no serious challenge to his dominance in 1958. And indeed he did not, but challenges can come in many forms—even forms that appear to be anything but serious.

And far from serious is exactly what Elvis Presley's greatest challenge in 1958 proved to be, for it came in the form of a brand-new force that came not to do battle with the hard-driving disciples of rock and roll, but rather to make light of the mission they took so seriously. It was the constellation *Novelty Merchant*, and in proposing silliness as an alternative to the serious business of rock and roll, it found an enormous audience. Where were the teenagers whose embrace of Elvis's raw sexual energy had seemed so revolutionary back in 1956? In 1958, they were listening to records like *Purple People Eater* and the *Chipmunk Song*.

No, it wasn't men with names like Como and Boone who knocked the rock and roll revolution subtly off course—it was men with names like **David Seville** and **Sheb Wooley**, and it was **Chipmunks** with names like Simon, Theodore, and Alvin. All they wanted to do was get some laughs and sell some records, these *Novelty Merchants*, but the enthusiasm with which America embraced them sapped the rock and roll revolution of its intensity. And it was that, along with the egalitarian spirit of

THE DOMINANT STAR
Elvis Presley
- #1 Hits this year: 2
- Weeks at #1 this year: 7
- #1 Hits in Career: 17
- Weeks at #1 in Career: 79

THE OPPOSING STAR
Sheb Wooley
- #1 Hits this year: 1
- Weeks at #1 this year: 6
- #1 Hits in Career: 3
- Weeks at #1 in Career: 6

WILDCARD
Domenico Modugno
- #1 Hits this year: 1
- Weeks at #1 this year: 6
- #1 Hits in Career: 1
- Weeks at #1 in Career: 6

the Memphis Draft Board, that sapped Elvis Presley of his and set the popstrological firmament on a path that would create a real necessity for the eventual British Invasion.

Call it disappointing or embarrassing, if you must, to have been born in a year when the average American record buyer did more damage to Elvis than Pat Boone ever did. But you could also take it as a challenge, setting for yourself the goal of **supporting causes that truly matter**, even when everyone else in your micro-generation tells you to **relax and have fun**.

Or you could console yourself with the knowledge that you were, at least, born in a year that chose the Wildcard **Domenico Modugno** over Dean Martin as its preferred, *auténtico* purveyor of *Volaré*—the record that launched the constellation *Eurosomething*.

WHAT'S YOUR SIGN?

1958 BIRTHDATES	BIRTHSTAR / BIRTHSONG	PAGE
Jan 1 - Jan 5	Pat Boone / April Love	108
Jan 6 - Feb 9	Danny and the Juniors / At The Hop	136
Feb 10 - Mar 16	Elvis Presley / Don't	255
Mar 17 - Apr 20	The Champs / Tequila	118
Apr 21 - Apr 27	The Platters / Twilight Time	253
Apr 28 - May 11	David Seville / Witch Doctor	280
May 12 - Jun 1	The Everly Brothers / All I Have To Do Is Dream	156
Jun 2 - Jul 20	Sheb Wooley / Purple People Eater	328
Jul 21 - Aug 3	Elvis Presley / Hard Headed Woman	255
Aug 4 - Aug 17	Ricky Nelson / Poor Little Fool	238
Aug 18 - Aug 24	Domenico Modugno / Volaré	235
Aug 25 - Aug 31	The Elegants / Little Star	152
Sep 1 - Sep 28	Domenico Modugno / Volaré	235
Sep 29 - Nov 9	Tommy Edwards / It's All In The Game	151
Nov 10 - Nov 16	Conway Twitty / It's Only Make Believe	312
Nov 17 - Nov 23	The Kingston Trio / Tom Dooley	199
Nov 24 - Nov 30	Conway Twitty / It's Only Make Believe	312
Dec 1 - Dec 21	The Teddy Bears / To Know Him Is To Love Him	305
Dec 22 - Dec 31	The Chipmunks / The Chipmunk Song	124

1959

The Year of Bobby Darin

The Massive and Lasting forces whose powers reach across the decades to affect us even today are rich material for popstrological inquiry, but the brilliant light of the brightest stars can also render equally interesting regions of the pop universe practically invisible to the popstrological eye.

The year of your birth was the first to demonstrate what popstrological wonders lie hidden from view when a blindingly bright star like Elvis Presley rules the universe, for this was the year in which the United States Army removed the king of rock and roll from his popstrological throne and created a momentary power vacuum into which some rather interesting things rushed. As one might expect in such a situation, there were pretenders to the throne—**Frankie Avalon** chief among them—who attempted to capitalize on Elvis's absence by capturing a portion of his core audience. But it was a truly Fresh and independent star who actually dominated this brief interregnum, and it was the expansion of two powerful and diametrically opposed new entities—the constellation *Storyteller* and the constellation *Speechless*—that constituted the year's most significant long-term popstrological development.

Bobby Darin was the man who warmed the popstrological throne for Elvis Presley in the year of your birth, gaining his position on the strength of *Mack The Knife*, his only #1 hit. And one might reasonably wonder what it says about Eisenhower-era America that it made a finger-snapping ode to a cold-blooded German murderer one of the biggest hit records in history, but popstrology's concern is what it says

about the innocent babies born in the Year of Bobby Darin.

Rest easy, though, children of 1959, for the Dominant Star in the year of your birth was more than just a glamorizer of violence. He was also a member of the constellation *Shape-Shifter*—a complicated man who was as unwilling to be defined by *Mack The Knife* as he was by earlier hits like 1958's *Splish Splash*. It is directly from Bobby Darin that the children of 1959 derive their tendency to **abhor and defy simplistic categorization schemes**. It's an attribute that sets the children of the Bobby Darin generation apart from many others, though perhaps the same could be said of their sometimes **slippery unwillingness to commit** firmly to a single one of the many faces they show to the world.

As complicated a man as Bobby Darin was, and as complex as his influence was on the generation born under his popstrological rule, the Opposing Star of 1959 gave the Bobby Darin generation a welcome ability to sometimes keep things simple. They were **Santo and Johnny**, the third-ever star to join the nonverbal constellation *Speechless* and the duo behind *Sleepwalk*, the song that launched a million sock-hop slow dances. Though Minor and Forgotten in the grand scheme of popstrological things, the Opposing Star of 1959 was nonetheless a significant force in a year that needed all the strong, silent types it could get, given the burst of activity within the chatty constellation *Storyteller*.

Like most of the great popstrological *Storyteller*s, **Johnny Horton** and Wildcard star **Lloyd Price** delivered

THE DOMINANT STAR
Bobby Darin
- #1 Hits this year: 1
- Weeks at #1 this year: 9
- #1 Hits in Career: 1
- Weeks at #1 in Career: 9

THE OPPOSING STAR
Santo and Johnny
- #1 Hits this year: 1
- Weeks at #1 this year: 2
- #1 Hits in Career: 1
- Weeks at #1 in Career: 2

WILDCARD
Lloyd Price
- #1 Hits this year: 1
- Weeks at #1 this year: 4
- #1 Hits in Career: 1
- Weeks at #1 in Career: 4

more than just great narratives in their 1959 hits. They delivered dead bodies, too, kicking off in *The Battle Of New Orleans* and *Stagger Lee* the popstrological trail of blood that continued into *Mack The Knife*. A grim portent, this, for the children of 1959? Probably not, for violence couched safely in fiction is violence couched safely in fiction. But given their birth in a year overflowing with excellent and entertaining narrative, the children of 1959 should expect, popstrology predicts, to find nothing in life so pleasing as lying on the couch, reading, watching, or listening to fictional tales of mayhem.

WHAT'S YOUR SIGN?

1959 BIRTHDATES	BIRTHSTAR / BIRTHSONG	PAGE
Jan 1 - Jan 18	The Chipmunks / The Chipmunk Song	124
Jan 19 - Feb 8	The Platters / Smoke Gets In Your Eyes	253
Feb 9 - Mar 8	Lloyd Price / Stagger Lee	257
Mar 9 - Apr 12	Frankie Avalon / Venus	97
Apr 13 - May 10	The Fleetwoods / Come Softly To Me	161
May 11 - May 17	Dave "Baby" Cortez / The Happy Organ	131
May 18 - May 31	Wilbert Harrison / Kansas City	179
Jun 1 - Jul 12	Johnny Horton / The Battle Of New Orleans	184
Jul 13 - Aug 9	Paul Anka / Lonely Boy	93
Aug 10 - Aug 23	Elvis Presley / Big Hunk O' Love	255
Aug 24 - Sep 20	The Browns / The Three Bells	112
Sep 21 - Oct 4	Santo and Johnny / Sleepwalk	276
Oct 5 - Nov 15	Bobby Darin / Mack The Knife	137
Nov 16 - Nov 22	The Fleetwoods / Mr. Blue	161
Nov 23 - Dec 13	Bobby Darin / Mack The Knife	137
Dec 14 - Dec 27	Guy Mitchell / Heartaches By The Number	234
Dec 28 - Dec 31	Frankie Avalon / Why	97

The Fourth Year of Elvis Presley

Popstrology is not a static discipline that seeks to establish and defend a fixed orthodoxy. Vigorous debate is actively encouraged within the popstrological community, and fresh perspectives on the power of the pop stars are openly welcomed. How else could popstrology hope to keep up with a universe of pop stars who are themselves so difficult to pin down as they adapt to changing times and generate new popstrological meaning in the process?

Certainly the year of your birth highlights the importance of open-mindedness and the danger of fixed ideas in the practice of popstrology, for 1960 was a year in which the effect of changing times made itself felt with startling clarity on the man who set those changes in motion, **Elvis Presley**. Indeed, the year of your birth can be seen, in a certain light, as the year in which the man who brought the pop-strological firmament into existence fell victim to his own creation.

Fresh from his compulsory service in the army, Elvis Presley returned to his kingdom in the year of your birth to reclaim the popstrological throne, but the pop universe to which he returned was rather different from the one he'd left behind. The constellation *Old Guard*—Elvis's old nemesis—was entering its second straight year of silence in 1960, and for the very first time, Elvis was the Dominant Star in a time of popstrological peace. The dominance of rock and roll—the revolutionary force that Elvis Presley personified—was now a taken-for-granted fact. Or was it?

The continuing strength of the constellation *Novelty Merchant* in 1960 strongly suggests that it was not. Arising initially when the forces of rock and roll declared an end to major combat with the forces of the status quo in 1958, the constellation *Novelty Merchant* gathered strength during Elvis's eighteen months in the army, remaining nearly silent in 1959, but exploding in 1960 with the arrival of not one but three new stars: **the Hollywood Argyles**, **Larry Verne**, and the year's Wildcard star, young **Brian Hyland**. As individuals, none of these Minor jokesters represented much of a threat to the raw and thrilling sound that initially brought Elvis to power, but their collective power was awesome indeed. For if the rise of silly joke songs as the most significant competition faced by rock and roll is not what encouraged Elvis Presley to let his guard down and drop his rebel's pose, then popstrologists do not know what did. And make no mistake: it was Elvis Presley himself, under the guidance of his manager, "Colonel" Tom Parker, who engineered his slide toward Las Vegas by way of Hollywood. His first post-army album, *Elvis Is Back!*, contained hints of the young king in songs like *Dirty, Dirty Feeling*, but soon to follow was *Are You Lonesome To-night?*, a #1 hit that marks, in popstrological terms anyway, the beginning of Elvis's theatrical phase. The king spent the rest of 1960 on a gospel album and on the sound track to *G.I. Blues*, which contained such disturbing portents as *Pocketful Of Rainbows* and *Wooden Heart*. Ahead of Elvis, from the vantage point of 1960, lay records like *Aloha Oe* and *In The Ghetto*, and films like *Harum Scarum* and *Clambake*. And behind him, needless to say, lay *Jailhouse Rock* and *Hound Dog*.

THE DOMINANT STAR
Elvis Presley
- #1 Hits this year: 3
- Weeks at #1 this year: 15
- #1 Hits in Career: 17
- Weeks at #1 in Career: 79

THE OPPOSING STAR
Percy Faith
- #1 Hits this year: 1
- Weeks at #1 this year: 9
- #1 Hits in Career: 1
- Weeks at #1 in Career: 9

WILDCARD
Brian Hyland
- #1 Hits this year: 1
- Weeks at #1 this year: 1
- #1 Hits in Career: 1
- Weeks at #1 in Career: 1

Elvis faced no overt resistance in 1960 from the year's Opposing Star, the Sexy and *Speechless* Canadian orchestra leader **Percy Faith**, but perhaps that wasn't such a good thing. The year of your birth may have been a time of popstrological peace, but along with peace often come peace's unfortunate handmaidens, **settledness and complacency**—the twin bugaboos of the fourth Elvis Presley generation. Indeed, as Elvis demonstrated in 1960 and as the children of that year continue to demonstrate, **some people are only at their best when they've got a battle to fight**.

WHAT'S YOUR SIGN?

1960 BIRTHDATES	BIRTHSTAR / BIRTHSONG	PAGE
Jan 1 - Jan 3	Frankie Avalon / Why	97
Jan 4 - Jan 17	Marty Robbins / El Paso	267
Jan 18 - Feb 7	Johnny Preston / Running Bear	256
Feb 8 - Feb 21	Mark Dinning / Teen Angel	143
Feb 22 - Apr 24	Percy Faith / Theme From "A Summer Place"	158
Apr 25 - May 22	Elvis Presley / Stuck On You	255
May 23 - Jun 26	The Everly Brothers / Cathy's Clown	156
Jun 27 - Jul 10	Connie Francis / Everybody's Somebody's Fool	164
Jul 11 - Jul 17	The Hollywood Argyles / Alley-Oop	182
Jul 18 - Aug 7	Brenda Lee / I'm Sorry	204
Aug 8 - Aug 14	Brian Hyland / Itsy Bitsy Teenie Weenie Yellow Polkadot Bikini	187
Aug 15 - Sep 18	Elvis Presley / It's Now Or Never	255
Sep 19 - Sep 25	Chubby Checker / The Twist	121
Sep 26 - Oct 9	Connie Francis / My Heart Has A Mind Of Its Own	164
Oct 10 - Oct 16	Larry Verne / Mr. Custer	318
Oct 17 - Oct 23	The Drifters / Save The Last Dance For Me	148
Oct 24 - Oct 30	Brenda Lee / I Want To Be Wanted	204
Oct 31 - Nov 13	The Drifters / Save The Last Dance For Me	148
Nov 14 - Nov 20	Ray Charles / Georgia On My Mind	120
Nov 21 - Nov 27	Maurice Williams and the Zodiacs / Stay	326
Nov 28 - Dec 31	Elvis Presley / Are You Lonesome To-night?	255

1961

The Year of Bobby Lewis

Popstrology is a science that is always hungry for fresh data—a science that seeks, whenever possible, to reveal the power of the pop stars by looking at the fullness of their careers. But the popstrological existence of some stars is so fleeting that they leave little evidence behind, and in these cases popstrologists must mine the truth from very small pieces of data indeed.

The year of your birth was a year that was dominated by one of these challenging stars, though **Bobby Lewis** wasn't the first Dominant Star to achieve that status despite having only a single #1 hit to his credit. Bobby Darin was the first to do that back in 1959, but Bobby Darin was a man whose sole #1 hit belied a fairly significant pop career. Bobby Lewis, on the other hand, was a star who exited the pop universe almost as quickly as he entered it, and 1961 was the first year in the popstrological era to be ruled over by a man whose biggest hit was effectively his only hit.

So what, then, can be said about the year of Bobby Lewis's extremely brief ascendancy? Do all the children of 1961 share the qualities of those born during the actual weeks of Bobby Lewis's run at the top of the charts? Do they all possess **fundamentally good hearts** yet still require reminding, on occasion, that **serving the needs of others can actually serve their own, too?** Perhaps some do, but given the relative weakness of Bobby Lewis's popstrological rule, it's more than likely that many do not.

To say that Bobby Lewis's popstrological rule was weak, however, is not to say that its weakness made it unimportant. For in popstrology as in politics, periods of weak rule can be fascinating times. **Pat Boone, Ray Charles, Lawrence Welk,** and **Chubby Checker** all finding room to work in a popstrological firmament guided by a very strong leader is almost impossible to imagine. But finding them working in the Year of Bobby Lewis makes absolutely perfect sense. Nineteen sixty-one was a time of **shifty and confusing power dynamics**, and in the context of the popstrological firmament, shifty and confusing times can be the ideal context for the nurturing of Fresh and innovative stars whose sounds may someday prove quite powerful indeed.

To a certain degree, 1961's Opposing Star can be classified in this latter group, for **the Highwaymen** represented the constellation *Folkie*, an entity that would prove phenomenally powerful as the sixties progressed. Yes, they were short-haired Wesleyan grads in suits and ties, and no, *Michael* (as in *"row your boat ashore"*) wasn't exactly *A Hard Rain's A-Gonna Fall*, but the squareness of the Highwaymen reflects a critical stage in the development of folk music, without which it might never have reached its Dylan-driven peak.

But for the clearest reflection of the Fresh wonders that arose under the weak but benevolent rule of Bobby Lewis on the popstrological throne, look to the year's Wildcard star, **the Shirelles,** the first all-female group ever to join the popstrological elite and therefore the first star to join the hugely important constellation *Les Girls*. Their rise provides a neat parallel to the success many in the Bobby Lewis generation will have at **blazing trails** and **knocking down barriers** in environments that give them even a little bit of room to run.

THE DOMINANT STAR
Bobby Lewis
- #1 Hits this year: 1
- Weeks at #1 this year: 7
- #1 Hits in Career: 1
- Weeks at #1 in Career: 7

THE OPPOSING STAR
The Highwaymen
- #1 Hits this year: 1
- Weeks at #1 this year: 2
- #1 Hits in Career: 1
- Weeks at #1 in Career: 2

WILDCARD
The Shirelles
- #1 Hits this year: 1
- Weeks at #1 this year: 2
- #1 Hits in Career: 17
- Weeks at #1 in Career: 79

WHAT'S YOUR SIGN?

1961 BIRTHDATES	BIRTHSTAR / BIRTHSONG	PAGE
Jan 1 - Jan 8	Elvis Presley / Are You Lonesome To-night?	255
Jan 9 - Jan 29	Bert Kaempfert / Wonderland By Night	196
Jan 30 - Feb 12	The Shirelles / Will You Love Me Tomorrow?	282
Feb 13 - Feb 26	Lawrence Welk / Calcutta	321
Feb 27 - Mar 19	Chubby Checker / Pony Time	121
Mar 20 - Apr 2	Elvis Presley / Surrender	255
Apr 3 - Apr 23	The Marcels / Blue Moon	217
Apr 24 - May 21	Del Shannon / Runaway	281
May 22 - May 28	Ernie K-Doe / Mother-In-Law	197
May 29 - Jun 4	Ricky Nelson / Travelin' Man	238
Jun 5 - Jun 11	Roy Orbison / Running Scared	243
Jun 12 - Jun 18	Ricky Nelson / Travelin' Man	238
Jun 19 - Jun 25	Pat Boone / Moody River	108
Jun 26 - Jul 9	Gary "U.S." Bonds / Quarter To Three	107
Jul 10 - Aug 27	Bobby Lewis / Tossin' And Turnin'	206
Aug 28 - Sep 3	Joe Dowell / Wooden Heart (Muss I Denn)	148
Sep 4 - Sep 17	The Highwaymen / Michael	181
Sep 18 - Oct 8	Bobby Vee / Take Good Care Of My Baby	317
Oct 9 - Oct 22	Ray Charles / Hit The Road Jack	120
Oct 23 - Nov 5	Dion / Runaround Sue	143
Nov 6 - Dec 10	Jimmy Dean / Big Bad John	139
Dec 11 - Dec 17	The Marvelettes / Please Mr. Postman	219
Dec 18 - Dec 31	The Tokens / The Lion Sleeps Tonight	308

The Year of the Four Seasons

The decline of a Massive star, even if gradual, creates a power vacuum in the universe of pop, and an extended period of chaos almost always follows before the first signs of a new order emerge. Those who practice the science of popstrology are quite naturally intrigued by periods when power is temporarily up for grabs before being grasped by a newly dominant force. But as fascinated as popstrologists are with instances of new and stable structures emerging in a disordered pop universe, they are even more fascinated when the stability of those structures proves to be an illusion.

In this respect, the year of your birth is quite fascinating indeed, for like 1970 and 1980, 1962 was a year in which a popstrologically Fresh force emerged to impose a short-lived order on the universe of pop in the wake of a giant's disappearance. In 1970, it was the Jackson 5 after the breakup of the Beatles, and in 1980, it was Blondie after the death of disco, but in 1962, it was **the Four Seasons** confidently assuming the popstrological throne after the effective disappearance of Elvis Presley.

Nineteen sixty-two was actually the second year to follow the end of Elvis Presley's dominant period, but it was the first in which a truly powerful star emerged to take his place. And that Dominant Star was no flash in the pan. The Four Seasons were a group whose utterly Fresh sound would prove to be a Lasting fixture in the popstrological firmament. Yet in retrospect, we can see that 1962 was very nearly the last year in which a group like the Four Seasons could hope to be anything other than a force of opposition to an as-yet-unseen power gathering across the Atlantic.

Who were they, these Four Seasons, and where did they come from? How did they manage to seize the popstrological throne in the year of your birth, and how does the fact that they did affect you and the other children of 1962? You could spend a lifetime pursuing a full and complete set of answers to these questions, but there is no question where your inquiry will begin: in Newark, New Jersey. It was there, on the banks of the Passaic, that the Four Seasons built their trademark sound out of pieces of doo-wop with a dash of Phil Spector thrown in. And it was there that they hatched their plot to launch the Jersey Invasion of 1962.

Along with **Connie Francis, the Shirelles,** and **Joey Dee and the Starliters,** the Four Seasons were part of a four-pronged attack by the constellation *Jersey Pride* in 1962—an attack that was but one half of a well-orchestrated pincer movement executed in partnership with the constellation *Outerborough*. The goal was to seize control of what seemed at that time to be the command-and-control center of the entire pop universe, 1613 Broadway, New York, New York, aka the Brill Building. With **Neil Sedaka** as their inside man, this blue-collar coalition of stars achieved its objective and assumed the mantle of popstrological power over the tepid resistance of the year's Opposing Star, **Bobby Vinton.** Vinton's hope was to reestablish the constellation *Old Guard* as the gravitational center of American pop, but he fell well short of his goal.

But if the Four Seasons and their compatriots hoped to usher in a lasting era of bridge-and-tunnel dominance, then they fell well short of theirs, too. Should they have been able to look at the

THE DOMINANT STAR
The Four Seasons
- #1 Hits this year: 2
- Weeks at #1 this year: 10
- #1 Hits in Career: 5
- Weeks at #1 in Career: 18

THE OPPOSING STAR
Bobby Vinton
- #1 Hits this year: 1
- Weeks at #1 this year: 4
- #1 Hits in Career: 4
- Weeks at #1 in Career: 12

WILDCARD
Mr. Acker Bilk
- #1 Hits this year: 1
- Weeks at #1 this year: 1
- #1 Hits in Career: 1
- Weeks at #1 in Career: 1

year's Wildcard star, **Mr. Acker Bilk,** and foresee what was about to happen? Probably not, for while Mr. Acker Bilk was British, he was as unrelated to the coming British Invasion as the Four Seasons were themselves, and even if they'd known what was being plotted three thousand miles across the Atlantic, there probably isn't much they could have done about it.

Among the children of the Four Seasons generation, one will find more than a few **all-American success stories,** but one will also find that even the most accomplished children of 1962 have difficulty banishing the **sense of grim foreboding** that takes some of the pleasure out of their every success.

WHAT'S YOUR SIGN?

1962 BIRTHDATES	BIRTHSTAR / BIRTHSONG	PAGE
Jan 1 - Jan 6	The Tokens / The Lion Sleeps Tonight	308
Jan 7 - Jan 20	Chubby Checker / The Twist	121
Jan 21 - Feb 10	Joey Dee and the Starliters / Peppermint Twist–Part I	139
Feb 11 - Mar 3	Gene Chandler / Duke Of Earl	119
Mar 4 - Mar 24	Bruce Channel / Hey! Baby	119
Mar 25 - Mar 31	Connie Francis / Don't Break The Heart That Loves You	164
Apr 1 - Apr 14	Shelly Fabares / Johnny Angel	157
Apr 15 - Apr 28	Elvis Presley / Good Luck Charm	255
Apr 29 - May 19	The Shirelles / Soldier Boy	282
May 20 - May 26	Mr. Acker Bilk / Stranger On The Shore	105
May 27 - Jun 30	Ray Charles / I Can't Stop Loving You	120
Jul 1 - Jul 7	David Rose / The Stripper	272
Jul 8 - Aug 4	Bobby Vinton / Roses Are Red (My Love)	318
Aug 5 - Aug 18	Neil Sedaka / Breaking Up Is Hard To Do	278
Aug 19 - Aug 25	Little Eva / The Loco-Motion	209
Aug 26 - Sep 8	Tommy Roe / Sheila	268
Sep 9 - Oct 13	The Four Seasons / Sherry	163
Oct 14 - Oct 27	Bobby "Boris" Pickett and the Crypt-Kickers / Monster Mash	252
Oct 28 - Nov 10	The Crystals / He's A Rebel	133
Nov 11 - Dec 15	The Four Seasons / Big Girls Don't Cry	163
Dec 16 - Dec 31	The Tornados / Telstar	309

1963

The Year of Jimmy Gilmer and the Fireballs

When times change dramatically, when strong and unfamiliar forces enter the pop-cultural arena and upset all of the taken-for-granted power structures—these are times that practically cry out for the interpretive power of popstrology. But popstrologists will tell you that it is the times of misleading calm that precede periods of dramatic unrest that sometimes yield the most fascinating popstrological material.

The year of your birth was one of those times, poised between the rock and roll revolution of the late 1950s and the British Invasion of the mid-1960s. It was the final year of flourishing for a wide range of popstrological species that would soon be rendered extinct, yet no one knew this at the time—not the pop stars marked for extinction and certainly not the white American teenagers whose tastes and longings were the popstrological firmament's animating force. It was the culture of these teens to which John Lennon was referring in 1970 when he described Americans prior to the arrival of the Beatles as "walking around in f*ckin' Bermuda shorts, with Boston crew cuts and stuff in [their] teeth." Broad though that generalization might have been about a time when a certain segment of Americans was busy marching on Washington and confronting George Wallace in the schoolhouse door, it has the unmistakable ring of popstrological truth. With the civil rights movement in full swing,

and the American advisory mission in Vietnam poised to expand, 1963 might be viewed in sociopolitical terms as a pot about to boil. In popstrological terms, however, the year of your birth was more like a groovy weenie roast at a carefree beach party.

Yes, 1963 was the Year of **Jimmy Gilmer and the Fireballs**—a star whose one and only #1 hit, *Sugar Shack*, is capable even to this day of causing otherwise clear-thinking adults to break out in dance moves reminiscent of a Frankie Avalon–Annette Funicello movie. In strictly lyrical terms, *Sugar Shack* probably encouraged thousands of creepy young men to believe that attractive waitresses yearn to date and marry their obsessively loyal customers. But in musical terms, the biggest hit of 1963 and the Dominant Star responsible for it spread nothing but youthful enthusiasm and joy.

Few songs in the popstrological canon can match *Sugar Shack* for the way it captured the vibe of a specific time and place, and the way it can take one back to that time and place in two bars or less. But the world that elevated Jimmy Gilmer and the Fireballs as its Dominant Star was not going to last much longer. The instrument of its undoing would not arrive until January of 1964, but the death of President Kennedy was an obvious portent of change, as was the subsequent rise of 1963's Opposing Star, a woman who was just what her record said she was: a **Singing Nun**.

Considering what lay ahead just a

THE DOMINANT STAR
Jimmy Gilmer and the Fireballs
- #1 Hits this year: 1
- Weeks at #1 this year: 5
- #1 Hits in Career: 1
- Weeks at #1 in Career: 5

THE OPPOSING STAR
The Singing Nun
- #1 Hits this year: 1
- Weeks at #1 this year: 4
- #1 Hits in Career: 1
- Weeks at #1 in Career: 4

WILDCARD
Kyu Sakamoto
- #1 Hits this year: 1
- Weeks at #1 this year: 4
- #1 Hits in Career: 1
- Weeks at #1 in Career: 4

few short weeks after 1963 came to a close, popstrologists can't help but feel wistful contemplating the popstrological firmament as it stood in the year of your birth. Historians must feel the same way when contemplating the Caribs of Hispaniola in early autumn of 1492, and paleontologists must feel something similar when contemplating the dinosaurs of the Yucatán on some fateful morning toward the end of the Cretaceous era. But just because the likes of Jimmy Gilmer went on about their business in blissful ignorance of a world-altering horror hurtling toward them through time and space, that doesn't mean that the Jimmy Gilmer generation will someday do the same. No, popstrology predicts that the children of 1963 will be a savvier bunch than the stars who ruled the universe of pop at the time of their birth. **Joyful and high-spirited? Sometimes. Naïve and doomed? Never.**

WHAT'S YOUR SIGN?

1963 BIRTHDATES	BIRTHSTAR / BIRTHSONG	PAGE
Jan 1 - Jan 5	The Tornados / Telstar	309
Jan 6 - Jan 19	Steve Lawrence / Go Away Little Girl	203
Jan 20 - Feb 2	The Rooftop Singers / Walk Right In	271
Feb 3 - Feb 23	Paul and Paula / Hey Paula	249
Feb 24 - Mar 16	The Four Seasons / Walk Like A Man	163
Mar 17 - Mar 23	Ruby and the Romantics / Our Day Will Come	275
Mar 24 - Apr 20	The Chiffons / He's So Fine	123
Apr 21 - May 11	Little Peggy March / I Will Follow Him	217
May 12 - May 25	Jimmy Soul / If You Wanna Be Happy	291
May 26 - Jun 8	Leslie Gore / It's My Party	173
Jun 9 - Jun 29	Kyu Sakamoto / Sukiyaki	276
Jun 30 - Jul 13	The Essex / Easier Said Than Done	154
Jul 14 - Jul 27	Jan and Dean / Surf City	192
Jul 28 - Aug 3	The Tymes / So Much In Love	313
Aug 4 - Aug 24	(Little) Stevie Wonder / Fingertips	328
Aug 25 - Sep 14	The Angels / My Boyfriend's Back	92
Sep 15 - Oct 5	Bobby Vinton / Blue Velvet	318
Oct 6 - Nov 9	Jimmy Gilmer and the Fireballs / Sugar Shack	172
Nov 10 - Nov 16	Nino Tempo and April Stevens / Deep Purple	306
Nov 17 - Nov 30	Dale and Grace / I'm Leaving It Up To You	135
Dec 1 - Dec 28	The Singing Nun / Dominique	288
Dec 29 - Dec 31	Bobby Vinton / There! I've Said It Again	318

1964

The First Year of the Beatles

I t was the year in which the British Invasion was launched, and as such it is a year that has taken on a shorthand significance akin to that of such historical watershed years as 1492 and 1929. But 1964 in popstrological terms was about more than just the arrival of a star so Massive that it redefined and realigned the entire pop universe. Without question, the central significance of 1964 can be found in its very label: the First Year of **the Beatles**. But 1964 did not play out quite as simply as it is often remembered, and the epic defeat of the old by the new was not the only popstrological battle that it witnessed.

There! I've Said It Again was the song that dominated the pop universe at the dawn of 1964. It was the third of four #1 hits by the Polish Prince, **Bobby Vinton**, who had joined the popstrological elite in 1962 as the first new star in four years to join the seemingly defunct constellation *Old Guard*. Vinton flourished in the strangely sedate world of the pre-Beatles sixties, driving home the point through his popstrological success that while rock and roll was here to stay, the rock and roll of Chubby Checker and Neil Sedaka was something that a throwback like Vinton stood a fighting chance against. Perhaps Perry Como and Pat Boone sat in their respective armchairs somewhere and watched the early weeks of 1964 unfold, thinking to themselves, "That punk Elvis Presley thought he had us beat, but look who's in the catbird's seat now."

And then it explodes. One minute the pop universe seems to be breaking their way, and the next minute the Beatles descend on America with their

funny hair and their funny accents and it's like the Big Bang of Elvis all over again. And to add insult to injury for the *Old Guard*, the Beatles conquer the world playing music inspired by and sometimes literally lifted from the very sources that Pat Boone *et al.* had tried to extinguish in the late 1950s: Little Richard, Chuck Berry, Fats Domino. The Beatles would take a popstrological breather in late 1964, during which Bobby Vinton would manage a farewell appearance, but the title of the song with which he did it says it all: *Mr. Lonely*.

Yes, the Beatles had driven a stake through the heart of that undead creature known as mainstream pop. Its death rattle could be heard in 1964 in the voices of **Louis Armstrong** and **Dean Martin**, who breathed their last as valiant warriors facing the British head-on. But outside the brief midsummer sorties by **the Beach Boys** and **the Four Seasons** and the almost inexplicable charge of the Canadian **Lorne Greene**, that was it for North American resistance to the British Invasion.

Well, North American male resistance, anyway, for the British Invasion did not defeat, but rather brought out the best in America's women and girls. Shining as the year's Opposing Star were **the Supremes**, too naïve or simply too damn excellent to shrink from the challenge of squaring off against the Beatles. The forces of the constellation *Les Girls* did heroic work in preserving a degree of respect for American pop in 1964, and they did it while locked in an intramural battle for the hearts and minds of America's teenage girls—a battle between the good-girl enticements of the Supremes' *Baby Love*

THE DOMINANT STAR
The Beatles
- #1 Hits this year: 6
- Weeks at #1 this year: 18+
- #1 Hits in Career: 20
- Weeks at #1 in Career: 54

THE OPPOSING STAR
The Supremes
- #1 Hits this year: 3
- Weeks at #1 this year: 8
- #1 Hits in Career: 12
- Weeks at #1 in Career: 22

WILDCARD
Louis Armstrong
- #1 Hits this year: 1
- Weeks at #1 this year: 1
- #1 Hits in Career: 1
- Weeks at #1 in Career: 1

and **the Dixie Cups'** *Chapel Of Love* and the tragic, bad-girl allure of **the Shangri-Las'** *Leader Of The Pack*.

They were born in the midst of a dramatic conquest of the popstrological firmament by a foreign invader, but what of it? Do the children of the first Beatles generation bear the mark of the conquerors, or the mark of the conquered? They probably bear the mark of something in between—of the type who **joins many battles in life** without winning any decisively but also **without ever being utterly defeated.**

WHAT'S YOUR SIGN?

1964 BIRTHDATES	BIRTHSTAR / BIRTHSONG	PAGE
Jan 1 - Jan 25	Bobby Vinton / There! I've Said It Again	318
Jan 26 - Mar 14	The Beatles / I Want To Hold Your Hand	101
Mar 15 - Mar 28	The Beatles / She Loves You	101
Mar 29 - May 2	The Beatles / Can't Buy Me Love	101
May 3 - May 9	Louis Armstrong / Hello, Dolly!	94
May 10 - May 23	Mary Wells / My Guy	321
May 24 - May 30	The Beatles / Love Me Do	101
May 31 - Jun 20	The Dixie Cups / Chapel Of Love	144
Jun 21 - Jun 27	Peter and Gordon / World Without Love	251
Jun 28 - Jul 11	The Beach Boys / I Get Around	101
Jul 12 - Jul 25	The Four Seasons / Rag Doll	163
Jul 26 - Aug 8	The Beatles / A Hard Day's Night	101
Aug 9 - Aug 15	Dean Martin / Everybody Loves Somebody	218
Aug 16 - Aug 29	The Supremes / Where Did Our Love Go	301
Aug 30 - Sep 19	The Animals / House Of The Rising Sun	93
Sep 20 - Oct 10	Roy Orbison / Oh, Pretty Woman	243
Oct 11 - Oct 24	Manfred Mann / Do Wah Diddy Diddy	216
Oct 25 - Nov 21	The Supremes / Baby Love	301
Nov 22 - Nov 28	The Shangri-Las / Leader Of The Pack	280
Nov 29 - Dec 5	Lorne Greene / Ringo	175
Dec 6 - Dec 12	Bobby Vinton / Mr. Lonely	318
Dec 13 - Dec 19	The Supremes / Come See About Me	301
Dec 20 - Dec 31	The Beatles / I Feel Fine	101

1965

The Second Year of the Beatles

The positive and negative impact of the pop stars on the population of mortals over whom they rule is the bread-and-butter focus of popstrology, but there are times when the most important popstrological vector of all is the impact that a tremendously successful pop star can have on its fellow pop stars, and even on itself.

In 1965, we have a year in which the critical importance of popstrological feedback is clearly on display. For in the year of your birth, in their second year as pop's sole and unchallenged superpower, **the Beatles** found themselves ruling the pop universe not just in their own name, but in the name of a British expeditionary force that had reached a sufficient size and scope to begin presenting problems to its leader even beyond those posed by the insane and unabating Beatlemania of the nation they invaded.

The Second Year of the Beatles was, in many ways, the final year of the Beatles as traditional pop stars and the first year of the Beatles as reinventors of what that term even meant. In 1964, they'd conquered the pop universe on the strength of personal charisma and sheer craftsmanship, playing American-inspired rock and roll better and with more passion than almost any American star of popstrological proportions had played it since 1959. In 1964, the girls screamed, the flashbulbs flashed, and the Beatles smiled for the cameras, but in 1965, while the girls and the flashbulbs screamed and flashed, the Beatles dropped their winning smiles and turned inward.

I Feel Fine was the Beatles song to which 1965 opened, but by year's end, the mood was rather different. *Help!* was

how John Lennon put it, with characteristic bluntness, while Paul's lament was naturally more melodic: *Yesterday*. The Beatles had had enough of the hysteria they'd created, but perhaps that wasn't the only thing that pushed them away from the universal appeal of *She Loves You* and toward the somewhat less accessible *I Am The Walrus*. Through the lens of popstrology, it seems clear that what forced the Beatles to reinvent themselves, and reinvent pop music in the process, was their need to escape an association with certain of their countrymen who were now their popstrological neighbors in the constellation *Britvasion*.

You do something new, it's very cool at first, and then it catches on. It's still cool for a while after other folks start doing it, but then something changes. Now there are some really uncool folks doing it, too, and instead of feeling cool yourself, you begin to feel: well, if you're a child of 1965, you probably know exactly how you begin to feel. **The Rolling Stones**, **Wayne Fontana and the Mindbenders**—even **Petula Clark** and **the Dave Clark Five** probably didn't bother the Beatles much as they rode the Beatles' coattails to popstrological stardom. But **Freddie and the Dreamers** and the year's Opposing Star, **Herman's Hermits**? No, the teenage Herman and his deeply unserious Hermits were probably too much for the Beatles to bear, and so they set about distancing themselves from the invasion they had once led so enthusiastically.

The Beatles would chart their own course through the remainder of the sixties, but if they took inspiration from anyone, it was probably from the man who inspired **the Byrds**, too: Bob Dylan. The powerful Wildcard star of

THE DOMINANT STAR
The Beatles
- #1 Hits this year: 5
- Weeks at #1 this year: 11+
- #1 Hits in Career: 20
- Weeks at #1 in Career: 54

THE OPPOSING STAR
Herman's Hermits
- #1 Hits this year: 1
- Weeks at #1 this year: 3
- #1 Hits in Career: 2
- Weeks at #1 in Career: 4

WILDCARD
The Byrds
- #1 Hits this year: 2
- Weeks at #1 this year: 4
- #1 Hits in Career: 2
- Weeks at #1 in Career: 4

1965 invented folk rock when they set a Dylan song to a rock and roll instrumental track, but the Beatles invented a whole series of new sounds and began to push the boundaries of pop by taking Dylan's dense, deep, and often inscrutable lyrics as inspiration for their own.

Will the children of 1965 all reach a point in their professional lives when they begin to loathe the crowd that surrounds them, and even to loathe themselves for being surrounded? Of course they will, everybody does. What sets the children of the second Beatles generation apart, popstrologically speaking, is their ability to **take that loathing and channel it into some rather positive reinvention.**

WHAT'S YOUR SIGN?

1965 BIRTHDATES	BIRTHSTAR / BIRTHSONG	PAGE
Jan 1 - Jan 9	The Beatles / I Feel Fine	101
Jan 10 - Jan 16	The Supremes / Come See About Me	301
Jan 17 - Jan 30	Petula Clark / Downtown	126
Jan 31 - Feb 13	The Righteous Brothers / You've Lost That Lovin' Feelin'	265
Feb 14 - Feb 27	Gary Lewis and the Playboys / This Diamond Ring	207
Feb 28 - Mar 6	The Temptations / My Girl	306
Mar 7 - Mar 20	The Beatles / Eight Days A Week	101
Mar 21 - Apr 3	The Supremes / Stop! In The Name Of Love	301
Apr 4 - Apr 17	Freddie and the Dreamers / I'm Telling You Now	167
Apr 18 - Apr 24	Wayne Fontana and the Mindbenders / Game Of Love	162
Apr 25 - May 15	Herman's Hermits / Mrs. Brown You've Got A Lovely Daughter	181
May 16 - May 22	The Beatles / Ticket To Ride	101
May 23 - Jun 5	The Beach Boys / Help Me Rhonda	101
Jun 6 - Jun 12	The Supremes / Back In My Arms Again	301
Jun 13 - Jun 19	The Four Tops / I Can't Help Myself	164
Jun 20 - Jun 26	The Byrds / Mr. Tambourine Man	113
Jun 27 - Jul 3	The Four Tops / I Can't Help Myself	164
Jul 4 - Jul 31	The Rolling Stones / (I Can't Get No) Satisfaction	270
Aug 1 - Aug 7	Herman's Hermits / I'm Henry VIII, I Am	181
Aug 8 - Aug 28	Sonny and Cher / I Got You Babe	289
Aug 29 - Sep 18	The Beatles / Help!	101
Sep 19 - Sep 25	Barry McGuire / Eve Of Destruction	227
Sep 26 - Oct 2	The McCoys / Hang On Sloopy	225
Oct 3 - Oct 30	The Beatles / Yesterday	101
Oct 31 - Nov 13	The Rolling Stones / Get Off Of My Cloud	270
Nov 14 - Nov 27	The Supremes / I Hear A Symphony	301
Nov 28 - Dec 18	The Byrds / Turn! Turn! Turn!	113
Dec 19 - Dec 25	The Dave Clark Five / Over And Over	137
Dec 26 - Dec 31	Simon and Garfunkel / Sounds Of Silence	284

1966

The Third Year of the Beatles

Nineteen sixty-six was dominated by the most powerful group the pop universe has ever seen, but it was dominated rather weakly in terms of quantifiable chart success. And yet in some ways, the Third Year of the Beatles reflects the true extent of the Beatles' popstrological power more clearly than any of the four separate years in which they were the popstrologically Dominant Star.

Two songs—*We Can Work It Out* and *Paperback Writer*—and five total weeks at #1 were all the Beatles managed in quantitative popstrological terms in 1966. This would be a monumental achievement, of course, for almost any other pop star, but for a group that had managed five #1 hits for more than eleven weeks a year earlier, it would seem to represent a significant decline in popstrological influence. But did it really? When one takes a closer look at the stars of 1966 whose competition kept the Beatles' dominance in check, one realizes that far from showing that the power of the Beatles was declining, they show the Beatles' power to shape the universe around them to be undiminished, or even increasing.

Nineteen sixty-six was not 1965. It was not a year in which the direct influence of the Beatles was manifested in a starmaking frenzy within the constellation *Britvasion*. No, the biggest Britvaders to work alongside the Beatles in 1966—**Petula Clark** and **the Rolling Stones**—were not new to the popstrological firmament in the year of your birth, and the only new stars who did join the constellation *Britvasion* that year were the relatively Minor **Donovan** and the absolutely Forgotten **New Vaudeville Band**. No longer was the most obvious indirect impact of the

Beatles their ability to drag others along on their coattails. In 1966, the most obvious indirect impact of the Beatles was the way in which they'd encouraged a wild array of Fresh new stars to follow their example and pull themselves up by their own bootstraps.

The Beatles were part of the constellation *Britvasion*, but the Beatles were also part of the constellation *Fresh Breeze*, and it is that aspect of their popstrological alignment that came to the fore in 1966 in the form of stars like **the Troggs** and **? and the Mysterians**. Along with **Nancy Sinatra, Lou Christie, the (Young) Rascals, the Mamas and the Papas**, and Donovan, those two groups were part of an astonishing burst of starmaking activity in the constellation *Fresh Breeze* in 1966. And better than any of those groups, the Troggs and ? and the Mysterians exemplified the new breed of band that came into existence only because the Beatles forced every would-be rock star back into the garage in 1964 to unlearn everything that pre-Beatles, early-sixties pop had taught them. As unpolished as they were popstrologically Fresh, these bands made the year of your birth quite possibly the most thrilling of all four Years of the Beatles.

And yet a star that was not Fresh but profoundly, uncannily, disturbingly Familiar also appeared in the popstrological firmament of 1966, and once again, it was a group whose rise would not have been possible without the influence of the Beatles. They were **the Monkees**, the Opposing Star of 1966, but soon to be the Dominant Star of 1967 in an act of patricide unparalleled in popstrological history.

Popstrological Freshness is indeed a

THE DOMINANT STAR
The Beatles
- #1 Hits this year: 2
- Weeks at #1 this year: 5
- #1 Hits in Career: 20
- Weeks at #1 in Career: 54

THE OPPOSING STAR
The Monkees
- #1 Hits this year: 2
- Weeks at #1 this year: 2
- #1 Hits in Career: 3
- Weeks at #1 in Career: 12

WILDCARD
Staff Sergeant Barry Sadler
- #1 Hits this year: 1
- Weeks at #1 this year: 5
- #1 Hits in Career: 1
- Weeks at #1 in Career: 5

powerful force in defining the generation born in the Third Year of the Beatles, but the countervailing influence of this most Familiar of all stars indicates that the children of 1966 will fulfill the **unlikely dual destiny** of being known for their **ability to recycle** just as much as for their marked **ability to create**.

And as for the influence of their birth year's Wildcard star—well, all popstrologists can say is that they hope the scary militarism of **Staff Sergeant Barry Sadler** will manifest itself in some very unexpected way, perhaps by inspiring the children of 1966 to support their local troops of Boy and Girl Scouts rather than their local militia.

WHAT'S YOUR SIGN?

1966 BIRTHDATES	BIRTHSTAR / BIRTHSONG	PAGE
Jan 1	Simon and Garfunkel / Sounds Of Silence	284
Jan 2 - Jan 15	The Beatles / We Can Work It Out	101
Jan 16 - Jan 22	Simon and Garfunkel / Sounds Of Silence	284
Jan 23 - Jan 29	The Beatles / We Can Work It Out	101
Jan 30 - Feb 12	Petula Clark / My Love	126
Feb 13 - Feb 19	Lou Christie / Lightnin' Strikes	125
Feb 20 - Feb 26	Nancy Sinatra / These Boots Are Made For Walking	287
Feb 27 - Apr 2	Staff Sergeant Barry Sadler / The Ballad Of The Green Berets	275
Apr 3 - Apr 23	The Righteous Brothers / (You're My) Soul And Inspiration	265
Apr 24 - Apr 30	The Young Rascals / Good Lovin'	259
May 1 - May 21	The Mamas and the Papas / Monday, Monday	214
May 22 - Jun 4	Percy Sledge / When A Man Loves A Woman	288
Jun 5 - Jun 18	The Rolling Stones / Paint It Black	270
Jun 19 - Jun 25	The Beatles / Paperback Writer	101
Jun 26 - Jul 2	Frank Sinatra / Strangers In The Night	286
Jul 3 - Jul 9	The Beatles / Paperback Writer	101
Jul 10 - Jul 23	Tommy James and the Shondells / Hanky Panky	191
Jul 24 - Aug 6	The Troggs / Wild Thing	311
Aug 7 - Aug 27	The Lovin' Spoonful / Summer In The City	211
Aug 28 - Sep 3	Donovan / Sunshine Superman	146
Sep 4 - Sep 17	The Supremes / You Can't Hurry Love	301
Sep 18 - Oct 8	The Association / Cherish	95
Oct 9 - Oct 22	The Four Tops / Reach Out I'll Be There	164
Oct 23 - Oct 29	? and the Mysterians / 96 Tears	88
Oct 30 - Nov 5	The Monkees / Last Train To Clarksville	235
Nov 6 - Nov 12	Johnny Rivers / Poor Side Of Town	266
Nov 13 - Nov 26	The Supremes / You Keep Me Hangin' On	301
Nov 27 - Dec 3	The New Vaudeville Band / Winchester Cathedral	239
Dec 4 - Dec 10	The Beach Boys / Good Vibrations	101
Dec 11 - Dec 24	The New Vaudeville Band / Winchester Cathedral	239
Dec 25 - Dec 31	The Monkees / I'm A Believer	235

The Year of the Monkees

Popstrology seeks the truth, pure and simple—the truth about the power of the pop stars, and the truth about the power of the mortals who decide which pop stars to embrace and which to shun. And if in this search for truth certain less-than-flattering truths about *ourselves* are revealed, then this is simply the nature of popstrology, a discipline that privileges honesty over ego-stroking.

Of all the years in the popstrological era, there is none—not even during the depths of 1980s *Reaganrock* —that goes as deeply to the root of a powerful and vaguely disappointing truth about human nature as the year of your birth does. And what is that truth? That we seem to care a lot less about truth than we do about pleasure.

Nineteen sixty-seven was the year that saw the first successful challenge to the three-year reign of **the Beatles** as popstrological dominators, but more important, 1967 was the year in which America embraced as its Dominant Star a made-for-TV rip-off of the Beatles themselves: **the Monkees**. It was not the first year in which powerful forces of legitimacy and artificiality did battle in the popstrological firmament, but it was the first year in which the forces of artificiality emerged as the hands-down winner.

The Monkees' alignment with the constellation *Artificial Ingredients* certainly marks the children of 1967 as a generation gifted at **deploying smoke and mirrors in the interest of career advancement**, and why should they not make use of this gift proudly? After all, the Monkees may have been fake, but there was nothing even a little

bit fake about their appeal. *I'm A Believer, (I'm Not Your) Steppin' Stone, Pleasant Valley Sunday, Daydream Believer*—you would be hard-pressed to find an honest person who can claim immunity to these and other gems that were written for the Monkees by some of the greatest songwriting talents of the day. Indeed, Carole King and Neil Diamond were but two members of an army of talented professionals who lifted the Monkees into the constellation **Regifted**, but is that further proof of the Monkees' illegitimacy, as some would have it, or is it just a brilliant illustration of the American genius for division of labor and mass production?

Very different answers to that question are likely to be heard from the children of 1967, for their popstrological legacy marks them as a generation likely to struggle with **questions over their own legitimacy**. Their birth year's Opposing Star is very much to thank for this, of course, for the Beatles were the group that made legitimacy the litmus test for rock and roll respectability in the first place. And 1967 was the year in which the Beatles made their opinion known regarding the compatibility of respectability and popstrological success when they chose not to release any singles from the decade's most influential album, *Sgt. Pepper's Lonely Hearts Club Band*.

Yes, the influence of the high and mighty Beatles injects a strong note of self-doubt into the lives of many members of the Monkees generation. "I'm happy being lovable, wholly unoriginal me, but should I be?" these self-doubting Monkees might say. Perhaps that's why so many children of 1967 follow the example of their birth year's Wildcard

THE DOMINANT STAR
The Monkees
- #1 Hits this year: 2
- Weeks at #1 this year: 10
- #1 Hits in Career: 3
- Weeks at #1 in Career: 12

THE OPPOSING STAR
The Beatles
- #1 Hits this year: 3
- Weeks at #1 this year: 3
- #1 Hits in Career: 20
- Weeks at #1 in Career: 54

WILDCARD
Bobbie Gentry
- #1 Hits this year: 1
- Weeks at #1 this year: 4
- #1 Hits in Career: 1
- Weeks at #1 in Career: 4

star, **Bobbie Gentry**, expressing their natural facility with the artificial in a completely respectable way by honing their craft as *Storyteller*s. Indeed, few and far between are the lucky children of the Monkees generation who feel totally at ease with their powerful yet potentially stigmatizing popstrological legacy.

WHAT'S YOUR SIGN?

1967 BIRTHDATES	BIRTHSTAR / BIRTHSONG	PAGE
Jan 1 - Feb 11	The Monkees / I'm A Believer	235
Feb 12 - Feb 25	The Buckinghams / Kind Of A Drag	112
Feb 26 - Mar 4	The Rolling Stones / Ruby Tuesday	270
Mar 5 - Mar 11	The Supremes / Love Is Here And Now You're Gone	301
Mar 12 - Mar 18	The Beatles / Penny Lane	101
Mar 19 - Apr 8	The Turtles / Happy Together	312
Apr 9 - May 6	Nancy and Frank Sinatra / Somethin' Stupid	287
May 7 - May 13	The Supremes / The Happening	301
May 14 - May 27	The Young Rascals / Groovin'	259
May 28 - Jun 10	Aretha Franklin / Respect	165
Jun 11 - Jun 24	The Young Rascals / Groovin'	259
Jun 25 - Jul 22	The Association / Windy	95
Jul 23 - Aug 12	The Doors / Light My Fire	147
Aug 13 - Aug 19	The Beatles / All You Need Is Love	101
Aug 20 - Sep 16	Bobbie Gentry / Ode To Billie Joe	170
Sep 17 - Oct 14	The Box Tops / The Letter	110
Oct 15 - Nov 18	Lulu / To Sir With Love	212
Nov 19 - Nov 25	The Strawberry Alarm Clock / Incense And Peppermints	297
Nov 26 - Dec 23	The Monkees / Daydream Believer	235
Dec 24 - Dec 31	The Beatles / Hello Goodbye	101

The Fourth Year of the Beatles

When people talk about the sixties, as people often do, they generally talk about the tumultuous events and trends that yanked America out of its Eisenhower-Camelot slumber and into a messier, more violent age. And when people talk about the sixties in this way, the year they talk about more than any other is the year of your birth, 1968. Not only was it a year like no other in postwar American history, but it was also a year that has been mythologized like no other in postwar American history.

It's easy to understand why. Look down a list of the historic figures and world events of 1968 and it's like looking at the lyrics of a Billy Joel song—Tet Offensive MLK, RFK and LBJ, Yippies Hippies DNC, Prague Spring and French May. There is no question that if you had a nickel for every time you've watched a video montage of images from 1968 set to the music of Buffalo Springfield's *For What It's Worth*, you'd have an awful lot of nickels, but in popstrological terms, none of this really matters. *For What It's Worth* came out in 1967, not 1968, and Buffalo Springfield never even made it to #1. But more to the point, the popstrological firmament had its own issues to deal with in 1968, and it reflected only dimly the turmoil that was taking place down on planet Earth.

Hello Goodbye was the #1 song that greeted the dawn of 1968, a year in which **the Beatles** would essentially stop saying hello to one another and start saying good-bye to the universe of pop. *Hey Jude* was the song that elevated them into position as the popstro-

logical firmament's Dominant Star for the very last time, and certainly the children of 1968 are the happier for it. Indeed, with all the potentially depressing vibrations associated with the stars of 1968, the re-assuring pick-me-up of *Hey Jude* is a true popstrological blessing in the lives of the fourth Beatles generation. The depressing vibrations in question derive mainly from **Otis Redding**, **the Doors**, and **Marvin Gaye**, but also from one fourth of the Beatles themselves. What do all these stars have in common? They are all members of the constellation *Tragic Demise*. They all exited the popstrological (and temporal) universe well before their time, which may explain why so many children of 1968 act as if they received **no parental guidance** at critical junctures in their social development.

As for the year's Opposing Star, there was nothing tragic about him, but there was an augury of something significant in his rise, and whether it was something significantly good or significantly bad depends on your taste. What made the rise of **Herb Alpert** so significant had nothing to do with Herb himself and everything to do with the man who wrote his breakthrough hit, *This Guy's In Love With You*. That man was Burt Bacharach, and though he'd been kicking around the margins of the popstrological firmament for years, it was not until the year of your birth that his Whitebread influence was truly felt and the imminent rise of the constellation *Lite & White* was foreshadowed.

But what of all that social upheaval going on in 1968? Was there really no sign of it at all in the popstrological firmament? No, there was *some* sign of it, in the form of **the Rascals**' *People Got*

THE DOMINANT STAR
The Beatles
- #1 Hits this year: 2
- Weeks at #1 this year: 11
- #1 Hits in Career: 20
- Weeks at #1 in Career: 54

THE OPPOSING STAR
Herb Alpert
- #1 Hits this year: 1
- Weeks at #1 this year: 4
- #1 Hits in Career: 2
- Weeks at #1 in Career: 6

WILDCARD
Jeannie C. Riley
- #1 Hits this year: 1
- Weeks at #1 this year: 1
- #1 Hits in Career: 1
- Weeks at #1 in Career: 1

To Be Free. The thing about *People Got To Be Free*, though, is that it was so groovy and upbeat that it was hard to tell what exactly it was saying the people needed to be free from, or needed to be free to do. Free to protest an unjust war on the streets of Chicago? Or free to wear short skirts and f*ck-me pumps to parent-teacher night, as the year's Wildcard star called for in your birth year's most direct commentary on American social strife in 1968?

No, the popstrological firmament in the year of your birth was nowhere near as tumultuous as the temporal world into which you came. And while it's probable that this fact made the fourth and final Beatles generation a bit more **detached from reality** than the average popstrological class, it probably also made the children of 1968 capable of **weathering life's storms with an inner calm** that can only come from not noticing the storms in the first place.

WHAT'S YOUR SIGN?

1968 BIRTHDATES	BIRTHSTAR / BIRTHSONG	PAGE
Jan 1 - Jan 13	The Beatles / Hello Goodbye	101
Jan 14 - Jan 27	John Fred and His Playboy Band / Judy In Disguise (With Glasses)	166
Jan 28 - Feb 3	The Lemon Pipers / Green Tambourine	205
Feb 4 - Mar 9	Paul Mauriat / Love Is Blue	221
Mar 10 - Apr 6	Otis Redding / (Sittin' On) The Dock Of The Bay	260
Apr 7 - May 11	Bobby Goldsboro / Honey	173
May 12 - May 25	Archie Bell and the Drells / Tighten Up	103
May 26 - Jun 15	Simon and Garfunkel / Mrs. Robinson	284
Jun 16 - Jul 13	Herb Alpert / This Guy's In Love With You	91
Jul 14 - Jul 27	Hugh Masekela / Grazing In The Grass	220
Jul 28 - Aug 10	The Doors / Hello, I Love You	147
Aug 11 - Sep 14	The (Young) Rascals / People Got To Be Free	259
Sep 15 - Sep 21	Jeannie C. Riley / Harper Valley P.T.A.	265
Sep 22 - Nov 23	The Beatles / Hey Jude	101
Nov 24 - Dec 7	The Supremes / Love Child	301
Dec 8 - Dec 31	Marvin Gaye / I Heard It Through The Grapevine	168

The Year of the Fifth Dimension

History is written by the winners, so the stories we hear of the past and the images we conjure of it always reflect a slanted and incomplete picture of what it was actually like to live through a given moment in history. Popstrology cannot hope to change this, of course, but popstrology can call attention to certain truths about our past that have been selectively edited from our collective memory.

The year of your birth provides one of the best opportunities for popstrologists to do just that, for 1969 was a year of unparalleled importance in the self-written cultural history of the baby-boom generation. But self-written histories are always to be mistrusted, particularly when written in the medium of movie and television sound tracks, and the children of this watershed year would do well to realize that while 1969 may indeed have been the year of Woodstock, it was also the Year of the **Fifth Dimension**.

They rose into position as the Dominant Star of 1969 on the strength of *Aquarius/Let The Sunshine In*, a medley of songs from the Broadway musical *Hair*. But the Fifth Dimension were not entirely new—they were the same group that had given the world *Up, Up And Away* less than two years earlier, and that's what made them such a perfect fit for *Aquarius*. *Hair* was a musical that served up the counterculture with enough popstrological Whitebread to make it palatable to mainstream audiences, and the Fifth Dimension pushed even farther in that direction. They may have joined the popstrological elite by proclaiming the dawning of the age of Aquarius, but the arrival of the Fifth Dimension heralded something rather

different: the dawning of the age of *Lite & White*.

There are those who call the founding of the constellation *Lite & White* by a group of African Americans ironic, but be that as it may, the formation of that mighty constellation in the final year of the sixties bestows upon the Fifth Dimension generation an **ability to find islands of blissful calm in times of trouble**. And while the line between blissful calm and stifling staleness may be a fine one, it's a line that anyone born in a year that saw the rise of **B. J. Thomas** and *Raindrops Keep Fallin' On My Head* is destined to walk.

But for all their Liteness and popstrological Whiteness, 1969's Dominant Star represented something else, too, the significance of which would become clear only with the further passage of time. Within the Fifth Dimension were the soon-to-be wife and husband Marilyn McCoo and Billy Davis, Jr., future popstrological *Spin-Offs* and one of only three undivorced couples in the constellation *Holy Matrimony*. Divorce rates skyrocketed within and without the popstrological firmament in the first decade of their young lives, but the children of 1969—and especially the double Fifth Dimensions born directly under the year's Dominant Star—possess an unmistakable knack for establishing **relationships capable of weathering the storms** that might tear weaker bonds asunder.

It is safe to say, though, that this powerful **potential for stability** will continually be tested, for 1969 was a year that saw more discord than it did harmony. Reduced for the second time to the status of Opposing Star, **the**

THE DOMINANT STAR
The Fifth Dimension
- #1 Hits this year: 2
- Weeks at #1 this year: 9
- #1 Hits in Career: 22
- Weeks at #1 in Career: 9

THE OPPOSING STAR
The Beatles
- #1 Hits this year: 2
- Weeks at #1 this year: 6
- #1 Hits in Career: 20
- Weeks at #1 in Career: 54

WILDCARD
Zager and Evans
- #1 Hits this year: 1
- Weeks at #1 this year: 6
- #1 Hits in Career: 1
- Weeks at #1 in Career: 6

Beatles focused most of their energy on preparing to break up, and this fact lingers like a grim portent over a generation otherwise inclined to **look on the bright side** and regard their **strong relationships** as unassailable. And if that ill omen leads some members of the Fifth Dimension toward a nearly **paralytic fear of what the future may hold**, it wouldn't be entirely surprising, considering the powerful, dystopian influence of **Zager and Evans** as their birth year's Wildcard.

WHAT'S YOUR SIGN?

1969 BIRTHDATES	BIRTHSTAR / BIRTHSONG	PAGE
Jan 1 - Jan 25	Marvin Gaye / I Heard It Through The Grapevine	168
Jan 26 - Feb 8	Tommy James and the Shondells / Crimson And Clover	191
Feb 9 - Mar 8	Sly and the Family Stone / Everyday People	289
Mar 9 - Apr 5	Tommy Roe / Dizzy	268
Apr 6 - May 17	The Fifth Dimension / Aquarius • Let The Sunshine In	159
May 18 - Jun 21	The Beatles / Get Back	101
Jun 22 - Jul 5	Henry Mancini / Love Theme From Romeo & Juliet	214
Jul 6 - Aug 16	Zager and Evans / In The Year 2525 (Exordium & Terminus)	331
Aug 17 - Sep 13	The Rolling Stones / Honky Tonk Women	270
Sep 14 - Oct 11	The Archies / Sugar, Sugar	94
Oct 12 - Oct 25	The Temptations / I Can't Get Next To You	306
Oct 26 - Nov 1	Elvis Presley / Suspicious Minds	255
Nov 2 - Nov 22	The Fifth Dimension / Wedding Bell Blues	159
Nov 23 - Nov 29	The Beatles / Come Together • Something	101
Nov 30 - Dec 13	Steam / Na Na Hey Hey Kiss Him Goodbye	295
Dec 14 - Dec 20	Peter, Paul and Mary / Leaving On A Jet Plane	251
Dec 21 - Dec 27	The Supremes / Someday We'll Be Together	301
Dec 28 - Dec 31	B. J. Thomas / Raindrops Keep Fallin' On My Head	307

The Year of the Jackson 5

Popstrology can sometimes be a subtle affair, requiring the most nuanced and painstaking analysis to reveal the hidden forces at work on an individual, a relationship, or an entire year in pop history. At times, however, one is confronted by popstrological forces so bold and so strong that they convey their meaning as plainly and obviously as the leather motorcycle jacket on George Michael's back.

The year that ushered in the seventies in all their strange musical glory provides a vivid example of the latter case, filled as it is with **stunning shifts in the balance of popstrological power**. It may not compare with 1964 for obvious drama, but in retrospect, the appearance of **the Jackson 5** coupled with **the popstrological end of the Beatles, the Supremes, and Simon and Garfunkel** signaled the start of a new era just as surely. This tidal shift in the popstrological currents marks 1970 as a crossroads year, transitional in nature yet striking in its own right for the sudden and powerful impact of the brothers Jackson.

Besides providing an optimistic, sugar-funk injection to **a year otherwise ripe with potential causes of mopery** (*viz.* the aforementioned breakups; Kent State; the deaths of Janis Joplin and Jimi Hendrix), the Jackson 5 can also take credit for helping to bring a powerful and generally positive popstrological entity back to life. Along with the year's other Fresh new sibling force, **the Carpenters**, the Jackson 5 reinvigorated the stagnant constellation *Gene Pool*, setting the scene for that constellation's epic zenith eight years later. The *Gene Pool* is well known for

its encouragement of strong family values, so the children of 1970 will tend to share a strong capacity to **give and receive unconditional love** and display **unshakable loyalty** to their closest friends and loved ones. They will also tend to descend rather easily into **slap fights, tattling, and bickering**, but then a degree of dysfunction is always to be expected in a familial context.

As neatly and attractively packaged as they were, the Jacksons represented not just a new aesthetic, but a newfound focus on aesthetics—a combination clearly reflected in the group's presence among the stars of the constellation *Hot Hairdo*. The Jacksons' look and massive popularity certainly contributed to rising Afros among African Americans but also may have played a role in that hairdo's dubious crossing of racial boundaries in the years to come.

Counterbalancing the lighthearted, youthful glee of the Jackson 5 was their Opposing Star, **Simon and Garfunkel**. Their farewell effort, *Bridge Over Troubled Water*, was 1970's single biggest hit, and it imbued those born in this year with a **potential for slightly melancholy gravitas**. When *Bridge Over Troubled Water* proved to be Simon and Garfunkel's last breath, so to speak, it placed on the otherwise carefree Jackson 5 generation the burden of being among the last to feel the direct influence of the constellation *Folkie* and the vaguely bummed-out attitude generally associated with it.

But the biggest stars rarely burn out without first casting off some of their energy into the pop universe. And indeed, in 1970 we see the first solo appearances of former Supreme **Diana Ross** and former Beatle **George**

THE DOMINANT STAR
The Jackson 5
- #1 Hits this year: 4
- Weeks at #1 this year: 10
- #1 Hits in Career: 4
- Weeks at #1 in Career: 10

THE OPPOSING STAR
Simon and Garfunkel
- #1 Hits this year: 1
- Weeks at #1 this year: 6
- #1 Hits in Career: 3
- Weeks at #1 in Career: 10

WILDCARD
The Guess Who
- #1 Hits this year: 1
- Weeks at #1 this year: 3
- #1 Hits in Career: 1
- Weeks at #1 in Career: 3

Harrison, heralding the birth of yet another new popstrological grouping: the constellation *Spin-Off*, an entity known to inspire the kind of ambivalence that comes with realizing that while life may always go on, we sometimes know that the best is already behind us.

Like the Jackson 5 themselves, the micro-generation born in this pivotal year **may exhibit enormous gifts at a tender age.** But the bright lights of youthful success can unmooor even the greatest of talents, so take heed, children of 1970, and never forget that for every Michael, there is also a Jermaine. Not to mention a Tito.

WHAT'S YOUR SIGN?

1970 BIRTHDATES	BIRTHSTAR / BIRTHSONG	PAGE
Jan 1 - Jan 24	B. J. Thomas / Raindrops Keep Fallin' On My Head	307
Jan 25 - Jan 31	The Jackson 5 / I Want You Back	189
Feb 1 - Feb 7	Shocking Blue / Venus	282
Feb 8 - Feb 21	Sly and the Family Stone / Thank You (Falettinme Be Mice Elf Agin) • Everybody Is A Star	289
Feb 22 - Apr 4	Simon and Garfunkel / Bridge Over Troubled Water	284
Apr 5 - Apr 18	The Beatles / Let It Be	101
Apr 19 - May 2	The Jackson 5 / ABC	189
May 3 - May 23	The Guess Who / American Woman	176
May 24 - Jun 6	Ray Stevens / Everything Is Beautiful	295
Jun 7 - Jun 20	The Beatles / The Long And Winding Road	101
Jun 21 - Jul 4	The Jackson 5 / The Love You Save	189
Jul 5 - Jul 18	Three Dog Night / Mama Told Me (Not To Come)	307
Jul 19 - Aug 15	The Carpenters / Close To You	116
Aug 16 - Aug 22	Bread / Make It With You	111
Aug 23 - Sep 12	Edwin Starr / War	293
Sep 13 - Oct 3	Diana Ross / Ain't No Mountain High Enough	273
Oct 4 - Oct 10	Neil Diamond / Cracklin' Rosie	142
Oct 11 - Nov 14	The Jackson 5 / I'll Be There	189
Nov 15 - Dec 5	The Partridge Family / I Think I Love You	248
Dec 6 - Dec 19	Smokey Robinson and the Miracles / Tears Of A Clown	267
Dec 20 - Dec 31	George Harrison / My Sweet Lord	178

1971

The Year of Carole King

Popstrologists are not immune to the feelings that many casual observers get when they look at our shared pop-cultural past and marvel at the baffling choices their fellow humans have sometimes made. After all, the list of now-appreciated geniuses who were ignored by those who came before us is at least as long as the list of now-derided lightweights who were embraced. On the other hand, there have been times in the past when the truly deserving and the richly rewarded were one and the same, and popstrologists encourage anyone trapped in the what-were-they-thinking mind-set to look back on these times with appreciative admiration.

Of all the years in the popstrological era, the year of your birth is perhaps the best example of a time when the judgment of those who came before us should be held up for praise rather than scorn. For 1971 was a year in which a woman who could easily have remained popstrologically invisible despite her foundational contributions to the universe of pop was enthusiastically and deservedly embraced instead. It was the Year of Carole King—a year ruled by the quintessential star in the constellation *Invisible Hand* and a year that saw the birth of a micro-generation more than willing to **invest its labor in the projects of others, even at the expense of its own public recognition.**

But mortal pop fans were not the only ones to embrace the Dominant Star of 1971, for no popstrological coronation was ever greeted with such enthusiasm *within* the popstrological firmament as Carole King's. If you run down the list of stars active in the pop universe of 1971, you can clearly see why, for it is difficult to find a star on that list who has never recorded a song written by Carole King. **Tony Orlando and Dawn**? Yes. **Rod Stewart** and **Isaac Hayes**? Yes and yes. **George Harrison** and **Paul McCartney**? As the Beatles, yes. And that is without even mentioning the profound debt of gratitude owed to Carole King by her fellow stars of 1971 **James Taylor** and **Donny Osmond**, whose only #1 hits were written by the woman who dominated the year of their popstrological emergence.

Yes, even Donny Osmond owed his popstrological existence to Carole King, so what then, you may ask, made him the Opposing Star of 1971? Rising into the popstrological firmament by covering a cover of one of Carole King's songs. Being as far removed from her substance-before-style vibe as is humanly possible. Being a dimple-cheeked boy from the constellation *Teen Idol* when she was a worldly wise woman of twenty-nine with more than a decade of toil in the constellation *Invisible Hand* already behind her. Suffice it to say that the popstrological vibrations generated by the Dominant and Opposing Stars of 1971 simply couldn't have been more different.

But clearly there was little in the way of overt resistance to Carole King in the year of her ascendancy. Indeed, the rather striking aesthetic counterpoint played by the year's Wildcard, Isaac Hayes, was the closest thing to discord in this year of feel-good harmony. There is one clear area of conflict visible in the lives of the Carole King generation, but it is a conflict generated by Ms. King herself in her double-sided #1 hit *It's Too Late/I Feel The Earth Move.*

THE DOMINANT STAR
Carole King
- #1 Hits this year: 1
- Weeks at #1 this year: 5
- #1 Hits in Career: 1
- Weeks at #1 in Career: 5

THE OPPOSING STAR
Donny Osmond
- #1 Hits this year: 1
- Weeks at #1 this year: 3
- #1 Hits in Career: 1
- Weeks at #1 in Career: 3

WILDCARD
Isaac Hayes
- #1 Hits this year: 1
- Weeks at #1 this year: 2
- #1 Hits in Career: 1
- Weeks at #1 in Career: 2

Love lost and passion regained in a little bit less than six and a half minutes is what that record managed. Powerful messages indeed for those seeking **romantic recovery, redemption, or rekindling**. But one must marvel also at the easy switch from heartbreak to horniness in the simple flip from A side to B. There are **undeniable therapeutic powers** in Carole King's sole entry in the popstrological canon as a performer, but for the micro-generation born under its influence, there may also be a tendency to grow all too comfortable in what might ultimately prove to be an **unfulfilling pattern of serial monogamy**.

WHAT'S YOUR SIGN?

1971 BIRTHDATES	BIRTHSTAR / BIRTHSONG	PAGE
Jan 1 - Jan 16	George Harrison / My Sweet Lord	178
Jan 17 - Feb 6	Tony Orlando and Dawn / Knock Three Times	243
Feb 7 - Mar 13	The Osmonds / One Bad Apple	244
Mar 14 - Mar 27	Janis Joplin / Me And Bobby McGee	195
Mar 28 - Apr 10	The Temptations / Just My Imagination (Running Away With Me)	306
Apr 11 - May 22	Three Dog Night / Joy To The World	307
May 23 - Jun 5	The Rolling Stones / Brown Sugar	270
Jun 6 - Jun 12	Honey Cone / Want Ads	183
Jun 13 - Jul 17	Carole King / It's Too Late • I Feel The Earth Move	199
Jul 18 - Jul 24	Paul Revere and the Raiders / Indian Reservation (The Lament Of The Cherokee Reservation Indian)	262
Jul 25 - Jul 31	James Taylor / You've Got A Friend	304
Aug 1 - Aug 28	The Bee Gees / How Can You Mend A Broken Heart	102
Aug 29 - Sep 4	Paul McCartney / Uncle Albert • Admiral Halsey	222
Sep 5 - Sep 25	Donny Osmond / Go Away Little Girl	244
Sep 26 - Oct 30	Rod Stewart / Maggie May	296
Oct 31 - Nov 13	Cher / Gypsys, Tramps & Thieves	122
Nov 14 - Nov 27	Isaac Hayes / Theme From Shaft	179
Nov 28 - Dec 18	Sly and the Family Stone / Family Affair	289
Dec 19 - Dec 31	Melanie / Brand New Key	229

The Year of Gilbert O'Sullivan

There have been numerous dramatic struggles for power in the pop universe—struggles for dominance between stars with radically different popstrological agendas. But there have also been times when the most significant conflict in the popstrological firmament wasn't between two stars, per se, but between two radically different moods represented by stars whose personal significance, in the grand scheme of things, is rather limited.

The year of your birth was one such year, for it was a year in which the critical power dynamics did not involve any of the truly Massive and Lasting names in the popstrological firmament. It was a year in which the interplay between the Dominant Star, **Gilbert O'Sullivan**, and his Opposing Star, **Johnny Nash**, was far from antagonistic, yet the conflict inherent in that interplay raises a significant question for those born in this year of emotional uncertainty: How will they deal with life's inevitable setbacks? Will they greet every bump in life's road with debilitating self-pity, or will they take their hard knocks with look-on-the-bright-side optimism?

This is the question that hangs over the heads of the children of 1972—a popstrological generation trapped between the competing and divergent lessons of Gilbert O'Sullivan's *Alone Again (Naturally)* and Johnny Nash's *I Can See Clearly Now*. Without question, you will find among the children of 1972 many who adhere fairly strictly to the popstrological advice seemingly offered by Mr. O'Sullivan: "When life hands you lemons, make sure everyone in the world knows about it. Make sure that no oppor-

tunity to mention it passes you by, and make sure to wallow in the delicious misery of it for as long as humanly possible." Less common are those who tend toward the other extreme, reflecting the example of Mr. Nash by emerging from every tragedy or deep-blue funk quickly and with a fresh-start spirit of nearly pharmaceutical proportions. Somewhat common are those who reside somewhere in the middle, but interestingly, most common of all are those who fluctuate seemingly without pattern between the Nashian and O'Sullivanian setback-response modes depending on the specific nature of the setback they suffer.

But the divergent philosophies of O'Sullivan and Nash were not the only powerful ideas competing for mind share when the children of 1972 came forth onto the earth. In fact, 1972 was a year filled with deeply felt proclamations from proponents of belief systems ranging from feminism and multiculturalism (**Helen Reddy, Three Dog Night**) to onanism and adultery (**Chuck Berry, Billy Paul**). As anyone who has spent much time around the children of 1972 can tell you, it's not all that uncommon for some of them to practice all of the above quite religiously. But what's even more uncommon is to find a child of 1972 who is not willing to stand up and proclaim his or her philosophy or lifestyle choice loudly and proudly.

And make no mistake, every possible philosophy and lifestyle choice has an adherent within the Gilbert O'Sullivan generation, up to and possibly including the lifestyle choice of the murderous rat-loving protagonist in the song that launched the Wildcard star of 1972 into the popstrological firmament, *Ben*.

THE DOMINANT STAR
Gilbert O'Sullivan
- #1 Hits this year: 1
- Weeks at #1 this year: 6
- #1 Hits in Career: 1
- Weeks at #1 in Career: 6

THE OPPOSING STAR
Johnny Nash
- #1 Hits this year: 1
- Weeks at #1 this year: 4
- #1 Hits in Career: 1
- Weeks at #1 in Career: 4

WILDCARD
Michael Jackson
- #1 Hits this year: 1
- Weeks at #1 this year: 1
- #1 Hits in Career: 10
- Weeks at #1 in Career: 23

WHAT'S YOUR SIGN?

1972 BIRTHDATES	BIRTHSTAR / BIRTHSONG	PAGE
Jan 1 - Jan 8	Melanie / Brand New Key	229
Jan 9 - Feb 5	Don McLean / American Pie	228
Feb 6 - Feb 12	Al Green / Let's Stay Together	175
Feb 13 - Mar 11	Nilsson / Without You	240
Mar 12 - Mar 18	Neil Young / Heart Of Gold	330
Mar 19 - Apr 8	America / A Horse With No Name	92
Apr 9 - May 20	Roberta Flack / The First Time Ever I Saw Your Face	160
May 21 - May 27	The Chi-Lites / Oh Girl	124
May 28 - Jun 3	The Staple Singers / I'll Take You There	292
Jun 4 - Jun 24	Sammy Davis, Jr. / The Candy Man	138
Jun 25 - Jul 1	Neil Diamond / Song Sung Blue	142
Jul 2 - Jul 22	Bill Withers / Lean On Me	327
Jul 23 - Aug 19	Gilbert O'Sullivan / Alone Again (Naturally)	245
Aug 20 - Aug 26	Looking Glass / Brandy (You're A Fine Girl)	210
Aug 27 - Sep 9	Gilbert O'Sullivan / Alone Again (Naturally)	245
Sep 10 - Sep 16	Three Dog Night / Black & White	307
Sep 17 - Oct 7	Mac Davis / Baby Don't Get Hooked On Me	138
Oct 8 - Oct 14	Michael Jackson / Ben	191
Oct 15 - Oct 28	Chuck Berry / My Ding-A-Ling	105
Oct 29 - Nov 25	Johnny Nash / I Can See Clearly Now	237
Nov 26 - Dec 2	The Temptations / Papa Was A Rollin' Stone	306
Dec 3 - Dec 9	Helen Reddy / I Am Woman	261
Dec 10 - Dec 30	Billy Paul / Me And Mrs. Jones	249
Dec 31	Carly Simon / You're So Vain	283

1973

The Year of Roberta Flack

When popstrologists look back to the middle years of the 1970s, they see a pop universe that was at once fragile and vital—vulnerable, as history would show, to a sound or aesthetic with imperial ambitions, but reveling for the meantime in the glorious chaos that only the absence of such a power could possibly create.

But when popstrologists look back specifically to the year 1973, they see a pop universe in which fragility and vitality were in play not just on a geopolitical level, but on an intimate level, too. For 1973 was a year whose Dominant Star made a career of expressing emotional and sexual fragility, but whose Opposing Star made a career out of something significantly more vital.

Roberta Flack ascended the popstrological throne in 1973 on the strength of *Killing Me Softly*, a song that accomplished the formidable task of matching or even surpassing the aching sincerity of her first #1 hit. Few would have thought *The First Time Ever I Saw Your Face* beatable in this category, yet Roberta Flack did more than just surpass herself with her second #1 hit. She also achieved a level of **sensitive-soul vulnerability** that would never again be approached in the balance of the popstrological era. No, never again would Roberta Flack's trademark vulnerability make its way into the highest reaches of the pop universe, unless you regard John Denver's *I'm Sorry*, Barry Manilow's *Mandy*, or David Soul's *Don't Give Up On Us* as expressing a vulnerability that is plausibly sincere. Most popstrologists do not, which is why most popstrologists agree that members

of the Roberta Flack generation are especially prone to being **reduced to puddles of emotion** by situations that might leave others as cold and hard as ice. Most popstrologists also agree that the children of 1973 cannot help but reflect in some fashion the **curious sexlessness** of Roberta Flack's otherwise passionate oeuvre. Yes, even her 1975 hit *Feel Like Makin' Love* could easily have been called *Feel Like Makin' Love (But Not Right Now)*, and this marks the Roberta Flack generation as one that, at the very least, will have difficulty achieving great love with those with whom they easily achieve great sex.

But counterbalancing all that is 1973's Opposing Star, **Grand Funk Railroad**—loud and proud purveyors of *Mustache Rock* and unapologetic spokesmen for the lifestyle traditionally associated with that constellation. "I am a sensitive and vulnerable soul," Roberta Flack might say, to which Grand Funk Railroad might reply, "That's great—*We're An American Band*." And what did it mean to be an American band in 1973 in GFR's particular sector of the pop universe? It meant all sorts of good things: liquor, groupies, trashed hotel rooms. It meant strumming more than just hearts with your fingers as you cut a swath through the "chiquitas from Omaha" and the "sweet, sweet Connie's from Little Rock." And most of all, it meant little time or inclination to feel love or regret along the way.

Or at least that's what Grand Funk Railroad would have us think it meant, and popstrologically speaking, that's all that matters. Born in a year when both **extremes in the sexual and emotional spectrum** were clearly on display, the children of 1973 may go

THE DOMINANT STAR
Roberta Flack
- #1 Hits this year: 1
- Weeks at #1 this year: 5
- #1 Hits in Career: 3
- Weeks at #1 in Career: 12

THE OPPOSING STAR
Grand Funk Railroad
- #1 Hits this year: 1
- Weeks at #1 this year: 1
- #1 Hits in Career: 2
- Weeks at #1 in Career: 3

WILDCARD
George Harrison
- #1 Hits this year: 1
- Weeks at #1 this year: 1
- #1 Hits in Career: 3
- Weeks at #1 in Career: 6

one way, and they may go another, but if they try to achieve a kind of equilibrium in those aspects of their lives, that equilibrium is likely to be rather dynamic indeed.

WHAT'S YOUR SIGN?

1973 BIRTHDATES	BIRTHSTAR / BIRTHSONG	PAGE
Jan 1 - Jan 20	Carly Simon / You're So Vain	283
Jan 21 - Jan 27	Stevie Wonder / Superstition	328
Jan 28 - Feb 17	Elton John / Crocodile Rock	194
Feb 18 - Mar 17	Roberta Flack / Killing Me Softly With His Song	160
Mar 18 - Mar 24	The O'Jays / Love Train	242
Mar 25 - Mar 31	Roberta Flack / Killing Me Softly With His Song	160
Apr 1 - Apr 14	Vicki Lawrence / The Night The Lights Went Out In Georgia	204
Apr 15 - May 12	Tony Orlando and Dawn / Tie A Yellow Ribbon Round The Ole Oak Tree	243
May 13 - May 19	Stevie Wonder / You Are The Sunshine Of My Life	328
May 20 - May 26	The Edgar Winter Group / Frankenstein	151
May 27 - Jun 23	Paul McCartney (and Wings) / My Love	222
Jun 24 - Jun 30	George Harrison / Give Me Love (Give Me Peace On Earth)	178
Jul 1 - Jul 14	Billy Preston / Will It Go Round In Circles	256
Jul 15 - Jul 28	Jim Croce / Bad, Bad Leroy Brown	132
Jul 29 - Aug 11	Maureen McGovern / The Morning After	227
Aug 12 - Aug 18	Diana Ross / Touch Me In The Morning	273
Aug 19 - Sep 1	Stories / Brother Louie	297
Sep 2 - Sep 8	Marvin Gaye / Let's Get It On	168
Sep 9 - Sep 15	Helen Reddy / Delta Dawn	261
Sep 16 - Sep 22	Marvin Gaye / Let's Get It On	168
Sep 23 - Sep 29	Grand Funk Railroad / We're An American Band	174
Sep 30 - Oct 13	Cher / Half-Breed	122
Oct 14 - Oct 20	The Rolling Stones / Angie	270
Oct 21 - Nov 3	Gladys Knight and the Pips / Midnight Train To Georgia	200
Nov 4 - Nov 17	Eddie Kendricks / Keep On Truckin'	197
Nov 18 - Nov 24	Ringo Starr / Photograph	293
Nov 25 - Dec 8	The Carpenters / Top Of The World	116
Dec 9 - Dec 22	Charlie Rich / The Most Beautiful Girl	264
Dec 23 - Dec 31	Jim Croce / Time In A Bottle	132

1974

The Year Without a Dominator

It can be said to a certain degree of the decade as a whole, but of all the years in the 1970s, none was as fabulously chaotic as the year of your birth. It was the Year Without a Dominator—the one and only year in the popstrological era in which no single star attempted to dominate the universe of pop. And glorious disorder, quite naturally, was the result. **John Denver** leading into **Roberta Flack** and **Paul Anka** into **Eric Clapton**? **Barbra Streisand** sandwiched between **Ringo Starr** and **Barry White**? When else but in the seventies could one have witnessed such sequences of glorious incongruity, and when else but in 1974 could one have witnessed so many of them?

This may be difficult for you to believe, but one prominent member of the critical establishment has actually called 1974 the worst year for pop music in American history, but that just goes to show you how easily one's mind can become corrupted by a false ideology like rock criticism. One likes to believe that a claim as patently absurd as this one about a year that produced both *Seasons In The Sun* and *Kung Fu Fighting* could never be taken seriously, but popstrologists find it troubling nonetheless, for what kind of message does it send the world about the children of 1974?

For their part, popstrologists make it a rule to steer clear of terms like "best" and "worst" when discussing the pop-musical past, but rules are made to be broken, and you'll have little difficulty finding a popstrologist who is willing to proclaim 1974 one of the best of all possible years in which to have been born. At least for those who are **comfortable going through life without a ruling philosophy** or any hope of finding one that's offered to them by their peers even remotely acceptable.

Yes, it is both a blessing and a curse to have been born during the only year in the popstrological era in which no single star rose to a position of dominance. Certainly no generation can match the birth class of 1974 for **open-mindedness, tolerance of alternative lifestyles, and respect for the rights of the individual**, but it can also be said that none can match them for **disunity of purpose**, either.

There are those in this world who chafe and bridle against any kind of dominating power, and then there are those who only thrive under the firm hand of an unquestioned leader. It should be abundantly clear by now which of these types is likely to be better represented among the children of 1974.

THE DOMINANT STAR
None

THE OPPOSING STAR
None

WILDCARD
None

WHAT'S YOUR SIGN?

1974 BIRTHDATES	BIRTHSTAR / BIRTHSONG	PAGE
Jan 1 - Jan 5	Jim Croce / Time In A Bottle	132
Jan 6 - Jan 12	Steve Miller / The Joker	232
Jan 13 - Jan 19	Al Wilson / Show And Tell	326
Jan 20 - Jan 26	Ringo Starr / You're Sixteen	293
Jan 27 - Feb 2	Barbra Streisand / The Way We Were	298
Feb 3 - Feb 9	Barry White (as Love Unlimited Orchestra) / Love's Theme	322
Feb 10 - Feb 23	Barbra Streisand / The Way We Were	298
Feb 24 - Mar 16	Terry Jacks / Seasons In The Sun	189
Mar 17 - Mar 23	Cher / Dark Lady	122
Mar 24 - Mar 30	John Denver / Sunshine On My Shoulders	141
Mar 31 - Apr 6	Blue Swede / Hooked On A Feeling	106
Apr 7 - Apr 13	Elton John / Bennie And The Jets	194
Apr 14 - Apr 27	MFSB / TSOP	230
Apr 28 - May 11	Grand Funk Railroad / The Loco-Motion	174
May 12 - Jun 1	Ray Stevens / The Streak	295
Jun 2 - Jun 8	Paul McCartney (and Wings) / Band On The Run	222
Jun 9 - Jun 22	Bo Donaldson and the Heywoods / Billy, Don't Be A Hero	145
Jun 23 - Jun 29	Gordon Lightfoot / Sundown	208
Jun 30 - Jul 6	Hues Corporation / Rock The Boat	186
Jul 7 - Jul 20	George McCrae / Rock Your Baby	226
Jul 21 - Aug 3	John Denver / Annie's Song	141
Aug 4 - Aug 10	Roberta Flack / Feel Like Makin' Love	160
Aug 11 - Aug 17	Paper Lace / The Night Chicago Died	246
Aug 18 - Sep 7	Paul Anka / (You're) Having My Baby	93
Sep 8 - Sep 14	Eric Clapton / I Shot The Sheriff	125
Sep 15 - Sep 21	Barry White / Can't Get Enough Of Your Love, Babe	322
Sep 22 - Sep 28	Andy Kim / Rock Me Gently	198
Sep 29 - Oct 12	Olivia Newton-John / I Honestly Love You	240
Oct 13 - Oct 19	Billy Preston / Nothing From Nothing	256
Oct 20 - Oct 26	Dionne Warwick and the Spinners / Then Came You	320
Oct 27 - Nov 2	Stevie Wonder / You Haven't Done Nothin'	328
Nov 3 - Nov 9	Bachman-Turner Overdrive / You Ain't Seen Nothing Yet	98
Nov 10 - Nov 16	John Lennon / Whatever Gets You Thru The Night	206
Nov 17 - Nov 30	Billy Swan / I Can Help	302
Dec 1 - Dec 14	Carl Douglas / Kung Fu Fighting	147
Dec 15 - Dec 21	Harry Chapin / Cat's In The Cradle	120
Dec 22 - Dec 28	Helen Reddy / Angie Baby	261
Dec 29 - Dec 31	Elton John / Lucy In The Sky With Diamonds	194

The Year of Elton John

The year previous may have appeared popstrologically chaotic, but its chaos was not without a certain logic. For it became clear in 1975 that the disorder of 1974 had simply been preparing the way for a new kind of ruler to ascend the popstrological throne—not a Dominant Star who would impose a new and rigorous order, but a Dominant Star who could make glorious disorder *function* as order.

And how perfectly fitting that the arranger of disorder who emerged as the Dominant Star of 1975 was the fabulously uncategorizable creature **Elton John**. With Elton as its king—or shall we say, monarch—the popstrological firmament suddenly made sense in a way that it hadn't since the demise of the Beatles. Nineteen seventy-five's popstrological veerings from **KC and the Sunshine Band** to **Captain and Tennille** and from **Olivia Newton-John** to **Earth, Wind & Fire** may appear at first glance to have been random and disorderly, but on closer scrutiny, one can clearly see the entire year as a deconstruction of Elton John himself, whose massive output in his mid-seventies heyday covered nearly all of the stylistic ground in which the aforementioned stars worked.

It was **a year of wild diversity**—a year in which nonconformity was the official popstrological credo, as evidenced by the significant activity in the constellation *Sui Generis*. Elton John was not the only one-of-a-kind star from that constellation of incomparables to work his magic in the pop universe of 1975, for under his benevolent and nonjudgmental rule two more icons of individuality emerged: the unstoppable **John Denver** and the inexplicable **Barry Manilow**.

When you consider that the children of the Elton John generation were born at a time when millions of Americans who had never been within fifty miles of a working farm were walking around humming about haystacks and flapjacks under the influence of John Denver's *Thank God I'm A Country Boy*, it should be no mystery why they are such **enemies of traditional boundaries and barriers** and such **nonsticklers for plausibility** in matters of identity construction.

Yes, the popstrological firmament of 1975 was a vibrant and ever-changing place, but not all of the changes afoot at the time were moving in the direction of glorious entropy. For well beneath the radar, a group with less innocent ambitions was doing its best to merge the diametrically opposed forces of *Mustache Rock* and *Lite & White* into a hybrid form with which it could rule the universe of pop. Six years later, a very different popstrological entity called *Reaganrock* would manage this seemingly impossible feat in dramatic fashion, but 1975's Opposing Star, **the Eagles**, managed only to soften what used to be the hard edge of their home constellation, *Mustache Rock*.

But the Eagles' efforts to seize power in a time of popstrological freedom also managed to mark some within the Elton John generation with a **tendency to reject the freewheeling ways** of their peers. The effect of **Van McCoy**, 1975's popstrological Wildcard and member of the *Disco Ball* vanguard, was probably enough to blunt that tendency in some, but insofar as the Eagles' failed power grab paved the way for the future empire of *Reaganrock*, it can safely be said that some **enemies of freedom** among the children of 1975 will enjoy a disturbing degree of success.

THE DOMINANT STAR
Elton John
- #1 Hits this year: 3
- Weeks at #1 this year: 7
- #1 Hits in Career: 6
- Weeks at #1 in Career: 15

THE OPPOSING STAR
The Eagles
- #1 Hits this year: 2
- Weeks at #1 this year: 2
- #1 Hits in Career: 5
- Weeks at #1 in Career: 5

WILDCARD
Van McCoy
- #1 Hits this year: 1
- Weeks at #1 this year: 1
- #1 Hits in Career: 1
- Weeks at #1 in Career: 1

WHAT'S YOUR SIGN?

1975 BIRTHDATES	BIRTHSTAR / BIRTHSONG	PAGE
Jan 1 - Jan 11	Elton John / Lucy In The Sky With Diamonds	194
Jan 12 - Jan 18	Barry Manilow / Mandy	216
Jan 19 - Jan 25	The Carpenters / Please Mr. Postman	116
Jan 26 - Feb 1	Neil Sedaka / Laughter In The Rain	278
Feb 2 - Feb 8	Ohio Players / Fire	242
Feb 9 - Feb 15	Linda Ronstadt / You're No Good	271
Feb 16 - Feb 22	Average White Band / Pick Up The Pieces	97
Feb 23 - Mar 1	The Eagles / Best Of My Love	149
Mar 2 - Mar 8	Olivia Newton-John / Have You Never Been Mellow	240
Mar 9 - Mar 15	Doobie Brothers / Black Water	146
Mar 16 - Mar 22	Frankie Valli / My Eyes Adored You	315
Mar 23 - Mar 29	Labelle / Lady Marmalade	202
Mar 30 - Apr 5	Minnie Riperton / Lovin' You	266
Apr 6 - Apr 19	Elton John / Philadelphia Freedom	194
Apr 20 - Apr 26	B. J. Thomas / (Hey Won't You Play) Another Somebody Done Somebody Wrong Song	307
Apr 27 - May 17	Tony Orlando and Dawn / He Don't Love You (Like I Love You)	243
May 18 - May 24	Earth, Wind & Fire / Shining Star	150
May 25 - May 31	Freddy Fender / Before The Next Teardrop Falls	159
Jun 1 - Jun 7	John Denver / Thank God I'm A Country Boy	141
Jun 8 - Jun 14	America / Sister Golden Hair	92
Jun 15 - Jul 12	Captain and Tennille / Love Will Keep Us Together	114
Jul 13 - Jul 19	Paul McCartney (and Wings) / Listen To What The Man Said	222
Jul 20 - Jul 26	Van McCoy / The Hustle	224
Jul 27 - Aug 2	The Eagles / One Of These Nights	149
Aug 3 - Aug 16	The Bee Gees / Jive Talkin'	102
Aug 17 - Aug 23	Hamilton, Joe Frank and Reynolds / Fallin' In Love	177
Aug 24 - Aug 30	KC and the Sunshine Band / Get Down Tonight	196
Aug 31 - Sep 13	Glen Campbell / Rhinestone Cowboy	113
Sep 14 - Sep 20	David Bowie / Fame	109
Sep 21 - Sep 27	John Denver / I'm Sorry	141
Sep 28 - Oct 4	David Bowie / Fame	109
Oct 5 - Oct 25	Neil Sedaka / Bad Blood	278
Oct 26 - Nov 15	Elton John / Island Girl	194
Nov 16 - Nov 22	KC and the Sunshine Band / That's The Way (I Like It)	196
Nov 23 - Dec 13	Silver Convention / Fly Robin Fly	283
Dec 14 - Dec 20	KC and the Sunshine Band / That's The Way (I Like It)	196
Dec 21 - Dec 27	The Staple Singers / Let's Do It Again	292
Dec 28 - Dec 31	Bay City Rollers / Saturday Night	100

The Year of Rod Stewart

Four score and seven years before the Gettysburg Address, the Founding Fathers brought forth a nation conceived in liberty and dedicated to the proposition that all men are created equal. Two hundred years into the grand experiment, liberty was all the rage in the nation they had founded, but liberty from the burden of conceiving children was perhaps it most popular expression. And as for equality—well, never was it clearer than in America's bicentennial year that all men are *not* created equal.

Yes, 1976 was a year in which freedom rang throughout this great nation and in the popstrological firmament as well, where the constellation *Disco Ball* had yet to become a tyrannical power. It was the pop universe at its democratic best, the year of your birth, with power being shared not quite equally, but certainly peacefully by all of the decade's major constellations. From the constellation *Shaking Booty*, there came *Love Machine (Part 1)* by the Miracles and from *Mustache Rock* there came *Rock 'N Me* by Steve Miller. From the constellation *Power Couple* there came *Don't Go Breaking My Heart* by Elton John and Kiki Dee, and from the deceptively sultry constellation *Lite & White*, there came both the weepy *If You Leave Me Now* by Chicago and the steamy *Afternoon Delight* by Starland Vocal Band. The sexual revolution was in full boom, and love was in the air. Up and down the AM dial, it was love and sex and sex and love, and up among the stars of the popstrological firmament, things were no different.

But to look at the state of popstrological affairs in 1976 and conclude that

the micro-generation born in that year must rank among the most **amorous and sexualized** would be a bit too simple—not inaccurate, necessarily, but definitely too simple. It's certainly true that 1976 was the Year of **Rod Stewart**, pop's ultimate white male seducer, but 1976 was a year defined not simply by the reign of its Dominant Star, but by a dialectic between Rod Stewart's hypersexuality and the hyposexuality of the year's Opposing Star, **Barry Manilow**.

Sometimes an immigrant is better able than a native to appreciate all that his new country has to offer, and in the year of your birth, Rod Stewart was an immigrant who did just that. He had left the U.K. definitively in 1975 to take up residence in America, and it's safe to say that he liked what he found when he got here. The European settlers of an earlier century saw the promise of America as residing in its ample virgin wildness, and so did Rod Stewart, only he meant it a bit more literally. Back in Scotland, Rod expressed his sexuality in folkish, countryish rock songs like *Maggie May*, about the emotional ambivalence surrounding his complicated relationship with a woman of a certain age. But here in the States, Rod let his inhibitions run wild, working his way toward the disco *Da Ya Think I'm Sexy?* by way of the slick and commercial *Tonight's The Night*. To paraphrase the basic gist of that song—1976's biggest: *"Don't you hesitate, my virgin child / Spread your wings and I'll come inside for a while."* Yes, Rod Stewart the Lovelorn had given way to Rod Stewart the Lustful, and his entry into the constellation *Shape-Shifter* was not far behind.

But then there is the interesting case

THE DOMINANT STAR
Rod Stewart
- #1 Hits this year: 1
- Weeks at #1 this year: 8
- #1 Hits in Career: 3
- Weeks at #1 in Career: 17

THE OPPOSING STAR
Barry Manilow
- #1 Hits this year: 1
- Weeks at #1 this year: 1
- #1 Hits in Career: 3
- Weeks at #1 in Career: 3

WILDCARD
C. W. McCall
- #1 Hits this year: 1
- Weeks at #1 this year: 1
- #1 Hits in Career: 1
- Weeks at #1 in Career: 1

of Barry Manilow, a man who could not have been created more unequal to Rod Stewart, but nonetheless a man with his own animal charms. It was a rather different audience that Barry made melt with songs like *Mandy* and this year's *I Write The Songs*, but no one can deny that that audience did melt. Barry Manilow was no Rod Stewart, but that's the whole point. He proved how sexy a popstrologically Not Sexy star could be to a certain segment of the world, and his presence in the pop universe of 1976 explains why the micro-generation born in that year may **not necessarily express its rampant sexuality** in the ways one normally expects. Particularly if they fall under the influence of the vehicular cryptosexuality of the year's Wildcard: the trucka-rap pioneer **C. W. McCall.**

WHAT'S YOUR SIGN?

1976 BIRTHDATES	BIRTHSTAR / BIRTHSONG	PAGE
Jan 1 - Jan 3	Bay City Rollers / Saturday Night	100
Jan 4 - Jan 10	C. W. McCall / Convoy	222
Jan 11 - Jan 17	Barry Manilow / I Write The Songs	216
Jan 18 - Jan 24	Diana Ross / Theme From Mahogany (Do You Know Where You're Going To)	293
Jan 25 - Jan 31	Ohio Players / Love Rollercoaster	242
Feb 1 - Feb 21	Paul Simon / 50 Ways To Leave Your Lover	284
Feb 22 - Feb 28	Rhythm Heritage / Theme From S.W.A.T.	263
Feb 29 - Mar 6	The Miracles / Love Machine (Part 1)	233
Mar 7 - Mar 27	The Four Seasons / December, 1963 (Oh, What A Night)	164
Mar 28 - Apr 24	Johnnie Taylor / Disco Lady	304
Apr 25 - May 1	The Bellamy Brothers / Let Your Love Flow	104
May 2 - May 8	John Sebastian / Welcome Back	277
May 9 - May 15	The Sylvers / Boogie Fever	303
May 16 - May 22	Paul McCartney (and Wings) / Silly Love Songs	222
May 23 - Jun 5	Diana Ross / Love Hangover	273
Jun 6 - Jul 3	Paul McCartney (and Wings) / Silly Love Songs	222
Jul 4 - Jul 17	Starland Vocal Band / Afternoon Delight	292
Jul 18 - Jul 31	Manhattans / Kiss And Say Goodbye	215
Aug 1 - Aug 28	Elton John and Kiki Dee / Don't Go Breaking My Heart	194
Aug 29 - Sep 4	The Bee Gees / You Should Be Dancing	102
Sep 5 - Sep 11	KC and the Sunshine Band / (Shake, Shake, Shake) Your Booty	196
Sep 12 - Oct 2	Wild Cherry / Play That Funky Music	323
Oct 3 - Oct 9	Walter Murphy and The Big Apple Band / A Fifth Of Beethoven	236
Oct 10 - Oct 16	Rick Dees and His Cast of Idiots / Disco Duck	140
Oct 17 - Oct 30	Chicago / If You Leave Me Now	123
Oct 31 - Nov 6	Steve Miller / Rock 'N Me	232
Nov 7 - Dec 31	Rod Stewart / Tonight's The Night	296

1977

The Year of Debby Boone

Popstrology is concerned with exploring both the causes and the ramifications of the victories a given star or a given sound enjoyed at a given moment in time. But popstrology is also concerned with exploring the causes and ramifications of failure, and most especially when failure is obscured by what appears from the outside to be victory.

In the year of your birth, **Debby Boone** and her allies in the constellation *Lite & White* defeated a ragtag coalition of forces representing the constellations *Shaking Booty*, *So-Soul*, and *Mustache Rock*. But popstrologists see the outcome of this contest as quite probably the most misleading victory in the popstrological era. For the ultimate winner of the battle of 1977 was not *Lite & White*, *Mustache Rock*, or the *Shaking Booty*—it was the one significant constellation that spent the majority of the year on the sidelines: the relatively small, seemingly unambitious, but clearly underestimated *Disco Ball*.

But the future course of popstrological events does not change the fact that this was the year in which the constellation *Lite & White* finally assumed the mantle of leadership in a pop universe it had influenced so greatly since the dawn of the 1970s. *Looks Like We Made It*, **Barry Manilow** sang, and it wasn't just his own success or the success of **Mary MacGregor**, **David Soul**, **Barbra Streisand**, and **Debby Boone** that gave his claim the ring of truth. For even nonresidents of Barry's home constellation—stars like **Fleetwood Mac** and even **the Eagles**—were sounding very *Lite & White* indeed in 1977. To be sure, this was still a year of tremen-dous popstrological diversity, but the rise of Debby Boone on the strength of the enormous hit *You Light Up My Life* made an otherwise weak consensus in the direction of Liteness & Whiteness an outright mandate. And it also bestowed upon the micro-generation born under the reign of Pat Boone's daughter an ability to **achieve power without causing pain**, and to **give pleasure without sparking passion**.

But a strong and much-needed balance to the influence of the constellation *Lite & White* on the children of 1977 can be found in the dissenting voice of the year's Opposing Star, **Stevie Wonder**, then fifteen years into his reign in the constellation *So-Soul* and very much at the top of his game. In combination with the sounds emanating from the irrepressible constellation *Shaking Booty* via **Rose Royce** and **KC and the Sunshine Band**, Stevie's *I Wish* and *Sir Duke* did much to counteract the slow-dance woodenness of *You Light Up My Life*, injecting the otherwise Whitebread Debby Boone generation with a **healthy dose of popstrological Soul**.

Yes, Debby Boone was the victor in the battle for popstrological dominance in 1977, but the spoils of battle do not always go to the victors, as a quick glance at the second half of 1977 clearly reveals. It was during Barry Manilow's midsummer reign, while the forces of *Lite & White* were celebrating their apparent victory and everyone else was busy watching the movies that launched **Bill Conti** and the Wildcard star **Meco**, that a family by the name of Gibb introduced its youngest member to the world, and in spectacular fashion. The transfer of his older brothers' loyalty to the *Disco Ball* in 1976

THE DOMINANT STAR
Debby Boone
- #1 Hits this year: 1
- Weeks at #1 this year: 10
- #1 Hits in Career: 1
- Weeks at #1 in Career: 10

THE OPPOSING STAR
Stevie Wonder
- #1 Hits this year: 2
- Weeks at #1 this year: 4
- #1 Hits in Career: 8
- Weeks at #1 in Career: 14

WILDCARD
Meco
- #1 Hits this year: 1
- Weeks at #1 this year: 2
- #1 Hits in Career: 1
- Weeks at #1 in Career: 2

had not seemed all that important at the time, but when Andy Gibb gained entry into the same constellation in July of 1977, and when folks got a chance to hear that new sound track album by **the Bee Gees**, it became clear that a popstrological coup d'état had taken place.

WHAT'S YOUR SIGN?

1977 BIRTHDATES	BIRTHSTAR / BIRTHSONG	PAGE
Jan 1	Rod Stewart / Tonight's The Night	296
Jan 2 - Jan 8	Marilyn McCoo and Billy Davis Jr. / You Don't Have To Be A Star	224
Jan 9 - Jan 15	Leo Sayer / You Make Me Feel Like Dancing	277
Jan 16 - Jan 22	Stevie Wonder / I Wish	328
Jan 23 - Jan 29	Rose Royce / Car Wash	272
Jan 30 - Feb 12	Mary McGregor / Torn Between Two Lovers	213
Feb 13 - Feb 19	Manfred Mann's Earth Band / Blinded By The Light	216
Feb 20 - Feb 26	The Eagles / New Kid In Town	149
Feb 27 - Mar 19	Barbra Streisand / Love Theme From "A Star Is Born" (Evergreen)	298
Mar 20 - Apr 2	Hall and Oates / Rich Girl	177
Apr 3 - Apr 9	ABBA / Dancing Queen	88
Apr 10 - Apr 16	David Soul / Don't Give Up On Us	290
Apr 17 - Apr 23	Thelma Houston / Don't Leave Me This Way	185
Apr 24 - Apr 30	Glen Campbell / Southern Nights	113
May 1 - May 7	The Eagles / Hotel California	149
May 8 - May 14	Leo Sayer / When I Need You	277
May 15 - Jun 4	Stevie Wonder / Sir Duke	328
Jun 5 - Jun 11	KC and the Sunshine Band / I'm Your Boogie Man	196
Jun 12 - Jun 18	Fleetwood Mac / Dreams	161
Jun 19 - Jun 25	Marvin Gaye / Got To Give It Up	168
Jun 26 - Jul 2	Bill Conti / Gonna Fly Now	130
Jul 3 - Jul 9	Alan O'Day / Undercover Angel	241
Jul 10 - Jul 16	Shaun Cassidy / Da Doo Ron Ron	116
Jul 17 - Jul 23	Barry Manilow / Looks Like We Made It	216
Jul 24 - Aug 13	Andy Gibb / I Just Want To Be Your Everything	170
Aug 14 - Sep 10	The Emotions / Best Of My Love	153
Sep 11 - Sep 17	Andy Gibb / I Just Want To Be Your Everything	170
Sep 18 - Sep 24	The Emotions / Best Of My Love	153
Sep 25 - Oct 8	Meco / Star Wars Theme	228
Oct 9 - Dec 17	Debby Boone / You Light Up My Life	108
Dec 18 - Dec 31	The Bee Gees / How Deep Is Your Love	102

The Year of The Bee Gees

There are those who doubt the power of popstrology to reveal personally meaningful insights by exploring the influence of the pop stars, and perhaps they always will. But if anyone questions the basic notion that the power of the pop stars extends well beyond their ability to sell records, they are either willfully ignorant or too young to have lived through a time when a single popstrological force utterly transformed our sociocultural reality.

The year of your birth offers an example of pop's **culturally transformative potential** that is perhaps even more striking than the First Year of Elvis Presley or the First Year of the Beatles. For while 1956 and 1964 were years dominated by popstrological giants that caused every other star of the time to question its place in the universe of pop, 1978 was a year dominated so completely by **the Bee Gees** and the constellation *Disco Ball* that there really was almost no place for any other star.

Who could have predicted that a low-budget film about a Brooklyn paint-store clerk would run riot over the pop-cultural landscape? Who could have predicted that this film and its sound track would transform three balding, hairy-chested Australians into popstrological emperors? Disco did not begin with the Bee Gees, and the Bee Gees did not begin with disco, but the combination of disco and the Bee Gees infected every aspect of American life in 1978 and brought a half decade of glorious discord in the popstrological firmament to a sudden end. In 1974, the pop universe didn't even have a Dominant Star, but four years later, it

was ruled by a star so dominant as to very nearly silence all dissent.

With **Yvonne Elliman, Donna Summer,** and of course the Bee Gees' own little brother, **Andy Gibb,** in full flower, 1978 was **a year of striking unity**—a unity established by conquest but maintained by overwhelming consensus. Indeed, in a year when the constellation *Disco Ball* loomed as large and as threatening, to some, as the Imperial Death Star, even those stars one might have expected to offer resistance to disco—stars like **Frankie Valli** and **the Rolling Stones**—instead fell under its powerful and glittery sway.

In 1978, the strongest voice of popstrological protest against disco and the wicked hedonism for which it stood came from the least likely of places: the traditionally nonconfrontational constellation *Oh . . . Canada.* It was the churchy, parental **Anne Murray** who stood up and became the Opposing Star in a year when no one else was brave enough to take the job. Disco's own excesses may ultimately have done more than Anne Murray did to bring the constellation *Disco Ball* crashing down, but that does not diminish the importance of her dissenting voice to those born in the popstrological Year of the Bee Gees. She may have sounded like a big, fat bummer at the time, but in being one, she endowed the children of 1978 with at least some slight sense that **just because the whole world seems to get behind something, it doesn't make it right.** And of course that same lesson was reinforced by 1978's Wildcard star, a popstrological *Power Couple* that most of the world got behind but that in many, many ways just wasn't right.

THE DOMINANT STAR
The Bee Gees
- #1 Hits this year: 4
- Weeks at #1 this year: 13
- #1 Hits in Career: 8
- Weeks at #1 in Career: 23

THE OPPOSING STAR
Anne Murray
- #1 Hits this year: 1
- Weeks at #1 this year: 1
- #1 Hits in Career: 1
- Weeks at #1 in Career: 1

WILDCARD
Barbra Streisand and Neil Diamond
- #1 Hits this year: 1
- Weeks at #1 this year: 1
- #1 Hits in Career: 1
- Weeks at #1 in Career: 1

WHAT'S YOUR SIGN?

1978 BIRTHDATES	BIRTHSTAR / BIRTHSONG	PAGE
Jan 1 - Jan 7	The Bee Gees / How Deep Is Your Love	102
Jan 8 - Jan 28	Player / Baby Come Back	253
Jan 29 - Feb 25	The Bee Gees / Stayin' Alive	102
Feb 26 - Mar 11	Andy Gibb / Love Is Thicker Than Water	170
Mar 12 - May 6	The Bee Gees / Night Fever	102
May 7 - May 13	Yvonne Elliman / If I Can't Have You	152
May 14 - May 27	Paul McCartney (and Wings) / With A Little Luck	222
May 28 - Jun 3	Johnny Mathis and Deniece Williams / Too Much, Too Little, Too Late	220
Jun 4 - Jun 10	John Travolta and Olivia Newton-John / You're The One That I Want	310
Jun 11 - Jul 29	Andy Gibb / Shadow Dancing	170
Jul 30 - Aug 5	The Rolling Stones / Miss You	270
Aug 6 - Aug 19	The Commodores / Three Times A Lady	129
Aug 20 - Sep 2	Frankie Valli / Grease	315
Sep 3 - Sep 23	A Taste Of Honey / Boogie Oogie Oogie	303
Sep 24 - Oct 21	Exile / Kiss You All Over	156
Oct 22 - Oct 28	Nick Gilder / Hot Child In The City	172
Oct 29 - Nov 4	Anne Murray / You Needed Me	237
Nov 5 - Nov 25	Donna Summer / MacArthur Park	300
Nov 26 - Dec 2	Barbra Streisand and Neil Diamond / You Don't Bring Me Flowers	299
Dec 3 - Dec 9	Chic / Le Freak	122
Dec 10 - Dec 16	Barbra Streisand and Neil Diamond / You Don't Bring Me Flowers	299
Dec 17 - Dec 30	Chic / Le Freak	122
Dec 31	The Bee Gees / Too Much Heaven	102

1979

The Year of Donna Summer

In the pop universe as well as the physical universe, no star shines forever. And when it comes time to go dark, some dim gradually, some fade quickly, and some explode dramatically, sending their mass spinning off into the popstrological void. Very occasionally, though, a Massive star neither fades nor explodes, but seems to disappear instantaneously at the very height of its brightness, as if suddenly sucked into a massive black hole.

In 1979, the year of your birth, the last of these scenarios was observed directly in the popstrological firmament for the very first time. And to make matters even more dramatic, it was not just any star that disappeared right before the world's eyes—it was the year's Dominant Star herself, the queen of disco, **Donna Summer**.

As the year of your birth opened, the constellation *Disco Ball* seemed not just strong, but unstoppable, having cut a swath through the culture at large and through the shattered remnants of constellations meekly represented in 1979 by the once-powerful **KC and the Sunshine Band** (from the constellation *Shaking Booty*) and **the Eagles** (from the constellation *Mustache Rock*). Did the fact of Ethel Merman recording a disco album in 1979 lead anyone associated with the *Disco Ball* to think about looking around for a place to take cover? Evidently not, for when disco collapsed, it took with it nearly every popstrological star who'd ever even experimented with it. Indeed, the final year of the 1970s was witness to one of the greatest mass-extinction events in the popstrological record, and experts still cannot agree on what exactly caused it.

But let us not allow the story of the

events surrounding Donna Summer's disappearance to keep us from appreciating the year of her reign on the popstrological throne—the year in which always-decadent disco entered its most truly decadent phase. Donna Summer's rich offerings to the disco inferno in 1979 were *Bad Girls* and *Hot Stuff*, and from the likes of **Anita Ward**, **Chic**, and **Rod Stewart** came *Ring My Bell*, *Le Freak*, and *Da Ya Think I'm Sexy?* Yes, you could say that sex was a popular theme in the popstrological firmament during the gloriously debauched year of your birth, just as **sex is a popular theme for you** and others in the Donna Summer generation. But sex was not just the theme of the stars in the constellation *Disco Ball* in 1979—it was also the theme of the group that some credit with precipitating disco's fiery crash.

They were called **the Knack**, and even if you later turned against them, if you were alive and could hear in 1979, you absolutely loved them the first time you heard them. Rarely before had anything as contextually Fresh blown into the pop universe from the constellation *Fresh Breeze*. With its stuttering power chords and its mostly inscrutable but definitely dirty lyrics, *My Sharona* was a song that excited the crowds, and to some degree, what it excited the crowds to do was burn all their disco records.

But maybe disco's death was inevitable. Maybe like all oversaturated pop-cultural phenomena, it was destined to buckle under its own weight or to collapse in the face of a challenger like New Wave. But even if disco *was* destined to buckle under its own weight, its collapse certainly wasn't delayed by the formation of the *Power Couple* featuring **Barbra Streisand and Donna**

THE DOMINANT STAR
Donna Summer
- #1 Hits this year: 2
- Weeks at #1 this year: 8
- #1 Hits in Career: 3
- Weeks at #1 in Career: 11

THE OPPOSING STAR
The Knack
- #1 Hits this year: 1
- Weeks at #1 this year: 6
- #1 Hits in Career: 1
- Weeks at #1 in Career: 6

WILDCARD
M
- #1 Hits this year: 1
- Weeks at #1 this year: 1
- #1 Hits in Career: 1
- Weeks at #1 in Career: 1

Summer. It may have seemed like a good idea at the time (although to whom is not quite clear), but in retrospect we can clearly see that something about that pairing brought an end to the popstrological career of disco's glorious queen.

WHAT'S YOUR SIGN?

1979 BIRTHDATES	BIRTHSTAR / BIRTHSONG	PAGE
Jan 1 - Jan 13	The Bee Gees / Too Much Heaven	102
Jan 14 - Feb 3	Chic / Le Freak	122
Feb 4 - Mar 3	Rod Stewart / Da Ya Think I'm Sexy?	296
Mar 4 - Mar 17	Gloria Gaynor / I Will Survive	168
Mar 18 - Mar 31	The Bee Gees / Tragedy	102
Apr 1 - Apr 7	Gloria Gaynor / I Will Survive	168
Apr 8 - Apr 14	Doobie Brothers / What A Fool Believes	146
Apr 15 - Apr 21	Amii Stewart / Knock On Wood	296
Apr 22 - Apr 28	Blondie / Heart Of Glass	106
Apr 29 - May 26	Peaches and Herb / Reunited	250
May 27 - Jun 2	Donna Summer / Hot Stuff	300
Jun 3 - Jun 9	The Bee Gees / Love You Inside Out	102
Jun 10 - Jun 23	Donna Summer / Hot Stuff	300
Jun 24 - Jul 7	Anita Ward / Ring My Bell	319
Jul 8 - Aug 11	Donna Summer / Bad Girls	300
Aug 12 - Aug 18	Chic / Good Times	122
Aug 19 - Sep 29	The Knack / My Sharona	200
Sep 30 - Oct 6	Robert John / Sad Eyes	195
Oct 7 - Oct 13	Michael Jackson / Don't Stop 'Til You Get Enough	191
Oct 14 - Oct 27	Herb Alpert / Rise	91
Oct 28 - Nov 3	M / Pop Muzik	212
Nov 4 - Nov 10	The Eagles / Heartache Tonight	149
Nov 11 - Nov 17	The Commodores / Still	129
Nov 18 - Dec 1	Barbra Streisand and Donna Summer / No More Tears (Enough Is Enough)	299
Dec 2 - Dec 15	Styx / Babe	300
Dec 16 - Dec 29	Rupert Holmes / Escape (The Piña Colada Song)	183
Dec 30 - Dec 31	KC and the Sunshine Band / Please Don't Go	196

The Year of Blondie

I t is natural for popstrological laymen and experts alike to find their greatest thrills in contemplating the dramatic cosmic storms that have occasionally raged in the pop universe. Those who are interested in drama on a smaller scale, however, would do well to study those periods of eerie quiet that often fall in between events of obvious popstrological drama.

The year of your birth was the first year of the 1980s, though some would say that it is more accurately viewed as the final year of the 1970s, given that the dominant force of the eighties was still not even a speck on the horizon. But popstrologists view the Year of **Blondie** almost as an epoch unto itself—a too-brief interregnum between the rule of the mighty constellation *Disco Ball* and the near-total hegemony of the constellation *Reaganrock*.

Appropriately enough, the group that sat atop the popstrological throne in this year of **calm between the storms** was perhaps the only group in the entire popstrological firmament to prove itself equally at home in both of the decades that it straddled. The very essence of **Blondie** is to be found in their affiliation with the constellation *Fresh Breeze*, and while they were the only representative of that constellation in this transitional year, one can see their influence clearly reflected throughout 1980, which stands with any other year in the popstrological era for **astonishing diversity**. Any year that opens with **KC and the Sunshine Band** and **Michael Jackson** and closes with **Kenny Rogers** and **John Lennon** is clearly a year that would see the birth of a micro-generation **more concerned**

with wild variety than with stable conformity, but there *is* no other year that began and ended that way, and only Blondie's own **refusal to work within prescribed limits** can explain the popstrological shape of 1980.

And yet the children of 1980 must also consider the role of their birth year's Opposing Star in the scheme of their generation's ongoing development. For while **Christopher Cross** when viewed alongside the other stars of 1980 appears quite rightly to be a vital contributor to the gorgeous mosaic, he appears as something rather less colorful when viewed up close. Taken on his own terms, the man behind the beautiful ballad *Sailing* represents popstrological Whitebread at its Whitebreadiest, without a hint of roughness or color. Along with **Olivia Newton-John** and Kenny Rogers, whose popstrological breakthrough came with the Lionel Richie–penned *Lady*, Christopher Cross represented the last great hurrah of the constellation *Lite & White*. But while it is certain that the strength of that popstrological entity in 1980 places certain limits on just how far the Blondie generation will follow its naturally adventurous spirit, the power of **Captain and Tennille's** *Do That To Me One More Time* suggests that the sexual arena, in any case, is not an area in which inhibition will rule the children of 1980.

Still, one cannot ignore the signs in the popstrological firmament of 1980 pointing toward an internal conflict within many of those born in this fascinating year—a conflict between their potential for wild strangeness and their desire to keep that strangeness within commonly accepted limits. Consider,

THE DOMINANT STAR
Blondie
- #1 Hits this year: 1
- Weeks at #1 this year: 6
- #1 Hits in Career: 4
- Weeks at #1 in Career: 10

THE OPPOSING STAR
Christopher Cross
- #1 Hits this year: 1
- Weeks at #1 this year: 1
- #1 Hits in Career: 2
- Weeks at #1 in Career: 4

WILDCARD
Kenny Rogers
- #1 Hits this year: 1
- Weeks at #1 this year: 6
- #1 Hits in Career: 1
- Weeks at #1 in Career: 6

for instance, the nearly self-cancelling strength of the constellation *Sui Generis* in 1980, as represented by **Queen** and **Billy Joel**. Even within that constellation of incomparables, it would be difficult to find two stars that generate popstrological vibrations as divergent as theirs, and yet, perhaps that is the entire point. Perhaps the one thing on which the children of 1980 can depend is that **every powerful instinct they possess, they also have the instinct to suppress.**

WHAT'S YOUR SIGN?

1980 BIRTHDATES	BIRTHSTAR / BIRTHSONG	PAGE
Jan 1 - Jan 5	KC and the Sunshine Band / Please Don't Go	196
Jan 6 - Feb 9	Michael Jackson / Rock With You	191
Feb 10 - Feb 16	Captain and Tennille / Do That To Me One More Time	114
Feb 17 - Mar 15	Queen / Crazy Little Thing Called Love	258
Mar 16 - Apr 12	Pink Floyd / Another Brick In The Wall	252
Apr 13 - May 24	Blondie / Call Me	106
May 25 - Jun 21	Lipps, Inc. / Funky Town	208
Jun 22 - Jul 12	Paul McCartney / Coming Up	222
Jul 13 - Jul 26	Billy Joel / It's Still Rock And Roll To Me	193
Jul 27 - Aug 23	Olivia Newton-John / Magic	240
Aug 24 - Aug 30	Christopher Cross / Sailing	132
Aug 31 - Sep 27	Diana Ross / Upside Down	273
Sep 28 - Oct 18	Queen / Another One Bites The Dust	258
Oct 19 - Nov 8	Barbra Streisand / Woman In Love	298
Nov 9 - Dec 20	Kenny Rogers / Lady	269
Dec 21 - Dec 31	John Lennon / (Just Like) Starting Over	206

The Year of Diana Ross and Lionel Richie

The popstrological code of ethics has its own version of a prime directive, devised to address the unlikely possibility that a working time machine will someday fall into the hands of a fully trained popstrologist. The rule is simple: don't mess with the past, because it might come back and bite you. And yet it is only human for a popstrologist with a healthy sense of curiosity to wonder whether he or she could alter the course of historical events if projected back to some critical juncture in popstrological time ...

But besides being potentially dangerous and officially banned, tinkering with popstrological space-time would also be extremely difficult, even for someone armed with a broad and deep knowledge of our pop-musical past. For how could anyone—even a time traveler transported back from the future—have convinced Americans in 1981 that their innocent embrace of **Diana Ross and Lionel Richie** would have such far-reaching implications? How could anyone have convinced them that it would tie in, somehow, to the rise of **REO Speedwagon**, or that the rise of REO Speedwagon represented the first step in the brand-new Reagan administration's covert effort to place the same distinctive stamp on the popstrological firmament that it sought more openly to place on the American economic and social fabric?

The duo that dominated this watershed year represented something far more important than anyone realized at

THE DOMINANT STAR
*Diana Ross
and Lionel Richie*
• #1 Hits this year: 1
• Weeks at #1 this year: 9
• #1 Hits in Career: 1
• Weeks at #1 in Career: 9

THE OPPOSING STAR
Dolly Parton
• #1 Hits this year: 1
• Weeks at #1 this year: 1
• #1 Hits in Career: 1
• Weeks at #1 in Career: 1

WILDCARD
REO Speedwagon
• #1 Hits this year: 1
• Weeks at #1 this year: 1
• #1 Hits in Career: 2
• Weeks at #1 in Career: 4

the time, though people certainly did realize that it represented something entirely new. Not only were the combined Diana Ross and Lionel Richie the first Dominant Star ever to hail from the constellation *Power Couple*, but they were also the first popstrological *Power Couple* to comprise two stars from the constellation *Spin-Off*. So what could possibly be ominous about either of these new developments? What could the world ever have to fear from a short-lived entity like a *Power Couple*, and what could be more hopeful or appropriate than two instigators of breakups pairing off with each other and finding happiness in one? From the perspective of 1981, anyway, the greatest significance of the year's Dominant Star seemed to stem from their affiliation with the constellation *Theme Singer*, and specifically from their affiliation with *Endless Love*, a film of few charms beyond its theme. But the perspective of 1981 was tragically warped.

Perhaps it was the blinding light of the year's Opposing Star, **Dolly Parton**, that made it difficult for Americans in 1981 to see what their Dominant Star was helping to bring about. Perhaps it was the sheer joy that she radiated that made them pooh-pooh the danger of a union that would serve to loose a solo **Lionel Richie** upon the universe of pop. At any rate, with Dolly Parton and a cadre of similarly Fresh and wildly diverse stars like **Kim Carnes, Kool and the Gang**, and **Rick Springfield** active in 1981, it probably seemed that the pop universe was in no danger of falling under the sway of a hegemonic power. So perhaps nothing could have made Americans in 1981 believe that Lionel Richie could somehow combine forces with 1980's Wildcard, REO Speedwagon, to help create a thing called *Reaganrock*, which would become the dominant, smothering constellation of the 1980s.

But that's how things played out. Among its other crimes against diversity, the constellation *Reaganrock* helped ensure that neither Dolly Parton, Kim Carnes, Kool and the Gang, or Rick Springfield would ever build on their popstrological breakthroughs, and if anything good is to come from that, it can only be to point the children of 1981 to an important lesson: **Never take your freedom for granted**. If you value it at all, you will commit yourself to **defending the interests of the weak** and to **questioning the motives of the powerful**, especially when the powerful seem to have no ill motives at all.

WHAT'S YOUR SIGN?

1981 BIRTHDATES	BIRTHSTAR / BIRTHSONG	PAGE
Jan 1 - Jan 24	John Lennon / (Just Like) Starting Over	206
Jan 25 - Jan 31	Blondie / The Tide Is High	106
Feb 1 - Feb 14	Kool and the Gang / Celebration	201
Feb 15 - Feb 21	Dolly Parton / 9 To 5	247
Feb 22 - Mar 7	Eddie Rabbitt / I Love A Rainy Night	259
Mar 8 - Mar 14	Dolly Parton / 9 To 5	247
Mar 15 - Mar 21	REO Speedwagon / Keep On Loving You	261
Mar 22 - Apr 4	Blondie / Rapture	106
Apr 5 - Apr 25	Hall and Oates / Kiss On My List	177
Apr 26 - May 9	Sheena Easton / Morning Train	150
May 10 - Jun 13	Kim Carnes / Bette Davis Eyes	115
Jun 14 - Jun 20	Stars On 45 / Medley: Intro "Venus" • Sugar Sugar • No Reply • I'll Be Back • Drive My Car • Do You Want To Know A Secret • We Can Work It Out • I Should Have Known Better • Nowhere Man • You're Going To Lose That Girl • Stars On 45	294
Jun 21 - Jul 18	Kim Carnes / Bette Davis Eyes	115
Jul 19 - Jul 25	Air Supply / The One That You Love	91
Jul 26 - Aug 8	Rick Springfield / Jessie's Girl	291
Aug 9 - Oct 10	Diana Ross and Lionel Richie / Endless Love	274
Oct 11 - Oct 31	Christopher Cross / Arthur's Theme (Best That You Can Do)	132
Nov 1 - Nov 14	Hall and Oates / Private Eyes	177
Nov 15 - Dec 31	Olivia Newton-John / Physical	240

1982

The Year of Paul McCartney and Stevie Wonder

They say that no one ever went broke underestimating the intelligence of the American public, but here's a corollary to that law: no one ever went broke overestimating the American public's weakness for too-easy solutions to difficult problems. It's an instinct that few of us are able to resist, but it's an instinct that can sometimes lead to trouble, and never was that more apparent than in the popstrological firmament in 1982.

The year of your birth was a **year of false starts** in may ways—a year filled with interesting sights and sounds that tried but failed to establish a firm base in the pop universe at a time when the constellation *Reaganrock* was still gathering the force it would need to extinguish the flame of popstrological invention. There was an uppity star from the constellation *Outback* called **Men at Work**, a hirsute and *Speechless* star from the constellation *Casio* called **Vangelis**, and a video-savvy star from the constellation *Storyteller* called the **J. Geils Band**. None of these stars would prove to be a Lasting presence in the popstrological firmament, but each of them made an effort to do so beginning in 1982. If nothing else, one can say that each of these stars set a fine example for the children of 1982 by attacking a difficult problem—how to achieve Lasting success—head-on, and without trying to find some trick or magic bullet.

The same cannot be said, however—for the man who brought this year's Dominant Star into being, Paul McCartney, who took a look at his piano one day and decided to craft a musical solution to the deeply rooted problem of racial strife and discord. America's bloodiest war was fought over it, and some of the most shameful chapters in its history revolved around it, yet it took an Englishman to help America see just how unnecessary all of its struggles over race really were. *Ebony and Ivory*—just like the *piano keys*! Now, why didn't we think of that? When you look today and see the peaceful racial harmony that rules throughout American society, you can thank Mr. McCartney for it. And when you look at the work of Stevie Wonder post-1982, you can do the same.

Yes, 1982 was the Year of **Paul McCartney and Stevie Wonder**, the ill-advised *Power Couple* that popstrologists believe was responsible for sapping Stevie Wonder's Soul and making *I Just Called To Say I Love You* possible. As Dominant Stars in the popstrological era go, few offer such stark lessons as this one. And certainly one of those lessons is a critical one for the children of 1982 to heed: **beware of simplistic answers when the questions you seek to answer are difficult**.

Obviously the key to applying that lesson is being able to tell the difference between something that is simplistic and something that is merely simple. For as the Opposing Star of 1982 ably demonstrated, there is great value in simplicity. **Joan Jett and the Blackhearts** rose into the popstrological firmament on the strength of one of the simplest, purest,

THE DOMINANT STAR
Paul McCartney and Stevie Wonder
- #1 Hits this year: 1
- Weeks at #1 this year: 7
- #1 Hits in Career: 1
- Weeks at #1 in Career: 7

THE OPPOSING STAR
Joan Jett and the Blackhearts
- #1 Hits this year: 1
- Weeks at #1 this year: 7
- #1 Hits in Career: 1
- Weeks at #1 in Career: 7

WILDCARD
Olivia Newton-John
- #1 Hits this year: 1
- Weeks at #1 this year: 3+
- #1 Hits in Career: 4
- Weeks at #1 in Career: 17

and most universal sentiments since *Let's Get It On*. It was a song called *I Love Rock 'N Roll*, and the power of the star who sang it is of great significance to the children of the Paul McCartney and Stevie Wonder generation. Without it, their unfortunate tendency to seek simplistic answers to life's toughest questions might not be counterbalanced by their occasional ability to get the answers right. And without it, they might overcompensate for their known weakness by lapsing into a habit of overthinking—a danger from which Joan Jett has luckily spared them.

WHAT'S YOUR SIGN?

1982 BIRTHDATES	BIRTHSTAR / BIRTHSONG	PAGE
Jan 1 - Jan 23	Olivia Newton-John / Physical	240
Jan 24 - Jan 30	Hall and Oates / I Can't Go For That (No Can Do)	177
Jan 31 - Mar 13	J. Geils Band / Centerfold	169
Mar 14 - May 1	Joan Jett and the Blackhearts / I Love Rock 'N Roll	193
May 2 - May 8	Vangelis / Chariots Of Fire	316
May 9 - Jun 26	Paul McCartney and Stevie Wonder / Ebony And Ivory	223
Jun 27 - Jul 17	Human League / Don't You Want Me	186
Jul 18 - Aug 28	Survivor / Eye Of The Tiger	302
Aug 29 - Sep 4	Steve Miller / Abracadabra	232
Sep 5 - Sep 18	Chicago / Hard To Say I'm Sorry	123
Sep 19 - Sep 25	Steve Miller / Abracadabra	232
Sep 26 - Oct 23	John Cougar / Jack & Diane	131
Oct 24 - Oct 30	Men At Work / Who Can It Be Now?	230
Oct 31 - Nov 20	Joe Cocker and Jennifer Warnes / Up Where We Belong	127
Nov 21 - Dec 4	Lionel Richie / Truly	264
Dec 5 - Dec 11	Toni Basil / Mickey	100
Dec 12 - Dec 31	Hall and Oates / Maneater	177

1983
The Year of Michael Jackson

Popstrology is not a science that traffics in gossip, but it is a science that's hungry for data. For this reason, popstrology holds that valid insights are sometimes to be gained through an exploration of the people who have shared a given pop star's bed through the years. But only sometimes. Most of the time, such an investigation can only serve to sidetrack the popstrologically curious on their quest for self-knowledge, and is better left to the proper authorities in some other field.

But to say that an inquiry into a pop star's amorous liaisons is popstrologically out of scope is certainly not to say that we should ignore the critical *professional* relationships in a pop star's life. Indeed, the year of your birth provides us with all the proof we need of how a seemingly small decision like who to sing a duet with can have a profound impact on the course of a pop star's career.

Nineteen eighty-three was the Year of **Michael Jackson**—the year in which the promise of his youth was gloriously fulfilled on an album that stands among the all-time greatest in pop-music history. One could pay the same compliment to Michael's 1979 album, *Off the Wall*, but *Thriller* was an accomplishment of another order. It didn't simply sell millions and millions of copies—it utterly dominated the pop-cultural landscape and obliterated the musical boundaries of the time. In 1983, you were as likely to hear *Billie Jean* on a radio station that played a lot of **Billy Joel** as on one that played a lot of **Eurythmics**, and that was saying something at the time.

Michael Jackson had been pushed in front of the public at the tender age of five and told never to lose their attention, and he succeeded beyond anyone's expectations. But in the year of your birth, the beloved former child star did something even more impressive: he came definitively into adulthood not a bit less beloved, and respected now to boot. To have been born during this slice of time is to have been marked perhaps not for greatness, but almost certainly for something **at least as great as what was predicted for you in your youth**, and that is no small gift.

But one can hardly expect the children of the Michael Jackson generation not to reflect a bit of what was to follow for the man who was their birth year's Dominant Star. Because most of them have probably not been singled out for worship at a very early age, most of them need not fear finding themselves singled out for revulsion later. But all of them need to understand what brought Michael Jackson down if they are to avoid the more modest downfall that awaits them if they repeat his mistakes.

And what was it that brought Michael Jackson down? You've probably heard at least one too many attempts to answer that question psychologically, but popstrologicaly the answer is rather simple. What brought Michael Jackson down was **naïve decision-making**—bad judgment born not of hubris but of innocence. Specifically, the bad judgment to form a popstrological *Power Couple* with Paul McCartney near the end of his year on the popstrological throne. This is what led to the utterly unique situation in 1983 as Michael

THE DOMINANT STAR
Michael Jackson
• #1 Hits this year: 2
• Weeks at #1 this year: 10
• #1 Hits in Career: 10
• Weeks at #1 in Career: 24

THE OPPOSING STAR
Paul McCartney and Michael Jackson
• #1 Hits this year: 1
• Weeks at #1 this year: 4
• #1 Hits in Career: 1
• Weeks at #1 in Career: 6

WILDCARD
Bonnie Tyler
• #1 Hits this year: 1
• Weeks at #1 this year: 4
• #1 Hits in Career: 1
• Weeks at #1 in Career: 4

became the first and only Dominant Star to participate directly in the formation of his own Opposing Star, the duo of **Paul McCartney and Michael Jackson**.

Stevie Wonder hadn't yet provided definitive proof of what many suspected, but neither had he proved that his Soul had *not* been sucked away following his *Power Couple*-ing with McCartney on 1982's *Ebony and Ivory*, and his example was there to be followed if only Michael had cared to. But perhaps Michael simply couldn't believe that any popstrological great, whether intentionally or not, could become the instrument of another's undoing. And perhaps the children of 1983 should take care to develop at least a bit of the **distrust and skepticism** that Michael Jackson hadn't developed by the year of their birth. Less than a month after their birth year ended, and less than two weeks after *Say Say Say* dropped from #1, Michael Jackson caught fire shooting a Pepsi commercial, and three months later, he made his first appearance in the strange uniform of some unknown foreign navy.

WHAT'S YOUR SIGN?

1983 BIRTHDATES	BIRTHSTAR / BIRTHSONG	PAGE
Jan 1 - Jan 8	Hall and Oates / Maneater	177
Jan 9 - Jan 29	Men At Work / Down Under	230
Jan 30 - Feb 5	Toto / Africa	310
Feb 6 - Feb 12	Men At Work / Down Under	230
Feb 13 - Feb 26	Patti Austin and James Ingram / Baby, Come To Me	96
Feb 27 - Apr 16	Michael Jackson / Billie Jean	191
Apr 17 - Apr 23	Dexy's Midnight Runners / Come On Eileen	142
Apr 24 - May 14	Michael Jackson / Beat It	191
May 15 - May 21	David Bowie / Let's Dance	109
May 22 - Jul 2	Irene Cara / Flashdance (What A Feeling)	114
Jul 3 - Aug 27	The Police / Every Breath You Take	254
Aug 28 - Sep 3	Eurythmics / Sweet Dreams	155
Sep 4 - Sep 17	Michael Sembello / Maniac	279
Sep 18 - Sep 24	Billy Joel / Tell Her About It	193
Sep 25 - Oct 22	Bonnie Tyler / Total Eclipse Of The Heart	313
Oct 23 - Nov 5	Kenny Rogers and Dolly Parton / Islands In The Stream	269
Nov 6 - Dec 3	Lionel Richie / All Night Long	264
Dec 4 - Dec 31	Paul McCartney and Michael Jackson / Say Say Say	223

1984

The Year of Prince

They say that history repeats itself, the first time as tragedy and the second as farce. Pop history, on the other hand, never truly repeats itself, but its past and its present do commingle—so often, in fact, that tragedy and farce are but two of many possible outcomes.

The power of the past to intrude on the popstrological present was never more apparent than in the year of your birth, a year dominated by a man who combined the power of three popstrologically invisible giants into one entirely new and entirely thrilling package. His name was **Prince**, and while he could be seen as a reincarnation of James Brown, Little Richard, or Jimi Hendrix if viewed from any single angle, taken head-on he was quite clearly a thing unto himself—a powerful interpreter of the past and a powerful new force in the constellation *Sui Generis*.

Imagine the chagrin of the *Reaganrock*ers watching this iconoclastic, dirty-minded little genius hold sway over a pop universe they had hoped to have pacified by 1984. Neatly packaged conformity was what they wanted, but raw and garish dissent is what they got, and not just from Prince, but also from a certain Club of British origin. Instead of seeing a new generation come forth into the world preprogrammed with a tendency to exhibit **middle-aged prosperity and compromise** well before its time, the powers behind the constellation *Reaganrock* saw the birth of a generation marked with the unmistakable stamp of a man whose feelings about corporate conformity are not fit to print in a family publication.

But perhaps it would be going too far to suggest that the children of 1984

constitute a micro-generation destined to **rise up against their Soul-sucking masters**. Prince may have done all he could to point them in that direction, but make no mistake: while Prince wore the crown in 1984, behind the scenes the popstrological firmament was still under the thumb of the forces represented by the year's Opposing Star, **Lionel Richie**.

Yes, one would be foolish to underestimate the influence of *Reaganrock* on the children of 1984, even though the Dominant Star of their birth year stood foursquare against that constellation's system of values. **Phil Collins, Kenny Loggins, Billy Ocean**—each of these *Reaganrock* giants made an appearance during the popstrological Year of Prince, significantly **dampening the natural funkiness** of the popstrological class of 1984 and suggesting that they may ultimately possess more **ambition to resist established orders** than actual ability to do so.

And we dare not forget that 1984 was the year in which the results of the proxy battle waged unwittingly by Paul McCartney on behalf of the *Reaganrock*ers became tragically clear. Many heard *Ebony And Ivory* in 1982 and feared for **Stevie Wonder**'s popstrological Soul, but the full, Soul-sucking impact of his ill-considered *Power Couple*-ing with Mr. McCartney was not confirmed until 1984, with the release of Mr. Wonder's *I Just Called To Say I Love You*. And as for the combination of McCartney and **Michael Jackson** in the *Power Couple* that ruled the pop universe as the Year of Prince began, well, its fiery aftermath speaks for itself.

THE DOMINANT STAR
Prince
- #1 Hits this year: 2
- Weeks at #1 this year: 7
- #1 Hits in Career: 4
- Weeks at #1 in Career: 10

THE OPPOSING STAR
Lionel Richie
- #1 Hits this year: 1
- Weeks at #1 this year: 2
- #1 Hits in Career: 4
- Weeks at #1 in Career: 10

WILDCARD
Culture Club
- #1 Hits this year: 1
- Weeks at #1 this year: 3
- #1 Hits in Career: 1
- Weeks at #1 in Career: 3

As thrilling as Prince's mastery of the popstrological past was, the impact of the past as personified by Paul McCartney was anything but thrilling for fans of Stevie Wonder and Michael Jackson. Without question, the children of 1984 possess the potential to be anything they wish—one need look no farther than the year's Wildcard, **Culture Club**, to see that. But their popstrological legacy is clearly more complicated than that, indicating not just a **generational independent streak** more than a mile wide, but also a tendency, not necessarily unconquerable, to be their own worst enemies.

WHAT'S YOUR SIGN?

1984 BIRTHDATES	BIRTHSTAR / BIRTHSONG	PAGE
Jan 1 - Jan 14	Paul McCartney and Michael Jackson / Say Say Say	223
Jan 15 - Jan 28	Yes / Owner Of A Lonely Heart	329
Jan 29 - Feb 18	Culture Club / Karma Chameleon	134
Feb 19 - Mar 24	Van Halen / Jump	316
Mar 25 - Apr 14	Kenny Loggins / Footloose	210
Apr 15 - May 5	Phil Collins / Against All Odds	128
May 6 - May 19	Lionel Richie / Hello	264
May 20 - Jun 2	Deniece Williams / Let's Hear It For The Boy	325
Jun 3 - Jun 16	Cyndi Lauper / Time After Time	203
Jun 17 - Jun 30	Duran Duran / The Reflex	149
Jul 1 - Aug 4	Prince / When Doves Cry	257
Aug 5 - Aug 25	Ray Parker, Jr. / Ghostbusters	246
Aug 26 - Sep 15	Tina Turner / What's Love Got To Do With It	311
Sep 16 - Sep 22	John Waite / Missing You	319
Sep 23 - Oct 6	Prince / Let's Go Crazy	257
Oct 7 - Oct 27	Stevie Wonder / I Just Called To Say I Love You	328
Oct 28 - Nov 10	Billy Ocean / Caribbean Queen	241
Nov 11 - Dec 1	Wham! / Wake Me Up Before You Go-Go	322
Dec 2 - Dec 15	Hall and Oates / Out Of Touch	177
Dec 16 - Dec 31	Madonna / Like A Virgin	213

The Year of Madonna

The goal of popstrology is to foster self-knowledge by revealing the hidden power of the pop stars to influence our mortal lives. Sometimes, though, a pop star is so intent on expressing her own power that there is little left hidden for popstrology to reveal.

There is no better example of a star whose popstrological meaning requires little professional training to perceive than Madonna Louise Ciccone, and the year of your birth was the year in which her power was unambiguously revealed. Yet 1985 was also a year in which the most significant popstrological development of all had very little to do with the year's Dominant Star. For while 1985 is recorded officially as the Year of Madonna, it was also the year in which the forces of the constellation *Reaganrock*, and the stifling blandness for which they stood, reached the absolute peak of their nearly hegemonic power.

Yet despite the powerful forces that were arrayed against her, it would be foolish to underestimate the influence of Madonna on those born in the year of her ascendancy. Assaying the precise nature of that influence, on the other hand, is no easy task. Madonna's alignment with the constellation *Shape-Shifter*, after all, makes it nearly impossible to pin down exactly what it is that these children of 1985 stand for, though **self-awareness** and a facility for **manipulating the perceptions of others** are pretty good guesses. It would also be reasonable to guess that **single-mindedness in the pursuit of success** is an ideal that many of them will strive to embody, even at the risk of being **branded as power-hungry monsters**. But it is beyond the powers of popstrol-ogy to identify a clear and simple destiny for the members of the Madonna generation, other than to say that if Madonna in the year of their birth could be even a little bit like a virgin, then **surely they can be anything they choose**.

In sharp contrast to Madonna, 1985's Opposing Star demonstrated that there are other ways to achieve a position of power than by writhing on the floor in a wedding dress and commanding the world to watch. Masking their popstrological ambition behind a deceptively unassuming exterior, square-jawed, fist-pumping **Huey Lewis and the News** put themselves forward as blue-collar purveyors of ham-and-eggs rock and roll, and the world believed them. But in retrospect we can see that the rise of Huey Lewis and the News was the critical step that lifted the constellation *Reaganrock* to a position of imperial dominance. And thus was the Madonna generation's natural tendency toward **brazen individuality** tempered with a **willingness to conform** to the expectations of the establishment when their pursuit of power calls for it.

But not everything happening in the pop universe of 1985 was about a contest of power, for we can see in the year's Wildcard, **USA for Africa**, a shining example of pure popstrological selflessness. Or can we? Was there, perhaps, just a wee bit of muscle-flexing at work in that unprecedented summit of American pop powers? It would be difficult to say no in answer to that question, and that's a perfectly fitting note on which to end a brief popstrological exploration of a generation to whom the word "no" is both unfamiliar and almost totally meaningless.

THE DOMINANT STAR
Madonna
- #1 Hits this year: 2
- Weeks at #1 this year: 5
- #1 Hits in Career: 7
- Weeks at #1 in Career: 15

THE OPPOSING STAR
Huey Lewis and the News
- #1 Hits this year: 1
- Weeks at #1 this year: 2
- #1 Hits in Career: 3
- Weeks at #1 in Career: 6

WILDCARD
USA for Africa
- #1 Hits this year: 1
- Weeks at #1 this year: 4
- #1 Hits in Career: 1
- Weeks at #1 in Career: 4

WHAT'S YOUR SIGN?

1985 BIRTHDATES	BIRTHSTAR / BIRTHSONG	PAGE
Jan 1 - Jan 26	Madonna / Like A Virgin	213
Jan 27 - Feb 9	Foreigner / I Want To Know What Love Is	162
Feb 10 - Mar 2	Wham! / Careless Whisper	322
Mar 3 - Mar 23	REO Speedwagon / Can't Fight This Feeling	261
Mar 24 - Apr 6	Phil Collins / One More Night	128
Apr 7 - May 4	USA For Africa / We Are The World	315
May 5 - May 11	Madonna / Crazy For You	213
May 12 - May 18	Simple Minds / Don't You (Forget About Me)	285
May 19 - Jun 1	Wham! / Everything She Wants	322
Jun 2 - Jun 15	Tears For Fears / Everybody Wants To Rule The World	305
Jun 16 - Jun 29	Bryan Adams / Heaven	90
Jun 30 - Jul 6	Phil Collins / Sussudio	128
Jul 7 - Jul 20	Duran Duran / A View To A Kill	149
Jul 21 - Jul 27	Paul Young / Everytime You Go Away	330
Jul 28 - Aug 17	Tears For Fears / Shout	305
Aug 18 - Aug 31	Huey Lewis and the News / The Power Of Love	207
Sep 1 - Sep 14	John Parr / St. Elmo's Fire (Man In Motion)	247
Sep 15 - Oct 5	Dire Straits / Money For Nothing	144
Oct 6 - Oct 12	Ready For The World / Oh Sheila	260
Oct 13 - Oct 19	a-ha / Take On Me	90
Oct 20 - Oct 26	Whitney Houston / Saving All My Love For You	185
Oct 27 - Nov 2	Stevie Wonder / Part-Time Lover	328
Nov 3 - Nov 9	Jan Hammer / Miami Vice Theme	178
Nov 10 - Nov 23	Starship / We Built This City	294
Nov 24 - Nov 30	Phil Collins and Marilyn Martin / Separate Lives	128
Dec 1 - Dec 14	Mr. Mister / Broken Wings	236
Dec 15 - Dec 31	Lionel Richie / Say You, Say Me	264

The Year of Whitney Houston

To achieve a full and complete appreciation of a star in the popstrological heavens, it is rarely sufficient to consider only the vibrations created by that star at the zenith of her powers. By ignoring all that came before and all that was to follow, a snapshot from a single moment in time often fails to capture a pop star's true significance, particularly if that snapshot captures her in what appears to be a moment of shining perfection.

To look back at the year of your birth is to look back at precisely such a moment, for the Year of **Whitney Houston** was a year dominated by a vibrant young star as bright and Fresh as anything the pop universe had seen in years. Whitney simply made jaws drop—because of her voice, because of her looks, and because of her sheer and evident life force. Her ascendancy to the popstrological throne in the year of your birth was all the more thrilling for occurring at the very peak of the constellation *Reaganrock*'s imperial power. Distracted, perhaps, by their efforts to stamp the excitement out of rock and roll, the powers behind that mighty constellation failed to keep an exciting new star from rising within a very different style. Suffice it to say that within the context of a year visited by the likes of **Starship**, **Mr. Mister**, and **Billy Ocean**, a belting diva with Whitney's youthful spirit was a true breath of Fresh air.

But in sharp contrast to a figure of Freshness and youthful brilliance who'd still not reached the peak of her powers, the Opposing Star of 1986 was a popstrologically Familiar figure of ancient brilliance that had long since passed the peak of its powers. That star was **Boston**, former legends of *Mustache*

Rock whose continued existence was but a rumor in 1986, a whispered legend passed among a shrinking tribe of El Camino drivers who'd come of age under 1976's *More Than A Feeling*. Boston drifted into the popstrological firmament like a ghost ship in the year of your birth, reminding the world (and you) that while youth will be served, so too will the demands of aging.

But the children of 1986 will surely want to know how Whitney Houston's eventual descent into tabloid land might impact their own lives. If one is to address the question, one must first ask what it was about the seemingly perfect Whitney that made that decline possible. Was it lack of self-esteem? If one listened to *Greatest Love Of All* in 1986, as one could scarcely avoid doing on an almost daily basis, one might have thought megalomania to be the biggest danger Whitney Houston would one day face. But if one goes back and listens to it today, one hears the not-so-faint note of wishful thinking, of overcompensating, in Whitney's expression of self-regard. And if one listens to the sugary, irresistible *How Will I Know*, one hears Whitney saying, almost literally, "I have no faith whatsoever in my own judgment, particularly when it comes to matters of the heart."

And perhaps it was Whitney's poor judgment in matters of the heart that sowed the seeds of her partial undoing, but there is no reason to think that this legacy will manifest for the girls and boys of the Whitney Houston generation in anything more serious than **a string of bad boyfriends and girlfriends** they will have to work their way through. In Whitney's own case, there was the popstrological influence of her

THE DOMINANT STAR
Whitney Houston
- • #1 Hits this year: 2
- • Weeks at #1 this year: 5
- • #1 Hits in Career: 7
- • Weeks at #1 in Career: 13

THE OPPOSING STAR
Boston
- • #1 Hits this year: 1
- • Weeks at #1 this year: 2
- • #1 Hits in Career: 1
- • Weeks at #1 in Career: 2

WILDCARD
Falco
- • #1 Hits this year: 1
- • Weeks at #1 this year: 3
- • #1 Hits in Career: 1
- • Weeks at #1 in Career: 3

own Birthstar working against her as well, for all the children of Stevie Wonder run the risk of being parted with their popstrological gifts if they are unable to smell trouble. In your case, **choose your intimates wisely**, or get advice from a wise adviser, and all should be well in the end.

WHAT'S YOUR SIGN?

1986 BIRTHDATES	BIRTHSTAR / BIRTHSONG	PAGE
Jan 1 - Jan 11	Lionel Richie / Say You, Say Me	264
Jan 12 - Feb 8	Dionne Warwick and Friends / That's What Friends Are For	320
Feb 9 - Feb 22	Whitney Houston / How Will I Know	185
Feb 23 - Mar 8	Mr. Mister / Kyrie	236
Mar 9 - Mar 15	Starship / Sara	294
Mar 16 - Mar 22	Heart / These Dreams	180
Mar 23 - Apr 12	Falco / Rock Me Amadeus	158
Apr 13 - Apr 26	Prince / Kiss	257
Apr 27 - May 3	Robert Palmer / Addicted To Love	245
May 4 - May 10	Pet Shop Boys / West End Girls	250
May 11 - May 31	Whitney Houston / Greatest Love Of All	185
Jun 1 - Jun 7	Madonna / Live To Tell	213
Jun 8 - Jun 28	Patti LaBelle and Michael McDonald / On My Own	202
Jun 29 - Jul 5	Billy Ocean / There'll Be Sad Songs (To Make You Cry)	241
Jul 6 - Jul 12	Simply Red / Holding Back The Years	285
Jul 13 - Jul 19	Genesis / Invisible Touch	169
Jul 20 - Jul 26	Peter Gabriel / Sledgehammer	167
Jul 27 - Aug 9	Peter Cetera / Glory Of Love	117
Aug 10 - Aug 23	Madonna / Papa Don't Preach	213
Aug 24 - Aug 30	Steve Winwood / Higher Love	327
Aug 31 - Sep 6	Bananarama / Venus	99
Sep 7 - Sep 13	Berlin / Take My Breath Away	104
Sep 14 - Oct 4	Huey Lewis and the News / Stuck With You	207
Oct 5 - Oct 18	Janet Jackson / When I Think Of You	190
Oct 19 - Nov 1	Cyndi Lauper / True Colors	203
Nov 2 - Nov 15	Boston / Amanda	109
Nov 16 - Nov 22	Human League / Human	186
Nov 23 - Nov 29	Bon Jovi / You Give Love A Bad Name	107
Nov 30 - Dec 6	Peter Cetera and Amy Grant / The Next Time I Fall	117
Dec 7 - Dec 13	Bruce Hornsby and the Range / The Way It Is	184
Dec 14 - Dec 31	The Bangles / Walk Like An Egyptian	99

The Year of U2

More than once in the popstrological era, the universe of pop has been ruled by a star or group of stars that wielded such fantastic power that resistance to it was truly futile. But every empire that rises must eventually fall, and in the popstrological firmament, empires have rarely fallen as a result of an enormous and formidable foe rising suddenly to oppose them. There have been times, in fact, when a single, solitary voice of dissent has found an audience and grown into a rolling tide of resistance that toppled the existing order from its very foundations. On the other hand, there have also been times when a voice of popstrological dissent has carried only as far as a whisper in a whirlwind.

The year of your birth was, alas, an example of the latter phenomenon. It was a year in which a star with the courage, charisma, and credentials to make a meaningful stand against the brutal empire of its time achieved a position of real power only to find not one ally prepared to rally to its noble but ultimately quixotic cause.

That courageous and charismatic star was **U2**, the Irish rock band that never met a high-minded cause it didn't like, and that brutal empire was the constellation *Reaganrock*, the entrenched enemy of thrills and experimentation then entering its seventh year as the dominant popstrological force of the 1980s. On paper, this was exactly the matchup you were looking for if you were rooting against the *Reaganrock*ers or simply rooting for a good fight. It's not that U2 were the most powerful star to go up against the empire since it was established in

1981—far from it. In each of the preceding four years, in fact, a star much more Massive than U2 had gone mano a mano with the constellation *Reaganrock* and come out on top, but **Michael Jackson**, Prince, **Madonna**, and **Whitney Houston** were only interested in individual achievement. U2 were interested in starting a revolution.

And so Bono and the boys rushed headlong into the popstrological firmament of 1987 without regard for the formidable lineup of *Reaganrock*ers arrayed before them. Perhaps **Gregory Abbott, Cutting Crew**, and **Bob Seger** weren't much to worry about, weakly affiliated as they were with the empire, but **Starship** and **Huey Lewis and the News**—these were *Reaganrock* stalwarts. Yet U2 managed to silence them with *With Or Without You* and *I Still Haven't Found What I'm Looking For*, two quiet yet deeply sincere ballads from the same album that contained the explicitly rebellious *Bullet The Blue Sky*. Goliath was down on his knees, and everything was in place to finish the giant off, if only someone with the same ambition as U2 could step in to deliver the coup de grâce.

That someone, however, was not going to be **Tiffany** or **Kim Wilde**. They were sweet and charming, and they were not *Reaganrock*ers, but uninspired sixties cover tunes simply weren't going to do the job. But that's all **Billy Idol** had to offer, too. Here was a man who was nominally a punk rocker, yet he established himself as 1987's Opposing Star by betraying whatever shred of punk idealism he possessed to record an old Tommy James song and leave U2 twisting in the wind. **Los Lobos** were just passing through to pay tribute to Ritchie

THE DOMINANT STAR
U2
- #1 Hits this year: 2
- Weeks at #1 this year: 5
- #1 Hits in Career: 2
- Weeks at #1 in Career: 5

THE OPPOSING STAR
Billy Idol
- #1 Hits this year: 1
- Weeks at #1 this year: 1
- #1 Hits in Career: 1
- Weeks at #1 in Career: 1

WILDCARD
Club Nouveau
- #1 Hits this year: 1
- Weeks at #1 this year: 2
- #1 Hits in Career: 1
- Weeks at #1 in Career: 2

Valens; Madonna, Whitney, and Michael were still just looking out for number one; and **Belinda Carlisle** was just a bit too spaced out to be of much use. History would show that 1987's Wildcard star, **Club Nouveau**, had a small hand in the eventual downfall of *Reaganrock* by introducing the first real hint of hip-hop into the popstrological firmament, but even their relatively inspired cover song did nothing to help U2 create a viable alternative to the dominant order in the year of your birth. One hopes that the children of 1987 never find themselves brutally subjugated by a regime that is any more repressive than your average nuclear family or dead-end workplace. For **try though a few of them may**, it is unlikely that the children of the U2 generation will have what it takes to **bring their subjugation to an end**.

WHAT'S YOUR SIGN?

1987 BIRTHDATES	BIRTHSTAR / BIRTHSONG	PAGE
Jan 1 - Jan 10	The Bangles / Walk Like An Egyptian	99
Jan 11 - Jan 17	Gregory Abbott / Shake You Down	89
Jan 18 - Jan 31	Billy Vera and the Beaters / At This Moment	317
Feb 1 - Feb 7	Madonna / Open Your Heart	213
Feb 8 - Mar 7	Bon Jovi / Livin' On A Prayer	107
Mar 8 - Mar 14	Huey Lewis and the News / Jacob's Ladder	207
Mar 15 - Mar 28	Club Nouveau / Lean On Me	126
Mar 29 - Apr 11	Starship / Nothing's Gonna Stop Us Now	294
Apr 12 - Apr 25	Aretha Franklin and George Michael / I Knew You Were Waiting (For Me)	166
Apr 26 - May 9	Cutting Crew / (I Just) Died In Your Arms	134
May 10 - May 30	U2 / With Or Without You	314
May 31 - Jun 6	Kim Wilde / You Keep Me Hangin' On	324
Jun 7 - Jun 13	Atlantic Starr / Always	96
Jun 14 - Jun 20	Lisa Lisa and Cult Jam / Head To Toe	209
Jun 21 - Jul 4	Whitney Houston / I Wanna Dance With Somebody (Who Loves Me)	185
Jul 5 - Jul 25	Heart / Alone	180
Jul 26 - Aug 1	Bob Seger / Shakedown	278
Aug 2 - Aug 15	U2 / I Still Haven't Found What I'm Looking For	314
Aug 16 - Aug 22	Madonna / Who's That Girl	213
Aug 23 - Sep 12	Los Lobos / La Bamba	211
Sep 13 - Sep 19	Michael Jackson / I Just Can't Stop Loving You	191
Sep 20 - Oct 3	Whitney Houston / Didn't We Almost Have It All	185
Oct 4 - Oct 10	Whitesnake / Here I Go Again	323
Oct 11 - Oct 17	Lisa Lisa and Cult Jam / Lost In Emotion	209
Oct 18 - Oct 31	Michael Jackson / Bad	191
Nov 1 - Nov 14	Tiffany / I Think We're Alone Now	308
Nov 15 - Nov 21	Billy Idol / Mony Mony	188
Nov 22 - Nov 28	Bill Medley and Jennifer Warnes / The Time Of My Life	229
Nov 29 - Dec 5	Belinda Carlisle / Heaven Is A Place On Earth	115
Dec 6 - Dec 31	George Michael / Faith	231

The Year of George Michael

There were no popstrologists around at the time to explain what was happening, but any close observer of the pop universe could see that it was something big. Thirty-two years had passed since the dawn of the popstrological era, but judging from the strange developments in the popstrological firmament, you couldn't be sure from week to week whether you were still in 1988, or whether you'd been transported back to 1958, '68, or '78. *Teen Idol*s were cropping up alongside aging ex-Beatles and desiccated **Beach Boys**. **Cheap Trick** was back, seemingly from the dead, and the last living remnant of the constellation *Lite & White* was playing cheek-by-jowl with a group attempting to resurrect the ghost of Lynyrd Skynyrd and the constellation *Mustache Rock*. Yes, the end of times was approaching, popstrologically speaking, and presiding over it all was a young man who looked and acted for all the world like the lost love child of Elvis Presley and Freddie Mercury.

There was one more partial year yet to come, but the Year of **George Michael** was the last full year in the popstrological era, and the near-dead and undead stars of the popstrological firmament seemed to know it. Yet amid the time-warp craziness of farewell performances by the likes of **George Harrison** and **Chicago**, something of great significance to the contemporary world was quietly taking place. It had been seven years since the first shot in the *Reaganrock* revolution was fired, and by 1988 it seemed as if the dominant constellation of the 1980s would never lose its grip on power. Yet it did just that in 1988—the constellation *Reaganrock*, worn down by four consecutive years of challenges from **Michael Jackson**, Prince, Madonna, and U2, quietly laid down its arms before a ragtag army of teenage girls and metalheads led by the newly butched-up former frontman of Wham!, George Michael.

There were no celebrations in the streets and no ringing of church bells when it happened, though, and it's perfectly understandable why. **Phil Collins** was still lurking about, after all, and **Richard Marx**, the year's Opposing Star, seemed only to be gaining power. *Reaganrock* hadn't gone away—it had simply abandoned its overt goal of suppressing all that was raw and thrilling, perhaps because that goal had already been achieved. Indeed, listening to a song like *The Flame*, one can't help but be struck by how completely outrocked even Cheap Trick was in 1988 by *Reaganrock*'s own Billy Ocean—a powerful commentary on the state of rock and roll in the late 1980s if ever there was one.

But this is not to take away from the accomplishment of the coalition that accepted the *Reaganrock*ers' surrender. Many had tried before them, but none had succeeded, and there is a powerful lesson in the way they overcame their differences to unite in the pursuit of a noble cause. After all, George Michael cooperating in any endeavor with **Guns n' Roses**, the year's Wildcard star, seemed almost unthinkable from the vantage point of 1988, but cooperate they did, and the fall of the empire was the result. Popstrological politics makes strange bedfellows, it seems, and it is probably safe to say that the children of the George Michael generation will

THE DOMINANT STAR
George Michael
• #1 Hits this year: 4
• Weeks at #1 this year: 7+
• #1 Hits in Career: 4
• Weeks at #1 in Career: 11

THE OPPOSING STAR
Richard Marx
• #1 Hits this year: 1
• Weeks at #1 this year: 1
• #1 Hits in Career: 3
• Weeks at #1 in Career: 4

WILDCARD
Guns n' Roses
• #1 Hits this year: 1
• Weeks at #1 this year: 2
• #1 Hits in Career: 1
• Weeks at #1 in Career: 2

acquaint themselves with some strange bedfellows of their own, but there is more to their legacy than that. The children of 1988 bear the unmistakable mark of a man whose fascination with himself knew no bounds, a man who brought a Diana Ross–like drive to his pursuit of solo greatness. But the clear **potential for narcissistic self-regard** that exists within the George Michael generation is nicely counterbalanced by a **willingness to form coalitions** when there is some greater good to be achieved.

WHAT'S YOUR SIGN?

1988 BIRTHDATES	BIRTHSTAR / BIRTHSONG	PAGE
Jan 1 - Jan 2	George Michael / Faith	231
Jan 3 - Jan 9	Whitney Houston / So Emotional	185
Jan 10 - Jan 16	George Harrison / Got My Mind Set On You	178
Jan 17 - Jan 23	Michael Jackson / The Way You Make Me Feel	191
Jan 24 - Jan 30	INXS / Need You Tonight	188
Jan 31 - Feb 13	Tiffany / Could've Been	308
Feb 14 - Feb 20	Exposé / Seasons Change	157
Feb 21 - Mar 5	George Michael / Father Figure	231
Mar 6 - Mar 19	Rick Astley / Never Gonna Give You Up	95
Mar 20 - Apr 2	Michael Jackson / Man In The Mirror	191
Apr 3 - Apr 16	Billy Ocean / Get Outta My Dreams, Get Into My Car	241
Apr 17 - Apr 30	Whitney Houston / Where Do Broken Hearts Go	185
May 1 - May 7	Terence Trent D'Arby / Wishing Well	136
May 8 - May 21	Gloria Estefan and the Miami Sound Machine / Anything For You	154
May 22 - Jun 11	George Michael / One More Try	231
Jun 12 - Jun 18	Rick Astley / Together Forever	95
Jun 19 - Jun 25	Debbie Gibson / Foolish Beat	171
Jun 26 - Jul 2	Michael Jackson / Dirty Diana	191
Jul 3 - Jul 16	Cheap Trick / The Flame	121
Jul 17 - Jul 23	Richard Marx / Hold On To The Nights	219
Jul 24 - Aug 20	Steve Winwood / Roll With It	327
Aug 21 - Sep 3	George Michael / Monkey	231
Sep 4 - Sep 17	Guns n' Roses / Sweet Child O' Mine	176
Sep 18 - Oct 1	Bobby McFerrin / Don't Worry Be Happy	226
Oct 2 - Oct 8	Def Leppard / Love Bites	141
Oct 9 - Oct 15	UB40 / Red Red Wine	314
Oct 16 - Oct 29	Phil Collins / Groovy Kind Of Love	128
Oct 30 - Nov 5	The Beach Boys / Kokomo	101
Nov 6 - Nov 12	Escape Club / Wild Wild West	153
Nov 13 - Nov 26	Bon Jovi / Bad Medicine	107
Nov 27 - Dec 3	Will To Power / Baby I Love Your Way • Freebird	325
Dec 4 - Dec 17	Chicago / Look Away	123
Dec 18 - Dec 31	Poison / Every Rose Has Its Thorn	254

The Year of Paula Abdul

They say that all good things must come to an end, but they never say that all good things must end well. Indeed, few good things ever do, at least if judged by the standards of how well they started.

Consider the popstrological era itself, which began in April 1956 in the blinding flash of light and thrilling explosion of sound that marked the rise of Elvis Presley. Thirty-three and a third years later, it came to an end in the year of your birth with the quiet, plaintive sound of *Right Here Waiting*, by **Richard Marx**. In with a bang, out with a whimper, as they say, but the anticlimactic end of the popstrological era shouldn't seem all that surprising. Long before the constellation *Reaganrock* set out in the 1980s to sap rock and roll of all that was raw and thrilling, America had demonstrated its willingness to embrace the likes of Air Supply and Pat Boone as warmly as the Beatles and the Stones. Indeed, the 450 stars in the popstrological firmament reflect the full, glorious breadth of America's sometimes impeccable and sometimes inexplicable taste in popular music, and so, in microcosm, do the stars that were active in the year of your birth.

From **Prince** to **Poison** and from **Milli Vanilli** to **Richard Marx**, the lineup of stars that graced the popstrological firmament in 1989 left relatively little pop-musical ground uncovered, at least by the somewhat stilted standards of the late-late eighties. Remember, grunge wasn't even a speck on the horizon at this time, so to say that **Bon Jovi** and **Roxette** represented nearly the full spectrum of what guitar-driven rock with any hope of chart success sounded like in 1989 would not be going too far.

Somewhere, a young MC Hammer and Vanilla Ice were laying the groundwork for their respective assaults on the pop charts in 1990, but within the popstrological era itself, the lip-synched, *Eurosomething* rapping of Milli Vanilli was about as close as anything ever came to breaching the secret hip-hop defense shield erected by the constellation *Reaganrock*.

No, 1989 didn't rock, in the truest sense of the word, and it didn't shake, rattle, or roll either. It did bump and grind a bit to the New Jack Swing of the year's Wildcard star, **Bobby Brown**, but mostly it just swayed gently to every possible variety of sweeping ballad, and bounced lightly to the pure, irresistible pop of the year's Dominant Star, **Paula Abdul**.

How fitting, in a way, that in its final, partial year, the popstrological firmament should be ruled sweetly and benevolently by a fresh-faced young woman who applied herself to the task of achieving pop stardom with the work ethic and unselfconscious enthusiasm of the head cheerleader she used to be. Give the kids something they can dance to and something nice to look at—that was her credo, and God bless her for it. Any number of stars in the popstrological firmament probably saw themselves as artists or poets, but how many of them really pulled it off? How many pop stars struggling to make their music "relevant" simply ended up producing something didactic and gloppy like *The Living Years*, by **Mike and the Mechanics**, 1989's Opposing Star? That preachy song about the importance of patching things up with your aging parents before they kick the bucket certainly found an audience among baby-boomers just beginning to ponder

THE DOMINANT STAR
Paula Abdul
- #1 Hits this year: 2
- Weeks at #1 this year: 5
- #1 Hits in Career: 2
- Weeks at #1 in Career: 5

THE OPPOSING STAR
Mike and the Mechanics
- #1 Hits this year: 1
- Weeks at #1 this year: 1
- #1 Hits in Career: 1
- Weeks at #1 in Career: 1

WILDCARD
Bobby Brown
- #1 Hits this year: 1
- Weeks at #1 this year: 1
- #1 Hits in Career: 1
- Weeks at #1 in Career: 1

their own mortality, but luckily for the children of 1989, their essence is more strongly defined by *Forever Your Girl*, Paula Abdul's sweet and irresistible statement of eternal fidelity. "I know I was forever my ex-boyfriend's girl, too," you could imagine Paula saying, "but this time's different, baby."

Some would say that those born in the Year of Paula Abdul are bound to be **more naïve than worldly wise**, and are probably **prone to privileg-ing style over substance**. There's probably a grain of truth to those views, but one could just as easily say that the children of 1989 simply embrace the value of **keeping things simple** and of focusing more of their energy on **spreading joy** than on spreading any super-serious gospel. And if there is a better and truer way in which a micro-generation could reflect the fundamental power of pop music, it's hard to know what it would be.

WHAT'S YOUR SIGN?

1989 BIRTHDATES	BIRTHSTAR / BIRTHSONG	PAGE
Jan 1 - Jan 7	Poison / Every Rose Has Its Thorn	254
Jan 8 - Jan 14	Bobby Brown / My Prerogative	111
Jan 15 - Jan 28	Phil Collins / Two Hearts	128
Jan 29 - Feb 4	Sheriff / When I'm With You	281
Feb 5 - Feb 25	Paula Abdul / Straight Up	89
Feb 26 - Mar 18	Debbie Gibson / Lost In Your Eyes	171
Mar 19 - Mar 25	Mike and the Mechanics / The Living Years	232
Mar 26 - Apr 1	The Bangles / Eternal Flame	99
Apr 2 - Apr 8	Roxette / The Look	274
Apr 9 - Apr 15	Fine Young Cannibals / She Drives Me Crazy	160
Apr 16 - May 6	Madonna / Like A Prayer	213
May 7 - May 13	Bon Jovi / I'll Be There For You	107
May 14 - May 27	Paula Abdul / Forever Your Girl	89
May 28 - Jun 3	Michael Damian / Rock On	135
Jun 4 - Jun 10	Bette Midler / Wind Beneath My Wings	231
Jun 11 - Jun 17	New Kids On The Block / I'll Be Loving You Forever	238
Jun 18 - Jun 24	Richard Marx / Satisfied	219
Jun 25 - Jul 1	Milli Vanilli / Baby Don't Forget My Number	233
Jul 2 - Jul 8	Fine Young Cannibals / Good Thing	160
Jul 9 - Jul 15	Simply Red / If You Don't Know Me By Now	285
Jul 16 - Jul 29	Martika / Toy Soldiers	218
Jul 30 - Aug 5	Prince / Batdance	257
Aug 6 - Aug 26	Richard Marx / Right Here Waiting	219

BIRTHSTARS

- ? and the Mysterians
- ABBA
- Gregory Abbott
- Paula Abdul
- Bryan Adams
- a-ha
- Air Supply
- Herb Alpert
- America
- The Angels
- The Animals
- Paul Anka
- The Archies
- Louis Armstrong
- The Association
- Rick Astley
- Atlantic Starr
- Patti Austin and James Ingram
- Frankie Avalon
- Average White Band
- Bachman-Turner Overdrive
- Bananarama
- The Bangles
- Toni Basil
- Bay City Rollers
- Beach Boys
- The Beatles
- The Bee Gees
- Archie Bell and the Drells
- The Bellamy Brothers
- Berlin
- Chuck Berry
- Mr. Acker Bilk
- Blondie
- Blue Swede
- Gary "U.S." Bonds
- Bon Jovi
- Debby Boone
- Pat Boone
- Boston
- David Bowie
- The Box Tops
- Bread
- Bobby Brown
- The Browns
- The Buckinghams
- The Byrds
- Glen Campbell
- Captain and Tennille
- Irene Cara
- Belinda Carlisle
- Kim Carnes
- The Carpenters
- Shaun Cassidy
- Peter Cetera
- Peter Cetera and Amy Grant
- The Champs
- Gene Chandler
- Bruce Channel
- Harry Chapin
- Ray Charles
- Cheap Trick
- Chubby Checker
- Cher
- Chic
- Chicago
- The Chiffons
- The Chi-Lites
- The Chipmunks
- Lou Christie
- Eric Clapton
- Petula Clark
- Club Nouveau
- Joe Cocker and Jennifer Warnes
- Phil Collins
- Phil Collins and Marilyn Martin
- The Commodores
- Perry Como
- Bill Conti
- Sam Cooke
- Dave "Baby" Cortez
- John Cougar
- Jim Croce
- Christopher Cross
- The Crystals
- Culture Club
- Cutting Crew
- Dale and Grace
- Michael Damian
- Danny and the Juniors
- Terence Trent D'Arby
- Bobby Darin
- Dave Clark Five
- Mac Davis
- Sammy Davis, Jr.
- Jimmy Dean
- Joey Dee and the Starliters
- Rick Dees and His Cast of Idiots
- Def Leppard
- John Denver
- Dexy's Midnight Runners
- Neil Diamond
- Mark Dinning
- Dion
- Dire Straits
- The Dixie Cups
- Bo Donaldson and the Heywoods
- Donovan
- The Doobie Brothers
- The Doors
- Carl Douglas
- Joe Dowell
- The Drifters
- Duran Duran
- The Eagles
- Earth, Wind & Fire
- Sheena Easton
- The Edgar Winter Group
- Tommy Edwards
- The Elegants
- Yvonne Elliman
- The Emotions
- Escape Club
- The Essex
- Gloria Estefan and the Miami Sound Machine
- Eurythmics
- The Everly Brothers
- Exile
- Exposé
- Shelly Fabares
- Percy Faith
- Falco
- Freddy Fender
- The Fifth Dimension
- Fine Young Cannibals
- Roberta Flack
- Fleetwood Mac
- The Fleetwoods
- Wayne Fontana and the Mindbenders
- Foreigner
- The Four Seasons
- The Four Tops
- Connie Francis
- Aretha Franklin
- Aretha Franklin and George Michael
- John Fred and His Playboy Band
- Freddie and the Dreamers
- Peter Gabriel
- Marvin Gaye
- Gloria Gaynor
- J. Geils Band
- Genesis
- Bobbie Gentry
- Andy Gibb
- Debbie Gibson
- Nick Gilder
- Jimmy Gilmer and the Fireballs
- Bobby Goldsboro
- Lesley Gore
- Grand Funk Railroad
- Gogi Grant
- Al Green
- Lorne Greene
- The Guess Who
- Guns N' Roses
- Hall and Oates
- Hamilton, Joe Frank and Reynolds
- Jan Hammer
- George Harrison
- Wilbert Harrison
- Isaac Hayes
- Heart
- Herman's Hermits
- The Highwaymen
- Buddy Holly and the Crickets
- Hollywood Argyles
- Rupert Holmes
- The Honey Cone
- Bruce Hornsby and the Range
- Johnny Horton
- Thelma Houston
- Whitney Houston
- The Hues Corporation
- The Human League
- Tab Hunter
- Brian Hyland
- Billy Idol
- INXS
- Terry Jacks
- The Jackson 5
- Janet Jackson
- Michael Jackson
- Tommy James and the Shondells
- Jan and Dean
- Joan Jett and the Blackhearts
- Billy Joel
- Elton John
- Elton John and Kiki Dee
- Robert John
- Janis Joplin
- Bert Kaempfert
- KC and the Sunshine Band
- Ernie K-Doe
- Eddie Kendricks
- Andy Kim
- Carole King
- The Kingston Trio
- The Knack
- Gladys Knight and the Pips
- Buddy Knox
- Kool and the Gang
- Labelle
- Patti LaBelle and Michael McDonald
- Cyndi Lauper
- Steve Lawrence
- Vicki Lawrence
- Brenda Lee
- Lemon Pipers
- John Lennon
- Bobby Lewis
- Gary Lewis and the Playboys
- Huey Lewis and the News
- Gordon Lightfoot
- Lipps, Inc.
- Lisa Lisa and Cult Jam
- Little Eva
- Kenny Loggins
- Looking Glass
- Los Lobos
- The Lovin' Spoonful
- Lulu
- M
- Mary MacGregor
- Madonna
- The Mamas and the Papas
- Henry Mancini
- The Manhattans
- Barry Manilow
- Manfred Mann
- The Marcels
- Little Peggy March
- Martika
- Dean Martin
- The Marvelettes
- Richard Marx
- Hugh Masekela
- Johnny Mathis and Deniece Williams
- Paul Mauriat
- C. W. McCall
- Paul McCartney (and Wings)
- Paul McCartney and Michael Jackson
- Paul McCartney and Stevie Wonder
- Marilyn McCoo and Billy Davis, Jr.
- Van McCoy
- The McCoys
- George McCrae
- Bobby McFerrin
- Maureen McGovern
- Barry McGuire
- Don McLean
- Meco
- Bill Medley and Jennifer Warnes
- Melanie
- Men at Work
- MFSB
- George Michael
- Bette Midler
- Mike and the Mechanics
- Steve Miller
- Milli Vanilli
- The Miracles
- Guy Mitchell
- Domenico Modugno
- The Monkees
- Mr. Mister
- Walter Murphy and His Big Apple Band
- Anne Murray
- Johnny Nash
- Ricky Nelson
- New Kids on the Block
- The New Vaudeville Band
- Olivia Newton-John
- Nilsson
- Billy Ocean
- Alan O'Day
- The Ohio Players
- The O'Jays
- Roy Orbison
- Tony Orlando and Dawn
- Donny Osmond
- The Osmonds
- Gilbert O'Sullivan
- Robert Palmer
- Paper Lace
- Ray Parker, Jr.
- John Parr
- Dolly Parton
- The Partridge Family
- Paul and Paula
- Billy Paul
- Peaches and Herb
- Pet Shop Boys
- Peter and Gordon
- Peter, Paul and Mary
- Bobby "Boris" Pickett and the Crypt-Kickers
- Pink Floyd
- The Platters
- Player
- Poison
- The Police
- Elvis Presley
- Billy Preston
- Johnny Preston
- Lloyd Price
- Prince
- Queen
- Eddie Rabbitt
- The (Young) Rascals
- Ready for the World
- Otis Redding
- Helen Reddy
- REO Speedwagon
- Paul Revere and the Raiders
- Debbie Reynolds
- Rhythm Heritage
- Charlie Rich
- Lionel Richie
- The Righteous Brothers
- Jeannie C. Riley
- Minnie Riperton
- Johnny Rivers
- Marty Robbins
- Smokey Robinson and the Miracles
- Jimmie Rodgers
- Tommy Roe
- Kenny Rogers
- Kenny Rogers and Dolly Parton
- The Rolling Stones
- Linda Ronstadt
- Rooftop Singers
- David Rose
- Rose Royce
- Diana Ross
- Diana Ross and Lionel Richie
- Roxette
- Ruby and the Romantics
- Staff Sergeant Barry Sadler
- Kyu Sakamoto
- Santo and Johnny
- Leo Sayer
- John Sebastian
- Neil Sedaka
- Bob Seger
- Michael Sembello
- David Seville
- The Shangri-Las
- Del Shannon
- Sheriff
- The Shirelles
- Shocking Blue
- Silver Convention
- Carly Simon
- Paul Simon
- Simon and Garfunkel
- Simple Minds
- Simply Red
- Frank Sinatra
- Nancy Sinatra
- Nancy and Frank Sinatra
- The Singing Nun
- Percy Sledge
- Sly and the Family Stone
- Sonny and Cher
- David Soul
- Jimmy Soul
- Rick Springfield
- The Staple Singers
- Starland Vocal Band
- Edwin Starr
- Ringo Starr
- Stars on 45
- Starship
- Steam
- Ray Stevens
- Amii Stewart
- Rod Stewart
- Stories
- The Strawberry Alarm Clock
- Barbra Streisand
- Barbra Streisand and Neil Diamond
- Barbra Streisand and Donna Summer
- Styx
- Donna Summer
- The Supremes
- Survivor
- Billy Swan
- The Sylvers
- A Taste of Honey
- James Taylor
- Johnnie Taylor
- Tears for Fears
- The Teddy Bears
- Nino Tempo and April Stevens
- The Temptations
- B. J. Thomas
- Three Dog Night
- Tiffany
- The Tokens
- The Tornados
- Toto
- John Travolta and Olivia Newton-John
- The Troggs
- Tina Turner
- The Turtles
- Conway Twitty
- Bonnie Tyler
- The Tymes
- U2
- UB40
- USA for Africa
- Frankie Valli
- Vangelis
- Van Halen
- Bobby Vee
- Billy Vera and the Beaters
- Larry Verne
- Bobby Vinton
- John Waite
- Anita Ward
- Dionne Warwick and Friends
- Dionne Warwick(e) and the Spinners
- Lawrence Welk
- Mary Wells
- Wham!
- Barry White
- Whitesnake
- Wild Cherry
- Kim Wilde
- Will to Power
- Deniece Williams
- Maurice Williams and the Zodiacs
- Al Wilson
- Steve Winwood
- Bill Withers
- Stevie Wonder
- Sheb Wooley
- Yes
- Neil Young
- Paul Young
- Zager and Evans

? AND THE MYSTERIANS

What's shtick for some is gestalt for you.

There are those today who regard your Birthsong, *96 Tears*, as a record of seminal importance—a garage-rock milestone that justifies granting your Birthstar a label that is the ultimate accolade in certain hipster circles: proto-punk. Perhaps they're right to invest this Minor and Forgotten star with such historical meaning, but it hardly matters from a popstrological perspective. What lies at the root of your popstrological legacy, and what truly lies, we suspect, at the root of your Birthstar's hero status among rock-history freaks, starts with their name—undoubtedly one of the coolest to be found among the stars of the popstrological firmament. A cool-ass name like ? and the Mysterians is a lot easier to come up with than to live up to, but your Birthstar lived up to theirs. To this day, no one can say with absolute certainty who ? really is: the former Rudy Martinez, who legally changed his name to a punctuation mark, or the space alien he actually claims to be. And whoever ? is, the really amazing thing isn't that he never took off his trademark shades and managed to keep his identity a secret during your Birthstar's extremely brief heyday, but that he's never revealed himself as part of some publicity-generating stunt in the years since. To

this day, the man whose friends call him "Q" remains a bit of a question mark, and so might you. You may or may not be the type to **cultivate an air of mystery**, but you probably are the type to be **totally and genuinely committed** to whatever air it *is* that surrounds you, and to **attract a loyal cult following** on the basis of that commitment.

CONSTELLATION
➤ Fresh Breeze

BIRTHSONG
➤ *96 Tears* Oct 23–29, 1966

ABBA

You may play in Peoria, but not everyone wants to be seen as a Peorian.

It is no mean feat to earn even a single #1 hit in America, which is why even the most Minor and Forgotten stars in the popstrological firmament are worthy objects of contemplation. But when a star as Massive and Lasting as ABBA earns just a single #1 hit, it's worthy of a full-scale investigation. ABBA, after all, are not just any star in the

constellation *Tip of the Iceberg*—they are, by some estimates, the biggest-selling pop group in Earth history. So how to explain the relative cold shoulder America turned to the bright and shiny Swedes the rest of the world found so impossible to resist? Well, patriotism, in part (see: Starland Vocal Band), but also fear—a profound and entirely reasonable fear of losing our vast edge in pop-music coolness over the notoriously dorky nations that made ABBA their gods. Americans could thrill to ABBA in the privacy of their bedrooms and automobiles, but to let that guilty secret be reflected in the kind of public displays of affection seen elsewhere in the world? To let that secret be revealed by allowing ABBA their rightful place in *our* popstrological firmament? Well, maybe the kids in Chile, Taiwan and the Benelux nations didn't have an image to keep up, but we Americans surely did. Time and the power of nostalgia eventually removed the taint of shame from those Americans who secretly worshiped your Birthstar, but don't

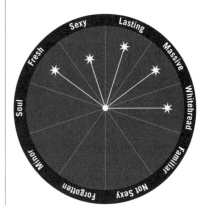

be surprised if you find yourself **treated as a guilty pleasure** before being **embraced as a beloved treasure**.

CONSTELLATIONS
- ➤ Tip of the Iceberg
- ➤ Eurosomething
- ➤ Holy Matrimony
- ➤ Fresh Breeze

BIRTHSONG
- ➤ *Dancing Queen* Apr 3–9, 1977

GREGORY ABBOTT
You are the exception that proves the rule.

The constellation *Reaganrock* is rightly associated first and foremost with Yuppies, but just as no history of that crowd would be complete without a brief discussion of the African-American Yuppie subtype known as Buppies, no discussion of the 1980s' dominant popstrological force would be complete without mentioning your Birthstar. Gregory Abbott's Buppie credentials were impeccable: he was young, he was handsome, he was well dressed, and he held advanced degrees from both Stanford and Berkeley. He was like a dream come true for a constellation looking to diversify and reduce its trade deficit with the black community in one fell swoop. By admitting Gregory Abbott into its big tent, the dominant constellation of the eighties increased its minority membership by

50 percent and for the first time embraced a star whose sound would be accepted in what radio programmers were beginning to call the "urban" format. *Shake You Down* was too much of a pop gem to fit neatly into the style known as "Quiet Storm," but what made it perfect for *Reaganrock* was that it was in the same general neighborhood—a neighborhood that was to 1970s funk and soul roughly what a Peter Cetera ballad was to 1970s *Mustache Rock*. If you're going to walk up to an attractive stranger and say, "Girl [or boy], I wanna *Shake You Down*," it will help to be as suave and seductive as your Birthstar, but if all you want to do is **thrive as an outsider among the powerful insiders**, you've got that covered, popstrologically.

CONSTELLATION
- ➤ Reaganrock

BIRTHSONG
- ➤ *Shake You Down* Jan 11–17, 1987

PAULA ABDUL
You move with grace, but your mobility may not always be upward.

In the old days, they used to talk about "A-list" celebrities versus "B-list" celebrities, and the distinction was as hard and fast as the line between "celebrity" and "nobody." But sometime within the last generation, or maybe even within the last handful of years, that all began to change, and the career arc of Paula Abdul is as clear an illustration as can be found of the New Blurriness that characterizes modern celebrity life. Chapter One of her career, in which she went from being a Laker Girl (C-list) to Janet Jackson's choreographer (B-list) to a member of the popstrological elite (A-list) wasn't so noteworthy, since everyone has to start somewhere. And because it's a time-honored truism that there's nowhere to go from the top but down, it was also unremarkable when Chapter Two saw Paula slip from the height of fame as an international pop star to being a largely forgotten nine- or ten-hit wonder in a troubled marriage to a washed-up former Brat Packer. No, the part of Paula Abdul's career that highlights the fluid unpredictability of our celebrity-driven culture has been Chapter Three, in which her unambiguously B-list status as an "I used to be on the A-list" celebrity has somehow made her the perfect judge of which no-list nobodies should have an artificial A-list status bestowed upon them on *American Idol* before descending quickly to the B-/C+ range of the celebrity spectrum. There may be as **many ups as downs on your path through life**, child of Paula Abdul, but your **willingness to ride them out** may be your greatest gift.

CONSTELLATION
➤ Royal Court

BIRTHSONGS
➤ *Straight Up* Feb 5–25, 1989
➤ *Forever Your Girl* May 14–27, 1989

BRYAN ADAMS
You may find yourself drawn to fire and ice, but your true comfort zone lies right in the middle.

A touch of danger, a hint of the forbidden. If you find yourself inexorably drawn to people and situations possessing those qualities, that's the unmistakable influence of your Birthstar, Bryan Adams, a rock and roller so completely lacking in outlaw qualities that many of those born under his influence will struggle to **shed the earnest likability** that is their strongest popstrological inheritance. It's a natural tendency, but an uphill battle, for while yours is not the only Birthstar with dual residence in the constellations *Reaganrock* and *Oh . . . Canada*, it is certainly the star most perfectly at ease with the resulting double dose of inoffensiveness. And why shouldn't Bryan Adams be at ease? He may inspire little in the way of passion, but he plays the same vital role in the universe of pop that his native Canada plays in global politics: he's an effective space-filler incapable of making enemies. So go ahead and fight that popstrological legacy if you wish, but just as the constellation *Reaganrock* might have wielded its power in a more frightening fashion without your Birthstar's Canadian influence, so might **your own moderating influence** spare the world from **the imperial ambitions of others**.

CONSTELLATIONS
➤ Reaganrock
➤ Oh . . . Canada
➤ Tip of the Ice Cube
➤ Theme Singer

BIRTHSONG
➤ *Heaven* Jun 16–29, 1985

A-HA
Your mastery of two dimensions will take you far, but attention to a third might take you farther.

In MTV's infancy, a dash of good looks and a head of interesting hair were enough to launch a synth-pop act to stardom, but by 1985 we demanded more from our Casio-wielding idols—we demanded special effects! Enter a-ha, who caught the last ride on the dying New Wave thanks to the video for a catchy, unidiomatic muddle of a song called *Take On Me*, in which lead singer Morten Harket was transformed from just another pretty face to just another pretty face rendered in jumpy crayon squiggles. The effect was an aesthetic and technological astonishment at the moment of its unveiling, but the trip from innovation to cliché is startlingly short in the age of video, and predictably enough, the F/X gimmick that fueled your Birthstar's rise was soon showing up in ads for minivans and maxipads. Unwilling or unable to wow us with greater feats of visual wizardry thereafter, your Fresh but Forgotten Birthstar retired, popstrologically speaking, to the lonely Norwegian pavilion in the constellations *Casio* and *Eurosomething*, from which position they impart upon you a certain **sulky but undeniable sexiness**, a **susceptibility to seasonal affective disorder**, and a tendency to **rely on bells and whistles**, even when conditions call for guitars.

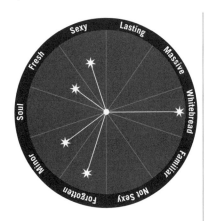

CONSTELLATIONS
➤ Casio
➤ Eurosomething

BIRTHSONG
➤ *Take On Me* Oct 13–19, 1985

AIR SUPPLY
It's not getting you to talk about your feelings that's the problem. It's getting you to stop.

They say you can't live on love alone, but try telling that to Air Supply. Sometimes they were lost in it and sometimes they were out of it, but always they were utterly and completely obsessed with it. Lucky for them, their monomania tapped into an almost unquenchable American demand for just the kind of schmaltz they were so adept at supplying. In an eighteen-month run at the start of the Reagan era, your Birthstar achieved near-total airwave saturation with *seven* epic ballads of pleading, smothering love, including *Lost In Love, All Out Of Love,* and of course your Birthsong, *The One That You Love,*

which captures in all its queasy glory that bargaining stage ("I might stop calling if you were to sleep with me one last time") through which so many breakups seem to pass. It's unlikely that very many of us would actually have wanted to *experience* love at the hands of your decidedly Unsexy Birthstar, but then it's not at all clear that the Australian avatars of male sensitivity were even as interested in making love as they were in talking about it. Perhaps the thing that those born under the influence of Air Supply should keep in mind above all is that while **good communication is an absolute necessity** in any romantic relationship, sometimes **a little less conversation and a little more action** is what the situation calls for.

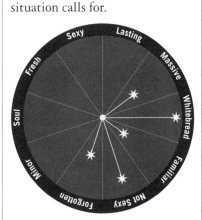

CONSTELLATIONS
➤ Lite & White
➤ Outback
➤ Tip of the Ice Cube

BIRTHSONG
➤ *The One That You Love* Jul 19–25, 1981

HERB ALPERT
You are the servant who becomes the master without forgetting where you started.

There's only one way to control your economic destiny, and that's to control the means of production. It's a lesson from Marx that most pop stars learn too late or never, but your Birthstar recognized it from the very beginning. That's why Herb Alpert and his friend Jerry Moss pooled their resources and put their initials on a record label of their very own in 1962. Founding A&M Records did more than just make your Birthstar a mint and allow him to make any kind of record he pleased, be it a mariachi jazz number (*The Lonely Bull*), a schmaltzy Bacharach love ballad (*This Guy's In Love With You*), or a sultry disco instrumental (*Rise*). It also put his hands on the very controls of the starmaker machine and earned him a place in the constellation *Invisible Hand* for making possible the popstrological rise of stars like the Carpenters, Billy Preston, Captain and Tennille, Styx, the Human League, the Police, Simple Minds, Bryan Adams, Falco, UB40, and Miss Janet Jackson. Your Birthstar helped create in you the makings of **a champion for alienated laborers,** though whether you apply this gift as a **hardened socialist,** an **enlightened capitalist,** or simply as a **workplace writer of scathing memos to management** is entirely up to you.

CONSTELLATIONS
➤ Invisible Hand
➤ Speechless

BIRTHSONGS
➤ *This Guy's In Love With You* Jun 16–Jul 13, 1968
➤ *Rise* Oct 14–27, 1979

AMERICA
In the desert, you can't remember your name, unless it's really easy to remember.

In the spring of 1972, the following conversation was played out a million times over as your Birthstar's first single was storming up the pop charts: "Hey, did he just say 'The heat was hot'?" "Yeah, I think he did." "Man, that Neil Young's really slipping, isn't he?" But *A Horse With No Name* wasn't a Neil Young song. It certainly sounded just *like* a Neil Young song, but would Neil Young really describe heat as "hot" and a desert as being filled with birds and plants "and rocks and things"? You hated to think so. So if this jangly, inarticulate, and irresistible tune didn't come

from the rock-poet laureate of Canada, where did it come from? It came from America, of course, the band and the country. It took some nerve to do it, and it made a thousand bar bands kick themselves for not doing it first, but it was only right that this should be the band to take the name America in the early 1970s. Their sound sat in a magical sweet spot just on the *Lite & White* side of *Mustache Rock*, though it's probably on the other side of that divide where their biggest popstrological impact can be seen. For if you think that the sound and the name of your Birthstar didn't play a profound role in the rise of the Eagles, then you give Don Henley and Glenn Frey far too much credit. Your Birthstar endowed you with an ability to **inspire followers greater than your following**, and with the liberating knowledge that your words **don't have to make sense to sound right**.

CONSTELLATION
➤ Lite & White

BIRTHSONGS
➤ *A Horse With No Name* Mar 19–Apr 8, 1972
➤ *Sister Golden Hair* Jun 8–14, 1975

THE ANGELS
There are other ways to lead than by example.

They were the first group of white girls to join the constellation *Les Girls*, and in some histories of the girl-group movement, their significance seems to start and stop right there. But since white girls like Carole King, Cynthia Weil, and Ellie Greenwich helped invent the girl-group sound, your Birthstar's skin color is of no real popstrological relevance. As is often the case with groups whose impact was limited to a single hit song, what *is* significant about the Angels is to be found in the message of your Birthsong, *My Boyfriend's Back*. For the generation of young women who would later struggle to make gender equality a reality, this song marked the completion of a dubious course in psychosexual development overseen by the early-sixties girl groups—a course in which they were encouraged to give their hearts to the kind of fine young rebels who never wrote letters home and whose most useful function in life was to beat up the weaker young men who dared to express a romantic interest in their girlfriends while they were away in the army. You may find in life that many of your own **central themes have come to be discredited**, but time can't touch the **charming sincerity** with which you continue to express them.

CONSTELLATIONS
➤ Les Girls
➤ Jersey Pride

BIRTHSONG
➤ *My Boyfriend's Back*
Aug 25–Sep 14, 1963

THE ANIMALS
You are the first mover content not to be the biggest shaker.

If you were a mainstream pop singer like Bobby Vinton, or even a young rock and roller like Jimmy Gilmer, the arrival of the Beatles in January 1964 hit you like a punch to the gut. By the middle of that year, though, when you peeked out and saw Dean Martin sitting at #1, you began to wonder if the worst was over. Then came the uppercut to the jaw, in the form of the Animals, who hinted at an entirely different line of attack from the forces of the constellation *Britvasion*. Musically, the significance of songs like *Don't Let Me Be Misunderstood* and *House Of The Rising Sun* was their roots in American blues rather than early rock and roll. But the popstrological significance of that distinction was more than musical, for your Birthstar represented only the first, probing attack by a long line of British blues-rockers to follow. The Rolling Stones, Cream, Led Zeppelin—all were products of the same forces that launched your Birthstar, a group whose Lasting impact was extended by serving as the *Launching Pad* for the minor but meaningful career of Eric Burdon. As a popstrological Animal—and that's exactly what you are—you have the talent and power to **finish jobs that are started by others**, and the extremely rare willingness to **let bigger beasts dine** on the fruits of your labor.

CONSTELLATIONS
➤ Britvasion
➤ Launching Pad

CELEBRITY
➤ **Keanu Reeves** (9/2/64) is a popstrological Animal.

BIRTHSONG
➤ *House Of The Rising Sun*
Aug 30–Sep 19, 1964

PAUL ANKA
Your beauty may fade, but your savvy will linger on.

Regrets? He's had a few, but writing the lyrics to *My Way* was not among them. Nor was writing a theme song for the man who replaced Jack Paar on the *Tonight Show*, and then negotiating a deal for the tune that paid him a hundred bucks every night Johnny Carson took the stage over the next thirty-two years. And your Birthstar certainly can't regret his prescient decision (at the age of nineteen) to buy back the masters of hits like *Diana*, *Lonely Boy*, *Puppy Love*, and *Put Your Head On My Shoulder*, thereby giving himself permanent control over lucrative reissues of his early catalog. In business he was infallible, from his early days as a self-made teen idol to his lucrative later years as a medallion-wearing Vegas headliner. So when the end draws near, and he turns to face life's final curtain, he'll have earned not only a pile of cash, but also the right to say he did things his way. Oh, except for that time when he changed the lyrics of his 1974 #1 hit *(You're) Having My Baby* to "*you're having* our *baby*" in deference to women's-lib advocates who got all over his case for that song's sexist title and lyrics (*"do ya feel my seed inside ya, growin'?"*). A Massive and Lasting star with unlikely dual residence in the constellations *Teen Idol* and *Invisible Hand*, the mighty Paul Anka bestows upon those born under his influence an **independent streak a mile wide** and, if they're lucky, just the smallest dose of his **natural business acumen.**

CONSTELLATIONS
➤ Teen Idol
➤ Invisible Hand
➤ Oh . . . Canada

CELEBRITY
➤ **Kevin Spacey** (7/26/59) is a child of Paul Anka.

BIRTHSONGS
➤ *Diana* Sep 9–15, 1957
➤ *Lonely Boy* Jul 13–Aug 9, 1959
➤ *(You're) Having My Baby* Aug 18–Sep 7, 1974

THE ARCHIES
You are a lightning rod for criticism with unassailable popular appeal.

It's difficult to understand why anyone would rail against the phoniness of a group as manifestly phony as the cartoon Archies, but that's exactly the kind of thing rock critics get paid to do. And did they ever kick and scream when a song "performed" by Archie and Jughead and the rest of the Riverdale gang went to #1 in the autumn of 1969! The real target of the critics' ire wasn't an innocent group of cartoon teens, of course, but the Great Satan they called bubblegum and his faithful servant, Don Kirshner—the brains behind the music of the Monkees and the Archies. The critics, however, might just as well have spent their time doing what the rest of the country did, which was watch the show, hum the tunes, and argue over who was hotter, Betty or Veronica. The popstrologically Massive Archies were not just lovable, they were also extremely danceable, thanks to the songwriting support of Kirshner's brilliant

Brill Building worker bees. Remember the lesson of your Birthstar when your critics' barbs are getting you down: **you'll catch more flies with honey and sugar than you ever will with vinegar.**

CONSTELLATION
➤ Artificial Ingredients

CELEBRITY
➤ **Marc Anthony** (9/16/69) is a child of the Archies.

BIRTHSONGS
➤ *Sugar, Sugar* Sep 14–Oct 11, 1969

LOUIS ARMSTRONG
You may no longer be relevant, but that doesn't mean you can't be timely.

How great an impact did the arrival of the Beatles have on the popstrological firmament? For three and a half solid months following their arrival, the American pop universe was so fundamentally shaken that it had no idea what to offer in response, until, like a crashed computer rebooting into DOS, it offered something from deep within its memory banks: the voice of Louis Armstrong. Your Birthstar was born long before popstrology could have much to say about his individual destiny, so perhaps it was the precise timing of his birth—July 4, 1900—that explains how he came to bear more personal responsibility for shaping the course of twentieth-century American music than Elvis and the Beatles combined. It was Louis Armstrong in his late-career mode as charming, light entertainer who earned a #1 hit with *Hello, Dolly!* in 1964, but it was Louis Armstrong the young trumpet player who revolutionized jazz by turning it into an improvisational art form with his recordings of the 1920s and '30s. Upon his popstrological arrival at the age of sixty-three, he became by far the oldest member of the constellation *Old Guard*, but your Birthstar's popstrological essence is perhaps more directly tied to the timing of his arrival and to his being the single most Massive star in the constellation *Tip of the Iceberg*. **It won't be long before you seem like ancient history** to the younger generation, child of Louis Armstrong, but years from now, when it seems your time has come and gone, you, too, may be called upon to tap into your vast experience and rescue that generation in its time of need.

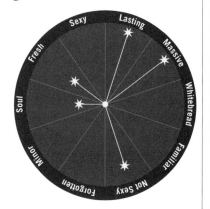

CONSTELLATIONS
➤ Old Guard
➤ Tip of the Iceberg

BIRTHSONG
➤ *Hello, Dolly!* May 3–9, 1964

THE ASSOCIATION
When the summit is in sight, will you have what it takes to leave your base camp?

In movies, music, dance, literature—in nearly every creative pursuit—there is a thin stratum of unknown but nonetheless *paid* professionals: ballerinas dancing in the Branson *Nutcracker*, actors simulating hemorrhoid pain on television, and unsigned rock bands thrilling crowds in the dozens in their local pubs and nightclubs. To aspiring stars making ends meet by waiting tables or selling office supplies, this minor-league success might look awfully nice, but to the minor-leaguers themselves, it can seem more frustrating than outright failure. Which is why, if you ever find yourself in an analogous bind, you should seek out the guidance of your Birthstar. Did the Association hang it up after packing L.A. clubs for months without landing a recording contract? Did they pack it up after shopping a complete, self-financed album that included not just *Along Comes Mary* but also the eventual #1 hit *Cherish* to dozens of major labels without finding a taker? No, they didn't. And though some would say that the rather soft impact they had on the universe of pop is partly to blame for the Liteness and Whiteness of the decade to follow, don't let that criticism deter you. **Hard work is no guarantee of success**, child of the Association, but **no one succeeds who stops pursuing success** in the face of that last, big hurdle.

CONSTELLATION
➤ Neither/Nor

CELEBRITY
➤ **Pamela Anderson** (7/1/67) is a child of the Association.

BIRTHSONGS
➤ *Cherish* Sep 18–Oct 8, 1966
➤ *Windy* Jun 25–Jul 22, 1967

RICK ASTLEY
For Achilles it was one heel, but for you it could be both feet.

It's an age-old problem every pop frontman or frontwoman who doesn't play an instrument faces: What to do with the rest of the body while singing? Ballad singers have it easy. They're not expected to do much except make faces and move their hands a bit, and except for the odd aberration like Celine Dion's sternum thump, that's mostly all they do. As for singers of straight-ahead rock, they have a rich tradition to tap into—a diverse repertoire of moves developed by the likes of Elvis Presley, Mick Jagger, Jim Morrison, Joe Cocker, Robert Plant, and David Lee Roth. But what about singers of bright, poppy dance music? Well, for them, there is little option but to dance, and therein lay the problem for your Birthstar, the briefly Massive Rick Astley. Rick did all he could to stand behind a 1950s microphone whenever possible and to wear suits or sports coats he could reasonably claim restricted his movement. But in the end, even he had to bust a move eventually, and when he did . . . well, let's just say it made Rick and everyone else wish he'd taken up the guitar. Try to **develop a wide range of talents**, children of Rick Astley, for no matter how great your strengths, **life has a way of exposing your weaknesses**.

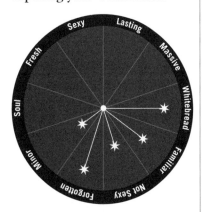

CONSTELLATIONS
- ➤ Britsuasion
- ➤ Casio

BIRTHSONGS
- ➤ *Never Gonna Give You Up* Mar 6–19, 1988
- ➤ *Together Forever* Jun 12–18, 1988

ATLANTIC STARR
You don't necessarily need to cook alone, but too many chefs will spoil the soup.

How many individuals can combine to form a viable popstrological entity? USA for Africa pushed the theoretical limit out past forty, but that group was formed under ideal laboratory conditions. Had even a fraction of its constituent parts ever been forced to share a tour bus or divvy up backstage dressing rooms, the results would have confirmed in dramatic fashion that a pop group with more than seven members is inherently unstable. There are exceptions to this rule, of course, but Atlantic Starr was not one of them. Your Birthstar had nine members just a few years before you were born, and though the Sylvers and Earth, Wind & Fire managed to thrive at that size, those groups were bound together by genetics in the former case and cultlike vegetarianism in the latter. Your Birthstar had no such magical glue, and so it flew apart shortly after attaining the lower reaches of the pop charts in 1983. There were, however, three brothers in the original lineup of Atlantic Starr, and while their talent alone was not enough to earn them membership in the constellation

Gene Pool, their determination to learn from their mistakes enabled them to soldier on. And so, with one unrelated drummer and a long string of female singers, the Lewis brothers pursued popstrological success at a much safer size, eventually making their breakthrough with the lovely soul ballad *Always*. **Some situations afford safety in numbers**, child of Atlantic Starr, but **your success may depend on knowing which ones don't**.

CONSTELLATION
- ➤ Neither/Nor

BIRTHSONG
- ➤ *Always* Jun 7–13, 1987

PATTI AUSTIN AND JAMES INGRAM
Hard work may take you far, but achievement alone cannot open all doors.

One can imagine the dismay among the megastars of the constellation *Power Couple* upon your Birthstar's admission to their ranks in early 1983: "Patti who? James who?" In a popstrological neighborhood of Streisands, Richies, and Newton-Johns, after all, the names Austin and Ingram sounded a little, well, unimpressive. Yes, commoners like Kiki Dee had been granted entry in the past, but only as sponsored guests of bona fide and recognizable stars like Elton John. But beyond their relative anonymity, it was also the circumstances of Patti Austin and James Ingram's arrival that raised eyebrows among the elite. *Baby, Come To Me* was over a year old, you see, before it began its rise to the top of the charts—an utterly dead record miraculously resurrected by the producers of *General Hospital* as a new love theme for their newly Laura-less Luke. And it was only the insatiable demands of smitten soap opera fans that got your Birthsong re-released and your Birthstar a spot in the constellation *Regifted*. Over time, Ms. Austin and especially Mr. Ingram would win the grudging respect of their fellow *Power Couple*s through their yeoman work in duos and trios with the likes of Michael Jackson, Michael McDonald, Linda Ronstadt, and

John Tesh, but don't be surprised if you **never quite attain the insider status** that's always **just barely beyond your reach**.

CONSTELLATIONS
➤ Power Couple
➤ Regifted

BIRTHSONG
➤ *Baby, Come To Me*
Feb 13–26, 1983

FRANKIE AVALON
When they've had too much of a very good thing, they'll turn to you for relief.

The King and his pelvis were safely out of sight in the U.S. Army when a new breed of teen idol was rushed off the assembly line to take his place. Clean and well groomed in sweaters and slacks, Frankie Avalon and his ilk recorded ballad after ballad and exuded a kind of sexless sexiness that made parents of teenage girls breathe a whole lot easier. Which is not to say that your Birthstar wasn't dishy in his own right—it's just that Frankie knew his role and played it to perfection, assisting immeasurably in the National Hormone Suppression Program of the late-fifties/early-sixties not only with his musical persona but also with his fruitless pursuit of Annette Funicello's virginity in innumerable Beach Blanket movies. **Doing the bidding of the profit-minded establishment** may be a natural tendency for you and others born under the

influence of the constellation *Thanks, Dick*, but it's within your power not to let that tendency define you. As the popstrological child of a star who did all he could to keep the generation gap from opening too quickly, you also have within you an **undeniable gift for building bridges**, and not because you aren't hot enough to burn them.

CONSTELLATIONS
➤ Teen Idol
➤ Thanks, Dick

BIRTHSONGS
➤ *Venus* Mar 9–Apr 12, 1959
➤ *Why* Dec 28, 1959–Jan 3, 1960

AVERAGE WHITE BAND
You may indeed be a product of your environment, but that doesn't mean it's the only one in which you can thrive.

Calling themselves the Average White Band and playing American soul music was a cute enough joke to pretty much guarantee steady bookings in their native Scotland, but a funny thing happened to your Birthstar on their way to becoming just another bar band playing for pints of lager and plates of haggis: these Average White Lads unexpectedly tapped into a force vastly greater than themselves, unleashing their inner Earth, Wind & Fire on a deeply funky instrumental called *Pick Up The Pieces*. From the first time anyone heard it, your Birthsong was one of those tunes that sounded as if it had existed from the beginning of time, and while you may not know it by name, you know its groove like you know your own phone number. The success of your Birthstar did more than establish a funky new direction for the constellation *Speechless*—it also proved once and for all the principle that a *Shaking Booty* really is color-blind and that you can't judge a soul by its cover. Not every child of the Average White Band will display a **popular appeal that transcends demographic barriers**, but the potential is there for those who **don't let their roots dictate their limits**.

CONSTELLATIONS
➤ Speechless
➤ Shaking Booty

CELEBRITY
➤ **Drew Barrymore** (2/22/75) is a child of the Average White Band.

BIRTHSONG
➤ *Pick Up The Pieces*
Feb 16–22, 1975

BACHMAN-TURNER OVERDRIVE
You are the one who runs with the wolves without necessarily joining the pack.

If you want to become a Mormon, you'll have to give up alcohol, smoking, caffeine, recreational drugs, a sizable chunk of your annual income, and a year of your teenage children's lives, but two things you won't ever have to give up are your mustache and your love of *Mustache Rock*. Which explains why converting to Mormonism forced Randy Bachman to leave his first band in 1970 (see: the Guess Who) but didn't prevent him from forming a new band, your Birthstar, in very much the same popstrological vein just two years later. Bachman-Turner Overdrive is what Randy called the group, in a stroke of naming brilliance inspired by a trucking magazine, and though BTO was the only group ever to have achieved prominence within the

minor subgenre of straight-edge *Mustache Rock*, they were good enough to make you find that fact regrettable. *Let It Ride*, *Takin' Care Of Business*, and your Birthsong, *You Ain't Seen Nothing Yet*, are beer-drinkin' classics created without the slightest help from beer, and therein lies the key to your pop-strological legacy. For while far too many of us allow our lifestyle to become the sum total of our life's achievements, yours is a popstrological legacy that indicates a rare capacity, in this day and age, for **not defining yourself purely in terms of what you consume**, or don't consume.

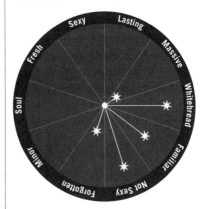

CONSTELLATIONS
➤ Mustache Rock
➤ Spin-Off

BIRTHSONG
➤ *You Ain't Seen Nothing Yet*
Nov 3–9, 1974

BANANARAMA

Some make a fetish of hard work and originality, but you make a fetish of things that the world actually cares about.

They were thin, they were pretty, and in the original tradition of the great sixties girl groups, they weren't going to risk their nails on something ridiculous like a guitar string. No, manual labor definitely wasn't for Bananarama—they left that kind of thing to girl *bands* like the Go-Go's and the Bangles. And though it can be argued that musical talents equal to or exceeding your Birthstar's can be found in your local karaoke bar on any given Tuesday night, there was no such *thing* as karaoke in early-eighties London, so the girls in Bananarama had no *choice* but to hire actual recording studios when they felt like singing along to the oldies. Quite appropriately, your Birthstar's popstrological breakthrough came via their 1987 cover of Shocking Blue's *Venus*, just as their early career had been built on covers of minor sixties classics like *He Was Really Sayin' Somethin'* and *Na Na Hey Hey (Kiss Him Goodbye)*. With polished looks and vaguely coordinated hand motions, Bananarama were a stylistically perfect choice to revive the hibernating constellation *Les Girls*. And though becoming the first new member to join that group since 1977 was probably the closest your Birthstar ever came to blazing a trail, their success should serve to remind you that in life as in pop, **pleasing presentation and good taste can easily compensate for a lack of original genius**.

CONSTELLATIONS
➤ Les Girls
➤ Britsuasion

BIRTHSONG
➤ *Venus* Aug 31–Sep 6, 1986

THE BANGLES

You are the type who defies stereotypes, except maybe not all the time.

It took five years from the arrival of Elvis Presley before the first girl group gained entry into the popstrological elite, but it took more than *thirty* years before the first girl *band* did it. That band was the Bangles, four real musicians and real songwriters who happened to be women and who followed the typically male route from garage to greatness after meeting through a "Bandmates Wanted" ad in an L.A. alternative weekly. But as proud as you may wish to feel about being born under the first and *only* all-female group in the popstrological firmament to actually play their own instruments, you would be mistaken to believe your Birthstar made it all the way to the top of the popstrological heap without compromising even a little bit. You can check out 1983's *All Over the Place* for a taste of their pre-makeover pop brilliance, but never forget it was a tarted-up and teased-out Bangles with Susanna Hoffs in the Diana Ross role who gained national prominence with a song by Prince (who had a way of sidling up to the cuties) and a place in the popstrological elite with an undeniably catchy but also somewhat cringe-inducing step away from the Byrds-meet-Big Star style that won them their earliest fans. To **overcome obstacles that cause others to stumble** is a gift within reach of all popstrological Bangles, but you may have to **compromise something of yourself** to grasp it.

CONSTELLATION
➤ Les Girls

BIRTHSONGS
➤ *Walk Like An Egyptian* Dec 14, 1986–Jan 10, 1987
➤ *Eternal Flame* Mar 26–Apr 1, 1989

TONI BASIL

You are the type who is ready for the world even before the world is ready for you.

As difficult as this may be for someone of your generation to believe, there was a time in ancient media history when music and television were utterly distinct businesses, when executives in both industries could watch a Betamax tape of nubile cheerleaders bouncing around to a ridiculously catchy pop tune and not have any idea what they were supposed to do with it. MTV, you see, was just a twinkle in Bob Pittman's eye in 1980, so *Mickey*—the song and the video—remained stranded on a videocassette-only release called *Word Of Mouth* for more than two years before fueling your Birthstar's belated popstrological rise. But, like any thwarted visionary with bills to pay, your Birthstar used the intervening months well, honing her technical skills and helping to establish the very aesthetic of the MTV revolution by directing videos like Talking Heads' *Once In A Lifetime*. And so it was that Toni Basil, who go-go danced on *Shindig* in the sixties and played a prostitute in *Easy Rider* in the seventies, finally took a leading role in a decade-defining pop-cultural enterprise and earned a place in the popstrological constellation *Invisible Hand* for her role in forcing the acceptance of her chosen medium. **Good things may come to those who wait,** but the lesson of your Birthstar is that **how you spend your time while waiting** might determine how good those things will be.

CONSTELLATION
➤ Invisible Hand

BIRTHSONG
➤ *Mickey* Dec 5–11, 1982

THE BAY CITY ROLLERS

Most grow into a taste for mint or cinnamon, but some never lose their taste for bugglegum.

Perhaps the lads from Edinburgh never found the time to borrow *Lolita* from the public library, or perhaps they really thought that pretty faces, cool haircuts, and head-to-toe tartan was a formula for achieving popstrologically Lasting success. Either way, the Bay City Rollers could have used a lesson in the risks associated with staking their success on the attentions of the *Tiger Beat* editorial staff and on the steady affections of the fickle creature that is the American preteen girl. It sure did work for a little while, though, as millions of girls in training bras went mad about plaid and the stutter-step rhythm of S-A-T-U-R-D-A-Y night. Like all first crushes, Rollermania was intense but brief. Within eighteen months of their anointment as America's most kissable new stars, Alan, Derek, Eric, Woody, and Les were at least two crushes old for members of their "loyal" fan base, whose school binders now proclaimed their 4-ever love for boys named Shaun and Andy. But don't let your popstrological legacy lead you into mopery, for while you may frequently find yourself **sparking momentary passion** in people who then **cast you aside like yesterday's news,** someday you will surely find that special someone who never tires of your trademark shtick.

CONSTELLATION
➤ Teen Idol

CELEBRITY
➤ **Tiger Woods** (12/30/75) is a Bay City Roller.

BIRTHSONG
➤ *Saturday Night* Dec 28, 1975–Jan 3, 1976

THE BEACH BOYS

When the water gets rough, will you still be able to stay afloat?

With a 1969 B-side called *Never Learn Not To Love*, your Birthstar brought an unknown pop songwriter named Charles Manson closer to the popstrological firmament than is pleasant to contemplate. But while it's easy to cast judgment on Beach Boy Dennis Wilson for his dubious choice of social acquaintances, it's important to remember that by 1969, his band was effectively without the services of its own resident madman, Dennis's brother Brian. Brian Wilson was the emotionally unstable pop genius whose talents made the Beach Boys more than just a good-time surf band. A popstrological *Fresh Breeze* if ever there was one, the Beach Boys introduced an entirely new sound into the pop universe with early hits like *Surfin' Safari*, but without Brian pushing them into deeper waters with his songwriting and production, your Birthstar might have lasted no longer than Jan and Dean. Songs like *In My Room* and *California Girls* typified the sunny-but-sophisticated sound that the Beach Boys used to preserve some popstrological dignity for male American pop groups in the midst of the British Invasion. But Brian Wilson's crack-up in the years immediately following his masterworks—the album *Pet Sounds* and the single *Good Vibrations*—set your Birthstar adrift, and 1988's *Kokomo* is a clear reflection of just how far they'd fallen since their 1960s heyday. Take care in life not to **stake your legitimacy on the gifts of others**, child of the Beach Boys, for **a ship with a flimsy rudder** is little better in the long run than a ship with no rudder at all.

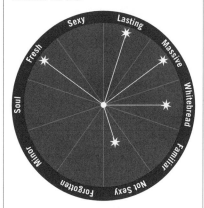

CONSTELLATIONS
➤ Fresh Breeze
➤ Theme Singer

CELEBRITIES
➤ **Courtney Love** (7/9/64) was born under the song *I Get Around*. **Todd Bridges** (5/27/65) and **Brooke Shields** (5/31/65) are also popstrological children of the Beach Boys.

BIRTHSONGS
➤ *I Get Around* Jun 28–Jul 11, 1964
➤ *Help Me, Rhonda* May 23–Jun 5, 1965
➤ *Good Vibrations* Dec 4–10, 1966
➤ *Kokomo* Oct 30–Nov 5, 1988

THE BEATLES

"When we got here, you were all walking around in f*ckin' Bermuda shorts, with Boston crew cuts and stuff in your teeth."

Thus spake John Lennon with his trademark soft touch from the vantage point of 1970, the year that marked the end of the band that led rock and roll's reconquest of the United States. The point that John was trying to make was that the Beatles represented something utterly new on the pop-cultural landscape of 1964 America, and while he cast his analysis in terms of outward style, he knew long before the rest of the world did that your Birthstar's world-altering impact had little to do with how they looked, and wasn't even just about how they sounded. What set the Beatles apart from everything that came before them is the same thing that underlies the essence of their popstrological influence on you: the seriousness of their purpose. Before the Beatles, a raw and thrilling rendition of *Twist And Shout* may have been the peak of what a rock band could hope to achieve, but after the Beatles, the standard was something intensely personal, like *A Day In The Life* or *Hey Jude*. Before them, even the best rock and roll was ultimately still just dance music, but after them, rock and roll came to be seen, for good and for ill, as something approaching a legitimate art form. Perhaps the Beatles, like most male pop groups, started out as teenagers looking to have a good time and score with chicks, but by the time you were born, they were young men whose motivation clearly lay elsewhere. John, Paul, George, and Ringo were young men who displayed their passion and sought their fulfillment first, last, and always through work, and that approach to life is clearly reflected in the enormous cohort of thirty- and forty-something humans born under their popstrological influence. **Careerism is the guiding force** in the lives of popstrological Beatles, occasionally as something to reject, but usually as something to embrace. And while **a passionate commitment to work may take you far**, child of the Beatles, take care to **tame your go-it-alone instincts**, for the **greatness of what you achieve in groups** may outweigh the personal fulfillment you derive from what you do on your own.

CONSTELLATIONS
➤ Sui Generis
➤ Britvasion
➤ Shape-Shifter
➤ Launching Pad

➤ Hot Hairdo
➤ Fresh Breeze
➤ Royal Court

CELEBRITIES
➤ **Matt Dillon** (2/18/64), **MCA** (8/5/64), **Trent Reznor** (5/17/65), **Krist Novoselic** (5/16/65), **Will Smith** (9/25/68), **Vanilla Ice** (10/31/68), **Parker Posey** (11/8/68), and **Owen Wilson** (11/18/68), among many others, are popstrological children of the Beatles.

BIRTHSONGS
➤ *I Want To Hold Your Hand* Jan 26–Mar 14, 1964
➤ *She Loves You* Mar 15–28, 1964
➤ *Can't Buy Me Love* Mar 29–May 2, 1964
➤ *Love Me Do* May 24–30, 1964
➤ *A Hard Day's Night* Jul 26–Aug 8, 1964
➤ *I Feel Fine* Dec 20, 1964–Jan 9, 1965
➤ *Eight Days A Week* Mar 7–20, 1965
➤ *Ticket To Ride* May 16–22, 1965
➤ *Help!* Aug 29–Sep 18, 1965
➤ *Yesterday* Oct 3–30, 1965
➤ *We Can Work It Out* Jan 2–15 and Jan 23–29, 1966
➤ *Paperback Writer* Jul 3–9, 1966
➤ *Penny Lane* Mar 12–18, 1967
➤ *All You Need Is Love* Aug 13–19, 1967
➤ *Hello Goodbye* Dec 24, 1967–Jan 13, 1968

➤ *Hey Jude* Sep 22–Nov 23, 1968
➤ *Get Back* May 18–Jun 21, 1969
➤ *Come Together/Something* Nov 23–29, 1969
➤ *Let It Be* Apr 5–18, 1970
➤ *The Long and Winding Road* Apr 5–18, 1970

THE BEE GEES
You are committed to the relationships others feel sentenced to.

They say that we share 99.4 percent of our DNA with chimpanzees, and not much less with starfish and flatworms, so perhaps biology really isn't the only thing that makes us who we are. Yet even if you look around at your siblings and wonder how you could come from the same planet, much less the same womb, there's no denying that you began your life as closely related to them as the members your Birthstar did to one another. Sure, Barry, Robin, and Maurice Gibb shared strikingly similar looks, but they were not the products of early experiments in cloning. And yes, they shared obvious and prodigious musical talents, but no one pushed them into performing together as children. Neither nature nor nurturing destined the Gibb brothers to become the most powerful force ever to rise in the constellation *Gene Pool*—they managed that feat entirely on their own, through hard work and a determination to grow together rather than apart. If a British journalist named Nik Cohn hadn't fabricated a 1975

New York magazine article called "Tribal Rites of the New Saturday Night," the movie *Saturday Night Fever* would never have been made and the Bee Gees would never have reached their lamé-and-chest-hair apotheosis. But if the Bee Gees themselves hadn't worked through their differences to reunite after a 1969 breakup, they never would have reached the popstrological heights at all. **Sibling rivalry, sibling worship, and sibling indifference** may be experienced in equal portions by popstrological Bee Gees, but even those without any siblings at all will rise or fall according to **connections they may not have chosen, but have nonetheless chosen to preserve**.

CONSTELLATIONS

➤ Gene Pool
➤ Outback
➤ Disco Ball
➤ Royal Court
➤ Invisible Hand

CELEBRITIES

➤ **Casey Affleck** (8/12/75), **Ashton Kutcher** (2/7/78), and **Norah Jones** (3/30/79) are all popstrological children of the Bee Gees.

BIRTHSONGS

➤ *How Can You Mend A Broken Heart* Aug 1–28, 1971
➤ *Jive Talkin'* Aug 3–16, 1975
➤ *You Should Be Dancing* Aug 29–Sep 4, 1976
➤ *How Deep Is Your Love* Dec 18, 1977–Jan 7, 1978
➤ *Stayin' Alive* Jan 29–Feb 25, 1978
➤ *Night Fever* Mar 12–May 6, 1978
➤ *Too Much Heaven* Dec 31, 1978–Jan 13, 1979
➤ *Tragedy* Mar 18–31, 1979
➤ *Love You Inside Out* Jun 3–9, 1979

ARCHIE BELL AND THE DRELLS

You're not the type to shirk your duty, but you are the type to cover your *ss.

The son of a senator's son could choose for himself whether to risk his hide in Vietnam, and a politically ambitious Rhodes Scholar could choose a path that kept his intact while also preserving his future career prospects. But an aspiring pop star with no family connections and no student deferment didn't have the luxury of choice that our forty-fourth and forty-third presidents had. When Archie Bell of Houston, Texas, got drafted, he knew he'd be putting not only his life but his future popstrological viability on the line, so before shipping out for combat duty in late 1967, your Birthstar went into the stu-

dio for what he knew could be the very last time. Maybe the knowledge that *Tighten Up* could be his only shot at immortality explains why Archie and his Drells had it all working, but whatever the reason, your Birthstar managed to record one of the funkiest #1 hits of all time that day. As it turned out, Archie Bell did get shot in Vietnam, though fortunately not so badly that it threatened his life. He was laid up in a West German hospital on the day that you were born, enjoying his newfound residence in the constellation *Fresh Breeze* and perhaps congratulating himself for displaying the good sense he passed down to you of **preparing diligently for every contingency—of planning for the worst** when all that others do is hope for the best.

CONSTELLATIONS

➤ Fresh Breeze
➤ Texstyle
➤ So-Soul

BIRTHSONG

➤ *Tighten Up* May 12–25, 1968

THE BELLAMY BROTHERS

As part of a whole, you may be greater than you are as a part.

David Bellamy wrote a song called *Spiders and Snakes*, which sold three million copies for Jim Stafford in 1974, and David's royalty checks from that song funded the next phase in his career as a would-be solo pop star. But then something strange and magical happened. David's big brother Howard, musically talented but less, um, ambitious, got up onstage to do a sound check one day in his capacity as a Jim Stafford roadie, and his singing was overheard by Stafford's manager, who was also David's manager, and who suddenly realized that Howard had the perfect voice for a song he'd been given from—get this—another *roadie* (this one for Neil Diamond). The chills are almost too much for even trained popstrologists to bear when they think about this, but within a few months, not only had the biological Bellamy Brothers begun a long and wonderful career performing *together*, but the success of their #1 song *Let Your Love Flow* had enriched one of Howard's roadie-brothers as well. They would eventually join the constellation **Shape-Shifter** after reinventing themselves as bona fide country stars via the brilliantly titled *If I Said You Had a Beautiful Body Would You Hold It Against Me*, but on the day that you were born, they were glorious avatars of the constellation **Mustache Rock**'s Eagles-influenced, country-tinged softness. The **power of brotherly love** is not limited to blood relatives, or even to men, as its **critical role in your life** should one day confirm.

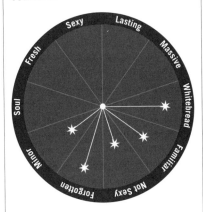

CONSTELLATIONS

➤ Gene Pool
➤ Shape-Shifter
➤ Mustache Rock
➤ Country Cousins
➤ Invisible Hand

BIRTHSONG

➤ *Let Your Love Flow*
  Apr 25–May 6, 1976

BERLIN

Your ambition may write checks that your body of work can't cash.

In a scene midway through *Top Gun*, the sexual tension built up in the film's first act is finally released as the screen heats up with the sight of shapely, naked torsos rising and falling sensuously with passing waves of effort and intensity. And then *after* the beach volley-ball scene, Tom Cruise puts his shirt on, leaves his buddies, and goes over to Kelly McGillis's bungalow for some perfunctory soft-core writhing to the strains of Berlin's *Take My Breath Away*. In truth, your Birthsong was about the only sexy thing in a romantic subplot pointedly lacking in the hot-spark chemistry of the man-to-man relationships in *Top Gun*, and it became a runaway make-out hit in the late summer of 1986. *Take My Breath Away* sent your Birthstar on a whiplash ride from the dying L.A. New Wave scene to the highest reaches of the pop universe, but just as Maverick lost his beloved Goose after flaming out in Iceman's jet wash, your Birthstar went into a flat spin of their own after their rapid ascent on Tom Cruise's tail. Bearded Kenny Loggins used *Danger Zone* from the same film to cement his Lasting place in the constellation **Theme Singer**, but the band that gave *Top Gun* its beard faded quickly into the land of bands that nostalgic cable channels seek to reunite. **Aligning yourself with the big guns** may pay

certain dividends, child of Berlin, but those dividends may offer you **no defense against collateral damage**.

CONSTELLATIONS
➤ Theme Singer
➤ Casio

BIRTHSONG
➤ *Take My Breath Away*
Sep 7–13, 1986

CHUCK BERRY
Even someone with the powers of a god may someday find himself playing the clown.

If you think Elvis was a threat to the forces of the Establishment in the mid-1950s, try to remember that Elvis only *sounded* black. Presley was packed off to the army at the height of his powers, but Chuck Berry was sentenced to two years in federal prison at the top of his, on dubious charges of transporting a minor across state lines. Your Birthstar created guitar-based rock and roll almost single-handedly—its sound, its structure, the way that it's performed on stage. His famous recordings of the 1950s—*Maybellene*; *Roll Over Beethoven*; *Brown Eyed Handsome Man*; *Back In The U.S.A.*; *Johnny B. Goode*; *Rock and Roll Music*; *Never Can Tell*—changed music history, yet like the works of that other establishment nightmare, Little Richard, they were routinely kept from the top of the pop charts by the likes of Pat Boone, Guy Mitchell, and a toned-down,

sweater-clad Elvis. Almost twenty years after his true heyday, Chuck Berry finally entered the popstrological firmament through an unlikely door, with a naughty 1972 novelty song called *My Ding-A-Ling*. And therein lies an interesting lesson for those born under a star more Massive than all the other stars of the constellation *Tip of the Iceberg* combined: if you're not content to **let achievement be its own reward**, there's **no telling what you may be reduced to** in your quest for acceptance by the broad mainstream.

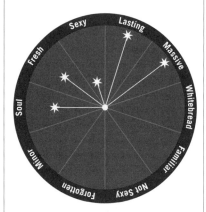

CONSTELLATIONS
➤ Tip of the Iceberg
➤ Sui Generis
➤ Novelty Merchant

CELEBRITIES
➤ **Eminem** (10/17/72) and **Snoop Dogg** (10/20/72) are Chuck Berrys born under the song *My Ding–A–Ling*.

BIRTHSONGS
➤ *My Ding-A-Ling*
Oct 15–28, 1972

MR. ACKER BILK
You are the strange fruit from not-so-strange shores.

If you'd told a random American music fan in 1962 that a British act would soon achieve total dominance of the pop universe and inspire a generation of future pop stars to take up an instrument and join a band, he might have scratched his head as he tried to picture throngs of teenagers practicing clarinets in bowler hats and waistcoats. This unlikely image would have popped into his head because the single, solitary Briton to have reached the top of the American charts as of 1962 was your Birthstar, Mr. Acker Bilk, a middle-aged jazz clarinetist dressed in the throwback garb of an Edwardian dance hall player. As popular as his instrumental smash *Stranger On The Shore* was, however, your vision of Ackerbilkmania could not come to pass. Instead, your Birthstar would have to content himself with a slightly more modest place in the pop universe, as a Minor and utterly Forgotten

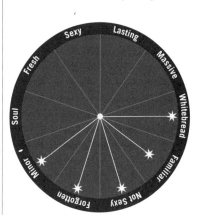

star in the constellation *Speechless* and as the first, false hint of the British Invasion to come. Yet take note of the absolute anti-perfection in your popstrological Starchart, for it marks you as an individual **unaided by eye-popping natural gifts** but also **unburdened by lofty expectations.**

CONSTELLATION
➤ Speechless

BIRTHSONG
➤ *Stranger On The Shore* May 20–26, 1962

BLONDIE
You have the power to hold disaster at bay, but not to prevent it if you go it alone.

Imagine how different history might have been if only your Birthstar had become the leader of a movement rather than just a one-time blast from the constellation *Fresh Breeze*. Would the dominant force of the 1980s have even had a chance to rise? Perhaps not, for Blondie certainly seemed to offer an alternative path out of the ruins of the constellation *Disco Ball* than combining the worst of *Mustache Rock* and *Lite & White* and calling it *Reaganrock*. "Look," Blondie seemed to be saying, "we can kill off the seventies without killing everything that was great about them. We can take a bit of punk, a bit of disco, and a bit of reggae and make it sound great without totally bastardizing the original

forms. We can even try a bit of this thing they're calling 'hip-hop' and use it somehow to keep New Wave from being completely taken over by hair-sprayed British keyboardists." But whether the average American band wasn't listening to Blondie or whether the average American simply never got the chance to listen to the bands that did hardly matters. Your Birthstar's vision of an eclectic yet mainstream-friendly future in the pop universe fell victim to the Strategic Dullness Initiative just a few short months after the namesake of the constellation *Reaganrock* took office. **No one likes the type who says "I told you so,"** children of Blondie, but if you **work on getting your message across** more effectively, you won't find yourself having to say it quite so often.

CONSTELLATIONS
➤ Fresh Breeze
➤ Royal Court
➤ Theme Singer

CELEBRITIES
➤ **Elijah Wood** (1/28/81) and **Julia Stiles** (3/28/81) are Blondies.

BIRTHSONGS
➤ *Heart Of Glass* Apr 22–28, 1979
➤ *Call Me* Apr 13– May 24, 1980
➤ *The Tide Is High* Jan 25–31, 1981
➤ *Rapture* Mar 22–Apr 4, 1981

BLUE SWEDE
What sounds like gibberish to some may feel like genius to you.

What in heaven's name possessed a group of Swedes to grunt like B-movie cannibals over the opening of a B. J. Thomas song is anyone's guess, but somehow, in some utterly inexplicable way, it worked. Somehow an endlessly repeated chant of *"ooga-chucka, ooga-ooga"* was exactly what *Hooked On A Feeling* needed in order to be transformed from a forgotten pop trifle into a pathologically unforgettable pop classic. There was precedent for your Birthstar's accomplishment in popstrological history, though not since the Marcels tacked their *"bomb buppa bomb"*s onto the front of *Blue Moon* had a group secured a place among pop's immortals purely on the strength of a string of vocal nonsense. But there was no precedent at the time for what was to become of your Birthsong twenty-five years after its moment of pop-strological dominance, when it rose again like a dormant virus to spread via *Ally McBeal* and the Internet as the musical accompaniment to that 3-D dancing baby, a pop-culture artifact with a strangely evil allure even greater than that of *Hooked On A Feeling*. If you find that your own **greatest accomplishment** in life comes not as a result of pure originality but through **adding your original spin to the work of others**, feel free to credit the Minor and Forgotten *Eurosomething* star who did just that at the moment of your birth.

CONSTELLATION
➤ Eurosomething

BIRTHSONG
➤ *Hooked On A Feeling*
Mar 31–Apr 6, 1974

GARY "U.S." BONDS
If genius is in the eye of the beholder, then your gift is in getting yours beheld.

Hoping to get the record some airplay, Legrand Records slapped the name of the fictitious group "U.S. Bonds" on the debut single by a local unknown named Gary Anderson. *New Orleans* ended up such a big hit that

Gary was lucky just to get his first name onto his future records. The record that made Gary "U.S." Bonds a household name, however, came just a bit later, in an impromptu late-night studio session with a well-lubricated Church Street Five and a dozen or so rowdy, clapping teenagers. The loose and raucous *Quarter To Three* was the apotheosis of the "Norfolk sound," a calypso/R&B blend created by Legrand's Frank Guida. *Quarter To Three* made Gary "U.S." Bonds a star twice in his lifetime—first by going to #1 in 1961 and then again by being one of the favorite songs of a young Bruce Springsteen, who engineered a second act in Gary's career with a comeback album in the early eighties. Twice boosted onto the charts by unseen geniuses, your Birthstar bestowed upon you the **power to attract powerful friends** by being in **the right place at the right time**.

CONSTELLATION
➤ Fresh Breeze

BIRTHSONG
➤ *Quarter To Three*
Jun 26–Jul 9, 1961

BON JOVI
Sometimes when you're alone, all you do is think, "Where is everybody?"

Did the boys in the band look at the picture of a wet, black Hefty bag that replaced their chosen cover for *Slippery When Wet* and wonder to themselves, "How much blacker can it get?" They certainly didn't need to, for the album that fueled Bon Jovi's rise needed no help from soft-core porn to sell millions—it succeeded on the strength of a big ol' pair of hits instead. *Livin' On A Prayer* and *You Give Love A Bad Name* were brilliant pop anthems from what was supposed to be a metal band, and therein lay their appeal. All of a sudden, a genre carefully tuned to the tastes and desires of adolescent boys had found something to offer their sisters and girlfriends as well. Thus was the era of hair-metal begun in earnest, and though the members of your Birthstar would probably point to other factors in explaining their success, it is of popstrological significance to you that (a) Jon Bon Jovi was arguably hard rock's all-time biggest cutie pie and (b) his band's first three #1 hits were cowritten and produced by a man named Desmond Child, the same man who turned a marginal Latin teen idol into the monster known as Ricky Martin. The constellation *Jersey Pride* was never prouder than when it admitted your Birthstar to its ranks, and you should be proud, too, even if your greatest achievements will be dismissed by some as simple products of your surface appeal.

CONSTELLATIONS
➤ Jersey Pride
➤ Hot Hairdo

BIRTHSONGS
➤ *You Give Love A Bad Name* Nov 23–29, 1986
➤ *Livin' On A Prayer* Feb 8–Mar 7, 1987
➤ *Bad Medicine* Nov 13–26, 1988
➤ *I'll Be There For You* May 7–13, 1989

DEBBY BOONE
When it's nature versus nurture, you choose not to take sides.

She was the biological child of Pat Boone and the popstrological child of his opposite, Elvis Presley. Yet somehow the sweet, shiny apple that was Debby Boone didn't fall far from either tree. Like Dad, she looked and sounded whiter than the whitest Whitebread, yet just like Elvis, she exploded onto the pop-cultural landscape and knocked the musical status quo from its tracks. *You Light Up My Life* ruled the pop universe for ten solid weeks in the autumn of your birth, a span eclipsed in the popstrological era only by your Birthstar's *own* Birthsongs, *Don't Be Cruel/Hound Dog*. What's more, in a year often mistakenly assumed to fall within the reign of the constellation *Disco Ball*, it was this Ultra-Brite icon of the constellation *Lite & White* who was the dominant popstrological force of 1977. So what caused Debby to reject the pop stardom that was hers and step instead into the skin of a Christian Contemporary singer? It might be tempting to chalk that up simply to Boone family values, but it can just as easily be seen as a conscious effort to avoid the classic trap so many popstrological Elvises fall into when they watch their inner spark get sucked out of them as they bend their career ambitions to the needs of the Establishment. Beautiful but not Sexy, Massive but not Lasting, your uniquely powerful Birthstar bestows upon you not just **a tendency to be**

pulled by competing influences, but the **strength of character** not to let any one of them win.

CONSTELLATIONS
➤ Lite & White
➤ Gene Pool
➤ Hot Hairdo
➤ Theme Singer
➤ Royal Court

CELEBRITY
➤ **John Mayer** (10/16/77) is a child of Debby Boone.

BIRTHSONG
➤ *You Light Up My Life* Oct 9–Dec 17, 1977

PAT BOONE
Like Elvis with a stick up his *ss, but like Elvis nonetheless.

In the 1950s, two handsome young white men began their careers making the black sound of early rock and roll safe for the lily-white pop charts. Both were steeped in religion and gospel music as boys, and both were raised in the segregated South, but one important barrier did separate them in childhood: a set of railroad tracks. On the wrong side of the tracks in Tupelo, Mississippi, were the Presleys, whose boy Elvis would go on to become, well, you know. On the right side in Nashville were the Boones, whose boy Pat would go on to become, well, your somewhat tight-*ssed Birthstar. Pat Boone was actually the near equal of Elvis Presley in terms of chart success in the mid-1950s, though his racial-barrier-preserving, teenage-virginity-respecting image was everything that Elvis's was not. It probably goes without saying that **electrifying charisma and raw sex appeal** are *unlikely* attributes for a popstrological child of Pat Boone to possess, yet **drab blandness and crippling sexual inhibition** need not be your portion, either. Your Birthstar did battle against all things raw and thrilling from his perch in the constellation *Old Guard*, but unless you've got a particular bone to pick with some up-and-coming sexpot, his legacy to you may be as benign as your **unfailingly polite demeanor and impeccable grooming**.

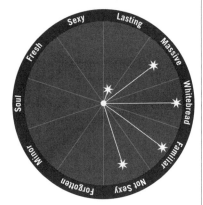

CONSTELLATION
➤ Old Guard

CELEBRITIES
➤ **Frances McDormand** (6/23/57), **Ray Romano** (12/21/57), and **Matt Lauer** (12/30/57) are popstrological Pat Boones.

BOSTON
The loyalty of your fans is unshakable, but be careful what you do with it.

You still see them occasionally at the mall or in the tire store, the proud but shattered remnants of the once-great nation of Boston fans. They pledged their unswerving allegiance back in 1976 to a band that managed only one more album in the ten years following their monumental debut, and if fan abandonment were a crime, Boston's leader, Tom Scholz, would be serving a life sentence. While the MIT-educated perfectionist tinkered and futzed with your Birthstar's third album, millions of the group's fans fell into the grip of bands like Toto in their vain search for an effective Boston substitute. Indeed, some popstrologists believe that without the diaspora of frustrated Boston fans in the early eighties, the rise of the constellation *Reaganrock* might not have been possible. A few true-blue Boston loyalists stood firm over the years, waiting for more of the feeling that *More Than A Feeling* gave them back in high school, yet for them it was as maddening as it was pleasing to plop 1986's

Third Stage onto their Technics turntables and not be able to tell the difference between it and 1976's *Boston*. The single *Amanda* earned your Birthstar a belated but entirely appropriate ticket into the dormant constellation *Mustache Rock*, from which they bestow upon you a **throwback appeal** that almost counterbalances your **control-freak tendencies** and your **stubborn insistence on not being rushed**.

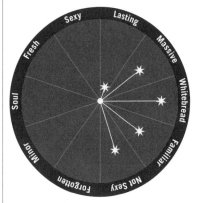

CONSTELLATIONS
➤ Mustache Rock
➤ Tip of the Ice Cube

DAVID BOWIE
You lead by impressive example, but will the same be true of your followers, and theirs?

David Bowie was instrumental in creating both glam rock and New Wave, and he wrote and/or produced enough decade-defining songs in the 1970s (*Walk On The Wild Side, All The*

Young Dudes, *Lust For Life*) to qualify for entry into the constellation *Invisible Hand* on that basis alone. But by far the most significant long-term contribution your Birthstar made to the future course of pop has little to do with music, at least for most of those who emulate it. By the time your Birthstar made his popstrological breakthrough in 1975, he was inhabiting his third or fourth significant artistic and aesthetic incarnation, and in transforming himself from a hippie singer/songwriter to the Thin White Duke via Ziggy Stardust, David Bowie essentially invented self-conscious pop reinvention. And this, perhaps even more than his incredible body of work, is what may prove to be his most Lasting impact. For without Bowie's example to guide her, would we have Madonna? Professional investors paid $55 million in a historic 1997 bond issue for the right to David Bowie's future publishing royalties, but to the extent that someone like Britney Spears claims Madonna as an influence in inspiring her own so-called reinventions, it might be said that

we are all paying for his past redefinition of what a *Shape-Shifter* should be. **Your ability to match style with substance is not in question**, child of David Bowie, but before you go building an army of followers, please **be aware of how difficult that trick is to pull off.**

CONSTELLATIONS
➤ Shape-Shifter
➤ Invisible Hand
➤ Fresh Breeze

BIRTHSONGS
➤ *Fame* Sep 14–20 and Sep 28–Oct 4, 1975
➤ *Let's Dance* May 15–21, 1983

THE BOX TOPS
You have the power to inspire cultish worship without ever becoming a household name.

*T*he Letter probably ranks third or fourth on the all-time list of short-hand-for-the-sixties sound track tunes, right between *Light My Fire* and *For What It's Worth*. Yet as deeply ingrained in your brain stem as it is, there's an excellent chance that you know almost nothing about the group that sang your Birthsong. On the other hand, there is an excellent chance that you spent your college years and beyond listening to groups like the Replacements, who worshiped openly in the cult of your Birthstar, or more accurately in the cult of your Birthstar's lead singer, Alex Chilton. Chilton was only sixteen

when he growled out his famous line about buying a ticket for an "aeroplane," back in 1967, and he never had another hit even approaching the scale of *The Letter*. But ask any indie-rock enthusiast to talk about his later work in Big Star—*September Gurls*, *In The Street* (source of the opening theme for *That Seventies Show*)—and you're going to get an earful. As a popstrological child of a Minor but Lasting star in the constellation *Launching Pad*, you possess an **undeniable ability to speak to and for your generation**, yet still it must be said that **your most loyal fans may have yet to be born.**

CONSTELLATIONS
➤ Underage
➤ Launching Pad

CELEBRITY
➤ Liev Schreiber (10/4/67) is a child of the Box Tops.

BIRTHSONG
➤ *The Letter* Sep 17–Oct 14, 1967

BREAD

Easy does it. That's it. Just like that.

When groups of accomplished, white-male musicians gathered in your childhood and resolved, as they often did, to leave all hints of roughness behind, it was your Birthstar's example they were often emulating. The rise of Bread had an enormous impact within the music industry, but it also marked the popstrological dawn of an important *sociocultural* archetype: the sensitive seventies guy. If Bread were a man, he'd have soft hands and a beard. He'd be in touch with his feminine side, and he wouldn't dream of touching yours until he was assured that you'd still respect him in the morning. This may seem at odds with the apparent message of your Birthsong, but don't let the title fool you: *Make It With You* was a sheep in wolf's clothing—a hand-holder of a song that, like Bread's other big hit, *Baby I'm-A Want You*, showed less interest in making "it" than in making it *through* the emotional trials of a long-term, committed relationship. To the oppositional Breads among you who've been working so hard and for so long to **cultivate a spicy persona** and **sow your wild oats**, perhaps it's time to **reap the Whitebread**. As the child of the fourth and quintessential star in the constellation *Lite & White*, your natural comfort zone is in

territory that **soothes and sustains** rather than shocks and awes.

CONSTELLATION
➤ Lite & White

CELEBRITIES
➤ **Jim Courier** (8/17/70) and **Malcolm-Jamal Warner** (8/18/70) are popstrological children of Bread.

BIRTHSONG
➤ *Make It With You*
Aug 16–22, 1970

BOBBY BROWN

Mixing business with pleasure is fine, until your pleasure become everyone else's business.

Believe it or not, there was a time when your Birthstar was something more than Mr. Whitney Houston, a time when he got more ink in *Billboard* than in the *National Enquirer*. In fact, Bobby Brown was a fast-rising star in the constellation *Fresh Breeze* following the 1988 release of *Don't Be Cruel*,

the multiplatinum album that introduced mainstream audiences to a hip-hop-inflected R&B style called New Jack Swing and conquered skeptics' predictions of Bobby's failure outside the boy band New Edition. So what was it that derailed your Birthstar's career? If this were VH1's *Behind the Music*, we'd say "personal demons," but popstrology seeks clear-eyed self-knowledge untempered by euphemism. Still, popstrology also believes discretion is the better part of valor where libelis concerned, so let us leave is at that. Your Birthsong provided a vital (and danceable) reminder that it is not only your right but your *prerogative* to **resist this thing called social control**, but, boy, is it a slippery slope from there. As a child of the once-mighty Bobby Brown, it's only natural that you'll **indulge your taste for the wild side** now and then, but never forget that **it is also your prerogative to exercise restraint** of the kind that he never did.

THE BROWNS
You are the blue-plate special of grits and coq au vin.

They pursued the Southern route to stardom, working their way up from Little Rock to Nashville on live radio programs like "Barnyard Frolics" and "Louisiana Hayride." But Maxine, Bonnie, and Jim Ed (yes, Jim Ed) Brown's ascent stalled just short of its goal, and by 1959, a workaday life on the margins of country success seemed all the Browns could hope for. But then something strange and marvelous happened. Through a wrinkle in the fabric of popstrological space-time, a sinking country star was suddenly and unexpectedly catapulted into the highest reaches of the *pop* universe thanks to the power of a Massive star from a completely different dimension. That star was Edith Piaf, the legendary French chanteuse whose 1945 hit, *Les Trois Cloches*, had somehow made its way to the ears of young Jim Ed back in high school in Pine Bluff, Arkansas. On the brink of quitting the music business entirely, the Brown siblings instead recorded the Little Sparrow's song as *The Three Bells*, and its dramatic suc-

cess made them not only the second star in the constellation **Gene Pool**, but also the first and still the most *continental* star in the constellation **Country Cousins**. As the child of a star whose rise requires the popstrological equivalent of advanced string theory to explain, you too may find yourself **challenging traditional boundaries** and enjoying your greatest successes when **hard work and serendipity** collide.

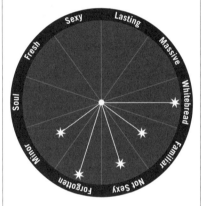

CONSTELLATIONS
➤ Country Cousins
➤ Gene Pool

BIRTHSONG
➤ *The Three Bells*
Aug 24–Sep 20, 1959

THE BUCKINGHAMS
You are the hard-shelled survivor who weeps over lost pen caps.

Maybe those erratic ups and downs of yours are merely chemical, but maybe the explanation lies in your Birthstar, the Buckinghams, and

in the ode to unhealthy emotion management that is your Birthsong. *Kind Of A Drag* was the song that dominated the pop universe at the moment of your birth, and "kind of a drag" is precisely the nonchalant phrase it offered up as a valid emotional response to being cheated on and abandoned by a romantic partner. Now, most of us feel that it's "kind of a drag" when the beer runs out, but gut-wrenchingly painful when someone we love does, and so we simply laugh at the Buckinghams for their go-with-the-flow posing in the early days of the free-love movement. But most of us don't have to deal, as you do, with having been born under the Buckinghams' popstrological influence. For you, their legacy can be felt **every time your mood swings**, or every time your **emotion meter gets stuck inappropriately** in one particular setting. Having been lifted to stardom on the strength of their emotional dishonesty, you might think your Birthstar would have bestowed upon you that same dubious gift, but while that's entirely possible, it's

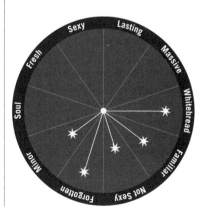

even more likely that they're to blame (or thank) for that **depth of feeling you can't seem to resist sharing** at every possible opportunity.

CONSTELLATION
➤ Neither/Nor

CELEBRITIES
➤ **Kurt Cobain** (2/20/67) was a Buckingham, born under the song *Kind of a Drag*. **Benicio Del Toro** (2/19/67) and **Lili Taylor** (2/20/67) still are.

BIRTHSONG
➤ *Kind Of A Drag*
Feb 12–25, 1967

THE BYRDS
Sometimes it's not the words you say, but the way that you say them.

The Byrds were by no means alone in mining pop hits out of the Bob Dylan catalog, but their rendition of *Mr. Tambourine Man* was the most important Dylan cover of all time. Before your Birthstar took that song and set it to a rock-and-roll instrumental track, Dylan covers had always been acoustic, and had always stayed within the accepted stylistic boundaries of folk. But the Byrds did something more than just earn themselves a place in the constellation *Fresh Breeze* with their first #1 song—they created the very genre called folk rock. With four decades of pop music reflecting its influence now behind us, the sound of jangly electric guitars over lush harmonies and a rock-and-roll rhythm section doesn't seem revolutionary, but it hit the universe of pop as hard in 1965 as the Beatles did in 1964. Without the Byrds, you don't get *Turn! Turn! Turn!, Eight Miles High*, and *So You Want To Be A Rock And Roll Star*, and you obviously don't get CSN&Y and the Flying Burrito Brothers. But you probably also don't get Simon and Garfunkel, the Eagles, and R.E.M., among others, and that's critical to understanding your own place in life. **Your gifts might have gone unnoticed** were it not for the genius of others, but for someone who **stands on such giant shoulders**, child of the Byrds, **you'd be surprised how many will follow in your footsteps**.

CONSTELLATIONS
➤ Fresh Breeze
➤ Folkie
➤ Launching Pad

CELEBRITY
➤ **Ben Stiller** (11/30/65) is a Byrd.

BIRTHSONGS
➤ *Mr. Tambourine Man*
Jul 20–26, 1965
➤ *Turn! Turn! Turn!*
Nov 28–Dec 18, 1965

GLEN CAMPBELL
Your train may take the long way, but it'll get you to your destination.

One of the few non-songwriting members of the constellation *Invisible Hand*, Glen Campbell can be heard playing guitar on half the records made in L.A. in the late fifties and early sixties. But in the Upstairs-Downstairs world of the record industry, an in-demand sideman who earns a fine living is never going to sit at the big table with the stars, no matter how indispensable his talents to their success. The Beach Boys even invited Campbell to join their group as a full member following Brian Wilson's breakdown, except that by "full member" they meant everything but an equal share in the royalties. After responding to their generous offer with a polite "screw you," your Birthstar proceeded to work his way up on his own, via hits like *Wichita Lineman, Galveston*, and *By The Time I Get To Phoenix*. And while his signature hit and first #1, *Rhinestone Cowboy*, may have sounded vaguely autobiographical, in reality there was precious little compromisin' on the road to Glen's horizon. A popstrological icon of the **working man made good** (good enough, even, to fall prey to the vices of the rich), your

Birthstar bestows upon you an **ability to shine in supporting roles,** but a **limited tolerance** for making them the sum total of your life's work.

CONSTELLATIONS
➤ Invisible Hand
➤ Country Cousins

BIRTHSONGS
➤ *Rhinestone Cowboy* Aug 31–Sep 13, 1975
➤ *Southern Nights* Apr 24–30, 1977

CAPTAIN AND TENNILLE
While others simply pretend, you want a love that will last to the end.

With divorce rates sky-rocketing and the sexual revolution in full bloom, it was dark days ahead for the American marriage in the mid-1970s. But then came Captain and Tennille, a walking, talking advertisement for wedded bliss who burst on the scene like a Whitebread super-nova in 1975. She with her shiny hair and perfect teeth, and he with a captain's hat that spoke of limitless nautical possibilities—if you were a white, married, suburban adult in the mid-seventies, they were exactly the couple you wished you could be part of. And notwithstanding the title of their irresistible debut #1, *Love Will Keep Us Together,* you somehow knew that love alone was not what kept that smile on Toni Tennille's face. No, theirs was a physical as well as a spiritual union of the souls, a fact well attested to in their second #1, *Do That To Me One More Time,* and in the fact that theirs is one of only three marriages represented in the constellation **Holy Matrimony** to survive intact to this very day. **The rewards of settled monogamy** are a driving force in the lives of most Captain and Tennilles—sometimes as a horror to run from, sadly, but more often than not as an ideal to strive for.

CONSTELLATIONS
➤ Lite & White
➤ Holy Matrimony

CELEBRITY
➤ **Tobey Maguire** (6/27/75) is a Captain and Tennille born under the song *Love Will Keep Us Together.*
➤ **Christina Ricci** (2/12/80) was born under the song *Do That To Me One More Time.*

BIRTHSONGS
➤ *Love Will Keep Us Together* Jun 15–Jul 12, 1975
➤ *Do That To Me One More Time* Feb 10–16, 1980

IRENE CARA
You could really have it all, if someone showed you where to find it.

When Hollywood comes to its senses and gets back to making movies that feature dances of liberation atop taxis, cafeteria tables, and blast furnaces, one can only hope that your Birthstar will be called out of retirement to provide their theme songs. Irene Cara's star was launched by the 1980 film *Fame,* a movie in which she not only starred, but for which she recorded not one but *two* Oscar-nominated songs. And though neither the song *Fame* nor *Out Here On My Own* managed to earn your Birthstar her popstrological stripes, she seized her next opportunity to do so three years later with a #1 hit theme song from what is still the definitive American film about female welders-by-day/exotic-dancers-by-night. But for all that *Flashdance* did for barefoot lobster dinners and the under-appreciated art of pole dancing, it failed to propel your Birthstar to greater heights of achieve-ment. For a brief moment, Irene Cara seemed to enjoy money-in-the-bank status as the closest female counterpart to Kenny Loggins in the popstrological constellation *Theme Singer*, but her rapid disappearance from popstrological view suggests that those born under her influ-ence should **take care not to be too passive** in matters of career, for the ability **to create oppor-tunities for yourself** is a better long-term bet than merely **seiz-ing those that others hand you**.

CONSTELLATION
➤ Theme Singer

CELEBRITY
➤ **Michelle Branch** (7/2/83) is a child of Irene Cara.

BIRTHSONG
➤ *Flashdance (What A Feeling)* May 22–Jul 2, 1983

BELINDA CARLISLE
The more you change your outside, the more it's what's inside that counts.

To those who knew and loved her in her first incarnation, there was something about the emergence of Belinda Carlisle as a solo artist that brought to mind the scene at the end of *The Stepford Wives* when we come to realize that our spirited heroine has been murdered and replaced by a mindless, compliant sexbot. This is not to suggest that your Birthstar was either (a) a mechanical replacement of her former self or (b) less than fully complicit in her late-eighties makeover. It's just that there was something *missing* from Belinda the second time around—some-thing more than just the extra pounds she'd carried in her hard-partying days as the lead singer of the fabulous Go-Go's. Sure, her newfound cheekbones looked great on MTV, but where was her *spark?* Where was the infectious life force that made her former

band so completely irresistible? Some Birthstars offer gifts and others offer challenges; yours offers both: the gift of **enormous verve and personality** and the challenge of achieving **main-stream appeal** without having those **gifts surgically removed**.

CONSTELLATION
➤ Spin-Off

BIRTHSONG
➤ *Heaven Is A Place On Earth* Nov 29–Dec 5, 1987

KIM CARNES
Your thumb is so green that you may sow the seeds of your own undoing.

You were born during a fascinating period in popstrological history—a period that witnessed an astonishing flowering among popstrological forces that would soon be swept into the ash heap of history by the rise of the con-stellation *Reaganrock*. But don't blame the hegemony of *Reaganrock* for the end of your Birthstar's briefly Massive career, for Kim Carnes was a victim of her own popstrological creation: a *Fresh Breeze* powerful enough to knock her off her feet. Prior to the spring of your birth, Kim Carnes was known for a Miracles cover (*More Love*) and a Kenny Rogers duet (*Don't Fall In Love With A Dreamer*), and if you'd been told then that she was des-tined for a popstrological break-through, you'd have guessed it would place her in the constellation *Lite & White*. But then came *Bette Davis Eyes*, straight from left field. Kim Carnes's God-given bourbon-and-Pall Malls voice was a perfect match for the lyric, but it was the utterly unexpected synthesizer sound—more Gary Numan than Christopher Cross—that made your Birthsong so alluring. Perhaps wisely, Kim Carnes never bothered to try recapturing the strange magic of her nine-week #1 hit, but popular memory of *Bette Davis Eyes* also made it impossible for her to build on her popstrological success in her vastly less interesting native style. Your Birthstar bestows upon you **many natural strengths**, child of Kim Carnes, but **your greatest success may not come from playing to them**. Decide for yourself whether that success is worth it.

CONSTELLATIONS
➤ Fresh Breeze
➤ Casio

CELEBRITY
➤ **Jamie-Lynn DiScala** (5/15/81) is a child of Kim Carnes.

BIRTHSONG
➤ *Bette Davis Eyes* May 10–Jun 13 and Jun 21–Jul 18, 1981

THE CARPENTERS
You may be miles from anyone's idea of edgy, but your power to win a passionate and loyal audience cannot be denied.

The brother-sister duo with the million-dollar smiles and the optimistic sound established themselves and the constellation *Lite & White* as a major force in the pop universe of the early 1970s. If you are one of the many Carpenters out there straining to get as far away as possible from your Whitebread roots, do at least pause to appreciate the relatively rare combination of popstrological qualities in your Birthstar. It is true that pop stars don't come any more Whitebread than Richard and Karen Carpenter, yet their sound was quite Fresh indeed in the early seventies. And let us not ignore that innocent, mild, yet undeniable sexiness, confusing though it must have been to fans of such nearly identical-looking members of the constellation *Gene Pool*. The exceptionally uncommon Fresh/Sexy/Whitebread nexus practically leaps out of the Carpenters' Starchart, and it creates strong potentials for **wholesome creativity and adventurousness** and perhaps for a little **testing of the conventional boundaries** that figure so prominently in the lives of you and your Whitebread ilk.

CONSTELLATIONS
➤ Gene Pool
➤ Lite & White
➤ Tragic Demise

CELEBRITY
➤ **Jennifer Lopez** (7/24/70) is a Carpenter born under the song *Close To You*. **Kevin Smith** (8/2/70), **M. Night Shyamalan** (8/6/70), and **Tyra Banks** (12/4/73) are also children of the Carpenters.

BIRTHSONGS
➤ *Close To You* Jul 19–Aug 16, 1970
➤ *Top Of The World* Nov 25–Dec 8, 1973
➤ *Please Mr. Postman* Jan 19–25, 1975

SHAUN CASSIDY
You are the carpenter who specializes in prefabricated homes.

e was only the third popstrological star young enough to be born within the popstrological era, and not only were the two who came before him (Michael J. and Donny O.) also connected to famous brothers, but the Birthstar of your Birthstar was Santo and Johnny (see: 1959), who were—hold onto your hats—*brothers*. The point is that it wasn't just nepotism that made Shaun Cassidy's career: it was popstrological manifest destiny. Still, a darker soul than he might have squandered that destiny in pre-fame bitterness while half-brother David rose to *Partridge Family* superstardom alongside Shaun's real mom, Shirley Jones. But Shaun Cassidy's soul was more blond than it was dark. He was cute, he could sort of sing, and unlike David, he didn't suffer from the why-won't-they-take-me-seriously's. Your good-natured Birthstar simply waited his turn, and verily it came to him at the advanced age of eighteen, when *Da Doo Ron Ron* on the pop charts and *The Hardy Boys Mysteries* on the airwaves gave him what popstrologists call the *Tiger Beat* double whammy: dual residence in the constellations *Teen Idol* and *Hot Hairdo*

to go with his career-making place in the constellation *Gene Pool*. Great teeth, great hair, and hordes of teenage fans may not be the birthright of Shaun Cassidy's popstrological progeny, but the **ability to succeed beyond where talent alone might take them** probably is.

CONSTELLATIONS
➤ Teen Idol
➤ Gene Pool
➤ Hot Hairdo

BIRTHSONG
➤ *Da Doo Ron Ron*
Jul 10–16, 1977

PETER CETERA
You are the glorious butterfly who's reluctant to emerge from the cocoon.

What Michael McDonald and Lionel Richie were to the Doobie Brothers and the Commodores, Peter Cetera was to Chicago: the man who found his true voice while teaching his former group how *not* to rock. It took your Birthstar seventeen albums with Chicago before he worked up the nerve to go solo, but when he finally did, his timing couldn't have been more perfect. The year was 1986, the constellation *Reaganrock* was in its ascendancy, and Kenny Loggins was simply too busy to record every single movie sound track, which left *Karate Kid, Part II* to Cetera and his *Glory Of Love*. And if your Birthsong's bombastic

Whitebread grandeur seems indistinguishable from Chicago's 1982 #1 *Hard To Say I'm Sorry,* it only goes to show you (a) the degree to which Cetera had transformed his former group by the end of his tenure and (b) the enduring appeal of a full-tilt, over-the-top power ballad in the hands of an uninhibited master. If you sometimes feel like renting the entire film oeuvre of Ralph Macchio and staying up all night to watch it, that's just popstrology at work. Because like your Birthstar himself, you are the type who understands **the importance of the word "sometimes" in the edict that less is sometimes more**.

CONSTELLATIONS
➤ Spin-Off
➤ Reaganrock
➤ Theme Singer

BIRTHSONG
➤ *Glory Of Love* July 27–
Aug 9, 1986

PETER CETERA AND AMY GRANT
You might actually be a saint, but to someone you're a sinner.

It's extremely difficult to imagine Peter Cetera as a defiler of a pious and virtuous young woman, but that's exactly how many of Amy Grant's biggest fans saw him when he tempted her into a popstrological *Power Couple* in late 1986. Ms. Grant wasn't a pop singer, you see—she was a singer of gospel and Christian Contemporary with a devout following that bought her records in the millions and viewed her move away from their chosen genre as a true fall from grace. You are too young to remember, but as powerful as the constellation *Reaganrock* was in the 1980s, its watered-down sound was still demon rock and roll to some, and not just a lunatic fringe. Or at least not a small lunatic fringe. These were the years, after all, in which Jerry Falwell's Moral Majority was at the apex of its powers, and devotees of his brand of Christianity viewed Ms. Grant's crossover as a grim portent indeed. And perhaps their fears were well founded, for not three months after you were born, the taint of sin was shockingly revealed even within the holy confines of the Praise the Lord Ministries, whose leader Jim Bakker provided America with what historians may someday call the first great scandal of the modern media age. As a child of Peter Cetera and

Amy Grant, you are **unlikely to be viewed as an iconoclast**, and yet your **capacity for toppling dubious icons** through **seemingly innocent actions** is popstrologically unquestionable.

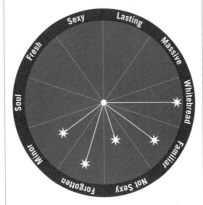

CONSTELLATIONS
➤ Power Couple
➤ Reaganrock

BIRTHSONG
➤ *The Next Time I Fall*
Nov 30–Dec 6, 1986

THE CHAMPS
They say a picture's worth a thousand words, but so is a single word in just the right context.

If you've ever attacked a problem with every weapon in your arsenal only to find the solution at the moment you stopped looking, that's the influence of your Birthstar at work. Like thousands of bands who never managed to rise from obscurity, the Champs earned their living on the prom-and-wedding circuit while dreaming of something more. Yet for all their hard work, it was a two-chord groove intended as a

between-set filler that turned them into legends. When the crowds started dancing during the breaks more enthusiastically than during their sets, the Champs were inspired to record the throwaway number they called *Tequila*. Your Birthsong, of course, became an instant classic that will probably be inducing Pee-wee Herman dance moves at wedding receptions long after anyone reading these words has breathed their last. But more than that, the rise of your Birthstar marked the rise of a new and instrumental force (literally and figuratively) in the popstrological firmament: the constellation *Speechless*. Unlike your Birthstar, you may not always prefer to **let your actions speak louder than your words**, but it's a near popstrological certainty that the words you do speak are powerful enough to **elicit enthusiastic support**.

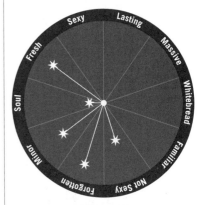

CONSTELLATIONS
➤ Fresh Breeze
➤ Speechless

BIRTHSONG
➤ *Tequila* Mar 17–Apr 20, 1958

GENE CHANDLER

Napoleon crowned himself emperor, and look where it got him.

The Founding Fathers believed that titles of European nobility had no place in American society because they set one man above another in a way that was corrosive to the democratic spirit. That's why they decided to call the commander in chief "Mr. President" rather than "Your Excellency," and that's why they would have warned the other members of the Chicago doo-wop group called the Dukays about the risks of letting legal issues arising from a label switch lead them to put *Duke Of Earl* out under the name of their lead singer. Sure enough, no sooner had your Birthsong begun its climb up the charts than Gene Chandler (née Eugene Dixon) began wearing a top hat and monocle and calling himself simply "the Duke." Chandler managed to seize the Dukays' rightful place in the popstrological firmament, but his Dukedom was short-lived. Within a year, he was plain old Gene Chandler

again, a fallen aristocrat toiling away in the 1960s Chicago soul scene alongside heroes of the working class like Curtis Mayfield. Those born under the influence of the Gene Chandler putsch will tend to **struggle with issues of power**—always **craving it**, always **taking it**, or maybe just always **losing it**.

CONSTELLATION
➤ Doo-Wop

CELEBRITIES
➤ **Sheryl Crow** (2/11/62) and **Jon Bon Jovi** (3/2/62) are both Gene Chandlers.

BIRTHSONG
➤ *Duke Of Earl* Feb 11– Mar 3, 1962

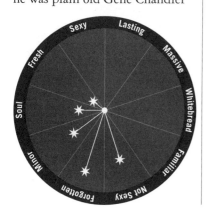

BRUCE CHANNEL

Why struggle for a fifty-cent word when your mind is filled with nickels and pennies?

Pretend it's a test on the back of a matchbook and fill in the blanks: *She's so _____, I'm gonna make her _____.* Good, now try this one: *Come on, baby, let's give it a _____, I wanna know if you'll be my _____.* Congratulations! You've just completed half the lyrics to your Birthstar's one and only pop hit and qualified yourself for admission into the American School of Rock and Roll Songwriting! If you're saying to yourself, "Gee, that entrance exam seems a bit too simple," then you're missing the point, because the very motto of the ASRRS is

"Keep It Simple, Stupid" and the entire curriculum is geared toward purging your memory of songs like *You're So Vain* and filling it instead with songs like *Hey! Baby.* (Your Birthsong was a favorite of the Beatles, after all, and look where it got them.) Bruce Channel carved out a modest but respectable career (and a quiet spot in the constellation *Invisible Hand*) post-1962 by writing songs for the likes of Jerry Lee Lewis, Alabama, and The Band, but even he found it difficult to recapture the simple perfection of *Hey! Baby* once he began consciously trying to do so. Those born under this Fresh but Forgotten star in the constellation *Texstyle* should always remember that it's a **slippery slope from complex to complicated.**

CONSTELLATIONS
➤ Texstyle
➤ Invisible Hand

CELEBRITY
➤ **Matthew Broderick** (3/21/62) is a Bruce Channel.

BIRTHSONG
➤ *Hey! Baby* Mar 4–24, 1962

HARRY CHAPIN

Not every story has a moral, but you're doing your best to change all that.

He was a deeply sincere and politically conscious singer-songwriter who dedicated himself in the years before his *Tragic Demise* on the Long Island Expressway to wiping out world hunger. Yet the greatest social change to which your Birthstar contributed was right here at home, where an entire generation of baby boomers just getting around to having kids in 1974 heard *Cat's In The Cradle* and swore to themselves that they'd not repeat the mistakes their own parents had made in raising them. And kudos must be given to those former sixties kids for attempting to break the eternal chain of transgenerational dysfunction. But just as one could knock Harry Chapin for **leaving no head unhammered** in your Birthsong ("*My son was just like me!*" Get it?!), these well-meaning boomers were **not the types to let their efforts go unheralded**. BABY ON BOARD signs, quality time, even the term "parenting" itself—these are cultural markers of your childhood that can be traced directly to the influence of your Birthstar. Though an absent father to his own popstrological children, your Birthstar remains a powerful force in the didactic wing of the constellation *Storyteller*, bestowing upon you not just the power of conviction, but **a tendency to share** those convictions at the drop of a hat.

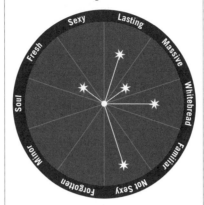

CONSTELLATIONS
➤ Storyteller
➤ Tragic Demise

BIRTHSONG
➤ *Cat's In The Cradle*
Dec 15–21, 1974

RAY CHARLES

It's fine to be a jack of all trades as long as you are the master of one.

Yes, he was one of soul music's founding fathers, and yes, his star sits at the very center of the constellation *So-Soul*, but you might be surprised to know that, according to Willie Nelson at least, Ray Charles did more for country music in his 1960s heyday than any man or woman you might normally associate with that genre. Indeed, your Birthstar's popstrological legacy, and a large part of his commercial success, can be traced to his all-embracing attitude toward music. He made his name and his critical reputation on undiluted R&B records like *What'd I Say*, but he spent his childhood immersed in the sounds of jazz, blues, gospel, and country, and it was his 1962 album *Modern Sounds in Country and Western Music* that yielded his biggest popstrological hit, *I Can't Stop Loving You*. Ray Charles has said, "There's only two kinds of music as far as I'm concerned: good and bad," and it is probably that philosophy that made him, by some measures, the third most successful pop star of the 1960s after Elvis Presley and the Beatles. Of course, that philosophy could have been disastrous in the absence of good taste and brilliant execution, but Ray Charles had little problem with either of those. It is only in his popstrological children that the **tendency to drift away from core competencies can sometimes lead to trouble**. On the other hand, the **unwillingness to be pigeonholed** can be a key underpinning of success for those born under this Massive and massively Soulful star, provided they can avoid the pitfalls of dilettantism.

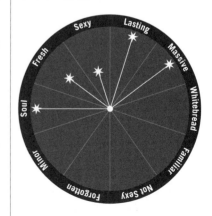

CONSTELLATION
➤ So-Soul

CELEBRITIES
➤ **Allison Janney** (11/19/60), **Wynton Marsalis** (10/18/61), **Ally Sheedy** (6/12/62), and **Paula Abdul** (6/19/62) are children of Ray Charles.

BIRTHSONGS
➤ *Georgia On My Mind* Nov 14–20, 1960
➤ *Hit The Road, Jack* Oct 9–22, 1961
➤ *I Can't Stop Loving You* May 27–Jun 30, 1962

CHEAP TRICK
You are the giver of sanctuary in times of teen trouble.

You are roaming the grounds of a suburban American high school at lunchtime in 1979, and the popstrological battle lines are clearly visible. For the popular crowd out on the quad, disco rules unchallenged, but for their mortal enemies in the parking lot, it is Ozzy who rocks and disco that emphatically Sucks. The only thing these two groups can agree on is their shared disdain for the freaks out behind the gym, for whom disco is dead, Ozzy is a joke, and the Clash is the Only Band That Matters. On this battleground of warring teenage tribes, there is only one place where you might find **an island of relative tolerance**: in the band room, where a motley group of future dropouts, rock stars, and software entrepreneurs sits reading guitar magazines and listening to Cheap Trick. Their sole #1 hit was a forgettable power ballad that came many years after their pop-anthem heyday (think *Surrender* and *I Want You To Want Me*), but in that heyday Cheap Trick occupied a crucial, peacemaking niche in the social universe of American teens and bestowed upon them a **powerful social neutrality** and a non-threatening charm **as appealing to jocks and geeks as to stoners and freaks**.

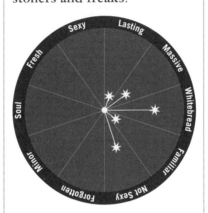

CONSTELLATION
➤ Tip of the Ice Cube

BIRTHSONG
➤ *The Flame* Jul 3–16, 1988

CHUBBY CHECKER
Crowds may be putty in your hands, but who is the putty-master and who is the putty-master's master?

There were a thousand dances with names and theme songs in the early sixties, but there was only one Twist, and Chubby Checker was its king. The man behind the throne, however, was the ubiquitous kingmaker Dick Clark, who knew that a mainstream re-recording of the obscure R&B tune *The Twist* would be a smash hit after he watched the dance it inspired take off on *Bandstand*. Dick handpicked Ernest "Chubby" Evans to sing the song after his other protégés, Danny and the Juniors, failed to move quickly enough, and Dick's wife added the name Checker to "Chubby" to complete the takeoff on "Fats Domino." The rest was history, as the Twist went on to become the Macarena of its time, embraced enthusiastically by American teens in 1959 and then again by swinging middle-aged adults in 1961, to the utter mortification of their teenage children (See: Joey Dee and the Starliters). Perhaps the star with the most to be grateful for in the constellation *Thanks, Dick*, your Birthstar bestows upon you a tendency to **align yourself with deceptively benevolent leaders**—a potential danger given your obvious

power to win legions of eager followers.

CONSTELLATION
➤ Thanks, Dick

BIRTHSONGS
➤ *The Twist* Sep 19–25, 1960, and Jan 7–20, 1962
➤ *Pony Time* Feb 27–Mar 19, 1961

CHER
If you can't help wearing your vulnerability on your sleeve, the trick is never to wear sleeves.

She married Greg Allman for nine days and she inspired three generations of drag queens and counting, but the only boy who could ever reach her was a dinky Italian guy with a Prince Valiant haircut and a bearskin vest. That much could be seen in the tears that flowed from Cher's eyes when Sonny Bono died—tears that served as a poignant reminder that a mere and vulnerable mortal actually resides within your Birthstar's mythic bodily form. This was something many of us had forgotten over the years, as we watched Cher continually disappear and reappear in ever more impressive physical form to bedazzle yet another generation of pop fans. But whatever feats of aesthetic renewal your *Shape-Shifter* Birthstar has in store for the remaining decades of the twenty-first century, always remember that you were born at a time when she bared not just her flesh in those Bob Mackie dresses, but her God-given nose and a bit of her soul as well. In a string of early-seventies hits that earned her a place in the constellation *Storyteller*, your formerly gawky and awkward Birthstar staked her claim as patron saint of picked-on misfits and ostracized mongrels. **Never fear rejection**, popstrological children of Cher, but as you gain wider and wider acceptance, **never forget that you've experienced it**, either.

CONSTELLATIONS
➤ Shape-Shifter
➤ Storyteller
➤ Spin-Off

BIRTHSONGS
➤ *Gypsys, Tramps & Thieves* Oct 31–Nov 13, 1971
➤ *Half-Breed* Sep 30–Oct 13, 1973
➤ *Dark Lady* Mar 17–23, 1974

CHIC
Some stand on giant shoulders, but you provide them.

If ever style and substance battled it out to a glorious draw, it was in the case of your Birthstar, whose brief heyday lifted disco to new heights just moments before its crash. They were Fresh, they were Sexy, they were Massive—yet who could have known the true extent of their power? Who could have known that Chic would emerge, Obi-Wan Kenobi–like, popstrologically *stronger* following their death as an active group? The force that was so strong in your Birthstar can be felt in the countless classics that one or both of Nile Rodgers and Bernard Edwards, the braintrust of Chic, produced following your Birthstar's demise. But even if they hadn't put their unmistakable stamp on songs like *We Are Family*, *I'm Coming Out*, *Let's Dance*, and *Like A Virgin*, among many others, your Birthstar would still shine as one of the most important stars in the constellation *Invisible Hand* purely on strength of one world-altering contribution to musical history. That contribution was the long and funky instrumental breaks that made *Good Times* a favorite record of the chatty Bronx club DJs who invented hip-hop. When the Sugar Hill Gang used *Good Times* as the basis for *Rapper's Delight*, the

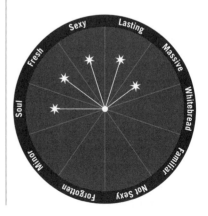

popular revolution was born, and your popstrological fate was sealed. The **movers and shakers may someday forget your name**, child of Chic, but there's **no limit to the moving and shaking** you'll continue to inspire.

CONSTELLATIONS
➤ Invisible Hand
➤ Disco Ball

BIRTHSONGS
➤ *Le Freak* Dec 3–9 and 17–30, 1978, and Jan 14–Feb 3, 1979
➤ *Good Times* Aug 12–18, 1979

CHICAGO
You may not deliver thrills, but you sure deliver value.

True to the needs of the album-oriented rock (AOR) format that launched them, the first four releases by the band called Chicago comprised three double albums and one *quadruple* album. That's *ten* LPs in a little less than thirty months, and if you factored that into your Birthstar's already staggering album-sales figures, you might find that in terms of sheer tonnage, Chicago shipped more vinyl than any other American rock band in the 1970s. Not bad for a group that could've walked through O'Hare Airport at the height of their success without attracting so much as a single screaming fan. That's not because their fans didn't love them, but because total subjugation of individual ego to the collective good of the group was the rule in Chicago, even to the point of using a logo rather than a picture of the band on all of their albums. It would turn out in the end, of course, that the incredibly accomplished and hardworking musicians who had chosen so admirably to prosper as seven anonymous dwarves had been harboring a would-be Snow White in their midst all along. Peter Cetera was his name, and as soon his name became well known to those who loved his high tenor voice, he was asked to leave a hive that was perfectly happy not to have a queen. **"Team player" may sound like faint praise** sometimes, but **find the right team to play with** and you'll realize your true power.

CONSTELLATIONS
➤ Launching Pad
➤ Lite & White

BIRTHSONGS
➤ *If You Leave Me Now* Oct 17–30, 1976
➤ *Hard To Say I'm Sorry* Sep 5–18, 1982
➤ *Look Away* Dec 4–17, 1988

THE CHIFFONS
Yours is the hand that helps the helping hands by graciously accepting their helpful handouts.

It was hard to listen to the *"hare Krishna, hare Rama"* chorus of *My Sweet Lord* and not conclude that George Harrison had stolen from the *"doo-lang doo-langs"* of the Chiffons in writing his 1970 hit. But as a matter of law and of popstrology, *He's So Fine* wasn't really your Birthstar's to lose. You see, the Chiffons had been handed stardom practically on a silver platter in the autumn of 1962, when a struggling songwriter named Ronnie Mack sold *He's So Fine* on the promise that he had a group ready to record it right away. Mack then contacted the only group he knew in New York, and within months, his gift had made four Bronx teenagers the fourth star to join the ascendant constellation **Les Girls** and the eighth to join the constellation **Regifted**. The Chiffons scored one more major hit with *One Fine Day*, a Goffin/King gem with the Chiffons' vocals plopped over a Little Eva demo. But with Ronnie Mack tragically dead (cancer, age twenty-five) and Little Eva releasing records of her own (e.g., *The Loco-Motion*), there were no popstrological gifts for your Birthstar to unwrap, and they faded gently into obscurity. Whether you're a **pathologically self-reliant** oppositional Chiffon or a Chiffon whose **every step is aided by a helping hand**, the lesson of your Birthstar is the same: there's **nothing wrong with being showered with gifts**, just as long as you've got a few gifts of your own.

CONSTELLATIONS
➤ Les Girls
➤ Regifted

CELEBRITIES
➤ **Quentin Tarantino** (3/27/63) and **Conan O'Brien** (4/18/63) are popstrological Chiffons.

BIRTHSONG
➤ *He's So Fine* Mar 24–Apr 20, 1963

THE CHI-LITES
You are a builder of emotional walls with hidden doors.

There's a wonderful scene in the fourth season of *The Sopranos* in which an emotional Tony, moved to tears in his Chevy Suburban while listening to your Birthsong, resolves to express certain pent-up emotions openly and honestly. That he expresses those emotions by savagely beating his state

assemblyman on the floor of an ex-mistress's bathroom is beside the point. The important thing is that Tony reconnected with the group who proved in his youth that the new male sensitivity was not the sole province of the constellation *Lite & White*. That was the vital role the Chi-Lites played in their early-seventies heyday: they were the *So-Soul* option for men who were ready and willing to get in touch with their feelings, but not if it meant listening to groups like Bread. Aside from the requisite foray into social commentary with 1971's *(For God's Sake) Give More Power To The People*, your Birthstar focused its energies almost exclusively on fare such as *Let Me Be The Man My Daddy Was*; *Coldest Days Of My Life*; *Have You Seen Her*; and, of course, *Oh Girl*—all of them songs that explored **masculine emotions** without consigning them to men's "feminine side." If you're a male child of the Chi-Lites yourself or just someone who loves one, it's important always to remember that something can **touch your feelings without being touchy-feely**.

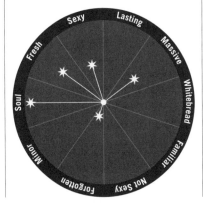

CONSTELLATION
➤ So-Soul

CELEBRITY
➤ **The Notorious B.I.G.** (5/21/72) was a Chi-Lite.

BIRTHSONG
➤ *Oh Girl* May 21–27, 1972

THE CHIPMUNKS
Your appeal is as strong as it is unreal.

Simon, the quiet one, and Theodore, the other quiet one, lent the group a certain stability with their calm and steady background presence, but it was Alvin—irrepressible, ADHD-afflicted Alvin—whose life spark made the Chipmunks great. To give sole credit for your Birthstar's considerable success to Alvin, though, would be to ignore the crucial role played by David Seville, the "fourth Chipmunk" and Alvin's long-suffering foil. Yes, David Seville, aka Ross Bagdasarian, created the Chipmunks from scratch, fulfilling the helium-induced vision first hinted at in *Witch Doctor* and launching the first popstrological star in the constellation *Artificial Ingredients*. But more than that, he stood by his sometimes insufferable creation through all the ups and downs of the decades that followed. Would the Chipmunks have survived the social, political, and musical upheaval of the sixties and seventies with their original lineup intact had Seville not been there to shepherd them through? Sadly, David Seville died before your Birthstar's glorious punk and country reinventions of the 1980s and '90s earned them a spot in the constellation *Shape-Shifter*, but he surely watched with pride from somewhere as his son and daughter engineered that feat. **Let others dismiss you as a lightweight**, child of the Chipmunks, for somewhere deep inside your middle-aged skin lies an **eternal six-year-old** whose unsinkable spirit has seen you through more discouraging attacks than that.

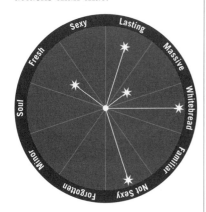

CONSTELLATIONS
➤ Novelty Merchant
➤ Artificial Ingredients
➤ Shape-Shifter

CELEBRITY
➤ **Susanna Hoffs** (1/17/59) is a child of the Chipmunks.

BIRTHSONG
➤ *The Chipmunk Song*
   Dec 22, 1958–Jan 18, 1959

LOU CHRISTIE
We all hit bottom, but not everyone bounces so high.

The former Lugee Alfredo Giovanni Sacco was a rising young star with two solid hits under his belt and a spot in Dick Clark's Caravan of Stars when he got called up to active duty from the army reserves in 1964. One day, he's making gold records and flirting on the tour bus with a cute girl from Detroit named Diana Ross. The next day, he's guarding gold bricks at Fort Knox and sharing a bunk with a young man in skivvies. It wasn't Vietnam, but it still must have felt like an inescapable quagmire to Lou Christie. When Lou finished his tour, he faced the double challenge of restarting a stalled career and doing it in a world permanently changed by the Beatles. It was a triumph of self-confidence, great songwriting, and an infectious sound that was equal parts Frankie Valli and Martha Reeves that earned popstrological immortality for Lou with the 1966 hit *Lightnin'*

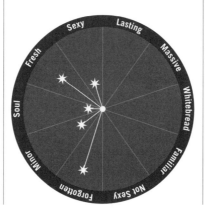

Strikes, a beloved gem that landed him in the constellation *Fresh Breeze* and continues to support his career as a hirsute heartthrob on the oldies concert circuit. **Overcoming setbacks** comes naturally to the children of Lou Christie, as does a **weakness in the knees for popstrological Supremes.**

CONSTELLATION
➤ Fresh Breeze

BIRTHSONGS
➤ *Lightnin' Strikes*
   Feb 13–19, 1966

ERIC CLAPTON
How many ships must a man jump from before he decides to swim?

An album called *History of Eric Clapton* came out when your Birthstar was only twenty-seven, and already it was difficult to squeeze a responsible overview of his career onto a single vinyl disk. Eric Clapton had, after all, quit his first famous band (the Yardbirds) before he was twenty and his second (John Mayall's Bluesbreakers) when he was twenty-one. He launched the farewell tour of his third (Cream) at twenty-three, and he had finished with his fourth (Blind Faith) and his fifth (Derek and the Dominos) by the time he was twenty-six. Even without the thirty-plus years as a solo act that followed his popstrological arrival in 1974, Eric Clapton would qualify for membership in the constellation *Tip of the*

Ice Cube, and the fact that he earned his only #1 hit with a song written by the popstrologically invisible Bob Marley only drives that point home further. There are many aspects of your wife-coveting, heroin-kicking, child-eulogizing Birthstar's career that may be reflected in you and in the rest of his popstrological children, but an admirable trait most of you share is a desire to **let your accomplishments speak for themselves**. And while pursuit of your goals may leave **a trail of broken relationships behind you**, perhaps you are simply one of those who take longer than others to **learn how to be alone**.

CONSTELLATIONS
➤ Tip of the Ice Cube
➤ Spin-Off

CELEBRITY
➤ **Ryan Phillippe** (9/10/74) is an Eric Clapton.

BIRTHSONG
➤ *I Shot The Sheriff*
Sep 8–14, 1974

PETULA CLARK
When the world hangs its head, you say, "Chin up, luv."

According to legend, Petula Clark got her big break during a rehearsal for a radio show in 1942, when a German air raid darkened the BBC studios and she sang in order to calm the nerves of the gathered cast and crew. Soon your preteen Birthstar was singing patriotic songs on her very own radio show, "Pet's Parlour," and establishing herself as an icon of hope and pluckiness during England's finest hour. It was two decades later, though, during the blitzkrieg of the British Invasion, that Petula Clark made her mark on this side of the Atlantic. And once again, she was cast in the role of a morale booster—not to a war-weary nation, but to a generation of young Americans deeply troubled by the uncoolness of their own suburban lives. With a style that was more Las Vegas than Liverpool, the music of Petula Clark held a strong appeal for the older set, but popstrologically speaking, her core audience was anyone young and bored enough to believe that things really could be great if only they could just grow up and get away from their stultifying surroundings. Movie shows, late-night cafes, gentle bossa novas—sophisticated delights like these exert a strong pull even on **oppositional Petula Clarks who take pleasure in exposing the world's many shortcomings** rather than in glossing them over. So even if you have settled for a love not quite as wide as the sky, count yourself fortunate for **taking pleasure in many things that are much more easily attained**.

CONSTELLATION
➤ Britvasion

CELEBRITIES
➤ **Diane Lane** (1/22/65) and **Chris Rock** (2/7/66) are popstrological children of Petula Clark.

BIRTHSONGS
➤ *Downtown* Jan 17–30, 1965
➤ *My Love* Jan 30–Feb 12, 1966

CLUB NOUVEAU
You may not have the strength to tear down barriers, but you might have the power to encourage those who do.

You couldn't make it into the popstrological firmament as a genuine hip-hop act—you just couldn't. Blondie, Falco, and Milli Vanilli rapped on their #1 records, but beyond that, hip-hop—the first truly revolutionary sound to arise since rock and roll itself—was almost entirely inaudible in the highest reaches of the pop universe in the 1980s. Almost. Before the decade was over, Bobby Brown would fight his way to the top with a hip-hop/R&B hybrid known as New Jack Swing, but the group that gave the popstrological firmament its first hint of the coming revolution was your Birthstar, Club Nouveau. It was the simplest thing in the world—a beat—that differentiated their remake of *Lean On Me* from the classic Bill Withers original, but what a difference it made. That beat—*boom-boom CHICK a-dukka boom-boom CHICK*—under an otherwise faithful rendering of *Lean On Me* represented the first breach of the constellation *Reaganrock*'s secret hip-hop defense shield, and it made Club Nouveau the one and only star in history to join the constellation *Fresh Breeze* on the strength of a song someone else made famous first. Some fight the power regardless of their chances of winning, but **you choose your**

battles wisely, child of Club Nouveau, preferring the **modest rewards of incremental success** to the dangerous lure of total victory.

CONSTELLATIONS
➤ Fresh Breeze
➤ Invisible Hand

BIRTHSONG
➤ *Lean On Me* Mar 15–28, 1987

JOE COCKER AND JENNIFER WARNES
Sometimes two wrongs actually do make a right.

Jennifer Warnes was a hard-working pro with a lovely voice, but director Taylor Hackford was never going to let someone with zero name-recognition (despite a minor hit in *The Right Time Of The Night*) record the theme song for his film *An Officer and a Gentleman*. Joe Cocker, on the other hand, had star power to burn, even thirteen years after his electrifying, starmaking performance of *With A Little Help From My Friends* at Woodstock. But the decade-plus of hard living following his 1969 triumph that had pushed his already raspy voice into undreamt-of regions of ravaged brilliance had also made Joe a bit iffy when it came to staying on his feet and rendering his lyrics intelligible. And so it was that one of the most unlikely yet wonderfully symbiotic pairings in the popstrological firma-

ment was formed and your extraordinarily hopeful legacy created. Any couple whose complementary strengths also serve to prop up each other's weaknesses is impressive, but a popstrological *Power Couple* that does that without also sowing the seeds of some or other evil is downright mind-blowing. **Your weaknesses may play a bigger role than your strengths** as you make your way through life, but you've also been blessed popstrologically with an inborn understanding of a lesson most others must learn the hard way: that **the perfect partner isn't necessarily the one that looks perfect on the outside.**

CONSTELLATIONS
➤ Power Couple
➤ Theme Singer

BIRTHSONGS
➤ *Up Where We Belong* Oct 31–Nov 20, 1982

PHIL COLLINS

You are the 'umble toiler who puts the "class" in "working class."

It's easy to imagine your Birthstar at nineteen, a full head of hair spilling down over his eyes, drumming away dutifully behind the mask-wearing prog-rock shaman Peter Gabriel and thinking to himself, "Geez, what I wouldn't give to do a Temptations song, just *once*." But as the junior member of the band Genesis in the early seventies, and as a product of the British class system, Phil Collins knew his place, and his place was behind the drum kit with his mouth shut. Even after Peter Gabriel quit Genesis, your Birthstar let his bandmates audition more than four hundred potential lead singers before clearing his throat and saying, "Y'know, I wouldn't mind 'avin' a go at it." Once he took over the reins, Phil Collins led his bandmates gradually but inexorably toward the lucrative mainstream, and toward the accessible hits that were the first Genesis songs most fans ever encountered. By the mid-1980s, Phil Collins had become the British near-equivalent of Huey Lewis, riding high in the constellation *Reaganrock* and brimming with such confidence and musical competence that it was frankly as hard to dislike him as it was to avoid him. But it is your Birthstar's willingness to endure a **slow, steady slog** to greatness that most clearly affects those born under his popstrological influence. For while many *say* that they are **willing to work hard for what they earn,** few show your capacity to **work so long and hard in the shadows** before emerging into the light.

CONSTELLATIONS
➤ Reaganrock
➤ Spin-Off
➤ Britsuasion
➤ Theme Singer

BIRTHSONGS
➤ *Against All Odds* Apr 15–May 4, 1984
➤ *One More Night* Mar 24–Apr 6, 1985
➤ *Sussudio* Jun 30–Jul 6, 1985
➤ *Groovy Kind Of Love* Oct 16–29, 1988
➤ *Two Hearts* Jan 15–28, 1989

PHIL COLLINS AND MARILYN MARTIN

Your storybook romances may all be like *Cinderella*, but without the final scene.

"All right, Kenny, I will prove it. Go ahead—pick any one of your backup singers and watch—I'll make 'er into a star." Is that how it all started? As a bet with Kenny Loggins over just how big a star Phil Collins had become since releasing his first solo album outside Genesis? We may never know for certain, but popstrologists can still say with confidence that whether Collins meant to or not, the message he sent to the rest of the world when he elevated a true and total unknown into the highest reaches of the pop universe by joining her in a popstrological *Power Couple* was that if he could do this, he could do anything. Not that Marilyn Martin acquitted herself as an amateur on your Birthsong, *Separate Lives*—far from it, in fact. But to think that the world would ever have known her name had she not been tapped by the British demigod of *Reaganrock* to join him on that wonderfully bitter Stephen Bishop breakup song is probably fantasy. Like the Greek gods whose couplings with mortals rarely left those mortals better off for the experience, Phil Collins's fling with Ms. Martin didn't endow her with any popstrological powers of her own. And while the children of this unprecedented popstrological experiment may find themselves all too often in **brief but emotionally fulfilling relationships characterized by dramatic power imbalances**, they clearly have a leg up on the children of those equally matched *Power Couple*s whose dramatic collisions were far more popstrologically troubling than emotionally fulfilling.

CONSTELLATIONS
➤ Power Couple
➤ Theme Singer

BIRTHSONG
➤ *Separate Lives* Nov 24–30, 1985

THE COMMODORES
People change, people grow, but few accept this as well as you.

If your own family or circle of friends has faced a similar situation, then you know how difficult it can be for even a close-knit group of people to accept with grace and dignity that one of their own has chosen to pursue an alternative lifestyle. Yet that's exactly what the Commodores managed to do

when they finally came to terms with Lionel Richie's true musical orientation. Oh sure, the road to acceptance probably passed through all the usual stages, from denial ("But what about *Brick House*, Lionel? You *love* that song!") to anger ("Damn, Lionel, you're a Commodore*, not a Carpenter!") to bargaining ("Well, what if you went and worked with Kenny Rogers for a bit? Would that help you get it out of your system?"). But a period of adjustment was to be expected from a band that started out with booty-shakers like *Machine Gun* and *Slippery When Wet* only to see their leader gravitate toward tearjerkers like *Three Times A Lady*, *Sail On*, and *Still*. The important thing is that in the end, the Commodores encouraged Lionel Richie to go out and pursue his awesome dream of Whitebread superstardom with their blessing, and though their own career never quite recovered from it, your Birthstar's loss was *Reaganrock*'s gain. **Love that does not judge or waver**—isn't that what we're all looking for? It's certainly what you've got to offer, if you can

bring yourself fully in touch with your popstrological potential.

CONSTELLATIONS
➤ So-Soul
➤ Launching Pad

BIRTHSONGS
➤ *Three Times A Lady* Aug 6–19, 1978
➤ *Still* Nov 11–17, 1979

PERRY COMO
Everyone may need a hug now and then, but not everyone wants one as often as you.

He was a fifty-something holdover in a cozy cardigan whose middle-of-the-road style was everything that rock and roll wasn't. Whereas rock and roll promised sex, excitement, and change, your Birthstar's brand of pop promised cocoa and Scrabble and a goodnight kiss from Mom and Dad on your way upstairs. Maybe that's why the first generation of teens exposed to Elvis Presley was reluctant to give up Perry Como completely. In the early months of a new era, records like *Hot Diggity*, *Catch A Falling Star*, and your Birthsong, *Round And Round*, held their own against vastly more rebellious fare, and while they might not have been cool, they really didn't need to be. They were the popstrological equivalent of a reassuring light left on in the kitchen after the sock hop, along with a note that reads *Hi, honey, how was the dance?* Like the well-raised brood of a fifties TV dad,

the popstrological children of Perry Como have **a wild side to compete with anyone's**, but they've also got the sense and good manners to **know when and when not to show it**.

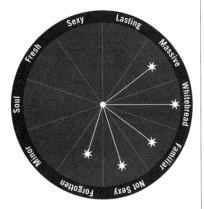

CONSTELLATION
➤ Old Guard

BIRTHSONG
➤ *Round And Round*
Apr 6–12, 1957

BILL CONTI
You are the motivational speaker who motivates without speaking.

A kid who grows up as a bassoon player probably never gets to hit the winning home run in the bottom of the ninth inning. What he does get, however, is a lot of time during orchestra practice to daydream about what it might feel like and to compose in his mind the stirring combination of Aaron Copland and the *1812 Overture* that would play while he sent the ball sailing over the fence. That's how your Birthstar, Bill Conti, knew exactly what to write when he was handed the job

of scoring Sylvester Stallone's *Rocky*. His previous sound track experience had been in the high-brow vein of Italian films like *The Garden of the Finzi-Continis*, but in 1976, he wrote a musical theme that helped turn a sentimental little boxing picture into a sociocultural phenomenon. *Gonna Fly Now (Theme From* Rocky*)* didn't just earn Bill Conti a place among the popstrological elite—it gave a popstrologically Massive gift to all humanity in the form of easily hummable shorthand for challenge and achievement against long odds. From his perch in the constellation *Theme Singer*, your Birthstar endows you with a **natural gift for stirring the emotions** and for instilling in others **the heart of a lion when no mere eye of a tiger will do**.

CONSTELLATIONS
➤ Theme Singer
➤ Speechless

CELEBRITY
➤ **Liv Tyler** (7/1/77) is a popstrological Bill Conti.

BIRTHSONG
➤ *Gonna Fly Now* Jun 26–Jul 2, 1977

SAM COOKE
Sin may shorten your life, but it needn't threaten the immortality of your soul.

His voice was a silky-smooth marvel, and if his singing didn't melt you, his unbelievable good looks would. He was Sam Cooke, former lead singer of a gospel group called the Soul Stirrers and one of the most soul-stirring talents in the history of pop. He earned just one #1 hit in his late-1950s, early-1960s heyday, though his long list of classic near-misses (*Wonderful World* and *Twistin' The Night Away*, to name only two) places his star squarely among the deceptively Massive forces of the constellation *Tip of the Iceberg*. Yet who knows how much greater his legacy might have been but for the events of December 11, 1964, when Los Angeles police found Sam Cooke dead on the office floor of the Hacienda Motel, shot three times in the chest by the motel's manager, Bertha Franklin. The authorities ruled Cooke's death a case of justifiable homicide, and indeed all available evidence suggested some rather serious misbehavior on his part. Yet even as the lurid details of the case were becoming common knowledge, some 200,000 fans—most but not all of them black—turned out in the streets of L.A. and Chicago to mourn the passing of a man whose legacy even then seemed worthy of transcending the scandal that gave the constellation

Tragic Demise its second incredibly brilliant star. Like your Massive and Lasting Birthstar, your greatest **contributions may lie hidden from view**, but so, unfortunately, may **the seeds of your eventual undoing**.

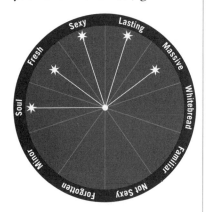

CONSTELLATIONS

➤ Tip of the Iceberg
➤ Tragic Demise
➤ So-Soul

BIRTHSONG

➤ *You Send Me* Dec 2–15, 1957

DAVE "BABY" CORTEZ

Why call it a rooster when you have the opportunity to call it a cock?

The late 1950s were a time when an instrumental tune called *Rumble* was banned from *American Bandstand* on fears that its title alone might inspire impressionable youth to go to war with switchblades and zip guns. Yet it was also a time when Ward Cleaver could be "hard on the Beaver" without raising an eyebrow in the CBS Standards and Practices division and a tune called *The Happy Organ* could rise, as it were, to the top of the pop charts without sparking a controversy. Were the ears of America really so deaf to double entendre in the year of your birth? Rest assured that they weren't, at least not in the halls of America's high schools, where your Birthsong earned many appreciative snickers from the sophisticated young humorists who filled out call slips at the local public library in the names of Messrs. Dick Hirtz, Jack Doff, and Rod Guzinya. But the pop-strological significance of Dave "Baby" Cortez goes beyond his hero-status among high school sophomores, for prior to his appearance in the constellation *Speechless*, churches and ball games were the only places you heard the instrument that gave your Birthsong its name. Try to imagine the sixties without the organ as a staple of rock and roll and you'll see why the popstrological children of Dave Cortez have as strong a likelihood of being **forgotten innovators** as **mischievous euphemizers**.

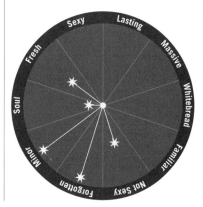

CONSTELLATION

➤ Speechless

BIRTHSONG

➤ *The Happy Organ*
May 11–17, 1959

JOHN COUGAR

You'll never forget where it is that you come from, and you'll never let anyone else forget it, either.

In contrary fashion to the wanna-die-in-a-small-town ethos of his heyday, your Birthstar began his drive to stardom as a would-be city slicker, but New York proved too much for the man. So after being dropped by the record label that saddled him with the name "Johnny Cougar," your Birthstar caught the midnight train to Muncie, and he never looked back. Indeed, John Mellencamp *cum* Cougar *cum* Cougar Mellencamp *cum* Mellencamp (again) set out with single-minded determination to become to his home state of Indiana what Bruce Springsteen was to New Jersey. True, the title of semiofficial State Troubadour is not generally *campaigned* for quite so openly, but no one can deny that it's a title your Birthstar earned through his moving and grooving portraits of Hoosier compromise (*Jack & Diane*), Hoosier suffering (*Rain On The Scarecrow*), Hoosier haplessness (*Authority Song*), and, very occasionally, Hoosier happiness (*Cherry Bomb*). Too hard and a tad too political to be a **Reaganrock**er, your

Birthstar resides in the constellation *Tip of the Ice Cube* and imbues those born under his influence with not only a **tendency toward hometown boosterism**, but also considerably **greater internal resources** than what appears on the surface.

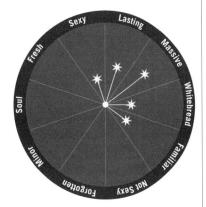

CONSTELLATION
➤ Tip of the Ice Cube

CELEBRITY
➤ **Kieran Culkin** (9/30/82) is a popstrological child of John Cougar.

BIRTHSONG
➤ *Jack & Diane* Sep 26–Oct 23, 1982

JIM CROCE
You are a teller of tales, some of them true.

A clichéd piece of advice all aspiring writers hear at some point is that they must "write what they know," and that the best way for them to gain knowledge is to go out and "experience life." It'll take you a lot longer than getting an MFA, but if you buy into the argument, the kind of life experience you're looking for is exactly the kind that singer-songwriter Jim Croce got in his ten-plus years as an ad salesman, soldier, jingle singer, teacher, construction worker, and truck driver before becoming a bona fide pop star. And at the end of your ten years, you'll have not only loads of experience, but also the wisdom to reject the simplistic formula that started you on your quest and write about whatever the hell you want. Did Jim Croce hang out in south-side bars and Times Square pool halls with men who kept guns in their pockets and razors in their shoes? No, but Jim Croce did know a thing or two about life, and he had an easygoing way about him that made songs like *Bad, Bad Leroy Brown* and *You Don't Mess Around With Jim* credible, even coming from a devoted family man who lived in rural Pennsylvania. That great enemy of promising pop careers—the charter flight—placed your *Storyteller* Birthstar in the constellation *Tragic Demise* even before *Time In A Bottle* became his second #1 hit,

but his popstrological legacy found immortality through you. Success may follow from your **eagerness to suck up all the experience you can**, children of Jim Croce, but it will take more creativity than that to succeed over the long haul.

CONSTELLATIONS
➤ Storyteller
➤ Tragic Demise

CELEBRITY
➤ **Monica Lewinsky** (7/23/73) is a child of the *Storyteller* Jim Croce.

BIRTHSONGS
➤ *Bad, Bad Leroy Brown* Jul 15–28, 1973
➤ *Time In A Bottle* Dec 23, 1973–Jan 5, 1974

CHRISTOPHER CROSS
You are the flavor of the month who turns out to be vanilla.

Technically speaking, halfway between the moon and New York City puts you approximately 125,000 miles above the earth, in a deep, dark void where the temperature hovers near absolute zero. It's a tough nut to crack, this central metaphor of *Arthur's Theme (Best That You Can Do)*, until you realize that it can only refer to the hopelessly stranded feeling that overcame your pale and husky Birthstar when he sensed the aesthetic imperatives that this new thing called MTV would be imposing.

Indeed, Cross's star burned out well before innovations like Carnie Wilson's Slim-O-Vision made MTV safe for unskinny pop stars, but let us not weep for a man who managed *five* Grammys, *two* #1 singles, and one multiplatinum album in the span of just *eighteen months*. At the apex of his brief career, Christopher Cross was a force of popstrological Freshness every bit as Massive as the Sexy stars of 1980 like Blondie and Kenny Rogers. In fact, Cross was briefly the brightest star in the constellation *Lite & White*, and if there is a further popstrological explanation to be found for the brevity of his career, it is in the dramatic disappearance of this once-powerful force as it was sucked into the maw of the newly dominant constellation *Reaganrock*. Your Birthstar's career reminds us that **nothing lasts forever**, and **substance will sometimes fail to triumph over style**, but those are lessons you've probably learned already.

CONSTELLATIONS
➤ Lite & White
➤ Theme Singer

CELEBRITIES
➤ **Macaulay Culkin** (8/26/80) and **Ivanka Trump** (10/30/81) are popstrological children of Christopher Cross.

BIRTHSONGS
➤ *Sailing* Aug 24–30, 1980
➤ *Arthur's Theme (Best That You Can Do)* Oct 11–31, 1981

THE CRYSTALS
Judge not the misdeeds of others, for you might someday find yourself covering up your own.

When Milli Vanilli were exposed as talent-free lip-synchers, the scandal rocked the pop universe, and if you were one of those who joined in the laughter and jeering that accompanied their public humiliation, you might want to sit down and brace yourself for some news about your own popstrological legacy that might be difficult to swallow: the Crystals, your Birthstar, didn't sing a note on the recording of your Birthsong. Not one note. They had sung on earlier hits like *Uptown*, and they would sing again on later ones like *Then He Kissed Me* and *Da Doo Ron Ron*, but rightful credit for *He's A Rebel* belongs to a group of girls called the Blossoms, whom producer/Svengali Phil Spector used to record your Birthsong in L.A. while his hotter property, the Crystals, were back in New York. Some who discover this truth have been known to reject their "sham" Birthstar and seek out the truth of their essence in their "birth" Birthstar, but while that's perfectly understandable, it's popstrologically insupportable. The "official" Crystals are the star who ruled over your birth, and if their residence in the constellation *Artificial Ingredients* disappoints you, try to remember that it could always be worse. Instead of feeling tragic or guilty, resolve instead to make the most ethical use you can of **your ability to act as a figurehead** for the good works of others.

CONSTELLATIONS
➤ Les Girls
➤ Artificial Ingredients
➤ Outerborough

CELEBRITY
➤ **Demi Moore** (11/10/61) is a child of the Crystals.

BIRTHSONG
➤ *He's A Rebel* Oct 28–Nov 10, 1962

CULTURE CLUB

If there's more to you than meets the eye, perhaps it's time that all changed.

Native Americans have always attached tremendous social prestige and cultural importance to individuals who blur the sharp line between male and female. The term you will generally hear them use today for these natural healers and peacemakers is *wintke*, from the Lakota *winyanktehca* for a "man who lives as a woman." Sadly, a far less polite term was often heard among non-Natives when your Birthstar first revealed its *wintke* to America in 1984. Boy George inspired a great deal of initial confusion and a great deal of professed revulsion, too, though much of that was clearly just masking some difficult-to-process feelings of attraction. After all, despite a look (porkpie hat, dreadlocks) that could inspire a series called *Queer Eye for the Queer Guy*, Boy George was beautiful in a way that no one could help noticing, though some had trouble admitting. As a popstrological child of a Club whose Culture was extremely challenging even to those who embraced their Fresh and often wonderful sound, your best self may be revealed when you **wear your inside on the outside**— when you expose your **inner strangeness** even if it **upsets certain settled conventions**.

CONSTELLATIONS
➤ Britsuasion
➤ Tip of the Ice Cube

BIRTHSONG
➤ *Karma Chameleon*
Jan 29–Feb 18, 1984

CUTTING CREW

You might not fit in with the jocks, but they'll still pick you for their team.

When a band leaves as small a mark on the pop universe as your Birthstar did, popstrologists have to cast a wide net in their search for meaning. Indeed, if all popstrologists had to work with in the case of Cutting Crew was their background and the evidence of their sole #1 hit, it would be difficult even to say which region of the popstrological firmament they should occupy. They were a mix of Brits and Canadians, after all, so neither the constellation *Britsuasion* nor the constellation *Oh . . . Canada* could take them in. And *(I Just) Died In Your Arms* was a song with a sound that a lot of different constituencies might have laid a claim on, from the moussed and mascara-ed male fans of D.O.A. to the moussed and mascara-ed female fans of Mr. Mister. Thankfully, if one scratches the surface a bit, the true alignment of your Birthstar is revealed in their minor coke-is-bad hit *Mirror And A Blade*, and in their work as an opening act for the groups that sang *We Built This City* and *Hip To Be Square*. Yes, that's right, it is the mighty constellation *Reaganrock* to which Cutting Crew belongs, and while they may not reside anywhere as near its excitement-depleted core as Starship and Huey Lewis and the News certainly do, your Birthstar nonetheless endows you with an ability to **endear yourself to the dominant power** of your day, yet possibly **without completely alienating those who oppose it**.

CONSTELLATION
➤ Reaganrock

BIRTHSONG
➤ *(I Just) Died In Your Arms*
Apr 26–May 9, 1987

DALE AND GRACE

Carpe diem, because your *diems* of glory may be numbered.

They were young, they were in love, and they were at the top of the pop charts as they stood on the steps of their Dallas hotel on Friday, November 22, 1963. Dale Houston and Grace Broussard had met just a few months earlier, but the chemistry between them—musical and otherwise—had been immediate. Their first recording session had produced a hit record, and almost immediately they embarked on a whirlwind romance/promotional tour that pushed *I'm Leaving It Up To You* to #1. While they waved at the passing motorcade on that beautiful November morning, their smash single was probably playing on a thousand radio stations nationwide, and their personal and professional prospects looked very bright indeed. A few minutes later, however, that motorcade passed through Dealey Plaza, and President John F. Kennedy was killed. A few hours later, pop radio went absolutely silent for three full days, and a few weeks later, the Beatles appeared and rendered the sound of your Birthstar popstrologically obsolete. And a few months later, Dale and Grace, the couple *and* the duo, broke up acrimoniously in Fargo, North Dakota. Through a negative lens, one might look at your popstrological makeup and say that for you, all joy will be fleeting, but it would be more accurate to say simply that **nothing lasts forever**—that the moment **you finally feel comfortable** is the moment when **the biggest change lies just around the corner**.

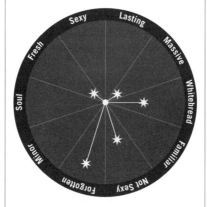

CONSTELLATION
➤ Neither/Nor

BIRTHSONG
➤ *I'm Leaving It Up To You*
Nov 17–30, 1963

MICHAEL DAMIAN

Ahead of you lies a path to success, if you make the proper turn at each of its many crossroads.

Few stars prove the meaninglessness of the label "one-hit wonder" better than Michael Damian, whose popstrological impact may have been Minor, but whose pop-cultural connectedness is deeply fascinating. For starters, your Birthstar is the final star to join the small but important constellation **Thanks, Dick**. He was invited onto *American Bandstand* in 1982 to lip-synch his single *She Did It*, and though that record went absolutely nowhere, his "performance" captured the attention of the producers of *The Young and the Restless*, the soap opera where he would spend the next twenty-plus years portraying "rock star" Danny Romalotti. What's more, the song that would fuel your Birthstar's Rick Springfieldian rise into the pop-strological firmament (and prevent Donny Osmond's *Soldier of Love* from reaching #1) was *Rock On*, a cover of a minor 1974 hit by British teen idol David Essex. The highlight of Essex's career was starring in the London production of the American pseudo-religious musical *Godspell*, and Damian would go on to star in the Broadway production of the British pseudo-religious musical *Joseph and the Amazing Technicolor Dreamcoat*—a role that would later be taken over by none other than Donny Osmond in one of his many attempts to recapture his teen-idol glory. Will you **make your way to the top of the heap**, child of Michael Damian? It's certainly possible, but whether or not you reach your destination, **the journey is certain to be interesting**.

DANNY AND THE JUNIORS

With friends like yours, who even cares about enemies?

In 1957 Philadelphia, Dick Clark could make you a star in a single afternoon on his newly national *American Bandstand*. He was the man with the keys to the kingdom, but how would you get him to open the doors? Well, for starters you needed a record with a good beat that you could dance to. Next, you needed to be young, clean-cut, and preferably white. Oh, and if by chance your song *just happened* to be recorded, pressed, distributed, published, or promoted by one of the dozens of companies in which Dick held a financial stake, well then maybe that wouldn't hurt either. One group of harmonizing teens who passed muster on all counts was Danny and the Juniors, four local high-schoolers with a catchy tune called *Do The Bop*, which Clark had them re-record as *At The Hop* in his first act as mentor and benefactor. By putting the boys on *Bandstand*, America's Oldest Living Teenager and Most Deceptively Packaged Powerbroker not only guaranteed your Birthstar's rise

into the popstrological firmament, but he also launched the small but powerful constellation *Thanks, Dick*. As a popstrological child of Danny and the Juniors, you've probably learned that on the road through life, **many hands will reach out to help you**. But you've probably also learned that, on closer examination, some of **those hands are more like meathooks**.

TERENCE TRENT D'ARBY

When they come to crucify the loudmouths, you'd do well to keep yours shut.

The rock press giveth and the rock press taketh away, but rarely as quickly in succession as in the case of your Birthstar. Terence Trent D'Arby was anointed on arrival as pop's Next Big Thing, and with good reason. *Wishing Well*, his first single, wasn't just your average blast from the constellation *Fresh Breeze*. Your Birthsong would have sounded Fresh (and oddly at home) in almost any decade, but in the context of the late-1980s, it sounded the way the first rush of air must feel when the doors of a crowded elevator open after eight hours stuck between floors in an August blackout. But there was a problem. Terence, it turns out, was a bit of an a**hole. Or at least he came off as one in the press, and what's the difference, ultimately? If you get your history from VH1, your Birthstar's fall from grace is a straightforward morality tale in which he calls his own debut album "the greatest since *Sgt. Pepper*," then pays the ultimate price for his blasphemy. But Terence Trent D'Arby didn't die or go into exile after the commercial failure of his next album. He's alive and well and now called Sananda Maitreya, and he didn't go into European exile till after the commercial failure of his *third* album, which was even better than his first and almost as good as the one he began giving away on the Internet in 2002. You have the **potential to produce astonishing work** for **no one's satisfaction but your own**, but if you yearn for bigger audiences, **take care not to offend** those who would control their opinions.

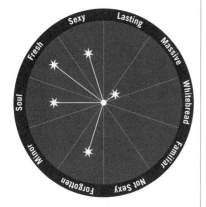

CONSTELLATIONS
- ➤ Fresh Breeze
- ➤ So-Soul
- ➤ Hot Hairdo

BIRTHSONG
- ➤ *Wishing Well* May 1–7, 1988

BOBBY DARIN
Resist expectations and keep throwing curveballs.

Bobby Darin wasn't the first to swing the signature tune from Bertolt Brecht and Kurt Weill's darkly cynical *Threepenny Opera*—credit for that idea goes to the great Louis Armstrong. But it was Darin's *Mack the Knife* that became the definitive version, and it was a big enough hit to cement him in many people's minds as the consummate cool-cat crooner. But the Bronx-born Darin was no mere lounge act. His knack for keeping people guessing first showed up in his shift from *Splish Splash*–singing rock and roll teen idol to finger-snapping Vegas headliner, and it continued to show itself through phases as a writer-performer of folk, protest-folk, folk-rock, and even country-western music. Moving freely in and out and back and forth among these diverse genres, Darin established himself as the third star in the intriguing constellation *Shape-Shifter*, and he might have shifted even more had heart disease not placed him in the constellation *Tragic Demise* in 1973 at the age of thirty-seven. Like your ambitious Birthstar, you, too, have a **distaste for comfortable ruts**—a tendency to **seek out challenges** even when things are clicking, **and a talent for pulling it off**.

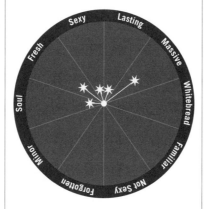

CONSTELLATIONS
- ➤ Shape-Shifter
- ➤ Outerborough
- ➤ Tragic Demise
- ➤ Royal Court

BIRTHSONG
- ➤ *Mack The Knife* Oct 5– Nov 15 and Nov 23– Dec 13, 1959

DAVE CLARK FIVE
Like a false security blanket, the sense of calm you engender may be deeply misleading.

Your Birthstar first arrived on American shores in the same month as the Beatles, with a near-#1 hit called *Glad All Over*. And though their popstrological breakthrough wouldn't come until the week of your birth almost two years later, their role in the developing universe of pop was made clear in that first brush with greatness, when the Dave Clark Five served to reassure those unnerved by Fab Four hysteria that as invasions go, this British one wasn't going to be all that scary. With a reassuring squareness that seemed pleasing to teens without inflaming their passions, your Birthstar brought a feeling of security to those prone to entertaining worst-case scenarios—a feeling that seemed fully justified by the subsequent arrival of Peter and Gordon, Freddie and the Dreamers, and Herman's Hermits. By the time you were born, of course, the Rolling

Stones had shown the constellation **Britvasion** to be every bit as dangerous as originally feared (at least to the popstrological status quo), but for a brief little while there, your not-so-Minor but largely Forgotten Birthstar calmed the nerves of a nation's nervous Nellies. Like a warmly lit but securely locked window on a cold winter's night, your **power to give hope and cheer is not quite equaled by your ability to deliver it.**

CONSTELLATIONS
➤ Britvasion
➤ Tip of the Ice Cube

BIRTHSONG
➤ *Over And Over* Dec 19–25, 1965

MAC DAVIS
Your gift for saying the right thing is matched only by your gift for saying the wrong thing.

When you tell your friends that your Birthstar is Mac Davis, maybe try to get them interested in the classic Elvis tunes he wrote in the late sixties—*In The Ghetto* and *A Little Less Conversation*. Or talk about his sensitive-dad classic *Watching Scotty Grow* and his family favorite *I Believe In Music*. Just try to avoid talking about your actual Birthsong, that's all. As great as *Baby Don't Get Hooked On Me* sounded in 1972, it really, really hasn't aged well, and even if you manage to convince your friends that Mac Davis was one of the most charming and likable characters in the pop-cultural landscape of the mid-1970s, they still might not be able to get past lyrics like *"Don't start clinging, baby, 'cause I can't breathe."* And if their twenty-first-century sensitivities are tweaked by that one, how will they feel about *"It's warm where you're touching me, woman-child"*? Taken out of context with the rest of his career, your Birthsong hardly sounds like the work of the wry and self-deprecating character Mac Davis was, but that shouldn't surprise you, given your own **tendency to stir the pot with well-intentioned political incorrectness.** Just be sure to **surround yourself with**

people who can appreciate the humor in a song like *It's Hard To Be Humble*—otherwise, you've got some tedious and lonely days ahead of you.

CONSTELLATIONS
➤ Invisible Hand
➤ Hot Hairdo
➤ Texstyle

BIRTHSONG
➤ *Baby Don't Get Hooked On Me* Sep 17–Oct 7, 1972

SAMMY DAVIS, JR.
The ground you break will be entirely your own.

He began his six-decade showbiz career at the age of four, as "Silent Sam, the Dancing Midget," and there are those who feel that Frank Sinatra treated him just like that in their Brat Pack heyday. But your Birthstar was no man's mascot—not even the man who gave him entrée into the white mainstream. Yes, he was *famously* ingratiating, but his persona contained enough threatening elements to make his monumental success more surprising than that of such polished racial-boundary crossers as Sidney Poitier and Harry Belafonte. Your Birthstar got himself excommunicated by Sinatra twice, once for his loud mouth in 1959 and later for his massive drug habit in the 1970s, and he got himself uninvited to John F. Kennedy's inauguration for marrying a white woman in 1960. Whether by converting to

Judaism, by supporting Richard Nixon, or by consorting with unsavory pornographers, Sammy Davis, Jr. did almost everything in his power to keep from earning anyone's unambivalent embrace—black, white, liberal, conservative, or otherwise. And yet, it was Sammy Davis, Jr. more than any other African American entertainer who forced the integration of formerly segregated venues such as Las Vegas, and who broke down America's most meaningful barrier of all by earning ungodly sums of money while doing it. Though he hated the song personally, it's difficult to imagine anyone other than your Birthstar singing about "groovy lemon pies" in *The Candy Man* and earning his way into the popstrological elite as a result. And it's equally hard to imagine his popstrological children allowing their own **eagerness to please** to rob them completely of their **sometimes inspiring and sometimes maddening individuality**.

CONSTELLATIONS
➤ Sui Generis
➤ Old Guard

CELEBRITY
➤ **Selma Blair** (6/23/72) is a child of Sammy Davis, Jr.

BIRTHSONG
➤ *The Candy Man* Jun 4–24, 1972

JIMMY DEAN
You are a natural storyteller with an irresistible sizzle.

Unless you are a country-music-hating vegetarian who never watched *The Muppet Show*, then you've probably been touched by your Birthstar's influence in more ways than you know. On his own musical terms, Jimmy Dean left a relatively small mark on the pop universe, scoring just a single #1 hit with *Big Bad John* and a couple of minor hits with spoken story-songs in much the same vein (e.g., *P.T. 109)*. But his charm and easy manner made him a natural for TV, where he extended his pop-cultural influence and earned a spot in the constellation *Invisible Hand* by nurturing the careers of numerous rising country stars and of an offbeat genius from Baltimore by the name of Jim Henson, who created Rowlf the piano-playing dog for Dean's weekly variety show. But it is probably on your breakfast plate and around your hips or midsection where you have forged the strongest ties to your Birthstar, the founder and namesake of a pork-sausage empire that made him the first and still-reigning king of country singers—turned—meat sales-

men (sorry, Kenny Rogers). Like your popstrologically Minor but gastronomically Lasting Birthstar himself, you possess a gift for **nurturing both the body and the spirit** and an **ability to keep up an entertaining patter** while you are doing it.

CONSTELLATIONS
➤ Storyteller
➤ Invisible Hand
➤ Texstyle

BIRTHSONG
➤ *Big Bad John* Nov 6–Dec 10, 1961

JOEY DEE AND THE STARLITERS
Where socialists and socialites dare to mingle, there you'll be.

Two of history's biggest trendsetters are responsible for the career of your Birthstar. The first was Karl Marx, who wrote a catchy little piece called the *Communist Manifesto* in 1848 and inspired a generation of Russians to cast off their chains and oust the czar. The second was Chubby

Checker, who ignited a revolution of his own with his 1959 smash, *The Twist*. The historical/popstrological convergence of these two heavyweights occurred outside New York City's Peppermint Lounge one night in 1961, when Prince Serge Obolensky, an ousted Russian aristocrat and seventy-one-year-old bon vivant, pulled a couple of friends out of his limo and said "Come, ladies, let's do ze tweest!" A gossip column ran the story the next day and ignited a worldwide resurgence among the middle-aged set of a dance craze that had been passé among teenagers for nearly two years. Really. Joey Dee was the bandleader at the now-famous Peppermint Lounge, and he knew enough to strike while the iron was hot. Within weeks, Joey Dee and the Starliters had a #1 hit in the can and a star in the constellation *Jersey Pride*, thanks to *Peppermint Twist*, the Birthsong of a popstrological cohort whose **startling business acumen** stems from a **keen sense of timing** and the **ability to mine gold from seemingly incompatible elements.**

CONSTELLATION
➤ Jersey Pride

CELEBRITY
➤ **Axl Rose** (2/6/62) is a child of Joey Dee and the Starliters.

BIRTHSONG
➤ *Peppermint Twist* Jan 21–Feb 10, 1962

RICK DEES AND HIS CAST OF IDIOTS

Genius is something you either have or you don't, but greatness is something you can reach out and grab.

It's not that Rick Dees found the crank-calls-and-fart-sounds format too confining for his gifts, and it's not that he grew tired of greeting the public at local comedy clubs and auto dealerships. It's just that Rick Dees wanted *more* than a drive-time DJ on local Memphis radio could expect to have. He wanted *zanier* crank calls and *larger* car dealerships to open, and he wanted to wish a "Happy Hump Day" to an audience in the millions, not just the thousands. So Rick Dees rolled out his secret, career-boosting weapon in 1976—a novelty record called *Disco Duck*, which, though it fell two notches below Weird Al's weakest on the scale of satiric cleverness, hit the pop universe with such impeccable timing that it rocketed straight to #1. So different was the radio industry of a generation ago that

your Birthstar was fired from his post for discussing his own record on the air (imagine that, Howard Stern), but when *Duck* began to fly, he was quickly hired by a local competitor whose parent company later promoted him to their L.A. flagship station, KIIS-FM. As ageless as Dick Clark and seemingly twice as nice, the host of the internationally syndicated "Rick Dees' Top 40 Countdown" made the most of his ascent into the popstrological firmament, and he bestows upon you a similar ability to **parlay simple needs and even modest gifts** into the precise degree of greatness to which you aspire.

CONSTELLATIONS
➤ Had to Be There
➤ Novelty Merchant
➤ Disco Ball

BIRTHSONG
➤ *Disco Duck* Oct 10–16, 1976

DEF LEPPARD

You are the popular pioneer who prefers the label "poppülr pïoneer."

If archaeologists in some distant future unearth from the ruins of a twentieth-century American high school a three-ring binder with phrases like "Mötley Crue," "Def Leppard," and *Gunter glieben glauchen globen*" hand-inked on its cover, they will probably assume that it belonged to a dyslexic Scandinavian exchange student. How could they possibly guess that this Germanic Esperanto was in fact the second language of the millions of American teens who called themselves "metalheads" in the 1980s? By creatively respelling their original name, Deaf Leopard, in 1978, your Birthstar repopularized the naming conventions pioneered by Led Zeppelin and Blue Öyster Cult, but don't blame Def Leppard for the hair-metal excesses of some bands who followed their lead. Def Leppard were a transitional form in the evolutionary history of heavy metal, a full step away from the satanic pretensions of Judas Priest, but several steps short of the poofy ridiculousness of Poison. With an enlightened policy toward occupational therapy and a flawless sound crafted by the man who would later produce and marry Shania Twain, the band with the one-armed drummer joined the constellation *Tip of the Ice Cube* as the most likable metal band not to hail from New Jersey, and they endowed you with a **greater interest in democracy than demonology** and an ability to **stay away from the kind of trouble into which your example often leads others**.

CONSTELLATIONS
➤ Tip of the Ice Cube
➤ Britsuasion

BIRTHSONG
➤ *Love Bites* Oct 2–8, 1988

JOHN DENVER

You are the city slicker who feels more at home with fuzzy little critters.

He made you think of good things, like gorp and Smokey the Bear. He made you want to pick up litter along the Appalachian Trail, or maybe just sit by a stream and say, "Hey, a raccoon—far out!" To children growing up in the seventies, he looked and sounded like the Have a Nice Day button come to life, but to the millions of adults who bought records like *Rocky Mountain High* and *Take Me Home, Country Roads*, he was more than just a great song-writer and unlikely fashion icon. With his bowl cut, granny glasses, and down vest, John Denver was the symbol of an extremely attractive lifestyle—a sincere, sensitive, and outdoorsy lifestyle that pointed many children of the sixties toward their futures as taxpaying, Patagonia-wearing Volvo owners and card-carrying members of the Sierra Club. There never was before and there never will be again a star quite like John Denver, whose aesthetic and musical uniqueness place him squarely in the middle of the constellation *Sui Generis*, among the pop universe's other unrepeatable greats. **Appreciate the wonders of nature** and **embrace the embarrassingly sincere goofball** within you, children of John Denver, for that is the path you will hike to happiness.

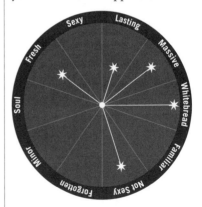

CONSTELLATIONS
➤ Sui Generis
➤ Lite & White
➤ Hot Hairdo
➤ Tragic Demise

CELEBRITIES

➤ **Alyson Hannigan** (3/24/74), **Hilary Swank** (7/30/74), and **Angelina Jolie** (6/4/75) are popstrological children of John Denver.

BIRTHSONG

➤ *Sunshine On My Shoulders* Mar 24–30, 1974
➤ *Annie's Song* Jul 21–Aug 3, 1974
➤ *Thank God I'm A Country Boy* Jun 1–7, 1975
➤ *I'm Sorry/Calypso* Sep 21–27, 1975

DEXY'S MIDNIGHT RUNNERS

You are the natural leader unafraid of ditching your followers.

"Right, then. I've got some good news and some bad news." So began the band meeting called by Kevin Rowland, the all-powerful leader of Dexy's Midnight Runners, in early 1982. "The good news is, I'm dropping the fitness theme, so you can hand in your tracksuits and stop jogging to rehearsals." "Oh, cheers, that's great, Kev!" "Yeah, well, the bad news is, you're all sacked. I'm going with a sort of Irish ragamuffin look for next year, and I'm afraid I'll be replacing you lot with a bunch of scruffy fiddlers." Kevin's decision certainly was bad luck for the newly unemployed Runners, who would barely miss out on the band's coming moment of pop-strological glory, but this wasn't the first and it wouldn't be the last purge-and-costume-change in the history of Dexy's Midnight Runners. Indeed, shortly after your Birthstar's brand of Celtic soul reached its musical and aesthetic zenith with *Come On Eileen*, Kevin Rowland once again fired most of his band, and he also ditched the sandals and dirty overalls that made them briefly famous. Clean cut in preppy golf gear, the next lineup of DMR would begin your Birthstar's slide back into obscurity, and cement their Minor but memorable position in the constellation *Shape-Shifter*. All the world's a stage, and most of us are merely players, but you're more like the **writer-director of a series of one-act costume dramas**.

CONSTELLATIONS

➤ Shape Shifter
➤ Britsuasion
➤ Fresh Breeze

BIRTHSONG

➤ *Come On Eileen* Apr 17–23, 1983

NEIL DIAMOND

You never count your money while you're sitting at the table, but mostly because there's too much to count.

Ten million white American housewives can't be wrong, though it took their hipster children twenty years and the cowardly shield of irony to catch up to what their moms already knew in the early 1970s. But that was just fine with Neil Diamond, because the royalties he earns from jokey tribute bands are just as real as those he earns from the heartfelt admirers who've made him one of the all-time biggest-selling American male pop stars. And make no mistake about it: earning royalties is something Neil Diamond does about as well as any human ever has. Forget the rest of his massive catalog and consider just how many times in your life you've heard *I'm A Believer*, *Red Red Wine*, and *Sweet Caroline*. Every time you did, a fractional cent or two was being added to a running tally of Neil Diamond's royalty earnings, and between the arrival of his first, 73¢ check from BMI in 1966 and his fifty-fifty divorce settlement in 1996, those many millions of fractional-cents helped him amass a fortune in excess of $300 million. Many people think of Barry Gibb when they think of white men with less-than-godlike looks who willed themselves to sex-symbol status on the strength of other-worldly talent and a hairy chest exposed by a shirt unbuttoned to the solar plexus, but that was Neil's look first, and a critical component of his Massive appeal. It may be your talent or it may be your looks, and in some rare cases it may be both, but whatever it is that underlies your success wouldn't serve you half as well without your popstrological ability to **exploit your gifts to their fullest possible commercial potential.**

CONSTELLATIONS
➤ Outerborough
➤ Invisible Hand
➤ Hot Hairdo

CELEBRITY
➤ **Matt Damon** (10/8/70) is a Neil Diamond.

BIRTHSONGS
➤ *Cracklin' Rosie* Oct 4–10, 1970
➤ *Song Sung Blue* Jun 25–Jul 1, 1972

MARK DINNING
You may not be the kind to laugh at a funeral, but you may be the kind to spy a business opportunity.

In the early rock and roll era, it wasn't just songs with suggestive lyrics that got banned. For instance, a novelty song called *Transfusion* was banned because the topic (blood transfusions) was deemed "not a joking matter," and even an *instrumental* tune called *Rumble* was banned simply on the basis of its inflammatory title. Against that backdrop, it's not surprising that Mark Dinning's *Teen Angel* was banned from many radio stations at the time of its release. Its subject matter (stalled car, railroad tracks) was shocking to many, and in making your Birthsong into a legendary smash hit, your Birthstar did two things: (1) he proved the futility of censorship in the age of rock and roll; and (2) he created an entirely new subgenre of pop by exposing the marketability of romantic death songs. *Last Kiss*, *Tell Laura I Love Her*, *Moody River*, *Ebony Eyes*, and *Leader Of The Pack* were the most notable follow-ups

to *Teen Angel*, the sole and legendary offering from a Forgotten star who bestowed upon those born under his influence an **incurable romanticism** that is deeply entangled with their **mile-wide morbid streaks**.

CONSTELLATION
➤ Storyteller

CELEBRITY
➤ **Meg Tilly** (2/14/60) is a child of Mark Dinning.

BIRTHSONG
➤ *Teen Angel* Feb 8–21, 1960

DION
You've constructed yourself on the examples of others, but that doesn't mean those examples were constructive.

The powerful effect of the early-sixties girl groups on the teenage baby boomers who listened to them is a well-known fact. But less well known is the powerful effect of certain young male artists, typified by your Birthstar, on that generation's psychosexual development. Indeed, the Marvelettes, Shelly Fabares, and the Shangri-Las may have taught America's girls how to fall for the wrong kind of guy, but Dion DiMucci was the one who introduced them to that guy in the first place. First with the Belmonts and later on his own, Dion embodied and promulgated a male ideal that made songs like *It's My Party* and *Leader Of The Pack* possible.

Tough on the outside but squishy-soft on the inside, quick to betray in romance but quicker to wallow in self-pity at the first hint of being betrayed, the young men your Birthstar portrayed in songs like *The Wanderer* and *Runaround Sue* may or may not have borne much resemblance to the heroin-addicted and future folk-singing Dion himself, but they did capture the imagination of a generation that would later sleep around and divorce at unprecedented rates. Perhaps true **narcissistic personality types** are born and not made, but more than a few popstrological Dions have **made themselves in the image of those types**, or have **found themselves drawn to those who do.**

CONSTELLATIONS
➤ Outerborough
➤ Doo-Wop
➤ Teen Idol
➤ Tip of the Ice Cube

BIRTHSONG
➤ *Runaround Sue* Oct 17–30, 1961

DIRE STRAITS
The esteem in which you hold others need not determine the esteem in which you hold yourself.

If you're like most people, you define yourself all too often by who you aren't rather than by who you are. You let the ever-shifting list of the people and things you find ridiculous and laughable be the only declarative statement you make to the world about your values and beliefs. If it's your goal to change this, then let popstrology help by exploring what Dire Straits was doing with *Money For Nothing*. It was easy enough in 1985, and it would be easy enough now, to call it merely ironic that a song satirizing the values of the music-video age rose to prominence mostly because of its music video. But that would be missing the real point of what Mark Knopfler, the leader of your Birthstar, was doing with your Birthsong. He wasn't just trying to have his cake and eat it too—he was trying to confirm his superiority to just about everyone and everything while doing so. Knopfler's superiority to the appliance-store lunkheads who called video stars "little faggots"; to the simpletons who laughed with them; to the intellectuals who laughed at them; to the "little faggots" themselves—these were the ideas that dominated the pop universe at the moment of your birth, which is why you could do worse than to **narrow the list of those you oppose** down to just the name of your Birthstar. Imagine the power in being an oppositional Dire Straits, in being the kind of person who says, "**I will not allow myself to feel smug and superior** simply because I have **a natural gift for derision.**"

CONSTELLATIONS
➤ Britsuasion
➤ Reaganrock

BIRTHSONG
➤ *Money For Nothing*
Sep 15–Oct 5, 1985

THE DIXIE CUPS
You may not offer liberation, but you put a good face on incarceration.

For sexually active young women in the early-1960s, the famous question Carole King and the Shirelles posed—*Will You Love Me Tomorrow?*—was of more than just popstrological importance. For up until the year of your birth, when the birth-control pill was finally made available to them, the likely consequence of one night's sweetly given love was the same for those women as it had been for their mothers and grandmothers before them: marriage within the next nine months to the young man they gave it up to. It would be easy, perhaps, to say that your Birthstar did little more than perpetuate a prefeminist, patriarchal myth with your Birthsong, *Chapel Of Love*, but that was never their intention. Like their fellow stars in the constellation *Les Girls*, the Dixie Cups spoke directly and honestly to the fears, hopes and dreams of their fellow young women, who, if they couldn't yet conceive of a young adulthood unburdened by motherhood, could at least dream of eternal freedom from loneliness and a lifetime of wedded bliss begun under blue skies and among singing birds. **You may not be the type to alter anyone's consciousness**, child of the Dixie Cups, but there's something to be said for **propping up morale**, even among those destined for disappointment.

CONSTELLATIONS
➤ Les Girls
➤ Gene Pool

CELEBRITY
➤ **Courteney Cox** (6/15/64) is a popstrological Dixie Cup.

BIRTHSONG
➤ *Chapel Of Love*
May 31–Jun 20, 1964

BO DONALDSON AND THE HEYWOODS
Some have difficulty accepting a helping hand. You don't.

When adults force children to sell chocolate bars or candles in support of their marching bands and drama clubs, they often dangle a pretty good prize as incentive to the go-getters who try to sell the most. And yet the go-getter who wins always seems to be the kid who gets Mom and Dad to go sell all his crap for him down at their place of employment. That's the kind of kid Bo Donaldson was, only Bo's mom didn't work in a bank or an auto dealership and Bo wasn't trying to win a bike or a skateboard. Bo's mom worked for Dick Clark, and the prize Bo Donaldson had his eyes on was popstrological immortality. First by getting them a spot on Dick Clark's "Caravan Of Stars" tour as an opening act, and then by getting them a spot on Dick Clark's *Action '73* TV show as regular guests, Mrs. Donaldson put her boy and his Heywoods in a position to aim for the popstrological firmament. But while her boss's unseen hand clearly explains your Birthstar's presence in the constellation *Thanks, Dick*, it isn't Bo's mom that explains their dual residence in the constellation *Regifted*. That alignment—as rare as a two-headed gift horse—stems from the fact that *Billy, Don't Be A Hero*, your Birthsong, probably should have been a #1 for Paper Lace, except Bo Donaldson and the Heywoods hastily covered their song and beat them to the top of the charts with it in the summer of '74. **Some people must to be told never to look a gift horse in the mouth**, but not you. **You receive gifts with grace and frequency, but can you learn to give as well as you get**?

CONSTELLATIONS
➤ Thanks, Dick
➤ Regifted
➤ Storyteller

BIRTHSONG
➤ *Billy, Don't Be A Hero*
Jun 9–22, 1974

DONOVAN

You have the good taste to know that crunchy and smooth are not necessarily incompatible.

Everyone from Tommy James to the Monkees tried out a flower-child pose at one point or other in their 1960s careers, but your Birthstar was the real thing, and not just some free-love-seeking poser. When Donovan came back from India after meeting the Maharishi with the Beatles, he renounced drugs and began preaching transcendental meditation. And when he grew tired of being a cog in the pop machinery, he didn't retire to Laurel Canyon or a tax retreat in Monaco, but to the remote desert near Joshua Tree National Monument, where he raised his children (Ione Skye of *Say Anything* and Donovan Leitch, Jr. of the band Nancy Boy) in full countercultural splendor. The **patchouli-scented neo-hippies** you ran with or ran from in college managed to mimic the aesthetics of your Birthstar's biggest fans, but they missed his core popstrological values entirely. For no human who subjects herself to the endless jammery of the Grateful Dead shows respect for the Freshness and pop craftsmanship of Donovan, just as the popstrological children of Donovan who **abandon their individuality** to the political or aesthetic dictates of the crowd show no respect for the **free-thinking eccentricity** that is their natural birthright.

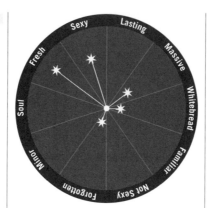

CONSTELLATIONS
➤ Fresh Breeze
➤ Britvasion
➤ Tip of the Ice Cube

BIRTHSONG
➤ *Sunshine Superman*
Aug 28–Sep 3, 1966

THE DOOBIE BROTHERS

You are the shot of whiskey with a white-wine chaser.

If you've seen *Gimme Shelter*, then you know that a group of Hells Angels providing "security" at Altamont beat a man to death with pool cues not twenty feet from Mick Jagger's feet. But what you may not know is that those same Hells Angels may have been humming a Doobie Brothers' song to themselves while they did it. The Doobies were practically the Hells Angels' house band in Southern California from 1969 to 1972, and it was the Angels' loyal support as much as anything that kept them going long enough to gain eventual entry into the constellation *Mustache Rock* with 1975's *Black Water*. By then, of course, the Brothers Doob had left the roughest figures in their early history behind in favor of a denim-clad crowd whose greatest joy derived not from cracking skulls but from cracking open beers and shouting, "Bring on the *doobies*, man!" But who could've imagined then that your Birthstar's greatest transformation still lay ahead, when the addition of the soulful and bearded Michael McDonald yanked them definitively away from their popstrologically mustached roots. *What A Fool Believes* was a pop-soul gem that might have mystified the Hells Angels back in 1969, but in 1979 it refreshed a nation fed mostly on disco, and it bestowed upon you an **ability to smooth rough edges** that is surprising, given your **deep-down affinity for the roughest of crowds**.

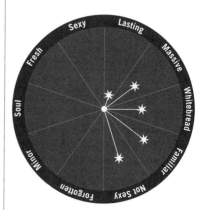

CONSTELLATIONS
➤ Mustache Rock
➤ Launching Pad

BIRTHSONGS

➤ *Black Water* Mar 9–15, 1975
➤ *What A Fool Believes* Apr 8–14, 1979

THE DOORS

Even some icons start out as iconoclasts.

Maybe you're saying to yourself, "Cool, I'm a *Door*," as if your newfound connection to Jim Morrison might explain that deep-down star quality of yours that's so sadly lost on others. Or depending on where you come down on the whole genius poet–versus–pretentious a**hole debate, you might be saying, "Oh, crap, a *Door*," instead. But the latter reaction would be as misplaced as self-satisfaction over your popstrological legacy. For while there may indeed be some among your popstrological ilk whose destiny, for good or for ill, is written in a trippy mix of Nietzsche, Blake, and Huxley filtered through bourbon and mescaline, most children of the Doors will find their connection to your Birthstar elsewhere. For them as for you, there is probably more to be learned in the mundane fact that Jim Morrison, the young Dionysus who mesmerized a generation with lyrics about funeral pyres and mystic heated wine was just a regular American kid trying to reject his mundane upbringing by crowning himself the Lizard King. That's what being the son of a rear admiral in the U.S. Navy could do to a kid

in the antiestablishment sixties, and while your own parents may not have given you something quite so easy to rebel against, it probably explains your own lifelong mission to **rise above deeply uncool roots** and to **write your own part in life's drama**, even if it means erasing your past.

CONSTELLATIONS

➤ Fresh Breeze
➤ Tragic Demise

CELEBRITY

➤ **Matt LeBlanc** (6/25/67), **Phillip Seymour Hoffman** (7/23/67), and **Deion Sanders** (8/9/67) are children of the Doors.

BIRTHSONGS

➤ *Light My Fire* Jul 23–Aug 12, 1967
➤ *Hello, I Love You* Jul 28–Aug 10, 1968

CARL DOUGLAS

You are the venerable master of a strange and funky dojo.

Carl Douglas never pretended to be an actual martial-arts master. He probably knew who Bruce Lee was, for instance, but if you'd asked him back in 1974 to name the five elements of animal-style kung fu, he probably would have guessed chicken, pork, beef, shrimp, and fish. All Carl wanted to do was shake some booties and sell a couple of records, yet he did much more than that one day in 1974 while killing a little extra studio time at the end of a recording session. By unwittingly combining the lethal power of kung fu with the irresistible charm of proto-disco on that fateful day, this out-of-shape Jamaican soul singer launched his star into the highest reaches of the pop universe and set off one of the silliest dance crazes of all time. And so it was that at the moment of your birth, Americans by the millions were grunting "Hunh!" and shouting "Hii-YAH" while chopping their arms in the air in a sort of funky hybrid of the bump and tai chi. It was as glorious a rise into the constellation *Had to Be There* as the pop universe has ever seen, and though you may never spark a trend as huge and as strange as Carl Douglas did, at least now you may understand your lifelong interest in **combining the seemingly incompatible** and your **inability to resist cheap**

take-out and the films of Quentin Tarantino.

CONSTELLATIONS
➤ Novelty Merchant
➤ Had to Be There
➤ Shaking Booty

BIRTHSONG
➤ *Kung Fu Fighting*
Dec 1–14, 1974

JOE DOWELL
The bigger they come, they harder they fall when you give 'em das boot.

Elvis Presley may have been the King of Rock and Roll, but in head-to-head competition it was Joe Dowell who emerged as the undisputed King of Rock *und* Roll. That's right, your Birthstar not only scored the first (though not the only) German-language #1 hit in the popstrological era, but he beat Elvis Presley's competing version of the same song to the top of the American charts. Give credit to his Nashville manager, Shelby Singleton, Jr., for hearing *Wooden Heart (Muss I Denn)* in the Elvis movie *G.I. Blues* and racing Dowell's version of the pop-ified German folk song out before RCA could ship Presley's as a U.S. single. Without that quick thinking on Singleton's part, Elvis himself might have become your Birthstar, backed by tuba and accordion and crooning in the soothing Hessian dialect. And while **you might think it more appealing** to be born under a star such as Elvis, in your heart of hearts do you really think that you—**eccentric, salt-of-the-earth you**—could have been born under anything other than a Minor and Forgotten star in the idiosyncratic constellation *Had to Be There*?

CONSTELLATION
➤ Had to Be There

BIRTHSONG
➤ *Wooden Heart (Muss I Denn)* Aug 28–Sep 3, 1961

THE DRIFTERS
You may know what production means, but do you know what "means of production" means?

They were a kind of grown-up Menudo, in which old members were swapped out for new ones not when they entered an awkward hormonal phase, but when they came to realize that 0 percent equity and a salary of $100 a week was a bit of a raw deal for the public-facing talent of a hugely successful business enterprise. From 1953 to 1956, the original lineup of the Drifters established themselves as R&B giants, recording one of the very first rock and roll records (*Money Honey*) and launching the solo career of the legendary Clyde McPhatter. When McPhatter left the group, he sold his 50 percent ownership stake in the Drifters' name and copyrights to his sole partner, the group's manager, George Treadwell. And from that point forward, Treadwell used the Drifters as his private cash cow, turning them into a kind of temporary employment agency for up-and-coming talents like Ben E. King and Rudy Lewis. Indeed, if you weren't a member of the Drifters between 1953 and 1963, you were nobody in the world of R&B. But even if you *were* a member, you got nothing but pride and a modest paycheck out of smash hits like *There Goes My Baby*, *This Magic Moment*, *Some Kind Of Wonderful*, *Up On The Roof*, *On Broadway*, and your Birthsong, *Save The Last Dance For Me*. Like most children of stars in the constellation *Tip of the Iceberg*, your **surface achievements may not reflect the depths of your abilities**, and until you're in a position to profit from those achievements, **this may always remain the case**.

CONSTELLATIONS
➤ Tip of the Iceberg
➤ Launching Pad

BIRTHSONG
➤ *Save The Last Dance For Me* Oct 17–23 and Oct 31–Nov 13, 1960

DURAN DURAN
Master your medium and you've mastered your message.

One can only hope that the video director for Duran Duran's *Hungry Like The Wolf* preserved some of the notes he scribbled down in advance of the historic shoot (*Bar scene: spill drink? knock over table? YES! Note to Simon: cheekbones, cheekbones!*). The cocktail napkin on which fateful words like those were written belongs in a museum somewhere, not just because they were instrumental in launching

your Birthstar, but because they helped to shape the very age we live in. For who knows what direction the infant medium of music videos might have taken without Duran Duran's influence? Would videos have become largely instructional pieces, filled with fingerboard close-ups demonstrating proper chord technique rather than with models crawling around in the Sri Lankan mud? Would Christopher Cross have ruled the eighties alongside an MTV-nurtured generation of pop stars who rose to fame on the strength of their musicianship alone? Thankfully, we'll never know what the template for success in the age of video might have looked like without this aesthetically gifted star from the constellation *Casio*, whose additional place in the constellation *Hot Hairdo* only adds to the allure of its already rare combination of Fresh, Sexy, and Whitebread aspects. **Giving the people what they want** is not a gift that's unique to you, child of Duran Duran, but giving it to them **before they even know they want it** may be.

CONSTELLATIONS
➤ Britsuasion

➤ Casio
➤ Hot Hairdo
➤ Theme Singer

BIRTHSONGS
➤ *The Reflex* Jun 17–30, 1984
➤ *A View To A Kill* Jul 7–20, 1985

THE EAGLES
Your wings are strong, but sometimes you prefer to float on a rising current of hot air.

Benjamin Franklin wanted America's national symbol to be the turkey, and we can all appreciate the symbolism of a top-of-the-food-chain raptor winning out over a wily, forest-dwelling game bird. But what symbolic meaning is attached to those other Eagles, who can rightfully lay claim to being America's national *musical* symbol? Objectively, the Eagles are the most popular American rock band of all time, having sold more total albums than any American pop group and more copies of *Their Greatest Hits (1971–1975)* than any album in American history. But what does this signify? There are those who might say that the victory of the Eagles is really a case of the turkeys having won out in the end—of mainstream America affirming once and for all its preference for white meat over red, for the mild over the gamy. Popstrologists, for their part, refrain from making such judgments, but even they cannot help but note that your Birthstar, like the turkey, was a creature whose ancestral ties to a wilder past became obscured over time as it grew to reflect the American fondness for easy digestibility. The Eagles produced a brand of music that was both easy to digest and compatible with Whitebread, but there can be no question that they belong in spirit to the constellation *Mustache Rock*, even though they brought that constellation far closer to *Lite & White* than its early fans would ever have thought possible. **You may not set out to swim in the mainstream**, child of the Eagles, but **you never know where the currents will take you.**

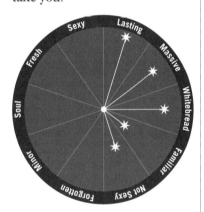

CONSTELLATIONS
➤ Mustache Rock
➤ Launching Pad

BIRTHSONGS
➤ *Best Of My Love*
  Feb 23–Mar 1, 1975
➤ *One Of These Nights*
  Jul 27–Aug 2, 1975
➤ *New Kid In Town*
  Feb 20–26, 1977
➤ *Hotel California* May 1–7, 1977
➤ *Heartache Tonight*
  Nov 4–10, 1979

EARTH, WIND & FIRE
Some are merely players on the stage of life, but you're more like a Vegas spectacular.

In their onstage regalia, your Birthstar looked less like a pop group than like a band of Afrocentric astronauts, and while George Clinton went on and on about visits from the mothership, if any funk-fueled group from the seventies could have actually built and launched a working spaceship, it would have been Earth, Wind & Fire. Right from the beginning, they showed the potential and the desire to be more than just your average band. They meditated together, they ate their vegetarian meals together—they even had Doug Henning on retainer as an in-house magician. They had the means, the motivation, and the opportunity to conquer any challenge, but the challenge they set for themselves was simple: to shake more booties and blow more minds in their live performances than any band that ever lived. Whether they accomplished that goal is a matter of your perspective and your taste, but one thing is certain: no star of their era worked much harder than they did at shining so bright. For you to see what *your* life can truly be, look no farther than the legacy of your strange and wonderful Birthstar, a deserving member of the constellation *Tip of the Iceberg*, who bestowed upon you an unmistakable **eagerness to please** and the

rare ability to do just that **without compromising your own taste or values.**

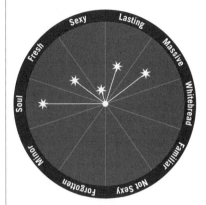

CONSTELLATIONS
➤ Shaking Booty
➤ Tip of the Ice Cube

BIRTHSONG
➤ *Shining Star* May 18–25, 1975

SHEENA EASTON
You may start them out with sugar, but you'll finish them with spice.

Three-year-olds understand everything they hear, but they do take things rather literally. So it's entirely possible that in 1984, if you happened to hear your Birthstar on the radio singing about the rising temperature within her "sugar walls," you simply understood her to be describing an overheated candy store. At the very least, you couldn't have appreciated the popstrological significance to you of a naughty little song written by a naughty little artist then known as Prince. Sheena Easton's performance of *Sugar Walls* was a revelation. To all who heard it, it became immediately clear that the seemingly sweet and innocent girl behind *Morning Train* and *For Your Eyes Only* had a bit more savvy upstairs, and a bit more ambition downstairs, than anyone had previously imagined. In fact, it became clear that your Birthstar was the Scottish second coming of Olivia Newton-John, albeit brunette and on a less Massive scale. Later attempts at self-reinvention as an old-fashioned torch singer confirmed your Birthstar's rightful place among the stars of the constellation *Shape-Shifter*, the clear source of her impact on the microgeneration of **quick-change artists**, **dirty-minded sweethearts**, and **sweethearts of the dirty-minded** born under her popstrological influence.

CONSTELLATIONS
➤ Shape-Shifter
➤ Britsuasion

CELEBRITY
➤ **Jessica Alba** (4/28/81) is a child of Sheena Easton.

BIRTHSONG
➤ *Morning Train* Apr 26–May 9, 1981

THE EDGAR WINTER GROUP
Next to your unique intensity, everything looks like a pale imitation.

In the early 1970s, a future popstrologist overheard the following snippet of conversation between two teenage neighbors repairing an El Camino in their front yard: "Hey, man, did you know Edgar Winter was an *albino?*" "I don't care what he is, man—that f*cking albino rocks!" And indeed he did. In a year that was dominated popstrologically by *Killing Me Softly* and *You're So Vain*, the Edgar Winter Group—the aforementioned albino plus a pair of remnants from the *Hang On Sloopy* McCoys—pledged its allegiance to the constellation *Mustache Rock* and to the bourbon and testosterone for which it stood. Their instrumental 1973 #1 hit *Frankenstein* (named for the dozens of splices necessary to cut its lengthy drum solos and "jazz explorations" to fit on a 45 rpm single), became easily the purest example of early-'70s American hard rock ever to dominate the popstrological firmament. But the popstrological legacy of your Minor but Lasting Birthstar is made even more interesting by virtue of being the hands-down *loudest* star ever to join the nonsinging constellation *Speechless*. In settings that call for a six or a seven, you may have a **hard time turning yourself down from eleven**, but though your **pedal-to-the-metal attitude may be too much for some**, rest assured that **it won't be for everyone**.

CONSTELLATIONS
➤ Speechless
➤ Mustache Rock

BIRTHSONG
➤ *Frankenstein* May 20–26, 1973

TOMMY EDWARDS
You are the old dog who yearns to learn new tricks.

By 1958, even the mighty stars of the constellation *Old Guard* could see that their anti-Elvis battle was a lost cause, and Minor lights of a bygone era like Tommy Edwards were destined for oblivion. But then a little thing called stereo came along, which prompted the reissue and re-recording of earlier mono albums like the one that included your Birthstar's 1951 hit, *It's All In The Game*. But if the lucky timing of this technological breakthrough explains why Tommy Edwards eventually became the inaugural star in the constellation *Regifted*, it was anything but luck that fueled his unlikely rise. Rather than redoing your Birthsong in its original, pop-standard arrangement as expected, Tommy Edwards had the savvy to update it as a rock and roll ballad, and in so doing he used the last chance he'd ever have at greatness to record a #1 hit. It wasn't as dramatic or ridiculous a move as Ethel Merman doing a disco album in 1979, but when Tommy Edwards entered the popstrological firmament in the year of your birth, he scored a victory for all supposed dinosaurs with a **willingness to evolve**. Whether you're the baby-boomer CEO of a hip-hop label or simply a middle-aged master of IM and iPods, thank your Birthstar each time you **defy your age by embracing the style of a younger generation**.

CONSTELLATIONS
➤ Regifted
➤ Old Guard

CELEBRITY
➤ **Tim Robbins** (10/16/58) is a popstrological Tommy Edwards.

BIRTHSONG
➤ *It's All In The Game* Sep 29–Nov 9, 1958

THE ELEGANTS
You are the economic genius whose genius is in your economy of effort.

A young genius born during the same week as you once captured the essential spirit of all popstrological Elegants in a song he wrote called *Don't Stop 'Til You Get Enough*. When you grooved to that song in 1979, you probably wouldn't have felt the least bit queasy to think that you shared a certain life-philosophy with a young and handsome mammal like Michael Jackson, and it shouldn't bother you now. Popstrology allows as much room for variation among individuals of the same basic makeup as genetics does, and the popstrological impulse that manifested as an attitude of "Don't stop anything, because it's *never* enough" in Michael is just as likely to have manifested in you as an attitude of **"Why not just quit while I'm ahead?"** The Elegants, you see, are actually the popstrological firmament's **shining beacon of minimal effort**. The Staten Island teens recorded *Little Star* in 1958, and they never recorded another hit again, choosing instead to milk your Birthsong for all it was worth on the equivalent of a career-long oldies tour that began even before their style of music could be considered the least bit old. They didn't stop till they got enough, but their ambition was rather limited, and whether you're a **type-A go-getter or a complacent bystander**, the influence of your Birthstar is surely there, informing your decision each time that alarm clock rings and you have to choose whether or not to hit "Snooze."

CONSTELLATIONS
➤ Doo-Wop
➤ Outerborough

CELEBRITY
➤ **Michael Jackson** (8/29/58) is a child of the Elegants.

BIRTHSONG
➤ *Little Star* Aug 25–31, 1958

YVONNE ELLIMAN
Your name may not be found among the greats, but it may be found in their Rolodexes.

What really holds the fabric of popstrological space-time together is not the brightness of its most Massive stars, but the combined strength of many Minor stars whose power resides largely in their Kevin Bacon–esque connectedness. Your Birthstar is a case in point. Draw three points representing such musically and popstrologically diverse stars as the Bee Gees,

Helen Reddy, and Eric Clapton, and the shortest route you'll find between any of them is through Yvonne Elliman. She was Mary Magdalene in the original London cast of *Jesus Christ Superstar* (in which she sang what became one of Helen Reddy's biggest hits, *I Don't Know How To Love Him*). She was Clapton's backup singer on *I Shot The Sheriff* and throughout his post-heroin comeback tour. And, of course, she was the voice behind the only Bee Gees song on the *Saturday Night Fever* sound track not sung by the Bee Gees themselves, *If I Can't Have You*. Follow the secondary connections from there to such invisible powers as Bob Marley and Andrew Lloyd Webber and such popstrological powers as John Travolta and Air Supply, and you begin to appreciate on a deeper level why your Birthstar's legacy to you is the ability to **draw your power from your network of powerful friends.**

CONSTELLATION
➤ Disco Ball

BIRTHSONG
➤ *If I Can't Have You*
May 7–13, 1978

THE EMOTIONS
You may not be a saint, but next to the real sinners you look pretty pure.

As children, they called themselves the Heavenly Sunbeams, and no name could have been more appropriate. Heck, even the coked-up hordes at Studio 54 had to feel a bit of the divine light shining when the soaring gospel harmonies of the Emotions came pouring down on them. The smash hit *Best Of My Love* was one of the biggest, most spine-tingling songs of the disco era, and it came from a group whose core values couldn't have been more different from what that era symbolized. The Emotions were a rotating cast of Hutchinson sisters, usually Sheila, Wanda, and Jeanette, but sometimes sister Pam or a close family friend when one of the others was out on maternity leave. Maurice White of Earth, Wind & Fire is the one who crafted their sound to suit the dance floor, but it is probably a Higher Entity who deserves credit for the raw material that made your Birthstars one of the most virtuous stars in the constellation *Disco Ball* and one of the grooviest in the constellation *Gene Pool*. **Family values** may or may not run strong in you and your popstrological brethren, but what does is a natural ability to **preserve your ideals while pleasing crowds** that might not necessarily share them.

CONSTELLATIONS
➤ Les Girls
➤ Gene Pool
➤ Disco Ball

BIRTHSONG
➤ *Best Of My Love*
Aug 14–Sep 10 and
Sep 18–24, 1977

ESCAPE CLUB
You seem to mean what you say, though it's not always clear what you mean to be saying.

According to your Birthstar, there's a political critique buried somewhere within the song that lifted them into the popstrological firmament in the week of your birth. But it should not be taken as a refutation of their claim to say that if *Wild, Wild West* was meant to be political, it *sounded* about as political as *Girls Just Want To Have Fun*. But this was still the 1980s, the era of **Reaganrock**. And as effective as that constellation was in preventing any radical new *sounds* from flourishing in the decade of your birth, it was even more effective at stifling any vocal criticism of the social forces that supported its reign. So maybe just throwing phrases like "safe sex" and "Ronnie's got a big gun" around within a poppy, infectious dance tune *did* send some kind of political message, relatively speaking. But even if it did, it was probably your Birthsong's use of the phrase "headin' for the nineties" that made it too thrilling to resist in 1988, perhaps in the same way that "Headin' for the '10s" might do for you at the midpoint of your college career. **The line between deeply coded subversion and meaningless drivel** can be difficult to draw sometimes in the world of pop music, but your popstrological gift may be to **walk that line in life itself**, and to please broad audiences while you do it.

CONSTELLATION
➤ Britsuasion

BIRTHSONG
➤ *Wild, Wild West* Nov 6–12, 1988

THE ESSEX
You are the caged bird whose keeper can't appreciate your singing.

I t's a strict code they live by in the United States Marines, and nowhere in their famous hierarchy of loyalty (God, Country, Corps) is there any room for undying commitment to a pop group. This was the difficult truth that five singing leathernecks from Camp Lejeune, North Carolina, had to swallow in 1963, when routine transfers put an end to their popstrological moonlighting as the Essex. They were fortunate enough to miss Vietnam by a couple of years, but unfortunate enough to serve in the branch of the military that was the least likely to treat them like the pop stars they briefly became. Today, a chart-topping pop group on active duty would be milked for every ounce of PR they could provide, but either the early sixties was a less cynical time in the military-recruiting business or the draft simply made that kind of thing unnecessary. Either way, by the time the members of the Essex got the chance to reunite, the Beatles had rendered their sound obsolete, and the bright, sassy gem that is your Birthsong, *Easier Said Than Done*, became the sole artifact of their brief popstrological reign. So **embrace the security of traditional institutions** if you like, Essexes, but never forget that they were **not designed to foster your growth as an individual**.

CONSTELLATION
➤ Neither/Nor

CELEBRITY
➤ Edie Falco (7/5/63) is a popstrological Essex.

BIRTHSONGS
➤ *Easier Said Than Done* Jun 30–Jul 13, 1963

GLORIA ESTEFAN AND THE MIAMI SOUND MACHINE
You are the one who wears the pants in your relationships, or who doesn't but doesn't seem to mind.

Y ou may be too young now to worry about the secret to a happy and lasting marriage, but someday that will change, and rather than spending a fortune on self-help books or therapy when it does, remember to consult the example of your Birthstar, one of only three stars in the constellation *Holy Matrimony* to include a still-married husband and wife. What is it that Gloria Estefan and the Miami Sound Machine would tell you is the key to keeping a marriage on an even, happy keel? The same thing Captain and Tennille would tell you: effective power-sharing. And what is effective power-sharing, in the context of a heterosexual marriage, anyway? It's the establishment of an arrangement in which the wife holds the actual power, but the husband is allowed to preserve the appearance of power. From the day in 1975 when eighteen-year-old Gloria Fajardo met her future husband, Emilio Estefan, Jr., at an audition for his South Florida wedding band, a slow process of attrition began that resulted in the happy couple's being the band's only permanent members by the time of their popstrological rise. And though by that time it was Gloria Estefan's voice and persona that were the driving force of what used to be her husband's group, it was Emilio Estefan's happy lot in life to be wealthy, happily married, and known universally as the one-man Sound Machine. Even **unequal partnerships have their compensations**, and your popstrological gift may be to find out firsthand.

CONSTELLATIONS
➤ Holy Matrimony
➤ Tip of the Ice Cube

BIRTHSONG
➤ *Anything For You*
May 8–21, 1988

EURYTHMICS
Some try to have it all and fail, and you will succeed by heeding their example.

They might have looked at the example of Marilyn McCoo and Billy Davis, Jr. and convinced themselves that they, too, could combine marriage with pop stardom, but they didn't. Instead, Annie Lennox and Dave Stewart looked at the overwhelming weight of evidence in the constellation *Holy Matrimony* and decided to end their romantic attachment entirely before making their run at greatness. Could they have achieved all they did without making this eminently reasonable decision? Perhaps. A synthesizer-driven married duo with the dominant wife front and center and the (apparently) submissive husband lurking in the background had ruled the pop universe once before, but perhaps the example of Captain and Tennille gave your Birthstar a completely different set of reasons to pursue a different course. But who's to say that Annie and Dave could even have made it as a couple if they'd given up on pop music instead of on love? It's certainly fun to imagine Annie in her bright-orange crew cut working the register at a mom-and-pop

bookstore while Dave checks inventory in the back, but it's less fun to imagine the pop universe of the 1980s without the hugely Fresh and camera-friendly Eurythmics. *Sweet Dreams (Are Made Of This)* was just the *Tip of the Ice Cube* for your Birthstar—a group that brought British aloofness back to the constellation *Casio* after its brief flirtation with Kim Carnes, and a group that showed its popstrological children that while **career and personal fulfillment may sometimes go hand in hand**, the safest course of action may be to **pursue them separately**.

CONSTELLATIONS
➤ Fresh Breeze
➤ Casio
➤ Britsuasion
➤ Tip of the Ice Cube
➤ Launching Pad

BIRTHSONG
➤ *Sweet Dreams (Are Made Of This)* Aug 28–Sep 3, 1983

THE EVERLY BROTHERS

The ties that bind may bind you more tightly than others.

Harmony was a huge part of rock and roll right from the beginning, but the sunny major chords of doo-wop would never have given us Simon and Garfunkel, the Beatles, or the Byrds. To get those groups, you first had to have the Everly Brothers, whose ringing close-harmonies introduced a whole new sound into the rock and roll vocabulary—the sound of Appalachia, set to driving acoustic guitars. Don and Phil Everly began performing together professionally when they were just little boys, and even after stardom hit, they shared everything: a driving work ethic, a dozen gold records, a crippling addiction to speed. They were the first stars in the hugely important constellation *Gene Pool* *and* the first members of that constellation to split up, which they did publicly and acrimoniously in 1973. A decade of estrangement ended for the Everly Brothers with forgiveness and reunion in 1984, but your Birthstar's legacy to you reflects the full complexity of their troubled yet incredibly powerful relationship. **Dissonance and harmony**—technically they're opposites, but as you may have learned in your own **strong-but-complicated relationships**, they're more like two sides of the same coin, each **inseparable from, and almost impossible to define without reference to, the other**.

CONSTELLATION
➤ Gene Pool

BIRTHSONGS
➤ *Wake Up Little Susie*
Oct 14–20, 1957
➤ *All I Have To Do Is Dream*
May 12–Jun 1, 1958
➤ *Cathy's Clown* May 23–
Jun 26, 1960

EXILE

When the curtain falls, you simply prepare for the second act.

Today you're likely to find your Birthstar's sole pop hit tucked into compilations labeled "disco," but that's only because it would be an even worse fit somewhere else. Easy to listen to but a bit too funky for **Lite & White**, kind of groovy but with a beat too inconsistent for the **Disco Ball**, *Kiss You All Over* was a hugely popular and Fresh-sounding hit that fit into no particular category, and perhaps that made it seem to Exile as if they'd found a formula for Lasting popstrological success. But they hadn't, and after failing to find a convincing follow-up to your Birthsong, they quickly found themselves facing oblivion. In the same situation, most pop groups either continue to fight the good fight until their labels cut them off, or they resign themselves to a lifetime of flogging their one big hit for every penny it's worth. Unsatisfied with those options, your Birthstar elected to pursue an unlikely Third Way to career salvation: they reinvented themselves as a country band. Other than the fact that *Kiss You All Over* was undanceable, there was little in Exile's repertoire to suggest their aptitude for country music, but as it turned out, they were damn good at it. Exiled from the world of pop after the year of your birth, but living like exiled despots with a fat Swiss bank account, Exile bestows upon those born under their influence remarkable **adaptability to changing situations** and a **stubborn refusal to let bad news be bad news**.

CONSTELLATIONS
➤ Shape-Shifter
➤ Country Cousins

BIRTHSONG
➤ *Kiss You All Over*
Sep 24–Oct 21, 1978

EXPOSÉ

You may not be the total package, but you may be the wrapping that goes around it.

They yanked the constellation *Les Girls* back to its singing-and-posing roots after the 1987 admission of the guitar-playing Bangles, but this was not the sum total of Exposé's accomplishments, for they also revived the long-dormant constellation *Artificial Ingredients* when they arrived on the popstrological scene in 1988. *Seasons Change*, you see, was not the first Exposé hit. The songs that put your Birthstar on the map were the mid-eighties dance-club hits *Point Of No Return* and *Come Go With Me*, but you can consult the case of a woman named Martha Wash if you're interested in what can become of dance-club hit-makers once the aesthetic imperatives of wider pop stardom come into play. Prior to the recording of the album that launched your Birthstar into the popstrological firmament, all three of Exposé's original members were summarily fired by the man who manufactured and controlled the group, Lewis Martinee, who quickly restaffed with three talented and, yes, lovely replacements. With only one of the three in place, your Birthsong was recorded, and once the other two assumed their positions, Exposé's earlier dance hits were then re-recorded and made into top-ten pop hits. **You may win an ardent following as an upholder of traditions**, child of Exposé, but **how many people will you have to hold down** to do it?

CONSTELLATIONS
➤ Les Girls
➤ Artificial Ingredients

BIRTHSONG
➤ *Seasons Change* Feb 14–20, 1988

SHELLY FABARES

Just because you can do something doesn't mean you should.

When Ricky Nelson launched his pop career by picking up a guitar and singing at the end of an episode of *Ozzie and Harriet*, network executives on both coasts sat up as one and exclaimed, "Holy crap—why didn't we think of that?" But television is a medium that rewards imitation more than it does originality, and so it was that your popstrological legacy was formed when the teenage actress who portrayed Mary Stone on *The Donna Reed Show* was ushered into an L.A. recording studio and told to start singing. As Shelly Fabares would be the first to admit, she sang just well enough not to embarrass herself, but with some serious studio help, that was plenty good to earn a spot among the stars of the constellation **Regifted**. There were follow-ups to *Johnny Angel* by your Birthstar—*Johnny Loves Me* and (for a nominal change of pace) *Ronnie, Call Me When You Get A Chance*—but your Birthstar soon left the world of pop behind her, both professionally and matrimonially, by giving up singing and by divorcing the record-producing legend Lou Adler and then returning to the familiarity of television in the cast of *One Day at a Time* and *Coach* and as the wife of *M*A*S*H*'s Mike Farrell. The **versatility to move in many worlds** is one aspect of your popstrological legacy, but the good sense to **choose the one that suits you** is another.

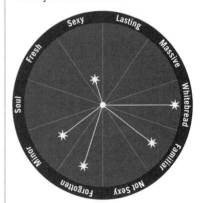

CONSTELLATION
➤ Regifted

BIRTHSONG
➤ *Johnny Angel* Apr 1–14, 1962

PERCY FAITH

You are the master of foreplay (and fiveplay and six . . .).

Without suggesting that Elvis's sex appeal was slipping in 1960, it must be said that he was outdone in the loin-stirring department that year by a balding, sixty-two-year-old orchestra conductor. Percy Faith wasn't the kind of sexy you looked at—he was the kind of sexy you *did something* about. And at the moment of your birth, you can be assured that tens of thousands of Americans were doing something about the feelings his instrumental *Theme From "A Summer Place"* brought on. Your Birthsong had the power to get Sandra Dee to sacrifice a national treasure—her onscreen virginity—to Troy Donahue in the film from which it came, so just try to imagine the effect it had on those less committed to defending theirs. Not that America's grown-ups were immune to Percy Faith's seductive magic. Indeed, for every stalemated teen couple that was tipped over the edge by your Birthstar during his nine-week popstrological reign, there were probably two sets of parents back at home letting their own defenses slip to the strains of your Birthsong and a glass of Harvey's Bristol Cream. He was the Sexiest and most Massive star ever to join the constellation *Speechless*—a Whitebread Barry White for a vastly less soulful time who bestowed upon his popstrological

children **a contagious knack for charting a course** and **going all the way to its conclusion.**

CONSTELLATIONS

➤ Speechless
➤ Theme Singer
➤ Oh . . . Canada

CELEBRITY

➤ **Linda Fiorentino** (3/9/60), **Courtney B. Vance** (3/12/60), **Jennifer Grey** (3/26/60), and **Brian Setzer** (4/10/60) are all children of Percy Faith.

BIRTHSONG

➤ *Theme From "A Summer Place"* Feb 22–Apr 24, 1960

FALCO

Like a dark horse from left field, your success depends on the element of strange surprise.

The bus accident that killed your Birthstar in 1998 went largely unnoticed in the English-speaking world, but in the Strasses and Allees of his native Vienna, February 6, 1998, will

always be remembered as the Day Der Musik Died. Falco was already a hero among the teutonic Volk for his unlikely appearance on the American pop charts with *Der Kommissar* in 1983, but he earned his people their place in the popstrological sun by rising all the way to #1 in 1986 with *Rock Me Amadeus*, a German-language tribute to that other famous Austrian. But the achievement did more than earn your Birthstar a place among the popstrological elite—it also earned him the unlikely distinction of scoring the first #1 pop single by a male rap artist. That's right—it wasn't Doug E. Fresh or Kool Moe Dee or Kurtis Blow or Run-D.M.C. but an Austrian in a powdered wig from the constellation *Eurosomething* who earned that distinction. On the strength of his strangely Fresh diphthongs and umlauts, your Birthstar beat hip-hop's founding fathers to the top of the pop charts and earned himself a place in the constellation *Had to Be There*, which is the clearest popstrological source of your **ability to annex unfamiliar territory** while leaving others to **scratch**

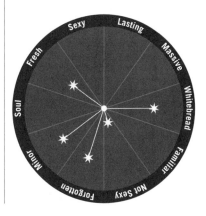

their heads in wonderment as to how you manage to pull it off.

CONSTELLATIONS
➤ Had to Be There
➤ Eurosomething
➤ Tragic Demise

BIRTHSONG
➤ *Rock Me Amadeus*
  Mar 23–Apr 12, 1986

FREDDY FENDER
They can lock you up, but they can't throw away the key to your success.

When your name is Paul McCartney, you can skate out of a place with hyper-tough drug laws like Japan even when you're caught with several ounces of a contraband herb. When your name is Baldemar Huerta, however, and you're caught with several *seeds* of the same plant in 1960 Louisiana, you're not going to be accorded the same preferential treatment. Your Birthstar served three years in Louisiana's notorious Angola State Prison in the early sixties—the same prison that once held Leadbelly—and if that's not the kind of backstory of which country music legends are made (or used to be made), nothing is. It took more than ten years for the man now calling himself Freddy Fender to establish himself as a country star following his stint in country prep school, and the song that did it for him is also the song that crossed over to rule the pop charts at the moment of your

birth. America had #1 hits sung in German, Japanese, and Italian before it ever had one sung in Spanish, as the second half of *Before The Next Teardrop Falls* was, but as a child of Freddy Fender, you probably don't need to ponder the popstrological triumphs of the former Axis powers to conclude that few crimes are so great as to render forgiveness impossible. Of course, as a child of Freddy Fender, you also don't need to be told that **the punishment doesn't always fit the crime,** though hopefully you've inherited from him an ability to **swallow bitter pills without becoming bitter yourself.**

CONSTELLATIONS
➤ Texstyle
➤ Country Cousins

CELEBRITY
➤ **Lauryn Hill** (5/25/75) and **Andre 3000** (5/27/75) are popstrological Freddy Fenders.

BIRTHSONG
➤ *Before The Next Teardrop Falls* May 25–31, 1975

THE FIFTH DIMENSION
Appearances can be deceiving—a fact you count on more than most.

Even before the tumultuous 1960s were over, a significant segment of the American public was ready to leave them behind, and like a popstrological dream come true, your Birthstar arrived in their moment of need to lift them *Up, Up And Away* from all that unrest in a "beautiful balloon." Ahhh, a balloon. What a soothing and utterly *perfect* image for what lay ahead in your Birthstar's career. A balloon is *soft*, after all, and a balloon is *light*, and while a balloon need not necessarily be *white*, there could be little doubt when listening to them on the radio that the members of the Fifth Dimension *were*. Except—guess what?—they weren't. All audible evidence to the contrary, the group with the jazzy Bacharachian softness that white people find so soothing was 100 percent black. Call it irony, if you like, that a group of African Americans gave rise to the mighty constellation *Lite & White*, but popstrologists see something far more interesting in it than mere irony: they see delicious payback to white America for co-opting ragtime, jazz, the blues, rock and roll, and everything else it found exciting in black culture in the twentieth century. But vengeful natures are not likely to be found among the ultimately inoffensive children of the Fifth Dimension. Far more likely are a **well-developed sense of irony** and the ability to **please the mainstream even while tweaking it**.

CONSTELLATIONS
➤ Lite & White
➤ Holy Matrimony
➤ Launching Pad
➤ Royal Court

CELEBRITY
➤ **Renée Zellweger** (4/29/69) and **P. Diddy** (11/4/69) are children of the Fifth Dimension.

BIRTHSONGS
➤ *Aquarius/Let The Sunshine In* Apr 6–May 17, 1969
➤ *Wedding Bell Blues* Nov 2–22, 1969

FINE YOUNG CANNIBALS
You surge ahead when others try to leave you behind.

The English Beat never approached a popstrological breakthrough during their early-eighties heyday, but they had a loyal cult following in the United States, and if you'd asked anyone within that following what they thought would become of Andy Cox and David Steele after the group's frontmen decided to jump ship, they'd have said, "Who?" The men who formed your Birthstar were completely anonymous even to some of their former group's biggest fans, any of whom would've bet that ship-jumpers Ranking Roger and Dave Wakeling would be the more popstrologically promising remnant of their beloved Beat. Turns out, though, that charismatic frontmen are sometimes more easily replaced than talented and ego-free songwriter/guitarists, because while General Public, the odds-on favorite among potential English Beat *Spin-Off*s, sputtered, Fine Young Cannibals soared on the strength of an exceptionally Fresh and vaguely retro sound and an exceptionally Fresh and vaguely retro frontman, Roland Gift. As the popstrological era wound to a close, your Birthstar provided the final contribution of the constellation *Fresh Breeze* to a pop universe

dominated by *Reaganrock*ers and teeny boppers. And in so doing, they blessed those born under their influence with a quiet kind of **conformity-resisting cool** to go along with their **keen survival instinct** and **knack for surpassing low expectations**.

CONSTELLATIONS
➤ Britsuasion
➤ Spin-Off
➤ Fresh Breeze
➤ Theme Singer

BIRTHSONGS
➤ *She Drives Me Crazy* Apr 9–15, 1989
➤ *Good Thing* Jul 2–8, 1989

ROBERTA FLACK
To say you feel like doing something is not the same as doing it.

The late sixties and early seventies saw the toppling of some fairly vulnerable social ideals—that sex was meant for marriage and that marriage meant "till death do us part" prominent among them. Soon, love without marriage would become just as socially acceptable as sex without love, but not before Americans embraced amid this confusion a pop star who seemed to sing almost exclusively of love without sex. Roberta Flack was a late-bloomer who'd worked as a schoolteacher and moonlighted in piano bars for years before making it as a professional musician, and in that aspect of her biography there are clear signs that her popstrological children would do well not to let go of their own **yearning for a creative outlet**, whatever **stultifying day job** they find themselves in. But perhaps those same children will be more interested to finally learn where the roots of their own **complicated attitudes toward sex** lie—in a body of popstrological work striking for its sexless sensuality. *The First Time Ever I Saw Your Face* and *Killing Me Softly With His Song* have more in common with chivalric chansons than with the work of Barry White, and even *Feel Like Makin' Love* concerns a sexual desire so theoretical, so highly conditional as to be effectively unfulfillable. For good or for ill, it may be part of your popstrological legacy to hear in a title like *Tonight, I Celebrate My Love* something functionally equivalent to *Let's Get It On*, but if so, it may be time for you to **simplify your romantic vocabulary** and **get back to certain long-cherished basics**.

CONSTELLATION
➤ Royal Court

CELEBRITY
➤ **Jennifer Garner** (4/17/72) is a child of Roberta Flack.

BIRTHSONGS
➤ *The First Time Ever I Saw Your Face* Apr 9–May 20, 1972
➤ *Killing Me Softly With His Song* Feb 18–Mar 17 and Mar 25–31, 1973
➤ *Feel Like Makin' Love* Aug 4–10, 1974

FLEETWOOD MAC
High performance, yes. Low maintenance, no.

If sixty minutes on the life of Shania Twain seems like fifty minutes too many, blame your Birthstar, because it's bands like Fleetwood Mac that made VH1's *Behind The Music* an hour-long show. Fleetwood Mac was a *ménage à cinq* in perpetual breakup mode during their 1970s heyday—pick any two members of the band circa 1977, and if they weren't sleeping together, then they probably weren't speaking to each other. Yet out of this interpersonal train wreck came one of the biggest albums of all time, *Rumours,* and a string of decade-defining hits like *Landslide, Rhiannon, Say You Love Me, Don't Stop*, and *Go Your Own Way*. While it cannot be said that the forces of relationship stability were *entirely* absent from the pop universe of the late 1970s (see: Captain and Tennille), they were most decidedly held at bay at the moment of *your* birth, when your combative, incestuous, and prolific Birthstar ruled from its perch among the deceptively Massive forces of the constellation *Tip of the Iceberg*. Your own personal life is **more likely to feature chaos than calm**, but to paraphrase Graham Greene, thirty years of warfare and terror under the Borgias gave Italy Michelangelo and the Renaissance, while five hundred years of democracy and peace gave Switzerland the cuckoo clock.

CONSTELLATIONS
➤ Tip of the Iceberg
➤ Holy Matrimony

BIRTHSONG
➤ *Dreams* Jun 12–18, 1977

THE FLEETWOODS
You are the dreamer who lives the dreamers' dreams.

The story of your Birthstar's rise reads like the plotline of a trigonometry-class daydream: three teens team up to write and perform a song for the senior class show; family and classmates proclaim, "Gee, you guys oughta record that!"; home-made tape is hand-delivered to local promoter via Greyhound bus; local radio picks up the record, and . . . well, you can see where this is headed. Suffice it to say that a million teenagers' ridiculous fantasies were given fresh new fuel by groups like the Fleetwoods, who managed a bootstraps rise from high school to the highest reaches of the pop universe on the strength of *Come Softly To Me*, and without assistance from the teen-idol machinery that produced contemporaries like Frankie Avalon. Short though their heyday may have been, your Birthstar stands as a powerful source of inspiration to the **self-made types** born under their influence—popstrological proof, if you like, that your childhood desire to **put on a show in your uncle's barn** was the first expression of your greatest strength.

CONSTELLATION
➤ Doo-Wop

CELEBRITY
➤ **RuPaul** (11/17/59) is a child of the Fleetwoods.

BIRTHSONGS
➤ *Come Softly To Me*
Apr 13–May 10, 1959
➤ *Mr. Blue* Nov 16–22, 1959

WAYNE FONTANA AND THE MINDBENDERS
It takes a natural winner to win when surrounded by quitters.

You can work your *ss off building a hometown following, and you can talk a record label into sending someone out to hear you play, but if you can't get your own band to show up for the big audition, you're generally going to join the ranks of popstrological also-rans. Unless you've got enough buddies from other local bands that you can grab a couple off their bar stools and hustle them up onstage so as not to miss your big chance. That's how Wayne Fontana came to find his Mindbenders and form the only member of the constellation *Britvasion* to meet meaningful resistance on American shores, where U.S. Customs agents detained them past the first two dates of their U.S. tour until they could produce written proof that they were important enough to be granted temporary work visas. Wayne Fontana would soon split to launch an unsuccessful solo career, while one of his audition-night rescuers would lead the Fontana-less Mindbenders to a near-#1 hit in 1966 with *A Groovy Kind of Love*, but the popstrological impact of the

cobbled-together group that is your Birthstar was limited to *Game of Love*, an immensely enjoyable record enlivened by the first popstrological appearance of Jimmy Page's guitar (but *just* his guitar, which he lent to the Mindbenders on the day they recorded your Birthsong). Minor and Forgotten though they may be, your Birthstar nevertheless bestows upon you an impressive **unwillingness to let opportunities slip through your fingers**, even if grasping them requires some **well-placed helping hands**.

CONSTELLATION
➤ Britvasion

BIRTHSONG
➤ *The Game Of Love*
Apr 18–24, 1965

FOREIGNER
Would you hang up your guns to be part of a winning battle?

So powerful was the constellation *Reaganrock* in the decade of your birth, that it's easy for us to think that the domination of palatably bland pseudo-rock in the 1980s was a historical inevitability. But it hardly seemed that way back in 1981, and popstrologists often wonder whether the constellation *Lite & White* might have managed to recapture the unthrilling territory REO Speedwagon had claimed for **Reaganrock** if Foreigner hadn't dropped a second enormous power ballad on an unsuspecting public later that same year. Your Birthstar's *Waiting For A Girl Like You* was just barely prevented from reaching #1 in the autumn of 1981 by Olivia Newton-John's last, sweaty hurrah, but it came close enough to make the point. The popstrological firmament of the 1980s would belong to middle-aged men ready to put their thrilling pasts behind them, and there was little anyone could do about it. It would take several more years for the group that rose to prominence as late-seventies arena rockers (*Hot Blooded, Feels Like The First Time*) to take their official place among the popstrological elite, but for their support of the cause at a critical time, they are rightly ranked among the founding fathers of **Reaganrock**. **You may have to wait longer than some**, child of Foreigner, but **keep supporting the winners, and you'll receive your rightful rewards eventually**.

CONSTELLATIONS
➤ Reaganrock
➤ Tip of the Ice Cube

BIRTHSONG
➤ *I Want To Know What Love Is* Jan 27–Feb 9, 1985

THE FOUR SEASONS
Yours is a voice that will not be silenced, or ever mistaken for foreign.

They were the godfathers of Italian-American soul, and though their roots were in old-school doo-wop, they left that style dead on a Newark street corner when they combined Frankie Valli's macho falsetto with Jersey-thick background vocals and a driving beat in the Spector/Motown style. Records like *Sherry* and *Walk Like A Man* epitomized the sound you couldn't refuse, a sound so strong and so popstrologically Fresh that even the mighty Beatles couldn't silence it. Indeed, the Four Seasons were one of only two American groups to enjoy significant chart success before, during, and after the mighty **Britvasion**, and they did it without abandoning their principles and converting to the Britvader look or the Britvader sound. And unlike the Beach Boys, the Beatles-surviving band that was to the Pacific Ocean what the Seasons were to the Passaic River, your Birthstar didn't depend for their success on the gifts of a single, psychotic genius. Too little Brian Wilson and too much sun turned the Beach Boys into a dried-out husk of a band well before their late-career comeback with *Kokomo*, but your Birthstar managed one of their most timeless hits with their comeback—*December, 1963 (Oh, What a Night)*. Perhaps you've had your share of foreign adventures, child of the Four Seasons, but it's your **mastery of the American idiom**, and your steadfast **refusal to see anything wrong with that**, that will always underlie your more successful ventures.

CONSTELLATIONS
➤ Jersey Pride
➤ Fresh Breeze
➤ Launching Pad
➤ Royal Court

CELEBRITY
➤ **Tommy Lee** (10/3/62), **Joan Cusack** (10/11/62), **Jodie**

Foster, (11/19/62), **Jon Stewart** (11/28/62), **Reese Witherspoon** (3/22/76), and **Jayson Blair** (3/27/76) are children of the Four Seasons.

BIRTHSONGS

- ➤ *Sherry* Sep 9–Oct 13, 1962
- ➤ *Big Girls Don't Cry* Nov 11–Dec 15, 1962
- ➤ *Walk Like A Man* Feb 24–Mar 16, 1963
- ➤ *Rag Doll* Jul 12–25, 1964
- ➤ *December, 1963 (Oh, What a Night)* Mar 7–27, 1976

THE FOUR TOPS

While others stare across their fences, you choose to enjoy your own green grass.

When Motown abandoned the struggling city from which it took its name, one group declined to join the move to sunnier, softer Los Angeles: the Four Tops. You might think that a group that had been together for ten years without a hit record before signing with Motown would think twice before letting hometown loyalty put an end to a professional relationship that had yielded two enormous #1 hits and numerous other classics like *Baby I Need Your Loving* and *Standing in the Shadows of Love.* But hometown loyalty probably wasn't the only thing on the minds of the Four Tops, who had watched Berry Gordy tear apart more than one great Motown group by launching one of its

members as a solo star. And if there was one thing that Levi Stubbs, Obie Benson, Lawrence Payton, and Duke Fakir felt more loyal to than Detroit, it was one another. Your Birthstar had only one significant hit after leaving Motown—*Ain't No Woman Like The One I've Got*—and what an appropriate farewell to the charts for a group that is the popstrological **patron saint of loyal stalwarts**. Not only did they never abandon Detroit, but the Four Tops never abandoned the Four Tops. It took the death of Lawrence Payton in 1996 to put an end to a record not approached by any other star in the popstrological firmament: forty-plus years of performing in their exact original lineup. **Stay true to your wonderful popstrological legacy**, child of the Four Tops, and **there's no reason it won't stay true to you.**

CONSTELLATION
- ➤ Hitsville

CELEBRITY
- ➤ **Jon Favreau** (10/19/65) is a child of the Four Tops.

BIRTHSONGS

- ➤ *I Can't Help Myself (Sugar Pie, Honey Bunch)* Jun 13–19 and Jun 27–Jul 3, 1965
- ➤ *Reach Out I'll Be There* Oct 9–22, 1966

CONNIE FRANCIS

We cannot choose our families, but we can choose when to follow their advice.

Concetta Franconero's dad gave her an accordion at the age of three in the hopes that she would master the instrument and one day open her own music school. It was a sweet and noble gesture from a man who would later morph into a hyper-controlling Svengali who dictated his daughter's every personal and professional move. Daddy Dearest turned his little girl into the international pop star Connie Francis (with some timely help from the likes of Arthur Godfrey, Ted Mack, and Dick Clark), but he appears to have done little for her self-esteem. With her doctors' help, she embarked on a decades-long addiction to prescription drugs while still in her teens, and her four marriages lasted a total of just six and a half years. Of course her total of three #1 hits (which doesn't even include her best-known songs, *Who's Sorry Now* and *Where The Boys Are*) would not be eclipsed by a solo woman until Diana Ross in 1976, but when you consider the sickening tragedy of her brutal rape following a 1974 concert in Long Island and a case of manic-depression that went undiagnosed before her institutionalization in 1981, you have to wonder whether a career as headmistress of Concetta's Accordion Academy wouldn't have been a better outcome for your Massive and massively tragic Birthstar. An ability to **smile through the pain** may be a valuable trait to possess, but it's better still to **choose your wishes carefully**, for their fulfillment may not bring you yours.

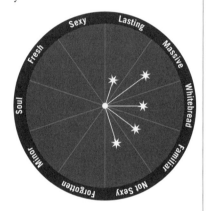

CONSTELLATIONS
➤ Thanks, Dick
➤ Jersey Pride
➤ Hot Hairdo

CELEBRITY
➤ **M. C. Hammer** (3/30/62) is a Connie Francis.

BIRTHSONGS
➤ *Everybody's Somebody's Fool* Jun 27–Jul 10, 1960
➤ *My Heart Has A Mind Of Its Own* Sep 16–Oct 9, 1960
➤ *Don't Break The Heart That Loves You* Mar 25–31, 1962

ARETHA FRANKLIN
Even the finest diamond can lose its beauty if placed in the wrong setting.

Many have bemoaned the way her raw, gospel voice was wasted on soulless show tunes in the flower of her youth, but to say that Columbia Records head Mitch Miller stifled Aretha Franklin's Soul is simply to say that he did his job. A well-known supporter of the constellation *Old Guard*, Miller was the man who nurtured the careers of Guy Mitchell and Doris Day, who declined to sign Buddy Holly, and who offered up Johnny Mathis as Columbia's answer to the burgeoning youth market. He was the man who had white people by the millions singing songs like *Be Kind To Our Web-Footed Friends* on his proto-karaoke television show *Sing Along With Mitch*, so it was only natural that he should feed Aretha Franklin a steady diet of Whitebread. But the years your Birthstar spent in the mainstream wilderness before becoming the Queen of Soul are quite instructive from a popstrological point of view. There was something magical about Aretha that the music industry simply cannot manufacture, but there is almost nothing that the music industry can't destroy, and it very nearly destroyed your Birthstar before she ever recorded *Respect*, *Chain Of Fools*,

(You Make Me Feel Like A) Natural Woman, or any of the other songs that made her an anchor star in the constellation *So-Soul*. It must be said, though, that Aretha *allowed* herself to be stifled in her youth, and she proved herself capable of mediocrity once again in late career, making the lesson that is central to your popstrological essence crystal clear: **Great though your gifts may be**, child of Aretha Franklin, **how and where you apply them may determine how far they take you**, and your judgment in that regard is far from infallible.

CONSTELLATIONS
➤ Tip of the Iceberg
➤ So-Soul

BIRTHSONG
➤ *Respect* May 28–Jun 19, 1967

ARETHA FRANKLIN AND GEORGE MICHAEL

The needs you serve may not only be your own.

For Aretha Franklin, being associated with a star on the rise was reason enough to participate, and for George Michael, it was clearly a no-brainer. Newly departed from Wham! and yearning for a little bit of respect, who better for him to join in a popstrological *Power Couple* than the Queen of Soul herself? In straightforward career terms, *I Knew You Were Waiting (For Me)* accomplished just what it set out to for the individuals involved: it moved George away from the teeny-bopper sound of Wham! and it extended the commercial viability of a late-career Aretha. In popstrological terms, however, it accomplished something else: it added yet another unlikely jewel to the crown of the constellation *Reaganrock*. You have to understand that in 1987, *Reaganrock* was powerful enough, and its network of operatives ubiquitous enough, that it could touch literally any-one—even Aretha Franklin. It was producer Narada Michael Walden, fresh from his "suc-cess" with Starship's *Nothing's Gonna Stop Us Now*, who did the deed in this case. Walden's drum-machine beats, synthe-sized *vroom*ing sounds, and chimey marimba notes never met a song they couldn't trans-form, even a song with soulful aspirations as obvious as your Birthsong's. George Michael would steer well clear of this sound in the Massive solo career that followed, but Aretha's pop-strological career ended with the song that ruled the universe at the moment of your birth, and let that be a lesson. **Alliances born of mutual self-interest** are the backbone of capitalist society, but **they rarely serve both sides equally**, and sometimes they **benefit those you have no interest in serving**.

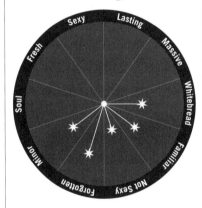

CONSTELLATIONS
➤ Power Couple
➤ Reaganrock

BIRTHSONG
➤ *I Knew You Were Waiting (For Me)*
Apr 12–25, 1987

JOHN FRED AND HIS PLAYBOY BAND

Even when the emperor wears his clothes, you have the courage to make fun of him.

Like everyone born in the fourth and final year of the Beatles' reign atop the popstrological firma-ment, you carry within you the mark of a group that changed the course of pop history and, some would say, of history itself. That mark, however, is pretty faint, for you were born under the direct rule not of the Beatles, but rather of a Louisiana party band whose popstrological rise was fueled by making fun of the Beatles. Which is not to say that *Judy In Disguise (With Glasses)* was exactly biting satire. It's just that your Birthsong captured the public's imagination, however briefly, purely by making light of the deepening seriousness of the Fab Four, whose transformation from the fresh-faced youngsters of *Love Me Do* to the trippy myste-rians of *I Am The Walrus* left cer-tain sunny segments of their fan base behind. After earning their place in the constellation *Novelty Merchant*, your Birthstar rather predictably dis-appeared from popstrological view, but as unselfconscious goofballs **unafraid of poking fun** at the pretensions of the high and mighty, they enabled those born under their brief rule to serve the critical, though sometimes underappreciated, social function of being either **givers or receivers of good-natured ribbing**.

CONSTELLATION
➤ Novelty Merchant

CELEBRITY
➤ **Mary Lou Retton** (1/24/68) is a child of John Fred and His Playboy Band.

BIRTHSONG
➤ *Judy In Disguise (With Glasses)* Jan 14–27, 1968

FREDDIE AND THE DREAMERS
You will thrive among heavyweights without being overly weighty.

Great artistic movements tend to be remembered for their fearless innovators and lasting geniuses, but for every Beethoven, Brahms, and Bach, there was probably a group called Gunther and the Glockenspiels who capitalized on the masters' popularity without quite matching their talent and sense of seriousness. Certainly this was true of the famed British Invasion of the 1960s, which brought to American shores not only the brilliant Beatles and unstoppable Stones, but also the deeply silly Freddie and the Dreamers. Frontman Freddie Garrity was equal parts Buddy Holly and Jerry Lewis, and his greatest contribution to the music scene of the mid-sixties wasn't even musical—it was a leaping, spastic "dance" memorialized in his group's minor hit *Do the Freddie*. During their brief heyday, your Birthstar occupied a joyful and uncomplicated corner of the constellation **Britvasion**—a constellation that got all the weighty self-importance it would ever need from its very first and largest star. The greatest gift your Birthstar bestows upon you is your capacity, perhaps long-repressed, for **unselfconscious silliness**. Its may not be the stuff of which your legend is eventually made, but it's **a rare and undervalued commodity** nonetheless.

CONSTELLATION
➤ Britvasion

CELEBRITY
➤ **Robert Downey, Jr.** (4/4/65) is a child of Freddie and the Dreamers.

BIRTHSONG
➤ *I'm Telling You Now* Apr 4–17, 1965

PETER GABRIEL
You may clearly be left of center, but that might not keep you from the middle of the road.

Someday, the music of your childhood will be edited down to a list of eighty to one hundred songs called "The Best Mix of the Clinton Years," and when it is, the biggest tragedy won't be that the teenage radio-listeners of tomorrow will assume everyone your age was crazy about the Spice Girls, but that the teenagers of tomorrow will fail to understand the fine but critical distinctions between being crazy about Mel B. and being crazy about Mel C. Distinctions like these are the stuff that popstrology is made of, for without them it might be impossible to tell the difference between you and someone born under the influence of Phil Collins. Phil Collins and Peter Gabriel were both middle-aged former lead singers of the prog-rock band Genesis who made their popstrological breakthroughs with mainstream-friendly sounds in the mid-1980s, but they couldn't have been more different. Where Collins was sweet, Gabriel was tart, and where Collins was dowdy, Gabriel was dashing. But if Peter Gabriel thought that his avant-garde past and his shamanistic bearing would keep him from being pulled into the maw of *Reaganrock*, he was gravely mistaken. No, he would never threaten Phil Collins's position as the British pillar of that constellation, and yes, he might have avoided it entirely if *In Your Eyes* hadn't become the song that launched a million hackneyed mix tapes, but the fact remains that your Birthstar joined the popstrological firmament as a *Reaganrock*er. **Those who know you best may understand your uniqueness**, child of Peter Gabriel, but **running with the dominant crowd may define you to everyone else.**

CONSTELLATIONS
➤ Spin-Off
➤ Reaganrock
➤ Britsuasion
➤ Tip of the Ice Cube

BIRTHSONG
➤ *Sledgehammer* Jul 20–26, 1986

MARVIN GAYE
One minute you make them wanna dance, and the next you make them wanna holler.

Considering his early career as a straight-ahead Motown hitmaker (*Ain't No Mountain High Enough*; *Ain't Nothin' Like The Real Thing*; *I Heard It Through The Grapevine*), who could have foreseen your Birthstar's 1971 battle to get his boss and brother-in-law Berry Gordy to release a highly personal album of original material called *What's Going On?* And considering the soulful and heart-wrenching political consciousness of that album, who could have foreseen follow-ups like *Let's Get It On* and *Sexual Healing*? He was a brilliant star in the constellation *Shape-Shifter* who had everything to live for and probably much more to give, so who could have foreseen a career cut short by a crippling coke habit and an unresolved family conflict that led to his shooting death at the hands of his own father in 1984? Feel free in your CD collection to exercise a preference for one

among the many Marvin Gayes—the Motown company man, the R&B Dylan, the shirtless icon of satin-sheet soul—but in your popstrological quest for self-knowledge, you'll need to focus your attention on all that went into making you the **complicated and contradictory** creature that you are.

CONSTELLATIONS
➤ Hitsville
➤ Shape-Shifter
➤ So-Soul
➤ Tragic Demise

CELEBRITIES
➤ **Marilyn Manson** (1/5/69), **Carson Kressley** (1/11/69), **Dave Grohl** (1/16/69), and **Jai Rodriguez** (6/22/77) are all Marvin Gayes.

BIRTHSONGS
➤ *I Heard It Through The Grapevine* Dec 8, 1968– Jan 25, 1969
➤ *Let's Get It On* Sep 2–8 and 16–22, 1973
➤ *Got To Give It Up, Pt. 1* Jun 19–25, 1977

GLORIA GAYNOR
Like a bouncing rubber ball, you may continually hit bottom, but you will never fail to bounce.

Several years ago, a young woman from a well-off Manhattan family was stood up at the altar with several hundred wedding guests already in their seats. In and of itself, it was hardly news, yet the event made all the

New York papers the next day. Why? Because the jilted bride-to-be got up and danced triumphantly to *I Will Survive* at a raucous reception that she refused to cancel in the face of her fiancé's dastardly act of cowardice. Gloria Gaynor didn't choose to become the patron saint of newly single women, but heaven knows that by doing so, your Birthstar guaranteed herself a loyal constituency until the end of popstrological time. She also established herself as a particularly beloved star in the constellation **Disco Ball**, bestowing upon those born under her influence a certain **indefatigable optimism** and the **enviable independence** to say, "Oh no, not I . . . " to so many of life's downers.

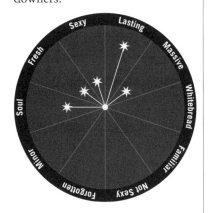

CONSTELLATIONS
➤ Disco Ball
➤ Jersey Pride

BIRTHSONG
➤ *I Will Survive* Mar 4–17 and Apr 1–7, 1979

J. GEILS BAND
Wherever you go, the sound of one hand clapping shall greet you.

Britney Spears, Internet porn, the Victoria's Secret catalog—there was none of that back in 1982. The only things that adolescent boys had to work with back then were the JCPenney insert in the Sunday newspaper and the scrambly soft core on late-night Cinemax. But then one day it happened—MTV flickered onto America's television screens, and within the space of a few hours, not only had America's boys witnessed Olivia Newton-John's *Physical*, but they'd also been treated to something by the J. Geils Band that looked like a brainwave-to-video transcription of the images that were already flashing through their minds every fifteen seconds or so. Intellectually, even these young men could probably recognize that *Centerfold* was meant to be a story of innocence lost, but for them your Birthsong was a story of experience gained, thanks to a video that featured a jaw-dropping parade of twenty-six-year-old high school girls in teddies who were obscured only occasionally by a skinny Mick Jagger type in spandex pants. Your Birthstar may be a Minor one in the grand scheme of pop, but they were the masters of a *very* appreciative audience segment in their day, endowing you with an **innate sense of age- and gender-appropriate entertainment** that might suit you

well in a field such as network television programming.

CONSTELLATION
➤ Storyteller

CELEBRITY
➤ **Justin Timberlake** (1/31/81) is a child of the J. Geils Band, born under the influence of the song *Centerfold.*

BIRTHSONG
➤ *Centerfold* Jan 31–Mar 13, 1982

GENESIS
Slow and steady wins the race to the middle, too.

The flashiest stars in the constellation **Shape-Shifter** are, of course, your Chers and your Olivia Newton-Johns—stars whose transmogrifications involved the revelation of edgier, or at least more scantily clad, personas. But a significant constituency within that constellation followed a rather different path, instead *dulling* their edges and ridding themselves of youthful idiosyncrasies and enthusiasms in their middle-age drift toward the rewards of the mainstream. And chief among flavor-shedding stars was Genesis, a driving force in the mid-eighties world of *Reaganrock* that got its start in the early-seventies world of arty English prog rock. Picture Nigel Tufnel in a druid outfit, delivering the ponderous, spoken-word opening of Spinal Tap's *Stonehenge*, and you'll come pretty close to picturing your Birthstar under the leadership of Peter Gabriel circa 1970. Biding his time behind the drums even then, though, was a young man named Phil Collins, whose cheerful charisma and love of American R&B would eventually take Genesis step by step toward popstrological immortality via the bouncy accessibility of *That's All* and your Birthsong, *Invisible Touch*. **A mastery of life's higher math** is quite clearly within your reach, child of Genesis, but your **comfort with common denominators** might dictate your path toward success.

CONSTELLATIONS
➤ Reaganrock
➤ Launching Pad
➤ Britsuasion
➤ Tip of the Ice Cube

BIRTHSONG
➤ *Invisible Touch* Jul 13–19, 1986

BOBBIE GENTRY
Sometimes the best part of your story is the part you leave out.

It was a story of repressed family drama—of hidden heartbreak and coded meanings exchanged over biscuits and blackeyed peas. But most of all, *Ode To Billie Joe* was a sultry Southern mystery whose unanswered questions were a national obsession at the moment of your birth. What did Billie Joe McAlister and the song's protagonist throw off the Tallahatchie Bridge? What made Billie Joe throw *himself* off the bridge just a few days later? According to a 1978 Robbie Benson television movie, the answers were (1) a rag doll; and (2) a simmering sexual-identity crisis of which said rag doll was somehow richly symbolic. That Bobbie Gentry herself co-wrote the script for this movie does little to satisfy skeptics, especially those still troubled by the role of the "nice young preacher" Brother Taylor. For them, the omigod-I'm-a-gay-man-in-a-redneck-world explanation for the events up on Choctaw Ridge has all the credibility that the magic-bullet theory does for Oliver Stone. File

your Birthsong alongside *You're So Vain* among pop's greatest unsolved mysteries, and be thankful to your Birthstar for endowing you with an **uncanny ability to hold an audience** by knowing **when to spill the beans and when to hold them in reserve.**

CONSTELLATIONS
➤ Storyteller
➤ Country Cousins

CELEBRITY
➤ **Carrie-Anne Moss** (8/21/67) is a child of Bobbie Gentry.

BIRTHSONG
➤ *Ode To Billie Joe* Aug 20–Sep 16, 1967

ANDY GIBB
If life were a sprint, you'd definitely reach the finish line first.

Someday science will allow every childbearing couple to create aesthetically perfect offspring by manipulating their combined DNA, but Hugh and Barbara Gibb had to do it the old-fashioned way: they just kept having sons until they had Andy. With his knee-buckling good looks and his brothers' songwriting talents backing him up, nineteen-year-old Andy Gibb staged an unprecedented display of youthful pop mastery in 1977–78, scoring three #1 hits with his first three releases. Could Andy's star have risen even higher? Perhaps, but Andy chose a prodigious cocaine habit over the chance to find out. With more time on this earth, would Andy have kicked that habit and tried again? Perhaps, but then, judging from the looks of the surviving Gibb boys, time also would have robbed Andy of his perfect, feathered mane and turned his chiseled features sharp and skeletal. These are the kind of questions that are critical for anyone born under the influence of the constellation *Tragic Demise* to ponder, and perhaps especially for you. For while your Birthstar unquestionably endowed you with **an ability to exploit the gifts that nature has given you**, do you have a plan for what you'll do when **time takes some of those gifts away**?

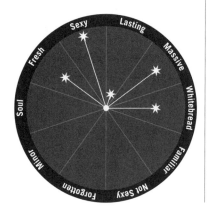

CONSTELLATIONS
➤ Gene Pool
➤ Outback
➤ Disco Ball
➤ Tragic Demise

BIRTHSONGS
➤ *I Just Want To Be Your Everything* Jul 24–Aug 13 and Sep 11–17, 1977
➤ *(Love Is) Thicker Than Water* Feb 26–Mar 11, 1978
➤ *Shadow Dancing* Jun 11–Jul 29, 1978

DEBBIE GIBSON
You are like the girl next door who will say nothing against the girl next door to her.

A lot of people tried to cast your Birthstar and her late-'80s companion in the constellation *Underage* as bitter rivals—as the Britney and Christina of their day. But to the frustration of those who yearn for a catfight whenever two women compete in the same arena, the battle between Debbie Gibson and Tiffany for the hearts, minds, and allowance dollars of America's preteen girls was a bit one-sided. Tiffany did her part, dating a New Kid on the Block and engaging in unilateral testing of theoretical hair-height limits, but your Birthstar never took the bait, and not just because her terminally flat hair forced her to. The fact is that supreme pop-tart status simply didn't interest Debbie Gibson, who saw herself not as the next Samantha Fox, but as the next Carole King. She wrote her own songs, she played her own instruments, and she even produced her own debut album. Debbie was the poster child for everything a well-raised teenager could achieve, if only she set her mind to justifying her parents' massive investment in music and voice lessons. Perhaps you've followed your Birthstar's lead and stayed safely away from **the swirling inferno of adolescent drama** that might otherwise consume you. But even if you're an oppositional Debbie Gibson who chooses instead to join the battle guns-a-blazin', you may soon decide that **conscientious objection is your more natural course**.

CONSTELLATIONS
➤ Underage
➤ Teen Idol

BIRTHSONGS
➤ *Foolish Beat* Jun 19–25, 1988
➤ *Lost In Your Eyes* Feb 26–Mar 18, 1989

NICK GILDER

The sound of sirens is a siren song to you.

They called John Hinckley a delusional madman, but Nick Gilder probably saw *Taxi Driver* too, and still he wrote a pop song that made the life of a teenage runaway/prostitute sound like a groovy way to meet boys. *Hot Child In The City* may not actually have inspired many underage record-buyers to flee the suburbs for the promised land of America's urban bus terminals, but it certainly fueled more than its share of misguided fantasies. In a way, though, part of the beauty of America in the seventies was its innocent prurience—its pre-Reagan willingness to embrace pop fantasies of murder (*The Night The Lights Went Out In Georgia*); madness (*Angie Baby*); prostitution (*Lady Marmalade*); adultery (*Me And Mrs. Jones*); road rage (*Convoy*); and nocturnal emissions (*Undercover Angel*). Like your Birthstar, the artists responsible for some of the above didn't create but rather exploited the public's titillation by some alluring social taboos, but don't try using that as a defense if you get entrapped in an FBI sting after typing the name of your Birthsong in an AOL chat room. *Hot Child In The City* was the song in everyone's ears at the moment of your birth, giving your Canadian Birthstar his only significant hit and giving those born under his influence a **tendency to flirt with danger**, or at least with fictional glamorizations of danger.

CONSTELLATION
➤ Oh . . . Canada

CELEBRITY
➤ **Justin Guarini** (10/28/78) is a Nick Gilder.

BIRTHSONG
➤ *Hot Child In The City* Oct 22–28, 1978

JIMMY GILMER AND THE FIREBALLS

The times may pass you by, but your timeless charms will still remain.

Very few of us have any business dancing in our swimsuits, especially those of us old enough to have been born under the influence of Jimmy Gilmer and the Fireballs. But try spinning your Birthsong, *Sugar Shack*, at your next pool party, then sit back and behold the glory of your friends' better aesthetic judgment falling by the wayside. Few songs in the pop canon have a power as inexorable as *Sugar Shack's* to compel such silly period dancing to break out (*My Sharona* comes to mind), but your Birthsong's power cannot be traced simply to its undeniably Fresh combination of chunky bass, proto-surf-guitar, and chirpy Hammond Solovox that legendary producer Norman Petty added to the track over the Fireballs' objections. No, the extraordinary power of your Birthsong and Birthstar can only be understood in the light of what followed their entry into the constellation **Royal Court** as the popstrological rulers of 1963. For as great as the British Invasion was for the long-term health and relevance of rock and roll, it also introduced a note of self-importance to the pop enterprise that marked the beginning of the end for unselfconscious party bands like Jimmy Gilmer and the Fireballs. **Light up the grill and swing your ample hips** whenever possible, for your popstrological strength lies in **giving and experiencing joy** without regard for **how goofy you look** while doing it.

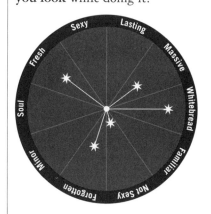

CONSTELLATION

➤ Royal Court

CELEBRITY

➤ **Brian Boitano** (10/22/63) is a child of Jimmy Gilmer and the Fireballs.

BIRTHSONG

➤ *Sugar Shack* Oct 6–Nov 9, 1963

BOBBY GOLDSBORO

Your favorite words in the English language are "Once more, with feeling."

His first real hit was *See The Funny Little Clown*, and it was an appropriate place to start for your Birthstar, whose collected works tend to fit neatly within the emotional framework of that song about a man who's laughing on the outside but—see if you can guess—*crying on the inside*. In a Bobby Goldsboro song, a man doesn't do something as mundane as fall in love with a girl or a car—a man does something big and meaningful like lose his virginity or his wife. Or, more accurately, a man in a Bobby Goldsboro song looks back with middle-aged wistfulness on losing his virginity or his wife, never failing to milk the recollection for every ounce of pathos it is worth. Yes, there were a few deviations from this formula for your Birthstar, but even his recording of the strangest Burt Bacharach song ever recorded, *Me Japanese Boy, I Love You*, tugged

rather hard on the sentimental heartstrings. It was nothing compared with *Honey*, though, which stands unchallenged as the most maudlin piece of work in the entire popstrological canon. To have been born under the influence of such a song and star is just as likely to have made you **numb to other people's feelings** as it is to have made you **compulsive about sharing your own**, but one gift it's almost certainly given you is an ability to **milk your stories for all they're worth**, whatever they may be.

CONSTELLATION

➤ Storyteller

CELEBRITY

➤ **Traci Lords** (5/7/78) is a child of Bobby Goldsboro.

BIRTHSONG

➤ *Honey* Apr 7–May 11, 1968

LESLEY GORE

When you cry, 50 percent of the whole world cries with you.

Where do girls learn about boys? From other girls, of course, and especially from girl pop stars. And so it was that America's booming population of teenage girls entered 1963 completely unprepared emotionally for the reality of romantic betrayal. Sure, there were hints of what boys were capable of in songs like *Will You Love Me Tomorrow?*, but before Lesley Gore came along, the message was mostly *He's So Fine* and *I Will Follow Him*. But with *It's My Party, She's A Fool, You Don't Own Me*, and *That's The Way Boys Are*, your Birthstar completed a protofeminist song cycle that paved the popstrological way for the more overtly liberated *Respect, I Am Woman*, and *I Will Survive*. Her most significant pop contribution as an adult were the lyrics to *Hot Lunch* (from the movie *Fame*), but it was as a seventeen-year-old girl from the northern suburbs that your Birthstar joined the constellation *Jersey*

Pride and awakened a generation of future feminists to the possibility that Johnny might not be the answer to their prayers, after all. **Stand up for what's yours emotionally**, children of Lesley Gore, and **the rest of the world will stand up with you**.

CONSTELLATIONS
➤ Jersey Pride
➤ Underage

BIRTHSONG
➤ *It's My Party* May 26–Jun 8, 1963

GRAND FUNK RAILROAD
Like a lead-footed driver in an era of cheap gas, you know but one speed—fast.

You could look back at the heyday of the American muscle car and wonder why anyone needed a three-thousand-pound hunk of iron that burned more fuel backing out of a driveway than a VW did driving all the way to Woodstock, but the answer should be obvious: the reason you needed a 360-horsepower 454 with the four-barrel carb and twin exhausts was to beat the other kids in town to the stadium ticket window the day that Grand Funk Railroad concert tickets went on sale. In 1971, your Birthstars sold out Shea Stadium faster than the Beatles did in 1965. Between 1970 and 1973, they were one of the top concert draws in the nation, and they sold close to 20 million albums without ever having a top-ten single. Along the way, their music helped define American hard rock, and their lifestyle helped create that genre's clichés. Look no farther than the lyrics of *We're An American Band* and the title of their 1974 album *All The Girls In The World—Beware!!* for insight into your Birthstar's deep artistic motivations and into your own **deep desire to let the good times roll**, buried though it may be under carefully applied layers of mature sophistication.

CONSTELLATION
➤ Mustache Rock

CELEBRITY
➤ **Gwyneth Paltrow** (9/28/73) is a child of Grand Funk Railroad.

BIRTHSONGS
➤ *We're An American Band* Sep 23–29, 1973
➤ *The Loco-Motion* Apr 28–May 11, 1974

GOGI GRANT
It's a futile job, but someone's got to do it.

No sooner had Elvis Presley fired the first popstrological shot in the rock and roll revolution than the forces of pop's establishment launched their first, stinging counterattack in the form of Gogi Grant. Had she been born ten years earlier, your now-Forgotten Birthstar might have enjoyed a popstrologically Lasting career in an era dominated by her middle-of-the-road ilk. But instead, Ms. Grant (*née* Audrey Arinsberg) faded rapidly from sight after knocking the King briefly from his throne in the summer of 1956 with her signature tune and one-and-only hit, *The Wayward Wind*. In retrospect, of course, it is easy to see your Birthstar as so much cannon fodder thrown at the unstoppable force that was Elvis Presley, but still it should be acknowledged that it was Gogi Grant, and not one of the more established *male* stars of the era, who became the inaugural star in the constellation *Old Guard*. Defenders of the pop status quo like Pat Boone and Perry Como enjoyed a great deal of success in the early years of the popstrological era, thanks in part to the sacrifices of your Birthstar, who bestows upon you a **willingness to take up causes that once were winners** and a **tendency to be underrewarded for your efforts**.

CONSTELLATION
➤ Old Guard

CELEBRITY
➤ **Sela Ward** (7/11/56) is a popstrological Gogi Grant.

BIRTHSONG
➤ *The Wayward Wind*
Jun 16–Jul 27, 1956

AL GREEN
You are the flip-flop artist who stands firm on principle.

Anyone would have been shaken by what transpired in Al Green's house on October 19, 1974, the day an ex-girlfriend interrupted his bath by pouring boiling-hot grits on his back before shooting herself dead with his own gun. On the other hand, not everyone would have taken the event as a crystal-clear signal that God intended him or her for the cloth. That's precisely how the soon-to-be-reverend Al Green took it, though, and so officially renounced pop superstardom and embraced a life in the church with an alacrity only a man who truly fears for his immortal soul could display. Yet despite your Birthstar's obvious sincerity in renouncing all things secular, the hands-down Sexiest soul singer of his generation did backslide occasionally over the coming decades, tantalizing his original fans with a secular soul record here and there among his many gospel recordings, but always flagellating himself for it afterward. Unique among the stars in the constellation *Shape-Shifter*, your Birthstar didn't so much evolve as lurch back and forth between two states in his deceptively Massive career, and for those born under his popstrological influence, this creates an interesting, doubled-edged legacy, ripe with the **potential to serve multiple masters**, but **filled with fear and guilt** about serving one too well.

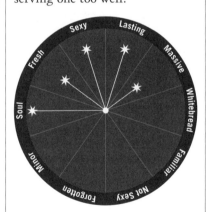

CONSTELLATIONS
➤ Shape-Shifter
➤ So-Soul
➤ Tip of the Ice Cube

BIRTHSONG
➤ *Let's Stay Together*
Feb 6–12, 1972

LORNE GREENE
When you hear your master's voice, do you wag your tail or bare your teeth?

His voice operated in a register most men can attain only after a pack and a half of cigarettes and a bad night's sleep. He couldn't sing, strictly speaking, but that hardly mattered, since Lorne Greene made his career strictly from speaking anyway. He was Canada's top radio newscaster in the 1940s and later starred as the patriarch of the Cartwright clan of bachelor ranchers on television's *Bonanza*. It was at the height of his fourteen-year run as Ben Cartwright that your Birthstar recorded a spoken-word story-song about an Old West gunslinger, and though it sounds like an unlikely song to hit #1 in a year otherwise dominated by John, Paul, and George, Lorne Greene's *Ringo* did indeed dominate the pop universe at the moment of your birth. And just as surely as that ponderous song about a frontier execution succeeded by the sheer force of Lorne Greene's vocal gravitas, you and others born under your Birthstar's deep and dramatic influence may find their own lives **shaped by commanding male authority figures**. Only the circumstances of your own life, however, can dictate whether this has manifested in you as an **irresistible attraction to the paternalistic** or a **distinct leaning toward the patricidal**.

CONSTELLATIONS
➤ Storyteller
➤ Oh . . . Canada

CELEBRITIES
➤ **Don Cheadle** (11/29/64) and **Marisa Tomei** (12/4/64) are popstrological Lorne Greenes.

BIRTHSONG
➤ *Ringo* Nov 29–Dec 5, 1964

THE GUESS WHO
Some people start parties, and others poop on them. You, however, do both.

They charged down from the windswept plains of Manitoba in 1970 with a loud and heavy sound that heralded the arrival of a powerful new force on the popstrological scene. They were the Guess Who, and their smash hit *American Woman* not only helped them beat the curse of the label "huge in Canada," but its clean and hard guitar attack and its Robert Plant–esque vocals also triggered the rise of the vital constellation *Mustache Rock*. Suddenly, all the bounty of America was theirs for the taking: chicks, Camaros, weed—you name it. One problem: lead guitarist Randy Bachman had converted to Mormonism, and like a fish allergic to water, he had to abandon the hard-livin' world that was his band's natural habitat. His departure spelled the eventual end of your Birthstar as a group, and it aligned them with the constellation *Launching Pad*, thanks to Bachman's later popstrological rebirth in Bachman-Turner Overdrive. But in their brief life span as a working band, your Birthstar bestowed upon you **the ability to inspire hedonistic abandon** and the **willpower to resist giving in to it yourself**.

CONSTELLATIONS
➤ Mustache Rock
➤ Oh . . . Canada
➤ Launching Pad

CELEBRITIES
➤ **Thom Filicia** (5/17/70) and **Tina Fey** (5/18/70) are Guess Whos born under the song *American Woman*.

BIRTHSONG
➤ *American Woman* May 3–23, 1970

GUNS N' ROSES
Some are troublemakers because they love the label, but you are a troublemaker because you love the trouble.

If f*cking in a Dumpster was your bag, then L.A. in the eighties was the place to be. Both inside and out back of the Whisky or the Troubadour on a given Saturday night, you could witness the most decadent expression of the rock and roll lifestyle the world has ever seen, and to the guys in bands like Poison and Warrant, your Birthstar must have seemed at first to be just another hog come to feed at the hair-metal trough. But they weren't. Axl, Slash, Izzy, Duff, and Steve were as interested as the next guys in the sex and the drugs, but when it came to the rock and roll, they were interested in the real thing, and if their shallower contemporaries had been clearheaded enough to recognize the danger that their raw, honest, and angry style represented, they'd have taken Guns n' Roses aside and said, "Dudes, shut UP—you'll ruin *everything*!" A few famous denizens of the Sunset Boulevard rock scene hung around long enough for Nirvana to come finish them off, but if it was grunge that finally killed hair metal, it was Guns n' Roses that struck the first, fratricidal blow. In the end, though, *Appetite for Destruction* was both the title of the brilliant album that launched Guns n' Roses into the constellation *Fresh Breeze* and a perfect summary of their professional philosophy. Your Birthstar died a messy and old-fashioned rock and roll death even before you entered grade school, but at birth they marked you as **one for the phony gasbags to watch** (and other enemies of truth and chaos, too).

CONSTELLATIONS
➤ Fresh Breeze
➤ Tip of the Ice Cube

BIRTHSONG
➤ *Sweet Child O' Mine* Sep 4–17, 1988

HALL AND OATES
When they say, "It'll never last," you say, "What do they know?"

Perhaps the popularity of their blue-eyed soul had something to do with the striking absence of brown-skinned soul in the pop-strological firmament of the 1980s, but primary responsibility for that has to rest with the constellation *Reaganrock*, an entity Hall and Oates steadfastly refused to join. At any rate, though, your popstrological legacy has very little to do with

how your Birthstar affected popular tastes and very much to do with how they defied conventional wisdom. For if ever there was a duo marked for certain breakup according to the Standard Rules of Pop, it was Hall and Oates. The psychic pressure applied upon your Birthstar by a public conditioned to expect the most telegenic member of any apparently unequal partnership to seek solo greatness was tremendous. But Daryl Hall—the tall, blond, cute one—never did dump John Oates—the short, goofy one in the fashion-defying mustache and natural perm. Was it mere loyalty that kept Mr. Hall from sending Mr. Oates off to join Sonny Bono, Jazzy Jeff, and Andrew Ridgeley on the island of popstrological left-behinds? Perhaps, but it seems more likely that there was much more "and" in Hall and Oates than anyone realized, all available evidence to the contrary. Many of us were born under the influence of groups that struggled to hide their inner discord, but you were born under one that hid the secret of its true inner harmony.

Congratulations, child of Hall and Oates, because it's a **rare and lovely popstrological gift** you possess of being able to **defy with quiet confidence the forces that tear so many relationships apart**.

CONSTELLATION
➤ Invisible Hand

BIRTHSONGS
➤ *Rich Girl* Mar 20–Apr 2, 1977
➤ *Kiss On My List* Apr 5–25, 1981
➤ *Private Eyes* Nov 1–14, 1981
➤ *I Can't Go For That (No Can Do)* Jan 24–30, 1982
➤ *Maneater* Dec 12, 1982–Jan 8, 1983
➤ *Out Of Touch* Dec 2–15, 1984

HAMILTON, JOE FRANK AND REYNOLDS
What's in a name? If you have to ask, then you may never understand.

The law-firm approach to naming a band works best when its members are recognizable stars (e.g., Crosby, Stills, Nash and Young) or when the combination somehow rolls off the tongue (e.g., Simon and Garfunkel). It is safe to say that "Hamilton, Joe Frank and Reynolds" did neither. Your Birthstar's name was clunky and strange to begin with, and it made even less sense considering that they continued to use it long after replacing name-partner Tommy Reynolds with a man named Alan Dennison. They could have followed Fleetwood Mac's lead and come up with something creative like "Dennison Ham," but instead they stuck to their guns and left their newest member off the masthead. And as a result, you'd be hard-pressed to find a more decisively Forgotten Birthstar in the entire pop universe, if only because no one could remember their name. Although they sounded every bit as good as the group America (now there's a name!), their understanding of brand identity lagged far behind that group's, as did their ability to leave a clearer and more Lasting mark on the universe of pop. As a popstrological child of HJF&R, you may have things well sorted out on a substantive level, but **pay more attention to packaging and presentation** than you normally do and **greater things might follow**.

JAN HAMMER
Just because you're the silent type doesn't mean you should remain silent.

The costume designer for *Miami Vice* did much more than spawn a dubious fashion trend when she dressed two TV cops in pastel T-shirts and crumpled Italian suits. She also bestowed an enormous gift upon future practitioners of her trade by creating a look that will still be used centuries from now as sartorial shorthand for the 1980s. But it was the lazy screenwriters of the future who received perhaps the greatest gift from *Miami Vice*, the show that demonstrated how five scenes' worth of difficult expository dialogue could easily be replaced with a ninety-second visual montage set to mood-appropriate pop music. *Miami Vice* brought the idiom of music videos to television dramas, and aside from the occasional pop song like Glenn Frey's *Smuggler's Blues*, it was the wall-to-wall instrumental score by your Birthstar that did the deed. Indeed, Jan Hammer's music was as much the star of *Miami Vice* as the clothes and Don "Freeze, pal" Johnson were, and probably more than Philip Michael "He ain't worth it, Tubbs!" Thomas was. If a DVD version of the complete *Miami Vice* is ever released that allows you to silence the dialogue, grab it immediately and you'll see how brilliant your Birthstar was at his job, and you'll understand why the double-edged gift he bestowed upon you is a **peerless ability to make your points nonverbally** and a **striking inability to do so otherwise**.

GEORGE HARRISON
You are the virtuoso freed from the limits of playing second fiddle.

He was called "the quiet one" when he was a Beatle, and when his influence pushed the band into experimentation with sitars and transcendental meditation, everyone said, "Ah, still waters run deep." But actually, George Harrison's waters weren't all that still, though they may have looked that way next to the roaring and roiling of Paul's and John's. It was George who first walked out on a Beatles recording session, after all, and George who first put out a solo album (*Wonderwall Music*, 1968). In fact, after a decade of adding his subtle instrumental genius to legendary hits by Lennon and McCartney while his own songs (e.g., *Here Comes The Sun*, *Something*) rarely made it onto the band's albums, George Harrison may have been the Beatle who was most enthusiastic about entering the constellation *Spin-Off* with his first solo #1 hit in 1970, *My Sweet Lord*. **An eagerness to jump from the sinking ship of a damaged relationship or other failing venture** is one influence your Birthstar bestows upon you, as is a tendency toward what some would regard as **flaky spiritualism**, but which popstrology regards as your true calling.

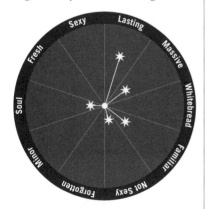

CONSTELLATIONS
➤ Spin-Off

CELEBRITY
➤ **Mary J. Blige** (1/11/71) is a child of George Harrison.

BIRTHSONGS
➤ *My Sweet Lord* Dec 20, 1970–Jan 16, 1971
➤ *Give Me Love (Give Me Peace On Earth)* Jun 24–30, 1973
➤ *Got My Mind Set On You* Jan 10–16, 1988

WILBERT HARRISON
Your name may be small when the credits roll, but the role that you play is large indeed.

You may never even have heard it, but in popstrological circles, the name Wilbert Harrison is often mentioned in the same breath as Elvis Presley or the Beatles. Why is such a Minor and Forgotten star as Wilbert Harrison so popstrologically significant? Because he saved rock and roll, that's why. You are flabbergasted, perhaps, to learn that a man you've never heard of performed such a heroic feat, but there are many different ways to be heroic. Was it heroic of the Irish to save civilization? Sure, but at the time, the anonymous Irish monks who copied and preserved manuscripts that were disappearing across the rest of Dark Ages Europe simply thought they were doing their job. They didn't know they were saving Western civilization by preserving its intellectual building blocks, and relatively anonymous musicians like your Birthstar probably felt the same way. Wilbert Harrison was just trying to make a living when he recorded *Kansas City*, but *Kansas City* and records like it ended up saving rock and roll by making their way to England, where a future invasionary force was being unconsciously prepared to reintroduce hard-driving, blues- and R&B–based rock and roll to a nation that had drifted into far less thrilling popstrological territory since Elvis went into the army. **Toiling in obscurity**, are you, child of Wilbert Harrison? That may be the way things stay, but you can rest assured that **your hard work is benefiting someone** more than it's benefiting you.

CONSTELLATION
➤ Invisible Hand

BIRTHSONG
➤ *Kansas City* May 12–25, 1959

ISAAC HAYES
Even if you're not great, you're bound to be complicated.

It's a long way indeed from *Hot Buttered Soul* to *Chocolate Salty Balls,* but your Birthstar's popstrological journey from Memphis, Tennessee, to South Park, Colorado, stands as an unmistakable testament to his Massive and Lasting impact. Even before Isaac Hayes had recorded a record of his own, he'd helped establish the very sound of 1960s R&B, as a session man at legendary Stax Records and as the co-writer of the Sam and Dave classics *Soul Man* and *Hold On! I'm Comin'*. But it was in the funky, spoken-word verses on his first two albums and on his classic (and only) #1 hit *Theme From "Shaft"* where Hayes had his greatest popstrological impact, laying the groundwork for what would later be called rap. When your Birthstar performed *Shaft* in shades and chains on national television on the night he was awarded the Academy Award for Best Score, this grandson of sharecroppers became the living popstrological embodiment of Black Power. Even more remarkably, your Birthstar established his identity to millions of middle-Americans as pop's baddest muthashutyourmouth without seeming either (*a*) terrifying or (*b*) harmless. And if

Isaac Hayes did not go so far as to bestow upon you a similar **ability to break boundaries while walking fine lines**, he probably did imbue you with the potential for **truly idiosyncratic career achievement**, or at the very least an **obsessive attraction** to a spooky television personality.

CONSTELLATIONS
➤ So-Soul
➤ Theme Singer
➤ Invisible Hand
➤ Hot Hairdo

CELEBRITY
➤ **Christina Applegate** (11/25/71) is an Isaac Hayes.

BIRTHSONG
➤ *Theme From "Shaft"* Nov 14–27, 1971

HEART
You'd never sell your soul for glory, but you might consider placing it in a blind trust.

In a more just pop universe, your Birthstar would have taken *Magic Man* or *Crazy On You* to #1 back in 1976 and then rested on their popstrological laurels as the only female-led star in the constellation *Mustache Rock*. But justice was not served in Heart's heyday, so sisters Ann and Nancy Wilson waited ten long years before leading their band to the popstrological heights—years that failed to diminish the brilliance of Ann's incomparable voice, but did much to expand

the proportions of her figure. So it was that in 1986, the trimmer, sexier Nancy became the new public face of Heart, while Ann—still gorgeous, but over-abundant by the brutal standards of the day—was pushed back behind a shrubbery. The videos that sold the songs that launched your Birthstar into the constellation *Reaganrock* made great use of Nancy's décolletage and perfect eighties hair, but when they showed Ann Wilson at all, they showed her in shadowy close-ups or in primitive versions of the Slim-O-Vision technology later perfected for Carnie Wilson. As a popstrological child of a star in the constellation *Shape-Shifter*, you are obviously capable of **clear-eyed pragmatism**, and that's a blessing in any calling. But unless you are pursuing a career in politics or entertainment, take great care, children of Heart, to ignore the **brutal lookist** that also lurks within you.

CONSTELLATIONS
➤ Reaganrock
➤ Shape-Shifter

HERMAN'S HERMITS

Some like a glass of fine red wine, but others prefer a cup of sweet, purple grape juice.

The Beatles transformed the pop universe as we know it and altered the very definition of what it meant to be a rock and roll band, but in cold, hard business terms, they did something just as important: they created a market. They created a market for bright and cheery British pop, and to the great good fortune of your Birthstar, they quickly left that enormous market behind as they followed their artistic vision into very different musical territory. It's been said that Herman's Hermits, who arrived on American shores in 1964 led by seventeen-year-old Peter Noone, were geared, groomed, and packaged to appeal to the middle-school set. But in truth, the audience Herman's Hermits served was the sizable segment of the American pop audience for whom the "*yeah, yeah, yeah*"s of *She Loves You* would always hold more appeal than the "*koo-koo ka-choo*"s of *I Am The Walrus*. Your Birthstar's American debut, *I'm Into Something Good*, appealed then as it appeals now to just about anyone with a pulse, and while the exaggerated Englishness of their two #1 hits made

them seem a bit too silly in the nation of their birth, it made them just silly enough to be embraced in America as the stylistic forerunners of the group that eventually made them obsolete: the Monkees. **Not everyone in this world can be taken seriously**, child of Herman's Hermits, but **you've got everything it takes to succeed** in a culture that values many things more highly than seriousness.

CONSTELLATION
- ➤ Britvasion

BIRTHSONGS
- ➤ *Mrs. Brown You've Got a Lovely Daughter* Apr 25–May 15, 1965
- ➤ *I'm Henry VIII I Am* Aug 1–7, 1965

THE HIGHWAYMEN

When fashions change, someone always gets left behind.

They were Wesleyan University frat brothers with the liberal-arts worldliness to sing folk songs in five languages and the Whitebread cluelessness to call

themselves the Clansmen. They meant their name to refer to their Scots-Irish repertoire, but luckily their first manager, a New Yorker named Greengrass, pointed out the problems it might present for a group of white boys planning to release a slave song from the Georgia sea islands as their first single. Thus did your Birthstar become "the Highwaymen," and thus did *Michael* (as in "row your boat ashore") become a #1 hit without sparking race riots. For a very brief moment in popstrological time, your Birthstar epitomized the earnest thoughtfulness of the constellation *Folkie*, and though they never actually recorded *I Gave My Love A Cherry*, it was precisely their brand of folk that the writers of *Animal House* were making fun of when they had John Belushi smash the guitar of a folkie doofus who did. But popstrological Highwaymen take note: those same writers were scrupulously true to the times they were depicting when they surrounded their folkie doofus on the stairs with a gaggle of adoring coeds. **The time and place in which you were regarded as hip** may

long since be gone, but there is a **time and a place for everything**, including squareness, stiffness, and whatever **outdated brand of appeal** you call your own.

CONSTELLATION
➤ Folkie

BIRTHSONG
➤ *Michael* Sep 4–17, 1961

BUDDY HOLLY AND THE CRICKETS

Your candle may someday burn out, but the light it casts will not fade away.

Contractual issues actually kept Buddy Holly's name off his only #1 single, but *That'll Be The Day* and a string of immortal classics that followed (*Maybe Baby, Peggy Sue, Everyday, Oh, Boy!*) put his fingerprints on almost every page in the history of rock and roll. The magnitude of your Birthstar's musical influence is incredible considering the shortness of his career, but just as incredible is the magnitude of his style influence, considering the way he looked. Seventies hipster-icon Elvis Costello gets credit for an assist, but it is your Birthstar who made what we'd call "geek chic" possible, by exuding utterly unaffected charisma in a boxy suit and chunky eyeglasses. The famous Iowa plane crash that took Buddy Holly's life did more than just give the world *American Pie*—it also froze in a state of near-perfection the brightest star in the popstrological constellations *Tip of the Iceberg* and *Tragic Demise*. **Your days may not be numbered** as his were, but the way to be true to your popstrological legacy is to **make the most of what time you have** by acting as if they were.

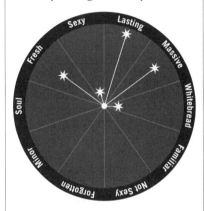

CONSTELLATIONS
➤ Tip of the Iceberg
➤ Tragic Demise
➤ Texstyle

BIRTHSONG
➤ *That'll Be The Day* Sep 23–29, 1957

HOLLYWOOD ARGYLES

Your broad liberal-arts education began before you even knew it.

Do the children of today have any idea how much cultural power the funny papers once had? Do they understand that television and movies once had special effects so laughably bad that the comics were the only place to go for convincing science fiction? As a child of the Hollywood Argyles, you at least are old enough to remember a time so media-deprived that *Blondie, Boner's Ark*, and *Family Circus* were the best thing going on a rainy Sunday afternoon, and you should also be able to appreciate how a nostalgic (and drunken) paean to a time-traveling cartoon caveman could resonate deeply enough with the American public of 1960 to become a #1 hit song. *Alley Oop* was the only song ever recorded by your Birthstar, who chose their name essentially at random from the intersection of L.A. boulevards where they recorded your Birthsong. And while those born under the Minor and Forgotten influence of the Hollywood Argyles **fight an uphill battle if gravitas is their goal**, they are greatly **prized as coworkers and driving companions** for their ability to make **huge stretches of idle time pass quickly and amusingly**.

CONSTELLATION
➤ Novelty Merchant

BIRTHSONG
➤ *Alley Oop* Jul 11–17, 1960

RUPERT HOLMES

You are the square peg who flourishes in a world of round holes.

His songwriting credits reach from Barbra Streisand to Britney Spears, but Rupert Holmes will forever be known for a kindhearted tale of attempted adultery called *Escape (The Piña Colada Song)*, a gem of such Lasting brilliance that decades from now, when all of us are too old to remember our names, we'll still be able to complete the musical phrase that begins *"If you like piña coladas . . . "* If you are truly committed to understanding the influence of the iconoclastic star who ruled the pop universe in the final weeks of the seventies, however, you should begin your quest by seeking out an earlier tune called *Timothy*—a minor 1971 hit for the Buoys. With *Timothy*, songwriter Holmes declared himself willing to tackle any and all subject matter, and it should go without saying that a man with the wit and nerve to craft a pop hit about cannibalism is a man worth watching. An absolute anchor in the constellation *Storyteller*, Holmes endows those born under his influence with the potential to **win friends and allies anywhere with candor and offbeat charm.** Consider Holmes's third career as a Tony-winning writer/composer (*The Mystery of Edwin Drood*) and you will begin to appreciate why **versatility and flexibility** are his further popstrological legacies to you.

CONSTELLATION
➤ Storyteller

BIRTHSONG
➤ *Escape (The Piña Colada Song)* Dec 16–29, 1979

THE HONEY CONE

You may not rule the world, but you do understand its ways.

Edna Wright was a Raelette, Shelly Clark was an Ikette, and Carolyn Wills would have been a Louette if Lou Rawls's backup group had had a name. Between them they'd put in a couple decades' worth of blue-collar service in the music business before making their popstrological ascent in 1971, so it's fair to say that the members of the Honey Cone didn't have all that much in common with the other residents of the popstrological neighborhood they moved into. The constellation *Les Girls*, after all, was home to cosseted princesses like the Supremes and wide-eyed teenagers like the Dixie Cups. It was home, simply stated, to a bunch of girls, and Edna, Shelly, and Carolyn definitely weren't girls. They were strong, black *women*, and you could hear it in songs like *While You're Out Looking For Sugar* and *Girls It Ain't Easy*, which in typical Honey Cone fashion could very easily have carried parenthetical subtitles like (*Mmm-hmmm*) or (*That's Right!*). It's easy to criticize many of the great girl groups for trafficking in the notion that salvation for women was to be found only in the arms of a strong and dominant man, but not the Honey Cone. They sang like women who longed for rescue *from* men as much as by them, and they bestowed upon their popstrological children an enviable **ability to outgrow romantic fantasies**, yet **without giving up on the dream of love** entirely.

CONSTELLATIONS
➤ Les Girls
➤ So-Soul

BIRTHSONG
➤ *Want Ads* Jun 6–12, 1971

BRUCE HORNSBY AND THE RANGE

You may not wish to join every club that will have you.

The Academy of Popstrological Arts and Sciences (TAPAS) has already drafted a letter waiting to be mailed to your Birthstar in response to the inevitable e-mail protesting his inclusion in the constellation *Reaganrock*. *Dear Mr. Hornsby,* it begins, *We would be happy to tell you what in the hell we are talking about.* It's a letter that's too long to summarize briefly, but its main points revolve around Mr. Hornsby's assertions that (*a*) your Birthsong was in fact "a critique of the socially unjust status quo in Reagan-era America"; and (*b*) he later "joined the Grateful Dead, for Christ's sake." As to the latter point, the legions of late-eighties/early-nineties Deadheads whose BMWs were purchased with Mom and Dad's supply-side dollars speak for themselves, but the former point is less easily deflected. In fact, while popstrologists acknowledge Mr. Hornsby's political intent on his only #1 song, they also know that it was pretty like a Windham Hill sampler, and that its mumbly lyrics—"*something something welfare lines . . . get a job . . . That's just the way it is*"—left it rather wide-open to misinterpretation. *We respect your music and your point of view, Mr. Hornsby,* the letter concludes, *but you wrote* Jacob's Ladder *for Huey Lewis and* The End Of The Innocence *for Don Henley, and our ruling stands. Best to the Range, etc., etc."* The road to a lot of places is paved with **good intentions**, child of Bruce Hornsby, so don't be surprised if **yours take you somewhere unexpected**.

CONSTELLATIONS
➤ Reaganrock
➤ Invisible Hand

BIRTHSONG
➤ *The Way It Is* Dec 7–13, 1986

JOHNNY HORTON

O, say, can you see the frightened Brits scatter before your approach?

The *Star-Spangled Banner* was written in 1814, but it took another 145 years before someone wrote a song about the War of 1812 that the average American could actually sing. That song, Johnny Horton's *The Battle Of New Orleans,* was a lighthearted portrayal of a good old-fashioned shootin' match, which was just the tonic Americans were yearning for at the height of the Cold War. Your Birthstar's one and only entry in the popstrological canon was so popular that the real question is, if President Eisenhower could add "under God" to the Pledge of Allegiance, why couldn't he have made your Birthsong the new national anthem? Can you even imagine how much more fun we'd be as a nation, and how much more *right* it would be on every level, if our winning Olympic athletes mounted the podium to a song about beans, bacon, and kicking British ass down the mighty Mississip'? Perhaps there'd even be a coin or a stamp dedicated to your briefly Massive but sadly Forgotten Birthstar, an early star in the constellation *Storyteller* who bestows upon you a **refreshing lack of sanctimony**, a **twisted form of Anglophilia**, and a **flair for bringing the past to life** in thrilling (if not entirely accurate) detail.

CONSTELLATION
➤ Storyteller

CELEBRITIES
➤ **Tom Arnold** (6/3/59), **Vincent D'Onofrio** (6/30/59), and **Suzanne**

Vega (7/11/59) are children of Johnny Horton.

BIRTHSONG
➤ *The Battle Of New Orleans* Jun 1–Jul 12, 1959

THELMA HOUSTON

Why be a slave to your needs when you can be their master instead?

When the Supremes sang *You Keep Me Hangin' On*, their lament referred to the withholding of romantic commitment, but when Thelma Houston sang *Don't Leave Me This Way*, she was looking for satisfaction of a more physical nature. Though at first listen it may have seemed a sort of pleading antithesis to Gloria Gaynor's *I Will Survive*, your Birthsong was, in fact, a fully empowered woman's straightforward appeal to the new code of etiquette that was taking hold amid the sexual revolution—a code that established the right of every woman to achieve the same measure of amorous closure expected by every man. Two years later, Anita Ward would take the Orgasmic Equity Movement to the next level with her demand for *unilateral* satisfaction in 1979's *Ring My Bell*, but it was your Birthstar who fired the movement's first popstrological shot, earning a spot in the constellation *Disco Ball* and bestowing upon those born under her influence with an unmistakable **tendency to stand up for what is theirs** but

perhaps to the point of engaging every opportunity for heated negotiation and **ignoring opportunities for self-satisfaction.**

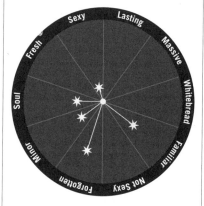

CONSTELLATION
➤ Disco Ball

BIRTHSONG
➤ *Don't Leave Me This Way* Apr 17–23, 1977

WHITNEY HOUSTON

You are the hothouse flower that yearns for the real dirt.

Destined by nature to be gorgeous and talented (she is Cissy Houston's daughter) and destined by nurture to be a pop megastar (she is Dionne Warwick's cousin and Clive Davis's pet project), Whitney Houston didn't *almost* have it all—she *had* it all. One of the true giants of the popstrological era and beyond, the only solo woman who would eventually eclipse her total number of #1 songs was Mariah Carey, and Mariah (among others) might not even have a career if Whitney

Houston hadn't single-handedly created the modern archetype of the belting pop diva. Sexy (still) and Fresh (upon arrival), Massive (duh) and Lasting (apparently), your Birthstar excels in every pop-strological aspect except the Whitebread/Soul dichotomy, where she rates an ambiguous N/A. Perhaps that explains the one obvious chink in Whitney's personal armor, which is her continuing weakness for a certain bad boy who once seemed to represent groovy street cred, but should have worn a sign saying "Unsafe Conditions Ahead." **Choose your intimates wisely**, Whitney Houstons, not because you should worry about being judged by their faults (you shouldn't), but because **they can nurture your weaknesses as well as your strengths.**

CONSTELLATIONS
➤ Royal Court
➤ Gene Pool
➤ Jersey Pride

BIRTHSONGS
➤ *Saving All My Love For You* Oct 20–26, 1985
➤ *How Will I Know?* Feb 9–22, 1986

- ➤ *Greatest Love Of All* May 11–31, 1986
- ➤ *I Wanna Dance With Somebody (Who Loves Me)* Jun 21–Jul 4, 1987
- ➤ *Didn't We Almost Have It All* Sep 20–Oct 3, 1987
- ➤ *So Emotional* Jan 3–9, 1988

THE HUES CORPORATION

You are the boat that floats upon a rising tide.

The death of disco was as rapid and dramatic as the extinction of the dinosaurs, and nearly as well documented, but the story of disco's birth is less often told because it's difficult to pinpoint musically, and because it happened years before John Travolta put on his famous white suit. But the birth of disco as a *popstrological* phenomenon can be traced directly and definitively to the week of your birth, in the summer of 1974. It's not something technical about the sound of *Rock The Boat*—beats per minute or anything like that—that marks it as the first #1 disco song. What gives your Birthsong that distinction is that it was launched directly from the dance floor to the highest reaches of the pop universe after being given up for dead by the label that released it. Listen to it today and it seems inconceivable that *Rock The Boat* wasn't instantly and universally recognized as a timeless classic, but indeed you would probably never have heard it had it not been for the eminent good taste of

patrons in New York City's largely black, Latin, and gay nightclubs of the mid-seventies. As a popstrological shareholder in the Hues Corporation, you draw considerable dividends from having been born during the launch of the mighty constellation *Disco Ball*, but any **megalomaniacal tendencies** you've developed as a result are probably well tempered by the **humility and willingness to share credit** you derive from your Birthstar's further placement in the constellation *Regifted*.

CONSTELLATIONS
- ➤ Disco Ball
- ➤ Regifted

BIRTHSONG
- ➤ *Rock The Boat* Jun 30–Jul 6, 1974

THE HUMAN LEAGUE

Where you lead, others will follow.

Their name evoked images of an Orwellian future in which bands of *Homo sapiens* with futuristic haircuts struggle to defeat the forces of machine-enforced con-

formity. And true to that spirit, the Human League were the first star in the popstrological heavens to put a human face on the electronic revolution that was transforming pop. Before their appearance, the stars in the constellation *Casio* were largely anonymous and shrouded in mystery—faceless wizards of a tool ominously called the synthesizer. Indeed, only a few years before you were born, synthesizers were intimidating contraptions the size of a Sperry Univac that seemed inoperable without an advanced degree in engineering. But with the rise of the Human League, the synthesizer came suddenly to be seen as an instrument that an attractive, even glamorous man or woman with limited technical or musical abilities could play with a single finger while looking stylish in heavy eyeliner and a loose-fitting shirt. **Mastering technology while looking fabulous** is not the only talent you may have inherited from your Birthstar, though. For in blazing the trail so many fellow stars of the constellation *Britsuasion* would later travel, the Human League

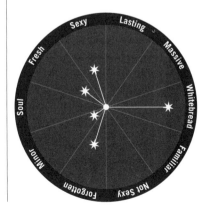

also endowed you with the ability to **ensure bigger rewards for your followers** than you take for yourself.

CONSTELLATIONS
➤ Casio
➤ Britsuasion

BIRTHSONGS
➤ *Don't You Want Me*
  Jun 27–Jul 17, 1982
➤ *Human* Nov 16–22, 1986

TAB HUNTER
Those who can, do, but sometimes so do those who can't.

It was the dawn of the teen idol era, when demand for young musical heartthrobs far exceeded supply, and movie star Tab Hunter was the total package: blond hair, a chiseled physique, and a teenage fan base eager to spend their allowances on rock and roll records. So who cared if he couldn't sing? When the head of Dot Records cold-called your Birthstar one day in 1957, the conversation went something like this: "Listen, Tab, can you carry a tune?" "Well, I'm not tone deaf if that's what you mean, but I'm not exac—" "That's great, kid! How'd you like to make a record?" Within weeks, the legions of teenage girls (and, as it turned out, boys) who kept Tab's picture under their pillows also had his #1 single on their turntables. *Young Love* fell within that genre of fifties music seemingly designed to convince otherwise happy, carefree teenagers

that their lives were not worth living in the absence of a devoted, monogamous soul mate, but that was a message America's teens were evidently more than ready to listen to. Not one to harbor Hasselhoffian illusions or ambitions, however, Tab gracefully retired his singing voice shortly after entering the popstrological firmament, in a fine example of the **humility, self-knowledge, and tender mercy** that are the special gifts of those born under this Birthstar.

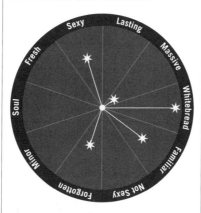

CONSTELLATION
➤ Teen Idol

CELEBRITY
➤ **Spike Lee** (3/20/57) is a child of Tab Hunter.

BIRTHSONG
➤ *Young Love* Mar 2–29, 1957

BRIAN HYLAND
You are a keen observer of fashion—too keen, perhaps, for some.

"Ah, how times have changed," you might say to yourself on hearing that your Birthsong

was almost shelved by Brian Hyland's record label because it broached the dangerous topic of skimpy swimwear. And you'd be right, considering that even an itsy-bitsy 1960 bikini would qualify as a muumuu by today's fashion standards. But what's much more interesting and popstrologically relevant about this story is that what saved *Itsy Bitsy Teenie Weenie Yellow Polkadot Bikini* from being self-censored into oblivion was the assurance given by its writers to the head of Kapp Records that your Birthsong was actually meant to be about a two-year-old girl. In other words, the fact that made your Birthsong morally acceptable in 1960 would probably render it morally *unacceptable* today. Go ahead—type "swimsuit AND little girl" into Google and see what horrors you dredge up from that reflecting pool of modern depravity called the Internet. Gone forever are the days when a song about a scantily clad toddler could rule the pop universe, and when a sixteen-year-old from Queens could ride such a song to a position of Forgotten greatness in the

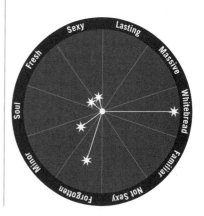

constellation *Novelty Merchant*. You, however, were born at a moment when both of these things not only could but actually did occur, which may explain why **your taste and values sometimes seem so out of step** with our rapidly changing modern times.

CONSTELLATIONS
- ➤ Novelty Merchant
- ➤ Underage
- ➤ Teen Idol
- ➤ Outerborough

BIRTHSONG
- ➤ *Itsy Bitsy Teenie Weenie Yellow Polkadot Bikini* Aug 8–14, 1960

BILLY IDOL
Anyone can strike a pose, but few can hold it as long as you.

I f he lives long enough, as he shows every sign of doing, your Birthstar may one day be the only living connection your children and grandchildren have to that bit of ancient history called punk rock. He'll be wheeled out onstage to receive a lifetime achievement award at the 2037 Grammys, and the crowd will come to its feet as Billy Idol pumps his bony fist and sneers his toothless sneer. And at that very moment, in a lonely English cemetery, Joe Strummer will roll over in his grave. Some of the original punks actually believed in the social and political significance of their ill-played, bare-bones rock, you see, but let's be honest: How

many kids wanted to dress up as Patti Smith for Halloween? The undeniable fact is that Billy Idol, with his spiky hair and lippy sneer, gave mainstream America all the punk it really wanted, and for that he was rewarded with a place among the popstrological elite (on the strength of a Tommy James song, no less) and a lifetime's worth of Robert Goulet–style cameo work as a self-mocking caricature of eighties pop culture. Like the fabulous Kenny Rogers, Billy Idol is that rare member of the constellation *Hot Hairdo* never to abandon the style that landed him there—an appropriate distinction for a star who bestows upon his popstrological children a **refusal to step out of character** and a **willingness to play to their greatest natural strengths**.

CONSTELLATIONS
- ➤ Britsuasion
- ➤ Hot Hairdo
- ➤ Tip of the Ice Cube

BIRTHSONG
- ➤ *Mony Mony* Nov 15–21, 1987

INXS
In the great sweep of history, not everyone gets to hold the broom.

T he death of frontman Michael Hutchence in 1997 was either lurid, suspicious, or simply sad, depending on your reading of the forensic evidence, but his band was popstrologically dead long before it joined the constellation *Tragic Demise*, and not of natural causes. It wasn't a breakup or a gradual loss of touch with popular tastes that did your Birthstar in—it was the greatest single incident of popstrological mass extinction since 1964: the Seattle Invasion. Nirvana, Pearl Jam, and the lesser soldiers of grunge swooped in just one year after the close of the popstrological era like avenging angels bent on ridding the pop universe of all things polished and bloated, and while your Birthstar didn't fall into either of those categories, one can hardly expect that both hair metal and the constellation *Reaganrock* could be brought to their knees without causing a bit of collateral damage. And there can be no question that that's what your Birthstar was, for during a period when the highest reaches of the pop universe were dominated by Starships and Ceteras, INXS managed to succeed by playing a brand of clean and Fresh guitar-based rock and roll that was in no danger of being confused with the work of, say, Bryan Adams. They were the final star in the constellation *Outback*, but their foreign passport could not spare them from a domestic conflict that did not involve them. You, too, may find yourself **in the wrong place at the wrong time**, child of INXS, but **don't let that stop you from enjoying your moment in the sun**.

CONSTELLATIONS
➤ Outback
➤ Tragic Demise
➤ Tip of the Ice Cube

BIRTHSONG
➤ *Need You Tonight*
Jan 24–30, 1988

TERRY JACKS
You may be surrounded by clowns, but no one will force their fun on you.

A mericans don't like to think about death, and when we do, we mostly like to think about it happening to other people. But the French are different. Their very national motto is a death wish, and when a French songwriter like Jacques Brel writes from the perspective of a dying man, he calls his song *The Dying*

Man, not *Seasons In The Sun*, and pulls no punches. He includes a spiteful verse directed at an old enemy, and he leads into his chorus with a line like *"When is it that one will put me in the hole?"* Granted, anyone asked to translate *Le Moribond* into English would have taken some liberties with the language, but perhaps not as many liberties as Rod McKuen, poet laureate of the flower-power generation, did. By the time McKuen got done with it, *Seasons In The Sun* had lost all of its Gallic bitterness and taken on a distinctly, well, American feel. The Canadian singer Terry Jacks may have recorded it and become your Birthstar, but his first plan was to get the Beach Boys to do it, and one can only imagine how fouled up you'd be if he'd pulled *that* off. Do you live each day as if it were your last, taking and **expressing childlike joy** in all of life's simple pleasures? No, we didn't think so. Do you roll your eyes at those who do? Yes, that's more like it. The Americanization of *Le Moribond* may have made it acceptable to America, but its true essence is likely to be seen in

those born under its influence—a popstrological generation **unafraid of emotional gravity**, or at least **reluctant to wear a cheery face** for no good reason.

CONSTELLATIONS
➤ Oh . . . Canada
➤ Storyteller

BIRTHSONG
➤ *Seasons In The Sun*
Feb 24–Mar 16, 1974

THE JACKSON 5
The relationships that matter most may be the ones you did the least to create.

P icture yourself in the kitchen of the Jackson house in Gary, Indiana, in early 1967. Jermaine is working on his hair upstairs while his dad barks at Jackie and Tito to stop arm-wrestling and start loading the car for tonight's gig over in Hammond. Rebbie and La Toya are watching TV with Little Randy while Marlon sits at the table, rearranging his vegetables and humming to himself quietly. Eight-year-old Michael is ignoring his dinner completely, but his mother lets it go since he's also keeping baby Janet amused by showing her his latest dance moves. Three years from now, the five oldest boys in this house will rule the pop universe more completely than any group since the Beatles, and twenty years from now, nearly every child in this family will be a household name. Through ups and downs unimaginable to most of us, the members of this family will support and stick up for one another almost without fail, yet thirty and forty years from now, the world will imagine the early Jackson household as a **simmering crucible of dysfunction**. Popstrologists, for their part, will neither support nor reject this view, but they most certainly will direct those born under the Jackson 5's influence to harken back to this time in their search for insight into their own crazy lives. **Has your family propped you up more than it's f*cked you up**, child of the Jackson 5, or has it done the opposite? Perhaps it's done both in equal proportion, but in any event, **it's almost certain to have made an indelible impression**.

CONSTELLATIONS

- ➤ Gene Pool
- ➤ Shaking Booty
- ➤ Hot Hairdo
- ➤ Launching Pad
- ➤ Underage
- ➤ Royal Court

CELEBRITIES

- ➤ **Heather Graham** (1/29/70), **Uma Thurman** (4/29/70), **Ethan Hawke**

(11/6/70), **Sean Hayes** (6/26/70), **Audra McDonald** (7/3/70), **Steven Page** (6/22/70), **Ed Robertson** (10/25/70), and **Tonya Harding** (11/12/70) are all children of the Jackson 5.

BIRTHSONGS

- ➤ *I Want You Back* Jan 25–31, 1970
- ➤ *ABC* Apr 19–May 2, 1970
- ➤ *The Love You Save* Jun 21–Jul 4, 1970
- ➤ *I'll Be There* Oct 11– Nov 14, 1970

JANET JACKSON

When the going gets crazy, the not-so-crazy get going.

Perhaps it was because she was young enough to fly under father Joe's punishing radar that she avoided becoming another La Toya or, for that matter, another Michael. Perhaps it was because she spent three years in the projects on *Good Times* that she got in touch with what some of us call reality. Or perhaps it was simply because she chose the right stylists, surgeons, and shrinks that Janet managed to keep a head on her shoulders that roughly resembled the one she was born with. Whatever the reasons, from the moment your Birthstar arrived on the scene, it was clear that the pop universe had been given the gift of the first Jackson since Rebbie who could be embraced without feeling even slightly creepy about it. Janet

Jackson managed only one of her astonishing ten career #1 hits within the popstrological era, placing her Sexy and Lasting star squarely among the deceptively Massive forces of the constellation *Tip of the Iceberg*. And despite all the fuss that surrounded your Birthstar's exposure of her nipple-brooch on national television, it can still be said safely that the beloved baby sister of the constellation *Gene Pool* bestows upon her popstrological brood an enviable ability to **flourish amid dysfunction** and to **carve a relatively unique place for themselves** within territory well traveled by others.

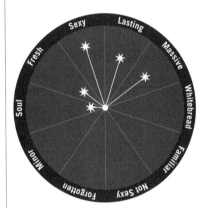

CONSTELLATIONS

- ➤ Gene Pool
- ➤ Tip of the Iceberg

BIRTHSONG

- ➤ *When I Think Of You* Oct 5–18, 1986

MICHAEL JACKSON

Your potential is limitless, but that's not so much a compliment as an intimidating fact.

The tipping point seemed to come in 1984, when Michael Jackson reemerged publicly at the American Music Awards just months after forming a popstrological *Power Couple* with Paul McCartney and subsequently catching fire on the set of a Pepsi commercial. Dressed in the sequined uniform of some exotic foreign navy and clutching a pint-size Emmanuel Lewis on his lap like a ventriloquist's dummy, your Birthstar appeared for the very first time to have moved beyond the realm of standard superstar eccentricity and into some new plane of being. There had been earlier warning signs, of course. Michael had, after all, made his solo debut with 1972's *Ben*, a touching ballad about the love of a sensitive boy for a homicidal rodent. But it was easy to dismiss that bit of strangeness in light of the thrilling Freshness and sheer genius of what was to come: *Off the Wall* (1979) and *Thriller* (1983), both of which deserve consideration for any short list of the greatest pop albums of all time. There would be many more #1 hits for your Birthstar after 1984, but never again would the question "What's up with Michael Jackson?" convey a straightforward interest in his musical career. Indeed, no life has been examined more closely and with less good faith than his, and though popstrology teaches us to examine the totality of our Birthstars' lives and careers for insights into ourselves, sometimes popstrology draws a line and says, "Enough." **Public attention will almost certainly play a strong role in your life,** perhaps because you crave it, despise it, or simply display a knack for earning it. But what that attention will do to you is anyone's guess. Love, adulation, worship, pity, disappointment, fear, revulsion—your Birthstar has inspired just about every possible human feeling in his lifetime, and so might you, but try to **forget his continuing slide toward Neverland,** if you can. Your Birthstar's influence hasn't turned you into a genius pop craftsman and it almost certainly won't turn you into whatever he is today.

CONSTELLATIONS
- ➤ Sui Generis
- ➤ Royal Court
- ➤ Spin-Off
- ➤ Gene Pool
- ➤ Underage

CELEBRITY
- ➤ **Mya** (10/10/79) is a child of Michael Jackson.

BIRTHSONGS
- ➤ *Ben* Oct 8–15, 1972
- ➤ *Don't Stop 'Til You Get Enough* Oct 7–13, 1979
- ➤ *Rock With You* Jan 6–Feb 9, 1980
- ➤ *Billie Jean* Feb 27–Apr 16, 1983
- ➤ *Beat It* Apr 24–May 14, 1983
- ➤ *I Just Can't Stop Loving You* Sep 13–19, 1987
- ➤ *Bad* Oct 18–31, 1987
- ➤ *The Way You Make Me Feel* Jan 17–23, 1988
- ➤ *Man In The Mirror* Mar 20–Apr 2, 1988
- ➤ *Dirty Diana* Jun 26–Jul 2, 1988

TOMMY JAMES AND THE SHONDELLS

You've got the rare gift of giving as good as you get.

Tommy James was a seventeen-year-old aspiring pop star from Michigan whose career was going nowhere until his amateurish, three-year-old recording of *Hanky Panky* was pulled from the bargain bin by a Pittsburgh DJ and became a bootleg smash. The Shondells, for their part, were four lads chosen almost at random by Tommy after he hustled to Pittsburgh sans the original Shondells, who declined to join their childhood pal on his Steeltown folly. Both stories are classic examples of the kind of events that populated the constellation *Regifted* with stars, but don't let them convince you that your Birthstar was luckier than they were good. Though Tommy and his Shondells were dismissed in their time by the rock cognoscenti as purveyors of worthless bubblegum, *Hanky Panky* sounds to objective ears every bit as Fresh and unsophisticated as *Wild Thing*, a song from the same year that some credit with sparking a garage-rock revolution. And if *Crimson And Clover* was good enough for Joan Jett, it should be good enough to convince those who roll their eyes at Tiffany and Billy Idol scoring consecutive 1987 #1s with Tommy James covers that your Birthstar, a unique dual member of the constellation *Invisible Hand*, is as gifted and giving a star as the constellation *Regifted* has ever seen. **It's better to give than to receive**, as the saying goes, but your Birthstar's gift to you is to believe that **it's better still to do both**.

CONSTELLATIONS
➤ Regifted
➤ Invisible Hand

CELEBRITY
➤ **Bobby Brown** (2/5/69) is a child of Tommy James and the Shondells.

BIRTHSONGS
➤ *Hanky Panky* Jul 10–23, 1966
➤ *Crimson and Clover* Jan 26–Feb 8, 1969

JAN AND DEAN
Yours is a voice that may yet change history, as long as someone else tells you what to say with it.

Shouts of "*Gold!*" set California on its path toward joining the United States, but what made it the most populous state in the nation were further shouts of "*Action!*" "*Free Love!*" "*Venture Capital!*" and, perhaps most important, "*Two girls for every boy!*" That was the immortal opening line of your Birthsong, *Surf City*, which was itself the opening popstrological salvo in the California Invasion of the early-1960s. In this respect, Jan and Dean were pioneers of a sort, but it must be noted that the duo behind *Honolulu Lulu*, *Dead Man's Curve*, and *Little Old Lady From Pasadena* were in no danger of achieving greatness before a friend they'd made on the local music scene offered them your half-written Birthsong. That friend, Brian Wilson, was the unstable genius behind the Beach Boys and the true innovator in your Birthstar's chosen field, and it's his vital contribution to Jan and Dean's rise that explains their presence in the constellation *Regifted*. They may not have written all of their own lines, but your Birthstar was still the first to deliver the sun-and-fun sales pitch to a generation of restless American youth. And in so doing, they bestowed upon you an ability to appreciate that **it's better to be gifted than good**, and better to be a madman's follower when he's still just known as an eccentric genius.

CONSTELLATIONS
➤ Regifted
➤ Tip of the Ice Cube

BIRTHSONG
➤ *Surf City* Jul 14 –27, 1963

JOAN JETT AND THE BLACKHEARTS

Beneath your tough exterior lies, well, an even tougher interior.

She had rock-star charisma to rival anything the pop universe had ever seen, and she rocked hard and unapologetically in a popstrological moment otherwise dominated by the likes of Air Supply, Christopher Cross, and Lionel Richie. Just imagine the power Joan Jett could have possessed, if only she'd chosen to seize it. With her smoldering looks and equally smoldering hooks, Joan Jett had the entire population of America's young men (and an uncertain percentage of its women) eating out of her hand. All she had to do was tart it up just the *tiniest* bit, and she would have ruled them like a goddess. But there would be no flouncy hair and flirty winks from Joan Jett—only a look that said, "Come hither and I'll kick your ass." By refusing to bend to commercial convention and adopt a more feminized persona, your Birthstar did more than just leave room for the future career of Courtney Love; she also stayed true to her popstrological orientation as a woman who really did love rock and roll more than she loved being a pop star. Children of this briefly Massive star from the constellation *Fresh Breeze* would do well to remember their Birthstar's example, for while mainstream **success may require serious compromise**, a **dash of rebellion** might earn you a cult following.

CONSTELLATION
➤ Fresh Breeze

CELEBRITIES
➤ **Kelly Clarkson** (4/24/82) and **Kirsten Dunst** (4/30/82) are children of Joan Jett and the Blackhearts.

BIRTHSONG
➤ *I Love Rock 'N Roll* Mar 14–May 1, 1982

BILLY JOEL

What's a burden to some is motivation to you.

Except for perhaps a brief moment in 1977, it was never truly cool to like Billy Joel, and yet Billy Joel has sold more albums in his career than every American male pop star other than Elvis. But Billy Joel's career is a testament to more than just the commercial irrelevance of uncoolness—it's also a testament to the incredible power of uncoolness as a creative force in someone talented enough to exploit it. If Billy Joel had been born cool, after all, he might still have had a brush with popstrological greatness as a sixteen-year-old high school dropout playing piano on 1964's *Leader of the Pack*, but he'd never have developed the yawning inferiority complex that runs throughout his incredible body of work. He'd never have been plagued by the kind of self-doubt that he veiled so thinly in songs that cast him either as a lovably simple romantic (*Just The Way You Are, An Innocent Man*) or as a cocky, pugilistic mutt (*My Life, It's Still Rock And Roll to Me, Uptown Girl*). And he'd almost certainly never have recorded the autodidactic epic *We Didn't Start the Fire* in order to prove that he really did read the *New York Times* and the *Daily News*. Billy Joel made it out of Hicksville, Long Island, through talent and sheer determination, but if he'd actually been any cooler than the rest of us shlubs, we might never have learned his name, and you might never have developed your tendency to **achieve success not despite but because of the burdens that you bear**.

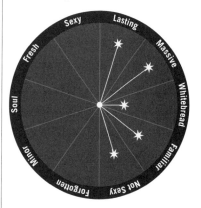

CONSTELLATION
➤ Sui Generis

CELEBRITY
➤ **Jason Schwartzman** (6/26/80) and **Michelle Kwan** (7/7/80) are children of Billy Joel.

BIRTHSONGS
➤ *It's Still Rock And Roll To Me* Jul 13–26, 1980
➤ *Tell Her About It* Sep 18–24, 1983

ELTON JOHN
You are the type who succeeds by playing against type.

His father, Stanley, wanted young Reginald Dwight to follow his footsteps into the British military, but Reg always was a bit of a mama's boy. It was Shirley Dwight's Elvis records that sparked his interest in rock and roll, and it was her uncritical maternal devotion that made it possible for that interest to become an ambition. How many words of discouragement would it realistically have taken to break the spirit of a soft, bespectacled boy dreaming of rock superstardom? One imagines not very many, but then again, this was a boy with the tenacity to keep wearing a pair of Buddy Holly–style eyeglasses until he ruined his twenty-twenty vision by getting his eyes to adjust to their strong prescription. Rearrange his DNA or his childhood environment just the littlest bit, and perhaps Reginald

Dwight would have become an RAF fighter pilot instead of Elton John, and perhaps your Birthstar would be Barry Manilow or Captain and Tennille. But leave things as they are, and you remain quite clearly the child of one of brightest stars in the popstrological firmament and perhaps the quintessential member of the constellation *Sui Generis*—a balding, brilliant, soccer-club-owning, princess-adoring homosexual with a toler-ance for gay-bashing rappers and an incomparable ear for pop hooks. There may not be a crea-ture quite so **strange, success-ful, and resplendent** hiding inside you, child of Elton John, but only in **the safety of entirely nonjudgmental rela-tionships** are you likely to find out for sure.

CONSTELLATIONS
➤ Sui Generis
➤ Royal Court
➤ Britsuasion

BIRTHSONGS
➤ *Crocodile Rock* Jan 28–Feb 17, 1973
➤ *Bennie And The Jets* Apr 7–14, 1974
➤ *Lucy In The Sky With Diamonds* Dec 29, 1974–Jan 11, 1975
➤ *Philadelphia Freedom* Apr 6–19, 1975
➤ *Island Girl* Oct 26–Nov 15, 1975

ELTON JOHN AND KIKI DEE
As every showman knows, it's more important to be loved than to be believed.

In early 1976, Elton John put his Massive career in jeopardy by acknowledging in a *Rolling Stone* interview that he was a "bisexual." It was a bold move for a pop star to make in those days, and it came as quite a shock to the millions of fans who had never suspected, even for a minute, that Elton might be the type to sleep with women. Did becoming chair-man of a fourth-division English football club and form-ing a popstrological *Power Couple* with Kiki Dee later that same year add much credibility to his rather dubious claim? No, not really. The world was fairly comfortable in its understand-ing of who Elton John was, so the only thing those moves did was provide some excellent sing-along material to Watford City fans and opponents and to American motorists of every stripe. And while imaginative football chants like "El-ton John is a homo-sex-u-al" may have grown somewhat stale in the years since your birth, the popstrological Freshness of

Don't Go Breaking My Heart has proven itself to be utterly timeless. As long as the car radio or something like it continues to exist, enthusiastic duets of *"When you were down / I was your clown"* will continue to break out on America's roadways between friends, lovers, and family members, without regard to gender or singing ability, and that's as joyful a popstrological legacy as one could possibly hope for. Some fake beards are more convincing than others, but that shouldn't matter to you, since **artifice is as unnecessary to your straightforward appeal as subtext is to your straightforward message**.

CONSTELLATIONS
➤ Power Couple
➤ Britsuasion

BIRTHSONG
➤ *Don't Go Breaking My Heart* Aug 1–28, 1976

ROBERT JOHN
There is no map for the path that you must follow.

When the writers of *The Brady Bunch* needed a new direction for the show in the face of the younger Bradys' rapidly declining cuteness, their solution was revealed via the deus ex machina of the Bradys' hidden musical talents. The bright, bubblegum brilliance of *It's A Sunshine Day* and *Keep On* would later come to define the glorious Brady sound, but true fans will remember that it all began with a draggy and hopelessly sincere ballad, *We Can Make The World A Whole Lot Brighter*—nominally by Greg, but really by Mr. Robert John. What was your Birthstar doing working for a bunch of kids who'd reached their professional peak in their early teens? Well, he was doing his damnedest to avoid the same fate for himself, that's what. As a twelve-year-old, he had made the lower reaches of the charts under the name Bobby Pedrick, Jr. (*White Bucks and Saddle Shoes*, 1958), and his dream of even greater achievements sustained him through the next twenty years hauling bricks (literally) and writing songs for failing sitcoms. **Dogged persistence** and a **sense of pride not easily injured** are the popstrological gifts bestowed on you by a star whose stubborn **refusal to become a footnote** finally paid off in 1979, when he earned his spot in the constellation *Lite & White* with the junior high slow-dance classic *Sad Eyes*.

CONSTELLATION
➤ Lite & White

BIRTHSONG
➤ *Sad Eyes* Sep 30–Oct 6, 1979

JANIS JOPLIN
You take all things in moderation, including moderation itself.

In 1986, Jon Bon Jovi sang of a rock star who could only tell the day by the bottle that he drank, and that goes to show you just how tame the world of rock had become by the time you were in your teens. Back in your Birthstar's day, the pills you took made it damn-near impossible to tell what bottle you were drinking, but who the hell cared what day it was anyway? "Sex, drugs, and rock and roll" was no empty cliché in the late 1960s—it was a way of life and a revolutionary philosophy, and Janis Joplin was its leading female exponent. Sex? Her string of conquests ranged, rather impressively, from Kris

Kristofferson to Dick Cavett. Drugs? Why yes, and always a bottle of bourbon at hand to smooth out the rough edges. Rock and roll? *Mercedes Benz, Piece Of My Heart, Get It While You Can*, and your Birthsong, the posthumous #1 hit *Me And Bobby McGee*, are howling, time-capsule classics. But what does all this mean for you, a popstrological child of the most raggedy star in the constellation *Hot Hairdo* and the first woman to join the constellation *Tragic Demise*? Hopefully just that **your desire to live life to the fullest is difficult to repress**. And if it is, why try? It wasn't heavy drinking from the cup of life that killed Janis Joplin, and with **the barest hint of discretion** it won't kill you, either.

CONSTELLATIONS
➤ Tip of the Iceberg
➤ Sui Generis
➤ Tragic Demise
➤ Hot Hairdo
➤ Texstyle

BIRTHSONG
➤ *Me And Bobby McGee*
Mar 14–27, 1971

BERT KAEMPFERT
You easily separate sh*t from shinola, but can you tell shinola from a diamond in the rough?

I f all he'd accomplished outside his own recordings was composing the music for Frank Sinatra's only #1 hit in the popstrological era, your Birthstar might still have qualified for entry into the constellation *Invisible Hand*. But *Strangers In The Night* is not the reason why his star resides there, and why the pop universe as we know it might never have come to be without his influence. Bert Kaempfert's world-altering impact came in 1961, when he hired four raw and hungry lads from Liverpool to play backup on a Tony Sheridan record he was producing in Hamburg. He didn't sign them to a real contract because he didn't think they were ready, and he didn't put their real name on the single he let them cut after the Sheridan session, because he thought the name "the Beatles" wouldn't sound as nice to Germans as "the Beat Brothers." Your Birthstar may have passed on the chance to play a bigger role in popstrological history, but his obscure recording (*Ain't She Sweet/Cry For A Shadow*) of the Not-Yet-Fab Four did help history on its way by reaching the ears of an English record-shop owner named Brian Epstein. **Missed opportunities** might haunt some popstrological children of Bert Kaempfert, but those less prone to regret might learn to **relish the more**

sublime satisfaction of providing such opportunities to others.

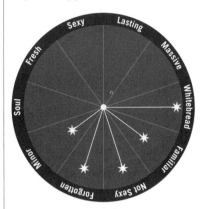

CONSTELLATIONS
➤ Invisible Hand
➤ Speechless
➤ Eurosomething

CELEBRITY
➤ **Julia Louis-Dreyfus** (1/13/61) and **Wayne Gretzky** (1/26/61) are popstrological children of Bert Kaempfert.

BIRTHSONG
➤ *Wonderland By Night*
Jan 9–29, 1961

KC AND THE SUNSHINE BAND
You are the hardworking hedonist with a two-track mind.

P rior to 1975, most people regarded it as an expression of pain, but for Harry Wayne Casey, the sound "Owww!" was an expression of unbridled joy. It was a sound to accompany not a stubbed toe but a shaken booty, a sound to signify the pure, funk-fueled joie de vivre that he and his incomparable Sunshine Band spread throughout the pop universe of the 1970s. And who wouldn't enjoy life if he or she lived it by your Birthstar's example? Any day that KC did a little dance and made a little love was an okay day by his standards, and quite frankly, that's a set of priorities that a lot of us could stand to get behind. Perhaps Harry Wayne would have brought the same level of enthusiasm and the same vocabulary of "awws" and "uh-huh"s to his work regardless of what profession he chose, but luckily for all of us he chose music over bus driving. Children of KC and the Sunshine Band, it is not just your destiny but your popstrological responsibility to carry on the legacy of the brightest star in the constellation *Shaking Booty*—to show the rest of us through your **groovy exuberance** that **life's simple pleasures are also its greatest** and that it's always better to *get* down than to stay down.

CONSTELLATION
➤ Shaking Booty

BIRTHSONGS
➤ *Get Down Tonight* Aug 24–30, 1975
➤ *That's The Way (I Like It)* Nov 16–22 and Dec 14–20, 1975
➤ *(Shake, Shake, Shake) Your Booty* Sep 5–11, 1976
➤ *I'm Your Boogie Man* Jun 5–11, 1977
➤ *Please Don't Go* Dec 30, 1979–Jan 5, 1980

ERNIE K-DOE
One man's trash may well be your treasure.

Local popularity in the live-music hotbed of New Orleans guaranteed your Birthstar a fine living even if his fame grew no farther, but Ernie K-Doe (*née* Kador) was not content to remain popstrologically invisible. Still, raw desire absent wit and resourcefulness will get you exactly nowhere, so Ernie applied his considerable wits to the problem at hand and dug up the resource he needed in the rejects pile of a songwriting friend and budding genius named Allen Toussaint. It was there that your Birthstar found his ticket to immortality in the form of *Mother-In-Law*, a song with relatively little musical merit, but more than enough cultural resonance to launch him into the constellation *Novelty Merchant*. But it is in Ernie K-Doe's connection to the man who placed him in the constellation *Regifted* that things get really interesting, for through the work of Allen Toussaint, a direct pop-

astrological line can be drawn from your Birthstar to such diverse pop-cultural figures as Glen Campbell, Nona Hendryx, and Bob Eubanks. Many owe their success in life to **standing on the shoulders of giants**, but **a knack for finding suitable shoulders on not-quite giants** may explain the roots of yours.

CONSTELLATIONS
➤ Novelty Merchant
➤ Regifted

BIRTHSONG
➤ *Mother–In–Law* May 22–28, 1961

EDDIE KENDRICKS
Keep your ear to the ground and you'll be the first to hear the stampede.

After leaving the Temptations, the group for which he sang such legendary hits as *The Way You Do The Things You Do* and *Just My Imagination (Running Away With Me)*, it took a couple of years for Eddie Kendricks to find his ticket to popstrological immortality, but he knew it the second he found it. It was a song called *Keep On Truckin' (Part 1)*, and the power he recognized in it had nothing to do with its sound. What your Birthstar recognized was that almost any song with this title would have an enormous pop-cultural tailwind behind it thanks to the almost unexplainable grip that the mere phrase "keep on truckin'" had on the American imagination in the early 1970s. Go back to 1968, and it had only about as much cultural currency as the phrase "bee's knees," but then a strange, dirty-minded cartoonist named R. Crumb resurrected this bit of pre-WWII blues slang by attaching it to a drawing of a Kilroy-esque character with enormous feet in the first issue of his now-famous comic book *Zap*. Soon thereafter, and for no obvious logical reason, that image and phrase could be found gracing everything from head-shop windows to kindergartners' T-shirts. Indeed, the phrase "keep on truckin'" had nothing to do with eighteen-wheelers initially, and perhaps it was your Birthstar who sparked the crossover and

thereby set the stage for America's strange, mid-seventies fascination with long-haul trucking. **Anyone can spot a trend** when it's staring him in the face, but not everyone is as gifted as you at **spotting a trend while there's still time to turn it to your personal advantage**.

CONSTELLATIONS
➤ Spin-Off
➤ So-Soul

BIRTHSONG
➤ *Keep On Truckin'*
Nov 4–17, 1973

ANDY KIM
No job is too small when your ambition is large.

Andrew Joachim of Montreal was the rare teenager to possess the talent, wits, and ambition to pursue his rock and roll dreams seriously. Just sixteen years old and intent on landing a gig as a professional songwriter, he hopped a train to New York City, where he fell under the wing of the Brill Building legend Jeff Barry (of Barry-Greenwich fame). By the time he was twenty-one, the rechristened Andy Kim was a plugged-in veteran of the New York pop scene and a minor pop star in the making. He had solid hits in the late sixties with *How'd We Ever Get This Way* and *Baby, I Love You*, and he eventually scored a #1 hit with 1974's *Rock Me Gently*. But it was as the songwriter he originally set out to be that your

Birthstar earned his fortune and his membership in the constellation *Invisible Hand*. In 1969, Andy wrote a silly little trifle of a song with his friend and mentor, Barry—for a Saturday morning cartoon show, of all things. That little trifle, called *Sugar, Sugar*, sold more than thirteen million copies, earning your Birthstar a healthy popstrological endowment to fall back on even if his own star had failed to rise. **You may not be immune to the allure of the spotlight**, child of Andy Kim, but don't be surprised if **your greatest rewards are earned in the shadows**.

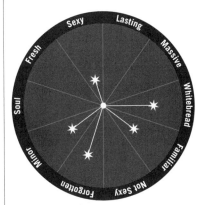

CONSTELLATIONS
➤ Invisible Hand
➤ Oh . . . Canada

BIRTHSONG
➤ *Rock Me Gently* Sep 22–
Sep 28, 1974

CAROLE KING

The list of those you've helped fills volumes, but don't let your own ambitions fall by the wayside.

A decade of toil in the constellation *Invisible Hand* explains why Carole King's Starchart reflects an impact more Massive and Lasting than those of most pop stars with just a single hit as a performer. Long before she was Carole King the popstrological queen of 1971, Carole Klein was just another piano-playing Jewish soul sister living in 1950s Brooklyn and dating another future pop star (Neil Sedaka). Then she was Carole King the songwriter, studio helper of pals Simon and Garfunkel and one half of Goffin-King, the husband-and-wife team behind #1 hits for the Shirelles (1961), Bobby Vee (1961), family babysitter Little Eva (1962), Steve Lawrence (1963), Donny Osmond (1971), and Grand Funk (1974). Later divorced and on her own, Carole dashed off another pop masterpiece or two for others (including *Natural Woman* for Aretha Franklin and *You've Got A Friend* for James Taylor), all before finally becoming a pop star in her own right fully ten years after writing her first #1 hit. **Leaving the spotlight to others** might carry you just as far as it carried your Birthstar, but **don't be afraid to put yourself center stage** and see what good might come of it.

CONSTELLATIONS
➤ Invisible Hand
➤ Royal Court
➤ Outerborough

CELEBRITY
➤ **Tupac Shakur** (6/16/71) was a popstrological Carole King.

BIRTHSONGS
➤ *It's Too Late/I Feel The Earth Move* Jun 13–Jul 17, 1971

THE KINGSTON TRIO

An out-of-date haircut is no reason to hang your head.

They might not have liked to acknowledge it, but the passionately political (and deeply self-serious) fans of 1960s protest folk owed the very existence of their beloved movement to three guys in crew cuts and candy-striped shirts. In their music as in their physical appearance, the group that honed its act in frats and sororities of Stanford University betrayed little discomfort with the sociopolitical status quo of the late 1950s. As for the *popstrological* status quo, though, the Kingston Trio altered that forever by introducing the astonishingly Fresh sound of a hundred-year-old folk song into the American pop mainstream of 1958. Your Birthstar's version of *Tom Dooley* may have focused more on moody atmosphere than on the details of the syphilis-tinged love quadrangle found in the original, but that little trade-off, and the Trio's banjo-backed harmonies, made possible the mammoth hit that launched their Massive career. And without the enormous profits that your Birthstar's Massive career generated, it is impossible to imagine Dylan, Baez, Ochs, *et al.* getting the major-label contracts that led to the records that helped define the 1960s. Not the first but certainly the most important star in the constellation *Folkie*, the Kinston Trio claim residence in a total of *five* important constellations, from that they bestow upon their popstrological progeny a networker's dream of **dense connections to greatness** that more than make up for a **lack of natural coolness**.

CONSTELLATIONS
➤ Folkie
➤ Fresh Breeze
➤ Tip of the Iceberg
➤ Storyteller
➤ Hot Hairdo

CELEBRITY
➤ **Jamie Lee Curtis** (11/22/58) is a child of the Kingston Trio.

BIRTHSONG
➤ *Tom Dooley* Nov 17–23, 1958

THE KNACK
You are the breath of fresh air on which a window may shut.

In July of 1979, a near-riot broke out on West Fifty-seventh Street in Manhattan when tickets went on sale to see the Knack play Carnegie Hall. Even there, so close to the epicenter of the still-strong disco craze, the hysteria was that intense for a group that owed its entire appeal to sounding and looking like everything that disco was not. All you needed was to hear a few bars of *My Sharona* to know that a powerful new force was rising in the constellation *Fresh Breeze*, and that the reign of the mighty *Disco Ball* would someday actually end. Ultimately, however, America's infatuation with your Birthstar died almost as quickly as disco itself. Victims of their own success and of a fanatical "Knuke the Knack" T-shirt-and-button campaign, your Birthstar didn't

stick around long enough to fill the popstrological vacuum they'd helped to create by pushing disco to the brink, leaving that honor to the briefly resurgent forces of *Lite & White* and the eventual pioneers of that thing called *Reaganrock*. A **look and an attitude that fall outside the norm** may just be **enough to get you noticed,** children of the Knack, but if long-term relevance is your goal, be prepared to **define yourself on your own terms** rather than just in opposition to others.

CONSTELLATION
➤ Fresh Breeze

CELEBRITY
➤ **Pink** (9/8/79) is a child of the Knack.

BIRTHSONG
➤ *My Sharona* Aug 19– Sep 29, 1979

GLADYS KNIGHT AND THE PIPS
You joined the choir to sing, but they won't stop preaching to you.

The gospel-trained voice of Gladys Knight in her early-seventies heyday was a marvelous instrument to behold, but try to tune it out, because it's the Pips whose influence you should be concerned about on your journey toward popstrological truth. Listen to their performance on *Midnight Train To Georgia*, and you can easily imagine what it would be like to have the Pips sitting behind you in a crowded movie theater. Whatever Gladys Knight sings about, there are the Pips with an editorial comment of their own. If Gladys says dreams don't always come true, the Pips say "*Uh-uh, no, uh-uh,*" and if Gladys says she hopes to join her man on his midnight train to Georgia, the Pips say "*I KNOW you will.*" Sometimes they clarify, sometimes they amplify, and sometimes they outright testify, but one thing the Pips *never* do is disagree. And therein lies the problem, for the popstrological children of Gladys Knight and the Pips find themselves all too often seated in the amen chorus or surrounded by one. Either way, you run the risk of what military analysts call "incestuous amplification," which occurs when you listen only to the **opinions of those already in lock-step agreement with you.** Affirmations and support from your nearest and dearest are gifts you shouldn't even consider discarding, but **avoid situations ripe for miscalculation** by finding an outside opinion before **convincing yourself of the righteousness** of your own.

CONSTELLATIONS
➤ So-Soul
➤ Tip of the Ice Cube

BIRTHSONG
➤ *Midnight Train To Georgia* Oct 21–Nov 3, 1973

BUDDY KNOX
You are the tiny oak that spreads a thousand acorns.

Frank Sinatra was the first and Elvis Presley was the next to show the world the power a pop star could wield over crowds of young women. But a pop star with the talent, looks, and charisma of Sinatra or Elvis comes along maybe once per generation. What really changed everything, and what provided the fuel for the explosion of rock and roll, was the dawning realization that a young man like Buddy Knox could produce the same effect, albeit on a

smaller scale, simply by learning a few chords on the guitar and writing a song as absurdly simple as *Party Doll*. Your Birthsong was the first in the popstrological era to be written by the star who performed it, and if it sounds like the kind of unsophisticated plea for sex that a the fifteen-year-old boy might write, that's because your Birthstar was only fifteen when he wrote it. But if the next four decades of pop history proved anything, it was the timeless power of unsophisticated pleas for sex written by and for American teenagers. And it all started with your Minor and Forgotten Birthstar, whose rise from a West Texas farm to the top of the popstrological heap charted a course that millions of rock and roll dreamers still seek to follow. It also imbued those born under his influence with the power to **overcome modest beginnings** and to **inspire revolutionary change while leading by example**.

CONSTELLATION
➤ Texstyle

BIRTHSONG
➤ *Party Doll* Mar 30–Apr 5, 1957

KOOL AND THE GANG
From boo-hoo to ya-hoo, you are the master of emotions beyond just your own.

If your faith in popstrology is shaky, if you find yourself questioning the dramatic power of the pop stars, make your way to the nearest catering hall some Saturday afternoon this June, and watch a well-oiled wedding or bar mitzvah band at work. For these are the lay practitioners of the popstrological arts—the humans who get paid to use music to control the emotional course of joyous but highly charged events that always threaten to veer off into disaster. Bridesmaids crying at the bathroom mirror, groomsmen barfing in the yard, thirteen-year-old kids filled with Manischewitz—these professionals have seen it all and played through it all, and they will tell you how time and again they have made order out of chaos by calling on the strength of their patron saint and your Birthstar, Kool and the Gang. Indeed, they could even prove to you that, when push comes to shove, there's nothing they need to get through a wedding, and little they need to get through a bar mitzvah, other than *Jungle Boogie*, *Ladies Night*, *Fresh*, *Get Down On It*, *Cherish*, *Joanna*, and, of course, their secret weapon, *Celebration*. To be born under the influence of the most effective forced-fun anthem in all the pop canon is a double-edged gift, for **an ability to**

whip crowds into a frenzy is a dangerous power in irresponsible hands, and for every popstrological Kool and the Gang who possesses **the power of mind control**, there is another who is just **especially susceptible to it.**

CONSTELLATIONS
➤ Tip of the Ice Cube
➤ Jersey Pride

CELEBRITY
➤ **John Walker Lindh** (2/9/81), the "American Taliban," is a child of Kool and the Gang.

BIRTHSONG
➤ *Celebration* Feb 1–14, 1981

LABELLE
You play to your strengths rather than to others' weaknesses.

What our modern era lacks in imagination it tends to make up for with explicitness, as can easily be seen by comparing the mid-1970s *Lady Marmalade* of your Minor but

Lasting Birthstar with the 2001 *Lady Marmalade* of the superstarlets Mya, Pink, Christina, and Lil' Kim. The pornographic effectiveness of the latter-day remake is much to be admired on purely technical grounds, but it's an open question whether it even approached the sexiness of the original. After all, back in 1975 you didn't sit alone in the dark *watching* a song like *Lady Marmalade*—you *danced* to it among a bunch of your fellow humans. In an era dominated by audio and not video, you might not have seen the group called Labelle at all, but if you did, you'd have seen a trio that featured Patti LaBelle, Nona Hendryx, and Sarah Dash in silvery eye shadow and Uhura-esque spacesuits that revealed very little but hinted at scenarios rather more interesting than a roomful of barely legal strumpets in Victorian hooker outfits. Comparing Labelle's glorious original version of your Birthsong to the in-your-face remake is like comparing the delicious frisson of "*Voulez-vous coucher avec moi?*" to the blunt effectiveness of "*Hey buddy, you wanna f*ck?*" And

while some are moved much more by the latter than they are by the former, the **best romantic targets for you** will be those who **prefer the thrill of the alluring** to the **straightforward pull of the merely lurid.**

CONSTELLATION
➤ Disco Ball

BIRTHSONG
➤ *Lady Marmalade* Mar 23–29, 1975

PATTI LABELLE AND MICHAEL MCDONALD
Your parents probably aren't cool now, but they once may have been.

If someone had told you in 1976 of a plan to unite the lead singer of the Doobie Brothers with the voice behind *Lady Marmalade* on a duet performance of a Burt Bacharach song, you might have struggled to keep your head from exploding. What forces would such a collision of the constellations *Mustache Rock, Shaking Booty,* and *Lite & White* produce? Who would be careless enough to try and find out? If someone told you in 1986 of a plan to do the same thing with Michael McDonald and Patti LaBelle, on the other hand, you might simply have shaken your head and said, "Yeah, that figures." What happened in that ten-year span that could change the perceived ignorance, and perceived threat, of your Birthstar so dramatically? Well,

Reaganrock happened, and when it did, an awful lot of the strangeness and diversity that characterized the seventies disappeared from the pop universe. The minions of the 1980s' dominant constellation would have cited your Birthstar's exceptionally non-threatening appearance, of course, as evidence that the pop universe was a safer place for the banishment of all that was raw and thrilling, but that probably rings false to you. After all, haven't you had that feeling for some time now that **you were born in the wrong place** or the wrong time—that something much greater, or at least **something more exciting, could have been yours**? Without trying to make you feel any worse, all popstrology can say to that is, "Yes, it certainly could have."

CONSTELLATIONS

➤ Power Couple
➤ Spin-Off
➤ Reaganrock

CELEBRITIES

➤ **Mary-Kate and Ashley, the Olsen twins** (6/13/86), are children of Patti LaBelle and Michael McDonald.

BIRTHSONG

➤ *On My Own* Jun 8–28, 1986

CYNDI LAUPER
Do they love you for your character, or for the character you play?

There were rumors—unsubstantiated rumors—that might explain your Birthstar's unusual behavior. Rumors that Captain Lou Albano was no mere manager of big-time wrestlers, but an actual sea captain who had raised Cyndi as his own after finding her swaddled in a bassinet in front of his houseboat on the Gowanus Canal. Rumors that Cyndi was a performance artist with a degree in semiotics from Brown who was perpetrating a high-concept put-on inspired by Andys Warhol and Kaufman. Popstrologists lend little credence to either rumor, though, preferring a less dramatic explanation for Cyndi Lauper's impossible Brooklyn-Queens accent, her Betsey Johnson–meets–bag lady fashions, and her initially charming but eventually cringe-inducing embrace of professional wrestling. They see, quite simply, fear. They see Cyndi's fear that her music alone was not enough to sustain her popularity, and her misguided belief that her exaggerated *Outerborough* persona was the keystone of her success. Strangely Sexy and eccentrically Soulful, your Birthstar might have been more Lasting if she'd possessed the tiniest fraction of Madonna's shape-shiftiness. But, alas, she didn't, and her shtick wore out long before her talent ever did. **The world will accept you quirks and all,** child of Cyndi Lauper, but always remember: **it's the eccentric they love, and not the eccentricities.**

CONSTELLATIONS

➤ Outerborough
➤ Casio

BIRTHSONGS

➤ *Time After Time* Jun 3–16, 1984
➤ *True Colors* Oct 19–Nov 1, 1986

STEVE LAWRENCE
You may not create your own good luck, but you're creative enough to do something good with it.

It would be easy enough to look at the career of Steve Lawrence and say, "Right place, right time," but it would only be two thirds right. To be sure, 1950s Brooklyn was a great place to be if you were young, Jewish, and musically talented, as half the members of the constellation *Outerborough* could tell you. But the former Sidney Leibowitz owes his decades-long career not just to being *in* the right place at the right time, but to being the right *man* for his place and time. Someone else would have won the talent contest whose first prize was a spot on a local TV show if your Birthstar hadn't, but would that someone else have kept that spot when the show became the first incarnation of the nationally broadcast *Tonight Show?* Would that someone else have won the heart of a fellow guest named Eydie Gorme and made her his wife/singing partner for the next half century? He was handsome and clean-cut without being an uptight stiff, and he could sing both pop standards and rock and roll without seeming phony to audiences in either genre. And while the planets may not have aligned themselves for you quite as neatly as they did for your Birthstar, your popstrological profile indicates an ability to **find the good in**

any situation and, through your own charm and talent, **make it into something great**.

CONSTELLATION
➤ Outerborough

BIRTHSONG
➤ *Go Away, Little Girl*
Jan 6–19, 1963

VICKI LAWRENCE
They say revenge is a dish best served fried.

D o you find the movie *Deliverance* more terrifying than *The Exorcist*? Do the words "possum" and "outhouse" make you anxious? If so, you might be suffering from tinshackophobia—the fear of things associated with the rural South. The diagnosis shouldn't be surprising, considering your birth under the influence of Vicki Lawrence and the song *The Night The Lights Went Out In Georgia*. Your Birthstar spent her own childhood deep in the heart of Burbank, and she rose to minor celebrity on the nearby set of *The Carol Burnett Show*. But it hardly mattered that a song about lust, murder, and wrongful execution was as strange a fit for Vicki Lawrence as *Folsom Prison Blues* would have been for Harvey Korman. Your Birthsong was a creepy, atmospheric gem, and what it lacked in clarity and narrative credibility it made up for by tapping into deep reserves of latent tinshackophobia in early-seventies America. *The Night The Lights Went Out* was your

Birthstar's first and last foray into the pop-musical universe, but it earned her a lasting spot in the constellation *Storyteller*, from which she imparts to you both the **wholesome appeal** of a local kid made good and a carpetbagger's **willingness to profit in foreign territory**.

CONSTELLATION
➤ Storyteller

CELEBRITY
➤ **Pharrell Williams** (4/5/73) is a child of Vicki Lawrence.

BIRTHSONGS
➤ *The Night The Lights Went Out In Georgia* Apr 1–14, 1973

BRENDA LEE
Sometimes even big things come in small packages.

S he was five feet tall in socks and saddle shoes and weighed about ninety pounds, but if you close your eyes and listen to her records from the late 1950s, you'll know you're hearing a heavyweight. Voices as great as your Birthstar's may come from performers of all sizes, but they almost never come from a performer so young. Brenda Lee was fifteen years old and already five years into a professional recording career when she had her first #1 single with 1960's *I'm Sorry*, but if you assume that her earlier efforts were kid stuff, track down the rockabilly singles *Bigelow 6–200* and *Miss Dynamite* to see how mistaken you are. She was the founding star in the constellation *Underage*, but she is also one of the few stars from that constellation that you might be happy to listen to today, and therein lies a key to understanding her popstrological essence. For Brenda Lee was not some scary 1950s version of LeAnn Rimes. It wasn't cloying precociousness but a true voice for the ages that launched her into the popstrological firmament, and it wasn't gimmickry but her truly Massive standing in the world of early-sixties pop that had the Beatles opening for *her* while touring England. Not many performers enter their sixth decade in show business, period, but almost none do it having started as young as Brenda Lee did. **Yours is a**

voice that commands respect, and while **you may not have achieved greatness at a tender age**, your popstrological legacy suggests that **you won't achieve obsolescence anytime soon**.

CONSTELLATIONS
➤ Underage
➤ Country Cousins

CELEBRITIES
➤ **Chuck D** (8/1/60) **and David Duchovny** (8/7/60) are Brenda Lees.

BIRTHSONGS
➤ *I'm Sorry* Jul 12–Aug 1, 1960
➤ *I Want To Be Wanted* Oct 18–24, 1960

LEMON PIPERS
It's perfectly fine to bluff your way to the top, but be careful not to overplay your hand.

Perhaps at some point in your professional life, you've found yourself in the position your Birthstar was in circa 1967—technically employed and still on the payroll, but so totally unproductive as to stretch the definition of the word "working" beyond its normal limits. Several years and zero hits into their contract with Buddah Records, the Lemon Pipers received a visitor from the central office sent to "suggest" that they record a song he'd written called *Green Tambourine*. Apparently oblivious to their precarious position, your Birthstar took a listen and then exercised

their sovereign creative right by politely declining. And there should have ended the Lemon Pipers' career, except that Paul Leka, the visitor from New York, decided to let the boys know that they were going to be dropped from their label if they stuck to their guns. "Let's hear that one more time," someone must've said, and soon enough *Green Tambourine* sounded good enough to the boys in the band that they recorded what was soon to become your Birthsong and assumed their place among the popstrological elite in the constellation *Regifted*. You are who you are because someone saved your Birthstar's life, popstrologically speaking. You can honor their legacy by **never, ever looking a gift horse in the mouth**.

CONSTELLATION
➤ Regifted

CELEBRITY
➤ **Sarah McLachlan** (1/28/68) is a child of the Lemon Pipers.

BIRTHSONG
➤ *Green Tambourine* Jan 28–Feb 3, 1968

JOHN LENNON

Yours is a voice that demands to be heard, though perhaps sometimes it should simply request.

He was one of pop's true and undisputed greats, and in a business that tends to save its biggest rewards for carefully managed personas, John Lennon was simply and adamantly a *person*—a real and sometimes hard-to-take person who was as committed to his own views as he was unconcerned about their popularity. But be wary of congratulating yourself too much on your popstrologically undeniable potential for greatness, for very few conscience-of-my-generation types manage to get through life without their **principled idealism** coming off at least occasionally as **strident self-righteousness**. And very few people who watch **cults of genius** form around them avoid attracting the occasional admirer who is a bit *too* **admiring for comfort**. John Lennon was, quite famously, the cinnamon to Paul McCartney's sugar, or the vinegar to his oil, if you prefer. And therein lies an important lesson for those born under the influence of this powerful popstrological *Spin-Off*: cinnamon and vinegar are wonderful ingredients, but their appeal taken straight cannot compare with their appeal in the company of softer complements.

CONSTELLATIONS
➤ Spin-Off
➤ Tragic Demise

BIRTHSONGS
➤ *Whatever Gets You Thru The Night* Nov 10–16, 1974
➤ *(Just Like) Starting Over* Dec 21, 1980–Jan 24, 1981

BOBBY LEWIS

In a world that's dog-eat-dog, it's sometimes worth remembering that you're actually a human.

Maybe spending his first twelve years in an orphanage gave him a natural kinship with underdogs and outsiders, or maybe he was simply born with a good heart. Whatever the reason, the milk of human kindness flowed strongly in your Birthstar, as he showed one night in early 1961 when he took four nervous white boys aside backstage at the Apollo Theater to calm their nerves with a much-needed pep talk. Several weeks later, on the brink of abandoning his own dream of stardom and returning defeated to his native Detroit, Bobby Lewis took one last stab, walking into the offices of Beltone Records, where one of those same young men from the Apollo sat noodling at the piano. Ritchie Adams was his name, and though the song he'd just written might have been a hit for anyone, *Tossin' And Turnin'* had far too much good karma behind it *not* to become a hit when your Birthstar took a crack at it. Bobby Lewis's name may have faded quickly from memory following his meteoric rise into the constellation *Royal Court*, but for those born under his reign as the popstrological king of 1961, the lesson of his example bears constant reinforcement: **hard-nosed selfishness may have gotten you this far**, but your greatest success may depend on accepting that occassionally in life, and *very* occassionally in a brutal industry like showbiz, **good deeds are actually rewarded** rather than punished.

CONSTELLATION
➤ Royal Court

BIRTHSONG
➤ *Tossin' And Turnin'* July 10–Aug 27, 1961

GARY LEWIS AND THE PLAYBOYS
You get by with a little help from other people's friends, too.

As Gary Lewis has sometimes told the story, he and his band were "discovered" by the mega-producer Snuff Garrett while they were playing a gig at Disneyland, but somehow Snuff Garrett's version has the greater ring of truth. According to him, the sequence of carefully managed events that took your Birthstar from theme-park obscurity to popstrological immortality began with a phone call from Gary's dad, Jerry. Yes, *that* Jerry Lewis, a man who worked so excruciatingly hard for every laugh he ever earned that he was determined to spare his own son the same indignity. Jerry Lewis's "kids"—the disabled cutie pies on his muscular dystrophy telethon—were often asked to wobble across the stage under their own limited power, but Jerry's actual child had no such demands placed upon him. He was launched into the constellation **Regifted** thanks to Snuff Garrett's heroic overdubbing on *This Diamond Ring* and to Dad's pull with Ed Sullivan, whose show gave young Gary and his Playboys priceless national exposure. Gary would later blame his being drafted for the derailment of his pop career, but his severe case of musical dystrophy was going to catch up with him sooner or later. **Everybody's got their crutches** in life, but given your popstrological legacy, it may be especially **challenging for you to stand independently without yours.**

CONSTELLATION
➤ Regifted

BIRTHSONG
➤ *This Diamond Ring*
Feb 14–27, 1965

HUEY LEWIS AND THE NEWS
In a world that is dominated by nouvelle cuisine, you are a cheeseburger and a basket of fries.

The formula for turning your hardworking bar band into a massively successful pop juggernaut goes like this: get a good-looking frontman, develop solid musical chops, and then get the planets to align themselves as they did for Huey Lewis and the News in 1983. That was the year that Huey and the boys rose to fame on the strength of their multiplatinum album *Sports,* and not coincidentally, it was also the year that the Chrysler Corporation introduced the first minivan in the United States. The American love affair with both products began almost immediately, as the minivan and Huey Lewis both satisfied the increasingly practical demands of the baby-boom generation. What the boomers needed in their vehicles circa 1983 was ample storage space and room for five, and what they needed as compensation for the feelings of emasculation that came standard with those new vehicles was someone to provide a steady stream of straight-ahead, fist-pumping rock and roll that sounded good at a reasonable volume in their minivan's tape deck. Enter Huey Lewis, standard-bearer in the *Reaganrock* revolution and voice of a settled and prosperous generation whose official anthem he eventually provided with his 1986 hit *Hip To Be Square*. Like your Birthstar, **your natural position in life is far away from the *avant garde*,** so if that's where you've set your sights, **be aware of how far you'll have to travel**.

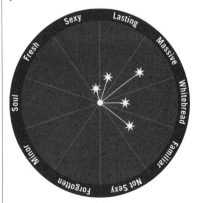

CONSTELLATIONS
➤ Reaganrock
➤ Theme Singer

GORDON LIGHTFOOT

You needn't be an enormous fish in order to feel cramped in a small pond.

If you want to know how helpful the label "Big in Canada" is when it comes to achieving success in the United States, just ask groups like Sloan, April Wine, or Chilliwack, or ask Ian and Sylvia, the 1960s Canadian folk duo who set your Birthstar on his slow path to popstrological greatness. Chances are excellent that you've never heard of them, but Ian and Sylvia Tyson were the first to appreciate Gordon Lightfoot's songwriting talents, and they were big enough in Canada at the time to share a manager with the Americans Peter, Paul and Mary, who gave Lightfoot his first taste of success by covering two of his songs in 1962. And while all that did was help make your Birthstar Big in Canada himself, that status was just enough to keep Gordon Lightfoot in the music business until he could achieve something bigger. Nineteen seventy-one's *If You Could Read My Mind* was the hit that finally made your Birthstar's name south of the border, and subsequent covers of that song by such popstrological luminaries as Glen Campbell, Olivia Newton-John, Johnny Mathis, Don McLean, and Jeannie C. Riley cemented his qualifications for the constellation **Invisible Hand**, which he entered upon scoring his first and only #1 hit as a performer in 1974—the bluesy gem *Sundown*. **It may be hard to get from where you are to wherever it is you're hoping to go**, but your popstrological legacy suggests that **you have what it takes to make that journey**.

CONSTELLATIONS

➤ Oh . . . Canada
➤ Invisible Hand
➤ Folkie

CELEBRITY

➤ **Derek Jeter** (6/24/74) is a child of Gordon Lightfoot.

BIRTHSONG

➤ *Sundown* Jun 23–29, 1974

LIPPS, INC.

If you still haven't found what you're looking for, try looking closer to home.

At the age of twenty, Steven Greenberg packed up his self-produced record and went to L.A. to become a star. At twenty and a half, he came back home with his tail between his legs, defeated for the moment but still convinced that his destiny lay far away from dreary Minneapolis. Fast-forward nearly ten years, and finally the pieces were falling into place for Steven. He'd found himself a knockout frontwoman in Cynthia Johnson, Miss Black Minnesota 1976, and his song *Funkytown* was about to explode. The moment was rapidly approaching when the man behind your Birthstar would have not just the motive but also the means and opportunity to make a move to a town that was right for him. So where did Steven Greenberg go when *Funkytown* earned Lipps, Inc. a bundle of money and the final new spot in the constellation *Disco Ball*? Nowhere. You see, while Steven was plotting his escape all those years, a group that Cynthia sang with on weekends called Flyte Time (later simply The Time) and a twenty-one-year-old kid from the other side of town called Prince had turned Minneapolis into a rather funky town in its own right. And so it was that Steven Greenberg and Cynthia Johnson became the George and Mary Bailey of pop, helping keep chilly Minnesota hot and bestowing upon their popstrological children a **relentless wanderlust** they **needn't wander far** to satisfy.

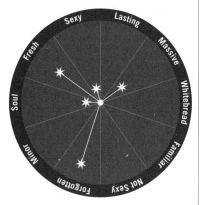

CONSTELLATIONS
➤ Disco Ball
➤ Casio

CELEBRITY
➤ **Venus Williams** (6/17/80) is a child of Lipps, Inc.

BIRTHSONG
➤ *Funkytown* May 25–Jun 21, 1980

LISA LISA AND CULT JAM
Some prefer to go it alone, but you prefer your strength in numbers.

Her older brother forbade her to travel to Brooklyn without a chaperone for an audition with a group called Full Force, but in keeping with the rich tradition of sixteen-year-old girls and their attitude toward sound advice from elders, Lisa ignored him completely. As it turns out, her brother needn't

have worried, for the talented group of producer-performers she was meeting with in Brooklyn would not only launch Lisa "Lisa Lisa" Velez to popstrological immortality, but they would do it by surrounding her with a protective army of young men to rival the size of the president's Secret Service detail. A year before you were born, they were "Lisa Lisa and Cult Jam with Full Force featuring Paul Anthony and Bowlegged Lou," but *All Cried Out* never made it to the top of the charts, and their official name on the two irresistible hits that did in 1987 was simply Lisa Lisa and Cult Jam. Your Birthstar's near-breakthrough as L.L. Cult J. w/ F.F. feat. P.A. and B.L. helped open the door, though, to the enormous conglomerations you see on today's hip-hop singles charts, just as your Birthstar's connection to the world of mid-eighties breakdancing helped crack the constellation *Reaganrock*'s impermeable hip-hop defense shield. **How far might your own talents take you,** child of Lisa Lisa and Cult Jam? Perhaps quite far indeed,

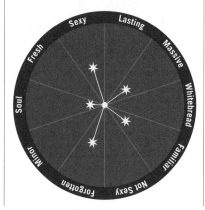

but it is safe to say that they'll take you farther if you can **line up an army of supporters behind you.**

CONSTELLATION
➤ Outerborough

BIRTHSONGS
➤ *Head To Toe* Jun 14–20, 1987
➤ *Lost In Emotion* Oct 11–17, 1987

LITTLE EVA
The most effective résumé is the one you never have to bother writing.

In the long history of pop music, no one was ever in a righter place at a righter time than Eva Narcissus Boyd. The future "Little Eva" was seventeen years old and fresh off the turnip truck from North Carolina when a Brooklyn neighbor hooked her up with the gig of a lifetime, working as a nanny for a hardworking Manhattan couple named Gerry Goffin and Carole King. Did the legendary songwriters negotiate the terms of Eva's compensation up front ("We'd like to offer you $35 a week, Eva, plus a week's bonus at Christmas and one ticket to pop immortality"), or did they simply surprise Eva with the biggest tip in the history of the child care industry when they let her earn a few extra bucks by singing the demo for a new song they'd written about a nonexistent dance called the Loco-Motion? When their boss Don Kirshner ended up releasing the demo as a single, he bestowed popstrological immortality upon Little Eva *and* the dance she invented to fit your Birthsong. Talent and charisma may or may not be part of your genetic mix, but your popstrological heritage certainly bestows upon you something vastly more valuable: a **willingness to start at the bottom** and an ability to **work your way up at break-neck speed.**

CONSTELLATION
➤ Regifted

BIRTHSONG
➤ *The Loco-Motion*
Aug 19–25, 1962

KENNY LOGGINS
While others clamor for the spotlight, you're the one who's always there when the final credits roll.

The skinny guy in the beard and the jumpsuit didn't exactly ooze charisma, but if you were a movie producer in the mid-1980s, nothing screamed money in the bank like Kenny Loggins, the most powerful star in the con-stellation *Theme Singer* and the man behind top-ten sound-track hits from the films *Caddyshack* (*I'm Alright*), *Top Gun* (*Danger Zone*), and, of course, *Footloose*. These films detailed the struggles of handsome young rebels to dance freely, golf sarcastically, and fly deadly fighter jets stylishly, and they called for precisely the kind of catchy, rockin'-but-not-*too*-rockin' style that Loggins was born to deliver. He may never have inspired much in the way of passion among his fans, but Kenny also offended no one, giving him that critical combination of qualities that is the hallmark of the stars in the constellation *Reaganrock*. Your path to success may take you in almost any direction, but wherever it leads, you will be at your best when you **leave the beauty contest to others** and **focus your energies on delivering the goods**.

CONSTELLATIONS
➤ Theme Singer
➤ Reaganrock
➤ Tip of the Ice Cube

BIRTHSONG
➤ *Footloose* Mar 25–Apr 14, 1984

LOOKING GLASS
When greatness thrusts itself upon you, will you be willing to embrace it?

The question still remains unanswered: Was it that your Birthstar *couldn't* grab their chance at Lasting stardom, or was it that they *wouldn't*? Here was the problem: Looking Glass were trying to be New Jersey's answer to Led Zeppelin, yet somehow they'd gone into the studio in 1972 and come out sounding like Van Morrison. The song they'd recorded was a groovy and not-at-all-heavy gem called *Brandy (You're A Fine Girl)*, a #1 single that suddenly had this hardworking bar band playing to audiences in the thousands rather than the dozens. Booming bass and loud guitars they could handle in a live venue, but the smooth vocals and lush production of *Brandy* were a bit of a problem outside the studio. Perhaps they could have hired some horn players and remade themselves in the mold their newfound fans were expecting, but whether it was by choice or by necessity, Looking Glass stuck to their stock-in-trade instead, which was heavy, early-seventies rock of a sort that doomed them to a somewhat Fresh but extremely Minor and Forgotten corner of the constellation *Jersey Pride*. To avoid your Birthstar's fate, you'll need to **nip misperceptions about you in the bud**, or **work a bit harder than is your habit** in order to live up to them.

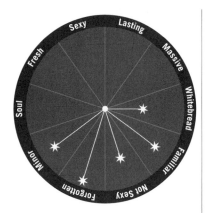

CONSTELLATION
➤ Jersey Pride

BIRTHSONG
➤ *Brandy (You're A Fine Girl)* Aug 20–26, 1972

LOS LOBOS
You honor the past without living in it.

Don McLean called it the Day the Music Died, a beautiful turn of phrase that is a historical and popstrological falsehood. February 3, 1959, was the day that four *young men* died—a twenty-one-year-old pilot and three rising pop stars named Buddy Holly, Ritchie Valens, and J. P. Richardson, aka "the Big Bopper." But it was decidedly *not* the day their music died, for the pop universe has a way of honoring its tragically dead. Holly got his honors in *American Pie* and the Bopper got his through his protégé, Johnny Preston. And though it took nearly thirty years for Ritchie Valens to get his, he eventually did via Los Lobos' cover of his 1958 hit, *La Bamba*. But you would do yourself a great disservice if you limited your popstrological awareness of your Birthstar to their posthumous memorial to Ritchie Valens. Though popstrologically invisible, the ongoing pop career of Los Lobos includes some unique and amazing work (e.g., 1983's *Will the Wolf Survive?* and 2003's *Good Morning Aztlán*) that falls well outside both the pop *and* "Latin" mainstreams but is accessible enough to make you wish that it didn't. Members of the constellation *Fresh Breeze* as much for the songs you don't know as for the one you do, your Birthstar marks you as the type to be **underestimated and all too frequently pigeonholed**, but also to possess the **hidden reserves** necessary to rise above that tendency.

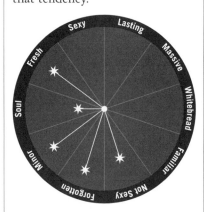

CONSTELLATION
➤ Fresh Breeze

BIRTHSONG
➤ *La Bamba* Aug 23–Sep 12, 1987

THE LOVIN' SPOONFUL
Some principles are worth defending, but how will you know which ones?

Put yourself in the shoes of Zal Yanovsky, a resident alien in the United States and the guitarist for the fun-lovin' Lovin' Spoonful. It's 1967, and your band is at the peak of its success, but the San Francisco Police have you by the long hairs. They've got you cold for marijuana possession, and you've been presented with a Hobson's choice: identify your source or face deportation. What would *you* have done in the face of this dilemma? Would you have betrayed the principles of the drug-loving sixties counterculture whose embrace had been such a big part of your band's success, or would you have risked a return to the brutally repressive nation of . . . Canada? Apparently for Zal, exile in Ontario sounded worse than career suicide, so he named names and left San Francisco a free man. And sure enough, your Birthstar was subsequently boycotted out of existence by their high-and-mighty fan base. The other primary force in the Spoonful, John Sebastian, would go on to future popstrological success in his solo career, while poor Zal, in what some might call an ironic fulfillment of his moral-ethical destiny, ended up back in Canada anyway. **You can go home again,** popstrological children of the Lovin'

Spoonful, **but perhaps not at a time of your choosing.**

CONSTELLATIONS
➤ Tip of the Ice Cube
➤ Launching Pad

CELEBRITY
➤ **Halle Berry** (8/14/66) is a Lovin' Spoonful.

BIRTHSONG
➤ *Summer In The City*
Aug 7–27, 1966

LULU
Hold on to your dreams—they may be the best thing that you've got.

Can you recall an exhilarating moment in your youth, when the future lay spread out before you like a wonderful adventure story waiting to be written? When compromise and mediocrity were unthinkable options in life and when the only love worth feeling was the kind of love you'd write across the sky? Can you recall how you felt when life hit you in the face like a frying pan a few years later and you found yourself in a crappy job and

waste-of-time relationship with yet another bad boyfriend or girlfriend? Well, imagine how your Birthstar felt when she exchanged the adolescent idealism of *To Sir With Love* and an onscreen crush on the elegant Sidney Poitier for real-life marriage to Maurice Gibb. Did Lulu (born Marie McDonald McLaughlin Lawrie) let this precipitous fall from the heady heights keep her from soldiering on? No, she didn't. She may never have approached the top of the pop charts after joining the constellation *Theme Singer* in 1967, but your Birthstar did at least divorce the second-homeliest Gibb and become a beloved figure on the British pop-cultural scene. There may indeed be **a time in life for closing the book** on youthful aspirations, but your Birthstar bestows upon you **the gift of not knowing when that is.** And though you may choose to blame her for your feeling that **life, or perhaps just romance, always falls short of expectations,** you should thank her, at least, for your **wide-eyed belief that someday things will be different.**

CONSTELLATIONS
➤ Theme Singer
➤ Britvasion

CELEBRITIES
➤ **Julia Roberts** (10/28/68) and **Lisa Bonet** (11/16/68) are popstrological Lulus.

BIRTHSONG
➤ *To Sir With Love*
Oct 15–Nov 18, 1967

M
You want anonymity? You got it.

Robin Scott clearly believed that there would be other pop hits in his future—hits more deserving, perhaps, of carrying his given name on their record sleeves. So he chose to use the pseudonym M on a weightless little ditty he'd written called *Pop Muzik.* Perhaps he was shy of staking his reputation on a song whose lyrics went no deeper than *"shooby-dooby doo-wop,"* but in fact the powerful message in *Pop Muzik* was unmistakable. This was the first overtly electronic #1 hit in pop history, and its pops and bing-bong sounds seemed to be saying, nonverbally, "Here's what the future sounds like." Indeed, were it not for his desire to remain personally anonymous, Robin Scott might well have become known as the Alexander Graham Bell of 1980s synth pop—a lofty honorific befitting the first star in those eighties powerhouses known as the constellations *Casio* and *Britsuasion.* Minor and

Forgotten yet important in his way, M ruled the pop universe just long enough to give rise to a popstrological micro-generation of **diffident innovators** and **unsung revolutionaries**.

CONSTELLATIONS
➤ Casio
➤ Fresh Breeze
➤ Britsuasion

BIRTHSONG
➤ *Pop Muzik* Oct 28–Nov 3, 1979

MARY MACGREGOR
When your cup runneth over, you're already thinking about a refill.

When a man dreams of having two women at once, we call him normal, but when a woman does it, we call her . . . well, we call her a name that betrays the continuing power of the hegemonic patriarchy your Birthstar set out to challenge with her steamy, feminist hit *Torn Between Two Lovers*. Okay, it wasn't really steamy, and it wasn't exactly feminist in a way that 1970s feminists would recognize, but there certainly was something revolutionary about your Birthsong, and not just because it involved a woman confessing to the sin of adultery. No, Olivia Newton-John had already done that in *I Honestly Love You*, but what Olivia didn't have the nerve (or maybe even the inclination) to do was suggest that she be allowed to have her cake and eat it, too. By arguing that one lover maybe *shouldn't* be enough for one passionate, liberated woman, Mary MacGregor broke all the rules of adultery-confessional pop. And if she'd offered better advice on how to suggest such an arrangement, perhaps she would have sparked a social revolution. But what most women listening to your Birthstar knew was that speaking of "empty spaces" inside that only another man can "fill" was an approach unlikely to sit well with even the most sensitive of sensitive males. **Being in touch with your own wants and needs** is a trait you are truly lucky to possess, but **finding the language to convince others to meet them** may be a bigger challenge.

CONSTELLATION
➤ Lite & White

BIRTHSONG
➤ *Torn Between Two Lovers*
Jan 30–Feb 12, 1977

MADONNA
The more you change, the more you stay the same.

Her alignment with the constellation *Shape-Shifter* hardly bears mentioning, so thoroughly entrenched in our minds is the notion that she continually "reinvents" herself. But how much "reinvention" has there really been in Madonna's Massive and ongoing career? Was there ever really a time when anyone heard her latest record or saw her latest video and said to themselves, "Wow, this is a fundamentally different Madonna from any that I've seen before"? Probably not, for Madonna made it crystal clear from the very beginning that image manipulation was her game, and that sex was the tool she'd use to hold our attention. For a little while in the early 1990s, it even seemed as if your Birthstar had fostered a genuine academic subdiscipline, so taken with her were certain showy cultural critics. Indeed, to hear all the breathless talk of "gender subversion" and "boundary transgression," you'd almost have thought that David Bowie never existed. There are those, of course, who believe that "corporate strategy" and "brand equity" are equally appropriate terms to deploy in the practice of Madonna Studies, and most popstrologists would concede their point. But popstrologists would argue vehemently with anyone who tried to call your Birthstar cynical. Calculating, perhaps, but to be able to **calculate a formula for achieving a goal** you deeply believe in is hardly a fault. If you can apply yourself half as diligently to your pursuit of happiness as your Birthstar did to hers, child of Madonna, **the world will be your oyster. Some will look at you and say "genius"** while others will look at you and say "fake," but **as long as they're looking at you,** you're likely to feel okay about it.

CONSTELLATIONS
➤ Shape-Shifter
➤ Theme Singer
➤ Royal Court

BIRTHSONGS
➤ *Like A Virgin* Dec 16, 1984–Jan 26, 1985
➤ *Crazy For You* May 5–11, 1985
➤ *Live To Tell* Jun 1–7, 1986
➤ *Papa Don't Preach* Aug 10–23, 1986
➤ *Open Your Heart* Feb 1–7, 1987
➤ *Who's That Girl* Aug 16–22, 1987
➤ *Like A Prayer* Apr 16– May 6, 1989

THE MAMAS AND THE PAPAS
You are the nontraditional child of a nontraditional family.

Let's say you were a mechanical warrior sent back in time to remove the hippies from the very fabric of history. Where should you start? Perhaps by preventing the formation of the Mamas and the Papas. With tunes like *California Dreamin'* and *Go Where You Wanna Go,* they sowed the seeds of the druggy, West Coast, free-love vibe you are seeking to eliminate, but their influence extended even farther. The late "Mama" Cass Elliot was the veritable yenta of the counterculture, matchmaking into existence such quintessentially sixties groups as the Lovin' Spoonful and Crosby, Stills, Nash and Young. Even more critically, "Papa" John Phillips wrote *San Francisco (Be Sure To Wear Flowers In Your Hair)* and co-created the Monterey Pop Festival, launching pad for Jimi Hendrix and Janis Joplin. Destroy the elements of your Birthstar before they come together, and you destroy the sixties as we knew them, and you also alter the course of the seventies, eighties and nineties by keeping Mackenzie Phillips out of *American Grafitti* and *One Day at a Time;* Mackenzie's stepmom, Michelle, out of *Knots Landing;* and Michelle's daughter Chynna out of Wilson Phillips. Decide for yourself whether the world would be a better place on balance, but never doubt that your own strength, too, derives from the **dense and peculiar web of relationships** you weave.

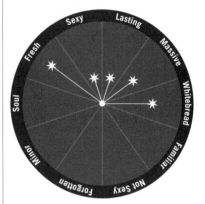

CONSTELLATIONS
➤ Holy Matrimony
➤ Invisible Hand
➤ Fresh Breeze
➤ Tip of the Ice Cube

CELEBRITY
➤ **Janet Jackson** (5/16/66) is a child of the Mamas and the Papas.

BIRTHSONG
➤ *Monday, Monday* May 1–21, 1966

HENRY MANCINI
The molds you don't fit are molds you don't need.

Ever wonder why you tried so hard as a kid to fit the mold of what everyone else considered cool? Ever wonder why it never quite worked? To the latter question, at least, popstrology can provide an answer, for in a year that history remembers for stars like Hendrix and the Who, you were born under a star more closely associated with William Shakespeare and Peter Sellers. Henry Mancini wrote and conducted countless famous instrumental scores, for movies like *Breakfast at Tiffany's* (from which *Moon River* came), *Days of Wine and Roses*, and *The Pink Panther*; and for television shows like *Peter Gunn*, *Newhart*, and *Remington Steele*. And though he didn't write but merely arranged and conducted his recording of your Birthsong, that fact does nothing to dim the brightest star in the estimable constellation *Speechless*. Time and again in his Massive Hollywood career, your Birthstar displayed the same gift you display on your best days: the **ability to express emotions in a way that encourages others to do the same**. And though it need not be true that you only do this by crying, this would not be entirely unexpected for someone born under a Birthsong that was to weepy,

star-crossed love what *Gonna Fly Now* was to cold-weather training and *Theme From "A Summer Place"* to attempted deflowering.

CONSTELLATIONS
➤ Speechless
➤ Theme Singer

BIRTHSONG
➤ *Love Theme From "Romeo & Juliet"* Jun 22–Jul 5, 1969

THE MANHATTANS
You may be a sinner, but you know when it's time to act like a saint.

T here's something in our DNA that gives us all an inborn gift for getting into trouble, but there's something in your popstrological profile that gives you the rare and enviable gift of sliding out of it just in the nick of time. You were born under the influence of a star called the Manhattans and a song called *Kiss And Say Goodbye*, the third in a series of four 1970s #1 hits to deal with the struggles of maintaining an adulterous relationship and the only one of the four to suggest an eminently reasonable way to keep those struggles from leading to disaster: quitting while you're ahead. *Me And Mrs. Jones*, *I Honestly Love You*, and *Torn Between Two Lovers* painted portraits of adulterers likely headed to an ugly day of reckoning, but your Birthsong painted the portrait of a man whose sense of self-preservation, if not his morals,

caused him to call a stop to his affair before things got truly out of hand. Was this the first time, and would it be the last time, that he would meet a mistress on the "saddest day of his life" to kiss and say good-bye? Likely not, but one would hardly expect an entirely honest protagonist in a song by a group from Jersey City that called itself the Manhattans. **Your moral compass may not point to true north**, but you know when it's pointing to trouble, child of the Manhattans, and unless you're completely out of touch with your popstrological gift, **you probably know how to steer clear** of it.

CONSTELLATIONS
➤ So-Soul
➤ Jersey Pride

BIRTHSONG
➤ *Kiss And Say Goodbye* Jul 18–31, 1976

BARRY MANILOW
Many will love you, but with a love that dare not speak its name.

In the mid-1970s, a health-food craze was sweeping the nation, and a generation of baby boomers deprived of almost nothing in childhood other than dietary fiber began ingesting some of the most fibrous, flavorless foods imaginable in tremendous quantities. They banished all that was fatty and delicious from their diets, but one thing they couldn't banish was their atavistic desire for schmaltz—a desire deeply ingrained even in those unfamiliar with the Yiddish word for chicken fat. We've all got it, that built-in need for something goopy and soothing, and in 1975, Barry Manilow was the only pop star on the planet ready and willing to supply it, without shame *or* irony. Okay, so songs like *I Write The Songs* (which he didn't even write) haven't exactly stood the test of time. Who cares? Americans clearly *needed* a song as patently ridiculous as that in 1976, and Barry Manilow was the guy who was brave enough to stand up and give it to them. He came and he gave without taking anything other than our self-respect, and whether you know it or not, he endowed you with an ability to **serve humanity's most basic needs with style,** and a willingness to do it **without expecting undying gratitude** in return.

CONSTELLATIONS
➤ Lite & White
➤ Sui Generis
➤ Outerborough

BIRTHSONGS
➤ *Mandy* Jan 12–18, 1975
➤ *I Write The Songs* Jan 11–17, 1976
➤ *Looks Like We Made It* Jul 17–23, 1977

MANFRED MANN
You are a polisher of rough diamonds and a finder of hidden gems.

They called it the British Invasion because the bands that launched it came from Britain, but in spirit and quite often in fact, the music they played came straight from America. Indeed, you could have found no bigger fans of great American pop music circa 1964 than those among the stars of the constellation *Britvasion,* whose fourth member was your Birthstar, Manfred Mann. Born Michael Lubowitz, the man whose stage name became the group name of the band originally called the Mann-Hugg Blues Brothers was a South African who trained as a jazz pianist but was pragmatic enough to apply his talents to pop upon arriving in England in the early sixties. But more than anything, Manfred Mann applied his good taste in American songwriting to the various pop entities (Manfred Mann, Manfred Mann's Chapter Three, Manfred Mann's Earth Band) that popstrology places under a single umbrella. The first Manfred Mann #1 was *Doo Wah Diddy Diddy,* an obscure girl-group tune by Jeff Barry and Ellie Greenwich, resurrected and turned into a classic by your Birthstar in 1964. The second was *Blinded By The Light,* written and first recorded in 1971 by Bruce Springsteen, who owes his closest connection to the popstrological firmament to your Birthstar. **Your own talents will take you far,** child of Manfred Mann, but **your gift for appreciating the talents of others will take you farther.**

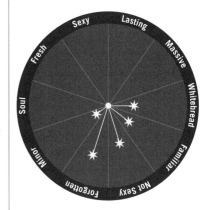

THE MARCELS
For every door that closes on you, another one shall open.

Your Birthstar gave the world two things it was ill-prepared for in 1961: a Rodgers and Hart standard transmogrified by the opening line *"Bomb buppa bomb, badang adang dang, ba-ding a dong ding,"* and a racially mixed lineup that made promoting *Blue Moon* on many national television programs out of the question. Luckily for the Marcels, radio still ruled the airwaves in those days, and the starmaking masters of that medium were free-thinking, free-spinning DJs like Porky Chedwick, who presided over the first "white" radio program on the East Coast to play exclusively "black" R&B and helped make your Birthstar's native Pittsburgh into a doo-wop hotbed that also gave rise to groups like the Skyliners and the (also racially integrated) Del-Vikings. In an immediate sense, it was New York's Murray the K who gave your Birthstar a heyday by playing *Blue Moon* twenty-six times on the air the very first day he heard it, but in the long run it was Chedwick, "the Daddio of the Raddio," who gave the

Marcels many future paydays by creating almost single-handedly the oldies radio format, which became the only place your popstrologically Forgotten Birthstar could be found after 1961. Perhaps **you've faced a glass ceiling or two** in your own life, child of the Marcels, but if you've emulated your Birthstar, you've found that **there are almost always other routes to the top.**

CONSTELLATION
➤ Doo-Wop

CELEBRITIES
➤ **Eddie Murphy** (4/3/61) **and Vincent Gallo** (4/11/61) are children of the Marcels.

BIRTHSONG
➤ *Blue Moon* Apr 3–23, 1961

LITTLE PEGGY MARCH
You are the unquestioned *meister* of your own destiny.

Maybe it was because she learned their language, or maybe it was because she

pushed a button in their national psyche with the title of her signature hit, *I Will Follow Him*. Whatever the reason, it was the Germans who really went bonkers for your Birthstar, who peaked in America at the age of fifteen but became an icon of Massive proportions in the strange parallel universe of Europop. Over here, Peggy March songs like *I Wish I Were A Princess*, *My Teenage Castle (Is Crumbling Down)*, and *Johnny Cool* fell commercially and popstrologically flat. But over there, where the magician David Copperfield is revered as a *Sex Gott* and David Hasselhoff was the first human invited to sing on the toppled Berlin Wall, little Margaret Battavio from Lansdale, Pennsylvania, spent the 1960s and '70s winning the Baden-Baden *Shlagerfestspiele* and raking in the deutsche marks with albums like *Hey, Das Ist Musik Für Mich*. And if those accomplishments alone do not impress, consider this: in the 1980s, Peggy March wrote songs that got actual Europeans to spend actual European money on records by Audrey Landers (of

Landers Sisters "fame") and by Jermaine Jackson and Pia Zadora. Outside of a Mentos ad, one rarely sees lives as **spookily charmed** as your Birthstar's, which is why her legacy to you is an ability to **thrive where others might fear or simply prefer not to tread**.

CONSTELLATION
➤ Underage

BIRTHSONG
➤ *I Will Follow Him*
Apr 21–May 11, 1963

MARTIKA
You are certainly filled with the promise of youth, but can you deliver on all you promise?

Alas, Martika, we hardly knew ya. You came along with your gypsy looks and your crafty hooks just barely in time to make your presence felt, and far too late for us to learn who you really were. You were an alumna of *Annie* and *Breakin' 2: Electric Boogaloo*—this much we knew—but we suspected you were something more than the Latina Debbie Gibson some had called you. And Prince thought so, too, for he took you under his wing, if that's what he calls it, shortly after your popstrological arrival. "How far might she go?" was the question we asked ourselves, but now we only ask, "Where has she gone?" And when our friends say, "Who?" we say, "Martika—the youthful face of things to come." And

when they say, "*Who?*" we say, "Never mind." Martika, you were born in the Year of the Fifth Dimension, and now it seems that's exactly where you've gone. A generation born under your influence now comes of age wondering what to make of their birth under your woefully Forgotten star, and what should we tell them, Martika? That the 450th and final star to join the popstrological firmament simply **peaked to soon and should serve as a warning** to them not to do the same? We'd like to tell them that **the promise of youth need not become a faded memory**, as it has for so many of us, but we await further input from you on this matter, Martika. Wherever you are.

CONSTELLATIONS
➤ Neither/Nor

BIRTHSONG
➤ *Toy Soldier* Jul 16–29, 1989

DEAN MARTIN
You soar with the eagles when you wish, but generally you prefer to remain unflappable.

There are fewer and fewer people living today who can manage a cocktail and a cigarette with true grace, let alone a microphone, too. But doing all three of these things while singing and cracking jokes was no more difficult than breathing for your Birthstar, who made his career as much on his well-lubricated, easygoing cool as on his voice or acting ability. Indeed, if the Rat Pack embodied the American ideal of swinging affability circa 1960, it was Dean Martin who embodied that quality within the Rat Pack, even more than Frank Sinatra. It's fascinating, from a popstrological point of view, that your Birthstar managed his popstrological breakthrough when he did—in the midst of the British Invasion and just barely before everything he stood for was about to be declared anathema by the increasingly powerful youth culture of the sixties. But if ever there was a star who was perfectly at ease being consigned to the realm of television variety shows and Las Vegas casinos, it was Dean Martin. If we can believe his unauthorized biographer, Nick Tosches, Dean Martin was perfectly at ease with just about everything because he was what Italians would call a *menefreghista*—a guy who doesn't give a flying f*ck about anything at all. That would certainly explain his ability to accept obsolescence with good cheer and to withstand ten years of professional collaboration with Jerry Lewis. And perhaps it would also explain your own striking ability to **bear life's ups, life's downs, and even life's unbearable annoyances** without losing your poise, or at least **without caring whether you stumble.**

CONSTELLATION
➤ Old Guard

BIRTHSONG
➤ *Everybody Loves Somebody*
  Aug 9–15, 1964

THE MARVELETTES
New flavors come, and new flavors go. And you oughta know.

They say Motown was like a family in the early days, but if it was, it was a family in which favor was granted unequally and the pecking order was determined not by age but by star power. In other words, Motown was a family very much like the Jacksons, and if the Supremes were its

shiny baby Janet, your Birthstar was its forgotten eldest daughter, Rebbie. It was the Marvelettes who gave Hitsville its very first #1 single with *Please Mr. Postman*, but despite that and several creditable follow-ups (*Playboy, Beechwood 4-5789*), your Birthstar was soon swept aside by boss Berry Gordy to make room for his darling Supremes. The great Smokey Robinson made a pet project of churning out songs for the Marvelettes throughout the 1960s, but instead of his best efforts or the attentions of the legendary Holland-Dozier-Holland team, your Birthstar was left to scratch for songs from up-and-comers like Norman Whitfield and Ashford and Simpson, back when they still had a lot of up-and-coming to do. Gems like *Don't Mess With Bill* and *Too Many Fish In The Sea* reminded the world of your Birthstar's gifts during this period, but by and large your Birthstar became a case of **slow death by corporate neglect.** But knowledge is power, so don't let it happen to you. Where favorites are played, **you may**

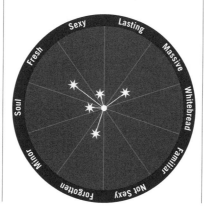

occasionally get locked out, but only if you let **the key to your happiness** remain in the hands of others.

CONSTELLATIONS
➤ Les Girls
➤ Underage
➤ Hitsville

BIRTHSONG
➤ *Please Mr. Postman*
  Dec 11–17, 1961

RICHARD MARX
When the mighty become the fallen, you'll still be left standing.

Thirty-three and a third years after the Big Bang of *Heartbreak Hotel*, the popstrological era came to a close with the gentle whimper of *Right Here Waiting*, and there's no sense in hiding from it. There's no sense in blaming your Birthstar for it, either, for Richard Marx didn't *create* the late 1980s—he simply thrived within them, generating the simulacrum of rock then craved by the forty-something baby boomers whose teenage longings had launched Elvis Presley. Indeed, within the rather stilted framework of the constellation *Reaganrock*, your Birthstar was a relatively Fresh and exciting presence. Relatively. And compared with some of the songs he helped bring into being as a backup singer for Lionel Richie, his own songs, like *Don't Mean Nothin'* were almost a bracing shot of real rock and roll. Almost. But even if your

Birthstar wasn't the type to question authority, he certainly didn't fear those who did. With the survival instinct he inherited from his own Birthstar, Bobby Vinton, Richard Marx has managed a hugely successful and ongoing career following the demise of *Reaganrock*, earning a spot in the constellation *Invisible Hand* through his songwriting efforts for Barbra Streisand, Kenny Rogers, Luther Vandross, *NSYNC, and Josh Groban, among others, and endowing those born under his influence with an enviable **ability to shape their talents to the needs of their environment**, no matter how much that environment might change.

CONSTELLATIONS
➤ Reaganrock
➤ Invisible Hand

BIRTHSONGS
➤ *Hold On To The Nights*
  Jul 17–23, 1988
➤ *Satisfied* Jun 18–24, 1989
➤ *Right Here Waiting*
  Aug 6–26, 1989

HUGH MASEKELA
The world may not beat a path to your door, but you might beat a path to theirs.

Today they'd call what your Birthstar did world music, but in 1968 they just called it jazz. But the way we label things has changed a lot since the late 1960s, hasn't it? Today, for instance, you probably wouldn't see an album by a black South African trumpet player given a title like *The Americanization Of Ooga-Booga*, but in the late 1960s that was just a cute and clever way for Hugh Masekela's record label to call attention to his exotic roots and fabulous hybrid sound. Indeed, if you think that Paul Simon was the one to introduce the sound of Afropop to mainstream America, think again, because that distinction would be more accurately bestowed upon your Birthstar, or perhaps upon his first wife, the legendary Miriam Makeba. *Grazing In The Grass* isn't one of the tunes that our collective cultural memory (read: television) tells us to associate with the summer of 1968, and yet your Birthsong ruled the pop universe for four solid weeks, twice as long as *Hello, I Love You*. Though redone with high-speed vocals by the Friends of Distinction in the following year, it's the instrumental original that landed Hugh Masekela in the constellation *Speechless* in the summer of your birth, when he bestowed upon you **an outsider's appeal**

that may occasionally **outshine even that of wildly popular poseurs.**

CONSTELLATION
➤ Speechless

BIRTHSONG
➤ *Grazing In The Grass*
  Jul 14–27, 1968

JOHNNY MATHIS AND DENIECE WILLIAMS
You may not mate for life, but when you mate, you mate wisely.

Justice delayed may be justice denied when it comes to civil rights, but if you had sold as many records as Johnny Mathis had by the late 1970s, you might be inclined to see the late exercise of popstrological justice as a simple case of better late than never. Hits like *Chances Are, The Twelfth of Never,* and *Wonderful Wonderful* made Mathis the heir apparent to Nat "King" Cole as white America's favorite nonthreatening black singer, and the nine-year run of his *Greatest Hits* on the *Billboard* album charts set a mark eclipsed only by *Dark Side of the Moon*. Chuck Berry's belated admission into the popstrological elite was a symbolic victory over the forces of prejudice that kept him out during his 1950s heyday, but Johnny Mathis's was more like a victory for the constellation **Old Guard**, whose ranks he would have joined had he made it to the top during his. It was the formation of a ***Power Couple*** with honey-voiced Deniece Williams, the former Stevie Wonder backup singer and future popstrological star in her own right, that finally took Johnny Mathis to the highest reaches of the pop universe at the moment of your birth. And while the juxtaposition of her Soul to his Whitebread may have been what made this couple click, their later work on *Without Us*—the *Family Ties* theme song—makes fairly clear in which direction your Birthstar's balance was tipped. **The power you possess on your own may be considerable**, but the **power you enjoy in a truly complementary pair will be even greater**.

CONSTELLATION
➤ Power Couple

BIRTHSONG
➤ *Too Much, Too Little, Too Late* May 28–Jun 3, 1978

PAUL MAURIAT
Your *je ne sais quoi* is almost always à la mode.

In the pop-cultural as well as the geopolitical arena, the United States and France have often had difficulty finding common ground. We like each other's movies, but beyond that, things get pretty grim, as evidenced by their mocking embrace of Jerry Lewis as a comic genius and our dismissal of their treasured Marcel Marceau as just another annoying mime. This is the backdrop you have to keep in mind if you want to appreciate fully the accomplishment of your Birthstar, the first and last Frenchman ever admitted into the popstrological elite (unless you count the fabricator Fabrice Morvan of Milli Vanilli). It would be easy to say that Paul Mauriat simply pulled a fast one—that America couldn't have known from his instrumental #1 hit that he was French. But one listen to your Birthsong reveals the speciousness of that argument. You've never heard anything that sounded so damn French in your entire life as *Love Is Blue*, a moody love song enlivened by drums and Bacharachian horns but still vaguely depressing in a Renaissance-Faire puppet-theater

sort of way. Paul Mauriat never returned to the popstrological firmament after the summer of your birth, but his spot in the constellation ***Invisible Hand*** derives from having been there already, as the composer of the international hit *Chariot*, which became the #1 *I Will Follow Him* in Peggy March's loose English translation. **Savoir faire is everywhere apparent** in the lives of popstrological Paul Mauriats, even, or perhaps **especially, when they choose to remain *Speechless***.

CONSTELLATIONS
➤ Speechless
➤ Eurosomething
➤ Invisible Hand

CELEBRITY
➤ **Gary Coleman** (2/8/68) is a child of Paul Mauriat.

BIRTHSONG
➤ *Love Is Blue* Feb 4–Mar 9, 1968

C. W. MCCALL

You are a master of disguise with the lure of the Pied Piper.

There never really was a C. W. McCall, long-haul trucker and fearless runner of roadblocks. There was only Bill Fries, an Omaha adman with an ear for esoteric dialogue and his finger on the pulse of one of the strangest fads ever to grip the nation, even by the standards of the 1970s. For a brief period in 1975–76, the trucking/CB radio craze had millions of Americans creating "handles" for themselves—Beer Man, Pink Lady, Scooter Pie, etc.—and daydreaming about the glamorous life of the big-rig trucker. Really, it's true, and your Birthstar helped make it so with his smash hit, *Convoy*. But highway drivers should thank their lucky stars that "trucka rap" never found a lasting audience, considering the list of crimes that your Birthsong romanticized. Destruction of state property, resisting arrest, reckless driving, reckless endangerment, conspiracy to defraud the state bureau of weights and measures—tens of thousands of lives are lost every year in auto accidents, yet your Birthstar managed to make a song about lawless truckers run amok seem kinda cute, earning him a spot in three highly mischevious constellations. You are a **natural evangelist with a keen sense of your own powers,** child of C. W. McCall, but **be careful how and whom you manipulate,** for popstrological

hell hath no fury like a public embarrassed by its lapses in judgment.

CONSTELLATIONS

➤ Novelty Merchant
➤ Had to Be There
➤ Artificial Ingredients

BIRTHSONG

➤ *Convoy* Jan 4–10, 1976

PAUL MCCARTNEY (AND WINGS)

A two-piece puzzle is hard to put together with one piece missing.

Popstrology may seem to be a bit rough on Paul McCartney, but it doesn't mean to be. Yes, popstrologists lay a great deal of responsibility at the feet of your Birthstar for the aftereffects of his early-eighties forays into the constellation *Power Couple*, but popstrologists do not regard him as a malevolent force, per se. And they certainly don't take the John Lennon side in the debate over who the greatest Beatle was. John and Paul's bitter divorce

was like most bitter divorces in that neither party offered what could reasonably be called a fair portrait of the other or an objective postmortem of the failed relationship. John was just plain mean to suggest in *How Do You Sleep?* that Paul's post-Beatles music was Muzak, and Paul was just plain disingenuous to play the role of the upstanding good guy when discussing the Beatles' breakup. But John was good at being mean, and Paul was good at being disingenuous. There may be no more fitting way to describe the greatest partnership in pop-music history than to say that the whole was greater than the sum of its parts, and while even John must have known this on some level, it was Paul who did the most to prove it. Was there a friend, a lover, or a colleague in your past who brought out the best in you, despite your fundamental differences? You may spend the rest of your life trying to repeat that magic, child of Paul McCartney, for you are more aware than anyone that **you require a counterbalancing force to achieve true great-**

ness. Like your Birthstar, you may experience what most consider success on your own, but your **deep yearning for partnership** is unlikely to let you find happiness that way.

CONSTELLATION
➤ Spin-Off

CELEBRITY
➤ **Carson Daly** (6/23/73) and **Jessica Simpson** (7/10/80) are children of Paul McCartney (and Wings).

BIRTHSONGS
➤ *Uncle Albert/Admiral Halsey* Aug 29–Sep 4, 1971
➤ *My Love* May 27–Jun 23, 1973
➤ *Band On The Run* Jun 2–8, 1974
➤ *Listen To What The Man Said* Jul 13–19, 1975
➤ *Silly Love Songs* May 16–22 and Jun 6–Jul 3, 1976
➤ *With A Little Luck* May 14–27, 1978
➤ *Coming Up* Jun 22–Jul 12, 1980

PAUL MCCARTNEY AND MICHAEL JACKSON

Learning from your mistakes is smart, but learning from others' mistakes is smarter.

George Harrison was the Beatle who really believed in karma, but if Paul McCartney's forays into the constellation *Power*

Couple didn't make a believer out of him, too, then nothing ever will. In 1982, the man teams up with Stevie Wonder, the first bona fide genius he's worked with in over a decade, and what happens afterward? Stevie's popstrological Soul mysteriously disappears in the wake of *Ebony and Ivory*. Then not one year later, Paul teams up with another pop genius in Michael Jackson, and what happens afterward? Michael catches fire while shooting a Pepsi commercial just two weeks after *Say Say Say* ends its run at #1. But despite all that, Paul McCartney to this day holds it against Michael Jackson that he outbid Paul for the publishing rights to the Beatles song catalog after Paul explained the value of such ownership to him on the set of the video for your Birthsong. And Paul McCartney, for all anyone knows, harbors the dangerous belief even now that it might be kinda groovy to work on something with a young pop star like Alicia Keys, say, or Justin Timberlake. **Some people never learn,** and the consequences of that fact can be very great for certain others. But as a child of the

most combustible star in the constellation *Power Couple*, you have not only the gift but the responsibility to **break a dangerous cycle of dysfunction** by being the type of person who does.

CONSTELLATIONS
➤ Power Couple
➤ Spin-Off (2x)

BIRTHSONG
➤ *Say Say Say* Dec 4, 1983–Jan 14, 1984

PAUL MCCARTNEY AND STEVIE WONDER

You are the enduring optimist with a dangerous tendency to oversimplify.

Without the black keys, the white keys on a piano would pretty much be stuck playing *Twinkle, Twinkle, Little Star* and *Do Re Mi*. If you want anything more interesting than that—if you want *Yesterday*, for instance—you're going to have to get the two sets of keys working together, so it's hardly surprising that Paul McCartney would look at a keyboard and see in it a perfect metaphor for some aspect of his own life. But race relations? It's hard to ignore the fact that of the eighty-eight keys on a standard piano keyboard, only thirty-six are black while fifty-two are white—a ratio that is only a slim mathematical improvement over the U.S. Constitution's "three-fifths of a man" clause, which helped set the stage for the American Civil War. How Stevie Wonder, the most Soulful force in all the popstrological firmament, was convinced to participate in selling this metaphorical fantasy is certainly a relevant question, though perhaps more concerning to you should be the Soul-sucking effect that doing so had on his career. There would be no more *Superstition*s or even *Master Blaster*s from Stevie after *Ebony And Ivory*—instead, there would be *I Just Called To Say I Love You*. Why can't we all just get along? Because **deep-rooted problems** rarely have such **simple answers**—a lesson that the children of this particular *Power Couple* would do well to remember.

CONSTELLATIONS
➤ Power Couple
➤ Royal Court

CELEBRITIES
➤ **Leelee Sobieski** (6/10/82), **Tara Lipinksy** (6/10/82), and **Anna Paquin** (7/24/82) are children of Paul McCartney and Stevie Wonder.

BIRTHSONG
➤ *Ebony And Ivory* May 9–Jun 26, 1982

MARILYN MCCOO AND BILLY DAVIS, JR.
Would you wait for a love that was perfect if you knew it would save your soul?

The statistics on American marriages got pretty damn depressing in the decade of your birth, though not as depressing as the statistics on marriage within the popstrological elite. As of 1977, the constellation *Holy Matrimony* took in a total of nine married couples, and of those nine, only two remain married to this day. It was always pretty clear what kept Toni Tennille together with her Captain, but what allowed the other surviving popstrological couple, Marilyn McCoo and Billy Davis, Jr., to buck the national and popstrological divorce trends? What practical lessons from their marital success story can the rest of us apply to our own twisted relationships? It's simple: go out and find your soul mate. Is this an easy piece of advice to follow? No, but you can listen to your Birthsong and look at your Starchart to see the benefits. Marilyn and Billy met as members of the Fifth Dimension, the unlikely progenitor of the constellation *Lite & White*, but once they married and got a popstrological place of their own,

their Soul aspect practically reversed itself under the power of *You Don't Have To Be A Star*. It's not that you're incapable of making a lasting relationship out of something less, child of Marilyn McCoo and Billy Davis, Jr., but **hold out for something more** and you may find that **the wait was worth it**.

CONSTELLATIONS
➤ Holy Matrimony
➤ Spin-Off

BIRTHSONG
➤ *You Don't Have To Be A Star* Jan 2–8, 1977

VAN MCCOY
You are a doer of great works you had no intention of doing.

If you made your living as a dance instructor, the dawn of rock and roll in the mid-1950s cut into your business pretty dramatically, but there were just enough Twists, Ponies, and Mashed Potatoes in the decade that followed that if you were resourceful, you could make up for the revenue shortfalls in your Waltz and Fox-trot divisions. By the early 1970s, however, you were living in a popstrological era that was to American dance teachers what the Dust Bowl was to Oklahoma farmers. *Mustache Rock* was undanceable, *Lite & White* was hug-and-sway at best, and no one had to teach fans of *Shaking Booty* how to do the Bump. But then, just when it seemed all hope was lost, along came disco like a blessed rain in a drought-stricken land. For those who taught or simply loved couples dancing, *The Hustle* was a god-send and your Birthstar was its prophet. Suddenly the young folks who wanted to look good on the floor of their local night-club had to put in some time in a dance studio, and soon enough, variations like the Latin, the Line, and the New York Hustles had made your once moribund industry cultur-ally vital. No Van McCoy, no John Travolta in a white suit—it's probably that simple. He'd written for the Shirelles and Gladys Knight, among others, and he put the original Peaches together with Herb, which secured him a place in the con-stellation *Invisible Hand* and further reinforces the already strong indications that his pop-strological children are likely to create **ripple effects that travel farther than their own feet could carry them**.

CONSTELLATIONS
➤ Disco Ball
➤ Invisible Hand
➤ Tragic Demise

BIRTHSONG
➤ *The Hustle* Jul 20–26, 1975

THE MCCOYS
If you had to choose between lucky and good, wouldn't you choose a little of both?

In between the apocalyptic *Eve Of Destruction* and the melancholy *Yesterday*, America took a short break from popstrological bummers and elevated an irresistible trifle called *Hang On Sloopy* to the top of the charts in the autumn of 1965. The infectious, three-chord brilliance of your Birthsong was no accident—it was written, after all, by Bert Berns (*née* Russell), who also wrote *Twist And Shout* and *Brown-Eyed Girl*. What *was* essentially an accident, though, was the selection of the McCoys to record *Sloopy*. Bert Berns helped run Bang Records in New York, and he'd instructed one of his bands (the Strangeloves, who were remnants of the Tokens) to be on the lookout while out on tour for a group of fresh-faced teenagers with at least the musi-cal chops to play the undemand-ing *Sloopy*. The Strangeloves found what Berns was looking for in Dayton, Ohio, in the form of four boys working the prom-and-sock-hop circuit by night and going to high school by day. Within days of their discovery, the boys called the McCoys (future guitar hero Rick Derringer among them) found themselves in a New York recording studio, cutting the track that would take them to #1 and earn them a spot in the con-stellation *Regifted*. **Youth may be behind you**, child of the McCoys, but **your unsophisti-cated appeal will be with you for life**.

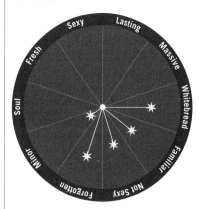

CONSTELLATION
➤ Regifted

BIRTHSONG
➤ *Hang On Sloopy*
    Sep 26–Oct 2, 1965

GEORGE MCCRAE

If you hope to climb the ladder, be sure to thank those who keep it standing.

He made his first run at pop stardom in the late sixties, and he fell so far short of his goal that he gave up the business entirely to be a stay-at-home dad. But the pressures of supporting a family compelled George McCrae to give it another shot in the mid-seventies, and perhaps it's because he wasn't simply trying to serve his own ego that he didn't think twice about poking his head into a studio at T.K. Records one day to hear what that kid Harry from the warehouse was working on in his free time. As it turned out, what Harry Wayne Casey—still a year short of his own *Shaking Booty* superstardom—was working on with his pal Richard Finch was the instrumental track to *Rock Your Baby*, which just happened to need a high-tenor voice like George McCrae's. And so it was that your Birthstar managed to rise into the constellation *Regifted* by befriending the brains behind KC and the Sunshine Band at a time when many would-be pop stars wouldn't have given them the time of day. So if your mother didn't teach you this already, let your Birthstar be the one to convince you that **it almost always pays to be nice to the support staff**, because you never know how much **your continued success may depend on them**.

CONSTELLATIONS
➤ Regifted
➤ Shaking Booty

BIRTHSONG
➤ *Rock Your Baby* Jul 7–20, 1974

BOBBY MCFERRIN

You march to the beat of your own private drummer.

Most boys go through a phase in which the source of their greatest amusement is the tremendous variety of sounds their own bodies can produce. Some boys retain this fascination well into adulthood, though few besides your Birthstar can be said to have translated it into something like art. An extremely minor though notably unique musician in the jazz category prior to 1988, Bobby McFerrin took musical self-sufficiency to a whole new extreme with the unlikely pop smash *Don't Worry Be Happy,* the only full-body a cappella recording ever to rule the pop universe. More than that, McFerrin managed to become a permanent darling of the left-leaning PBS crowd not just for his incredible vocal talent but for his refusal to allow then–Vice President George H. W. Bush to use *Don't Worry Be Happy* as his official campaign theme song. McFerrin's Bush-blocking efforts were fruitless, of course, thanks to Willie Horton and an ill-advised tank ride by Michael Dukakis, but still this truly odd member of the constellation *Had to Be There* bestows on those born under his influence not only **strong political convictions**, but also a gift for **strange and strangely pleasing bodily emanations**.

CONSTELLATION
➤ Had to Be There

BIRTHSONG
➤ *Don't Worry Be Happy* Sep 18–Oct 1, 1988

MAUREEN MCGOVERN

Ain't no building hot enough, ain't no shipwreck deep enough.

There have been plenty of disastrous films that spawned enormous pop hits, but only one true disaster film that accomplished the feat: *The Poseidon Adventure*, the upside-down-cruise-ship epic that launched your Birthstar into the constellation *Theme Singer*. The Hollywood force behind *Poseidon* was Irwin Allen, the legendary seventies disastermonger. But contrary to popular opinion, Irwin Allen wasn't really interested in making movies about earthquakes, sinking ships, and burning skyscrapers. He was interested in making movies about *people* in earthquakes, sinking ships, and burning skyscrapers, so each and every one of his epics focused on a band of flawed but sympathetic victims struggling to survive against impossible odds. And every one of his epics also had a *love theme*. Indeed, before she turned up her nose at such work in favor of a successful (and ongoing) career as a classy cabaret chanteuse, Maureen McGovern provided two of those love themes: your Birthsong, *The Morning After*, and *We May Never Love Like This Again* from *The Towering Inferno*. Minor and Forgotten though she may be, your Birthstar bestows upon you one or both of two powerful gifts: **a knack for finding romance in unlikely places,** and **a pathological need to paint a pretty picture of disastrous situations**.

CONSTELLATIONS
➤ Theme Singer
➤ Lite & White

BIRTHSONG
➤ *The Morning After*
Jul 29–Aug 11, 1973

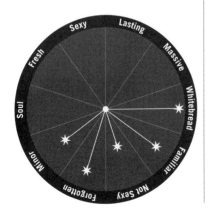

BARRY MCGUIRE

If you had a hammer, you'd probably beat the world over the head with it.

To put it into terms that someone who was born in but did not live through the sixties might appreciate, if Joan Baez or Phil Ochs were the Public Enemy of protest-folk, then Barry McGuire was its MC Hammer—an enthusiastic popularizer who became an object of ridicule within his own genre. It wasn't wrong, as such, to dismiss McGuire as a deeply inferior Dylan imitator; all you had to do was listen to *Eve Of Destruction* to agree with that label. But if your Birthsong lacked the soul and subtlety of *A Hard Rain's A-Gonna Fall*, it nonetheless managed to broadcast a list of Dylanesque sociopolitical gripes deep into the heart of the American suburbs, where soul and subtlety aren't necessarily the most effective approaches to consciousness-raising anyway. The eastern world really was explodin' at the moment of your birth, and most of the kids being asked to kill really weren't old enough for votin', so at the very least, Barry McGuire deserves credit for saying so in terms the average teenager could understand. But that is not to say that the pop-strological children of the most underappreciated lefty ever to rise in the constellation *Folkie* are either (*a*) lefties or (*b*) underappreciated. Indeed, your **dogmatic opinions** may fall anywhere and everywhere on the political spectrum, and it's almost certain that **your friends and relations have a very healthy appreciation** for how strongly you hold them.

CONSTELLATION
➤ Folkie

BIRTHSONG
➤ *Eve Of Destruction*
Sep 19–25, 1965

DON MCLEAN
What's gone for you is not forgotten.

The oral tradition in modern society isn't what it used to be, but you can still thank it for passing certain bits of cultural knowledge down to you across great distances in time. You owe your knowledge of what a Trojan horse and an Achilles' heel are to *The Iliad*, an epic poem composed more than two millennia ago, and you probably owe your knowledge of how Buddy Holly died to one composed back in 1970. Even today, just a few decades after it was first performed, *American Pie* contains references that are difficult for non–baby boomers to decipher, but you know your Birthsong's chorus better than you know your national anthem, and chances are that your children will, too. Yes, there are those for whom the title *American Pie* conjures images very different from a snowy field in 1959 Iowa, but don't hold Hollywood in too much contempt for that. Claymation *Sinbad* movies, after all, probably taught you what a Cyclops was long before you'd ever heard of *The Odyssey*, and if a teen sex farce leads the members of some future generation indirectly to Don McLean and Buddy Holly, well, that's just the way pop culture works. No one had invested February 3, 1959, with much transcendent meaning before Don McLean called it "the day the music died," and though you could blame your Birthstar

for his part in encouraging the baby boomers to invest their *entire* experience of rock and roll with such transcendent meaning, you could also thank him for investing you with a **desire to honor those who came before you** and **a gift for seeing the deeper significance** in what others see only as senseless tragedy.

CONSTELLATION
➤ Folkie

BIRTHSONG
➤ *American Pie* Jan 9–Feb 5, 1972

MECO
The force of something very strange is very strong in you.

It took years for the terms "*Star Wars*" and "geek" to be permanently joined together in popular parlance, but rest assured that the *Star Wars* geeks were there from day one in the summer of 1977. Without any Internet or *Entertainment Tonight* camera crews to guide or encourage them, they simply began showing up outside American

movie theaters day after day, show after show, practicing their light-saber moves and codifying the spelling of "Boba Fett." And your Birthstar was right there with them. Meco Monardo was his name, and after seeing *Star Wars* an uncountable number of times in its first week of release, this college roommate of Chuck Mangione and producer/arranger for Tommy James and Gloria Gaynor found himself humming the brilliant John Williams *Star Wars Theme* and thinking to himself, "Gee, if Walter Murphy can do it with Beethoven's *Fifth* . . ." And thus was born the third and final star to gain entry into the constellation *Speechless* by discofying an existing instrumental theme. It is Meco's connection to the roots of a world-changing cultural phenomenon that continues to perplex and amuse us, which explains his influential place in the constellation ***Had to Be There***, from which he bestows upon those born under his influence the potential to **popularize the obsessions of fringe subcultures** and the power to **perplex nearly as many people as you charm.**

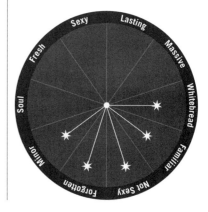

CONSTELLATIONS
➤ Had to Be There
➤ Speechless
➤ Disco Ball
➤ Theme Singer

BIRTHSONG
➤ *Star Wars Theme*
Sep 25–Oct 8, 1977

BILL MEDLEY AND JENNIFER WARNES
You are the kind who looks at the past with rose-colored glasses.

I f asked to describe the most recent vacation you took with your nuclear family, would you call it: (*a*) a simmering crucible of dysfunction, (*b*) a soul-sucking bore, (*c*) both, or (*d*) the time of your life? You're young enough today to answer honestly, but the hell of it is that even if the truth is (*a*), (*b*), or (*c*), you will someday convince yourself that it was actually (*d*). Such is the influence of that dangerous force called nostalgia—a force that can cast a glossy haze over events, even terrible events that once were sharply defined. Perhaps you'll resolve here and now to be **the rare individual who resists the pull of nostalgia** as you move past your youth, but considering your popstrological legacy, **it's going to be an uphill battle**. You were born, after all, under the influence of *(I've Had) The Time Of My Life*, the theme song from a film that made a family vacation in the Jewish Catskills of the early sixties seem

kinda sexy. Jennifer Grey's nose may have been the only genuine thing about *Dirty Dancing*, but your Birthsong itself was as irresistible as it was musically out of place in what was otherwise an attempt at a period piece. The duo of Jennifer "Never Met a Past-His-Prime Sixties Icon I Didn't Like" Warnes and Bill "the Low-Voiced One" Medley of the Righteous Brothers is your official Birthstar, but like many Minor stars in the constellation *Theme Singer*, this popstrological *Power Couple* takes a backseat in terms of influence to the film their work supported.

CONSTELLATIONS
➤ Power Couple
➤ Theme Singer

BIRTHSONG
➤ *(I've Had) The Time Of My Life* Nov 22–28, 1987

MELANIE
You may not speak Greek, but you probably know what "phallus" and "Sappho" mean.

S he was an unknown to most of the crowd who watched her play in the rain at Woodstock in 1969, but her performance and the song she later wrote about it, *Lay Down (Candles In The Rain)*, cemented her image as an icon of the flower-power set. *Lay Down* and other achingly sincere songs in the same vein—e.g., *Peace Will Come (According To Plan)*—explain your Birthstar's presence in the constellation *Folkie*, but it was a song that almost defies categorization which earned her a place among the popstrological elite. Whatever else it was, Melanie's *Brand New Key* was the kind of song the Germans, God love 'em, call an "ear worm." It burrowed its way into the cortex of all who heard it, quite against their will, and there it took root, doing whatever it is that a singsong nostalgia piece full of thinly veiled coital imagery does to the human brain. So what did its dominance of the pop universe at the moment of your birth do to you? Well, as a child of Melanie, you may be given to **leading public discussions of human sexuality**, but frankly, you may be just as likely to find them cringe-inducing. On the other hand, it is the rare Melanie indeed who has never formed a **fulfilling, pseudo-romantic relationship with a car, bike, or motorcycle** or at least felt a certain stirring inside when phrases like "precision engineered" and "interlocking mechanism" are spoken.

CONSTELLATION
➤ Folkie

CELEBRITY
➤ **Ricky Martin** (12/24/71) and **Taye Diggs** (1/2/72) are popstrological Melanies.

BIRTHSONG
➤ *Brand New Key* Dec 19, 1971–Jan 8, 1972

MEN AT WORK
You are the dingo in wallaby's clothing.

Helen Reddy, Olivia Newton-John, Andy Gibb, the Bee Gees, Rick Springfield—they all were model minorities who found brilliant success in America without calling overt attention to their foreign roots and without parading their quaint ethnic customs. And then along came Men at Work, the first antipodal invader with the cheek to wear their nation's trademark strangeness on their sleeves. *Who Can It Be Now?* could just as easily have been English, but *Down Under* was the Australian equivalent of *Say It Loud (I'm Black And I'm Proud)*. It terrified the powers-that-be to think what Australian Pride might do to the prized blandness of white America, but the Vegemite, as they say, was already out of the tin. Nativist forces did manage to prevent any future uppity stars from entering the constellation **Outback** (*viz.* Midnight Oil), but they could do nothing to prevent the likes of Paul Hogan, Foster's Lager, and Outback Steak Houses from joining the American pop-cultural mix. The forces of **restrained propriety may sometimes weaken your resolve**, child of Men at Work, but it's **hide the liquor and bar the door** when you let your true self walk about.

CONSTELLATION
➤ Outback

BIRTHSONGS
➤ *Who Can It Be Now?* Oct 24–30, 1982
➤ *Down Under* Jan 9–29 and Feb 6–12, 1983

MFSB
While others steal scenes, you work behind them.

The reason every Motown record from the 1960s sounds so damn tight and so damn similar is because the same handful of unheralded, non-royalty-earning studio musicians played nearly every note on every Motown release from Mary Wells to Michael Jackson. They called themselves the Funk Brothers, and what they did standing in the shadows of Motown was what your Birthstar did almost as anonymously at Philadelphia International, epicenter of the Philly Soul sound. For one brief, shining moment, however, the group of racially and chronologically integrated musicians whose *Invisible Hand* gave the sound of the O'Jays and the Spinners its distinctive *oomph* stepped out of the shadows and into the popstrological spotlight. Affectionately called the Mothers, Fathers, Sisters and Brothers (because that's exactly what they were), they became MFSB on the classic instrumental appropriately titled *TSOP* (for *The Sound Of Philadelphia*). Funky enough to become the theme song for *Soul Train*, your Birthsong was also grandiose enough to prefigure the coming sound of disco and to launch your working-class Birthstar into *four* popstrological constellations. **Glory hogs and spotlight grabbers** are occasionally found among oppositional MFSBs, but those who go with the flow of your Birthstar tend to find greater reward **working tirelessly in critical supporting roles**.

CONSTELLATIONS
➤ Speechless
➤ Shaking Booty
➤ Invisible Hand
➤ Theme Singer

BIRTHSONG
➤ *TSOP* Apr 14–27, 1974

GEORGE MICHAEL
You give to us your leather, then take from us your face.

When you can dump a partner like Andrew Ridgeley and trade up to Aretha Franklin in the space of a single year, you know your stock is on the rise. Your Birthstar certainly knew it in 1987, so after scoring his first post-Wham! hit (*I Knew You Were Waiting For Me*) alongside the Queen of Soul, he decided that perhaps he should be the next to wear that crown. The first order of business in the reinvention and Americanization of George Michael was to distance himself from the short-shorts and "Choose LIFE" shirts of his recent past. Butching up both his look and his sound, your Birthstar took the pop universe by storm with an album called *Faith,* whose four #1 hits earned him a spot in the constellation *Royal Court* as the dominant popstrological force of 1988. Surrounded by supermodels yet clearly more interested in his own Tom-of-Finland reflection, George Michael was an icon of **pansexual self-obsession** at a time when even Madonna had yet to strike that pose. And though he seemed to invite his own popstrological slide when he literally removed himself from his wildly popular videos, in his moment at the top, your Birthstar bestowed upon you a willingness to take a **valiant stand in support of your truest passions**. And in his later moment at the bottom, he shared with you the lesson that **discretion is always the better part of valor**, particularly if you choose to display your passion publicly.

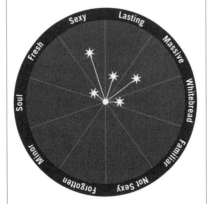

CONSTELLATIONS
➤ Spin-Off
➤ Royal Court
➤ Britsuasion

BIRTHSONGS
➤ *Faith* Dec 6, 1987–Jan 2, 1988
➤ *Father Figure* Feb 21–Mar 5, 1988
➤ *One More Try* May 22–Jun 11, 1988
➤ *Monkey* Aug 21–Sep 3, 1988

BETTE MIDLER
You are the Carmen Miranda who knows that bananas are not the only fruits.

The universe may never again give rise to another Jewish girl from Honolulu who's equal parts Judy Garland and Ethel Merman, but if it does, let's hope that girl finds her way to New York City, because where else are they going to appreciate her? At the very least, it's impossible to imagine a place and time other than Greenwich Village in the early seventies that could have incubated your Birthstar. Unless you think that some other moment in social and popstrological time—past, present, or future—could place the host of the *Tonight Show* in a gay bathhouse to catch a cabaret act that features renditions of both *Delta Dawn* and *Chatanooga Choo Choo*. Your Birthstar may not have reached #1 until 1988 with an overwrought ballad from an overwrought film about overwrought middle-aged women, but never mind, because Miss M was nearly twenty years into a substantial and unorthodox pop career by then. Her popstrological power emanates from the constellations *Sui Generis* and *Tip of the Ice Cube*, and from the **underappreciated eccentricity** that combination of affiliations implies. Your own **strange and quirky brilliance** may not play in Peoria, but **find your natural audience** and you'll win their love forever.

CONSTELLATIONS
➤ Sui Generis
➤ Tip of the Ice Cube

BIRTHSONG
➤ *Wind Beneath My Wings*
Jun 4–10, 1989

MIKE AND THE MECHANICS
The lure of the exotic is not the lure with which you fish.

In business and in politics, the 1980s were a great time to be a white man nearing middle age, but then what decade wasn't? Even the popstrological resurgence of that demographic group in the decade of your birth was not all that strange, considering that it had ruled relatively unchallenged in every decade of the twentieth century but for the seventies, the sixties, and the second half of the fifties. But the 1980s were nearing an end at the moment of your birth, as was the reign of the dominant constellation *Reaganrock*, giving Mike and the Mechanics precious little time to grab a slice of popstrological immortality. Lucky for them and significantly for you, they seized their last, best opportunity and ruled the pop universe briefly and weakly in the week of your birth. *All I Need Is A Miracle* is the Mike and the Mechanics song that seems to have earned a place in the expanded edition of the pop canon, but it's *The Living Years* that ruled the pop universe at the moment of your birth, marking you with **surprisingly grown-up concerns for one so young**. And though being born under the very last group of forty-something white guys to rule the pop universe may not sound like much of a gift, it has endowed you with the fascinating potential to **take advantage of doomed power structures** just before they are consigned to history's ash heap.

CONSTELLATIONS
➤ Reaganrock
➤ Britsuasion

BIRTHSONG
➤ *The Living Years*
Mar 19–25, 1989

STEVE MILLER
When they take away your downtime, they take away your soul.

If you are a rock and roll guitarist hoping to tap into the great and mystical depository of pop hooks, you can try to facilitate the process with certain popular herbs and elixirs, but in the end there is no substitute for time—vast swaths of unstructured time noodling on the sofa while waiting for the riff-keepers to speak through your callused, mortal hands. Ask Keith Richards or Joe Perry, and they'll tell you: they didn't sit down and *write* the hooks in *Satisfaction* and *Walk This Way*, and they didn't really *discover* them. What they did was clear their minds, loosen their fingers, and wait for those timeless riffs to discover *them*. Ask Steve Miller, too, for while he may not have channeled any one hook to rival the aforementioned two, the irresistible hooks in his body of work (*The Joker, Rock 'N Me, Jet Airliner, Take The Money And*

Run) bespeak frequent contact with the other side throughout his 1970s heyday. This, combined with a sometimes chubby, always unpretentious persona, made him a popular favorite among highway-drivin' rockers for the better part of three decades, and the only solo star aligned with the forces of the constellation *Mustache Rock*. **Sitting around waiting for inspiration to strike** won't lead to success in every field of work, but your popstrological profile certainly suggests that you **slow down and give it a try** sometimes.

CONSTELLATIONS
➤ Mustache Rock
➤ Texstyle

BIRTHSONGS
➤ *The Joker* Jan 6–12, 1974
➤ *Rock 'N Me* Oct 31–Nov 6, 1976
➤ *Abracadabra* Aug 29–Sep 4 and Sep 19–25, 1982

MILLI VANILLI
Come judgment day, you'll still be able to look yourself in the mirror, rather happily.

Someday they will make a smash-hit Broadway musical of your Birthstar's famous story, and the most uplifting scene of all will be when Milli and Vanilli first approach each other after meeting eyes across the floor of an L.A. nightclub, and they begin to sing: *"I like your braids / I like your moves / You stole my look / You stole mine, too!"* The show will end in tragedy, of course, as a lip-synching scandal turns them into the most ridiculed star in the pop universe and drives poor Milli (or is it Vanilli?) to his death. But in that first act, a critical and often overlooked side of your Birthstar's story will be told: the story of how two young men working the *exact same look* overcame the human instinct to destroy the competition. It really could have gone either way, but Milli and Vanilli chose love (albeit something close to self-love) over war in that moment, and in so doing they propelled themselves to the highest reaches of the pop universe by sheer force of aesthetic destiny. There never was and never will be another star in the pop universe exactly like the one that made you, but it's within your power to show the world what it lost when it banished your Birthstar to the popstrological wilderness. **Resist the poison of shame** if you can, child of Milli Vanilli, and **protect your peace-loving nature**. With the forces that will array themselves against you, **you'll need it**.

CONSTELLATIONS
➤ Artificial Ingredients
➤ Sui Generis
➤ Eurosomething
➤ Hot Hairdo
➤ Tragic Demise

BIRTHSONG
➤ *Baby Don't Forget My Number* Jun 25–Jul 1, 1989

THE MIRACLES
You are the Hootie-less blowfish or the Huey-less Newsie, except not at all pathetic.

The pop universe owes a significant percentage of its total mass to the anonymous members of the many creatively named backup units who completed the plural portion of their groups' names. But your Birthstar, the Miracles, were no mere Drells, Pips, or Heywoods. Yes, they had been reduced to "and the" status when Berry Gordy elevated their resident genius to a headline position in the 1960s, but they refused to let this change determine their fate. A piece of popstrological immortality came their way in 1970 as the second half of Smokey Robinson and the Miracles, but merely being part of the glue that binds the popstrological firmament together was not enough for them, so after Smokey's eventual departure, the Miracles vowed to defy historical precedent and shed some light of their own. And sure enough, four years later, with a new lead singer but their old egalitarian name, your Birthstar performed a popstrological miracle when the driving beat of *Love Machine (Part 1)* lifted them into the highest reaches of the pop universe. As a child of the first and only group of should've-been-left-behinds to take up residence among the ship-jumping stars of the constellation *Spin-Off*, you have as part of your popstrological legacy the **potential to rise from the ranks of the toiling masses**. What you do with that potential is entirely up to you, for you may well find that **life among the ranks of the spoiled masters isn't everything it's cracked up to be.**

CONSTELLATIONS
➤ Spin-Off
➤ Shaking Booty

BIRTHSONGS
➤ *Love Machine (Part 1)*
Feb 29–Mar 6, 1976

GUY MITCHELL
When all bow down to hail the King, you will be too brave, or too foolish, to join them.

Make no mistake, 1956 belonged to Elvis Presley and to the legions of teenagers he awakened to a world of musical and sexual possibilities. But the King did not rule unopposed in the first year of his popstrological reign, and your Birthstar was the valiant soldier of the unsexy status quo who provided him with his strongest challenge. The weapon that Guy Mitchell used to unseat Elvis from sixteen straight weeks atop the pop charts was an absolute classic of mid-fifties establishment pop called *Singing The Blues*. With its bouncy beat and ceaseless whistling, it was probably the least soulful rendering of a song with "blues" in the title that the pop universe has ever seen, but it sounded like heavenly respite to that portion of the American public shell-shocked by the year's earlier popstrological developments. View Guy Mitchell as the ultimate anti-Elvis if you must, but in preventing total victory for the King in the year of his debut,

your Birthstar did more than just bestow upon you a **tendency toward squareness**—he also helped make you into the **brave defender of establishment values** that you are. And while **you may not make fine distinctions** between kings who rule brutally and kings who rule soulfully, you will **oppose tyranny** in any form with **rigid and admirable consistency.**

CONSTELLATION
➤ Old Guard

CELEBRITIES
➤ **David Sedaris** (12/26/56) and **Katie Couric** (1/7/57) are popstrological children of Guy Mitchell.

BIRTHSONGS
➤ *Singing The Blues* Dec 8, 1956–Feb 8, 1957
➤ *Heartaches By The Number* Dec 14–27, 1959

DOMENICO MODUGNO

You are a true original with the power to break barriers and outshine imitators.

The formula for turning Italian food into American Italian food is simple: triple the portions and heap on the cheese. That's how the skimpy thing Italians call pizza became the three-meat, stuffed-crust behemoth we Americans adore, and in a sense, it's how a skinny little Italian named Domenico Modugno was almost thwarted in his climb to the popstrological mountaintop. Domenico won Italy's heart and the 1958 San Remo Festival of Music with his sweet and gentle *Nel Blu Dipinto Di Blu*, selling a *million* copies of the record in Italy alone. To make it in the States, however, he had to play David to a cheese-wielding Italian American Goliath by the name of Dean Martin. Dino's English-language cover of your Birthsong—retitled *Volaré*—may be the more familiar version to many of us today, but in 1958 it was your Birthstar who won an unlikely victory for **understated authenticity** by topping the U.S. charts with the first foreign-language #1 in the rock era and establishing a hard-won beachhead on the shores of American pop as the founding star in the constellation *Eurosomething*. Try to remember when the **layers of your public persona** seem to grow too thick that for you the path to happiness may lie in a **return to the simple things**.

CONSTELLATION
➤ Eurosomething

CELEBRITY
➤ **Jennifer Tilly** (9/16/58) is a Domenico Modugno.

BIRTHSONG
➤ *Volaré (Nel Blu Dipinto Di Blu)* Aug 18–24 and Sep 1–28, 1958

THE MONKEES

Some question the meaning of reality, but you question its value.

When aspiring popstrologists begin their formal training, the first star they are asked to contemplate is the Monkees. "What is it that defines the Monkees?" they are asked, and of course their answer is that the Monkees were artificial. "But were the Monkees *bad*?" the popstrological novices are then asked, and of course their answer is no—the Monkees were far from bad. And then comes the crucial question: "So were the Monkees *legitimate?*" And eventually a voice rises above the noisy debate to say, "Who cares?" The student who provides this clever answer is always praised for having read his or her orientation packet carefully and having learned that the word "legitimate" is a rock-critic term that all popstrologists strive to banish from their vocabularies. But then the master returns to the central thread of the discussion: "Who cares if the Monkees were legitimate?" he asks rhetorically. "A good half of those born under their popstrological influence, that's who." The point of the lesson is to remind those who hope to practice the science of popstrology that their first responsibility is not to themselves but to those they would serve. Legitimacy may not be an issue popstrologists like to talk about, but legitimacy most certainly is the ruling issue in the lives of popstrological Monkees. So count yourself lucky if you feel perfectly comfortable **basing your success on something others regard as less than real,** child of the Monkees. Perhaps your example will convince the

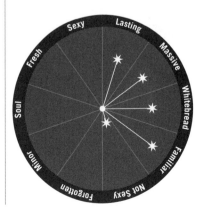

oppositional Monkees out there to ease up a bit and spare themselves the heartache of their **high-minded pursuit of legitimacy at any cost.**

CONSTELLATIONS
➤ Artificial Ingredients
➤ Regifted
➤ Royal Court

CELEBRITIES
➤ **King Ad-Rock** (10/31/66), **David Schwimmer** (11/2/66), **Lisa Lisa** (1/15/67), **Laura Dern** (2/10/67), and **Anna-Nicole Smith** (11/28/67) are children of the Monkees.

BIRTHSONGS
➤ *Last Train To Clarksville* Oct 30–Nov 5, 1966
➤ *I'm A Believer* Dec 25, 1966–Feb 11, 1967
➤ *Daydream Believer* Nov 26–Dec 23, 1967

MR. MISTER
When others might jump ship, you simply lean into your oar.

Did you ever have one of those days where everything just seemed to click? Where the stars and planets cooperated with the weather, your hair, and your blood-sugar level to create the sensation that the universe had something very good in store for you that day? No? That's too bad, because your Birthstar sure did just a year or so before you were born. Actually, just the *frontman* of your Birthstar,

Richard Page, did, but what he did about it helped make you who you are. The powers that combined forces to bless Richard Page were, appropriately enough, popstrological. Page had been laboring like a civil-service employee in the constellation *Reaganrock* for years, supporting the likes of Kenny Loggins, John Parr, and REO Speedwagon. But when two of that constellation's stars—Toto and Chicago—lost their frontmen in quick succession, it was Page they both invited to take over as theirs. It's a well-known fact that the dominant constellation of the 1980s took care of its own, but to be offered a lucrative position in two—okay, one and a half—hugely successful groups was beyond any good fortune that ever befell, say, Richard Marx. Which band did Richard Page choose? His own Mr. Mister, and his belief was duly rewarded as your Birthstar earned not one but two #1 hits in the next twelve months. **Some sell their talents to the highest bidder,** but when the bidding heats up, **you will realize the value of keeping ownership of yours.**

CONSTELLATION
➤ Reaganrock

BIRTHSONGS
➤ *Broken Wings* Dec 1–14, 1985
➤ *Kyrie* Feb 23–Mar 8, 1986

WALTER MURPHY AND HIS BIG APPLE BAND
What's sacrilegious imitation to some is fearless innovation to you.

If you've ever rosined a bow, cut a reed, or cleared a spit valve, then you are in a better position than most to appreciate the hero status your Birthstar enjoys among those reluctantly consigned in early adolescence to the social Siberia of the band or orchestra room. For Walter Murphy is the man who experienced in real life what you only dreamed of as a teenager, which was somehow translating your mastery of chromatic scales into a career as a bona fide pop star. The song that launched your Birthstar was an audacious disco variation on Beethoven's *Fifth Symphony*, and while it was not, strictly speaking, a cover song, it had the brilliant cover-song's magic of sounding both completely Familiar and completely Fresh at the very same time. And for all the *"Roll Over, Beethoven"* jokes your Birthsong spawned among critics, it was an unqualified popular smash in 1976 that got even bigger one year later when it was included on a little sound track album called *Saturday Night Fever*. For those born under the influence of Walter Murphy and his (nonexistent) Big Apple Band, **creating the new will begin with mastering the classics**.

CONSTELLATIONS
➤ Speechless
➤ Disco Ball

BIRTHSONG
➤ *A Fifth Of Beethoven*
Oct 3–9, 1976

ANNE MURRAY
No one likes a wet blanket, until they find their clothes are on fire.

The constellation *Disco Ball* was at its absolute zenith in the year of your birth. The pop universe pulsated steadily at 128 beats per minute, and with the likes of Barbra Streisand and Frankie Valli falling under disco's intoxicating spell, the party showed no signs of ending. But every party needs its pooper, and in 1978 that pooper was Anne Murray, your Birthstar. Before you go crying in your beer over just missing out on being a popstrological Donna Summer, try to remember that when the disco backlash finally came, even the Queen herself ended up repenting her sins and disavowing her fabulous crown. In that sense, your Birthstar was simply ahead of the curve for openly criticizing the hedonistic lifestyle with which disco had become associated and for offering an undanceable ballad as a musical alternative. Your Birthstar bestows upon you a powerful popstrological gift, but choose your moments to apply it wisely, for **your willingness to rain on popular parades** can be either **courageous or curmudgeonly** depending on the context and on your perspective.

CONSTELLATIONS
➤ Lite & White
➤ Oh . . . Canada

BIRTHSONG
➤ *You Needed Me*
Oct 29–Nov 4, 1978

JOHNNY NASH
When they say "partly sunny," do you think "partly cloudy"?

The Oval Office tapes from the morning following the 1972 re-election of Richard Nixon must surely have captured the president in a cheerful mood. . . .[11.4.72. 932] "What'd I tell you, Haldeman? Watergate shmatergate, am I right?" "Yes, sir, you certainly showed them, sir." "Say, Bob, what's that song playing on Rosemary's radio out there?" "Uh, that's the number-one song in the country today, Mr. President—*I Can See Clearly Now*, by Johnny Nash." "Hmmm . . . *dark feelings have disappeared*—I like that. It's got kind of a bossa nova feel, doesn't it, Bob?" "Yes, sir, something like that." "Well, let's see about getting this Nash fellow for the inaugural ball if we can. He's not Jewish, is he?" "Mmm, I suspect not, Mr. Pre—" "*Mmmm-mmm sunshiny day* . . .Well, let's get to work, Bob. Where's that [expletive deleted] Kissinger—I think it's time we had him straighten out this Vietnam mess once and for all." [END] Like a tropical sun at high noon, the brightness of your Birthstar **banished all shadows** from universe of pop during his four-week reign in the constellation *Fresh Breeze*. So why is it that not every popstrological child of Johnny Nash greets each new day with **boundless energy and fresh-start optimism**? Caffeine withdrawal mainly, but also because some who begin their lives on such a remarkable high note are **bound to be disappointed** by nearly all that follows.

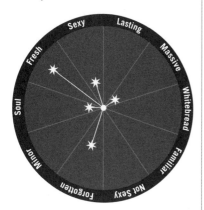

CONSTELLATIONS
➤ Fresh Breeze
➤ Texstyle

CELEBRITY
➤ Rebecca Romijn-Stamos (11/6/72) is a child of Johnny Nash.

BIRTHSONG
➤ *I Can See Clearly Now* Oct 29–Nov 25, 1972

RICKY NELSON
You are the lightweight with a surprisingly powerful punch.

With the full weight of the American Broadcasting Corporation behind him, it was an economic inevitability that the younger son of Ozzie and Harriet Nelson would sell a few records, but that ironclad guarantee didn't guarantee that he wouldn't stink. And he didn't stink—not by a long shot. Backed by some of the best song-writers and studio musicians of the late 1950s, Ricky Nelson scored hit after hit with a mix of ballads and rockabilly that only the most willful cynics could dismiss as the typical teen-idol pap. And while he certainly resides squarely in the constellation *Regifted*, that grouping of stars whose success was not so much earned by them as granted by others, your Birthstar set a musical standard of quality that has rarely if ever been matched by the long and continuing line of TV teens turned pop stars. He could have been little more than the Tori Spelling of pop, but instead he struck a blow for connected rich kids everywhere with his good taste and solid output, which did not come definitively to an end until 1985, when a plane crash in East Texas added his star to the constellation *Tragic Demise* and left the actress Tracy and the hair-metal purveyors Matthew and Gunnar Nelson without a father. **Play your connections** for all they're worth, children of Ricky Nelson, but if it's respect you're after, the trick is to **foster low expectations** and then **exceed them by miles.**

CONSTELLATIONS
➤ Regifted
➤ Teen Idol
➤ Tragic Demise

CELEBRITIES
➤ **Madonna** (8/16/58), **Angela Bassett** (8/16/58), and **Melissa Etheridge** (4/29/61) are popstrological Ricky Nelsons.

BIRTHSONGS
➤ *Poor Little Fool* Aug 4–17, 1958
➤ *Travelin' Man* May 29–Jun 4 and Jun 12–18, 1961

NEW KIDS ON THE BLOCK
You stand on the shoulders of giants, but giants stand on your shoulders, too.

The philosopher George Santayana said, "Those who cannot remember the past are condemned to repeat it." But what about those who are too young to remember the past—are they doomed, too? Perhaps it depends on how you define the term "doomed," but if you regard the boy-band explosion of your pre-teen years as a disastrous phenomenon, then perhaps the answer is yes. There can be no question, after all, that the Backstreet Boys, *NSYNC, *et al.* did not arise in a vacuum. They were inspired by and modeled quite consciously on the singing-and-dancing white boys who ruled the pop universe at the moment of your birth: New Kids on the

Block. A billion-dollar music-and-merchandise juggernaut in their late-eighties heyday, your Birthstar will probably serve as a model for many pop juggernauts to come, but they, too, were a product of history. The New Kids were created, groomed, managed, and owned by one Maurice Starr, a musical entrepreneur who first created New Edition as a blatant knockoff of the Jackson 5, then created your Birthstar as a blatant knockoff of both New Edition and the original Jackson 5 knockoff, the Osmonds. Somewhere on the island of lost boys within the constellation *Teen Idol*, Donnie, Danny, Jordan, Joey, and Jon are probably swapping tales of training-bra conquests with the Bay City Rollers, but while they continue to live in the past, you live at a **fascinating intersection of past, present, and future. Beware the power you possess,** child of the New Kids, for **you are not the only one who has to live with its potential effects**.

CONSTELLATIONS
➤ Teen Idol
➤ Tip of the Ice Cube

BIRTHSONG
➤ *I'll Be Loving You (Forever)* Jul 11–17, 1989

THE NEW VAUDEVILLE BAND

As hard as it is to understand yourself, it may be harder yet for others to understand you.

Even trained popstrologists sometimes go looking to the pop stars for answers only to return with more questions. And while sometimes those questions provide rich material for further popstrological inquiry, the question most experts confront when contemplating your Birthstar is, simply, "What the f*ck?" What, in other words, can possibly explain the rise and not-so-brief rule of a Rudy Vallée sound-alike group that would have sounded more at home in 1926 than it did in 1966—a group whose lead singer, for heaven's sake, went by the name of Tristram, Seventh Earl of Cricklewood? It's a **mystery of taste** inside a riddle about Brits wrapped in an enigma named Geoff Stephens, who wrote and recorded *Winchester Cathedral* on his own, then declined to participate in the relatively successful touring career of the guys he recruited into the fictitious New Vaudeville Band. Popstrology alone cannot explain how your Birthsong managed to stay atop the American pop charts longer than *Good Vibrations*, but it can say with a high degree of certainty that it couldn't have occurred at any time other than 1966—a year that was stirred up significantly by the forces of the constellation *Fresh Breeze* and visited not once but twice by two of your ruling houses, the constellations *Had to Be There* and *Artificial Ingredients.* Your **success in life may speak for itself,** but don't be surprised if it **tends to mystify** even those who had a hand in making it possible.

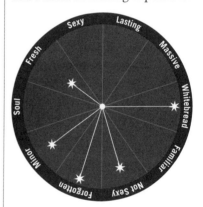

CONSTELLATIONS
➤ Had to Be There
➤ Artificial Ingredients
➤ Britvasion

BIRTHSONG
➤ *Winchester Cathedral* Nov 27–Dec 3 and Dec 11–24, 1966

OLIVIA NEWTON-JOHN

Beneath your sugary exterior lies a spicy interior, or so you'd like us to think.

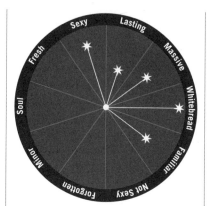

If Pat Boone had turned his *ss to the camera on *The Ed Sullivan Show* in 1957 and belted out *Da Ya Think I'm Sexy*, he might have approximated the impact Olivia Newton-John had on her fans when she cavorted in a leotard and sang about "getting horizontal" in the video for her 1981 single, *Physical*. Sure, her *Grease* makeover from saddle shoes and sweater sets to frizzy hair and f*ck-me pumps foreshadowed this transformation, but come on—that was just a movie! This was the real-life Olivia Newton-John—the radiant Australian good girl behind *Please Mister Please* and *Have You Never Been Mellow*—doing a *slo-mo shower scene*! A former country singer who then became a powerful force of mildness in the constellation *Lite & White*, Olivia Newton-John's further transformation in 1981 into an aerobicized sexpot cemented her placement among the mercurial stars in the constellation *Shape-Shifter*. Your Birthstar's unique and fascinating combination of affiliations makes her more than just the popstrological **patron saint of good girls who yearn to be bad** and of the boys (or girls) who love them for it—it also bestows upon you a **knack for surprising reinventions** and the **power to please almost any audience.**

CONSTELLATIONS

➤ Lite & White
➤ Shape-Shifter
➤ Country Cousins
➤ Outback

CELEBRITIES

➤ **Vanessa Carlton** (8/16/80), **Kelis** (8/21/80), **Barbara and Jenna Bush** (11/25/81), and **Britney Spears** (12/2/81) are all Olivia Newton-Johns.

BIRTHSONGS

➤ *I Honestly Love You* Sep 29–Oct 12, 1974
➤ *Have You Never Been Mellow?* Mar 2–8, 1975
➤ *Magic* Jul 27–Aug 23, 1980
➤ *Physical* Nov 15, 1981– Jan 23, 1982

NILSSON

You are the insider's insider, yet what's inside you is rarely known.

When John Lennon called him his favorite American singer, a great burden of public expectation might have been placed upon your Birthstar had he not been practically unknown to most who heard that quote. His truly remarkable voice could be heard on *Everybody's Talkin'* (from *Midnight Cowboy*), *Me And My Arrow* (from the brilliant play/animated special *The Point*), and perhaps most ubiquitously on the theme from *The Courtship of Eddie's Father*, yet even at the peak of his success as a singer, the name Harry Nilsson meant little to most of the record-buying public. Inside the business, however, his professional reputation was huge, having been built on his songwriting efforts for the Turtles, the Ronettes, Rick Nelson, and Three Dog Night, among many others. But though your Birthstar's clear affiliation in the universe of pop is with the great enablers of the constellation *Invisible Hand*, those born under his influence would do well to realize that that Harry Nilsson's sole #1 hit, *Without You*, was actually written by someone else. Like a flower that's dull to humans but psychedelic to bees, **your strength is often difficult for others to perceive,** but your contributions to the

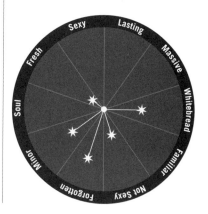

world need not be invisible if only you'd accept the help of others from time to time.

CONSTELLATION
➤ Invisible Hand

CELEBRITY
➤ Billy Joe Armstrong (2/17/72) is a child of Nilsson.

BIRTHSONG
➤ *Without You* Feb 13– Mar 11, 1972

BILLY OCEAN
You can be the best worker of all time and still never make it as employee of the month.

I f a new Mount Rushmore were to be carved into a cliff honoring the greatest stars of the constellation *Reaganrock*, then Huey Lewis, Phil Collins, and Lionel Richie would clearly fill slots one through three. Slot four, though, would be more of a question mark. In the end, there'd probably be a vote to choose between Kenny Loggins and Bryan Adams, but if they settled the question based on cold, hard numbers, that final slot would go to Billy Ocean, whose popstrological power in the mid-to-late eighties was quantitatively greater than that of Mr. Adams and Mr. Loggins combined. But two things would work against any grassroots campaign to see your Birthstar's face included in the monument: (1) the incredibly misleading message about *Reaganrock* that would be sent by featuring not one but *two* black faces among its pantheon and (2) the fact that Billy Ocean failed, despite undeniable good looks, to establish a visual identity as strong or as well suited to the stone-carver's art as that of the bearded Loggins or the pock-marked Adams. Keep your Birthstar's example in mind, children of Billy Ocean, next time you consider casting your lot with the popular crowd: if the **ruling class is not your place by birth**, it's **unlikely to become so** merely by dint of hard work.

CONSTELLATION
➤ Reaganrock

CELEBRITY
➤ Haley Joel Osment (4/10/88) is a popstrological Billy Ocean.

BIRTHSONGS
➤ *Caribbean Queen* Oct 28–Nov 10, 1984
➤ *There'll Be Sad Songs (To Make You Cry)* Jun 29–Jul 5, 1986
➤ *Get Outta My Dreams, Get Into My Car* Apr 3–16, 1988

ALAN O'DAY
Why wrestle with your inner demons when you can sleep with them instead?

I magination is the most powerful tool you possess, yet you sometimes feel ashamed to admit how much use you make of it. Take romance, for instance. Isn't it true that your most successful relationships have been with people you've never actually met? A psychotherapist might see this tendency as a major psychological hang-up, but the less judgmental science of popstrology invites you to view it as a gift bestowed upon you by your uniquely imaginative Birthstar. Alan O'Day was unafraid to admit his sexual preference, and his preference was for sexual partners of the noncorporeal variety. First as the writer of Helen Reddy's *Angie Baby*, and later as the writer-performer of *Undercover Angel*, O'Day gave the pop canon not one but two catchy #1 hits exploring the virtues of highly realistic, if slightly delusional, self-satisfaction. Your Birthstar lent new meaning to

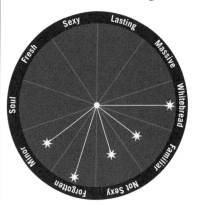

the constellation *Invisible Hand*, and the greatest way to celebrate his legacy is by **taking matters into your own hands**. Buy yourself some flowers, cook a nice meal, and see where the evening takes you—you just might find that **learning to love yourself really *is* the greatest love of all**.

CONSTELLATION
➤ Invisible Hand

BIRTHSONG
➤ *Undercover Angel* Jul 3–9, 1977

THE OHIO PLAYERS
Some people say that love takes time, but you're not "some people."

First of all, let us assure you that you are completely normal, at least for someone born under the popstrological influence of the Ohio Players. Yes, it can cause embarrassment at times, but isn't your ability to find sexual excitement in everyday activities like riding an elevator or buttering toast somewhat better than its polar opposite? Certainly your Birthstar thought so, and so they took it upon themselves in the mid-1970s to set things right every time the pop universe threatened to catch itself in a sexless rut. Consider this sequence atop the pop charts in early 1975: Barry Manilow, the Carpenters, Neil Sedaka . . . Ohio Players. Or in 1976: *Convoy, I Write The Songs, Do You Know*

Where You're Going To . . . Love Rollercoaster! Your Birthstar's timing was uncanny, and their music—well, their music could thaw permafrost. Any discussion of the cover art on Ohio Players albums like *Fire* or *Honey* or *Skin Tight* would risk things getting seriously out of hand, so suffice it to say that for those born under the funkiest of stars in the constellation *Shaking Booty*, **getting in the mood** is rarely going to be a challenge, though **getting others there as quickly as you could** sometimes prove to be.

CONSTELLATION
➤ Shaking Booty

BIRTHSONGS
➤ *Fire* Feb 2–8, 1975
➤ *Love Rollercoaster* Jan 25–31, 1976

THE O'JAYS
You say what you mean, and you mean what you feel.

Philadelphia was a hotbed of popstrological activity right from the beginning, with Dick Clark's idol-making years in the late 1950s. But the shining, popstrological apotheosis of the City of Brotherly Love didn't come until the early 1970s, when Kenny Gamble and Leon Huff established the record label that made the sound of Philly Soul famous. Gamble and Huff's Philadelphia International was a critical force in the gloriously diverse pop universe of the early 1970s, and your Birthstar was perhaps its greatest success. Backed by the house band (and future *Speechless* star) MFSB, the O'Jays joined the constellation *So-Soul* on the strength of one of the most beloved songs in the pop canon, *Love Train*, your Birthsong. So why is it, then, that as a person born under an irresistible anthem of globe-uniting love, you find yourself so often filled with **feelings toward your fellow humans that are far less charitable**? It's because you are the popstrological child not of a single song, but of the star that delivered that song—a star as capable of the never-forget bitterness of *Back Stabbers* and the missed-my-chance regret of *Use Ta Be My Girl* as of the universal

brotherly love of *Love Train*. **You're only human,** child of the O'Jays, but at least you're **capable of expressing the full range of human emotions,** which is more than some can say.

CONSTELLATIONS
➤ Tip of the Ice Cube
➤ So-Soul

BIRTHSONG
➤ *Love Train* Mar 18–24, 1973

ROY ORBISON
You take the good with the bad in life, though not always in equal portions.

At the height of what might have been a truly phenomenal career, Roy Orbison saw his wife, Claudette, die in a motorcycle accident and his two young sons killed when his Nashville home burnt to the ground. Given that his commercial fortunes declined dramatically at nearly the same time, one might be tempted to view your Birthstar as the popstrological equivalent of Job, the good and prosperous man whose world was shattered in order to settle a bet between God and Satan. But the pop universe isn't guided by any omnipotent force, let alone a jealous one. Its mysterious inner workings are driven by *human* achievement, *human* tragedy, and *human* caprice and folly, and those are the forces that buffeted your Birthstar throughout his roller-coaster,

three-decade career. And furthermore, while the biblical Book of Job features a Hollywood ending in which the protagonist's faith is restored and his previous wealth doubled by a merciful God, your Birthstar's story ends far more ambiguously, with his signature hit forever associated with a Julia Roberts hooker movie and his association with the troubling Traveling Wilburys his final musical legacy. **Into even the sunniest lives some rain must fall,** but that's cold comfort to the popstrological inheritors of a **fair amount of brilliance** and perhaps an **unfair amount of tragedy.**

CONSTELLATION
➤ Texstyle

CELEBRITY
➤ **Michael J. Fox** (6/9/61) and **Janeane Garofalo** (9/28/64) are popstrological Roy Orbisons.

BIRTHSONGS
➤ *Running Scared* Jun 5–11, 1961
➤ *Oh, Pretty Woman* Sep 20–Oct 10, 1964

TONY ORLANDO AND DAWN
Sometimes the luck of the draw is the best bet you've got.

Pop stars often say that being in a band is like being in a marriage, and the comparison seems apt. For just as some pop marriages implode despite having been entered into by individuals with a long history of friendship and a common set of beliefs and goals, others, like your Birthstar's, thrive despite being formed by near-total strangers. Tony Orlando and Dawn, you see, were the product of an arranged pop marriage. Actually, in an arranged marriage it's common for the bride and groom to meet at least once shortly before their wedding, but the arrangement that formed your Birthstar was even more extreme—more like a groom not meeting his bride until after the birth of their second child. *Candida* was the song that brought your Birthstar together, except not literally, since Tony Orlando recorded his vocals over those of Telma Hopkins and Joyce Vincent-Wilson without ever meeting them. To have predicted then that this hastily arranged collaboration would yield one of the defining groups of the early seventies and the second star of color in the constellation *Lite & White* would have been insane, but not as insane as predicting that the collaborators would enjoy a snappy chemistry that made their live act a hugely popular concert draw and their 1975–77 variety show a hugely popular TV hit. **Looking for love in all the wrong places**, children of Tony Orlando and Dawn? You just may have to **wait for it to come find you.**

CONSTELLATION
➤ Lite & White

BIRTHSONGS
➤ *Knock Three Times*
  Jan 17–Feb 6, 1971
➤ *Tie A Yellow Ribbon Round The Old Oak Tree*
  Apr 15–May 12, 1973
➤ *He Don't Love You (Like I Love You)* Apr 27–May 17, 1975

DONNY OSMOND
When the world laughs, it's laughing *with* you. Most of the time, anyway.

He was a national sensation by the time he was fourteen, with two #1 records under his belt and a devoted teen following. By nineteen he had it all: good looks, gobs of money, and a hugely popular television show.

But all Donny Osmond ever wanted was the one thing he could never have. No, not Marie—*credibility*. Donny Osmond's desire to be taken seriously as a musician was so great, so all-consuming, that it appears to have robbed him of all the joy he might have derived from his considerable showbiz success. The purple socks, the ice skates, the bubblegum remakes of classic pop hits, and the brazen imitation of the Jackson 5 that launched his star in the first place—America was always ready to love Donny for what he was, but we simply weren't going to take him seriously. Somewhere at this very moment, Donny Osmond is probably having a tuxedo fitted while plotting a Rod Stewart–like album of smoky pop standards—an album that the public will duly ignore. Don't let the object lesson of your Birthstar escape you, children of Donny Osmond: if you can't become the one you love, then **try to love the one you are**, because **plenty of others already do.**

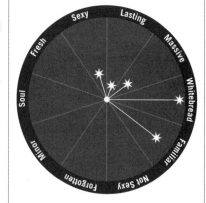

CONSTELLATIONS
➤ Gene Pool
➤ Spin-Off
➤ Underage
➤ Teen Idol

CELEBRITY
➤ **Jada Pinkett-Smith** (9/18/71) is a child of Donny Osmond.

BIRTHSONG
➤ *Go Away Little Girl*
  Sep 5–25, 1971

THE OSMONDS
Too many good apples can ruin the whole bunch for some, too.

Yes, they rose to prominence by copying every last detail of the Jackson 5 save for hairdos and skin color, but popstrologists view the rise of the Osmonds as a triumph of reproductive vigor and missionary zeal, not thievery; in other words, if it hadn't been bubblegum soul that the first family of Mormon America adapted to their needs, it would have been something else. There was but one kink in the family's otherwise perfect plan to colonize every corner of the known pop universe with fresh-faced Osmonds: the unexpected alacrity with which one of their own took the spotlight. You can see it clearly in pictures from the early-seventies: as Alan, Wayne, Merrill, and Jay work as hard to stay in step as four dutiful farmboys plowing the family plot, young Donny looks into the camera with wide-eyed yearning, as if to say "Please, America—please love me enough to free me from the collective." Who knows whether Donny would still trade his career for Michael Jackson's, as he surely would have in 1979 or 1983? What we do know is that the Osmond homestead in the constellation *Gene Pool* never felt quite comfortable to the family's brightest star, which may explain why successive waves of Osmond progeny have failed to expand their family's once formidable empire. The **importance of family ties** runs strong in you, child of the Osmonds, though whether those ties **support or suffocate** may depend on factors beyond Popstrology's reach.

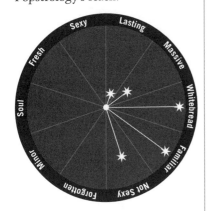

CONSTELLATIONS
➤ Gene Pool
➤ Underage
➤ Launching Pad

CELEBRITY
➤ **Johnny Knoxville** (3/11/71) is a child of the Osmonds, born under the song *One Bad Apple*.

BIRTHSONG
➤ *One Bad Apple* Feb 7– Mar 13, 1971

GILBERT O'SULLIVAN
You may not be the Godfather of Soul, but you're definitely on his Christmas list.

Who would have thought that a guy who cribbed his look from the Little Rascals and his sound from Paul McCartney and his name from the creators of the *Mikado* would end up a heroic champion of artistic originality? That an Irishman with a bowl cut, suspenders, and pants that ended at the knee would become a revolutionary force in the world of hip-hop? It all started with a massive #1 single that had Americans weeping to their AM radios in the summer of '72. *Alone Again (Naturally)* made your Birthstar a member of the constellation **Royal Court** as the popstrological king of 1972, and when it was sampled without permission on Biz Markie's 1991 album *I Need A Haircut,* it also made him the winner of a landmark copyright-infringement case that established the guiding legal principles regarding sampling. As a performer, your Birthstar was far from Sexy and heaven knows that he was Whitebread, but by getting James Brown and George Clinton paid for their foundational contributions to hip-hop, your Birthstar became a member of the constellation *Invisible Hand* and an indirect force of *ss-shaking funk and popstrological Soul. On the outside you may sometimes play the doofus, but on the inside you are nobody's dunce.

CONSTELLATIONS
➤ Royal Court
➤ Invisible Hand

CELEBRITIES
➤ **Ben Affleck** (8/15/72), **Cameron Diaz** (8/31/72), and **Chris Tucker** (8/31/72) are children of Gilbert O'Sullivan.

BIRTHSONG
➤ *Alone Again (Naturally)* Jul 23–Aug 19 and Aug 27–Sep 9, 1972

ROBERT PALMER
An offensive picture is worth a thousand offensive words.

Outside of a pair of popstrological giants (Madonna, Whitney Houston), women played a smaller role in the pop universe of the mid-1980s than they had at any time since the late 1950s, so you can see why an enlightened guy like your Birthstar, Robert Palmer, would feel motivated to do something to remedy the situation. What's harder to see, though, is how an enlightened guy like Robert Palmer could think that handing pretend guitars and drums to a group of sultry fembots and soliciting from them the least convincing air-band performance since The Partridge Family was going to *remedy* anything. Just weeks before your birth, the pop-strological firmament had grudgingly admitted Heart to its ranks—the third star in three *decades* to feature a woman playing her own guitar (after Joan Jett and A Taste of Honey). And now, here was your Birthstar trying to build on that small bit of progress with his "wry" commentary on the stereotypical role of women in music videos. Say this much for your Birthstar: in presenting America's girls with a truly laughable image of what they might grow up to be if they chose to pursue rock and roll as a career path, he may have inspired a generation of **fearsome female rebels** whose presence shall soon be made known. Of course, he may also have given rise to a generation of **outwardly classy but**

inwardly leering young men, whose appreciation of their pop-strological sisters will be somewhat twisted.

CONSTELLATIONS
➤ Reaganrock
➤ Britsuasion

BIRTHSONG
➤ *Addicted To Love*
Apr 27–May 3, 1986

PAPER LACE
Don't worry about your ignorance if it helps you follow your bliss.

In America, at least, it's a well-known historical fact that Al Capone was brought to justice not by the uniformed officers of the Chicago Police, but by the bespectacled accountants of the FBI. In England, however, they seem to have gotten Mr. Capone confused with John Dillinger or Bonnie and Clyde, at least to judge from your gloriously catchy but historically dubious Birthsong. *The Night Chicago Died* chronicled a deadly 1930s gun battle between Chicago cops and Al Capone's foot soldiers on the "East Side of Chicago"—a battle that never happened on a side of Chicago which, if it existed, would lie beneath the surface of Lake Michigan. But if your Birthsong failed to go through a rigorous fact-checking process prior to its release, it was probably because the British group Paper Lace was rushing to avoid having another potential American hit stolen from them the way *Billy, Don't*

Be A Hero was just weeks earlier by Bo Donaldson and the Heywoods. And maybe also because historically accurate lyrics about balance-sheet discrepancies would have lacked a certain, well, punch. At any rate, as a popstrological child of Paper Lace, **wading into unfamiliar waters** comes more easily to you than it does to others, for your great gift is to **let your enthusiasm take you places others might fear to go** without thorough preparation.

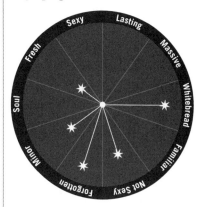

CONSTELLATION
➤ Storyteller

BIRTHSONG
➤ *The Night Chicago Died*
Aug 11–17, 1974

RAY PARKER, JR.
Be wise when choosing your friends, but be wiser when choosing your enemies.

Consciously or not, your Birthstar stole from the wrong guy when he lifted his hit song *Ghostbusters* almost measure for measure from *I Want a New Drug.*

Huey Lewis was no communist—he was the poet laureate of hippies-turned-yuppies and the red-blooded alpha dog of the constellation *Reaganrock*, and he wasn't about to share his intellectual property with some mere *Theme Singer*. There were probably other subsurface issues motivating Mr. Lewis—jealousy, for instance, over *Ghostbusters* being so much more fun and popular than *New Drug*, and also some misdirected self-loathing over Ray Parker, Jr. being an actual black soul singer. Whatever the reasons, Huey sued the daylights out of your Birthstar and forced a significant out-of-court settlement in the case. Based on current U.S. copyright law, the entire eighties oeuvre of Huey Lewis and the News will pass into the public domain sometime around the year 2100, at which time it will become perfectly safe, if you should live that long, to unearth and plunder a pop jewel like *Hip To Be Square*. Legally, anyway. For **who knows what power your sworn enemy might wield** from beyond the grave?

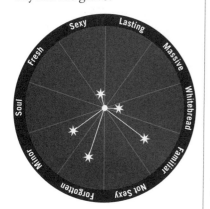

CONSTELLATION
➤ Theme Singer

BIRTHSONG
➤ *Ghostbusters* Aug 5–25, 1984

JOHN PARR
What looks like a moronic inferno to some may still be a blaze of glory for you.

In unsettled weather, a haunting electrical glow can sometimes be seen around elevated objects like the mast of a ship. Ancient Mediterranean sailors regarded the phenomenon as lucky, so they named it after their patron saint, Elmo, but they failed to appreciate the destructive power his "fire" would wield in modern times. It was Saint Elmo's fire, after all, that ignited the airship *Hindenburg* in 1938, and that's not the only flaming gasbag with which it's been associated. For *St. Elmo's Fire* was also the name of the 1985 film that brought together far too many members of the Brat Pack than any single movie ever should have. John Parr thought he'd caught his big break when he was asked to write and perform that movie's theme song, but how could a star as dim as his possibly survive a cinematic conflagration strong enough to launch the career of Demi Moore and prevent any of the thespians Lowe, McCarthy, Sheedy, Nelson, and Estevez from combining their powers again? A more experienced member of the constellation *Theme Singer* like

Kenny Loggins might have known better than to place himself in harm's way, but your Minor and Forgotten Birthstar took the only chance he might ever have gotten, and if he emerged from the experience quite scathed indeed, at least it cannot be said that he shrunk from the challenge. They say **discretion is the better part of valor**, but for the popstrological children of John Parr, discretion **may be a luxury they cannot afford.**

CONSTELLATIONS
➤ Reaganrock
➤ Theme Singer

BIRTHSONG
➤ *St. Elmo's Fire (Man In Motion)* Sep 1–14, 1985

DOLLY PARTON
Style and substance need not be at odds, unless you choose the wrong one to favor.

Popstrology is a science, but it's not rocket science. It takes years of training to become a practicing professional, but anyone with reasonable powers of observation and imagination can read the hidden meaning of the pop stars, as long as he or she can avoid being mesmerized by their outward personas. Your Birthstar presents a significant challenge, though, for few stars in the pop-strological era mesmerized the mortal public as completely as Dolly Parton did with her outward persona. The wigs, the accent, the outfits, and—yes, it must be said—the cleavage established your Birthstar immediately upon her crossover from country as what we call an icon, but what a shame if you were only to understand her that way yourself. There was and is absolutely nothing wrong with the wisecrackin', pop-singin', theme-park-ownin' Dolly Parton who ruled the pop universe at the moment of your birth, but there was a decade of brilliant and restrained country singing and songwriting that preceded that phase in Dolly's life, and it's that tradition to which she's returned in late career. The woman of style and substance who wrote *I Will Always Love You* and recorded a version of that song that actually *improves* with each listen has a wealth of **talent, grace, and understated elegance** to offer those born under her popstrological influence. But it may take a popstrological intervention to rescue those who have taken from their incredible Birthstar only the lesson of her most famous wisecrack: **"It takes a lot of money to look this cheap."**

CONSTELLATIONS
➤ Country Cousins
➤ Invisible Hand
➤ Theme Singer

CELEBRITY
➤ **Paris Hilton** (2/17/81) is a popstrological Dolly Parton.

BIRTHSONG
➤ *9 to 5* Feb 15–21, 1981

THE PARTRIDGE FAMILY
You live in a world others only dream of inhabiting. Too bad it's not real.

To look at *The Partridge Family* today is to realize how far our lip-synching standards have come in just a generation, yet despite some of the least convincing musical fakery in television history, runaways used to show up on Shirley Jones's Beverly Hills lawn in the early 1970s hoping she might adopt them into her television family. And who can blame them? Who *didn't* want to join Mrs. Partridge's misbegotten brood as they drove around the country in a custom-painted school bus performing at various state fairs and all-ages nightclubs? It's difficult to overstate how strongly the c'mon-get-happy allure of *The Partridge Family* tugged at the deepest yearnings of American kids trapped in desperately uncool families. And thanks to the magic of syndication, the myth of the average suburban family moonlighting as overnight pop sensations continues even today to plant itself in the minds of America's youth, creating massive psychological as well as popstrological effects. Yet only at the moment of your birth was the myth made so tantalizingly real, as *I Think I Love You*, another irresistible product of the constellation **Artificial Ingredients**, came to rule the pop universe. The **ability to guide (or misguide) the bored and disaffected** is a powerful gift indeed, but it's **not a power to be trifled with**, lest your too-zealous followers bring their devotion right to your front door.

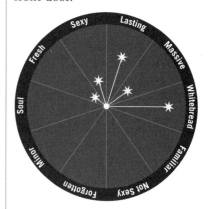

CONSTELLATIONS
➤ Artificial Ingredients
➤ Launching Pad

CELEBRITY
➤ Q-Tip (11/20/70) is a child of the Partridge Family.

BIRTHSONG
➤ *I Think I Love You*
Nov 15–Dec 5, 1970

PAUL AND PAULA
Arm candy is nice, but not if you can't eat it.

Hey, Paula was no masterpiece of songwriting or vocal technique, but like *I Got You Babe* two years later, it captured America's heart because it was performed by real-life lovers whose true romantic devotion could be felt in every note. Which would be lovely, if any of it were true. In fact, the young pair of Texans who sang your Birthsong were really named Jill and Ray, and they never even dated, but the folks at their record label understood a thing or two about marketing, and so the fiction of Paul and Paula was born. But as innocent as this little fib may sound to us today, the tragic aftermath of the Milli Vanilli scandal teaches us that any act of deception powerful enough to launch a star into the constellation *Artificial Ingredients* has the very strong potential to inflict psychic trauma on those it was intended to assist. How else to explain Ray "Paul" Hildebrand's nervous breakdown on the night of your Birthstar's big-time concert debut as part of the "Caravan of Stars"? Tour host Dick Clark himself filled in for one night by singing the "Paul" part alongside Jill "Paula" Jackson, but *"Hey, hey, Dickie"* just didn't have the same ring, and when Hildebrand's popstrological identity crisis failed to pass quickly, your Birthstar's short and deceptive career came abruptly to an end. You've probably already learned that **sham relationships have a way of collapsing** the moment they face a crisis; your challenge now is to let that hard-won knowledge **add no more than the proper dose of realism** to your dreams of storybook romance.

CONSTELLATIONS
➤ Artificial Ingredients
➤ Texstyle

CELEBRITY
➤ **Michael Jordan** (2/17/63) is a child of Paul and Paula.

BIRTHSONG
➤ *Hey, Paula* Feb 3–23, 1963

BILLY PAUL
Thou shalt not covet thy neighbor's wife, unless you really, really love her.

Considering the number of somebody-done-somebody-wrong songs in the history of pop music, it's amazing how few of them have been told from the perspective of the wrongdoer. Songs about the innocent *victims* of sexual infidelity are a dime a dozen in the pop canon, but until Billy Paul did it in 1972, not one star in the popstrological firmament had ever been rewarded with a #1 hit for actually owning up to committing the mortal sin of adultery. But the popstrological significance of your Birthstar may not be exactly what you think, and it's certainly different from that of stars like the Manhattans and Mary McGregor, who followed Billy Paul's confessional example in the years to come. For while *Me And Mrs. Jones* does describe an extramarital affair, it seems to describe one that might just be more genuinely hopeful and fulfilling than either of the relationships it threatens to upset. And while it's very easy for all of us to click our tongues and agree that it's just plain *bad* to be sexually unfaithful, how many of us would have good reason to hesitate before casting the first stone at Billy Paul? Indeed, your Birthstar is regarded by the nonjudgmental science of Popstrology as the patron saint of **potentially great relationships that begin in** inappropriate circumstances. So does this give you some kind of **free pass on philandering**, child of Billy Paul? If you're true to your Birthstar, you already know the answer to that question, and you'll only go **looking for** *true* **love in all the wrong places.**

CONSTELLATION
➤ So-Soul

BIRTHSONG
➤ *Me And Mrs. Jones*
Dec 10–30, 1972

PEACHES AND HERB
Like the true master of the shell game, you manage to mislead without ever displeasing.

The pop-soul duo that is your Birthstar took its supremely catchy name from the childhood nickname of Herb Fame's first partner, Francine "Peaches" Barker, but when a string of modest R&B hits for Peaches and Herb came to an end in the late sixties, Herb dumped Francine and quit the business altogether. When he reemerged in the late seventies, Herb knew he needed a new partner, but he also knew the value of a name. And so Mr. Fame (née Feemster) launched his audacious (and ongoing) Peaches-replacement scheme, quietly installing Linda Greene as the new (but not the final) Peaches. Together, Herbie and Linda (see, it doesn't really work) gave the world the exquisite *Shake Your Groove Thang* and the irresistible *Reunited*, one of the few great songs about *making* up to be found in the pop canon. From their place in the constellation *So-Soul* they bestow upon those born under their star **a warm and sexy grooviness** to balance out that **difficulty with maintaining truly honest relationships.**

CONSTELLATIONS
➤ So-Soul
➤ Hot Hairdo

BIRTHSONG
➤ *Reunited* Apr 29–May 26, 1979

PET SHOP BOYS
All the colors of the rainbow will align themselves behind your flag.

A certain segment of the population felt threatened from the moment they first heard your Birthstar's name. They weren't actually sure what a Pet Shop Boy was, but they were pretty sure they'd want to beat one up if they had the chance. Remember now, this was the summer of 1986 we're talking about. Ronald Reagan was the president, Madonna was just a girly sexpot, and the video for *Addicted To Love* was playing twenty-four hours a day on MTV. True, Tom Cruise's *Top Gun* did top the box office that summer, but believe it or not, people back then actually thought that beach-volleyball epic was about *fighter pilots*! The point is that it wasn't an easy environment for a couple of openly, um, *urbane* fellows to achieve success of popstrological proportions, yet that's exactly what your Birthstar did. Looking back at it now, it seems clear that you were born at a watershed moment in the history of

pop—a moment when the pop-strological closet doors were opened for the first time by men who wore no makeup or feather boas. **An easy acceptance of alternative lifestyles** comes naturally to popstrological Pet Shop Boys, as do strong feelings one way or another for **caustic wits and well-dressed Brits**.

CONSTELLATIONS
➤ Casio
➤ Britsuasion

BIRTHSONG
➤ *West End Girls* May 4–10, 1986

PETER AND GORDON

Money can't buy you love, but love could make you money.

When a young lady named Jane Asher dumped her boyfriend in 1968, it pretty much spelled the end of your Birthstar's brief recording career. Without suggesting that Jane's brother Peter and his childhood mate Gordon were lacking in charm and talent, it must be said that their success as the duo Peter and Gordon owed less to their own gifts than to the cast-off pop songs of Jane's ex-beau Paul and *his* childhood mate John. Yes, *that* Paul and John. You see, Peter and Gordon in their brief hey-day were a sort of outlet for the factory seconds of Lennon and McCartney, offering the world a creditable and successful simula-

tion of the originals until the demise of the Asher-McCartney romance cut off their source of throwaway #1 songs like *World Without Love*. But don't let the story of your *Regifted* Birthstar make you feel lame or inadequate. **Profiting from the genius of others** isn't like depending on the kindness of strangers—indeed, it's simply a mark of the **pragmatic good sense** that is your greatest popstrological inheritance.

CONSTELLATIONS
➤ Regifted
➤ Britvasion

BIRTHSONG
➤ *World Without Love* Jun 21–27, 1964

PETER, PAUL AND MARY

If you had a hammer, you'd sure try to do something socially constructive with it.

Want to bring some joy to the left-leaning, sixty-something white person in your life? Hook him up with

a couple pounds of Fair Trade coffee and a Peter, Paul and Mary CD. Watch the years peel away as he is transported back to a brief moment in the early 1960s when optimism was a viable political outlook and clean-cut collegians with acoustic guitars were the conscience of their generation. Charter members of the message-heavy constellation *Folkie*, even your Birthstar's apolitical offerings like *Puff The Magic Dragon* were subject to misguided countercultural analysis. And though the decade whose ethos they helped to define was nearly over before Peter, Paul and Mary officially joined the popstrological elite, like the other stars in the constellation *Tip of the Iceberg*, their sole #1 hit belies their Massive impact on the pop universe. Just because you're a popstrological child of Peter, Paul and Mary doesn't mean you'll be a **Whitebread, do-gooder liberal**, but liberal or conservative, it's almost certain that **an activist's heart** beats somewhere within you.

BOBBY "BORIS" PICKETT AND THE CRYPT-KICKERS

If you do not choose the path less followed, that doesn't mean it won't choose you.

A lot of kids grow up wishing their parents had cooler jobs than they really do—in a 7-Eleven, say, rather than in some stupid bank. But your Birthstar didn't have that problem, because his father managed the local movie theater, and Bobby Pickett spent every free moment of his early childhood there watching films about zombies, vampires, and creatures from the Black Lagoon. He'd mastered a dead-on Boris Karloff impression by the time he was nine, and though he went to Hollywood years later with dreams of being a movie actor, it was the Karloff shtick and his love of monster movies that ended up making him a star. Bobby and a pal wrote *Monster Mash* in about an hour and recorded it even quicker, and it went on to become the biggest novelty song of all time. To his everlasting credit, your Birthstar embraced his popstrological place in the constellation *Novelty Merchant* with wholehearted glee, and though he never reached #1 again, he became an indispensable mainstay of *The Dr. Demento Show* with gems like *Me And My Mummy*, *Star Drek*, and the unspeakably brilliant *King Kong (The White Man Done You Wrong)*. **Never question the value of your "unmarketable" talents,** child of Bobby Pickett, for they may be **more marketable than you think**.

CONSTELLATION
➤ Novelty Merchant

BIRTHSONG
➤ *Monster Mash* Oct 14–27, 1962

PINK FLOYD

Greatness lies beneath your surface, but you'll have to get off the sofa to unleash it.

A lot of old purists decry the crass commercialization that characterizes popular music today, but is there really any difference between, say, Britney Spears releasing a single on the Pepsi Web site and Pink Floyd's less publicized but equally profitable comarketing arrangement with the American marijuana industry in 1980? Not everyone knows it, but the release of *The Wall*—an album that required a certain blood-saturation of THC the way *House Of Wax* required 3-D glasses—was timed to coincide with a push by Northern California sensimilla growers to expand their market share in the wake of the paraquat fears of a nation previously hooked on Mexican weed. What did your Birthstar get out of the deal besides a huge vote of thanks from their captive—nay, sedentary—audience? They got the pop breakthrough that had eluded them throughout the 1970s despite having their legendary album *The Dark Side Of The Moon* spend seven *years* on the album charts. From their spot in the constellation *Tip of the Iceberg*, your Birthstar imbued you with a **willingness to make late-night snack runs** and **thoughts that are sometimes deeper than mere sequences of words can articulate**.

CONSTELLATIONS
➤ Tip of the Iceberg
➤ Britsuasion

BIRTHSONG
➤ *The Wall* Mar 16–Apr 12, 1980

THE PLATTERS
You are the outsider who dares to try to work your way in.

Their sound was smooth and polished, and though they were black, they were *nonthreatening* black, like the Ink Spots and Mills Brothers before them. And so it was that your Birthstar, the third-ever star to join the pop-strological elite, was drafted into service by anti-Elvis forces of the constellation *Old Guard*. But this was an alliance doomed to end badly for the one and only black group to enter the popstrological firmament in the 1950s—a group that sold millions of records and scored three #1 pop hits and one brilliant near-miss (*The Great Pretender*) between 1956 and 1959. Not even the Platters were immune to the double standards of the day. When the group's four male members were arrested on "morals charges" in August 1959, it shouldn't have been big news, considering that the criminal charges against them were eventually dismissed. But your Birthstar's commercial fate was sealed when the news spread quickly that the girls found working in their Cincinnati hotel room were white. Bookings

suddenly became more difficult, and radio stations began dropping the Platters from their rotations, and though garden-variety infighting and personnel changes helped hasten their eventual fade-out, your once-bright Birthstar offers a clear and important lesson to those born under their influence: while your **willingness to fit in** may take you far, **the more forced the fit, the more tenuous your success.**

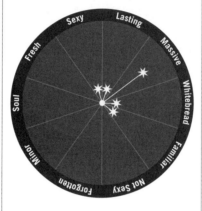

CONSTELLATION
➤ Old Guard

BIRTHSONGS
➤ *My Prayer* Aug 4–17, 1956
➤ *Twilight Time* Apr 21–27, 1958
➤ *Smoke Gets In Your Eyes* Jan 13–Feb 2, 1959

PLAYER
All the world's a stage, but not everyone's a Player.

Go ahead and say it to yourself a couple of times just for the thrill of it: "I'm a Player, I'm a *Player!*" Once you've gotten

that out of your system, though, you'll want to return to the potentially less ego-boosting task of unraveling exactly what this newfound aspect of your identity means. To be a Player in the popstrological sense, after all, bears little relation to being a player (or a "playa," for that matter) in the twenty-first-century colloquial sense. Unless a band that fell as quickly as it rose can in some way be compared to a person who seduces easily and then moves on, or unless the act of sneaking into the constellation *Lite & White* despite a sound that featured as much sultry bass as sweet harmony can somehow be compared to sex-fueled duplicity. But no, this would be far too much of a stretch to make in analyzing a group whose sole #1 hit, *Baby Come Back*, is a plea for romantic reconciliation that belongs squarely in the sensitive-guy section of the popstrological canon. And clearly it's your Birthsong—as well remembered as your Birthstar is Forgotten—that reveals the true essence of popstrological Players, whose **deep-down sweetness may,**

under the right set of circumstances, **pass for deep-seated sexiness**.

CONSTELLATION
▶ Lite & White

BIRTHSONG
▶ *Baby Come Back* Jan 8–28, 1978

POISON
Like a Log Cabin Republican, you're not the type to be bothered by cognitive dissonance.

No one will ever argue that *Unskinny Bop* and *Talk Dirty To Me* belong in the canon of pop's greatest songs, but if you take that as a knock against Poison, then you're missing the point. The fact is that the rise of your Birthstar marked the absolute zenith of eighties hair metal, and eighties hair metal was a cultural force that transcended mere music. Among other things, it filled the critical social function of drawing suburban white kids by the millions into the nation's stadiums and giving them something they could really pump their fists to, and that's something that the constellation *Reaganrock* had never really managed. And if it strikes you as ironic that many of those same kids would have called Boy George a fag just a few years earlier for wearing the same hair and makeup as Poison, then so be it. Because just like you, the fans of eighties hair metal were **perfectly at ease**

with such apparent contradictions—so much so, in fact, that they made treacly power ballads like *Every Rose Has Its Thorn* the genre's biggest hits, and they accepted as hyper-masculine what was essentially a drag act utterly devoid of camp. **Labels will no doubt be applied** to you, child of Poison, but you've got **the power to make them meaningless**.

CONSTELLATION
▶ Tip of the Ice Cube

BIRTHSONG
▶ *Every Rose Has Its Thorn* Dec 18, 1988–Jan 7, 1989

THE POLICE
Plays well with others, sure, but stays well with others? Maybe not.

"**G**ordy" or "Gordo" would have been the obvious choices, but when a childhood friend looked at Gordon Sumner's favorite bumblebee-striped sweater and dropped a vastly jazzier nickname on him

instead, the act had the effect of a lit match on dry wood. In that moment was born one of pop's greatest egos, and in that moment was it foreordained that this "Sting" would one day decide that his destiny did not include mortal bandmates called Stew and Andy. Decide for yourself whether the pop universe is a better place as a result of *Russians* and *Fields Of Gold* than it would have been with another two decades of *Roxanne*s and *So Lonely*s from the Police, but it's all academic anyway. Your Birthstar was a stellar explosion waiting to happen—a star so unstable that the mere fact of selling millions of records and sounding better than 99 percent of its contemporaries was never going to hold it together. A single entry at the top of the charts toward the end of a substantial career places your Birthstar in the constellation *Tip of the Ice Cube*, but it is their place in the constellation *Launching Pad*—that grouping of popstrological left-behinds—that explains why their popstrological children have such a strong **potential to**

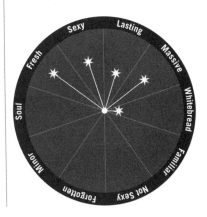

achieve collaborative great-ness, but may face great diffi-culty in making those collabo-rations last.

CONSTELLATIONS
➤ Tip of the Ice Cube
➤ Launching Pad

BIRTHSONG
➤ *Every Breath You Take*
Jul 3–Aug 27, 1983

ELVIS PRESLEY
"When the mode of the music changes, the walls of the city shake."

Plato said that in the first century BC, and two thousand years later, the fear of music's socially destabilizing potential was just as strong. But what was it that made some Americans tremble at the sight and sound of the young Elvis Presley? Was it really the music he was playing and the moves that he was making? Or was it the look in their sons' and daughters' eyes while he was doing it? Could they see even then what these grade-schoolers of 1956 might do to the world as the college students of 1966? For all that's been made of Elvis taking black music and making it safe for white teenagers, the real revolution he led was in taking teenage music and mak-ing it *unsafe* for their parents. They didn't start calling it the generation gap until the mid-1960s, but it's reasonable enough to trace the opening of

that divide to the social impact of the first and still the greatest star the popstrological firma-ment has ever seen. But what about those too young to have joined that particular revolu-tion? What popstrological gifts did the King of Rock and Roll bestow upon the innocent new-borns who entered the world under the rule of one of his *sev-enteen* songs that topped the pop universe for a total of *seventy-nine* weeks? Well, if raw sexu-ality and world-altering charisma are the answers you're hoping for, then you're confus-ing popstrology with genetics, though even genetics evidently can't make one Elvis from the seed of another. No, popstrolog-ically speaking we are as likely to draw from our Birthstars' weaknesses as we are from their strengths, and certainly yours is a star with as many well-docu-mented weaknesses as mind-boggling strengths. So which Elvis are you—a raw and thrilling newcomer, a sweater-wearing conformist, a leather-clad comeback kid, or a bloated and addled has-been? Maybe you've been all of these, or maybe you've been none, but whatever you are, popstrology tells us that it may not be *exactly* what you want or were meant to be, for if there's one thing shared by nearly all of the King's popstrological children, it is a vulnerability to seeing their considerable spirit sucked out of them as they bend themselves to the needs of the Establishment. There are other obvious lessons to

draw from the greatest star who ever walked the earth, but this may be chief among them: a life spark is a terrible thing to waste, and yours really may be one worth saving.

CONSTELLATIONS
➤ Sui Generis
➤ Royal Court
➤ Hot Hairdo
➤ Fresh Breeze
➤ Tragic Demise

CELEBRITIES
➤ Kim Cattrall (8/21/56), Carrie Fisher (10/21/56), Cameron Crowe (7/13/57), Chris Noth (11/13/57), Sharon Stone (3/10/58), Iris DeMent (1/5/61), and Ben Harper (10/28/61) are all popstrological children of Elvis Presley.

BIRTHSONGS
➤ *Heartbreak Hotel*
Apr 21–June 15, 1956
➤ *I Want You, I Need You, I Love You* Jul 28–Aug 3, 1956
➤ *Don't Be Cruel/Hound Dog* Aug 18–Nov 2, 1956
➤ *Love Me Tender* Nov 3–Dec 7, 1956

- ➤ *Too Much* Feb 9–Mar 1, 1957
- ➤ *All Shook Up* Apr 13– Jun 2, 1957
- ➤ *(Let Me Be Your) Teddy Bear* Jul 8– Aug 25, 1957
- ➤ *Jailhouse Rock* Oct 21– Dec 8, 1957
- ➤ *Don't* Feb 10–Mar 16, 1958
- ➤ *Hard Headed Woman* Jul 21–Aug 3, 1958
- ➤ *Big Hunk O' Love* Aug 10–23, 1959
- ➤ *Stuck On You* Apr 25– May 22, 1960
- ➤ *It's Now Or Never* Aug 15– Sep 18, 1960
- ➤ *Are You Lonesome To-night* Nov 28, 1960– Jan 8, 1961
- ➤ *Surrender* Mar 20–Apr 2, 1961
- ➤ *Good Luck Charm* Apr 15–28, 1962
- ➤ *Suspicious Minds* Oct 26–Nov 1, 1969

BILLY PRESTON

What others achieve through privilege, you achieve through merit.

Playing the organ in church behind the visiting gospel legend Mahalia Jackson got him noticed at the age of ten by the producers of the movie *St. Louis Blues*, and playing the young blues legend W. C. Handy in that movie got him noticed by the legendary Sam Cooke. Being taken by Cooke six years later to tour England along with the legendary Little Richard got him noticed by an up-and-coming group of future legends called the Beatles, who would cross his path again seven years later when George Harrison bumped into him at a concert by the legendary Ray Charles, who had taken Preston under his wing and brought him back on tour to England after hearing him sing *Georgia On My Mind* during a sound check on the set of *Shindig* in 1965. Those who only know the Billy Preston story from that point forward—the story of how an unknown twenty-two-year-old American organ player received equal billing with the Beatles on *Get Back* and then launched a solo career on the Beatles' own Apple label—can be forgiven for looking at your Birthstar's career and thinking, "It's good to have friends in high places." But the full story of Billy Preston's overnight success, which took the better part of two decades to achieve, points fairly clearly to gifts much greater than a knack for making good connections. The **potential to succeed through the help of well-placed friends** is a

popstrological gift you share with all of your fellow Billy Prestons, but **the skill and talent to realize that potential** is up to you to develop.

CONSTELLATION
- ➤ So-Soul

BIRTHSONGS
- ➤ *Will It Go Round In Circles* Jul 1–14, 1973
- ➤ *Nothing From Nothing* Oct 13–19, 1974

JOHNNY PRESTON
You are the star that falls so that others might rise.

Three rising stars lost their lives on the Day the Music Died, but the impact of that famous plane crash created popstrological reverberations that affected many others. Don McLean, Bobby Vee, and Los Lobos all owe their places in the popstrological firmament to the deaths of Buddy Holly and Ritchie Valens, but the death of passenger number three—J. P. Richardson, aka "the Big Bopper"—made possible the career of one musical giant and ended the career of another. Your Birthstar was the young protégé of Jape Richardson, who wrote *Running Bear* for him after hearing him sing in an East Texas nightclub. It's easy to sense the presence of the man behind *Chantilly Lace* in the big, rolling piano licks of your Birthsong, a truly irresistible piece of culturally insensitive old-time rock and roll. And perhaps there would have been more hits just like it for the *Regifted* Preston if his mentor hadn't developed a nasty cold in early February of 1959. Ritchie Valens earned his way onto that ill-fated flight by winning a coin toss with Buddy Holly's drummer, Tommy Allsup, but the sniffly Big Bopper got his seat by playing on the sympathies of Buddy Holly's bassist, a young man named Waylon Jennings. So yes, your Birthstar remains a Minor and nearly Forgotten star in the constellation *Storyteller* because of the events of February 3, 1959, but his career died so that country music's original outlaw might live, and that's how he bestowed upon you an ability—though not necessarily an eagerness—to **make personal sacrifices in the interest of the common good.**

CONSTELLATIONS
➤ Regifted
➤ Storyteller
➤ Texstyle

CELEBRITY
➤ **Greg Louganis** (1/29/60), **James Spader** (2/7/60), and

Robert Smigel (2/7/60) are all Johnny Prestons.

BIRTHSONG
➤ *Running Bear* Jan 12–Feb 1, 1960

LLOYD PRICE
You are the real deal who avoids the raw deal.

Dick Clark made Lloyd Price re-record it with a different set of lyrics before he'd air it on *American Bandstand*, but Dick Clark couldn't keep the unexpurgated version of *Stagger Lee* from becoming the first unapologetically black-sounding #1 hit by a black artist in the popstrological era. The raw, stomping New Orleans sound of your Birthsong was phenomenally Fresh and exciting to pop audiences who'd done little swimming outside the lily-white mainstream, but even more exciting was the notion of a pop song showing the nerve to cheer its homicidal protagonist on with a chorus of background singers shouting, "*Go, Stagger Lee! Go, Stagger Lee!*" There are whole books you can read about the significance of the Stagger Lee (or Stack-O-Lee or Stagolee) story in African American culture, but they will illuminate only part of your Birthsong's significance. For *Stagger Lee* firmly established a crucial popstrological trend by being the second story-song ending in death to emanate from the constellation *Storyteller*. *Tom Dooley* came before your Birthsong, but *Battle*

Of New Orleans, El Paso, Running Bear, Teen Angel, Big Bad John, Ringo, Ode To Billie Joe, I Shot The Sheriff, Papa Was A Rolling Stone, The Night The Lights Went Out in Georgia, and *Billy, Don't Be A Hero* all came after. **Situations may sometimes conspire to keep you down,** child of Lloyd Price, but **stick to your guns,** and success will follow.

CONSTELLATIONS
➤ Storyteller
➤ Fresh Breeze

CELEBRITY
➤ **Kyle MacLachlan** (2/22/59) is a popstrological Lloyd Price.

BIRTHSONG
➤ *Stagger Lee* Feb 9–Mar 8, 1959

PRINCE
You are the sum of many parts, none of them compliant.

Prince Rogers Nelson was born in June of 1958 under the reign of—we kid you not—the song *Purple People Eater,* and it's safe to say that few human beings have fulfilled their popstrological destiny quite as literally as he has. But long before he was even known as the Purple One, and long before he consumed, in his Princely fashion, such popstrological hotties as Martika, Sheena Easton, and Susanna Hoffs, your Birthstar devoured, digested, and assimilated the music, moves, and images of three men whose popstrological absence he would avenge by proxy: James Brown, Little Richard, and Jimi Hendrix. Crafting his own unique style from the raw material of theirs, Prince acted as champion for those missing giants, and brought them in spirit to the popstrological firmament when he earned the first of his four #1 hits in the popstrological era. Perhaps your Birthstar would have earned many more in the years that followed had he not become embroiled in the business battle that saw him forsake his very name and adopt as his moniker a glyph representing the words "F*ck you, Warner Brothers" in his obscure royal language. But once a crusader for justice, always

a crusader for justice, and it is your popstrological gift and curse to be unafraid of crusades. **You serve no master but your own conscience**, child of Prince, but your **tendency to see almost everything as a matter of conscience** may truly make you its slave.

CONSTELLATIONS
➤ Sui Generis
➤ Royal Court
➤ So-Soul
➤ Invisible Hand

CELEBRITY
➤ **Avril Lavigne** (9/27/84) is a popstrological child of Prince.

BIRTHSONGS
➤ *When Doves Cry* Jul 1– Aug 4, 1984
➤ *Let's Go Crazy* Sep 23– Oct 6, 1984
➤ *Kiss* Apr 13–26, 1986
➤ *Batdance* Jul 30–Aug 5, 1989

QUEEN
In a land of apples and bananas, you are the rare strange fruit who gains acceptance.

No foreign country has given our pop universe one-tenth as much popstrological mass as Great Britain has, but what may seem at first to be merely a consequence of speaking the same language must be something more, or we'd see a lot more Canadians among the popstrological elite, wouldn't we? What

Americans get from the Brits, and what we realize on some level we *need* from the Brits, is a regular dose of strangeness in the form of pop stars our own culture would have snuffed out before they ever had a chance to shine. How else to explain the American embrace of a group like Queen, a band that operated in more ways than one well outside the boundaries of what American bands of their era were allowed to be? Ask yourself this: if an American band circa 1976 were to have tried practicing *Bohemian Rhapsody* or *Bicycle Race* in their suburban garage, how long would it have taken before the neighbors came round with pitchforks? Even Queen were forced to play it relatively straight with *Crazy Little Thing Called Love* and *Another One Bites The Dust* in order to gain entry into the popstrological firmament, but how long would they have waited in vain had their entire career not been made understandable to Americans with the simple description, "Well, they're English"? **Flamboyant excess and unbridled eccentricity** may or may

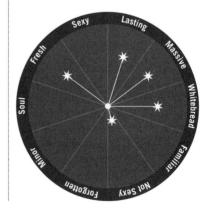

not be things your Birthstar passed on to you, but an ability to **prosper in foreign territory** and to **use your heritage to open doors** probably are.

CONSTELLATIONS
➤ Sui Generis
➤ Britsuasion

CELEBRITIES
➤ **Chelsea Clinton** (2/27/80) and **Ashanti** (10/13/80) are popstrological Queens.

BIRTHSONGS
➤ *Crazy Little Thing Called Love* Feb 17–Mar 15, 1980
➤ *Another One Bites The Dust* Sep 28–Oct 18, 1980

EDDIE RABBITT
You are the clever carpetbagger with the ability to pass for a local.

Immigrants to some cultures can take a lifetime to adapt to unfamiliar surroundings—years to master not just a new idiom, but also the deeply embedded codes that govern social conduct. But some cultures are easier to crack than others, and so it was that an enterprising kid from East Orange, New Jersey, managed to parlay smarts, talent, and a tailor-made real name into a promising country-music career just a few short months after packing up and heading south to Nashville. The secrets to his success? A subtle, affected twang in the voice, of course; a great-looking beard; and a quick mastery of country subject matter and song titling.

Working My Way Up To The Bottom was his first Nashville effort, and Elvis's *Kentucky Rain* was his first professional success. Then came *Every Which Way But Loose* and *Drivin' My Life Away*, both of them pop crossover hits that paved the way for the infectious *I Love A Rainy Night* and Eddie Rabbitt's entry into the popstrological elite in a highly unlikely pair of constellations: ***Country Cousins*** and ***Jersey Pride***. If the world knew the full truth of your origins, child of Eddie Rabbitt, you might be branded a phony, but there's precious little chance they'll ever see through **your well-rehearsed and frankly irresistible act**.

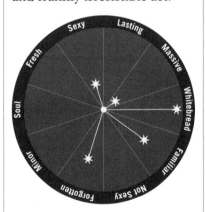

CONSTELLATIONS
➤ Jersey Pride
➤ Country Cousins

CELEBRITY
➤ **Josh Groban** (2/27/81) is an Eddie Rabbitt.

BIRTHSONG
➤ *I Love A Rainy Night* Feb 22–Mar 7, 1981

THE (YOUNG) RASCALS
Be careful what label you wish for, because you might just get it.

The last thing the Rascals wanted to be called was the "Young" Rascals, but the threat of a lawsuit by a prominent harmonica band forced the name change on them, so they put on knee britches and newsboy caps and made the best of it. But they also made it their single-minded mission to rid themselves of the infantilizing adjective, and perhaps that's what fueled their considerable success. Nineteen sixty-six was a banner year for the constellation ***Fresh Breeze***, but none of the stars who joined it that year was any Fresher, popstrologically speaking, than the then–Young Rascals. *Good Lovin'* was a cover song, but the energy your Birthstar brought to it made theirs the definitive version, and you would be hard-pressed to find more exuberant and soulful songs by a white American band of the sixties than *Groovin'* and *People Got to Be Free*. But you remember what it was like when all you wanted out of life was to stop being a kid, or at least to stop being seen as one, don't you? The Rascals got their wish in 1967, but perhaps they shouldn't have been in such a hurry to grow up. Grown-up ego clashes tore them apart fairly shortly after they reclaimed their grown-up name, and even three decades later, one of the Rascals couldn't even bring himself to stand on the same side of the stage as the other three when all four were inducted into the Rock and Roll Hall of Fame. **Retaining your connections to childhood innocence** may be the best path for you, child of the (Young) Rascals, because **adulthood, as you know, isn't all it's cracked up to be.**

CONSTELLATION
➤ Fresh Breeze

CELEBRITIES
➤ **Will Ferrell** (7/16/67), and **Dweezil Zappa** (9/5/68) are popstrological Rascals.

BIRTHSONGS
➤ *Good Lovin'* Apr 24–30, 1966
➤ *Groovin'* May 14–27 and Jun 11–24, 1967
➤ *People Got To Be Free* Aug 11–Sep 14, 1968

READY FOR THE WORLD
Some are born to lead, but you may have been born to follow.

In medals, sashes, and cummerbunds, they looked like Swedish diplomats at a state dinner, but with Jeri curls. But if their look was something original, their sound certainly wasn't. It was Prince who broke the ground and sowed the seeds of the funky musical style your Birthstar worked in at the time of your birth, and it was Prince protégés like the Time and Sheila E. who reaped the biggest rewards from what he had sown. Within this farming metaphor, Ready for the World were more like gleaners—the people who used to go through an already-harvested field to extract the last bit of food value before it was plowed under. Not that they sounded bad—far from it. It's just that your Birthstar's sound was of a moment that was about to pass, and they were quite unready for the world to tire of it. They made one run at a comeback in the early nineties with new outfits and new hairstyles in the mode of New Jack Swing, but even the brilliantly titled *Yo! That's A Lot Of Body* failed to find much of an audience. They called themselves Ready for the World, and insofar as they sounded exactly like something the world had already shown itself ready for, they were absolutely right. But if you were born under their influence, do not fail to heed their popstrological lesson:

Originality is not the only path to success, but **the path to success has a finite amount of room for loyal followers.**

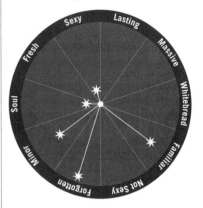

CONSTELLATION
➤ Hot Hairdo

BIRTHSONG
➤ *Oh Sheila!* Oct 6–12, 1985

OTIS REDDING
He went out at the top, leaving you with nowhere to go but down.

You were born under the influence of the first posthumous #1 hit in the popstrological era, though you are not alone among the popstrological orphans born in 1968. Jim Morrison and Marvin Gaye are both dead, after all, as are half the Beatles, but there's something especially poignant about a star whose *Tragic Demise* came before his popstrological children were even born. The plane crash that killed the great Otis Redding came just as his career was taking off, and for those born under his influence, the tragedy of his death isn't just that it came before he could achieve his full measure of greatness, but that it came before anyone could *question* his greatness. It was the white counterculture crowd, in particular, who adopted Otis Redding into their pantheon following his legendary performance at the Monterey Pop Festival, and that's a crowd that tends to its icons with a jealous zeal. Which is not to say that your Birthstar didn't deserve extreme admiration for recording one brilliant #1 hit, *(Sittin' On) The Dock Of The Bay*, and writing another, *Respect*, in a very short career. But admiration and constructing an unquestioning cult of perfection are two very different things, and when Otis Redding's fans chose the latter course, they unwittingly bestowed upon his popstrological children a **propensity for setting unrealistic expectations** to go along with their **gift of very nearly being able to meet them**.

CONSTELLATIONS
➤ Tragic Demise
➤ Invisible Hand
➤ Tip of the Ice Cube

BIRTHSONG
➤ *(Sittin' On) The Dock Of The Bay* Mar 10–Apr 6, 1968

HELEN REDDY
When you were just an embryo, women still had a long way to go.

Nothing in her personal or professional credentials suggested Helen Reddy as a feminist icon prior to 1972, but in that year she launched that movement's loudest salvo in the form of *I Am Woman*, a strident anthem of personal empowerment that took the women's-lib message out of the pages of *Ms.* and put it out where it could do some real consciousness-raising—on the AM airwaves. Some would say that the struggle for gender equity in the 1970s is a subject better suited to sociology than to Popstrology, but if you want to understand the false consciousness that the first-wave feminists were talking about, what better place to start than by looking at the songs they were raised on—the *Johnny Angel*s, the *It's My Party*s, and the *Will You Love Me Tomorrow*s? Yes, even the *female* stars of the early popstrological era were guilty of supporting the patriarchal power structures that worked to keep their sisters down, but your Birthstar put an end to all that, proving in the process that what pop hath wrought, pop, too, can put asunder. Cheering feminine strength (*I Am Woman*) and battling feminine illusions (*Delta Dawn* and *Angie Baby*), your Birthstar's popstrological legacy gives the women born under her influence **little excuse for falling into gender-stereotyped traps** and the men born under her influ-

ence **a healthy fear of setting them**.

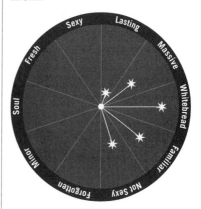

CONSTELLATIONS
➤ Outback
➤ Storyteller

BIRTHSONGS
➤ *I Am Woman* Dec 3–9, 1972
➤ *Delta Dawn* Sep 9–15, 1973
➤ *Angie Baby* Dec 22–28, 1974

REO SPEEDWAGON
For a seat at the table, would you sing for your supper?

Was it the natural result of creative evolution, or did REO Speedwagon cut a secret deal with the transition team of President-elect Ronald Reagan? We may not ever know the truth, but what we do know is this: (1) Just a few short weeks after the inauguration of our fortieth president, your Birthstar unveiled an awesome new weapon not previously seen in their arsenal—the power ballad; and (2) the launch of *Keep On Lovin' You* against the civilian population caught almost everyone by surprise, though it was not recognized until many months later as the first strike in a popstrological war against all things raw and thrilling. The role of the new administration in the whole affair remains unclear, but what *is* clear is that the rise of REO Speedwagon marked the rise of the new and Massively powerful constellation *Reaganrock*. While retaining aesthetic signifiers of rebellion like leather jackets and long male hairstyles, the *Reaganrockers* eschewed anything that was truly risky or threatening, and in doing so, they set an example that much of the U.S. population would follow throughout the 1980s. Are all popstrological children of REO Speedwagon willing to **reinvent themselves in the interest of profit**? Not necessarily, but nearly all will find their principles **surprisingly flexible when the lure of power is dangled** before them.

CONSTELLATION
➤ Reaganrock

BIRTHSONGS
➤ *Keep On Lovin' You*
Mar 15–21, 1981

➤ *Can't Fight This Feeling*
Mar 3–23, 1985

PAUL REVERE AND THE RAIDERS
You will not join clever conversations as often as your silly hats will start them.

It's only natural with the passage of time, but still it's sad to watch groups like your Birthstar fade from popular memory with each year of distance we gain on the 1960s. Oldies radio has done its part to keep the truth alive, but the millions of Americans who get their history from television would have a hard time believing that a party band in goofy Revolutionary War outfits not only flourished in the era of the Beatles and the Stones, but was more successful than almost every American male pop group of the late 1960s. How big were Paul Revere and the Raiders? Big enough to play themselves on an episode of *Batman*, that's how big. Dick Clark launched them by making them the house band on *Where the Action Is*, and hits like *Kicks* and *Just Like Me* made them famous, but it was a late-career change of pace that earned them their popstrological stripes. There was no precedent in the Raiders' upbeat catalog for the didactic and hokey *Indian Reservation (The Lament Of The Cherokee Reservation Indian)*, but one can hardly be surprised that your Birthsong was a hit. Heartfelt and grossly condescending white guilt, after all, was

as powerful an organizing principle in the lives of some baby boomers as was rock and roll itself, and the combination of the two was almost impossible to resist in 1971. **Sophisticated appeal is not a description that comes to mind** when one thinks of your Birthstar, but blessedly, **you're probably not the type to be bothered by that**.

CONSTELLATIONS
➤ Thanks, Dick
➤ Had to Be There
➤ Tip of the Ice Cube

BIRTHSONG
➤ *Indian Reservation*
Jul 18–24, 1971

DEBBIE REYNOLDS
When life gives you lemons, you make fresh, pink lemonade in a lovely glass pitcher.

Ask Carrie Fisher and she'll tell you that her mother always was a more complicated woman than *Singin' In The Rain* or *Tammy And The Bachelor* (the source of your Birthsong) would suggest. Back in 1957, though, baby Carrie was just an infant, and Debbie Reynolds the woman was totally inseparable in the public's mind from Debbie Reynolds the Hollywood persona. She was America's favorite girl-next-door—talented, funny, and adorable onscreen, and blessed with a *perfect* life offscreen. One only wishes that she had been a country singer/songwriter so that the striking *imperfection* of her life in ensuing years might have been chronicled in song. Who wouldn't have wanted to hear Debbie Reynolds apply the caustic wit she revealed in late-career movie roles to songs about losing husband Eddie Fisher to Elizabeth Taylor, or about hubbies two and three both leaving her nearly bankrupt? Alas, tunes like *Violet Jezebel* and *Mamas, Don't Let Your Babies Grow Up To Be Deadbeats* can exist only in our imagination, for you Birthstar let her singing career fall by the wayside after briefly ruling the pop universe at the moment of your birth and bestowing upon you a remarkable **ability to keep up appearances** even **when your world is crumbling** around you.

CONSTELLATIONS
➤ Old Guard
➤ Theme Singer
➤ Texstyle

CELEBRITY
➤ **Gloria Estefan** (9/1/57) and **Ethan Coen** (9/21/57) are popstrological children of Debbie Reynolds.

BIRTHSONG
➤ *Tammy* Aug 26–Sep 8 and Sep 16–22, 1957

RHYTHM HERITAGE

You're not the type to reinvent the wheel—you're the type to invent it in the first place.

Some people discount your Birthstar's dramatic 1976 achievement because others were so close to making a similar breakthrough at the very same time. But if Marconi and the Wright brothers can be called the inventors of radio and the airplane after barely beating their competition to the punch, then surely Rhythm Heritage deserve to be hailed as heroes for becoming the first star to join the popstrological elite by taking an existing catchy tune and "discofying" it. Yes, discofication was a technology waiting to explode in the mid-1970s, as the imminent arrival of Walter Murphy (*A Fifth Of Beethoven*) and Meco (*Star Wars Theme*) would attest. But the first time anyone successfully tapped into its awesome power was when producer Steve Barri

convened a group of studio musicians to record a dance version of the theme from his son's favorite TV show, *S.W.A.T.* Actual musicians (some of them future popstrological stars) may have participated in making your Birthsong, but don't let that confuse you: your Birthstar is not a band so much as a symbol—a symbol of the power of ideas and of the pioneers who give them tangible expression. Will **humankind's next generation of great achievers** be stocked with popstrological children of Rhythm Heritage? It wouldn't be surprising, given their **rapid response to great ideas** and the **strategic weapons** at their disposal.

CONSTELLATIONS
➤ Speechless
➤ Disco Ball
➤ Theme Singer

BIRTHSONG
➤ *Theme From "S.W.A.T."* Feb 22–28, 1976

CHARLIE RICH

They may love you, but they'll never understand you.

The man voted Entertainer of the Year for 1974 by the Country Music Association of America stood onstage at the 1975 CMA awards to announce that year's winner, but a funny thing happened when he opened the envelope and saw what was written inside. Instead of merely reading the name John Denver and stepping back from the podium, Charlie Rich reached into his pocket for a light and set the envelope on fire, right there onstage. Many observers thought your Birthstar had finally come unhinged, but those who knew him well saw his act for what it was: a somewhat **socially jarring yet undeniably principled stand against phoniness** by a man whose inner struggles and **powers of introspection** taught him that genuine pain and turmoil could never be cured by a mere dose of sunshine on down-vested shoulders. In a thirty-five-year career that ran from the rockabilly genius of *Lonely Weekends* to the countrypolitan splendor of *Behind Closed Doors*, the Soulful popstrological ***Shape-Shifter*** called the Silver Fox earned eleven #1 hits on the country charts and one crossover smash in your Birthsong, *The Most Beautiful Girl*. **Pleasing almost any audience** is hardly a challenge for the popstrological children of Charlie Rich, but remaining composed when their **invisible buttons get pushed** may very well be.

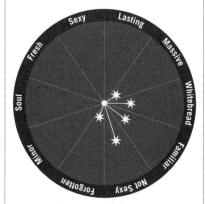

CONSTELLATIONS
➤ Shape-Shifter
➤ Country Cousins

BIRTHSONG
➤ ***The Most Beautiful Girl In The World*** Dec 9–22, 1973

LIONEL RICHIE

For you the excitement begins when the thrill is gone.

Lionel Richie had a dream, and it wasn't just to control his own musical destiny—it was to contribute to the establishment of a whole new popstrological reality. He tried to follow the progressive model at first, hoping to reinvent his former group, the Commodores, by introducing ballads like *Truly* and *Three Times A Lady* into their *Brick House*–dominated mix. But when the Commodores watched Lionel Richie engineer the rise of the white-and-mighty Kenny Rogers with *Lady* in 1980, they encouraged him to seek his bliss elsewhere, perhaps out of fear for where his increasing powers might lead them. And once freed from the tether of the Commodores, Lionel Richie did indeed see his awesome dream become reality as his patented brand of sweeping, Whitebread balladry fueled the rise of the mighty constellation *Reaganrock* and became, arguably, the defining sound of the 1980s. **Some people work within the system** to bring about change, while **others must strike out along a maverick's path** to see their revolutionary visions fulfilled. And if your Birthstar's lesson tells you anything besides which category you're best suited to, it should be that **even a dream of calm and moderation can spark a dramatic revolution.**

CONSTELLATIONS
➤ Spin-Off
➤ Reaganrock
➤ Invisible Hand
➤ Theme Singer

THE RIGHTEOUS BROTHERS

If you can't be in the skin you love, make them love the skin you're in.

B anish from your memory, if you can, the image and sound of Dionne Warwick, Hall and Oates, or Maverick and Goose singing *You've Lost That Lovin' Feelin'.* For if one black woman and two pairs of white guys can be called pale reflections of another pair of white guys, then that's exactly what those pretenders were in relation to your Birthstar, the Righteous Brothers. Bill Medley and Bobby Hatfield weren't actually brothers in either sense of the word, though they eagerly adopted their new name after some actual African Americans paid them what any blue-eyed soulsters would naturally regard as the ultimate compliment. And no one could dispute that they sounded righteous, though it must be said that their second-biggest hit, *(You're My) Soul And Inspiration*, did little more than rehash the unique vocal sound and Spector-produced splendor of their first. Nevertheless, this Lasting star in the constellation *Fresh Breeze* still stands as the most popstrologically Soulful group ever to emerge from Orange County, California, bestowing upon you an ability to **craft something Fresh from the blandest of ingredients** and to **defy all labels and expectations** in pursuit of your chosen people's approval.

CONSTELLATION
- ➤ Fresh Breeze

CELEBRITY
- ➤ **Robin Wright Penn** (4/8/66) is a Righteous Brother.

BIRTHSONGS
- ➤ *You've Lost That Lovin' Feelin'* Jan 31–Feb 13, 1965
- ➤ *(You're My) Soul And Inspiration* Apr 3–23, 1966

JEANNIE C. RILEY

"Judge not . . . " is your credo, except when it comes to yourself.

W hen your Birthstar said "men," it came out "min," and when she said "eyes," it came out "ahs." In New York or L.A., the accent might have been as big an impediment as Eliza Doolittle's Cockney lilt, but in Nashville, Tennessee, it was her ticket to pop immortality. Never in pop history has one voice been more right for one song than Jeannie C. Riley's was for *Harper Valley P.T.A.,* a crypto-feminist tale of a small-town Southern widow's defense of short skirts and f*ck-me pumps as appropriate parent/teacher-night attire. Yet rarely, too, in pop history has one star proven so uncomfortable with the song that was her bread and butter. America wanted to believe that your Birthstar really *was* the Hester Prynne–meets–Daisy Duke protagonist of *HVPTA,* and for a time she seemed willing to indulge the misconception and dress the part. Eventually, though, she sided with the meddling, small-town values her sole #1 hit derided and became, rather publicly, a born-again Christian. Jeannie's abdication did open up the role of *HVPTA*'s merry widow for the willing and fabulous Barbara Eden in the 1980 made-for-TV movie, but it also bestowed upon those born

under your Birthstar's influence with a **tendency to second-guess** themselves and a **willingness to leave behind** the source of their original popularity.

CONSTELLATIONS
➤ Storyteller
➤ Texstyle
➤ Country Cousins

CELEBRITY
➤ **Ricki Lake** (9/21/68) is a child of Jeannie C. Riley.

BIRTHSONG
➤ *Harper Valley P.T.A.* Sep 15–21, 1968

MINNIE RIPERTON
You are the honey bun whose sweetness will seem saccharine to some.

Detractors would probably cite its cloying lyrics, or the way that pressure builds inside your eyeballs when Minnie Riperton hits her ultrasonic high notes, but the *real* reason people make such wicked fun of your Birthsong, *Lovin' You*, is fear. That's right, fear over what might happen if they allowed even the *tiniest* amount of your Birthstar's guileless sincerity to penetrate their hard, hipster shells. Fear that they might suffer the same fate as Minnie's good friend Stevie Wonder, who fell so completely under her spell while producing *Lovin' You* that he actually put the sound of chirping birds in the background of the entire record. Not that Stevie

needed all that much pushing to go in that direction, but still, the impact of your Birthstar on Stevie Wonder and his post-1979 output (think: *I Just Called To Say I Love You*) is difficult to ignore, even if it doesn't compare to the direct Soul-sucking influence of Paul McCartney and *Ebony And Ivory*. Minnie Riperton died of cancer in 1979 at the age of 32, and while placement in the constellation *Tragic Demise* alone does not grant a popstrological star some kind of free pass on negative analysis, the Snow White of soul and her **sometimes grating but always well-meaning** progeny **deserve better in life** than to be derided by smart*ss hipsters.

CONSTELLATION
➤ Tragic Demise

BIRTHSONG
➤ *Lovin' You* Mar 30–Apr 5, 1975

JOHNNY RIVERS
Others make a fetish of freshness while you focus on tasty, reheated leftovers.

Perhaps you will look at the title of your Birthsong and say, "Never heard of it," but you surely wouldn't say the same thing about Johnny Rivers's other top-40 hits, like *Maybellene, Midnight Special, Baby I Need Your Lovin', The Tracks of My Tears*, and *Blue Suede Shoes*. For indeed, these are songs from the sound track of our lives—songs that helped shape the pop universe as we know it and songs that will be remembered for generations to come as being . . . sung by other people. No, your Birthstar isn't the man who made those famous songs famous, but he is a man who crafted a long and not-insignificant pop career out of recording cover versions of famous songs that sometimes sold as much and charted as high as the originals. If Johnny Rivers hadn't written his sole #1 hit himself, and if he hadn't been the first to record the song for which he's best known, *Secret Agent Man*, he might reside among the well-supported stars of the constellation *Regifted*. Instead, he is a member of the constellation *Tip of the Ice Cube*—a star whose sole #1 hit only hints at a sizable (though not truly Massive) career and who bestows upon you and others born under his influence a gift that may actually exceed the value of true artistic talent in our modern age:

an ability to **achieve success based more on good taste than on originality**.

CONSTELLATION
➤ Tip of the Ice Cube

BIRTHSONG
➤ *Poor Side Of Town* Nov 6–12, 1966

MARTY ROBBINS
The Italians say a good friend is easier to find than a good enemy. Well, maybe for them.

Your Birthsong, *El Paso*, is a simple story of frontier justice—of a Texas cowboy who guns down a perceived romantic rival, then dies at the hands of an avenging posse before he can reunite with his lovely señorita. But if you are inclined to look past the surface of things, it would not be unreasonable to read Marty Robbins's signature song as an allegorical fantasy in which he himself is the victim of the initial murder and the pop star Guy Mitchell is the cold-blooded cowboy who dies in a righteous hail of bullets. Why, you ask, would your NASCAR-

driving, *Grand Ol' Opry*–starring, country-music-legend of a Birthstar possibly bear a sublimated homicidal grudge against the tuxedo-clad stiff behind *Singing The Blues*? Because that song was originally recorded by Marty Robbins, and it was just beginning to climb the charts when his labelmate, Mitchell, talked Columbia Records into letting him record a competing version. Guy Mitchell's blander-than-bland version ended up eclipsing your Birthstar's and ruling the pop universe of 1956 for nine straight weeks. Though twice denied entry into the pop-strological firmament by Mitchell (who pulled the *exact same move* on Robbins again in 1957 with *Knee Deep In The Blues*), it was Marty Robbins who had the brighter career in the long run, which should serve to remind his **never-forgive, never-forget** progeny that while there's **nothing wrong with playing a fantasy vigilante**, the best revenge is always to live well, especially if you manage to **live better than your enemies**.

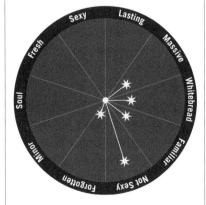

CONSTELLATIONS
➤ Country Cousins
➤ Storyteller
➤ Texstyle

CELEBRITIES
➤ **Michael Stipe** (1/4/60) and **Stanley Tucci** (1/11/60) are children of Marty Robbins.

BIRTHSONG
➤ *El Paso* Jan 4–17, 1960

SMOKEY ROBINSON AND THE MIRACLES
Corporate structures aren't for everyone, but they may be just right for you.

The term "company man" has always carried a strongly negative connotation, as if total devotion to a commercial enterprise necessarily required sacrificing one's individuality and freedom of thought, or even selling one's soul. But as generally defensible as that assumption might be, if ever one man defied it, it was Smokey Robinson, the heart and soul of your Birthstar and a big part of the reason they called Berry Gordy's business empire the "the Motown family." Was he a company man? He was the *quintessential* company man. Smokey hooked up with Berry Gordy before there even was a Motown or Tamla label, he married one of his own Miracles in 1963, and he named his kids Berry and Tamla. But along the way, he may have done more than any single person to create the early sound of the constellation *Hitsville* by writing *My Guy* for Mary Wells and *My Girl* for the Temptations and by writing, producing, and recording Miracles' hits like *Shop Around*, *You've Really Got A Hold On Me*, *I Second That Emotion*, *The Tracks Of My Tears*, and *Ooo Baby Baby*. **You may sometimes feel like a cog in the machine**, child of Smokey Robinson and the Miracles, but if the world needs your machine, then **the world needs big, strong cogs like you**.

CONSTELLATIONS
➤ Hitsville
➤ Tip of the Iceberg
➤ Launching Pad
➤ Invisible Hand

CELEBRITIES
➤ **DMX** (12/18/70) and **Tyson Beckford** (12/19/70) are children of Smokey Robinson and the Miracles.

BIRTHSONG
➤ *Tears Of A Clown* Dec 6–19, 1970

JIMMIE RODGERS
You look straight ahead and you try to act normal, but for some reason it never works.

To be perfectly honest, even popstrologists find it difficult at times to explain the strange and powerful influence of the pop stars. Take Jimmie Rodgers, for instance. What is it about him, or about his folkabilly classic, *Honeycomb*, that could possibly have provoked two officers of the Los Angeles Police Department to inflict a grievous head injury upon him after a routine traffic stop in 1967? If you prefer to accept the official police line that your Birthstar simply "fell," then fine. You can just go on about your life believing that you are the popstrological child of a mild and unproblematic star, Minor even in his time and Forgotten in our own. But if you harbor any nagging doubts about the good intentions of the LAPD, then perhaps you've discovered a way into exploring that little **"attitude problem"** you've struggled with through the years. As admirers of those who challenge

entrenched power structures, we hope that you will **continue to question authority** in your own special way. As responsible popstrologists, however, we hope that you will also **drive safely and obey the local traffic laws**, particularly when visiting the greater Los Angeles area.

CONSTELLATION
➤ Folkie

BIRTHSONG
➤ *Honeycomb* Sep 30–Oct 13, 1957

TOMMY ROE
When you've been paid by the hour, you appreciate the value of a dollar and the dangers of downtime.

By 1962, twenty-year-old Tommy Roe had given up his rock and roll dreams and taken a job soldering wires in an Atlanta GE plant. Then one day he got the call he'd only dreamt about from ABC/Universal, telling him that *Sheila*, a record he'd made fully two years earlier, was suddenly flying up the charts. "You gotta get on the road right now and promote this record!" they told him. "Gee, I'm sorry, sir, but I'm making seventy dollars a week here at the plant now, and that's pretty good mon—" "How's five grand cash up front grab you, kid? Kid?" "Uh, I'll go get my guitar." Tommy followed the money on that fateful day, and he never really stopped thereafter. The Buddy Holly-esque *Sheila* was the single that made him, but that sound soon gave way to the wildly successful yet critically reviled bubblegum pop of follow-up hits like *Jam Up And Jelly Tight* and his second #1, *Dizzy.* As a popstrological child of Tommy Roe, your success may also depend on your willingness to **follow the market wherever it may lead** and your clear-eyed ability to **appreciate a safety net without becoming trapped in it.**

CONSTELLATION
➤ Neither/Nor

BIRTHSONGS
➤ *Sheila* Aug 26–Sep 8, 1962
➤ *Dizzy* Mar 9–Apr 5, 1969

KENNY ROGERS
Say what you will for the flower of youth, but it's the late bloomer whose perfume is the sweetest.

He began his musical career in R&B in the late 1950s, then shifted to folk in the mid-sixties and even psychedelia in the late sixties. Finally, with few options remaining, he moved into country, and that's when he finally hit pay dirt. First came *Lucille* and *The Gambler,* and then came *Lady,* the crossover smash that resulted from a strategic (some would say *unholy*) alliance with Lionel Richie. Suddenly all that talent and persistence had paid off, making Kenny a pop star of truly Massive proportions. But let's be honest: it wasn't the music so much as the pure, unadulterated sex appeal of Kenny Rogers that made him the popstrological giant that he was. It didn't matter whether he was dressed in a Stetson hat and leather duster or in a snug three-piece suit with open-collar shirt—Kenny's impeccable hair and beard brought the whole look together. Prematurely gray like the "before" shot in a Just For Men ad, Kenny Rogers was the Sexiest Unskinny Middle-Aged White Man Alive for three years running in the early eighties, when his gravelly voice sent shivers through millions of women of a certain age. Living proof that **white-hot sexiness comes in all shapes and sizes,** your Birthstar bestows upon you a **quiet animal magnetism** that may be lost on many, but that

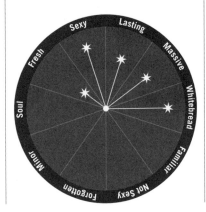

someone, somewhere, will appreciate in time.

CONSTELLATIONS
➤ Country Cousins
➤ Lite & White
➤ Hot Hairdo
➤ Texstyle

CELEBRITY
➤ **Christina Aguilera** (12/18/80) is a child of Kenny Rogers.

BIRTHSONG
➤ *Lady* Nov 9–Dec 20, 1980

KENNY ROGERS AND DOLLY PARTON
Like a grand-slam breakfast, you are not made for dainty appetites.

That the mighty Kenny Rogers and Dolly Parton had the potential to shine as bright in partnership as any star in the constellation *Power Couple* was obvious. What was less certain was whether Kenny could control himself long enough in a recording session with Dolly to emerge as a bull rather than a steer. One can easily imagine the scene: "Awww now, Kenny, c'mon, let's keep our hands to ourselves. Let's try and stay focused here, okay? All right now, let's take it from the t— *Kenny . . .* KENNY!" Once safely captured on tape, *Islands In The Stream* barreled its way to the top of the charts, confirming through its awesome power that the dynamic duo of

Country Cousins that formed your Birthstar might have ruled the whole pop universe if they'd really wanted to. But the alliance of the era's two most outsize sex symbols proved to be the last appearance either would make on the popstrological stage, and as if that weren't enough, the moment of your birth was given further significance by falling under the last of *fifteen* #1 songs written by the popstrological giant Barry Gibb. **Great achievements** by the popstrological children of Kenny Rogers and Dolly Parton, may frequently **come at the end of an era**. But if you let that sad fact dampen your **desire to grab the brass ring**, you'll give up your chance of getting it and dishonor your popstrological legacy, too.

CONSTELLATIONS
➤ Power Couple
➤ Country Cousins

BIRTHSONG
➤ *Islands In The Stream*
Oct 23–Nov 5, 1983

THE ROLLING STONES

"We are young men. We are not concerned with your petty morals."

When Keith Richards spoke those words in a London court appearance on drug charges in 1967, he may well have been speaking his mind, but he was also quoting his band's unofficial corporate motto. The Rolling Stones were the "bad boys" of the British Invasion, as we all know, but if you've always assumed that this was a label attached to them because of their bad-boy behavior, you've got it nearly backward. Long before Altamont, long before Brian Jones's "death by misadventure," long before their highly publicized brushes with the law, and long before being banned and unbanned from *The Ed Sullivan Show*, the Rolling Stones adopted the bad-boy label as part of a conscious and clever marketing strategy. It was the Stones' first manager, Andrew Loog Oldham, who came up with the brilliant "Would you let your daughter marry a Rolling Stone?" campaign that was used to differentiate your Birthstar from, while cleverly linking it to, the better-known Beatles long before most Americans had even heard of either group. In fairness, though, it's not as if it was Herman's Hermits that Oldham was trying to cast as menaces to polite society. Mick, Keith, and especially Brian had both the talent and natural inclination to live up to

the expectations their publicity created, but without the license to misbehave granted to them by their own brand identity, who knows what they'd have become? They later called themselves "the world's greatest rock-and-roll band," and fifteen years of mostly brilliant music in a forty-plus-year career sets a pretty high mark for any band to meet if they wish to claim that label for themselves. Many bands have surpassed your Birthstar in the bad-behavior department, on the other hand, but then the Stones never tried to claim sole ownership of that label. They were, however, the first significant pop star to embrace the label rather than try to live it down, and therein lies the central element of their popstrological legacy to you. You are no more likely than anyone else to **build your reputation on naughtiness or decadence**, child of the Rolling Stones, but whatever reputation it is that you set out to build, you have an inborn ability to **stay on message** and **meet or surpass the high expectations you set for yourself**.

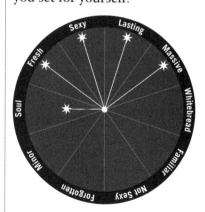

CONSTELLATIONS
➤ Britvasion
➤ Fresh Breeze

CELEBRITIES
➤ **Jack Black** (8/28/69), **Edward Norton** (8/18/69), **Christian Slater** (8/18/69), **Matthew Perry** (8/19/69), **Mark Wahlberg** (6/5/71), and **Noah Wyle** (6/4/71) are Rolling Stones.

BIRTHSONGS
➤ *(I Can't Get No) Satisfaction* Jul 4–31, 1965
➤ *Get Off My Cloud* Oct 31–Nov 13, 1965
➤ *Paint It Black* Jun 5–18, 1966
➤ *Ruby Tuesday* Feb 26–Mar 4, 1967
➤ *Honky Tonk Women* Aug 17–Sep 13, 1969
➤ *Brown Sugar* May 23–Jun 5, 1971
➤ *Angie* Oct 14–20, 1973
➤ *Miss You* Jul 30–Aug 5, 1978

LINDA RONSTADT
Once you earn your following, it's likely to follow you wherever you may go.

In places like Laurel Canyon and Mill Valley, there are pockets of holdovers living a lifestyle virtually untouched by time—a lifestyle they first adopted during Linda Ronstadt's heyday as the popstrological queen of early-seventies California rock. For the most part, though, the distinctive elements of their material culture—the faded denim and peasant blouses, the white wine and doobies—were absorbed into the left-hand side of the American mainstream as their fellow West Coast baby boomers evolved along with your Birthstar rather than remaining culturally frozen in the time of her first flourishing. And where did those evolutions lead Linda Ronstadt and the members of her natural fan base? From Hank Williams to Elvis Costello, and from Gilbert and Sullivan to Cole Porter and traditional Spanish *canciones*. If she had never made a record after 1974, your Birthstar would still be regarded as a popstrologically defining force of the 1970s simply for being the first to put Don Henley and Glenn Frey together in a recording studio. But as important as gestating the Eagles was to the future of the pop universe, leading a significant chunk of her generation on an eclectic journey out of youth and into middle age as tasteful musical grazers in the NPR/PBS mold may be Linda Ronstadt's most significant contribution to modern culture. As *Shape-Shifter*s go, your Birthstar was among the most consistently shifty, and she bestowed upon you a similar **ability to flourish in unlikely territory even after the bloom of youth has left you**.

CONSTELLATIONS
➤ Tip of the Ice Cube
➤ Shape-Shifter

BIRTHSONG
➤ *You're No Good* Feb 9–15, 1975

THE ROOFTOP SINGERS
Give a hungry man a fish, and you feed him for a day. Give him lots of fish, and you feed him for lots of days.

For white kids in coffeehouses from Berkeley to Cambridge, *Blowin' In The Wind* was the anthem of the civil rights movement, and *Walk Right In* was a silly pop song by a group whose name didn't deserve to be spoken in the same breath as Bob Dylan's. But to a certain seventy-nine-year-old man living in an unheated shack beside the railroad tracks in Memphis, the song that accomplished more direct, nonviolent action by far was your Birthsong. Gus Cannon, you see, was the former honky-tonk singer who wrote *Walk Right In* back in 1930, and when the Rooftop Singers unearthed and re-recorded it in 1963, they not only earned themselves a #1 hit and a place in the constellation *Folkie*, but they also earned Gus

Cannon a nice stream of royalties and a wave of recognition that got him his own recording contract. *Walk Right In* proved to be your Birthstar's only moment in the popstrological spotlight, but though its perky harmonies and jangly twelve-strings didn't sound much like protest folk, there are no specific instances in recorded pop history of a genuine protest song getting an old man's heat turned on and his banjo out of hock. Many people profess or strive to think globally and act locally, but Rooftop Singers like **you understand that local action will be effective and appreciated** pretty much regardless of what you're thinking about.

CONSTELLATION
➤ Folkie

BIRTHSONG
➤ *Walk Right In* Jan 20–Feb 2, 1963

DAVID ROSE
What others accomplish with bump-and-grind, you accomplish with smoke and mirrors.

Certain pieces of music become so indispensable to humanity that it is almost impossible to imagine existing without them. Without the theme from *Rocky*, what would you hum to yourself as you jogged on winter mornings? Without the themes from *The Twilight Zone* or *Psycho*, how would you indicate feelings of spookiness or jokey homicidal rage? And without your Birthsong, what would you sing as your loved one executed a clumsy but endearing striptease at bedtime? You may not be the one in a thousand adults of your age who actually looks good undressed, but your popstrological gift of **at least *feeling* smashingly good** in the act of undressing is much to be admired. Which is not to say that your popstrological legacy stops right there. No indeed, for the popstrological children of David Rose have seemingly limitless layers to reveal, tending, for instance to hold strong feelings for the work of both Judy Garland (one of David Rose's wives) and Michael Landon (whose *three* smash television series all featured prominent David Rose scores). But certainly the most admirable trait of those born under this critically important star in the constellation *Speechless* is that gift with the razzle-dazzle—that peerless

ability to satisfy their audience while always **leaving something to the imagination**.

CONSTELLATION
➤ Speechless

CELEBRITY
➤ **Tom Cruise** (7/3/62) is a child of David Rose.

BIRTHSONG
➤ *The Stripper* Jul 1–7, 1962

ROSE ROYCE
Odesmobile may be more like it, for you.

The record industry is notorious for its voodoo economics, so it wouldn't be surprising if your working-class Birthstar came out owing their record label 2.3¢ for each copy they sold of their hit single, *Car Wash*. It certainly wouldn't have surprised the members of Rose Royce, eight men and one woman who'd been working in the unglamorous trenches of the music business for many years before taking their brief turn in the spotlight. Highly accomplished road and session musicians with hard-earned, cool-ass nicknames like "Powerpack" and "Captain Cold," the members of your Birthstar were brought together and given their name by the legendary songwriter Norman Whitfield. Whitfield also gave them their ticket to pop immortality, in the form of the theme song from *Car Wash*, a trenchant cinematic exploration of 1970s ghetto life as seen through the knowing eyes of screenwriter Joel Schumacher (future director of *St. Elmo's Fire*). Rose Royce may never have repeated the booty-shaking success of their debut single, but you can be sure that they never stopped working, and as your Birthstar would be quick to remind you, there are fates in life **much worse than not being rich**, and paths to happiness that really do **begin with digging a ditch**.

CONSTELLATIONS
➤ Theme Singer
➤ Shaking Booty

BIRTHSONG
➤ *Car Wash* Jan 23–29, 1977

DIANA ROSS
When lightning starts shooting from your fingers, it may be time to leave the prom.

Was it really fair to accuse Diana Ross of stealing the spotlight from her fellow Supremes when the effect she has on spotlights is so clearly beyond her conscious control? Shoving the microphone away from Mary Wilson's face during an onstage reunion attempt in 1983? Okay, *that* was the conscious act of an unreconstructed diva, as was attempting a Supremes "reunion" tour seventeen years later alongside two women she'd never even met. But becoming a megastar in the first place—a star who reduced her former equals to "and the" status before leaving them adrift in the popstrological void as she single-handedly launched the brand-new constellation *Spin-Off*? As you can see in the earliest film clips of the Supremes onstage, *that* was simply inevitable. But what about you? As the popstrological child of Diana Ross, are you **destined to leave a trail of wreckage behind you** as you charge your way over life's highest mountains and through its deepest valleys? Not necessarily, though if you were brutally honest with yourself, you might see a **distinct pattern of self-ism** in many of your endeavors. And even if it gets you where you're heading in the end, be aware of your tendency to **leave some-**thing good behind in your never-ending **quest for something great**.

CONSTELLATIONS
➤ Hitsville
➤ Spin-Off

CELEBRITIES
➤ **Kelly Ripa** (10/2/70), **Ani Difranco** (9/23/70), and **Dean Ween** (9/25/70) are popstrological Diana Rosses.

BIRTHSONGS
➤ *Ain't No Mountain High Enough* Sep 13–Oct 3, 1970
➤ *Touch Me In The Morning* Aug 12–18, 1973
➤ *Theme From Mahogany (Do You Know Where You're Going To)* Jan 18–24, 1976
➤ *Love Hangover* May 23–Jun 5, 1976
➤ *Upside Down* Aug 31–Sep 27, 1980

DIANA ROSS AND LIONEL RICHIE

Your parts alone are greater than the sum of many wholes.

Prior to the emergence of the star known as Sinatra-Sinatra in 1967, the dynamics of a pop-strological power-coupling were understood only in theory, and even after the close observation of Streisand-Diamond (1978) and Streisand-Summer (1979), some popstrologists doubted whether the universe would ever see a truly explosive example of the phenomenon. Their doubts were laid permanently to rest in the year of your birth, when your Massive Birthstar took its place in the constellation *Power Couple*. The film *Endless Love* was the last and, it must be said, artistically the weakest installment in the underage–Brooke Shields soft-core trilogy. Yet thanks in very large part to a theme song that ruled the pop universe for nine solid weeks, it earned $33 million at the box office, and that lesson was not lost on executives in the music and movie industries. But the pop universe itself was also changed as a result of the experience, as the predictions of theoretical popstrologists were borne out in your Birthstar's incredibly massive yield. As the child of the first new star composed of two constellation *Spin-Off* members, staying satisfied in **long-term relationships may prove to be your greatest challenge**, but if popstrology tell us anything, it is that short-lived or not, **the relationships you do form are likely to be powerful**.

CONSTELLATIONS
➤ Power Couple
➤ Royal Court
➤ Spin-Off
➤ Theme Singer

CELEBRITIES
➤ **Beyoncé Knowles** (9/4/81) and **Nicole Richie** (9/21/81) are children of Diana Ross and Lionel Richie.

BIRTHSONG
➤ *Endless Love* Aug 9–Oct 10, 1981

ROXETTE

No mistake could compare with forgetting that mistakes are how we learn.

If you've ever traveled in Asia, you may have seen the street vendors who sell T-shirts printed with off-kilter English phrases like "Cool Patrol" and "Sport Team World Is Good!" You sort of know what they're getting at, but then again, maybe you don't. It's the same feeling you get from listening to the hits of your Birthstar, Roxette—hits packed with such lines as *"Her lovin' is a wild dog!"*; *"She's the heart of the fun-fair!"*; and *"She's tellin' all her secrets, IN A WONDERFUL BALLOON!"* From a purely musical perspective, it would be fair enough to say forget about the lyrics, since it was really their bright pop hooks and pleasant good looks that launched your adorable Swedish Birthstar into the constellation *Eurosomething*. But Roxette's lyrics are the key to understanding their powerful legacy to you. For while their lyrics were often beyond understanding for native speakers of the English language, Roxette were so confident and enthusiastic singing their cheery nonsense that no one really cared whether any of it made sense. And confidence, or the lack thereof, is indeed the ruling issue in the lives of popstrological Roxettes, whose best selves will always be found when they set aside their **fear of looking or sounding ridiculous** and give the world a chance to **love them despite their imperfections**.

RUBY AND THE ROMANTICS

A rose by any other name would smell as sweet, unless, perhaps, it had a name like "sh*tcake."

At the height of the dot-com madness in the late 1990s, *Saturday Night Live* ran a parody ad for a savings bank whose Web address was www.clownpenis.com, "because all the other names were taken." Perhaps everyone in America could laugh at the joke other than Ruby and the surviving Romantics. Back in 1963, you see, your Birthstar had been forced to adopt their name just as their first record was being readied for release, because a group with the same name as their old one had managed to crack the bottom of the charts just a few months earlier. So it was that *Our Day Will Come* went out under the newly contrived name Ruby and the Romantics, which sounded absolutely fine to the millions who enjoyed your groovy bossa nova Birthsong but never stopped sounding like "clownpenis" to the members of a group that had been called "the Supremes" just a few weeks earlier. If you could go back in time to 1962 Detroit and convince Berry Gordy to let Diana, Flo, and Mary to continue on as the Primettes, perhaps things might have worked out differently for your Minor and Forgotten Birthstar, but failing that, Popstrology suggests that in career-related matters, you **protect your good name** by **acting quickly before others steal your thunder.**

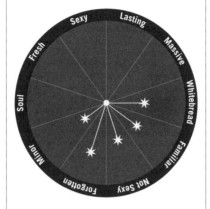

STAFF SERGEANT BARRY SADLER

Many will salute the courage of your convictions, but others will raise their hand in a very different gesture.

You didn't have to like the Vietnam War back in 1966 to dislike those self-righteous college kids with their peace signs and their *Blowin' In The Wind*. But if you *were* inclined toward either feeling, then you were going to *love* Staff Sergeant Barry Sadler and the phenomenally successful record that became the great anti-antiwar anthem of the 1960s. But warmongers and reactionaries were really just a small portion of your Birthstar's fan base, being outnumbered many times over by preteen boys who cared more about baseball cards than they did about politics and who still thought it might be cool to be a real army guy like the one who sang *The Ballad Of The Green Berets*. That's right, your Birthstar was a real soldier—a special forces combat veteran on active duty whose popstrological rise into the constellation **Had to Be There** began when a punji-stick sent him home from Vietnam. And had things gone better for the United States in Vietnam, who knows how much bigger your Birthstar might have become? As it was, though, Sergeant Sadler's views quickly became popstrologically untenable, and he returned, apparently, to performing the kind of hits he originally trained for. Your Birthstar may have bestowed upon you **the courage to stand by**

your values regardless of their **popularity**, but as the shadowy circumstances under which he was shot through the head while training Contras in Reagan-era Guatemala attest, **the price of unpopularity is greater in some contexts** than it is in others.

CONSTELLATIONS
➤ Had to Be There
➤ Hot Hairdo
➤ Tragic Demise

CELEBRITIES
➤ Tone-Lōc (3/3/66) and **Edie Brickell** (3/10/66) are children of Staff Sergeant Barry Sadler.

BIRTHSONG
➤ *The Ballad Of The Green Berets* Feb 27–Apr 2, 1966

KYU SAKAMOTO
You are like the elegant songbird stuffed in a pigeon-hole.

Domenico Modugno's *Volaré* retained its original Italian name (*Nel Blu Dipinto Di Blu*) in its subtitle, and the title of Bert Kaempfert's *Wonderland By Night* was a direct translation from the original German. Yet when Kyu Sakamoto's lovely Japanese ballad was released in the United States, his label didn't call it *Ue O Muite Aruko* or *I Look Up When I Walk*—they called it *Sukiyaki*. *Newsweek* compared it at the time to releasing *Moon River* in Japan with the title *Beef Stew*, but that's a bit of a gloss, isn't it? The reason *Wonderland By Night* wasn't

called *Der Wienerschnitzel*, and *Volaré* wasn't called *Spicy Meatball* was that offensive stereotypes of white Europeans became unfashionable in polite society far earlier than stereotypes of Asians did. Imagine *Georgia On My Mind* rechristened *Fried Chicken On My Mind* and you come closer to the spirit of what the powers-that-be did to Kyu Sakamoto, yet even this jaw-dropping act of cultural bias couldn't keep his great tune down. *Sukiyaki* propelled your Birthstar to his unique place as the only Asian member of the popstrological elite, and its melody resurfaced years later in both A Taste of Honey's English-language *Sukiyaki* and Slick Rick and Doug E. Fresh's *La-Di-Da-Di*. If people's **tendency to exoticize the new and unfamiliar** is in some way related to your personal or professional success, take care to ensure that your success is not undone by their **tendency to homogenize**, which may be even greater.

CONSTELLATION
➤ Tragic Demise

CELEBRITY
➤ **Johnny Depp** (6/9/63) is a child of Kyu Sakamoto.

BIRTHSONG
➤ *Sukiyaki* Jun 9–29, 1963

SANTO AND JOHNNY
You needn't speak a word to cause a lot of action.

Johnny Farina fell in love with the steel guitar listening to the radio as a kid, and after teaching himself to play it, he taught his older brother Santo the standard electric guitar so he'd have someone to play with. But the steel guitar was an instrument you heard only in country and Hawaiian music in the early 1950s, and demand for those two genres was uncertain at best in Santo and Johnny's native Brooklyn. If there was one thing your Birthstar needed in order to achieve popstrological viability, it was a way to fit their talents to rock and roll, and luckily for them, if there was one thing rock and roll needed, it was a way to take over the business of providing slow-dance music at high school sock hops from the Pat Boones of the world. Enter the rock-and-roll ballad, a musical form that met both of these needs. It would not be unreasonable to call your Birthsong, *Sleep Walk*, the greatest instrumental rock-and-roll ballad of all time, and because the Platters (*I Only Have Eyes For You*) belong officially to the constellation **Old Guard**, it is entirely reasonable, popstrologically speaking, to credit your Minor and Forgotten Birthstar with putting rock and roll in the frottage business. **Your moment in the sun may be brief**, child of Santo and Johnny, but **the joy that moment creates for others may be impossible to overstate**.

CONSTELLATIONS
➤ Speechless
➤ Gene Pool
➤ Outerborough
➤ Fresh Breeze

CELEBRITY
➤ **Jason Alexander** (9/23/59) and **Shaun Cassidy** (9/27/59) are children of Santo and Johnny.

BIRTHSONG
➤ *Sleep Walk* Sep 21–Oct 4, 1959

LEO SAYER
The journey of a thousand hugs begins with a single cuddle.

His given name was Gerard, and the nickname "Leo" was granted in honor of his generous mane, not his demeanor. For if your Birthstar was a lion, he was the snuggly stuffed lion you buy at the airport for your four-year-old niece. He was listed officially at five-four and 110 pounds soaking wet, but those figures belie his stature as a pop star in his native England. Over there, he'd enjoyed a successful pop career since his early-seventies days as a glam-rocker in full French-mime makeup. Over here, though, where that look runs afoul of a deep national aesthetic bias, Leo Sayer seemed to appear as if from nowhere in 1976 as a tiny, falsetto-singing oddity with the largest white-man Afro, proportionally, that Americans had ever seen. In truth, though, your Birthstar did cut a rather striking though not exactly Sexy figure with his stunning head of hair and his cute way of walking in four-inch platform shoes. If Kenny Rogers had sung *When I Need You*, the forty-something ladies in the audience might have fallen at his feet, but when your Birthstar did it, they yearned instead to hold him in their laps. And if that legacy explains your lifelong effort to **cultivate a persona more mysterious and alluring than cute and cuddly**,

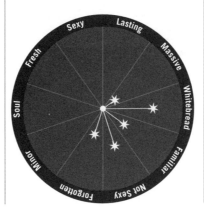

it would hardly be surprising. Never lose sight, though, of the fact that **good things come in all packages**, and that adhering to the **tyrannical standards of the mighty** is not the only road to success and happiness.

CONSTELLATION
➤ Hot Hairdo

BIRTHSONGS
➤ *You Make Me Feel Like Dancing* Jan 9–15, 1977
➤ *When I Need You* May 8–14, 1977

JOHN SEBASTIAN
You sing your own song with feeling, and you let your audience make of it what they will.

"Grown-up city kid returns to the tough neighborhood of his youth to tackle the biggest challenge of his life: teaching the kind of kids *he* was in high school." That was the premise for which your Birthstar was asked to write a theme song, and that's exactly what he did. John Sebastian—Lovin' Spoonful *Spin-Off* and hippie legend of Woodstock fame—wrote a sweet and playfully nostalgic tune about finding your true calling in a life you left behind. How could he have known that the writers of *Welcome Back, Kotter* would quickly change their show from a seriocomic fish-returns-to-water tale to a flimsy platform for catchphrase-spouting caricatures? Horshack's "Oooh, oooh, oooh," Washington's "Hi therrre,"

Barbarino's "What? What?" and "Up your nose with a rubber hose" were the pop-cultural coin-of-the-realm in 1976, and though they bore little relation in tone or spirit to the show your Birthsong seemed to describe, the disconnect did nothing to hinder the popularity of all things Kotter-related. If you weren't wearing an Uncle Sam T-shirt in the summer of '76, you were probably wearing one with the Sweathogs on it, and if you weren't humming the ridiculously good theme songs from *Rockford Files* or *Sanford and Son*, you were surely humming *Welcome Back*. **You may not control what becomes of your creations** once they leave your own hands, but being at ease with that fact may be the key to your success.

CONSTELLATIONS
➤ Spin-Off
➤ Theme Singer

BIRTHSONG
➤ *Welcome Back* May 2–8, 1976

NEIL SEDAKA
Talent, perseverance, and connections—the holy trinity of showbiz longevity—are your keys to success.

He began his career in lockstep with his high school sweetheart, Carole King, another nice, piano-playing Jewish kid from Brooklyn who could crank out catchy tunes in her sleep. Neil Sedaka landed a songwriting gig at Don Kirshner's Aldon Publishing, where he toiled alongside Carole and other Brill Building legends. But Neil broke out early from the constellation *Invisible Hand* by recording his own material, scoring his first #1 hit in 1962, then watching his successful career go cold and stay cold for more than a decade in the wake of the British Invasion. By 1975, however, the teenage fans who ate up his *Calendar Girl* and *Breaking Up Is Hard To Do* were the thirty-something adults behind the rise of the constellation *Lite & White*, a revolutionary force in the pop universe. Sedaka launched his massive comeback

from this softest of constellations with his hit ballad *Laughter In The Rain* and as the cowriter of the spectacular *Love Will Keep Us Together* for the über-Lite and über-White Captain and Tennille. Like your Birthstar, you too have the potential to **survive long dry spells by working hard and rolling with the punches**.

CONSTELLATIONS
➤ Outerborough
➤ Invisible Hand
➤ Lite & White

CELEBRITY
➤ **Sean Lennon** (10/9/75) is a popstrological child of Neil Sedaka.

BIRTHSONGS
➤ *Breaking Up Is Hard To Do* Aug 5–18, 1962
➤ *Laughter In The Rain* Jan 26–Feb 1, 1975
➤ *Bad Blood* Oct 5–25, 1975

BOB SEGER
You'd probably never sell your soul, but you can't control it once you've lent it.

His credentials in the world of blue-collar rock and roll are unassailable, so what is it that earned the Springsteen of Michigan a spot in the constellation of Richard Marx and Billy Ocean? It wasn't softness and polish, but rather a trait shared by many late-career entrants into the constellation *Reaganrock*: a willingness to compromise principles that once seemed rock-hard. Is it ironic that a song about that very topic is what cemented Bob Seger's *Reaganrock* status when it became the centerpiece of what may be the longest-running ad campaign in modern history? Maybe a little, but the tens of millions of Americans who know *Like A Rock* only as a song about pickup trucks have no idea that it's really a middle-aged man's lament over his compromised principles, and the admen who convinced Seger to bend his iron-clad no-endorsements rule knew that they wouldn't. The leader of the Silver Bullet Band turned down untold millions of sponsorship dollars from the folks who make Coors Lite, and when he gave his music to Chevrolet, he did so in the hopes that it might bolster the economic mainstay of his native Detroit. An honorable and principled move, certainly, but one that cemented the popstrological fate of a man whom the constellation **Reaganrock** had been hoping to claim ever since *Old Time Rock & Roll* became linked to the image of a Princeton-bound Tom Cruise in Ray-Bans and Jockey shorts. **You**

may not choose to feed the machine, child of Bob Seger, **but that doesn't mean that you won't be chosen to.**

CONSTELLATIONS
➤ Reaganrock
➤ Tip of the Ice Cube

BIRTHSONG
➤ *Shakedown* Jul 26–Aug 1, 1987

MICHAEL SEMBELLO

Some are born to stand in the spotlight, but you may be born to stand just outside it.

I t's not enough to be enormously talented—you also have to be willing to abandon your ego entirely if you want a career as a top-notch studio musician. And it's the extreme rarity of these two traits in combination that explains why the same handful of names crops up again and again on the credits of your favorite pop albums from any given era. But the qualities that make a great session instrumentalist can make it extremely difficult to break out of that role, or to leave a distinctive mark on the world when you do, which is why Michael Sembello found it so difficult to get his own record deal after fifteen years of deploying his guitar (and his songwriting) talents in support of Stevie Wonder, Michael Jackson, and Diana Ross, among others. It's also why he remained a virtual unknown even after scoring an enormous smash hit with

Maniac, arguably the rightful theme song from the movie *Flashdance*. Indeed, though his name may be more recognizable than that of the Jennifer Beals body double whose maniacal jackhammer thighs gave your Birthsong its motif, it was anonymous toil that got him his shot, and anonymous toil to which he returned after briefly making it. **Quiet accomplishment and the respect of your peers** are nothing to turn your nose up at, children of Michael Sembello, but **if it's the top of the marquee you're shooting for**, you'll have to ignore **your genius at filling the supporting role**.

CONSTELLATIONS
➤ Theme Singer
➤ Invisible Hand

BIRTHSONG
➤ *Maniac* Sep 4–17, 1983

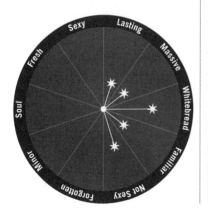

DAVID SEVILLE

You are the tinkerer whose tinkerings may encourage others to experiment.

What disco did for cocaine and the Beatles did for acid, your Birthstar did for helium, the true and timeless gateway drug for thrill-seeking American youth. How many young baby boomers began their substance-seeking ways while striving to simulate the *"walla walla bing bing"*'s of David Seville's *Witch Doctor* or the *"Me, I want a hula-hoop"*'s of his later creation, the Chipmunks? It's impossible to say. What is known is that while many kids had experimented with the noble gas at birthday parties prior to your Birthstar's rise, millions of these casual users did not develop serious habits until the former Ross Bagdasarian harnessed the hilarity-inducing power of a 45 rpm record played at 78 and brought it within the grasp of the recording arts and sciences. But the smash hit *Witch Doctor* was an event of more than just technological and sociological significance; it was also a popstrological milestone, for it brought into being the powerful constellation *Novelty Merchant*, a critical source of both silliness and strangeness in the years and decades to come. **Setters of trends** and **pushers of product** are frequently found among the popstrological children of your Birthstar, as are **natural jokers and stone-faced seriosos** who

lie at opposite ends of the spectrum in which your Birthstar made his living.

CONSTELLATION
➤ Novelty Merchant

BIRTHSONG
➤ *Witch Doctor* Apr 28–May 11, 1958

THE SHANGRI-LAS

You are the one who brings home to Mother the type one doesn't bring home to Mother.

For the girls who dreamed of wedding bells and soldier boys, there were the Dixie Cups and the Shirelles, but for the girls who dreamed of screeching tires and doomed-but-gorgeous gang leaders, there were the Shangri-Las. Their public image evoked Capri pants, white lipstick, and snapping gum, but while calling your Birthstar the girl group for bad girls would be right in spirit, it would be wrong in fact. After all, this quartet of good girls (two sets of sisters from the same Queens high school) were in the record business, and who do you think

buys more records—bad girls, or good girls with richly melodramatic fantasy lives and tangled psychosexual longings? So perfectly tailored to this latter audience segment was your Birthsong, *Leader Of The Pack*, that at the moment of your birth, millions of good girls the world over were entertaining morbid fantasies of glamorous teen widowhood and sad-hearted bad boys—of facing the question "Where's Jimmy?" and answering, "He's dead, Betty—tragically, handsomely *dead.*" If you've managed in life to make excellent and responsible decisions in the arena of romance, thank someone other than your Birthstar, for their strongest legacy to you, besides a gift for melodrama, is an **ability to overrule your better judgment** when matters of passion are in play.

CONSTELLATIONS
➤ Gene Pool
➤ Les Girls
➤ Underage
➤ Outerborough
➤ Hot Hairdo

BIRTHSONG
➤ *The Leader Of The Pack* Nov 22–28, 1964

DEL SHANNON
You are drawn to the light because it makes the darkness visible.

If you ever studied music, you learned that a minor chord is separated from a major chord in the same key by just one note, but no one ever needed to teach you what a huge difference that one note makes. It's programmed somewhere deep in our brainstems to experience a minor chord as a sign of distress, and to yearn with every fiber of our existence for the resolution of that distress in the shift to a sunny major chord. Your Birthstar's brain stem, though, may have been programmed a little differently. Legend has it that Del Shannon stopped his band midsong one night at the Hi-Lo Lounge in Battle Creek, Michigan, to have his organ player repeat over and over, to the audience's dismay, an ad-libbed sequence of minor chords. By the next night, Shannon (*née* Charles Westover) had written *Runaway* around that sequence, and his popstrological arrival in the constellation *Fresh Breeze* was assured. Yet as incredible as your Birthsong is, it's also emotionally draining in its way, especially considering the shakiness of its optimism when the minor chords of the verse resolve into the *wah-wah-wah-wah wuh-hun-der*s of the major-chord chorus. But perhaps this is our best insight into the emotional problems that Del Shannon treated for so long with alcohol before turning to the miracle of SSRIs

and adding his star to the constellation *Tragic Demise* by committing suicide while on Prozac in 1990. If the **sun feels nicest to you when it's disappearing behind dark clouds,** thank your Birthstar, and **stick to nature** if you try to change it.

CONSTELLATIONS
➤ Fresh Breeze
➤ Tragic Demise

CELEBRITIES
➤ **George Clooney** (5/6/61) and **Ving Rhames** (5/12/61) are Del Shannons.

BIRTHSONG
➤ *Runaway* Apr 24–May 21, 1961

SHERIFF
The bridges you burn may yet be the ones you follow to success.

How insatiable was the American public's demand for treacly power ballads by nominal rockers at the end of the 1980s? Insatiable enough to cause a dangerous shortage in domestic supply. How intent were the

forces of the constellation *Reaganrock* on maintaining their popstrological supremacy even as George Bush the Elder was assuming the reins of earthly power? Intent enough to dip into their strategic power-ballad reserves by resurrecting a six-year-old recording by an unknown group of Canadians and hoisting it to the top of the American pop charts. Even to call your Birthstar a band at that point in time would have been inaccurate, for Sheriff had turned in its badge four years earlier, and its lead singer was working as a Toronto bike messenger when *When I'm With You* shot to #1. The constellation *Oh . . . Canada* gained its final member with the rise of your Birthstar, and the constellation *Reaganrock* nearly did the same. And though Sheriff's inability to reunite even after a #1 hit suggests that you and your popstrological brethren are not the types to **set differences aside in the interest of mutual benefit,** it can safely be said that you *are* the types to **rush to the support of others in their time of need,** even if their need is ultimately self-serving.

CONSTELLATIONS
➤ Reaganrock
➤ Oh . . . Canada

BIRTHSONG
➤ *When I'm With You*
Jan 29–Feb 4, 1989

THE SHIRELLES
What lipstick and powder can't cover up, you find most interesting.

On a purely demographic basis, the arrival of your Birthstar on the popstrological scene was an event of tremendous significance, increasing the number of women in the popstrological firmament by 40 percent and the number of *black* women by 400 percent. But those numbers hide the real significance of being the first girl-group to join the popstrological elite. What the Shirelles represented, and what the constellation they founded stood for, was not only a sound that few could resist, but a much-needed dose of girl talk on the topic that mattered most: boys. Not that boys themselves weren't just as interested in eavesdropping on the girls' concerns, but the real gift of the stars in the constellation **Les Girls** was to their fellow girls. Despite spending millions of dollars on records in the late 1950s, America's teenage girls had been offered only the married Debbie Reynolds, the scary-intense Connie Francis, and the underage Brenda Lee as popstrological role models and girlfriends in the five years prior to your Birthstar's arrival. All that

would change, of course, but the Shirelles will always be remembered as the first voice of pre-protofeminism, and their popstrological children will always carry within them the knowledge that **sharing the personal**, while not always political, is almost always an effective way to form **lasting emotional connections**.

CONSTELLATIONS
➤ Les Girls
➤ Jersey Pride

CELEBRITY
➤ **George Stephanopoulos** (2/10/61) is a Shirelle.

BIRTHSONGS
➤ *Will You Love Me Tomorrow?* Jan 30–Feb 12, 1961
➤ *Soldier Boy* Apr 29– May 19, 1962

SHOCKING BLUE
A breeze always feels freshest where the air is stalest.

Outside of the BBC and the home of the William F. Buckleys, the best English spoken on planet Earth is spoken in the Netherlands, so it was hardly surprising that the first English-singing star to join the constellation *Eurosomething* should be Dutch. What was surprising, though, was that a group from a country most Americans associate with wooden shoes and wax-covered cheese should sound so Fresh—indeed, every bit as Fresh as the homegrown ruler of the year in which they rose, the Jackson 5. If you listen to Shocking Blue's *Venus*—which is to say, *not* Bananarama's *Venus*—you can hear distinct echoes of the Who and hints of Duane Eddy, yet you still can't find anything that sounds quite like it. Breaking down America's defenses against singers of English from the European mainland certainly was a major accomplishment, and it paved the way for the glorious ABBA and a-ha, among others. Yet the popstrological accomplishment that best defines the Forgotten Amsterdam quartet with a name like a late-night cable show is their status as the only *Eurosomething* star to hold dual citizenship in the constellation *Fresh Breeze*. **Don't let little things like your social, cultural, and ethnic background define you**, children of Shocking

Blue. Your popstrological legacy is a **passport that will carry you across any border** you choose.

CONSTELLATIONS
➤ Eurosomething
➤ Fresh Breeze

BIRTHSONG
➤ *Venus* Feb 1–7, 1970

SILVER CONVENTION
You were conceived in sin, but at a moment when no one seemed to mind.

Perhaps this scenario sounds familiar: (1) German producers cut a record with hired help and release it under the name of a fictitious group; (2) the record becomes a international dance hit; and (3) aesthetically pleasing individuals are produced to embody that fictitious group. Yes, the parallels to Milli Vanilli are striking, but your Germans didn't plan their deception from the start the way the Milli Vanilli Germans did, and the lovely ladies in sequined dresses they put forward

as the Silver Convention could actually sing their hit in live performances, which of course the lovely gentlemen in braided tresses could not. But more to the point, in an age before video, no one who grooved to your Birthsong in the discos of Europe and North America knew or cared much about who sang or didn't sing *Fly, Robin, Fly*. With a steady supply of cocaine and 128-beats-per-minute dance music, they'd have embraced a far more pernicious star from the constellation *Artificial Ingredients* and not felt the least bit dirty about it. Minor and Forgotten, but Sexy even if you couldn't see them, the "group" that ruled over your birth imbued you with quite a bit **more pleasing power than staying power**, but also with the enviable charm of **escaping untarnished from misdeeds and predicaments** that might bring others down.

CONSTELLATIONS
➤ Artificial Ingredients
➤ Disco Ball

BIRTHSONG
➤ *Fly, Robin, Fly*
   Nov 23–Dec 13, 1975

CARLY SIMON
Talent is nice, but nothing says "money in the bank" like money in the bank.

Take a pencil and write down three words that rhyme with "yacht." We get "dot," "pot," and "snot," but bonus points to you if you came up with either of Carly Simon's choices: "apricot" and "gavotte." *Qu'est-ce que c'est qu'une gavotte*, you ask? If you have to ask, then clearly you weren't raised in the wealthy and cultured milieu that taught your gorgeous and talented Birthstar lots of words like "milieu" and the name of many obscure French country dances. Carly Simon is the daughter of the Simon and Schuster fortune, you see, and signs of her ruling-class, media-elite background aren't difficult to spot: they're there in *You're So Vain*, her signature song about a Lear jet–flying boyfriend; they're there in the cozy Hollywood relationships that led to a string of seventies and eighties movie-theme hits like *Nobody Does It Better*, *Coming Around Again*, and *Let The River Run*; they're there in the savvy deals to sell ketchup and aspirin with *Anticipation* and *I Haven't Got Time For The Pain*; and they're there in the late-career dabbling as an author of children's books (published by . . . well, go ahead and guess). **Capital begets capital**, they say, but as a popstrological child of Carly Simon, you already know that. It's why you dedicate so much of your energy to **attaining** the status you were born to inhabit, even if it wasn't the status into which you were born.

CONSTELLATION
➤ Tip of the Ice Cube

BIRTHSONG
➤ *You're So Vain* Dec 31, 1972–Jan 20, 1973

PAUL SIMON
You may be a ship that drifts for a bit, but you'll eventually find a safe and interesting harbor.

Like Paul McCartney, your Birthstar joined the constellation *Spin-Off* in the wake of a breakup that was more like a divorce than a standard pop falling-out, and like Paul McCartney, your Birthstar had a kind of sad-sack vibe about him that many divorced men do. But Paul Simon was no Paul McCartney. Yes, he was a lonely musical divorcé with a deep-seated need for partnership, but Paul Simon didn't express that need in a series of toxic popstrological *Power Couple*s. In fact, after more than a decade of uneven

success as a solo act, Paul Simon found a perfectly healthy and indeed rather pleasing solution to his professional loneliness in a series of international collaborations that yielded, among other things, his enormous and incredible 1986 album, *Graceland*. The rejuvenating effect of his Southern Hemisphere sojourns on your Birthstar certainly makes one wonder whether Stevie Wonder and the world might have been spared *Ebony and Ivory* had Paul McCartney done something similar, but that question is in the realm of pure popstrological speculation. What matters to you is that expanding his horizons beyond his *Outerborough* roots worked for your Birthstar, cementing his status among the stars of the constellation *Tip of the Ice Cube* and belying the false insouciance of his popstrological breakthrough, *50 Ways To Leave Your Lover*. **You many not love to be alone,** child of Paul Simon, but your patience and good judgment will help you **avoid the pitfalls that others fall into** in their heedless quest for togetherness.

CONSTELLATIONS
➤ Spin-Off
➤ Tip of the Ice Cube
➤ Outerborough

BIRTHSONG
➤ *50 Ways To Leave Your Lover* Feb 1–21, 1976

SIMON AND GARFUNKEL
Even loveless marriages can produce lovely things.

If Lennon and McCartney were the once-perfect young couple who grew so far apart that they could never speak again, and if Sonny and Cher were the oddball pair whose genuine affection made for a rocky but life-long friendship even after their split, then Simon and Garfunkel were the couple whose entire marriage was marked by undercurrents of bitterness and mutual resentment—the couple who can barely manage to meet and be civil to each other every ten years or so for the sake of their loving kids. Like so many couples who fit that regrettable profile, your Birthstar came very close to breaking up before a little accident ended up keeping them together. The bundle of joy that prevented their breakup was the melancholy *Sounds Of Silence*, an acoustic non-hit from the ignored album *Wednesday Morning, 3 AM*, until producer Tom Wilson used Bob Dylan's session band to overlay the drums and electric guitar that transformed a *Folkie* flop into a folk-rock smash. The assisted birth of their first #1 explains your

Birthstar's residence in the constellation *Regifted*, an unlikely position, perhaps, for such a Massive and respected star, but a critical piece of your popstrological puzzle, for whether you are the product of a strained partnership or a participant in one, you should realize that **happy accidents are possible even amid the discord**.

CONSTELLATIONS
➤ Outerborough
➤ Folkie
➤ Regifted
➤ Launching Pad

CELEBRITY
➤ **Michael Imperioli** (1/1/66), **Mariah Carey** (3/27/70), **Queen Latifah** (3/18/70), **Lara Flynn Boyle** (3/27/70), and **Vince Vaughan** (3/28/70) are children of Simon and Garfunkel.

BIRTHSONGS
➤ *The Sounds Of Silence* Dec 26, 1965–Jan 1, 1966 and Jan 16–22, 1966
➤ *Mrs. Robinson* May 26– Jun 15, 1968
➤ *Bridge Over Troubled Water* Feb 22–Apr 4, 1970

SIMPLE MINDS
Your biggest accomplishment will earn many fans, though you may not be among them.

In the post–New Wave, pre-Alternative world of non-mainstream, non-American, mid-eighties rock, they were a kind of Scottish U2. But without the intervention of that genre's greatest cinematic supporter, it's safe to say that Simple Minds would have toiled in popstrological anonymity for the remainder of their pop career. John Hughes, who named one of his films after its Psychedelic Furs theme song (*Pretty in Pink*) and who featured groups like the Thompson Twins and Spandau Ballet prominently in another (*Sixteen Candles*), handed your Birthstar their ticket into the constellation *Regifted* by having them record the theme song to what many regard as the definitive document of white, upper-middle-class, 1980s teen angst: *The Breakfast Club*. Like most of Hughes's films, the movie that launched your Birthstar didn't so much preach against social stratification as argue for the situational crossing of social boundaries when true love, the chance to get laid, or, in this case, Saturday detention made it necessary. But it wasn't any strong feelings about the teenage caste system that caused your Birthstar's lead singer, Jim Kerr, to bad-mouth your "inane" Birthsong repeatedly after it earned Simple Minds their popstrological stripes. No, that was

simple and straightforward **pretentiousness** at work, an unfortunate aspect of your Birthstar's legacy, which, along with a **tendency to look a gift horse in the mouth**, forms a kind of negative counterpoint to your otherwise positive **tendency to practice, or at least to preach, the gospel of social equality**.

CONSTELLATIONS
➤ Britsuasion
➤ Regifted
➤ Reaganrock
➤ Theme Singer

BIRTHSONG
➤ *Don't You (Forget About Me)* May 12–18, 1985

SIMPLY RED
You might not have trouble winning some respect, but you may have trouble winning it from everyone.

For reasons of their own, the English have never let go of their obsession with making fun of Simply Red or, more accurately, with making fun of Simply Red's ginger-haired frontman. Jokes about inappropriate relations with rabbits predominate (try dropping the *Y* from the title of your Birthsong and replacing the first word of their other big hit, *Money's Too Tight To Mention*, with the word "Bunny's"), but everything's fair game when it comes to Mick Hucknall, who is to the Brits roughly what Michael Bolton is to us. It's easy to see why a band named for the color of its lead singer's hair might be singled out for ridicule, of course, but the fact that this never really bothered Americans suggests that there's something uniquely British at work in all the Simply Red–baiting. Is it simply a case of "We hate it when our countrymen become successful by trying to sound like black Americans"? Perhaps, but it really should be acknowledged that Mick Hucknall is a blue-eyed soulster who didn't make his name on covers of Sam Cooke and Percy Sledge songs. He made it by writing *Holding Back The Years*, which sounds like a lost gem from the Stax or Atlantic catalog of the early seventies if you just ignore the Sade-like production style. If only to correct the brutality of the British, American popstrologists defiantly place Simply Red among

the stars of the constellation *So-Soul*, and they hope this gives you the **emotional reserves** to withstand the many times **your peers will choose you as their easy target**.

CONSTELLATIONS
➤ Britsuasion
➤ So-Soul

BIRTHSONG
➤ *Holding Back The Years*
Jul 6–12, 1986

FRANK SINATRA
Feeling no pain may bring joy to some, but for you joy and pain go hand in hand.

Anyone interested in understanding Frank Sinatra, and particularly those born under his popstrological influence, should do themselves a favor and track down a copy of Gay Talese's famous 1966 *Esquire* piece, "Frank Sinatra Has a Cold." It's probably the best piece of music journalism ever written, and it will give you a better feel for your Birthstar than anything else you're likely to read and certainly anything you're likely to see on television. But as fascinating an exploration as it is of Frank Sinatra's legendary power in the world of show business—the topic that underlies nearly every joke you've ever heard about the man—Talese's piece is also notable for its succinct and elegant description of the forces that underlie Sinatra's popstrological essence: **loneliness and sensuality**. It's the powerful combination

of the two that animated your Birthstar's greatest work, and as Talese says of Sinatra's greatest work, "When blended with the dim light and the alcohol and nicotine and late-night needs, it became a kind of airy aphrodisiac." If you try to express loneliness and sensuality in the idiom of rock and roll, you get *Heartbreak Hotel*, an undeniably powerful work that nonetheless operates on an entirely different level from Sinatra's *One For My Baby (And One More For The Road)*, say, or *In The Wee Small Hours Of The Morning.* Let others repackage themselves to suit current fashions, child of Frank Sinatra. Your gift, and your burden, is to **prefer what's cool to what's hot**, and while **you may not feel quite yourself when unambiguously happy**, those who love you might not recognize you if you did.

CONSTELLATIONS
➤ Old Guard
➤ Tip of the Iceberg
➤ Jersey Pride

CELEBRITY
➤ **John Cusack** (6/28/66) is a Frank Sinatra.

NANCY SINATRA

They say that blood is thicker than water, but for you it may be even thickerer.

She was the eldest daughter of one of the most powerful men in America, but those who would paint her dad as the Godfather of Pop need only look at the career of Nancy Sinatra to see how wrong they are. For what kind of godfather would allow his daughter to parade around in public in go-go boots and a bikini? And what kind of godfather would allow his daughter to fall under the sway of a twisted genius like Lee Hazlewood? Perhaps, you might say, an absentee godfather overcompensating for his frequent absence by giving his grown daughter more latitude than he otherwise would have liked. Or perhaps a business-minded godfather forced to overlook the strangeness and embrace the economic value of an earner like Hazlewood, who wrote and produced Nancy's stupendous *These Boots Are Made For Walkin'* and then produced the father-daughter duet *Somethin' Stupid*, both for Frank's own Reprise record label. But while Nancy Sinatra's popstrological rise owed at least a little something to her daddy's name, if her daddy listened to the sheer insanity of her duet with Hazlewood on *Some Velvet Morning* and ended her popstrological career by saying,

"That's it, Nance—you're coming home, baby," he did nothing more than any caring father would have done in the same situation. You may not always like it, but **your family got you where you are and they kept you from being where you aren't**.

CONSTELLATIONS
➤ Gene Pool
➤ Fresh Breeze

CELEBRITY
➤ **Cindy Crawford** (2/20/66) is a child of Nancy Sinatra.

BIRTHSONG
➤ *These Boots Are Made For Walkin'* Feb 20–26, 1966

NANCY AND FRANK SINATRA

You are the feeler of warm feelings who's not quite sure what to do with them.

When Frank Sinatra asks you to sing a duet with him, you know it's an offer you can't refuse. Still, you have to be thinking: What's going to happen if I hit a wrong note or

step on one of the man's lines? That's why Bono and Kenny G were happy to record their parts thousands of miles away from Mr. Sinatra for his 1993 album, *Duets*, and it's why the only singer to have a bona fide pop smash in a duet with Frank was the one singer guaranteed not to quake in her boots when he entered the room: his pretty daughter Nancy. It's hard to be nervous around someone who taught you to sing your ABCs, and the vocal chemistry in your Birthsong, *Somethin' Stupid*, is undeniable. Yet how interesting it is that your father-daughter Birthstar chose to sing a song of *unrequited* love. Theirs was the first-ever #1 hit resulting from the pairing of independent, pop-strologically viable stars, and it was not the last time that such a pairing would hint at dysfunctional undercurrents. Indeed, by founding the constellation **Power Couple**, your Birthstar created a place for some of the most dysfunctional and damaging creations in the history of pop. But responsibility for those aberrations is not your Birthstar's. No, the legacy of

Nancy and Frank Sinatra's pairing to the children born under its influence is more gently dysfunctional: an **ability to feel deep, familial love**, and an **inability to express it in a head-on way**.

CONSTELLATIONS
➤ Power Couple
➤ Gene Pool

CELEBRITY
➤ **Liz Phair** (4/17/67) is a child of Nancy and Frank Sinatra.

BIRTHSONG
➤ *Somethin' Stupid* Apr 9–May 6, 1967

THE SINGING NUN

When they find themselves in times of trouble, confused souls may turn to you.

Late December back in '63 was a very special time indeed, separated by just a few weeks from the death of John F. Kennedy and the coming British Invasion. Perhaps only during this strange and vulnerable moment in popstrological time could a Belgian nun have ascended the American pop charts with a jaunty tune about a Catholic saint, sung in French, no less. Yes, your Birthstar really was a nun, and yes, she really sang, but beyond those facts, the Debbie Reynolds movie of the same name will do little to aid your exploration of the Singing Nun's deeper, more

complex life story. After achieving pop immortality and a place in the constellation *Had to Be There* with *Dominique*, Sister Luc-Gabrielle (*née* Jeanine Deckers) walked away from stardom and from her church. Indeed, an album honoring the birth control pill was the highlight of Ms. Deckers's post-convent career, which ended tragically in 1985 when she and her longtime female companion committed suicide in the face of a massive tax bill from the Belgian government relating to royalties Jeanine had donated in full to the Roman Catholic Church. **Follow your conscience wherever it leads**, popstrological children of the Singing Nun, but always remember that **no good deed goes unpunished**.

CONSTELLATIONS
➤ Had to Be There
➤ Sui Generis
➤ Eurosomething
➤ Tragic Demise

CELEBRITY
➤ **Brad Pitt** (12/18/63), **Jennifer Beals** (12/19/63), and **Benjamin Bratt**

(12/16/63) are children of the Singing Nun.

BIRTHSONG
➤ *Dominique* Dec 1–28, 1963

PERCY SLEDGE
Your heart may get broken, but your wounds will heal beautifully.

Reeling emotionally in the midst of a painful breakup, Percy Sledge, hospital-orderly-by-day, club-singer-by night, turned to his backing band and asked them between songs to play something—anything—besides the upbeat R&B they usually performed. And when they began to play, your Birthstar began to ad-lib the raw and heart-wrenching lyrics to what would eventually become one of pop's all-time classics, *When A Man Loves A Woman*. Perhaps at some point in your life you've written a poem or a journal entry in a similar state of mind, only to read it later and wish that you hadn't. Perhaps that's why Percy Sledge decided to give sole songwriting credit on your Birthsong to his bassist and organist, or perhaps it was merely his generosity of spirit. But either way, it meant that this Massive star in the constellation *So-Soul* would earn not a penny from the innumerable covers of *When A Man Loves A Woman* that have followed his original. This fact in no way weakens your popstrological tie to a certain Michael Bolton, who earned his sole #1 hit with your Birthsong in 1991, but looking on the bright side, it does mean that you still have a good chance of catching a live performance by your hardworking Birthstar in an affordable venue like Ville Platte, Lousiana's annual Smoked Meat Festival. In matters of business, **your judgment may be too hasty**, child of Percy Sledge, but in matters of the heart, your **unaffected honesty** will someday find a devoted audience.

CONSTELLATION
➤ So-Soul

BIRTHSONG
➤ *When A Man Loves A Woman* May 22–Jun 4, 1966

SLY AND THE FAMILY STONE
When all you do is serve others, it's difficult to serve yourself very well.

Frustrated by the demographic and stylistic divisions he saw in the pop landscape of the late sixties, a San Francisco Bay Area DJ named Sylvester Stewart set out to combine the best and banish the worst forces of his day in one single band that would feature men and women, black and white, playing an unheard-of thing called psychedelic soul in costumes that would make Liberace proud. On a purely aesthetic level, Sly and the Family Stone looked like nothing the pop universe had ever seen, and pop hits like *Dance To The Music*, *Everyday People*, *Everybody Is A Star*, and *Family Affair* all worked to further the same basic message: that people of wildly different stripes could do a lot better than just coexist peacefully if they'd only open their minds to the possibility. Sly Stone led by example, but it was an uphill battle, and in the end the enormity of his mission combined with his newfound weakness for demon coke to bring his Massive career screeching to a halt. It's unlikely, of course, that your own career arc will very closely resemble your Birthstar's, yet it's quite likely indeed that you also find yourself exhausted at times by **your struggle to be all things to all people**. Unless, that is, you're the oppositional type who has avoided your Birthstar's trap

by becoming a f*ck-'em-all lone wolf who looks out for number one first, last, and always. Either way, **stability and happiness for you probably lie somewhere in the middle**, in a place Sylvester Stewart never found during his brief but glorious heyday.

CONSTELLATION
➤ So-Soul

CELEBRITY
➤ **Jennifer Aniston** (2/11/69) is a child of Sly and the Family Stone.

BIRTHSONGS
➤ *Everyday People* Feb 9– Mar 8, 1969
➤ *Thank You (Falletinme Be Mice Elf Agin)/Everybody Is A Star* Feb 8–21, 1970
➤ *Family Affair* Nov 29– Dec 18, 1971

SONNY AND CHER
Just because it's over doesn't mean your work is done.

In November of 1987, Sonny and Cher appeared on *Late Night With David Letterman* and sang *I Got You Babe* together for the first time in more than a decade. Anyone who loved their records in the sixties or their variety show in the seventies took great pleasure in watching this happen, but this reunion was no mere nostalgia rush for you. You were born under the direct popstrological influence, after all, of the man and woman who founded the constellation *Holy Matrimony* in 1964 and reversed its hopeful vibrations with their very public divorce in 1974. Yet in your twenty-third year, Sonny and Cher returned to make amends for the popstrological impact of their failed marriage by showing the world that it's never too late to salvage a dysfunctional breakup. Yes, it had taken your Birthstar many years to get to the point of being civil to each other in public, but that only goes to show you how much work it takes to make a severed relationship succeed. And if you ever find yourself wondering whether it's worth the effort, consider this: five months after your Birthstar's popstrological reunion, Cher won her Oscar for *Moonstruck*, and the very next day, on April 12, 1988, Sonny was elected mayor of Palm Springs. **They say that breaking up is hard to do,** but that's not likely to faze you, child of Sonny and Cher. In breaking up and every other phase of your many relationships, you're the type to say that **if something's worth doing, it's worth doing right.**

CONSTELLATIONS
➤ Holy Matrimony
➤ Launching Pad

CELEBRITIES
➤ **Kyra Sedgwick** (8/19/65), **KRS-One** (8/20/65), and **Shania Twain** (8/28/65) are children of Sonny and Cher.

BIRTHSONG
➤ *I Got You Babe* Aug 8–28, 1965

DAVID SOUL
You have the right to remain face-less, but anything you sing can be held against you.

*S*tarsky and Hutch may seem an unlikely launching pad for a soothing star in the constellation **Lite & White**, but you shouldn't be all that surprised. Your Birthstar didn't play Starsky, after all, he played Hutch, the sensitive and soft-spoken cop who'd lecture a drug-dealing pimp about health food while Starsky was beating a confession out of him. It was a role that David Soul (*née* Solberg) earned after a decade of yeoman work on classic cop shows like *Ironside*, *Cannon*, and *The Rookies*, but if you are tempted to read your Birthstar as a simple 1970s precursor to David Hasselhoff, perhaps you should explore his initial attempt at stardom, which came in the late sixties as a folksinger in a full-face ski mask performing under the name the Covered Man. That's a true story, and it's unlikely ever to be repeated by another pretty-boy pop star yearning to have his music taken seriously, because as it turned out, audiences lost all interest in the Covered Man once he eventually removed his mask on *The Merv Griffin Show.* Be that as it may, your Birthstar's achingly sincere side finally found its creative outlet on *Starsky and Hutch* and in the constellation *Lite & White*, from which place in the pop-cultural landscape he bestowed upon those born under his influence the confidence of a **tough guy who doesn't act it** and the irresistible allure of a **sexpot who doesn't show it.**

CONSTELLATION
➤ Lite & White

CELEBRITY
➤ **Sarah Michelle Gellar** (4/14/77) is a child of David Soul.

BIRTHSONG
➤ *Don't Give Up On Us* Apr 10–16, 1977

JIMMY SOUL

More realistic than romantic, you focus on the bread and butter while others chase the sizzle.

James "the Boy Wonder" McCleese was a traveling, gospel-singing preacher by the tender age of seven, but it wasn't until he met Frank Guida at the age of eighteen that he exchanged one cool-*ss name for another and became the pop star known as Jimmy Soul. Guida was the man behind the raucous, calypso-influenced R&B sound of Norfolk, Virginia's Legrand label, best known for the records of Gary "U.S." Bonds. And it was Guida who gave your Birthstar both his name and his ticket to pop immortality with the song *If You Wanna Be Happy*, still the only tune in the history of pop to take a stand *against* pretty girls as worthy objects of matrimonial aspiration and still a tune as profoundly irresistible as it is politically incorrect. As influential as he was in the life of James McCleese, Frank Guida was only a minor starmaker, powerful enough to launch your Birthstar into the constellation *Novelty Merchant*, but not strong enough to expand on that accomplishment, despite worthy follow-up efforts like *My Baby Loves To Bowl*. Still, Jimmy Soul's impact can be seen day in and day out in the lives of his pop-strological progeny, **pragmatic defiers of convention like you** who know that **good things come in all kinds of packages**.

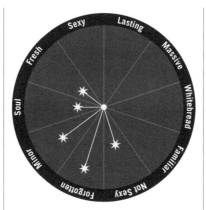

CONSTELLATION
➤ Novelty Merchant

CELEBRITY
➤ **Mike Myers** (5/25/63) is a child of Jimmy Soul.

BIRTHSONG
➤ *If You Wanna Be Happy* May 12–25, 1963

RICK SPRINGFIELD

Your charms may well lie hidden, like a diamond in the fluff.

He was the second heart-throb named Rick to step from the small screen to the pop scene, and like his forerunner Rick Nelson, he was a whole lot better than he had any right to be. If you were caught up in one of 1981's competing "cool" music scenes—punk, New Wave, hard rock, heavy metal—then your official stance on the Australian-born *General Hospital* hunk Rick Springfield was that he sucked. But in the safety and isolation of your car or bedroom, well out of sight and earshot of your friends, there is absolutely no way that you didn't belt out the lyrics and air-guitar the power chords to *Jessie's Girl* when it came on the radio. Springfield's clean, guitar-powered pop-rock sound was hardly new, but it sounded pretty damn Fresh in a summer otherwise dominated by Air Supply, *Endless Love*, and Christopher Cross. Rick Springfield's appearance in the constellation *Outback* reassured Americans that Australia could still supply something more substantial than air, and though follow-ups like *I've Done Everything For You* and *Human Touch* failed to establish him as a Lasting force in the universe of pop, your Sexy Whitebread Birthstar managed to bestow upon those born under his influence an undeniable **ability to defy easy categorization** and to **greatly exceed unduly low expectations**.

CONSTELLATION
➤ Outback

BIRTHSONG
➤ *Jessie's Girl* Jul 26–Aug 8, 1981

THE STAPLE SINGERS

The church of the dirty mind is not the only place you worship.

The constitutional separation of church and state is nothing compared with the carefully guarded line that separates gospel music from the secular world of pop. You can do one or you can do the other, but unless you're Al Green and willing to endure the painful and exhausting cleansing rituals, you really can't go back and forth. If anyone knew this, it was Roebuck "Pops" Staples, who left behind an almost thirty-year career in gospel in the 1960s by leading daughters Cleotha, Yvonne, and Mavis out of the bosom of the church and into the strange and uncertain world of pop. At first your Birthstar hewed somewhat close to their original path, with covers of secular message-songs like *For What It's Worth* and *Long Walk To D.C.*, and indeed their popstrological breakthrough came with 1972's decidedly funky but vaguely spiritual *I'll Take You There*. Soon enough, though, the Staple Singers closed the church door once and for all with 1975's *Let's Do It Again*, which was *not* about getting back into the Communion line for seconds on crackers and wine. If at some point in life you find yourself **yearning for spiritual meaning**, keep your popstrological legacy in mind and choose a faith that will accept your **inability to ignore the pleasures of the flesh**.

CONSTELLATIONS
➤ Gene Pool
➤ So-Soul

BIRTHSONGS
➤ *I'll Take You There*
  May 28–Jun 3, 1972
➤ *Let's Do It Again*
  Dec 21–27, 1975

STARLAND VOCAL BAND

Jarlsberg is fine for some, but it's American cheese that made this country great.

ABBA conquered Europe faster than Adolf Hitler, yet they managed only modest success here in the United States. Why? Good old-fashioned patriotism, that's why. ABBA were reaching their peak internationally in the summer of 1976, but at the height of our bicentennial celebration, Americans weren't about to let some foreign import conquer our domestic market. Especially when we had our own home-grown quartet of radiant and married white people in the form of the Starland Vocal Band, who took their place among the popstrological elite on precisely July 4, 1976, on the strength of *Afternoon Delight*, their timeless ode to *l'amour du jour*. The Starland Vocal Band's rapid rise into the constellations *Lite & White* and *Holy Matrimony* didn't sink the Swedish armada, but it did take the wind out of ABBA's sails. More important, it kept the skyrockets flying for two solid weeks past Independence Day, as kids across America were sent out to play in the midday heat so that Mom and Dad could enjoy a home-cooked lunch in peace, quiet, and privacy. It wouldn't be surprising if you discovered **a taste for foreign delicacies** in your adulthood, child of the Starland Vocal Band, but it would be a shame if you forgot that North American **Whitebread is what sustained you** until you did.

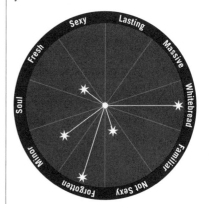

CONSTELLATIONS
➤ Lite & White
➤ Holy Matrimony

EDWIN STARR
When others say, "Let's foster a constructive dialogue," you say, "Let's cut through the crap."

The Vietnam era's most famous protest songs were written by men who also wrote *Imagine* and *A Hard Rain's A-Gonna Fall*, but the Vietnam era's *funkiest* protest song was written by a man who also wrote *Car Wash*. Norman Whitfield was his name, and among the many dozens of timeless late-sixties/early-seventies classics he wrote with his partner Barrett Strong was your Birthsong, *War*. It was written with the Temptations in mind, but when the suits at Motown decided to have that group stick to the more oblique social commentary of *Ball Of Confusion*, Whitfield and Strong handed it to Edwin Starr, a Minor and Forgotten star in the constellation *Hitsville*, but a star with a powerful legacy nonetheless. If your Birthsong were easier to play on the acoustic guitar or easier for crowds of white people to sing a cappella, it might have joined *Give Peace A Chance* and *Blowin' In The Wind* in the musical canon of the anti-Establishment left. But the fact that it

hasn't bears significantly on your popstrological legacy. For while a **current of idealism** may run strong and deep within you, so might an **aversion to those whose aching sincerity is too much on display**. What are high-minded ideals good for? Absolutely nothing, you might say, if your biggest joy is in preaching them to the choir.

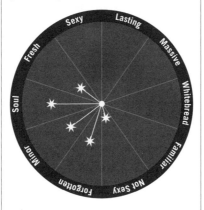

CONSTELLATION
➤ Hitsville

CELEBRITY
➤ **Jay Mohr** (8/23/70), **Macy Gray** (9/9/70), and **Debbie Gibson** (8/31/70) are children of Edwin Starr. **River Phoenix** (8/23/70) was, too.

BIRTHSONG
➤ *War* Aug 23–Sep 12, 1970

RINGO STARR
Just because you laugh through drama, it doesn't mean you're just a clown.

Most fans favored John, Paul, or George, but there's no question who the Beatles' own favorite Beatle was. It was Ringo, and if you've got an extra $500 laying about, you can purchase the proof in a copy of his beautiful *Postcards from the Boys*, a limited-edition collection of sweet and heartfelt cards sent to Mr. Richard Starkey by his famous bandmates through the decades. It's no accident that Sir Paul has no such collection of his own gathering dust in a drawer at home, just as it's no accident that the only musical project to which all four Beatles contributed post-breakup was your Birthstar's 1973 album, *Ringo*—the source of his two #1 hits. The man who replaced Pete Best on drums once proclaimed that he was "joost happy to be here," and that quote has become a shorthand way to refer to any lucky tagalong on someone else's gravy train. But don't let Ringo's willingness to embrace that persona convince you that it was truthful. Your Birthstar's self-effacing charm didn't just make the Beatles more personally likable than they would have been without him—it also kept them together longer than most groups of prodigiously talented

egomaniacs could possibly hope. Ringo's drumming was as **quietly spectacular** as his popstrological children can be on their best days—though those days may too often be spent **managing tantrums and pissing contests** with **easy humor and abundant goodwill**.

CONSTELLATION
➤ Spin-off

BIRTHSONGS
➤ *Photograph* Nov 16–24, 1973
➤ *You're Sixteen* Jan 20–26, 1974

STARS ON 45
Where others go to worship, you go to exhume.

I t was the summer of 1981, and after an eleven-year hiatus, the sound of the Fab Four once again ruled the airwaves. Only instead of John, Paul, George, and Ringo, this time the world had to settle for Bas, Hans, Jaap, and Okkie, the Dutch studio musicians behind your Birthstar. The phenomenon called Stars on 45 was not so much a band as a business plan, built around the notion that a half-dozen Beatles snippets re-recorded by anonymous impersonators and set to a relentless disco hand clap was just what the world needed six months after John Lennon's death. Perhaps the centers of your brain devoted to good taste are offended by your Birthstar's **spectacular creative vision**, but as a child of **the**

most entrepreneurial star in the popstrological firmament, it would be surprising if your rational side weren't saying, "Damn, that's brilliant." And it's hard to argue with the results. With a touch of *Sugar, Sugar* and a dash of *Venus* thrown in just for kicks, your Birthsong was an irresistible (and high-profit-margin) confection that not only ruled the pop universe longer than some of the songs it sampled, but created a market for future crammed-together medleys that only served to burnish further one of the brightest stars in the constellation *Had to Be There*. **Follow your instincts in matters of business**, children of Stars on 45, even if they tell you to **slaughter a few sacred cows**.

CONSTELLATIONS
➤ Had to Be There
➤ Artificial Ingredients
➤ Eurosomething

BIRTHSONGS
➤ *Medley: Intro "Venus"/Sugar Sugar/No Reply . . .* June 14–20, 1981

STARSHIP
Just because people believe it, that doesn't make it true.

I t's a point of fact that San Francisco was built on sand dunes and landfill, a foundation almost as shaky as your Birthstar's claim to have built it on rock and roll. But let us accept Starship's premise, for the moment, and explore some of its implications. First, the basics: your Birthstar's bold assertion rests on the band's ability to trace its lineage through singer Grace Slick back to the late-sixties heyday of her former group, the Jefferson Airplane. Okay, so that casts a bit of doubt on the validity of the "we" in *We Built This City*, but more to the point, what does it say about your Birthstar that their claim left all other surviving architects of the psychedelic sound, few and far between though they may have been, entirely out of the equation? And even setting that issue aside, what does it say about the state of the pop universe at the moment of your birth that it was regarded as even remotely reasonable for Starship to call what they were doing rock and roll? *Knee Deep In The Hoopla* was the name of the album that launched your Birthstar into the constellation *Reaganrock*, but **knee-deep in the *poopla* is where you might find yourself** all too often if you can't unburden yourself of the popstrological "gift" you have for **creating untenable situations with your "innocent" yet insupportable claims**.

CONSTELLATION
➤ Reaganrock

BIRTHSONGS
➤ *We Built This City*
Nov 10–23, 1985
➤ *Sara* Mar 9–15, 1986
➤ *Nothing's Gonna Stop Us
Now* Mar 29–Apr 11, 1987

STEAM
**Would you choose the poverty of
truth, or the wealth of unintended
consequences?**

You almost certainly know
your Birthsong, *Na Na
Hey Hey Kiss Him
Goodbye,* by heart, but
you've probably never heard of the
man who actually recorded it.
Gary DeCarlo was his name, and
in mid-1969 he had just finished
recording a set of songs that represented his serious artistic vision as
a singer/songwriter. All he needed
was a throwaway B-side for his
first single, so with the help of his
guitar player and producer, Gary
banged out a song so far beneath
him that surely no radio station in
the world would bother to play it.
Only this ridiculous trifle of
Gary's sounded better to his label

than anything he'd previously
recorded, and while most aspiring
stars would be thrilled to watch
any song of theirs become a #1 hit,
Gary DeCarlo wasn't. First he
refused to put your Birthsong out
under his real name, and then,
when *Na Na Hey Hey* exploded
while his "real" songs tanked,
Gary refused to join the touring
band cobbled together to play the
part of the fictitious "Steam."
Time and the steady stream of royalties that *Na Na Hey Hey* has
earned as part of the sports-arena
canon have probably softened
Gary DeCarlo's feelings about your
Birthsong over the years, but
hopefully in your own life you've
learned to be at peace with the fact
that your **deepest thoughts go
unappreciated** while your **mindless exercises pay your bills**.

CONSTELLATION
➤ Artificial Ingredients

CELEBRITY
➤ **Jay-Z** (12/4/69) is a child of
Steam.

BIRTHSONG
➤ *Na Na Hey Hey Kiss Him
Goodbye* Nov 30–Dec 13,
1969

RAY STEVENS
**What you once forswore, you may
someday just go ahead and do
again.**

Just when he thought he was
out, they pulled him back
in. Ray Stevens had spent
his early career in the shady
underworld of novelty songs, but
by the early seventies he'd gone
completely legit. "No more
songs like *Ahab The Arab,*" he
told himself, "from now on it's
only the sweetly sincere Ray
Stevens of *Communicate With Me,
America* and *Everything Is
Beautiful.*" But then a minor college fad for running naked
through public places caught
your Birthstar's attention, and he
couldn't resist taking a shot at
that last big score. *The Streak*
went all the way to #1, thanks in
part to a nationally televised
streaking incident on Oscar
night in 1974, and soon Ray had
slipped back into his old ways.
Driven by his pathological need
to be silly and supported by the
Muzak royalties from *Everything
Is Beautiful,* he has directed his
energies since 1974 into songs
like *I Need Your Help, Barry*

Manilow, and *Osama, Yo Mama*, reaffirming his rightful place in the constellation ***Novelty Merchant*** and bestowing on those born under his mismatched #1 hits a definite **ability to keep a straight face**, but greater success when they **allow themselves (and others) to smile**.

CONSTELLATIONS
➤ Novelty Merchant
➤ Lite & White

CELEBRITY
➤ **Jewel** (5/23/74) and **Alanis Morissette** (6/1/74) are children of Ray Stevens.

BIRTHSONGS
➤ *Everything Is Beautiful* May 24–Jun 6, 1970
➤ *The Streak* May 12–Jun 1, 1974

AMII STEWART
You probably excel at catching waves, but perhaps just barely before they break.

The most famous and successful examples of the musical phenomenon known as "discofication" were, of course, instrumentals: Meco's *Star Wars Theme*, Rhythm Heritage's *Theme From S.W.A.T.*, and Walter Murphy's immortal *A Fifth of Beethoven*. But most efforts to create popstrological hits out of discofied non-instrumentals fell as flat as Ethel Merman's 1979 disco album, Amii Stewart's pumped-up, full-tilt version of Eddie Floyd's 1966 hit *Knock on Wood*

being the rare exception. If she'd made her debut several years earlier, Amii Stewart might have had time to build on her early success and find further hits with the formula that earned her the next-to-last spot in the constellation ***Disco Ball***. But your Birthstar's rise came during what would prove to be the last days, or at least the last months, of disco, and a discofied *Light My Fire* was her final, failed effort to build on her Minor popstrological foothold before changing tastes made that style of grave-digging commercially untenable. Tall, gorgeous, and dressed like a drag queen's dream, she cut an imposing onstage figure in her brief heyday, like Grace Jones but without the element of danger. And by ruling the pop universe at the moment of your birth, she bestowed upon you a **knack for playing angles that others can't pull off**, but also a **sense of timing that leaves something to be desired**.

CONSTELLATION
➤ Disco Ball

CELEBRITY
➤ **Kate Hudson** (4/19/79) is an Amii Stewart.

BIRTHSONG
➤ *Knock On Wood* Apr 15–21, 1979

ROD STEWART
You're in our hearts and in our beds, but have you got what it takes for a committed relationship?

If the rest of the world wrote an open letter to the popstrological children of Rod Stewart, it might sound a little something like this: *Dear Rods: Why? Why did you make us fall in love with you? We don't loosen up our pretty French gowns for just anyone, you know. We thought we had something really special, and we're not just talking about the sex (although that was spectacular). Look, we're all grown-ups. We knew when we hooked up with you that we might not be able to satisfy you on our own, so it's not the wandering eye that gets us. Sure, sometimes we wish you would just accept the fact that people find you sexy and quit looking for reinforcement all the time, but you want to know what really bothers us? It's that you never wake us up just to talk to us anymore, and quite frankly, when you've told us lately that you love us, you sound sort of like . . . well, a soulless robot. Honestly, sometimes we think we should just swear off you and that model-shagging, talent-wasting, cash-flow-conscious Birthstar of yours! But then we hear* Maggie May *again, and we realize that a world without Rod Stewart and you is a world we'd hate to live in. Listen, we've got to take care of ourselves now, Rods. We can't just keep waiting for the "old" you to come back. So call us* **when you've achieved whatever it is you're still trying to achieve**, *okay? We'll be waiting.*

CONSTELLATIONS
➤ Royal Court
➤ Shape Shifter
➤ Hot Hairdo
➤ Spin-Off

CELEBRITIES
➤ **Winona Ryder** (10/29/71), **Brandy** (2/11/79), **Jennifer Love Hewitt** (2/21/79), and **Mena Suvari** (2/9/79) are popstrological Rod Stewarts.

BIRTHSONGS
➤ *Maggie May* Sep 26–Oct 30, 1971
➤ *Tonight's The Night (Gonna Be Alright)* Nov 7, 1976–Jan 1, 1977
➤ *Da Ya Think I'm Sexy?* Feb 4–Mar 3, 1979

STORIES
Give you any line, you'll cross it.

The early 1970s was a time of significant racial tension in the United States, though you wouldn't have known it from looking at the pop charts. While the Black Panthers called for race war in Oakland, and the opponents of forced busing rioted in Boston, the popstrological firmament witnessed a period of fabulous and unprecedented integration, as the funkiest Soul shared space peacefully with the whitest Whitebread. But if this broad vibrational context succeeded in spawning a generation that would make hip-hop the next great popstrological blurrer of racial lines, the specific moment of your birth succeeded in doing something far more interesting to you. For you were born under the influence of a star called Stories, whose existence was so ephemeral as to require you to focus closely on your Birthsong, and to look deeper than its "*Louie Loo*-eye"s for clues to your popstrological legacy. And what does your Birthsong tell you? Perhaps it tells you that for all of America's difficulty in dealing with issues of race, if it was willing to embrace a bunch of white guys singing about the "danger" of "tasting brown sugar" and telling their "brothers" that "there ain't no difference if you're black or you're white," it's willing to embrace just about anything. Perhaps your own **boundary-tweaking ways** have manifested themselves in some area far removed from race relations, but whatever your chosen field of endeavor, it's likely that your success will derive from **saying the things you're not supposed to**, even if people love to hear them.

CONSTELLATION
➤ Storyteller

CELEBRITY
➤ **Dave Chappelle** (8/24/73) is a child of Stories.

BIRTHSONG
➤ *Brother Louie* Aug 19–Sep 1, 1973

THE STRAWBERRY ALARM CLOCK
You may not be a groundbreaking original, but you thrive in ground that others break.

Let those wizened sixties survivors scoff at your "phony" psychedelic Birthstar. Let them rail against the silliness of the Strawberry Alarm Clock and extol the genius of Jimi Hendrix and the Jefferson Airplane. Just don't let the bastards get you down, that's all. They may be right in asserting that your bubblegum Birthstar had all the credibility of the Archies among the dropped-out, turned-on tastemakers of 1967, but remember: Hendrix never even had a #1 record, and when Grace Slick got one, it wasn't for *White Rabbit* but for *We Built This City*. The point is, in pop as in most other matters, Americans **turn a deaf ear to the concerns of the cultural elite**, and you'd do well to do the same in your own life. As a Strawberry Alarm Clock born in the Year of the Monkees, your popstrological profile bears the imprint of not one but two forces of artificiality, but it also bears the imprint of the genuine thrill those forces generated at the moment of your birth. Just as the nonsense phrase "incense and peppermints" sent millions of American preteens rifling through Grandma's hard-candy jar in search of their first hallucinogenic experience, **the highly convincing simulations** you produce at work or at home may be **functionally indistinguishable from the real thing** to the people whose opinions really matter.

CONSTELLATION
➤ Neither/Nor

BIRTHSONG
➤ *Incense And Peppermints*
Nov 19–25, 1967

BARBRA STREISAND
You are the scared little bunny in the skin of a lion.

Whose icon is she anyway? Who can lay the greatest claim on the little girl from Brooklyn who grew up to become La Streisand? Jewish women? Gay men? Gay Jewish men who impersonate women? The real answer, of course, is everyone and no one, for hers is a star that shines brighter than a thousand points of light—a star too Massive for the mere universe of pop to contain. And what should the rest of the world expect of the children born under your Birthstar's blinding glow? Great hair, great legs, and great voices? Personas for which the term "diva" seems a pale and inadequate description? No, popstrology rarely works so simply, and perhaps that's a good thing. What the science of the pop stars *does* tell us is that Barbra Streisand resides in one of the most interesting regions of the pop universe—among the broken-mold originals of the constellation *Sui Generis*. She rose to greatness not on the strength of talent alone, but on the strength of a potent and idiosyncratic *combination* of **talent, ego, and insecurity**, and therein lies the lesson her popstrological children should heed: **what we show on the outside is never quite what we are on the inside**, but success for you may depend on **showing more of the real you** than the rest of us typically dare.

CONSTELLATIONS
➤ Sui Generis
➤ Lite & White
➤ Outerborough
➤ Theme Singer

BIRTHSONGS
➤ *The Way We Were*
Jan 27–Feb 2 and
Feb 10–23, 1974
➤ *Love Theme From "A Star Is Born" (Evergreen)*
Feb 27–Mar 19, 1977
➤ *Woman In Love*
Oct 19–Nov 8, 1980

BARBRA STREISAND AND NEIL DIAMOND

When they try to blame you, they should probably be blaming themselves.

You can look at some popstrological *Power Couple*s and say "Yes, I see why A + B sort of needed to happen," or "Okay, I can see why the world thought it needed the particular C that A + B provided." But when you look at a coupling between pop giants like the one that occurred at the moment of *your* birth, sometimes all you can say is, "Oh God, no." That's exactly how people are going to react, too, when you tell them of your popstrological background, so it's best to prepare yourself for it mentally. The thing for you to remember, unless you decide simply to bury your newfound knowledge, is that every cloud has its silver lining, sort of. The combination of Barbra Streisand and Neil Diamond may seem like yet another unnatural pairing engineered by the greedy and heedless corporate machine, but it wasn't. It came about when a Louisville DJ noticed that Streisand had recorded *You Don't Bring Me Flowers* in the same key as the man who wrote it, Neil Diamond, and when that DJ started airing a handmade mix of the two versions, his audience went bonkers. Only when insatiable grassroots demand forced it to happen was a real-life duet by these two *Outerborough* giants arranged, so if someone tries to **make you feel like the mutant child** of a marriage that never should have happened, you be sure to tell him that you're actually the **mutant child of democracy in action**.

CONSTELLATIONS

➤ Power Couple
➤ Outerborough

CELEBRITIES

➤ **Clay Aiken** (11/30/78) and **Nellie Furtado** (12/2/78) are popstrological children of Barbra Streisand and Neil Diamond.

BIRTHSONG

➤ *You Don't Bring Me Flowers Anymore*
Nov 26–Dec 2 and Dec 10–16, 1978

BARBRA STREISAND AND DONNA SUMMER

Would it be worth all of your treasure to have just a moment's pleasure?

Queen of Disco she may have been, but for Donna Summer—or Donna Summer's handlers, anyway—to think that she could form a popstrological *Power Couple* with Barbra Streisand and emerge from the experience with her powers intact was the height of hubris, or chutzpah, as Ms. Streisand might say. It's not that Donna Summer couldn't hold her own on the actual recording of your Birthsong—indeed, she and Barbra belted it out to a near draw on the disco mini-opera *No More Tears (Enough Is Enough)*. But as Neil Diamond learned in 1978 after *You Don't Bring Me Flowers* went to #1, and Barry Gibb learned in 1980 after *Guilty* nearly did, Barbra Streisand in the disco era was like a popstrological succubus, providing momentary pleasure in her couplings but leaving her partners popstrologically spent in the aftermath. Donna Summer never had another significant hit after joining Ms. Streisand to form your Birthstar, and though there were certainly other factors at work in her rapid fall from prominence, the children of this dangerous dual star would do well to choose their partners carefully—to **resist the allure of star power** and **seek out less charged relationships**, which might ultimately be more fulfilling.

CONSTELLATIONS

➤ Power Couple
➤ Disco Ball

BIRTHSONG

➤ *No More Tears (Enough Is Enough)* Nov 18–Dec 1, 1979

STYX

If you were a poodle, your name might be Satan.

The cursed river called Styx conjures chilling images of hellfire, damnation, and eternally tortured souls, while the band called Styx conjures images of piano ballads, Japanese robots, and the incomparable stagecraft of frontman Dennis DeYoung. To all but a cynical few, this seems to be a serious disconnect, but what else would you expect from one of the most confused pop acts of the 1970s and '80s? Your Birthstar could never decide between prog rock and show tunes, you see, but frankly neither could a significant segment of late-seventies rock fans, who embraced Styx's internal conflict and the strange, delicate balance they struck between the rock hard, the syrupy soft, and the flat-out bizarre. Listen only to your Birthsong, *Babe*, and you might think your Styx was little more than REO Speedwagon with better voices. But set aside a weekend to plumb the depths of *Mr. Roboto*, and if you're the type who abhors bland uniformity, you'll say, *"Domo arigato*, Styx, *domo."* "Thanks for being a hell of a lot more interesting than Toto and Foreigner and April Wine, and thanks for endowing me with the **wacked-out but strangely lovable set of contradictions** that make me who I am."

CONSTELLATION

➤ Tip of the Ice Cube

BIRTHSONG

➤ *Babe* Dec 2–15, 1979

DONNA SUMMER

They call you angel in the morning, and devil in the evening.

Once upon a time, an ordinary girl from a good Christian family found herself adrift in central Europe after a failed marriage and a brief career in musical theater. At the mercy of the devious locals, she fell under the spell of a certain Giorgio Moroder, the Munich Mephistopheles, who delivered stardom to the girl but at a dear price: seventeen minutes of simulated orgasm on *Love To Love You Baby*. Her moral compass fully abandoned and her inner strumpet emphatically embraced, our heroine transformed herself into the shimmering Queen of Disco and led her loyal subjects on a giddy, four-year slide toward Sodom and Gomorrah (or at least from Sodom *to* Gomorrah). But then one day it happened: Donna Summer came no more. She'd met an old friend named Jesus, you see, and just like that she cast down her crown and turned her back on legions of heartbroken followers. Like a bar that loses its most colorful patron to the rigors of AA, the world of disco was never the same after your Birthstar's spiritual rebirth. But be thankful for the time she did spend ministering to the heathen, for it was under the glorious and decadent zenith of the constellation *Disco Ball* that you were born and endowed with the **power to lead by example**, both **into and away from temptation** in its many forms.

THE SUPREMES
**In sibling rivalries, there's rarely
one clear and happy winner.**

They were the most successful American pop group of the 1960s—a group whose twelve #1 hits in the popstrological era ranks behind only the totals of Elvis Presley and the Beatles. They sounded great, they looked amazing, and they were ripped apart and cast aside like yesterday's news when Berry Gordy made Diana Ross into a goddess and loosed her solo star into the pop universe. And if you think that explains why you've seen so many good things in your life crash and burn as a result of bulging egos, you may be right. But before you simultaneously applaud and console yourself for being a beloved genius occasionally undone by the naked ambition of others, consider the careers of Mary Wells and the Marvelettes—two among many Motown girl groups whose once-bright careers withered and died in the shadow of your light-hungry Birthstar. Pampered, cosseted, and showered with gifts from the genius songwriting team of Holland-Dozier-Holland, the Supremes were Daddy's do-no-wrong favorites in the Motown "family"—the beneficiaries of Berry Gordy's rank favoritism long before that same favoritism became their undoing. Gifted in their own right but popstrologically **Regifted** at the expense of many others, the brightest star in the constellation *Les Girls* bestows upon you a complex popstrological legacy that's as likely to manifest itself in **career triumphs intimately connected to the talents of others** as in **career setbacks tied to the same thing**.

SURVIVOR

In the right hands, even a blunt instrument can be extremely effective.

An endocrinologist could explain to you how the original *Rocky* and its stirring theme song, *Gonna Fly Now,* succeeded by subtly and safely manipulating the levels of dopamine, seratonin, and adrenaline in our systems. It doesn't take a medical expert, though, to identify the hormone at work in *Rocky III* and its theme song, *Eye Of The Tiger.* That testosterone is powerful stuff—it transformed Rocky Stallone from a lovable, side-of-beef palooka in *I* to a vengeful, chiseled action figure in *III,* and it fueled your Birthstar's rise from semi-obscure Chicago rock band to pumped-up popstrological superpower. Taken in moderate doses, testosterone can elevate your mood, sharpen your senses, and increase your self-esteem, which is why they will still be playing your Birthsong at live sporting events a hundred years from now. But as any heavy steroid user can tell you, too much testosterone can lead to things like jaundice, psychosis, gynecomastia, and *Rocky IV.* For the popstrological children of Survivor, an **ability to pump up the masses** may be your greatest gift, but **moderation of aggressive tendencies** is the sine qua non of social survival.

CONSTELLATIONS
➤ Theme Singer
➤ Reaganrock

BIRTHSONG
➤ *Eye Of The Tiger*
Jul 18–Aug 28, 1982

BILLY SWAN

If you hope to climb the ladder, you may have to do your share of carrying it first.

You might think that writer's royalties from a top-10 hit would be enough to support a young man for a while as he further developed his craft, but the fact is that it takes more than that before a songwriter can quit his day job. But in the end, that may have been a good thing for Billy Swan, who was financially unsteady enough even after writing the legendary Clyde McPhatter's 1962 hit *Lover Please* that he spent the next several years working as a security guard at Graceland and then as a janitor at Columbia Records in Nashville. It was in that second job that the fates conspired to place another hungry young musician named Kris Kristofferson before him, and that's who Billy gave his janitor's bucket to when he decided to quit himself. Several years later and now a budding star, Kristofferson returned the favor by hiring your Birthstar as his bassist—a job he still holds to this day. And a few years after that, Kristofferson gave Billy Swan an electric organ that he fiddled on one day and came up with *I Can Help,* a throwback little gem that would later be covered by both Jerry Lee Lewis and Swan's former boss Elvis Presley, but not before Swan himself used it to launch himself into the popstrological elite as one of the most obscure stars among the behind-the-scenes supporters of the constellation *Invisible Hand.* Your **early success may not be enough to build a career on,** child of Billy Swan, but your **willingness to return to the bottom** may be enough to get you to the top.

CONSTELLATION
➤ Invisible Hand

BIRTHSONG
➤ *I Can Help* Nov 17–30, 1974

THE SYLVERS

What you lack in the way of original genius you more than make up for in sheer enthusiasm.

I t would take the combined Carpenters, Bee Gees, and Jackson 5 to outnumber the Sylvers, a family so large that their parents figured it made more sense to turn them into a singing act and keep them on the road than it did to have all *nine* of them fighting for phone and bathroom privileges back home in Memphis. The Sylvers began as a quartet in the late sixties—a popular road act that gradually added siblings and built a résumé of moderate R&B hits before breaking through popstrologically in 1976 with the brilliant *Boogie Fever*. The largest and possibly the least dysfunctional star in the constellation **Gene Pool**, the Sylvers also occupy a well-deserved place in the joyful constellation **Shaking Booty** as well as in the constellation **Hot Hairdo**, thanks to Afros that challenged theoretical height limits circa 1976. Professionally, they never escaped the Jackson 5's long shadow, but in popstrological terms, the Sylvers exert a similar and infinitely less problematic influence. **If you find yourself wishing that your star could burn a little brighter**, just remember that fame has its price, so **be careful what you wish for**.

CONSTELLATIONS
➤ Gene Pool
➤ Shaking Booty
➤ Hot Hairdo

BIRTHSONG
➤ *Boogie Fever* May 9– May 15, 1976

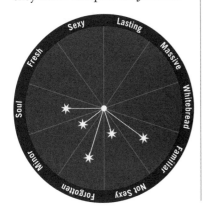

A TASTE OF HONEY

You will succeed by ignoring the path you're expected to follow.

M usically, it was one of disco's great triumphs, but the significance of your Birthsong and its timeless bass hook goes far beyond that. With apologies to Carly Simon, whose gentle strumming exists somewhere within the luxe production of *You're So Vain*, it's *Boogie Oogie Oogie* that represents the first *meaningful* instance in the popstrological era of a woman playing a guitar on her own #1 record. It may come as a shock to you that this achievement was not made until 1978, but wait—it gets worse. So powerful was the traditional logic of the pop-music industry—that attractive and talented women should focus on singing and leave the rest of the work to men—that if you put Carole King, Carly Simon, Karen Carpenter, Dolly Parton, Joan Jett, the Bangles, and Debbie Gibson in a room with Janice Marie Johnson and Hazel Payne of A Taste of Honey, that room would contain nearly every single woman in the popstrological firmament who ever played *any* instrument on her own pop hits. There were two (largely invisible) male members of A Taste of Honey in 1978, so while your Birthstar does not belong to the constellation *Les Girls*, they do stand as a truly unique and groundbreaking star in the constellation *Disco Ball* and in the pop universe as a whole. **Don't let others tell you what you can and cannot do**, Taste of Honeys. You'd be surprised what you can **achieve by ignoring conventional wisdom**.

CONSTELLATION
➤ Disco Ball

CELEBRITY
➤ **Fiona Apple** (9/17/78) is a popstrological Taste of Honey.

BIRTHSONG
➤ *Boogie Oogie Oogie* Sep 3–23, 1978

JAMES TAYLOR
Like all sensitive souls, you feel the sting of even the gentlest WASP.

Boarding school, heroin addiction, and a voluntary stay in a Berkshires mental hospital: if there were a High Church of Preppie Sensitivity, these would be its rites of ordination. The collected works of J. D. Salinger and Sylvia Plath would be its gospels, and the greatest hits of high priest James Taylor would form its hymnal. Most of the hits in that hymnal came during the period when your Birthstar burned most brightly, a brief span bracketed by the 1971 release of the definitive J.T. single *Fire and Rain* and his 1973 marriage/corporate merger with Carly Simon. Yet on the basis of those recordings alone (*Walking Man*, *Sweet Baby James*, *Carolina In My Mind*), James Taylor and the church he represents will continue to win converts with each new generation of white liberal-arts students, and the enduring appeal of his gorgeous, downbeat ballads will extend the already considerable power he wields from the constellation *Tip of the Ice Cube*. Brooklyn's own Carole King gave your Birthstar the song that became his only #1 hit, providing a wonderful example of the **ethnically nonexclusive appeal** of both his and **your brand of unique Whitebread Soulfulness**.

CONSTELLATION
➤ Tip of the Ice Cube

BIRTHSONG
➤ *You've Got A Friend*
Jul 25–31, 1971

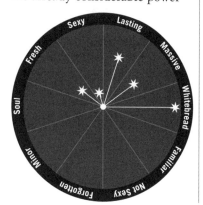

JOHNNIE TAYLOR
It's not called deception if all you do is exploit a misperception.

The constellation *Disco Ball* began its popstrological rise in 1974, but it was not until 1976 that it picked up any serious momentum. That was the year the disco phenomenon began to achieve pop-cultural saturation—the year that *New York* magazine published the fabricated article that inspired *Saturday Night Fever* and the year that the very word "disco" became powerful enough to make #1 hits out of a witless novelty song called *Disco Duck* and a nondisco R&B song called *Disco Lady*. That's right, your Birthsong is not a disco song. It certainly *talked* about disco, and its title will forever get it included in retrospectives of disco, but if you find yourself a copy and try hustling to it, you'll see what we mean. *Disco Lady* was a joy to listen to, but its double-platinum success, and your Birthstar's entry into the constellation *Regifted*, stemmed directly from the misdirected enthusiasm of a disco-crazed America. Johnnie Taylor later had a minor hit with a song called *I Could Never Be President*, but perhaps he was wrong about that. After all, he's the one who made you the type of person who is **embraced not so much for what you are, as for what you appear to be**.

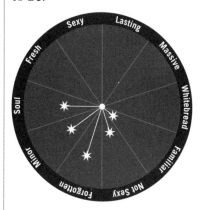

CONSTELLATIONS
➤ So-Soul
➤ Regifted

BIRTHSONG
➤ *Disco Lady* Mar 28–Apr 24, 1976

TEARS FOR FEARS

You take yourself seriously even if nobody else does.

If they were Scientologists, they'd have been "Cheers for Clears," and if they were EST graduates, they'd have been "Jeers for Pee-ers." But Roland Orzabal and Curt Smith weren't either of those things. They were believers in Arthur Janov's primal scream therapy, which preached the power of a really big tantrum (tears) to cure adult neuroses whose roots lay in childhood (fears). And if that explanation of your Birthstar's name gives you a new appreciation for a group with a name like Wham! then you are one of those **lucky enough to have escaped the pretentiousness** that is your Birthstar's greatest popstrological legacy. Not to say that their two 1985 #1 hits, *Shout* and *Everybody Wants To Rule The World* weren't fine and pleasant pop songs that could be enjoyed without mental strain. It's just that Curt and Roland (and *especially* Roland) would have been deeply disappointed to learn that most of us had no idea what they were singing about and weren't really all that interested in the meaning of the trippy imagery they worked so hard at stuffing into their music videos. One can only hope that your self-actualized Birthstar took the rapid end of their popstrological significance well, particularly since their legacy lives on through people like you whose **struggles with self-importance** so clearly reflect their own.

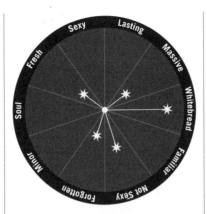

CONSTELLATION
➤ Britsuasion

BIRTHSONGS
➤ *Shout* Jun 2–15, 1985
➤ *Everybody Wants To Rule The World* Jul 28–Aug 17, 1985

THE TEDDY BEARS

You are the little acorn that becomes some kind of oak, anyway.

Legend has it that in order to pay for his first-ever session in a professional studio, the soon-to-be legendary Phil Spector needed $40 he didn't have, and his mom was only able to front him $30. Luckily for Phil, a high school friend named Annette Kleinbard came through with the balance, and luckily for Annette, Phil agreed to her one small condition: that she be made lead singer of his group. It was probably as wise an investment in her future as any young woman could possibly have made with ten dollars in 1958, and not just because Miss Kleinbard's voice is indeed the one you hear on *To Know Him Is To Love Him* every time your classic Birthsong plays. The Teddy Bears will always be known first and foremost as the group that launched the architect of the Wall of Sound, and while it's Phil Spector's future impact that explains their presence in the constellation *Invisible Hand*, your Birthstar also launched Annette Kleinbard on a successful, if decidedly more modest, career in the music industry. Some might say that the lyrics to *Gonna Fly Now (Theme From Rocky)*, her most prominent accomplishment, were utterly superfluous to that song's success, but royalty checks are royalty checks. And while you may have made much or little of it in your own life and career, you Birthstar's gift to you is in your **ability to parlay one small victory into a string of victories** to follow.

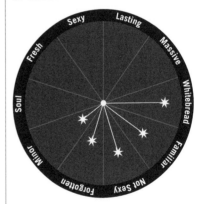

CONSTELLATIONS
➤ Invisible Hand
➤ Doo-Wop

BIRTHSONG
➤ *To Know Him Is To Love Him* Dec 1–21, 1958

NINO TEMPO AND APRIL STEVENS

Traditional mores may restrain you in public, but what you do in private is really your own business.

April Stevens (*née* Carol LoTiempo) could recite a recipe for pancakes and make it sound sexy, which explains how she and her brother Nino turned a tired standard like *Deep Purple* into an unlikely #1 hit in November 1963. But despite April's rather stirring vocal style, she and Nino fell quickly from the popstrological heights after attempts to repeat their *Deep Purple* success foundered. Instead of trying to sex up old chestnuts like *Tea For Two* and *Stardust*, what if your Birthstar had chosen songs in the vein of April's minor 1962 solo hit, *Teach Me Tiger*? If nothing else, *that* was a song that gave Miss Stevens something to work with by casting her in the role of a young virgin lobbying to be stripped of that status. And if April's loving brother Nino could write such a risqué song for her, then why not take the next logical step and sing it together? Because it would have provided a little bit more frisson than America was ready to handle, of course. Popstrologists given to idle speculation often wonder what strange forces might have been unleashed had your Birthstar not forced aficionados of disturbing brother-sister chemistry to wait another seven years for the Carpenters to add a comparably subtext-rich star to the constellation *Gene Pool*. But perhaps it's for the best, since by doing so, your Birthstar might have pushed **that undeniable je ne sais quoi** of yours even farther into **territory that others find inappropriate**.

CONSTELLATION
➤ Gene Pool

BIRTHSONG
➤ *Deep Purple* Nov 10–16, 1963

THE TEMPTATIONS

You may not write the message, but you certainly do stick to it.

The business of Motown Records was simple: manufacturing hits. In trying to make a superstar of Diana Ross, Berry Gordy himself lost sight of this mission, but the Temptations never did, and they stand as the true, shining triumph of the system that created the constellation *Hitsville*. They had thirty-eight hits in the pop top-forty—not just more than any other Motown artist, but more than any American group ever. And they were alone among the *Hitsville* stars in successfully navigating the transition from the mid-sixties to the early seventies by evolving from the glorious love poetry of Smokey Robinson (*My Girl*, *The Way You Do The Things You Do*) to the funk-fueled social commentary of Norman Whitfield (*Ball Of Confusion {That's What The World Is Today}*, *Papa Was A Rollin' Stone*). But beyond their quantitative achievements, your Birthstar embodied the original Motown ideal that the records, for good or for ill, mattered more than the people who made them. In an era when pop groups were beginning to be known as much for the personalities of their members as for their actual music, the Temptations remained essentially unknowable, other than through their incredible records. Various intrigues, upsets, and tragedies saw your Birthstar's lineup change almost annually during their late-sixties/early-seventies heyday, but in a group that had all five members singing lead on some of their records, the turmoil went largely unnoticed by the

record-buying public. **You may not be the island of stability some perceive you to be**, child of the Temptations, but perhaps you'd say that **what's behind the curtain hardly matters if what's out front is winning applause.**

CONSTELLATIONS
➤ Hitsville
➤ Launching Pad

CELEBRITY
➤ **Nancy Kerrigan** (10/13/69) is a Temptation.

BIRTHSONGS
➤ *My Girl* Feb 28–Mar 6, 1965
➤ *I Can't Get Next To You* Oct 12–25, 1969
➤ *Just My Imagination (Running Away With Me)* Mar 28–Apr 10, 1971
➤ *Papa Was A Rollin' Stone* Nov 26–Dec 2, 1972

B. J. THOMAS
Like bourbon and Fresca or peanut butter and bacon, you are a strange hybrid with undeniable appeal.

While your Birthstar hardly ranks among the greatest or most exotic stars of his era, he is nonetheless a figure of significant popstrological interest, for his rise to prominence would surely have been impossible without the post-Beatles gravitational distortions that blurred the lines between the parallel dimensions of country, R&B, and pop in the early 1970s. This was the era of countrypolitan and bubblegum soul, and it was an era uniquely open to your Birthstar's confusing mix of loyalties to Hank Williams, Tom Jones, and Wilson Pickett. How appropriate, then, to this moment in popstrological space-time that the #1 song at the dawn of the seventies was a piece of Burt Bacharach insta-Muzak (*Raindrops Keep Fallin' On My Head*) recorded by a man in a cowboy hat and boots. Only two other stars in the popstrological firmament share dual residency with B. J. Thomas in the constellations *Lite & White* and *Country Cousins*, and while your Birthstar may pale next to Olivia Newton-John and Kenny Rogers, the rest of us still watch with fascination as you and your popstrological ilk **create surprisingly pleasing blends from apparently incompatible elements.**

CONSTELLATIONS
➤ Country Cousins
➤ Lite & White
➤ Texstyle
➤ Theme Singer

BIRTHSONGS
➤ *Raindrops Keep Fallin' On My Head* Dec 28, 1969– Jan 24, 1970
➤ *(Hey Won't You) Play Another Somebody Done Somebody Wrong Song* Apr 20–26, 1975

THREE DOG NIGHT
Why fight for your share when there's plenty to go around?

On cold nights in the outback, Australian Aborigines sleep with their dogs to stay warm, and to describe a night so cold that one or two dogs just won't do, they use the phrase that gave your Birthstar its name. It's one of the coolest band names in pop-music history, and it was a wonderfully appropriate name for a group that America cuddled up to so enthusiastically in the early 1970s. Between 1969 and 1975, Three Dog Night released *twelve* gold albums and an astonishing string of top-forty singles, many of them by then-struggling songwriters like Harry Nilsson, Randy Newman, and Hoyt Axton. As early supporters of folks who later supported so many others, your Birthstar earned themselves an honorary spot in the constellation *Invisible Hand*, a fittingly **selfless achievement** for a group whose organizing concept was of three men sharing lead-singer duties equally, without any one of them being the dominant Dog. When Chuck

Negron—future author of the brilliantly titled drug-confessional *Three Dog Nightmare*—gradually became the group's vocal centerpiece in the mid-1970s, though, it spelled the end of your Birthstar. But as anyone who's ever slept with one dog (let alone three dogs) knows, what starts out as the coziest of co-sleeping arrangements almost inevitably falls apart through someone's jockeying for prime position. **Group dynamics may be tricky for you**, child of Three Dog Night, especially if you forget your good intentions and indulge the primal instinct to **hog the spotlight rather than share its warmth with others**.

CONSTELLATION
➤ Invisible Hand

CELEBRITIES
➤ **Beck** (7/8/70), **Corey Feldman** (7/16/70), **Shannen Doherty** (4/21/71), and **Sofia Coppola** (5/14/71) are Three Dog Nights.

BIRTHSONGS
➤ *Mama Told Me (Not to Come)* Jul 5–18, 1970
➤ *Joy to the World* Apr 11–May 22, 1971
➤ *Black & White* Sep 10–16, 1972

TIFFANY
A Pop Tart makes a tasty breakfast, but it won't carry you through the whole day.

The 450 stars in the popstrological firmament are incredibly diverse in terms of style, sound, and influence, but one quality unites them all: each and every one of them had the ability in their day to make Americans reach for their wallets. And yet prior to the rise of one Tiffany Darwish, no one had thought to shorten the distance between herself and popstrological immortality by undertaking her march to stardom in the place where America's wallets are most ready to be opened: its indoor shopping malls. Perhaps the stroke of genius that launched the promotional mall tour that launched your *Underage* Birthstar in 1987 should be credited to one of her handlers rather than to Tiffany herself, but it's certainly Tiffany who deserves the credit for making it work in her acid-washed jeans, boxy leather jacket, and stupendous head of 1980s hair. She launched the New Kids, she sued for legal emancipation from her mother, she posed for *Playboy*, she changed her hair—she did, in short, everything you can ask of a star angling to appear on VH1's *Behind the Music*, and when her career failed to reignite in the wake of that triumph, it only served to reinforce the lesson her early rise should already have taught you: **getting your product to market is an important step**, but if your product's not right for its time, **product placement alone will never sell it**.

CONSTELLATIONS
➤ Underage
➤ Teen Idol
➤ Hot Hairdo

BIRTHSONGS
➤ *I Think We're Alone Now* Nov 1–14, 1987
➤ *Could've Been* Jan 31– Feb 18, 1988

THE TOKENS
Your hands may not have always been clean, but you've probably washed them enough by now.

Your Birthsong was an instant classic that went on to become one of the most successful pop songs of all time, yet its true creator never saw a penny of its profits. But before you jump to any conclusions about your popstrological legacy, you should explore (via Rian Malan's brilliant 2000 exposé in *Rolling Stone*) the fascinating story of how a South African legend named Solomon Linda saw the Zulu chants on his 1938 recording *Mbube* bastardized and transmogrified into the *"whee-dee-dee-dees"* of *The Lion Sleeps Tonight*. In the exploitation of Solomon Linda, the Tokens were little more than accessories after the fact, and if there was penance to be paid for that crime, they paid it in full by spending the remainder of their career out of the limelight, toiling in the constellation *Invisible Hand* as producers for the likes of the Chiffons and Tony Orlando. Just how faithful were the post–*Lion Sleeps* Tokens to the cause of intellectual-property protection? Well, it was the former Tokens, operating as Bright Music Corporation, who pressed the famous plagiarism suit against George Harrison for lifting *My Sweet Lord* from *He's So Fine*, the Chiffons song to which Bright Music held

the copyright. As a popstrological Token, it's probably true that **you owe a tremendous debt to those who preceded you**, but it's probably also true that **you've found a way to pay it back.**

CONSTELLATIONS
➤ Outerborough
➤ Doo Wop
➤ Invisible Hand

BIRTHSONG
➤ *The Lion Sleeps Tonight* Dec 18, 1961–Jan 6, 1962

THE TORNADOS
When others try to steal your thunder, try to be ready with some lightning, too.

These days, any kid with a Mac and some shareware could do it, but in 1962, you had to be a true mad scientist to make a record that sounded like *Telstar*. Joe Meek, the brains and hands behind the studio creation called the Tornados, was a mad scientist's mad scientist, using everything from handmade compression and room-size pre-amps to battery-operated organs and wax-paper-covered combs to cook up the eerie and mesmerizing sound of your Birthsong. Indeed, though Meek's inspiration for the song was the first communications satellite to orbit the earth, the real-life Telstar was probably less advanced technologically than half the equipment in his North London recording studio. Sadly, *Telstar* was the only hit your

Birthstar was able to launch from its platform in the constellation *Speechless*. Five million copies of the record sold internationally, yet thanks to a frivolous plagiarism suit, *Telstar* netted the tragic geek-genius Joe Meek not one dime. He died penniless and by his own hand, the court decision that unfroze his rightful royalty payments coming too late to prevent his *Tragic Demise*. But take heart, children of the Tornados, and consider yourselves not cursed but rather popstrologically forewarned to **look up from your labors long enough to prevent others from claiming its fruits**.

CONSTELLATIONS
➤ Speechless
➤ Tragic Demise

BIRTHSONG
➤ *Telstar* Dec 16, 1962–Jan 5, 1963

TOTO
Yes, it is a pretty basket, but should you really put all your eggs into it?

It's a tale of two Totos—well, three if you go back to their late-seventies start as would-be *Mustache Rock*ers in the .38 Special mold. But let's set that proto-Toto aside and look at the two Totos of greatest concern to those born under their influence: the Massively successful, Grammy-sweeping Toto of 1983, and the bottom-feeding Toto of every year thereafter. What knocked your Birthstar off the popstrological radar so quickly post-1983? Was it the abuse that rock critics heaped on Toto out of all proportion to the band's objectionable qualities? No, that was something Toto was well accustomed to. What did Toto in was the loss of the real force behind their early-eighties success: a twenty-three-year-old actress named Rosanna Arquette. She was the guitarist's girlfriend, but she was the whole band's den mother and muse, bringing cookies to the studio late at night and inspiring their two biggest hits—*Rosanna*, obviously, but almost surely *Africa*, too. But the affections of young starlets can be fleeting—especially for veteran rock acts–turned–temporary superstars (remember Soul Asylum?). And when Ms. Arquette's ardor for Toto abated, so did Toto's will to go on. The popstrological children of these consummate *Reaganrock*ers would do well to **diversify their assets, emotionally speaking,** lest they expose themselves to catastrophic and unrecoverable losses.

CONSTELLATION
➤ Reaganrock

BIRTHSONG
➤ *Africa* Jan 30–Feb 5, 1983

JOHN TRAVOLTA AND OLIVIA NEWTON-JOHN
Whatever it is that you've got, it's what people think they want.

There is an element within the popstrological community that will always view the constellation *Power Couple* as home to some of the most damaging phenomena ever to arise in the pop universe, yet even those who hold this view find it as difficult to resist the allure of your Birthstar as the rest of the world did back in 1977. The movie *Grease* hit all the right buttons with its combination of fifties nostalgia and seventies sexual revolution, and the sight and sound of Olivia Newton-John acting and John Travolta singing offered a fish-out-of-water thrill to surpass even that of watching Gabe Kaplan and Jaclyn Smith on *Battle of the Network Stars*. But the fact that John Travolta really could sing and Olivia Newton-John really could sort of act was just icing on the cake, of course, because the foundation of their popstrological success was far more primal. Never before had the sexual longing of so many teenagers been focused so intensely on a single point in the popstrological heavens, and it's hard to imagine it ever happening again. Fresh, Sexy, and Whitebread in a way that few *Homo sapiens* could resist, your Birthstar bestowed upon you an ability to **create real sparks in professional settings,** but also a tendency to set somewhat **unrealistic expectations in the sexual arena.**

CONSTELLATIONS
➤ Power Couple
➤ Theme Singer

BIRTHSONG
➤ *You're The One That I Want* Jun 4–10, 1978

THE TROGGS
Keeping it simple is almost never stupid.

The Troggs' *Wild Thing* was the song that launched a thousand garage bands, and if your Birthstar had hung up their instruments after it launched them into the constellation *Fresh Breeze*, they'd still be able to point to a million anonymous cover versions and a handful of famous ones as proof of their Lasting popstrological significance. There were other, minor hits for the Troggs, and they continue to perform even to this day, but the only recording they've made since 1966 that truly burnished their popstrological star was of an intraband argument amid a failing recording session that was bootlegged out of the studio and passed around as "the Troggs Tapes." On it, various Troggs can be heard bickering hilariously in accents and language that are said to have inspired *This Is Spinal Tap*. But beyond the charm of St. Hubbins–esque gems like "You can't just put a bit o' f*ckin' fairy doost over the bastard!" the Troggs Tapes also offer critical insight into the secret of your Birthstar's success, and perhaps the key to yours. It's about four minutes in, right around the forty-third "f*ck," when the difficulty they were having getting anything good on tape is contrasted to the manner in which *Wild Thing* was recorded, without fussing, without tweaking,

"Just one take, and that's IT!" **Will your first effort always be your best**, child of the Troggs? Maybe not, but **the more thought you put into improving, the less likely you are to pull it off.**

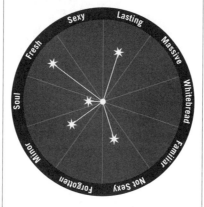

CONSTELLATION
➤ Fresh Breeze

BIRTHSONG
➤ *Wild Thing* Jul 24–Aug 6, 1966

TINA TURNER
You first act may be your longest, but your second will be your greatest.

If you spent the rest of your nights in a hyperbaric chamber, encased in soothing masques and slathered in the richest emollients, you'd probably still find yourself as you approached fifty looking and feeling the way human beings are meant to look and feel as they approach fifty: soft, droopy, and dog-tired. So how is it that Tina Turner looked so different from that in the year of your birth? Not surgery, surely, for she was looking too good for her age way back before cosmetic surgery could realistically have been involved. Tina was already thirty-three when she was blowing crowds away with her little-bit-easy, little-bit-rough routine on *Proud Mary*, and thirty-three was something very different back in 1971. And furthermore, if plastic surgery had developed the technology to do for the legs what it can clearly do for the nose, we'd have seen a lot more legs like Tina Turner's by now. So what, then, explains the apparent agelessness of your Massive, late-blooming Birthstar as she now approaches *seventy*? A deal with the devil, most likely, though not the standard sort. It was a deal with the devil in which Tina agreed to stay married to his good friend Ike Turner for nearly twenty years in exchange for emerging with her looks and her popstrological Soul completely intact. Only Frank Sinatra among the stars in the constellation *Tip of the Iceberg* waited longer to earn his popstrological stripes, but luckily for you, your Birthstar endowed you with **the capacity to endure far more than just a long wait** on your road to success.

CONSTELLATIONS
➤ Tip of the Iceberg
➤ Spin-Off

BIRTHSONG
➤ *What's Love Got To Do With It* Aug 26–Sep 15, 1984

THE TURTLES
Slow and steady can win the race, but only if you decide to join it.

A t the core of your Birthstar were Howard Kaylman and Mark Volman, two high school buddies who started out playing surf-guitar as the Crossfires, then switched to folk rock as the Tyrtles before achieving popstrological immortality with cheery pop rock as the (correctly spelled) Turtles. But fast-forward a few years ahead from *Happy Together*, and thanks to a soap opera that began when their manager ran off to Mexico with most of their money and their bassist's wife, Howard and Mark are legally enjoined from performing under the name Turtles or any form of their given names. And so they became the Phlorescent Leech and Eddie, members of the original Mothers of Invention and onstage witnesses to the Montreux debacle that inspired *Smoke On The Water* and the London debacle that led to Frank Zappa's temporary retirement. But Howard and Mark—now Flo and Eddie— stuck together throughout it all, eventually landing work as DJs and composers of music for children's cartoons. There are stars whose stories—whether triumphs, tragedies, or farces—follow a relatively clear and coherent narrative, but then there is your Birthstar, whose story travels a path from Dick Dale to the Care Bears by way of Bob Dylan. There's nothing wrong with **taking a journey without a reliable map**, as long as you're prepared, child of the Turtles, to **take a long and very strange trip**.

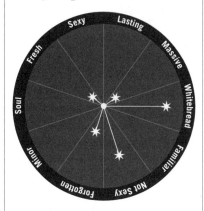

CONSTELLATION
➤ Tip of the Ice Cube

BIRTHSONG
➤ *Happy Together*
Mar 19–Apr 8, 1967

CONWAY TWITTY
You are the immutable constant with a hidden mutant past.

Y ou could be quite familiar with your Birthstar and still not know anything about the phase in his career that landed him among the popstrological elite. Sure, between 1965 and his death in 1993, he had *forty* #1 hits on the *country*-music charts, but if you only know the Conway Twitty of *Hello Darlin'*, *Tight Fittin' Jeans*, and *One Man Woman, One Woman Man*, then allow us to reveal the truth: the earliest star in the constellation **Country Cousins** was not a crossover fluke, but a bona fide *rock and roll* star in the 1950s, years before he scored his first Nashville hit. In fact, listen to a few bars of 1958's *It's Only Make Believe* and you might think you're hearing Elvis himself. Then take a good look at the name Conway Twitty next to the name of the title character in *Bye Bye Birdie* and you'll see proof of just how prominent a rock and roller your Birthstar once was. Twitty's transformation into a country-music demigod may have limited his direct popstrological impact, but it gave rise to a powerful force in the pop universe—the constellation **Shape-Shifter**. And it's from that hugely influential constellation that perhaps your strongest popstrological legacy derives: the **knack for personal reinvention** that's gotten you where you are, but which the **apparent solidity** of your current persona may not reveal to others.

CONSTELLATIONS
➤ Shape-Shifter
➤ Country Cousins

CELEBRITY
➤ **Megan Mullally** (11/12/58) is a Conway Twitty.

BIRTHSONG
➤ *It's Only Make Believe*
Nov 10–16, 1958

BONNIE TYLER

In a world where everyone has good taste, is good taste even worth having?

The dominant aesthetic of the early twenty-first century is everywhere and inescapable, from our Pottery Barn living rooms to our J. Crew wardrobes, but "clean lines" and "simple elegance" end where "soulless uniformity" begins, and if anyone out there is going to show us some way out of our minimalist trap, it's probably going to be someone like you—a popstrological child of Bonnie Tyler and of the least minimal #1 song of the popstrological era. There are #1 songs that are *longer* than *Total Eclipse Of The Heart* (well, only *Hey Jude*, *Light My Fire*, and *American Pie*), but there is no song that is *bigger*, and therein lies the fabulous essence of your popstrological legacy, which stems perhaps less from gravel-voiced Welsh beauty Bonnie Tyler than it does from the songwriter/producer who stood behind her, Jim Steinman. Steinman is also the man behind Meat Loaf, whose *I'd Do Anything For Love (But I Won't Do That)* may be the only example of Jim Steinman's insane pop dramaturgy you've ever experienced firsthand. But if that's the case, do yourself a favor and acquaint yourself quickly not just with your Birthsong but also with the Steinman/Loaf classics *Paradise By The Dashboard Light* and *Two Out Of Three Ain't Bad*. If those unapologetically bombastic epics don't explain why you are who you are, then hopefully they'll inspire you to become who you should be: the type who doesn't **climb over others on your way to the top**, but climbs to the top so you can **show others the way over it**.

CONSTELLATION
➤ Britsuasion

BIRTHSONG
➤ *Total Eclipse Of The Heart*
Sep 25–Oct 22, 1983

THE TYMES

Where the avant-garde go, there you'll be—about a step and a half behind.

From the vantage point of 1963, it would have taken true clairvoyance to predict the imminent and world-altering impact of the British Invasion. If you'd been asked to predict the shape of popstrological things to come back then, you probably would have put your money on the surf sound, the girl groups, or the stars of the constellation *Folkie* being the dominant force of the near future. One force you wouldn't have bet on, though, was the constellation *Doo-Wop*, which became the first constellation in the popstrological firmament to die a natural death of sonic obsolescence directly following the week of your birth. Indeed, so clearly of the past was the sound of the Tymes that popstrologists see their rise as one of the first documented cases of the "nostalgic deathwatch"—the same pop-cultural force that draws viewers by the millions to the final episodes of long-running television shows that have long since ceased to be watchable. If you've ever felt that same **yearning to be part** of the end of an era, it would be popstrologically fitting, as would that sense you've had so many times in life of having **gotten into something good on the ground floor**, but in a broken elevator.

CONSTELLATION
➤ Doo-Wop

CELEBRITY
➤ **Lisa Kudrow** (7/30/63) is a child of the Tymes.

BIRTHSONG
➤ *So Much In Love*
Jul 28–Aug 3, 1963

U2
It's not called a pose if it's your actual posture.

He mesmerized his future bandmates with his rock-star charisma on the day they first met in Adam Clayton's Dublin living room, and if he'd told them then that he could do the same thing to live audiences in the hundreds of thousands, they probably would have believed him. But if the mulletted kid then called Paul Hewson had told them that he'd grow up to be a legitimate player on the world *political* stage, too, they'd have probably said, "Ah, feck off." And yet, he would have been right, for while countless celebrities have flogged their causes on awards shows and in magazines down the years, only U2's leader can ring up the president of Nigeria and say "Obasanjo? It's Bono—I'm comin' over." But never forget that the scale of Bono's political relevance flows directly from your Birthstar's Massive and Lasting popstrological relevance. If U2 had packed it in creatively after becoming the pop universe's dominant star in the year of your birth, Bono might still be wandering the earth doing battle against injustice, but he'd be doing it on a significantly smaller scale, like some kind of upscale Irish Kwai Chang Caine. But because U2 followed 1987's *The Joshua Tree* with nearly two decades (and counting) of Fresh, innovative, and popular albums, Bono finds himself today the world's hippest ambassador-without-portfolio, and you find yourself imbued with the power to **build a life that's true to your ideals**, provided you remain **willing to sing for your supper**.

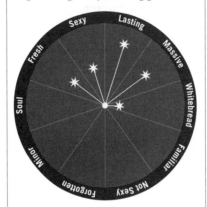

CONSTELLATION
➤ Royal Court

BIRTHSONGS
➤ *With Or Without You* May 10–30, 1987
➤ *I Still Haven't Found What I'm Looking For* Aug 2–15, 1987

UB40
You may not be Midas, but everything you touch will turn into something.

Some would call it a travesty, but to popstrologists it's just a brilliant illustration of pop's quirky, democratic ways that one of the most popular "reggae" songs in American history, objectively speaking, was written by Neil Diamond. Some would even go so far as to say that UB40's entire career is worthy of ridicule for being based almost entirely on the gimmick of reggae-fying other people's hits (e.g., *I Got You Babe, Can't Help Falling in Love*) in the way they reggae-fied your Birthsong, but popstrologists refrain from value-judgments of that sort. Besides, popstrologists know that your Birthstar *didn't* reggae-fy *Red Red Wine*—in fact, they'd never heard any version of the song other than a 1969 reggae version by the Jamaican singer Tony Tribe. So while it surely says something essential about UB40 that their taste in reggae songs led them to the doorstep of Neil Diamond, it's important to realize that what some would call the most lucrative musical gimmick since discofication was meant by your Birthstar as the sincerest form of flattery. A Phoenix DJ fueled UB40's popstrological rise by deciding to add *Red Red Wine* to his playlist four years after its initial release, and in so doing he confirmed the rightful place in the constellation *Regifted* of a star whose popstrological children share a double-edged tendency to **be credited with cleverness they may or may not actually possess**.

CONSTELLATIONS
➤ Britsuasion
➤ Regifted

USA FOR AFRICA
If you had a horn, you'd toot in the morning.

Yes, it raised a great deal of money for African famine relief, but more important, the gathering together of some forty American pop giants into the one-off super-group USA for Africa taught us to be thankful—not just for the many blessings we enjoy in this country, but for the suffering of millions of starving Ethiopians, whose plight made possible the greatest show of popstrological force the world may ever see. Huey, Michael, Lionel, Stevie, Willie, Bruce, Ray, and Cyndi singing *and* waiving their royalties in unison? Bob Dylan doing his famous Bob Dylan impression on tape? Let's see the homeless or the struggling American farmers draw that kind of star power. No, it took tragedy of a different order to engineer your Birthstar's rise, so take a moment out of your day to say thank you. "Thank you, hungry Ethiopians, for making *We Are The World* possible, for making us feel virtuous, and for dropping conveniently from view once we (and our pop stars) grew tired of shelling out for every single this-Aid and that-Aid." For those born under the reign of this Massive and unwieldy Birthstar, the challenge in life may be to **make the most of your good inten-**tions without **patting yourself on the back too much**.

CONSTELLATION
➤ Power Couple (20x)

CELEBRITY
➤ **Robert Iler** (3/2/85) is a child of USA For Africa.

BIRTHSONG
➤ *We Are The World*
  Apr 7–May 4, 1985

FRANKIE VALLI
Your arrival will be greeted like the return of the prodigal who never really left.

In the early sixties, the most powerful man in Newark wasn't a Soprano, he was a falsetto. And not just any falsetto but *il falsetto di tutti i falsetti*—Francis Casteluccio, aka Frankie Valli, frontman for the Four Seasons. Under the leadership of your Birthstar, the Four Seasons grew popstrologically Massive enough to survive even the Beatles, but don't let Valli's work as a solo artist fool you: his loyalty to his crew never wavered, and your Birthstar remains unique among all the stars of the constellation *Spin-Off* for never actually leaving his original group while pursuing a solo career. Indeed, it was Frankie's fellow Seasons who wrote and produced his spectacular solo signature hit, *I Can't Take My Eyes Off Of You*, and his first solo #1, *My Eyes Adored You*. And it was Frankie who led the Four Seasons into battle in 1976 to reclaim their popstrological turf with *December, 1963 (Oh, What A Night)*. Notwithstanding his alliance with the powerful head of the Gibb family on 1978's *Grease*, your Birthstar never abandoned the group that nurtured him, adding yet another stand-up star to the constellation *Jersey Pride* and imbuing those born under his influence with a gift for **asserting their independence** without ever having their **loyalty to friends and family** called into question.

CONSTELLATIONS
➤ Spin-Off
➤ Jersey Pride
➤ Theme Singer

CELEBRITY
➤ **Kobe Bryant** (8/23/78) is a popstrological Frankie Valli.

VANGELIS

In the game of life, you may belong in the pep band.

Far from the athletic type, Evangelos Odyssey Papathanassiou was the burly, hirsute type you might see enjoying a seafood lunch in his Speedo at an outdoor cafe in a Mediterranean beach town. Like the Greek hero Pheidippides, whose ancient exploits gave rise to the modern marathon, the man who called himself Vangelis would probably have dropped dead at the end of a twenty-six-mile run, but if an owlish orchestra conductor like Bill Conti could provide the rousing theme to the ultimate American boxing film, then why couldn't a Sasquatch-like synth player provide the stirring theme to the ultimate British running film? That's what the producers of *Chariots Of Fire* figured, anyway, and that's how your Birthstar got the chance to write the stirring score that won him an Oscar and inspired untold millions of hum-along slo-mo runs, chest out, head thrown back, and elbows flying. In life **there are sprinters and there are marathoners**, and you may even find yourself trying to be both. But if you find the race not all that rewarding, why not follow your Birthstar's example? **Conserve your energy for the finer things in life**, and choose the **reinvigorating power of an afternoon nap** over a **vigorous run along a windswept beach**.

CONSTELLATIONS

➤ Speechless
➤ Eurosomething
➤ Theme Singer
➤ Casio
➤ Hot Hairdo

BIRTHSONG

➤ *Chariots Of Fire* May 2–8, 1982

VAN HALEN

A little more conversation, a little less action, please.

If you were a female groupie chosen to provide backstage services to the band Van Halen during their late-seventies/early-eighties heyday, then certainly you hoped to be assigned either Eddie Van Halen or David Lee Roth himself. Alex Van Halen would be okay because (*a*) he was Eddie's brother and (*b*) he was the drummer, and as for husky bassist Michael Anthony—well, he wouldn't be your first choice, but at least he was in the band. After him, you could live with getting the band's current coke vendor or M&M sorter, but you hoped to avoid dropping too far down the ladder of managers and roadies from there—a distinct possibility in Van Halen's formal and hierarchical system of groupie management. But whatever your assignment, it was a big step up from Bad Company or Triumph to the most important American hard-rock act of your micro-generation—a group that popstrologists agree gave the world of ponderous mid-seventies arena rock just the dose of sophomoric hedonism it needed to transform itself into hair metal in the late 1980s. Like other stars in the constellation ***Tip of the Iceberg***, Van Halen's sole #1 hit belies a popstrological impact that was, shall we say, seminal. **Finding an *emotional* basis for personal relationships** is the greatest challenge Van Halen's popstrological progeny will face, because **the physical stuff is going to come easy**.

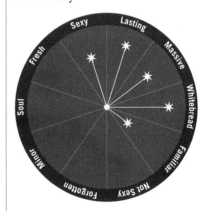

BOBBY VEE

You are the diligent understudy who understands that accidents really do happen.

For Don McLean, it was the Day the Music Died, but for fifteen-year-old Bobby Velline, it was the tragic day his star was born. The plane that crashed in an Iowa field on the night of February 3, 1959, was taking Buddy Holly, Richie Valens, and the Big Bopper north to Moorhead, Minnesota—to a show that the future Bobby Vee was planning to attend as a fan, but instead ended up performing in as the only local kid who could play the chords and sing the lyrics to every song his idol Buddy Holly had ever recorded. Within eighteen months of his tragic big break, this wholesome and handsome middle-American teenager was in the capable grip of the starmaker machine, and instead of singing *That'll Be The Day* in the shower, he was singing the Goffin/King gem *Take Good Care Of My Baby* on *American Bandstand*. Bobby Vee understood that **there is a time to mourn and a time to seize the day**. Will you be as ready as your Birthstar was to **set your qualms aside when opportunity finally knocks?**

CONSTELLATIONS
➤ Regifted
➤ Teen Idol

CELEBRITIES
➤ **James Gandolfini** (9/18/61) and **Joan Jett** (9/22/61) are popstrological children of Bobby Vee.

BIRTHSONG
➤ *Take Good Care Of My Baby* Sep 18– Oct 8, 1961

BILLY VERA AND THE BEATERS

Like Cyrano without the nose, your talent as a mouthpiece may be what makes your name.

Prime-time exposure alone can't explain your Birthstar's sudden rise from near-obscurity to popstrological immortality following the use of your Birthsong as the musical theme to the Michael J. Fox/Tracy Pollan breakup on *Family Ties*. Yes, *At This Moment* was a perfectly solid piece of blue-eyed-soul balladry that fit neatly into the dominant vibe of the constellation **Reaganrock**, but tens of thousands of Americans didn't write to NBC begging to know where they could buy it simply because it sounded good. They wrote because at the moment they heard it, they said to themselves, "Here is a song that expresses a universal human emotion better than I could ever hope to, a song that can become the new opening track on the mix tape I present to every boyfriend/girlfriend who dumps me." In the just-dumped mix-tape hit parade of the late-eighties, there was Peter Gabriel's *In Your Eyes* for those who clung to a last shred of hope, but *At This Moment* was the choice for the merely bereft, whose deputization of Billy Vera as spokesman for their feelings of heartsick disappointment was as responsible as Alex P. Keaton for lifting your Minor and Forgotten Birthstar to his place in the constellation **Regifted**. You may not be one whose **destiny is to star in the show**, child of Billy Vera, but

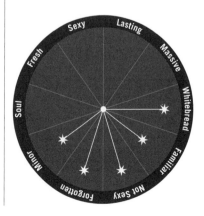

where would such stars be without the folks like you who **feed them their lines**?

CONSTELLATIONS
➤ Regifted
➤ Reaganrock

BIRTHSONG
➤ *At This Moment* Jan 18–31, 1987

LARRY VERNE
If you cannot be timeless, you can at least be timely.

Larry Verne himself was a hired gun, a guy with a great accent who worked down the hall from the real creative forces behind the 1960 novelty hit *Mr. Custer*: Fred Darian, Al de Lory, and Joe Van Winkle. They were the comic geniuses who conceived your Birthsong when one turned to the other and said, "Hey, you know what would be *hilarious*? A song about a frightened American soldier trapped in a losing battle on unfamiliar ground, outnumbered and surrounded by a hostile native

army bent on thwarting his people's imperialist ambitions!" Five or six (or forty-three) years later, *Mr. Custer* would have gone over like a lead balloon unless it were marketed as an allegorical protest song, but at the moment of your birth, Vietnam haunted only the French, "quagmire" was a rarely used word, and *Mr. Custer* was just cute enough to launch your Birthstar into the then-powerful constellation *Novelty Merchant*. Larry Verne himself faded quickly into obscurity after 1960, as did the gentlemen whose groundwork placed him in the constellation *Regifted*, but their legacy lives on in a brood of popstrological children whose **sense of humor might not be for everyone**, but whose **sense of timing is unassailable**.

CONSTELLATIONS
➤ Novelty Merchant
➤ Regifted

BIRTHSONG
➤ *Mr. Custer* Oct 10–16, 1960

BOBBY VINTON
Empires may fall, but savvy emperors can enjoy cushy exile.

Visit his theater in Branson, Missouri, and you'll find the blue-velvet curtain (what else?) on the main stage stitched with genuine fourteen-karat gold. Visit his Web site at www. bobbyvinton.com and you'll find

the gift shop frequently sold out of the Vinton Spirit Body Mist (4 oz./$7.00). Yes, the Stones and the Fab Four put an end to your Birthstar's run atop the early-sixties pop charts (he had four #1 hits from '62 to '64 and none thereafter), but they never threatened the true source of his power, which was his commercial hammerlock on a vast segment of the American pop audience whose tastes ran more to martinis than to marijuana. Bobby Vinton prospered through popstrologically lean years by packing nightclubs and theaters from Vegas to Atlantic City week-in and week-out, for four decades and counting. Some call him the biggest casualty of the British Invasion, but shed no tears for the Polish Prince. For in the end, he didn't just survive the Beatles, he handed them (via the Stones) the infamous business manager Allen Klein, and in so doing helped hasten their eventual downfall. Your Birthstar may have bestowed upon you a **vulnerability to the sneak attack**, but he also gave you the will and the patience to **exact your revenge by living well**.

CONSTELLATION
➤ Old Guard

CELEBRITY
➤ **Nicholas Cage** (1/7/64) is a Bobby Vinton.

BIRTHSONGS
➤ *Roses Are Red* Jul 8–Aug 4, 1962
➤ *Blue Velvet* Sep 15–Oct 5, 1963
➤ *There! I've Said It Again* Dec 19, 1963–Jan 25, 1964
➤ *Mr. Lonely* Dec 6–12, 1964

JOHN WAITE
You may think you've failed to grab the gold ring, but perhaps you've succeeded in dodging a bullet.

Popstrologists have put forth various theories to explain why your Birthstar was never allowed into the constellation *Reaganrock*, but a true consensus has yet to emerge. Some say that being young and British in the year of Culture Club's emergence was enough in itself to scare off the recruiters. Others say that John Waite's #1 hit was simply too good—that a lovely and thoughtful rock ballad free of Richiean schmaltz or Collinsian bombast represented a different kind of threat to the dominant constellation of the 1980s. But skeptics of this latter view point out that while *Missing You* was neither bland nor trite on its own terms, it did represent unmistakable movement in that direction relative to your Birthstar's earlier work in a group called the Babys—a trend that couldn't have been lost on the *Reaganrock*ers. Yet the dominant constellation of the eighties declined to admit John Waite into its ranks not only in 1984, but also, inexplicably, in 1991 after he fully and unambiguously embraced its signature look and sound with a group called Bad English and a song called *When I See You Smile*. Perhaps you, too, have **tried and failed to be accepted by the "in" crowd**, child of John Waite. Perhaps now you will understand why, and perhaps in time you will realize that **what appears to be failure** at the moment it happens can turn out, in retrospect, to have been a great success.

CONSTELLATION
➤ Britsuasion

BIRTHSONG
➤ *Missing You* Sep 16–22, 1984

ANITA WARD
Some may call you demanding, but it's the squeaky wheel that gets the scented body oil.

It never caught on as a feminist anthem the way that *I Am Woman* did, but some would say that *Ring My Bell* marked an equally important cultural milestone in the struggle for women's rights. Catchy, danceable, and refreshingly free of agitprop, your Birthsong laid out a highly practical road map to addressing some real-world gender issues. "Sit around on the couch while I do all the housework if you must," sang Anita Ward in her one and only hit song, "but when I get done, you're going to *ring my bell* all night." How effective was your Birthsong in empowering women to get their basic needs satisfied? There's no way to say for certain, but surely it deserves at least *some* of the credit for all the bell-ringing that went on in the late seventies, doesn't it? *Ring My Bell* has become a treasured part of the late-seventies pop canon, but your Birthstar herself—alas, she went as quickly as

she came. In her brief, bright reign in the constellation *Disco Ball*, however, Anita Ward bestowed upon those born under her influence a **degree of sexual self-awareness some might find intimidating** and a **keen understanding of what makes relationships work.**

CONSTELLATION
➤ Disco Ball

BIRTHSONG
➤ *Ring My Bell* Jun 24–Jul 7, 1979

DIONNE WARWICK AND FRIENDS
Many people wear a ribbon, but you remind them what it's for.

One year after half the known pop universe participated in a recording session to raise money for African famine relief, four middle-aged stars on the downward slope of their careers gathered to make a record in support of the American Foundation for AIDS Research. They were Dionne, Stevie, Gladys, and Elton—a double *Power Couple*, sure, but not a Mary among them (Elton being married to a woman at the time), and no Barbra, Bette, or Diana, either. To be fair, the charitable mission of *That's What Friends Are For* was a last-minute decision that kept a wider net from being cast for big-name stars. Yet and still, it pays to remember that in 1985,

nearly five years into a global epidemic, you might have had an easier time arranging a star-studded benefit for toddlers trapped in wells than for victims of AIDS. But regardless of how much or how little money your Birthstar managed to raise, their biggest contribution may have been simply in raising the topic of AIDS, however obliquely, in a way that didn't evoke fear and denial among the general public, and that was something remarkable in 1986. "That's what earplugs are for," you might say if forced to listen to your Birthsong too much, but "That's what legs are for" is what you might say the next time you're asked why you're always so willing to **stand up for important causes**, even before it **becomes fashionable to do so.**

CONSTELLATION
➤ Power Couple (2x)

BIRTHSONG
➤ *That's What Friends Are For* Jan 12–Feb 8, 1986

DIONNE WARWICK(E) AND THE SPINNERS
They say that opposites attract, but they never say what happens next.

At the moment of your birth, the pop universe witnessed a collision of popstrological Whitebread and Soul the likes of which it had never seen before and has seen only one time since. And while you probably have more practical questions than this regarding your popstrological legacy, you may be interested to know that the formation of your Birthstar helped to answer a critical question in popstrological theory: what happens when two forces of equal but opposite critical aspects collide? What the combination of Dionne Warwick(e) and the Spinners showed, and what the combination of Paul McCartney and Stevie Wonder later confirmed, is that the outcome of such incidents is rarely ever a compromise, and is almost always determined by subject matter. What if your Birthstar had tapped into Dionne's Bacharachian catalog for a song to perform together rather than choosing the groovy *Then Came You*? Would the fabulous Spinners have emerged from the union with their popstrological Soul as decisively sapped as Stevie Wonder's was in the wake of *Ebony and Ivory*? Most likely yes, but that's not the way things happened. Instead, it was Ms. Warwick(e) who was gifted with a bit of Soul after joining in this unlikely **Power Couple**, ending a five-year run without a hit, inspiring her to drop the lucky *e* she had added to the end of her last name on the advice of a numerologist in 1971, and freeing her to pursue other avenues of supernatural fulfillment. You **need not choose a logical partner** in order to form a strong relationship, but **awareness of your relative strengths and weaknesses** can help you defeat the logic of failure.

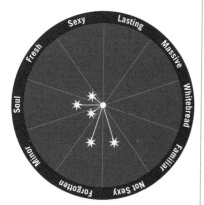

CONSTELLATION
➤ Power Couple

BIRTHSONG
➤ *Then Came You* Oct 20–26, 1974

LAWRENCE WELK
Your ability to elicit sighs of delight is matched only by your ability to elicit tears of boredom.

I t was the Television Show That Time Forgot, and it aired like clockwork every Saturday night from 1955 to 1982. For the generation that grew up on the big bands of the thirties and for-

ties, *The Lawrence Welk Show* was a blessed island of calm in a world gone mad for rock and roll. But for the innocent children and grandchildren forced to watch along with them, it was something closer to *The Island of Dr. Moreau.* The man at this generational flash point was an accordion-playing, Alsatian-accented North Dakotan who kicked off each number with "a vun and a two" and ended with a cheery "wunnerful, wunnerful," delighting the old folks and making the youngsters dream of watching paint dry. With his 1961 instrumental *Calcutta,* Welk earned a place in the popstrological constellation *Speechless*, and endowed those born under his influence with **an anachronistic charm** that may **separate them from their generational crowd** until such time as that generation is drawn to the early-bird hour at the local smorgasbord. More to the point, your Birthstar's trademark sound was called "champagne music," which may explain both the **giddy highs** with which you are sometimes greeted and the **headachy lows** some develop upon longer exposure.

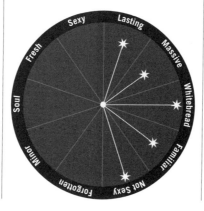

CONSTELLATIONS
➤ Speechless
➤ Old Guard

BIRTHSONG
➤ *Calcutta* Feb 13–26, 1961

MARY WELLS
You can rage against the machine, or you can walk away before your arm gets caught in the gears.

M otown Records didn't have a single top-ten hit until Mary Wells earned three in 1962, and it didn't have a #1 hit until Mary Wells earned one with *My Guy* in 1964. In fact, Motown didn't even *exist* until seventeen-year-old Mary Wells agreed to sign up as its first artist in 1960, so with all due respect to the songwriting geniuses who surrounded her there (Smokey Robinson, Holland/Dozier/ Holland), it's fair to say that, to some degree, Mary Wells made Motown as much as Motown made Mary Wells. So why, then, did your Birthstar jump ship for a big contract at a new label just as her star had reached a new peak? It's easy to see with the benefit of hindsight that this may have been the fateful step that kept her star from rising any higher, but it's also fair with the benefit of the same hindsight to wonder whether Mary Wells really had much choice. With the showy and resource-hungry Supremes looming over the horizon, could your Birthstar possibly have survived her popstrological rise any better than, say, the Marvelettes did? Perhaps she simply had dollar signs in her eyes, but it seems as likely from a popstrological perspective that what Mary really saw was the writing on the wall—that she simply understood at the tender age of twenty-one the cold, hard truth that you would do well to make your mantra: **No matter how much you serve the institution**, and no matter how much it seems to serve you, **institutions will serve themselves first**, even if it costs them your loyalty.

CONSTELLATIONS
➤ Hitsville
➤ Tragic Demise

BIRTHSONG
➤ *My Guy* May 10–23, 1964

WHAM!
There may be no I in "team," but there's definitely an m and an e.

A mericans have always granted greater aesthetic latitude to the English than we do to ourselves, and it's that extra degree of free-dom that made it possible for two Brits in short-shorts, white gloves, and tanning-parlor tans to emerge as stars in America in 1984. Wham!, as they called themselves, always with the exclamation point, was the sensational and grossly unequal partnership of Andrew Ridgeley and Yorgos Panayiotou, aka George Michael. But as irresistible a confection as *Wake Me Up Before You Go-Go* was, you might be tempted to decide upon learning that *Careless Whisper* was a George Michael record credited to Wham! only in North America that your Birthstar's popstrological significance begins and ends with acting as the springboard for the stubbled one's Massive solo career. In fact, popstrologists prefer to look at Wham! as living proof that **even grossly unequal partnerships offer certain compensations** to both parties. To the less-talented Mr. Ridgeley, Wham! obviously offered a brief taste of international celebrity and all the fringe benefits associated with it. But for Mr. Michael, this star in the constellation *Launching Pad* was more than just a stepping-off point—it was something to define himself against, both musically and aesthetically, as he undertook his solo rise. Lennon and McCartney they weren't, but Ridgeley and Michael nonetheless provide a powerful lesson in the **long-term value of discarded friendships** to those born under their popstrological influence.

CONSTELLATIONS
➤ Launching Pad
➤ Britsuasion

CELEBRITY
➤ **Scarlett Johansson** (11/22/84) is a child of Wham!

BIRTHSONGS
➤ *Wake Me Up Before You Go-Go* Nov 11–Dec 4, 1984
➤ *Careless Whisper* Feb 10–Mar 2, 1985
➤ *Everything She Wants* May 19–Jun 1, 1985

BARRY WHITE
When someone asks you "How do you take it?" your answer is, "I don't—I make it."

I t really shouldn't matter who you are or what your orientation is in matters of the heart; if the thought of the late, great Barry White cuddling up against you in satin jammies and grumbling sweet nothings in your ear doesn't make you feel a little bit tingly, there's something deeply wrong with you. A recitation of the song titles alone would be enough for some of us: *Can't Get Enough Of Your Love, Babe*; *Your Sweetness Is My Weakness*; *It's Ecstasy When You Lay Down Next To Me*; *I'm Gonna Love You Just A Little More, Baby*. "But wait," you may be saying, "can a man as ample as my Birthstar really be the most popstrologically Sexy star of the 1970s?" The answer, of course, is yes, for what on this earth is sexier than the ability to make others feel sexy? And what pop star, other than Percy Faith, has made as many people on this earth feel sexy as Barry White has? It makes perfect sense that your Birthstar credited his first (and wordless) #1 pop hit to the Love Unlimited Orchestra, for this Massive and massively Sexy star from the constellations *So-Soul* and *Speechless* was **a giver and not a taker**, and a believer, as you yourself may be on your best days, in **the power of love without limits**.

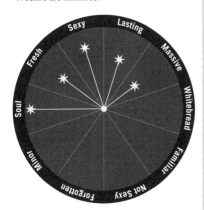

CONSTELLATIONS
➤ So-Soul
➤ Speechless

CELEBRITIES
➤ **Seth Green** (2/8/74) and

Jimmy Fallon (9/19/74) are children of Barry White.

BIRTHSONGS
➤ *Love's Theme* Feb 3–9, 1974
➤ *Can't Get Enough Of Your Love, Babe* Sep 15–21, 1974

WHITESNAKE
You certainly flirt with disaster, yet you seem to make out just fine.

Yes, the advent of the power ballad in 1981 launched the constellation *Reaganrock* and blurred the line separating hard rock from middle-aged pop, but the power ballad was a musical form that was flexible enough to suit practitioners on either side of that divide, as your Birthstar proved in 1987. One might think that a band with a name like Whitesnake and an album to their credit called *Slide It In* faced no danger of being drawn into the popstrological realm of Phil Collins and Lionel Richie. But eliminate the lead guitar from *Here I Go Again* and it's not impossible to imagine Richard Marx or even Peter Cetera adding it to his *Reaganrock* portfolio. But, thankfully, you can't remove the lead guitar from *Here I Go Again*, just as you can't remove a writhing Tawny Kitaen from the hood of the car in any of Whitesnake's late-eighties videos. Those two signifiers, and very little else, kept your Birthstar safely on the side of the would-be devils who called

their power ballads "metal," preventing the dominant constellation of the 1980s from claiming yet another aging remnant of the thrilling 1970s as one of its own. The course you chart through **life may take you over some rather slippery slopes**, but as a popstrological child of Whitesnake, you may just have the dexterity to **slither away from danger**, or toward it as your desire dictates.

CONSTELLATIONS
➤ Britsuasion
➤ Hot Hairdo

BIRTHSONG
➤ *Here I Go Again* Oct 4–10, 1987

WILD CHERRY
You may not give people what they expect, but you certainly give them what they want.

Throughout most of American history, when the white boys in public gatherings started referring to themselves loudly as "white boys," that was the signal for peace-loving folks of all colors to head for the exits. Yet for a brief moment in the year of your birth, your Birthstar changed all that with their famous anthem, *Play That Funky Music*. If they'd had their druthers, the group called Wild Cherry might have chosen to enter the popstrological firmament in the constellation *Mustache Rock*, but fate intervened to save them from barband obscurity and elevate them instead into their fascinating popstrological position as the next-to-last and second-least-likely star in the constellation *Shaking Booty* (after the Scottish Average White Band). Heaven knows they weren't the first group of white boys to take a crack at playing black music, but they were among the first to base their success on calling attention to what they were doing loudly and unapologetically. And therein lies the only truly troubling aspect of your Birthstar's popstrological legacy, for while they trumpeted their musical boundary-crossing with self-deprecating wit, the irresistible song they did it with was later appropriated and stripped of *all* wit by a certain Rob Van Winkle in his pre–*Ice Ice Baby* signature hit as Vanilla Ice. **Defying cultural conventions without causing offense** is a rare and magical gift you may have inherited from your Birthstar, but **beware of the example you set for others** whose touch may not be so deft.

CONSTELLATION
➤ Shaking Booty

BIRTHSONG
➤ *Play That Funky Music*
Sep 12–Oct 2, 1976

KIM WILDE
You've got everything it takes to be a success, but perhaps you're not alone in that.

I f someone had told you in 1987 that Kylie Minogue would still be a viable popstrological entity in the early part of the next century, your first reaction would have been disbelief, and your second would have been to wonder, "Why her and not Kim Wilde?" So similar in look, style, and sound were Kim and Kylie in the year of your birth that only Ms. Minogue's relative youth would have made her seem the more likely candidate to build a Lasting career on a foundation of lip gloss, hair spray, and sugary cover tunes. Perhaps it's because Kim Wilde never took up acting, or perhaps it's because she never took the prudent step of securing uninterrupted public attention through popstrologically lean times by becoming romantically involved with a string of tabloid-friendly pop stars. Whatever the reason, though, your Birthstar clearly failed to make the kind of career choices that can keep a star of less-than-stellar musical gifts popstrologically relevant. But we live in a day and age when it's never too late for a fallen star to turn it around, so who knows? If you travel to England anytime soon, you will find that your Birthstar has established a toehold on celebrity once again, as a television gardener and as an occasional guest star on programs like *Celebrity Detox Camp*, which takes celebrities of precisely Ms. Wilde's stature to Thailand for a week of televised fasting and colonic irrigation. Someone just like you will **achieve a measure of greatness** someday, child of Kim Wilde, and **if you figure out how**, that someone might be you.

CONSTELLATIONS
➤ Britsuasion
➤ Casio

BIRTHSONG
➤ *(You Keep Me) Hangin' On*
May 31–Jun 6, 1987

WILL TO POWER
There's a thin line between archaeology and grave-digging, but it's a line you dare to walk.

They say that Bob Rosenberg's own record label even begged him not to do it—begged him not to mess with the space-time continuum by combining the latent powers of Lynyrd Skynyrd and Peter Frampton into a single medley in 1988. But a man who names his band after a line from Nietzsche is a man who keeps his own counsel, and in the end, America proved Bob Rosenberg very, very right. Even through a haze of late-eighties synthesizer effects, the combination of *Freebird* and *Baby, I Love Your Way* had the irresistible power of a million burning Zippos, and for two short weeks at the end of the Reagan administration, it was the seventies all over again in America as the constellation *Mustache Rock* regained its popstrological ascen-

dancy. Your Birthstar played no encores to its sole #1 hit, and it has been rumored that they were later sucked back through the popstrological wormhole they'd created—back to the year 1975, where lucky time-travelers can find them out on the road as the opening act on Foghat's *Fool For The City* tour. But during their brief reign, they bestowed upon you a certain **anachronistic appeal** that derives from your ability to **make even stale Whitebread seem Fresh once again**.

CONSTELLATION
➤ Mustache Rock

BIRTHSONG
➤ *Baby, I Love Your Way/Freebird (Medley)*
Nov 27–Dec 3, 1988

DENIECE WILLIAMS
You have the power to win fans among those who truly have power.

It may be difficult for you to appreciate it now, but as you move deeper into your twenties and then into your thirties, you'll come to understand how fortunate you are to be born under the influence of Deniece Williams. For your Birthstar is more than just a Minor and relatively Forgotten member of the constellation *Theme Singer*. She is also the popstrological queen of making uncool men seem cool, and that's a gift of inestimable value in almost any career, if you can master it yourself. Actually, your Birthstar got her start supporting one of the coolest men of all time, Stevie Wonder,

but after leaving his backing group, she started to make her mission clear. For her next collaboration, Deniece Williams chose the old and hopelessly out-of-date Johnny Mathis, and her gorgeous and youthful voice proved such a perfect complement that it lifted the two of them into the constellation *Power Couple* in 1978. But it was singing *Let's Hear It For The Boy* on the *Footloose* sound track—over the scene in which the dumpy kid wins our heart by learning to dance—that established her independence and her popstrological legacy. Personally and/or professionally, **clumsy, oafish, or simply uncool** men are likely to play a significant role in your life, child of Deniece Williams. But unlike some of your peers, you may have what it takes to **make that role a positive one**.

CONSTELLATION
➤ Theme Singer

BIRTHSONG
➤ *Let's Hear It For The Boy*
May 20–Jun 2, 1984

MAURICE WILLIAMS AND THE ZODIACS
You might actually be tall, but you know the value of keeping it short.

In 1953, "rock and roll" and "doo-wop" weren't even terms in the American vocabulary, yet thirteen-year-old Maurice Williams had already written two of those genres' absolute classics. But what's more amazing than the fact that *Little Darlin'* and *Stay* sounded Fresh enough to become hits many years after they were written is that young Maurice Williams actually earned money from their success. You can count on one hand the number of naïve, young songwriting musicians who emerged from their first music-industry encounter in the 1950s with their copyrights intact, but Williams did, thanks to the advice of a good man named Ernie Young at Nashville's Excello Records. Young signed Maurice and his friends as the Gladiolas in 1956, and though their version of *Little Darlin'* was trounced on the mainstream pop charts by that of the Diamonds, a white group, Williams still got his author's royalties, which enabled him to keep his group around long enough to change their name and earn their popstrological stripes in the autumn of 1960. The Four Seasons, Jackson Browne, and Rufus would all score hits with longer versions of your Birthsong in later years, but at 1:39 in its glorious original form, it's easy to understand why the shortest #1 record in the popstrological era and the group that recorded it endowed those born under their influence with the wisdom to know that a valid substitute for lasting genius is to **always leave them wanting more**.

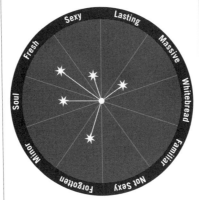

CONSTELLATIONS
➤ Doo-Wop
➤ Invisible Hand

BIRTHSONG
➤ *Stay* Nov 21–27, 1960

AL WILSON
You are the proof that good things can come from unexpected places.

If geography were destiny, Al Wilson would have been in a world of trouble, popstrologically speaking. When you think of hotbeds of soul, after all, you think of places like Philadelphia and Memphis, not places like Victorville and Chino. Those are places where your car breaks down driving between L.A. and Las Vegas, not places you go to launch your pop career. And yet, if your car happened to break down on Interstate 15 sometime in the early 1970s and you found yourself with some time to kill in Palmdale, you might have wandered into a nondescript nightclub and heard Al Wilson working like an up-and-comer almost fifteen years into his professional career, proving night after night that while Philly and Memphis might be the places where soul was made, it was in places far from the public eye where popstrological Soul was often earned. Your Birthstar made it to the lower reaches of the charts as far back as 1961, and he got a decent crack at stardom in the late sixties with *The Snake* on Bobby Goldsboro's Soul City label, but it was only after eight more years of blue-collar work in the literal and cultural desert that he recorded *Show And Tell*, the song that launched him into the constellation *So-Soul*, from which position in the popstrological firmament he bestows upon you the very **opposite gift of the flash in the pan**: an ability to **heat slowly and steadily** till the moment that you're finally ready to cook.

CONSTELLATION

➤ So-Soul

BIRTHSONG

➤ *Show And Tell* Feb 6–12, 1974

STEVE WINWOOD
Whatever your powers may be, they will someday prove pleasing to the powers that be.

No one ever spray-painted "Winwood Is God" on the streets of London, but your Birthstar was almost as central a player in the world of 1960s British blues and R&B as Clapton himself. From the Spencer Davis Group (*Gimme Some Lovin'*) to Traffic to Blind Faith to Ginger Baker's Air Force and back to Traffic again, keyboard prodigy Steve Winwood covered more than enough territory to enter the pantheon of Album-Oriented Rock legends, but that's a long way from the saturation-level popularity it takes to join the popstrological elite. To earn that status, your Birthstar had to wait until early middle age—the demographic sweet spot for Englishmen seeking entry into the constellation *Reaganrock* circa 1986. In his younger incarnations, Steve Winwood might have cringed at joining a constellation that stood for everything rock and roll was supposed to stand against, but as they say, if the shoe fits. *Higher Love* sounded uncannily like the slickly produced love child of

Lionel Richie's *All Night Long* and Phil Collins's *Sussudio*, and if *Back in the High Life* sounded like a Miller beer commercial waiting to happen, it wasn't lost on the folks at Anheuser-Busch, who swooped in prior to your Birthstar's next album to commission *Don't You Know What the Night Can Do?* for a Michelob campaign. Take care that the **freshness of your youth** does not **give way to slavish obedience to the status quo**, child of Steve Winwood. Unless, of course, you decide that the financial rewards are worth it.

CONSTELLATIONS

➤ Reaganrock
➤ Spinoff
➤ Britsuasion

BIRTHSONGS

➤ *Higher Love* Aug 24–30, 1986
➤ *Roll With It* Jul 24–Aug 20, 1988

BILL WITHERS
It's always better late than never, but you're the type who's better late than early.

Funny how life sneaks up on you, isn't it? How the wide-open vistas of your youth gradually narrow in your twenties to the point that your thirties and beyond feel more like a forced march than a glorious adventure? Well, if you've really managed to convince yourself that it's too late for someone like you to contemplate a total reinvention, just look to your Birthstar for a reminder of everything that's wrong with that assumption. Bill Withers was thirty-two years old before he ever set foot in a recording studio, and even after releasing a debut album with a hit as big as *Ain't No Sunshine*, your Birthstar could still be found hedging his bets and manufacturing toilet seats on a Boeing assembly line outside Seattle. Perhaps he feared that his best inspiration could only come while crafting the platform on which so many others find theirs, but more likely he was simply exhibiting caution, that great double-edged trait that maturity bestows upon us. But your Birthstar did eventually leave job security behind him, and the risk paid off with entry into the popstrological elite on the strength of *Lean On Me* and eventual membership in the constellation *Invisible Hand* on the strength not only of that song's 1987 return to #1, but of the classic *Just The Two Of Us*, credited to sax player Grover Washington, Jr., but written and sung by none other than Bill Withers. **Late bloomers** of the world unite! Follow your Birthstar's example and you have **nothing to lose but your chains**.

CONSTELLATIONS
➤ Invisible Hand
➤ So-Soul

BIRTHSONG
➤ *Lean On Me* Jul 2–22, 1972

STEVIE WONDER
Superstition can also be a good thing, depending on what threatening icons it makes you avoid.

We call it the blind leading the blind when one clueless soul leads another into trouble, but judging from the career of Stevie Wonder, it seems that the blind do just fine when leading themselves—it's when they fall under the sway of the sighted that things get iffy. A star at the age of eleven, the child prodigy behind *Fingertips (Part 2)* and *Uptight (Everything's Alright)* entered adulthood with

no one to answer to creatively but himself. And what he did with that freedom was simply become as Massive, Fresh, and Soulful a star as the universe of pop has ever seen. Before he was thirty, Stevie Wonder had written, performed, and produced some of the best pop music ever made, on legendary albums like *Talking Book, Innervisions, Fulfillingness' First Finale*, and *Songs In The Key Of Life*. And had he ended his career right there, those born under your Birthstar's influence might now walk the earth like giants. But he didn't. And whether you blame Paul McCartney or the auto accident that robbed Stevie of his sense of smell, you simply can't ignore the precipitous decline in Stevie Wonder's Freshness and popstrological Soul following his work on *Ebony And Ivory* (see: Paul McCartney and Stevie Wonder). It is songs like *I Just Called To Say I Love You* that remind us that even the godlike among us are actually mere mortals—a lesson you would do well to remember given your **enviable array of popstrological gifts** and your potential **inability to smell**

trouble in the form of those who might plunder them.

CONSTELLATIONS
➤ So-Soul
➤ Hitsville
➤ Underage

CELEBRITIES
➤ **Whitney Houston** (8/19/63), **Tori Spelling** (5/16/73), and **Joaquin Phoenix** (10/28/74) are children of Stevie Wonder.

BIRTHSONGS
➤ *Fingertips (Part 2)* Aug 4–24, 1963
➤ *Superstition* Jan 21–27, 1973
➤ *You Are The Sunshine Of My Life* May 13–19, 1973
➤ *You Haven't Done Nothin'* Oct 27–Nov 2, 1974
➤ *I Wish* Jan 16–22, 1977
➤ *Sir Duke* May 15–Jun 4, 1977
➤ *I Just Called To Say I Love You* Oct 7–27, 1984
➤ *Part-Time Lover* Oct 27–Nov 2, 1985

SHEB WOOLEY
Your greatest natural ally may be the law of unintended consequences.

He wanted to be a cowboy singing star, but his skills in the saddle and his rugged good looks actually got in the way. Sheb Wooley grew up on a farm in dust-bowl-era Oklahoma, and while his first love was music, he was also a local rodeo champion by age eleven. He hoped to become the next Gene Autry, but when he got to Hollywood in the late forties, he soon found himself being handed acting roles in movie westerns instead, and his career as a country-and-western singer stalled. He became a regular on the classic TV series *Rawhide*, but he never quit singing, and it was his reluctant decision to record a joke song he'd written called *The Purple People Eater* that foreshadowed the second act in Wooley's career. Embracing his knack for parody, Sheb Wooley developed a comic alter ego named Ben Colder, whose drunken parodies of country-music stars would eventually earn Wooley the showbiz stardom that had eluded him as a "legit" musician. **Your place on life's stage may not be quite where you intended** it to be, child of Sheb Wooley, but count yourself lucky. In a career that took him from *High Noon* to *Hee Haw*, your Birthstar embodied the ancient adage that **the key to survival is adaptability**, and so, in your own way, have you.

CONSTELLATION

➤ Novelty Merchant

CELEBRITIES

➤ **Prince** (6/7/58) and **Kevin Bacon** (7/8/58) are Sheb Wooleys, born under the influence of the song *Purple People Eater*.

BIRTHSONG

➤ *Purple People Eater*
Jun 2–Jul 20, 1958

YES

You are the smooth little acorn that falls from an old and twisted oak.

There was a time in rock history when a band could release an entire vinyl LP consisting of just two tracks, and even if those tracks averaged twenty-two minutes in length and had names like *Fish (Schindleria Praematurus)*, that band would be called "progressive" rather than "insane." This strange time was called the early 1970s, or at least it was for most of your Birthstar's ilk. Most prog rockers either faded quietly into obscurity or left their symphonic pretensions behind them when rock fashions changed, but the band called Yes just said no to that trend, and soldiered on well into the nineties as the sole survivors in an otherwise extinct genus of dinosaur rock. "But wait," you say, "my Birthsong is not a ponderous song-suite with a name like *And You and I: Cord of Life/Eclipse/The Preacher The Teacher/Apocalypse*." Okay, Yes did

once stray briefly from their tried-and-true formula. And yes, you could listen to your Birthsong and hear in its metallic *shweeks* and *chunka-chunk*s the familiar broken-toy sounds of a lot of eighties synth pop. But everything about *Owner Of A Lonely Heart* sets it apart from the oeuvre of your Birthstar, from its sound and length to the total lack of punctuation marks in its title. And so, though it would be going too far to call you the **simple-minded product of an intellectual bloodline**, it is true that **unpretentiousness and accessibility** are not entirely out of your reach.

CONSTELLATIONS

➤ Britsuasion
➤ Tip of the Ice Cube

BIRTHSONG

➤ *Owner Of A Lonely Heart*
Jan 15–28, 1984

NEIL YOUNG

For a brooding loner, you make quite a social impact.

It may be true that history is driven as much by chance as by any other logic, but if someone tries to tell you that it was anything other than the guiding hand of fate at work when Stephen Stills flagged down a familiar Pontiac hearse on the streets of L.A. in 1965, you tell them to shop their cockamamy theories somewhere else. Folk-singing Canadian émigré Neil Young was the driver of that hearse, and he'd barely crossed the city limits when this fellow he'd met up in Ontario recognized his distinctive ride and got him to pull over. Not just Buffalo Springfield, but really the whole country-rock revolution was born that day, and hard as it is to imagine the sixties without the Springfield or Crosby, Stills, Nash and Young, it's even harder to imagine every decade since then without the sound Neil Young's groups helped to create. Indeed, any time you hear a rock and roll song that has a certain *jangle*, it's fair to say that your Birthstar had a hand in making it possible. And even when you hear a jangly rock song that's particularly cheery, remember that you might not be hearing it at all but for the existence of a Canadian guitar player dark and gloomy enough to drive a hearse years before *Harold and Maude*. Ultimately **happier alone than in groups**, you are nonetheless **the type around whom movements may form**.

CONSTELLATIONS
➤ Oh . . . Canada
➤ Spin-Off
➤ Tip of the Ice Cube

BIRTHSONG
➤ *Heart Of Gold* Mar 12–18, 1972

PAUL YOUNG

Some are givers and some are takers, but you are the type who gives by taking.

The idea that songwriting is the underpinning of a pop star's legitimacy can be traced directly to the post-Beatles sixties, and so can the idea that legitimacy is a legitimate criterion by which to judge a pop star. The doctrine of legitimacy, if applied strictly, would rank Duran Duran over Frank Sinatra, and Vangelis over Louis Armstrong, so perhaps there is no reason to feel disappointed to learn that you were born under the influence of a star whose only discernible gift was for producing deeply felt remakes of other people's creations. It was a Hall and Oates cover that elevated Paul Young into the popstrological firmament, but it was covers of Marvin Gaye and the Four Preps that made him a huge star in England even before the success of *Everytime You Go Away*, and it was covers of Joy Division, Ann Peebles, Crowded House, Free, and the Chi-Lites that kept his relatively Minor star burning into the early nineties. In this respect, your Birthstar is much more closely related to Tom Jones than he is to Bob Dylan, but ask Bob Dylan or the dozens of writers behind the songs in your Birthstar's catalog how they feel when their royalty checks arrive in the mail, and you'll understand how legitimate a man like Paul Young is in their eyes. **You may not be the total package**, child of Paul Young, but **those you lean on for your missing pieces will be more than happy to have your business**.

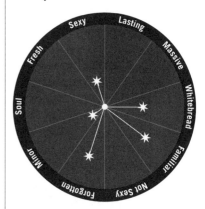

CONSTELLATION
➤ Britsuasion

BIRTHSONG
➤ *Everytime You Go Away* Jul 21–27, 1985

ZAGER AND EVANS

Some will call you a visionary, others a Cassandra. Some will simply call you "heavy."

Despite the impression that television might give, Hendrix, the Who, and the Jefferson Airplane were not the only sound of their generation. In fact, when a hundred thousand college students headed home from Woodstock, the song they probably listened to on the drive back to Long Island wasn't *Purple Haze*—it was the ponderous *In the Year 2525 (Exordium and Terminus)* by Denny Zager and Rick Evans, the biggest stars ever to emerge from the Lincoln, Nebraska, motel-lounge circuit. With their trippy dystopian visions of an armless, foodless future, Zager and Evans were like Nostradamus for bong smokers, and they ruled the pop universe absolutely in the summer of 1969. So why have you never heard of them? Blame the relentless efforts of the baby boomers to package and market a grossly incomplete "official" memory of their teenage years. With their talk of environmental collapse, human cloning, and the total disappearance of chewy foods, your Birthstar provided **powerful and thought-provoking subject matter** to a generation grappling with the urgent question of whether their entire universe might be, like, just a single atom in the fingernail of some giant creature somewhere. Yet like so many stars in the constellation *Had to Be There*, they've been nearly expunged from popular memory, the tragic victims of the what-were-we-thinking phenomenon. You too might someday **find yourself the unlikely master of a given moment in space-time**, but always remember that **instant fans can sometimes be fickle.**

CONSTELLATION
➤ Had to Be There

BIRTHSONG
➤ *In The Year 2525 (Exordium & Terminus)*
Jul 6–Aug 16, 1969

CONSTELLATIONS

Artificial Ingredients

I f performing under an assumed name or letting studio musicians record everything but the vocals on their hit singles was enough to qualify a pop group as artificial, then this would be the largest constellation in the pop universe by far, and it would include more "legitimate" names than you might expect. But entry into the constellation *Artificial Ingredients* actually required artifice of a much more substantial sort, such as outright deceit (**Milli Vanilli, the Crystals**), concocting an artificial story to abet your popstrological rise (**Paul and Paula, C. W. McCall**), or having real musicians who had nothing to do with a group's hit record assume that group's identity (**the New Vaudeville Band, Steam, Silver Convention**). Yet by far the most powerful members of this constellation of misleaders are two stars that no one ever thought were real (**the Chipmunks** and **the Archies**) and two that no one with any sense ever should have (**the Monkees** and **the Partridge Family**). But of course the question of what "real" even means in the context of popular culture is a valid one, especially considering how enjoyable the music of many of these very unreal stars is.

RELATIONSHIP ISSUES

They say that honesty is the foundation of any successful relationship, but considering how difficult it is to maintain a relationship once both parties reveal their true, dysfunctional selves, perhaps there's something to be said for those who stick to portraying the selves they'd rather be instead. On the other hand, children of the constellation *Artificial Ingredients* who can't keep up their act face a rockier transition than most when their outward personality gives way to the real and flawed person within, no matter how enjoyable that person may be.

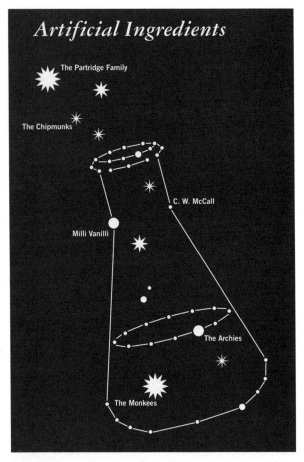

Artificial Ingredients

THE STARS
(*in order of appearance*):

1. The Chipmunks
2. The Crystals
3. Paul and Paula
4. The Monkees
5. The New Vaudeville Band
6. The Archies
7. Steam
8. The Partridge Family
9. Silver Convention
10. C. W. McCall
11. Stars on 45
12. Exposé
13. Milli Vanilli

Britsuasion

As the seventies neared their end, not a single new star had entered the popstrological firmament from Britain since 1975, and notwithstanding a prominent group of Australian brothers, the four years following the arrival of the Bay City Rollers were a period of all-American dominance in the pop universe. But then, just as the popstrological Year of Donna Summer was coming to a close, a strange creature named **M** appeared on the horizon. He couldn't have seemed like much of a threat to American hegemony at the time, but is it any accident that within one hundred days of his arrival, the Eagles, the Commodores, Donna Summer, Barbra Streisand, KC and the Sunshine Band, and Captain and Tennille *all* made their final popstrological appearances? Did the Britsuaders compensate by bringing us some truly strange and wonderful fruits in the years to come? Of course they did—they were British. But for every **Queen**, **Culture Club**, and **George Michael**, there was also a **Phil Collins**, **Robert Palmer**, or **Steve Winwood**—stars who fueled their rise into the popstrological firmament by masking their inner Britishness and pursuing the crafty strategy of aligning themselves with the constellation *Reaganrock.* Everyone talks about the British Invasion, and understandably so, for the stars who led it are among the most powerful the universe has ever seen. But if success is measured in numbers, it is not the stars of the constellation *Britvasion* but the far less flashy stars of the constellation *Britsuasion* who were the true conquerors of America.

RELATIONSHIP ISSUES

The dirty little secret we never talk about when we talk about relationships is the critical role of power in determining their success. Who holds it, who lacks it? It's not always true that one party does just one or the other, but especially in romantic relationships, it's almost never true that both parties share it equally. And certainly it's unlikely to be true in relationships involving children of the constellation *Britsuasion*, for their gift is to show great skill at gaining and preserving power, and without even seeming as if it were their intent to do so.

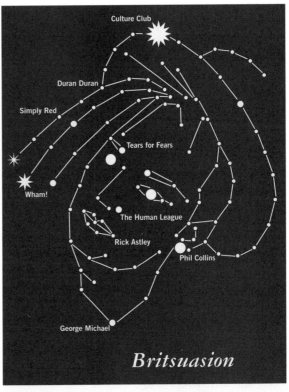

Britsuasion

THE STARS
(*in order of appearance*):
1. M
2. Queen
3. Pink Floyd
4. Sheena Easton
5. The Human League
6. Dexy's Midnight Runners
7. Eurythmics
8. Bonnie Tyler
9. Yes
10. Culture Club
11. Phil Collins
12. Duran Duran
13. John Waite
14. Wham!
15. George Michael
16. Simple Minds
17. Tears for Fears
18. Paul Young
19. Dire Straits
20. Robert Palmer
21. Pet Shop Boys
22. Simply Red
23. Genesis
24. Peter Gabriel
25. Steve Winwood
26. Bananarama
27. Kim Wilde
28. Whitesnake
29. Billy Idol
30. Rick Astley
31. Def Leppard
32. UB40
33. Escape Club
34. Mike and the Mechanics
35. Fine Young Cannibals

Britvasion

They called it the British Invasion, but if you'd asked the young invaders what their secret weapon was, each and every one of them would have given you the same answer: good old American rock and roll. It wasn't conquest but rather reconquest they sought. The only goal of these (mostly) boys from the Mersey and the Thames at the time was to reclaim the pop universe for the forces of real rock and roll, and if that meant banishing the likes of Bobby Vinton to the lucrative ash heap of Las Vegas history, then so be it. Which is not to say that all of the stars in the constellation *Britvasion* rose on the strength of a sound as raw and thrilling as that of **the Beatles**, **the Animals**, and **the Rolling Stones**. No, stars like **Herman's Hermits** and **Petula Clark** bore little resemblance to those fierce British warriors, yet they were embraced with nearly as much enthusiasm during this constellation's four-year reign. Only thirteen stars joined the constellation *Britvasion*, but the popstrological impact of this grouping cannot be overstated, for it was the British Invasion that sent American rock and roll bands scurrying back into the garage, where they took a page from the conquerors' book and began applying themselves to unlearning all of the sheen and polish that had crept into American pop in the years preceding the Beatles' arrival.

RELATIONSHIP ISSUES

There are those who take their time easing into new relationships, even to the point of masking their true intentions for fear of scaring someone off. And then there are the children of the constellation *Britvasion*, whose natural tendencies are closer to a blitzkrieg attack than to a quiet campaign for consensus. And while this approach has the clear potential to backfire, it also has the potential to expose and quickly undo whatever defenses the other party might needlessly erect to friendship, love, or creative partnership.

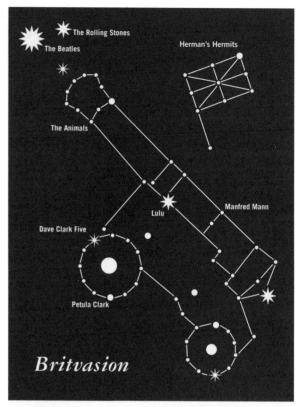

Britvasion

THE STARS
(*in order of appearance*):
1. The Beatles
2. Peter and Gordon
3. The Animals
4. Manfred Mann
5. Petula Clark
6. Freddie and the Dreamers
7. Wayne Fontana and the Mindbenders
8. Herman's Hermits
9. The Rolling Stones
10. The Dave Clark Five
11. Donovan
12. The New Vaudeville Band
13. Lulu

Casio

The constellation *Casio* does not include every star that made use of synthesizer magic in their music, but it does include all of those stars whose sound would be unrecognizable, and whose very existence would be difficult to imagine, without it. It began in the autumn of 1979, when a mysterious figure by the name of **M** rose suddenly and dramatically into the popstrological firmament on the strength of a song no garage band was going to imitate easily: *Pop Muzik*, the first #1 song in the popstrological era that was overtly electronic in origin. Soon enough, the popstrological firmament would be filled with *deet-deets*, *bing-bongs*, *shweeeeks*, and various other broken-toy sounds unimaginable to earlier generations of pop stars. There had been vacuum-tube tinkerers like the Tornados since the early 1960s, and there had even been synthesizer players since the early 1970s, but it was not until just before the dawn of the 1980s that computer-generated music became a popstrological force to be reckoned with and any kid in an average American town could walk into the local music store, hit the "Bossa Nova" and "Glockenspiel" buttons on a Baldwin Fun Machine, and proceed to make *Chopsticks* sound better and stranger than ever before.

RELATIONSHIP ISSUES

We all construct our public personas from parts not necessarily found in our true, inner natures, especially at the outset of our new relationships. But few of us are as comfortable doing it as those born under the constellation *Casio*. If that sounds like a backhanded compliment, though, it shouldn't. Knowing who you really are and deciding who you really want to be aren't quite the same thing, but unless you're a stickler for transparency, there's no reason why you shouldn't find happiness in a relationship with a child of this synthetic constellation who has decided to be something odd and charming.

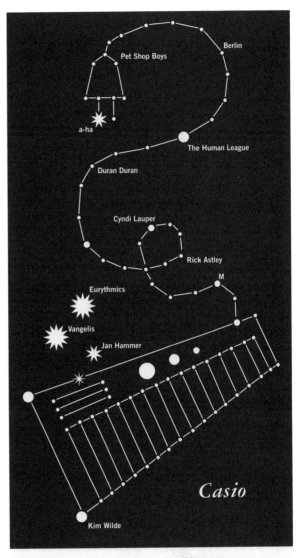

THE STARS
(*in order of appearance*):

1. M	6. Cyndi Lauper
2. Lipps, Inc.	7. Duran Duran
3. Kim Carnes	8. a-ha
3. Vangelis	9. Jan Hammer
4. The Human League	10. Pet Shop Boys
5. Eurythmics	11. Berlin
	12. Kim Wilde
	13. Rick Astley

Country Cousins

It is an enduring mystery why British, Irish, and even Swedish pop stars seem to lose their distinctive accents when singing, while American singers from anywhere south of Baltimore do not. But what is even more mysterious is how country music—a genre often indistinguishable from pop but for the twangs and drawls of the people who sing it—has lent so much to the universe of pop only to become so estranged from it in the modern era. This was not always the way, of course. The line between country and pop was crossed often enough in the 1960s and '70s to give rise to the constellation *Country Cousins*—a collection of stars whose original or eventual home was in the universe of country, but who nonetheless made their mark in the universe of pop. **Conway Twitty**, **Brenda Lee**, **Freddy Fender**—these and many other names on the roster of *Country Cousins* come straight from the country music pantheon, but if you are surprised to see the name **Olivia Newton-John** listed among them, consult your Country Music Association encyclopedia under the listing "Female Vocalist of the Year, 1974." Not a single new star entered the constellation *Country Cousins* after **Kenny Rogers**, **Dolly Parton**, and **Eddie Rabbitt** did so within four months of one another in 1980–81, and while you may not regard that as a tragedy, you might wish to revisit that opinion after you consider that REO Speedwagon brought the constellation *Reaganrock* to life the very week after Mr. Rabbitt's rise.

RELATIONSHIP ISSUES

Looking for love in all the wrong places is something we've all done at one time or another, but too often we overreact to our failure and let our list of the "right" places to look grow too narrow. Not so for the children of the constellation *Country Cousins*. More than most, they recognize the importance of keeping the gene pool diverse, so to speak, and they excel at finding love and friendship outside the social territory that is their natural habitat.

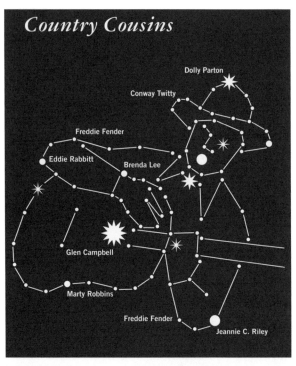

THE STARS
(*in order of appearance*):
1. Conway Twitty
2. The Browns
3. Marty Robbins
4. Brenda Lee
5. Bobbie Gentry
6. Jeannie C. Riley
7. B. J. Thomas
8. Charlie Rich
9. Olivia Newton-John
10. Freddy Fender
11. Glen Campbell
12. The Bellamy Brothers
13. Exile
14. Kenny Rogers
15. Dolly Parton
16. Eddie Rabbitt
17. Kenny Rogers and Dolly Parton

Disco Ball

How did disco rise from nowhere to achieve social, cultural, and popstrological domination almost overnight in the mid-1970s? The answer is that it didn't rise overnight. Like the Imperial Death Star in that far-away, long-ago galaxy, the constellation *Disco Ball* took a while to come together, and there was ample time and ample reason for those who might have stopped it to realize that something big might be afoot in the universe of pop. *Lite & White* and *Mustache Rock*, the dominant sounds of the time, were flat-out undanceable, and if the John Denvers and Grand Funk Railroads of those constellations had been students of pop history, they'd have looked at the defunct constellation *Folkie* and realized that undanceable entities tend to have a rather limited life span in the popstrological firmament. Popstrologists trace the roots of the constellation *Disco Ball* to the appearance of **the Hues Corporation** (*Rock The Boat*) in 1974, but they see the arrival of **Van McCoy** (*The Hustle*) as the event that truly changed the shape of things to come. Before *The Hustle*, it was easy to think that the constellation *Shaking Booty* was covering all of America's dancing needs, but the music emanating from that constellation was ultimately just too rhythmically challenging for white audiences, and so disco was born. And when **the Bee Gees** converted to disco, it was like Constantine converting to Christianity, for it lent the constellation *Disco Ball* a connection to an established popstrological power that paved the way to its world domination.

RELATIONSHIP ISSUES

The thing to keep in mind is that while disco may have disappeared from the pop charts, it never actually died. Disco simply went into hiding in the urban nightclubs where it originated until it could reemerge as a populist favorite once the world grew tired of *Reaganrock*. In a similar fashion, children of the constellation *Disco Ball* may find themselves all too often discarded and disavowed after brief but intense relationships, but eventually, they too will find themselves back in the warm embrace of those who begin to regret ever having let them go.

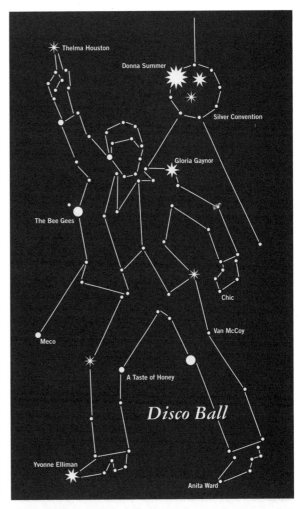

THE STARS
(*in order of appearance*):

1. The Hues Corporation	11. The Emotions
2. Labelle	12. Meco
3. Van McCoy	13. Yvonne Elliman
4. Silver Convention	14. A Taste of Honey
5. Rhythm Heritage	15. Donna Summer
6. Walter Murphy and His Big Apple Band	16. Chic
7. The Bee Gees*	17. Gloria Gaynor
8. Rick Dees and His Cast of Idiots	18. Amii Stewart
9. Thelma Houston	19. Anita Ward
10. Andy Gibb	20. Barbra Streisand and Donna Summer
	21. Lipps, Inc.

*While the Bee Gees made their first popstrological appearance earlier than any other star in the constellation *Disco Ball*, their transformation from vaguely folkie rock and rollers to disco purveyors did not come until 1976's *You Should Be Dancing*.

Doo-Wop

As basketball is to baseball, so was doo-wop to guitar-based rock and roll: it was a form that city kids could adopt with no more physical space than a stoop or a street corner and with practically no financial investment in equipment. It is no accident, in other words, that the state of Texas never launched a star into the constellation *Doo-Wop*, and it is no accident that the Bronx, Brooklyn, and Philadelphia did. Indeed, for every practitioner of this group vocal style that made it into the popstrological elite, there were a thousand others in the cities of the Northeast that didn't, and nearly all of them had brilliant names. In Pittsburgh alone, there were the Del-Vikings, the Smoothtones, and the El Capris, and in the "M" section of the national doo-wop directory there were the Mello-Kings, the Medallions, the Monotones, and the Moonglows. Of course not all of the stars in the constellation *Doo-Wop* had such mellifluous monikers, and not all of them came from east of the Mississippi, but none of them did neither, and stars like **the Elegants**, **the Marcels**, and **Maurice Williams and the Zodiacs** did both.

RELATIONSHIP ISSUES

In a society that prizes individual achievement above all else, it is a rare thing indeed to find someone who recognizes the unique power of collaboration, and the danger that individual ego poses to that power. In the context of relationships, the tendency to privilege cooperation over individual effort is generally a positive thing that those born under the constellation *Doo-Wop* bring to the table, but it can be problematic in pairings with partners who expect more than just a solid backup performance out of their friends, lovers, and colleagues.

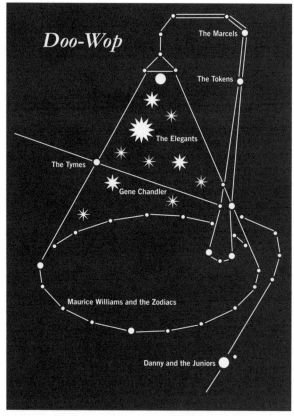

THE STARS
(*in order of appearance*):
1. Danny and the Juniors
2. The Elegants
3. The Teddy Bears
4. The Fleetwoods
5. Maurice Williams and the Zodiacs
6. The Marcels
7. The Tokens
8. Dion
9. Gene Chandler
10. The Tymes

Eurosomething

Americans folded like the French in the face of the British Invasion, and we've welcomed many Canadians, Australians, and Britons in the years since, but we tend to draw the line at popstrological invasion by foreigners who do not speak our language. Indeed, if you look through the ranks of the constellation *Eurosomething*—the collection of stars from the European continent who overcame America's popstrological barriers to immigration—you find only three (**Domenico Modugno, the Singing Nun**, and **Falco**) who sang in their native tongues. Four (**Bert Kaempfert, Paul Mauriat, Vangelis**, and **Jan Hammer**) didn't sing at all, one (**Milli Vanilli**) only lip-synched, and the remaining six were forced to sing in English to earn their popstrological stripes. But perhaps it wasn't only the language barrier that kept more stars from joining the constellation *Eurosomething*, for while some of those who did make it in were suave (**Domenico Modugno, Bert Kaempfert**) and some were sexy (**ABBA, a-ha**), others were more than a little bit "off," in that foreign-exchange-student sort of way. In the end, none of the stars in the constellation *Eurosomething* earned the unambivalent embrace of the American record-buying public, but all of them were too damn charming to be locked out entirely.

RELATIONSHIP ISSUES

One thing all of the stars in the constellation *Eurosomething* did was refuse to be constrained by the circumstances of their birth, and something similar can be seen in their popstrological children. Unafraid to follow their hearts even into unfamiliar territory, those born under the *Eurosomething* stars can occasionally create relationship magic with some rather unlikely partners. But their ability to stay in those relationships tends to vary quite a bit depending on how tightly they cling to their own cultural roots.

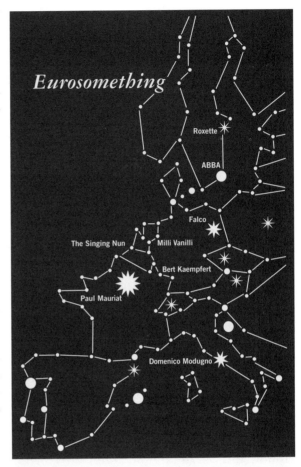

THE STARS
(*in order of appearance*):
1. Domenico Modugno
2. Bert Kaempfert
3. The Singing Nun
4. Paul Mauriat
5. Shocking Blue
6. Blue Swede
7. ABBA
8. Stars on 45
9. Vangelis
10. a-ha
11. Jan Hammer
12. Falco
13. Roxette
14. Milli Vanilli

KEY: *Their countries of origin*
1. Italy 2. Germany 3. Belgium
4. France 5. The Netherlands
6. Sweden 7. Sweden
8. The Netherlands 9. Greece
10. Norway 11. Czechoslovakia
12. Austria 13. Sweden 14. France and Germany

Folkie

The popstrological era is often mistakenly equated with what music historians would call "the rock and roll era." But for proof that the era that began with Elvis Presley was not only about rock and roll, one need look no farther than the stars of the small but influential constellation *Folkie*. Was *Tom Dooley* a rock-and-roll song? Were **Peter, Paul and Mary** rock and rollers? Clearly not, yet groups like **the Kingston Trio** and songs like *Puff The Magic Dragon* were critical cultural forces in the world of the 1950s and '60s, both to the sincere and often arrhythmic white collegians who embraced them and to the raucous party boys and girls who abhorred them. Indeed, even while the other kids were rockin' 'round the clock, a sizable contingent of young Americans was instead swaying gently to songs like *Michael* (as in *"row your boat ashore"*). Notably absent in this popstrological grouping of **Highwaymen** and **Rooftop Singers** are names like Bob Dylan, Joan Baez, and Phil Ochs, but Little Richard and Chuck Berry could tell you something about the difference between cultural significance and commercial reward, too. They just wouldn't try to write a folk song about it. Not every star in the constellation *Folkie* actually gained entry on the strength of a folk song, but even that fact shows you how intertwined folk music and rock and roll had become by the time *Folkie* stars like **Simon and Garfunkel**, **Melanie**, and **Gordon Lightfoot** made their popstrological breakthroughs.

RELATIONSHIP ISSUES

It can be easy in a relationship to fall into routines, including the routine of failing to express your deepest feelings with heartfelt sincerity. It would certainly be going too far to say that the children of the constellation *Folkie* are immune to this tendency, but it would not be going too far to say that they are the type to stand up and agitate against it. Indeed, passionate protest comes easily to those born under this deeply sincere constellation, so be prepared to have your consciousness raised and your authority questioned if you should find yourself involved with one.

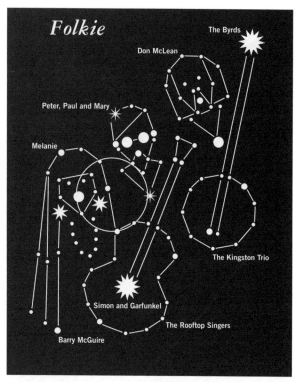

THE STARS
(in order of appearance):
1. Jimmie Rodgers
2. The Kingston Trio
3. The Highwaymen
4. The Rooftop Singers
5. The Byrds
6. Barry McGuire
7. Simon and Garfunkel
8. Peter, Paul and Mary
9. Melanie
10. Don McLean
11. Gordon Lightfoot

Fresh Breeze

Pop-music styles come and pop-music styles go, but the one pop-music style that's never out of date is the style that sounds almost nothing like everything else you're hearing at a given point in time. That's the style that unites the members of the constellation *Fresh Breeze*, a popstrological body that **Elvis Presley** brought into being at the very dawn of the popstrological era, but an entity that showed its stylistic nonexclusivity when **the Kingston Trio** breezed to the top of the pop charts in 1958 with a song about death by hanging that was every bit as Fresh as it was morose. *Quarter To Three* (**Gary "U.S." Bonds**), *Monday, Monday* (**the Mamas and the Papas**), *Tighten Up* (**Archie Bell and the Drells**), *I Love Rock 'N Roll* (**Joan Jett and the Blackhearts**), and *Sweet Child O' Mine* (**Guns N' Roses**)—many if not most of the #1 songs by the stars in the constellation *Fresh Breeze* will sound as thrilling fifty years from now as they do today, but if *Tom Dooley* doesn't sound particularly Fresh to you, remember that popstrological Freshness is all about context, and there was nothing contextually Fresher over the course of the popstrological era than the musical output of the stars in the constellation *Fresh Breeze*.

RELATIONSHIP ISSUES

There is nothing more captivating than the kind of charm that disarms your defenses because it's so far out of the ordinary. That's the kind of left-field charm that often blesses those born under the constellation *Fresh Breeze* with an ability to dive deep and quickly into new relationships, whether romantic or platonic. The thing about *Fresh Breeze*s, though, is that they are not the same as sustained winds, so look for more than just charm from a child of this constellation if you hope to make your voyage with him or her on the ship of love or friendship a long one.

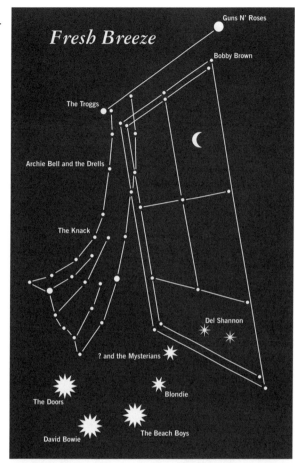

THE STARS
(*in order of appearance*):
1. Elvis Presley
2. The Kingston Trio
3. Lloyd Price
4. The Champs
5. Santo and Johnny
6. Del Shannon
7. Gary "U.S." Bonds
8. The Four Seasons
9. The Beatles
10. The Beach Boys
11. The Righteous Brothers
12. The Byrds
13. The Rolling Stones
14. Lou Christie
15. Nancy Sinatra
16. The (Young) Rascals
17. The Mamas and the Papas
18. The Troggs
19. Donovan
20. ? and the Mysterians
21. The Doors
22. Archie Bell and the Drells
23. Shocking Blue
24. Johnny Nash
25. David Bowie
26. ABBA
27. Blondie
28. The Knack
29. M
30. Kim Carnes
31. Joan Jett and the Blackhearts
32. Dexy's Midnight Runners
33. Eurythmics
34. Club Nouveau
35. Los Lobos
36. Terence Trent D'Arby
37. Guns N' Roses
38. Bobby Brown
39. Fine Young Cannibals

Gene Pool

They say that America is a nation without an aristocracy, but if that's true in some technical sense, it's clearly false in every other, for ours is a country that has time and again shown its willingness to suspend its critical faculties and put its trust in our most prominent families. And not just in politics, but in pop music, too, for would we have given stars like **Donny Osmond** and **Shaun Cassidy** anywhere near as much attention as we did if they had just been Donny Doe and Shaun Smith? Some of the stars in the constellation *Gene Pool* are popstrological legacies, but most are family acts that rose entirely on their own merits, with one of those key merits being the fact that they were family acts. And what is it about a family act that we find so appealing? Is it the thrill of unmistakably similar voices singing in harmony, or is it the challenge of figuring out how one family could produce so much harmonious talent while our own produced something far less impressive? As long as parents have been able to make money off their musically talented offspring, there have been brother, sister, and brother-and-sister acts, but in the popstrological era, the power of the stars in the constellation *Gene Pool* is difficult to overstate. For is it even possible to imagine the shape of the pop universe without the influence of the **Jackson 5, the Bee Gees**, and the stars related to them by blood?

RELATIONSHIP ISSUES

Families are wonderful things, but families can also f*ck you up, and the same can be said for what families can do to your relationships. It would be both inaccurate and unfair to say that the children of the constellation *Gene Pool* are any more likely than the rest of us to let their families get in the way of their friendships and romantic relationships, but it *would* be fair to say that they are much more likely to exhibit behavior in those relationships that is directly traceable to the twisted influence of the families that raised them.

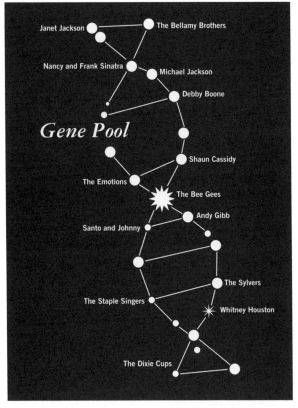

THE STARS
(*in order of appearance*):
1. The Everly Brothers
2. The Browns
3. Santo and Johnny
4. Nino Tempo and April Stevens
5. The Dixie Cups
6. The Shangri-Las
7. Nancy Sinatra
8. Nancy and Frank Sinatra
9. The Jackson 5
10. The Carpenters
11. The Osmonds
12. The Bee Gees
13. Donny Osmond
14. The Staple Singers
15. Michael Jackson
16. The Bellamy Brothers
17. The Sylvers
18. Shaun Cassidy
19. Andy Gibb
20. The Emotions
21. Debby Boone
22. Whitney Houston
23. Janet Jackson

KEY: *Their genetic bonds*
1. brothers 2. brother and sisters
3. brothers 4. brother and sister
5. sisters and cousin 6. two sets of sisters 7. daughter (of Frank Sinatra) 8. father and daughter
9. brothers 10. brother and sister
11. brothers 12. brothers
13. brother (of the Osmonds)
14. father and daughters
15. brother (of the Jackson 5)
16. brothers 17. brothers and sisters 18. son/ half brother (of Shirley Jones/ David Cassidy of the Partridge Family) 19. brother (of the Bee Gees) 20. sisters and sometimes a cousin 21. daughter (of Pat Boone) 22. cousin (of Dionne Warwick) 23. sister (of Michael Jackson)

Had to Be There

There are hundreds of songs in the popstrological canon that sound dated—songs like *At The Hop* or *Tie A Yellow Ribbon Round The Old Oak Tree*, for instance, which are nearly impossible to listen to as anything other than nostalgic time capsules. But then there are songs like *In The Year 2525 (Exordium & Terminus)* by **Zager and Evans** and *Disco Duck* by **Rick Dees and His Cast of Idiots**—songs that are almost impossible to listen to period, or at least songs that are impossible to listen to without shaking your head and wondering how they ever could have been #1 hits. Indeed, try as you may to understand the popstrological success of the stars in this constellation, you cannot do it without resorting to the logic of the phrase, "Well, I guess you *Had to Be There*." You really did have to be there in the mid-1970s to understand why *Convoy* (**C. W. McCall**) and *Kung Fu Fighting* (**Carl Douglas**) weren't regarded as ridiculous joke-songs, and you really, *really* had to be there in the early sixties to understand how **Joe Dowell** and **the Singing Nun** gained entry into the popstrological firmament on the strength of a cover of a half-German Elvis song and a French-language tribute to Saint Dominic. Some of the songs that emanated from this constellation have more than novelty value to recommend them, yet still they are songs that could not have been created in just any social-historical context. Even those of us who lived through and enjoyed some of the songs by the stars of the constellation *Had to Be There* have a hard time believing that we ever really *were* there, yet who can deny the fun of asking and attempting to answer the eternal question, "What were we thinking?"

RELATIONSHIP ISSUES

We've all been in relationships that seemed like a good or at least a plausible idea at the time we entered into them, only to decide shortly thereafter that they were anything but. The children of the stars in the constellation *Had to Be There* may not be any more likely than the rest of us to find themselves shaking their heads over some of their partnering decisions, but they certainly are more likely than the rest of us to be the cause of such head-shaking, especially when paired with partners who carefully guard their public images.

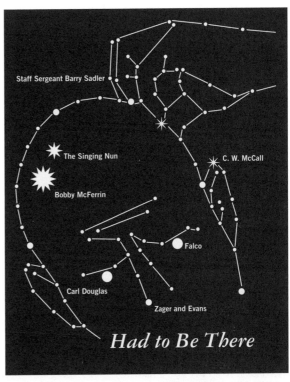

Staff Sergeant Barry Sadler
The Singing Nun
Bobby McFerrin
C. W. McCall
Falco
Carl Douglas
Zager and Evans

Had to Be There

THE STARS
(*in order of appearance*):
1. Joe Dowell
2. The Singing Nun
3. Staff Sergeant Barry Sadler
4. The New Vaudeville Band
5. Zager and Evans
6. Paul Revere and the Raiders
7. Carl Douglas
8. C. W. McCall
9. Rick Dees and His Cast of Idiots
10. Meco
11. Stars on 45
12. Falco
13. Bobby McFerrin

Hitsville

There was a time in pop history when you could hear a record for the very first time and have a pretty good chance of guessing where it was recorded. The sounds of Chicago, Memphis, Philadelphia, Muscle Shoals, and even L.A. were easy to recognize in an era when individual record labels really did have their own individual sounds, but for every music fan living today who can still pick out the sound of an old Chess, Atlantic, Stax, or Columbia record, there are approximately three million who can pick out the sound of an old Motown record. Berry Gordy, the starmaker behind the constellation *Hitsville*, ran several separate labels out of the Detroit headquarters from which this constellation takes its name, but whether it was a **Marvelettes** record on Tamla, a **Supremes** record on Motown, or a **Temptations** record on Gordy, every record that left the *Hitsville* factory had that unmistakable, racial-boundary-crossing "sound of young America." This was the sound that **Mary Wells** and **Marvin Gaye** helped to make famous, though in truth it was a sound largely created by an unsung group of studio musicians called the Funk Brothers and a handful of not-quite-unsung songwriter/producers called Smokey Robinson, Holland-Dozier-Holland, and Norman Whitfield.

RELATIONSHIP ISSUES

They called it "the Motown Family," and rightly so, for within the Motown family, favor was both given and taken away, individuality was often stifled, and rifts were sometimes papered over without being healed. But what family doesn't have its share of dysfunction? When you start a new relationship, whether romantic or platonic, you know that time will expose certain foibles and neuroses in your partner that are not at first apparent. When you start a new relationship with a child of the constellation *Hitsville*, though, you can be especially certain of this, and especially certain into what general category those foibles and neuroses will fall.

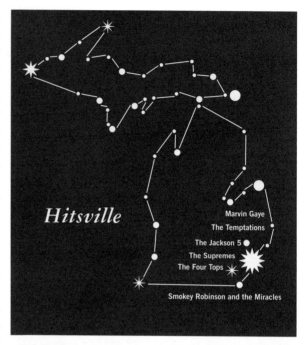

Hitsville

Marvin Gaye
The Temptations
The Jackson 5
The Supremes
The Four Tops
Smokey Robinson and the Miracles

THE STARS
(*in order of appearance*):

1. The Marvelettes
2. Stevie Wonder
3. Mary Wells
4. The Supremes
5. The Temptations
6. The Four Tops
7. Marvin Gaye
8. The Jackson 5
9. Edwin Starr
10. Diana Ross
11. Smokey Robinson and the Miracles*

* Smokey Robinson and the Miracles were not the last star from the Motown label to join the popstrological firmament, but the membership rolls of this constellation were closed when Berry Gordy abandoned Motown's Hitsville U.S.A. headquarters for Los Angeles in 1972.

Holy Matrimony

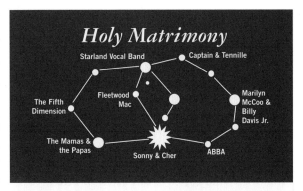

Few married couples would have the courage to try it even in a relatively undemanding professional context, but ten couples in the popstrological era were brave enough to try combining the rigors of maintaining a happy and healthy marriage with the rigors of pop superstardom. Statistically speaking, the average marriage between unfamous Americans stands a 50 percent chance of ending in divorce, but we expect greater-than-average performance from our pop stars, and they rarely disappoint. Fully seven of the ten marriages represented in the constellation *Holy Matrimony* ended in divorce, some of them quite publicly. But as **Sonny and Cher**, the original popstrological divorcés, showed us, the failure of a marriage need not always mean the total failure of a relationship. John and Christine McVie of **Fleetwood Mac**, after all, still perform together as amiably as any two members of that group ever did, and while John and Michelle Phillips of **the Mamas and the Papas** do not, their union did give the world one third of Wilson Phillips. And while the team batting average of the constellation *Holy Matrimony* may leave something to be desired, there can be no disputing that one of its stars, **the Captain and Tennille**, is as bright a beacon of marital bliss as can be found anywhere in the known universe.

RELATIONSHIP ISSUES

It's a bit of a cliché to say that fear of commitment is a common impediment to romantic attachment, but that doesn't mean it's not true. Thank heavens for the children of the constellation Holy Matrimony, though, for while the rest of us may let our knowledge of divorce statistics and our own bitter experience hold us back, they do not hesitate to dive right in. And not just in romance, either, for you would have a hard time finding anyone more ready to make their work friends their best friends than those born under the influence of this constellation of stars without boundary issues.

THE STARS
(*in order of appearance*):
1. Sonny and Cher
2. The Mamas and the Papas (John and Michelle Phillips)
3. The Fifth Dimension (Marilyn McCoo and Billy Davis, Jr.)
4. Captain and Tennille (Daryl Dragon and Toni Tennille)
5. Starland Vocal Band (Bill and Taffy Danoff, John Carroll and Margot Chapman)
6. Marilyn McCoo and Billy Davis, Jr.
7. ABBA (Bjorn Ulvaeus and Agnetha Fältskog, Benny Andersson and Anni-Frid Synni-Lyngstad-Fredriksson-Andersson)
8. Fleetwood Mac (Christine and John McVie)
9. Gloria Estefan and the Miami Sound Machine (Gloria and Emilio Estefan, Jr.)

KEY: *Their marriage outcomes*
1. divorce 2. divorce 3. going strong 4. going strong 5. divorce, divorce 6. going strong 7. divorce, divorce 8. divorce 9. going strong

Hot Hairdo

People say that the advent of music videos in the early 1980s placed a dangerous new emphasis on aesthetic presentation among the pop stars, and on hair in particular, but if you think that the girl groups of the early sixties and the king of rock and roll himself didn't spend a prodigious amount of time tending their high and sculpted or perfectly pomaded hairstyles, you're kidding yourself. Among the stars in the constellation *Hot Hairdo*, you will find trendsetters who helped make their 'dos the hot hairdos of their day (**the Beatles, John Denver**), and you will also find those who merely reflected with perfection hairdos that were already extremely hot (**Staff Sergeant Barry Sadler, the Sylvers, Tiffany**). You will also find some who sported hairdos that no magazine editor of the day would have called fashionable but were nonetheless extremely popular (**Vangelis**) or just undeniably white-hot (**Kenny Rogers**). What unites the stars in the constellation *Hot Hairdo* is that they made their hair a critical element of their graphic presentation. **Isaac Hayes** without his shaved dome? **Janis Joplin** without her unkempt mane? **Neil Diamond** without his visible chest hair and **Leo Sayer** without his whiteman Afro? It is as hard to imagine these scenarios as it is to imagine the aesthetic history of Western civilization in the modern age without the influence of stars like **Elvis Presley, the Supremes, Duran Duran,** and **Bobby Brown**.

RELATIONSHIP ISSUES

Anyone who's the least bit honest about romantic relationships will admit that good looks are important, but that's not the same thing as saying it's important for one's romantic partner to have a "good look." For the children of stars in the constellation *Hot Hairdo*, though, the two ideas may be inseparable, as those who become involved with them are likely to find out.

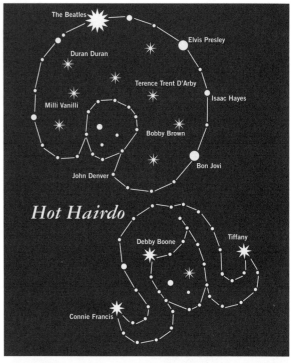

Hot Hairdo

THE STARS
(*in order of appearance*):

1. Elvis Presley
2. The Kingston Trio
3. Connie Francis
4. The Beatles
5. The Supremes
6. The Shangri-Las
7. Staff Sergeant Barry Sadler
8. The Jackson 5
9. Neil Diamond
10. Janis Joplin
11. Rod Stewart
12. Isaac Hayes
13. Mac Davis
14. John Denver
15. The Sylvers
16. Leo Sayer
17. Shaun Cassidy
18. Debby Boone
19. Peaches and Herb
20. Kenny Rogers
21. Vangelis
22. Duran Duran
23. Ready for the World
24. Bon Jovi
25. Whitesnake
26. Tiffany
27. Billy Idol
28. Terence Trent D'Arby
29. Bobby Brown
30. Milli Vanilli

KEY: *Their signature 'dos*
1. slick pompadour 2. collegiate crew cut 3. rock-hard Gidget flip 4. various: mop tops to bushy beards 5. various: beehives to Jackie-O's 6. high helmets 7. G.I. Joe 8. high Afros 9. bushy upper torso 10. styled with a fork 11. rocker-soccer shag 12. Black Powerdome 13. tight male perm 14. bowl of oats 15. sky-high Afros 16. white-guy Afro 17. feathered perfection (male) 18. feathered perfection (female) 19. braids and beads 20. gray 'n' groomed 21. head-to-toe coverage 22. bleached and pyramidal 23. Jeri curls 24. big yet manly 25. bigger yet still manly 26. working girl 27. Bart Simpson 28. long braids 29. the Fade 30. long braids (extended version)

Invisible Hand

There are stars so bright that none of their achievements are hidden from view, and then there are the stars of the constellation *Invisible Hand*, whose popstrological import cannot be fully appreciated without reference to the behind-the-scenes work they did in support of others. Remove the first and fourth members of *Invisible Hand* from history, and you lose *My Way* and *Little Darlin'*. Remove the second and fifth, and you lose the Wall of Sound and quite possibly the Beatles. Not every member of this critical constellation has songwriting credits to match those of **Carole King** or **Isaac Hayes**, and not every member even earned his or her place by writing songs, but every single member of the constellation *Invisible Hand* earned at least one #1 hit of his or her own as a performer and also made some nonperforming contribution without which the pop universe as we know it might not exist.

RELATIONSHIP ISSUES

Sometimes you can tell from the outside what makes a great relationship work, whether it's runaway sexual chemistry or well-matched codependency. But more often than not, the thing that makes certain relationships last is invisible to the outside world. Are the children of the constellation *Invisible Hand* more likely to be supportive and selfless friends, lovers, and colleagues than the rest of us? Perhaps, but they are also more likely to have their support and selflessness go unnoticed, especially by partners whose need for attention is greater than their capacity to give it.

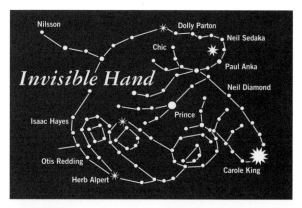

1. Paul Anka
2. The Teddy Bears
3. Wilbert Harrison
4. Maurice Williams and the Zodiacs
5. Bert Kaempfert
6. The Tokens
7. Jimmy Dean
8. Bruce Channel
9. Neil Sedaka
10. The Mamas and the Papas
11. Tommy James and the Shondells
12. Paul Mauriat
13. Otis Redding
14. Herb Alpert
15. Three Dog Night
16. Neil Diamond
17. Smokey Robinson and the Miracles
18. Carole King
19. The Bee Gees
20. Isaac Hayes
21. Nilsson
22. Bill Withers
23. Gilbert O'Sullivan
24. Mac Davis
25. MFSB
26. Gordon Lightfoot
27. Andy Kim
28. Billy Swan
29. Van McCoy
30. Glen Campbell
31. David Bowie
32. The Bellamy Brothers
33. Hall and Oates
34. Alan O'Day
35. Chic
36. Dolly Parton
37. Lionel Richie
38. Toni Basil
39. Michael Sembello
40. Prince
41. Bruce Hornsby and the Range
42. Club Nouveau
43. Richard Marx

KEY: Just some of their invisible contributions
1. wrote *My Way* 2. included Phil Spector, architect of the Wall of Sound 3. saved rock and roll 4. Maurice Williams wrote *Stay* and *Little Darlin'* 5. got the Beatles heard by Brian Epstein 6. made *He's So Fine* and therefore *My Sweet Lord* happen 7. helped launch countless country careers and also the Muppets. 8. his #1 hit introduced the Beatles to the harmonica, which led to *Love Me Do* 9. wrote *Stupid Cupid* and *Love Will Keep Us Together* 10. made the sixties happen 11. covers of their records launched Tiffany and Billy Idol 12. wrote music of *I Will Follow*, which launched Little Peggy March 13. wrote *Respect* 14. cofounded A&M Records 15. didn't write songs, but recorded early songs by famous songwriters 16. wrote songs like *I'm A Believer* and *Red Red Wine* 17. wrote *My Girl* and *My Guy* 18. wrote *Will You Love Me Tomorrow* 19. wrote all of Andy Gibb's #1s, and also #1s by Yvonne Elliman and by Kenny Rogers and Dolly Parton 20. wrote Sam and Dave's *Soul Man* and *Hold On! I'm Comin'* 21. wrote songs like Three Dog Night's *One* 22. wrote and sang Grover Washington, Jr.'s *Just The Two Of Us* 23. filed lawsuit that established unauthorized sampling as copyright infringement 24. wrote *In The Ghetto* and *Watching Scotty Grow* 25. played on nearly every early-seventies record on Philadelphia International 26. Wrote Dylan's *Early Morning Rain* and Marty Robbins's *Ribbon Of Darkness* 27. cowrote *Sugar Sugar* 28. gave a struggling Kris Kristofferson his janitor's job 29. put Peaches together with Herb 30. played on half of all records made in L.A. in the early 1960s 31. produced and/or wrote for T. Rex and Iggy Pop; made Madonna possible 32. David Bellamy wrote *Spiders & Snakes* 33. Daryl Hall wrote Paul Young's #1 hit *Everytime You Go Away* 34. wrote Helen Reddy's #1 hit *Angie Baby* 35. made the record that made *Rapper's Delight* possible; produced half of all early-to-mid-eighties stars 36. wrote *I Will Always Love You* 37. launched Kenny Rogers by writing *Lady* 38. helped define what music videos were 39. played on most of Stevie Wonder's greatest records 40. wrote songs for Sheena Easton, the Bangles, Martika 41. wrote Huey Lewis and the News's *Jacob's Ladder* 42. created En Vogue, which in turn helped create TLC, SWV, Destiny's Child 43. wrote (and writes) songs for Barbra Streisand, Luther Vandross, Josh Groban

Jersey Pride

For the most part, the British invaders of the mid-1960s came from northern cities like Manchester, Newcastle, and, of course, Liverpool—places that occupy the same cognitive territory in the minds of cosmopolitan Londoners that the great state of New Jersey does in the minds of most Manhattanites. And while it's certainly easier to imagine living in a pop universe without the stars of the constellation *Jersey Pride* than a universe without the Beatles and the Rolling Stones, why would you want to try? Even without Bruce Springsteen ever earning a #1 hit, the Garden State produced more (and more important) popstrological stars by far than the island of Manhattan ever did. And while the stars of the constellation *Jersey Pride* may not have invaded anything, they took bridges, tunnels, and turnpikes in fantastically diverse popstrological directions, making critical contributions to the girl-group sound (**the Shirelles**) and to such other big-hair-based genres as disco (**Gloria Gaynor**), hair metal (**Bon Jovi**), and even country (**Eddie Rabbitt**). And of course one native New Jerseyan (**Frank Sinatra**) can possibly be credited with building the pop-cultural foundation of the world we inhabit by becoming the very first modern pop star.

RELATIONSHIP ISSUES

We use the term "inferiority complex" as if it were always a bad thing, but is there anything wrong, pragmatically speaking, with entering into a relationship feeling as if you've got something to prove? Those who are born under the influence of the constellation *Jersey Pride* may swagger with confidence on the outside, but on the inside they tend to possess a degree of humility that can make them ideal and dependable friends, lovers, and colleagues.

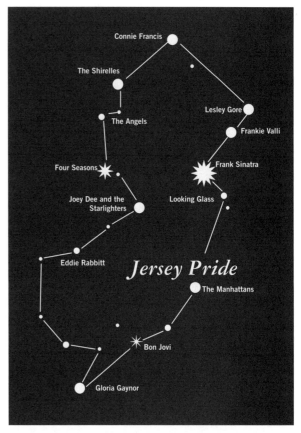

THE STARS
(*in order of appearance*):
1. Connie Francis
2. The Shirelles
3. Joey Dee and the Starliters
4. The Four Seasons
5. Lesley Gore
6. The Angels
7. Frank Sinatra
8. Looking Glass
9. Frankie Valli
10. The Manhattans
11. Gloria Gaynor
12. Kool and the Gang
13. Eddie Rabbitt
14. Bon Jovi

Launching Pad

Ours is a society that has elevated the importance of the individual to unprecedented heights, and perhaps much of what makes our culture great stems from this fact. But our focus on individual achievement also means that we have a tendency to leave some pretty great things behind, and nowhere is that more clear than in the collection of marvelous left-behinds that can be found in the constellation *Launching Pad*. Not every star in this constellation was abandoned by one of its members in the interest of pursuing individual glory. Some dissolved amicably, and some flew apart without any one member being more to blame than any other. But whatever the reasons that caused them to throw off a critical piece of their popstrological mass, it is sobering to contemplate the constellation *Launching Pad* and ask yourself whether the public interest was served by their doing so. Would you choose the solo career of Lionel Richie over another decade of the *Brick House* **Commodores**? What about Sting versus **the Police**, or ten more years of **the Beatles** versus the combined solo careers of Lennon, McCartney, Harrison, and Starr? It hardly matters which you'd choose, of course, for what's done is done. Of the eighteen stars in the constellation *Launching Pad*, only **Chicago** and **Genesis** managed a popstrological return after the definitive departure of their defining members, so pining away for the long-awaited reunion of the true **Van Halen** is pining that might be better directed elsewhere.

RELATIONSHIP ISSUES

When you begin to realize that a relationship can no longer stay afloat, are you the type to jump from the sinking ship, or do you leave the lifeboats to others and remain on board until the water swallows you up? The children of the constellation *Launching Pad* are almost certain to have followed the latter course at some point in their relationship careers, so if you get involved with one and then decide to jump ship yourself, at least you'll know that you won't be the first. If, on the other hand, you find yourself sticking around till the bitter end, at least you'll know that you won't be alone.

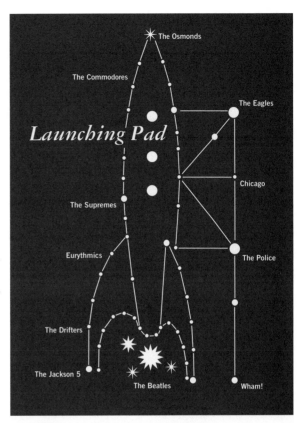

THE STARS
(*in order of appearance*):
1. The Drifters
2. The Four Seasons
3. The Beatles
4. The Supremes
5. The Temptations
6. The Byrds
7. Sonny and Cher
8. Simon and Garfunkel
9. The Lovin' Spoonful
10. The Box Tops
11. The Fifth Dimension
12. The Guess Who
13. The Jackson 5
14. The Partridge Family
15. Smokey Robinson and the Miracles
16. The Osmonds
17. The Eagles
18. The Doobie Brothers
19. Chicago
20. The Commodores
21. The Police
22. Eurythmics
23. Van Halen
24. Wham!
25. Genesis

KEY: *The stars they launched*
1. Clyde McPhatter, Ben E. King
2. Frankie Valli 3. John Lennon, Paul McCartney, George Harrison, and Ringo Starr
4. Diana Ross 5. Eddie Kendricks
6. Crosby, Stills and Nash (and Young), Flying Burrito Brothers
7. Cher 8. Paul Simon 9. John Sebastian 10. Alex Chilton
11. Marilyn McCoo and Billy Davis, Jr. 12. Bachman-Turner Overdrive 13. Michael Jackson
14. David Cassidy 15. The Miracles 16. Donny Osmond
17. Don Henley, Glenn Frey
18. Michael McDonald 19. Peter Cetera 20. Lionel Richie 21. Sting
22. Annie Lennox 23. David Lee Roth 24. George Michael
25. Phil Collins, Peter Gabriel

Les Girls

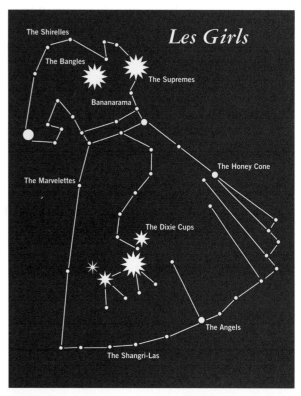

It began with the arrival in 1961 of four fresh-faced girls from New Jersey called **the Shirelles**. They were the very first all-female group to join the pop-strological firmament, and their breakthrough opened a floodgate. In a little less than four years, they would be joined in the constellation *Les Girls* by seven more stars, each of them brilliant in their own way, and one of them, **the Supremes**, more brilliant than anything America would muster for another ten years at least. But it is the collective accomplishment of the girl groups, and especially these early girl groups, that is most impressive of all. For before their arrival, American girls looking to the pop stars for guidance in matters of the heart had to choose between the stiff, parental advice of Pat Boone and the deep dysfunction of Connie Francis. But for all that the stars of the constellation *Les Girls* did to raise the sometimes false consciousness of their fellow girls, let's not ignore the service they rendered to boys, too. Before the girl groups, did boys really know that emotionally distant rebels were more attractive to young women than average-looking goofballs and even clean-cut jocks? Did boys even suspect that if they promised to do right by a girl tomorrow, they could probably get what they wanted tonight? Perhaps on some level they did, but the stars of the constellation *Les Girls* gave their suspicions the force of popstrological truth.

RELATIONSHIP ISSUES

It is said that women are, in some fundamental and possibly physiological way, more attuned to emotions and social dynamics than men. Perhaps they are, yet the majority of the stars in the constellation *Les Girls* made a career out of doling out some rather dubious relationship advice. Popstrology is not so literal as to decree that those born under this constellation's influence are doomed to repeat the mistakes suggested by many of their Birthstars, but anyone involved romantically or platonically with a child of *Les Girls* would do well to realize that their partner's way of thinking will clearly reflect a strong feminine influence, for good or for ill.

THE STARS
(*in order of appearance*):
1. The Shirelles
2. The Marvelettes
3. The Crystals
4. The Chiffons
5. The Angels
6. The Dixie Cups
7. The Supremes
8. The Shangri-Las
9. The Honey Cone
10. Silver Convention
11. The Emotions
12. Bananarama
13. The Bangles
14. Exposé

Lite & White

Some constellations were brought into being suddenly and dramatically in a blast of pop-strological turmoil and rebellion, but this one came on just a bit more quietly, as soft as a summer breeze and as fresh as a ten-year-old Twinkie. The sound of *Lite & White* spawned format changes on FM radio stations throughout the country, as they geared their playlists to suit Americans' evident appetite for the safe and soothing sounds of stars like **the Carpenters** and **the Fifth Dimension**. Yes, the Fifth Dimension, for the group that founded this constellation was also the group that proved that Liteness is color blind and that Whiteness is more a state of mind than a state of being. By the time **Christopher Cross** and **Air Supply** were completing this collection of mellow pop stars, the music emanating from this constellation had established almost total hegemony in previously music-free settings such as doctors' waiting rooms, telephone on-hold loops, and, of course, elevators. But do not mistake the early-eighties demise of the constellation *Lite & White* for the demise of either Liteness or Whiteness, for it was out of the ashes of this popstrological entity and its antithesis, the constellation *Mustache Rock*, that the dominant force of the 1980s arose: the mighty and dreaded constellation *Reaganrock*.

RELATIONSHIP ISSUES

The double-edged relationship effect of the constellation *Lite & White* is to give those born under the influence of its stars an ability to blend initially with just about anyone, but a tendency to grow gradually more difficult to take over the course of time. Indeed, without other popstrological influences to spice up the situation, *Lite & White*s will tend to lose their initial appeal over time except to the least adventurous of partners.

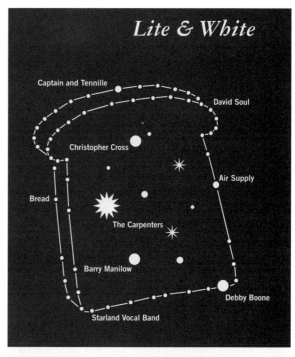

THE STARS
(*in order of appearance*):
1. The Fifth Dimension
2. B. J. Thomas
3. Ray Stevens
4. The Carpenters
5. Bread
6. Tony Orlando and Dawn
7. America
8. Maureen McGovern
9. Barbra Streisand
10. John Denver
11. Olivia Newton-John
12. Barry Manilow
13. Neil Sedaka*
14. Captain and Tennille
15. Hamilton, Joe Frank and Reynolds
16. Starland Vocal Band
17. Chicago
18. David Soul
19. Debby Boone
20. Player
21. Anne Murray
22. Robert John
23. Christopher Cross
24. Kenny Rogers
25. Air Supply

* Neil Sedaka first entered the popstrological firmament long before any other star in this grouping, but his rebirth into the constellation *Lite & White* did not come until 1975.

Mustache Rock

In April of 1970, Canadian journeymen **Guess Who** combined faded denim and straight-ahead guitar rock with the shaggy hairstyles of the departing Beatles to herald the birth of the constellation *Mustache Rock*. Enormous belt buckles, long hair, maybe a white guy with an Afro—these and, of course, a range of fabulous mustache styles were the aesthetic signifiers that united the stars of this small but significant constellation. But *Mustache Rock* was more than just a look—it was the sound of a lifestyle. Led in spirit by the likes of **Grand Funk Railroad** early on, the purveyors of *Mustache Rock* provided a slow but steady drip of guitar-driven hard rock that stood in stark contrast to the sounds emanating from places like the constellations *Lite & White*. The most powerful band in this constellation, **the Eagles**, is also the most popular American pop group of all time, and though they pushed *Mustache Rock* in a significantly softer direction beginning in 1975, it is nonetheless estimated that between 1970 and 1977, more beer was consumed to the sound of *Mustache Rock* than to the sounds of the stars in the constellations *Lite & White* and *Disco Ball* combined. Well into the 1980s, when some former *Mustache Rock*ers like Don Henley had forsaken their scrappy look and sound for something significantly less kick-ass, the late-arriving **Boston** resurrected this dormant constellation, and the apparently time-traveling **Will To Power** extended its renaissance and brought the ghosts of rock gods Lynyrd Skynyrd and Peter Frampton into the popstrological firmament with their medley of *Freebird* and *Baby I Love Your Way*.

RELATIONSHIP ISSUES

Say what you want about *Mustache Rock*, but it was a constellation that loved to party, and therein may lie a central problem for those who fall under the influence, so to speak, of the stars in this grouping. When the supply of excitement is high, all is well, but relationships involving *Mustache Rock*ers all too often end when the initial high of romantic (or platonic) infatuation wears off.

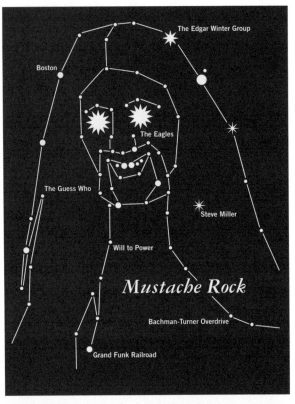

THE STARS
(in order of appearance):
1. The Guess Who
2. The Edgar Winter Group
3. Grand Funk Railroad
4. Steve Miller
5. Bachman-Turner Overdrive
6. The Eagles
7. The Doobie Brothers
8. The Bellamy Brothers
9. Boston
10. Will to Power

Novelty Merchant

At the dawn of the popstrological era, it seemed that the decisive battle over the future course of the pop universe was the one between the Elvis Presley and the constellation *Old Guard*, but no sooner had Elvis defeated the reactionary forces of the status quo than the rock-and-roll revolution faced a threat of a very different nature: an outbreak of silliness in the constellation *Novelty Merchant*. Novelty songs have been around for centuries, slipping in and out of fashion like a sometimes-dormant virus to which no musical genre is truly immune. But never in recorded history has there been an epidemic of novelty songs like the one that struck the pop universe in the late 1950s and early '60s. It began with **David Seville**'s helium-tinged *Witch Doctor*, a song that led directly to **Sheb Wooley**'s *Purple People Eater* and to **the Chipmunks**. By 1962, *Monster Mash* had given the constellation *Novelty Merchant* its eighth star in little more than four years, and with an opportunistic *Old Guard* infection in the form of Bobby Vinton then appearing, it was by no means clear whether rock and roll really was here to stay. Only the magic pill of the deeply serious Beatles brought an end to this constellation's period of flourishing, and it is certainly no coincidence that the outbreak of *Novelty Merchant*ism that gave this constellation its final five stars began almost immediately after the Beatles' breakup.

RELATIONSHIP ISSUES

Humor may be the single most important factor in keeping human relationships healthy and happy. It lightens the mood, it relieves stress, it can even make you live longer—that's why they say "laughter is the best medicine." But let's not forget that the source of that last bit of wisdom is *Reader's Digest*, a periodical whose appeal tends to be limited to bored ten-year-olds and socially isolated senior citizens. The point is that there's a big difference between conditioned laughter and the genuine article, and while no one can question the willingness of those born under the constellation *Novelty Merchant* to try for the latter, their ability to deliver the goods may vary according to the proven ability of their individual Birthstars.

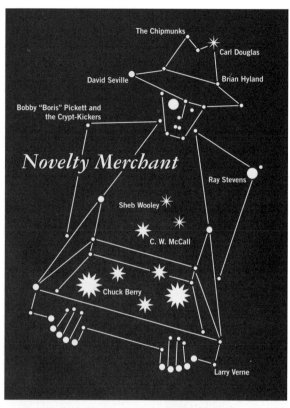

THE STARS
(*in order of appearance*):
1. David Seville
2. Sheb Wooley
3. The Chipmunks
4. The Hollywood Argyles
5. Brian Hyland
6. Larry Verne
7. Ernie K-Doe
8. Bobby "Boris" Pickett and the Crypt-Kickers
9. Jimmy Soul
10. John Fred and His Playboy Band
11. Ray Stevens
12. Chuck Berry
13. Carl Douglas
14. C. W. McCall
15. Rick Dees and His Cast of Idiots

KEY: *Their novelty songs*
1. *Witch Doctor* 2. *Purple People Eater* 3. *The Chipmunk Song* 4. *Alley-Oop* 5. *Itsy Bitsy Teenie Weenie Yellow Polkadot Bikini* 6. *Mr. Custer* 7. *Mother-In-Law* 8. *Monster Mash* 9. *If You Wanna Be Happy* 10. *Judy In Disguise (With Glasses)* 11. *The Streak* 12. *My Ding-A-Ling* 13. *Kung Fu Fighting* 14. *Convoy* 15. *Disco Duck*

Oh...Canada

If you meet someone who looks and sounds as if he might come from Buffalo but he tells you he's not even an American, you might ask him which foreign country he comes from. And if he says, "Canada," the deflated tone of your response is likely to match the name of this constellation: *Oh...Canada*. From the American perspective, there's something vaguely wrong with the fact that Canada considers itself to be an independent nation, but never underestimate the cultural and popstrological distance that separates our two countries. Canadians are nicer than us, they're funnier than us, and heaven knows they're less dangerous than us, but these are not the qualities of which pop greatness is generally made, at least not in the United States. Up in Canada, you can be as nice, funny, and undangerous as you like and still have a shot at domestic stardom thanks to government content regulations mandating that a bit more than a third of all the music a Canadian radio station plays be Canadian in origin. But if you are a Canadian wanting to break into the popstrological elite, your path must run through the United States, where your choices are either to become believably American (**Paul Anka**, **Bryan Adams**) or to mask your Canadian-ness with something like the commanding gravitas of a **Lorne Greene**, the moody broodiness of a **Neil Young**, or the *ss-kickin' hardness of a **Guess Who**.

RELATIONSHIP ISSUES

None of us is completely immune to the appeal of the bad boy or the bad girl; it's simply part of human nature to flirt with danger when looking for love. But it's also part of human nature to outgrow a taste for the wild side and to choose, for good or for ill, to settle down with someone *nice*, someone *safe*—someone very much like yourself, but just a little bit different. This is where the children of the constellation *Oh...Canada* come in, for though wildness is not their forte, mildness that falls just short of actual blandness is.

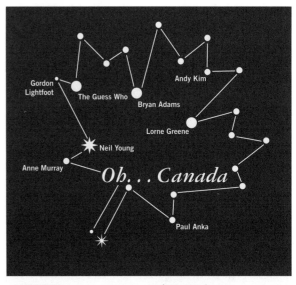

THE STARS
(*in order of appearance*):
1. Paul Anka
2. Percy Faith
3. Lorne Greene
4. The Guess Who
5. Neil Young
6. Terry Jacks
7. Gordon Lightfoot
8. Andy Kim
9. Nick Gilder
10. Anne Murray
11. Bryan Adams
12. Sheriff

Old Guard

In the beginning, there was Elvis Presley, and it was good. Except that it wasn't all that good for the stars who ruled the smooth, sedate, and sexless universe of the pre-popstrological era. Stars like **Pat Boone** and **Perry Como** were commercial powerhouses who looked and sounded exactly the way most of white America wanted its pop stars to look and sound, and they weren't about to take Elvis's challenge to their livelihood sitting down. *Heartbreak Hotel* was the song that opened the popstrological era, and when it ended its two-month reign at #1, the forces of the status quo immediately responded with **Gogi Grant**, who became the second star in the entire popstrological firmament and the founding star in the constellation *Old Guard*. Through the remainder of 1956 and over the course of 1957, other forces of the *Old Guard* were sent forth into battle against the army of the young king, and while it might appear on the surface that they failed, Elvis's victory over the constellation *Old Guard* was perhaps not total. It is true that the pop universe would never again fall under the sway of a star like **Guy Mitchell**, but it is also true that the pop universe would never again be ruled by the Elvis Presley of *Hound Dog* and *Jailhouse Rock*. After 1958, the constellation *Old Guard* was mostly reduced to recruiting nostalgia acts, but the raw and exciting rock and roll of the young Elvis also went into hibernation until January of 1964.

RELATIONSHIP ISSUES

People change, people grow, and sometimes change and growth are good things. But in the context of a preexisting relationship, change and growth can sometimes be perceived as threats to stability. Are those born under the influence of the constellation *Old Guard* more likely than the rest of us to stifle growth and change in their friends, lovers, and colleagues? Perhaps, but there are plenty of people out there who stifle it in themselves first, and who make excellent partners for the children of the *Old Guard*.

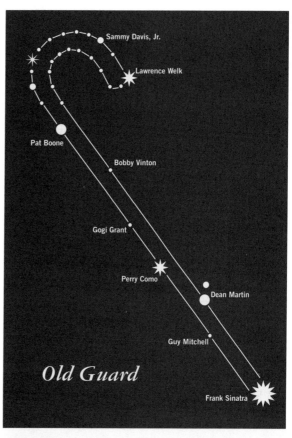

THE STARS
(*in order of appearance*):
1. Gogi Grant
2. The Platters
3. Guy Mitchell
4. Perry Como
5. Pat Boone
6. Debbie Reynolds
7. Tommy Edwards
8. Lawrence Welk
9. Bobby Vinton
10. Louis Armstrong
11. Dean Martin
12. Frank Sinatra
13. Sammy Davis, Jr.

Outback

I t's the curious wildlife that initially earned Australia its reputation for strangeness, but never mind the wombat and the duck-billed platypus—have you ever spent much time around Australians? They're really not the Canadians of the Southern Hemisphere, that's for sure, but the funny thing is, you'd hardly know it by looking at their pop stars. Or at least you'd hardly know it from looking at the stars they launched into the popstrological firmament. The fact that Australia managed to produce **Air Supply** and AC/DC roughly contemporaneously suggests that America did not get to sample from the full breadth of that country's pop-music bounty, for if you look down the list of stars in the constellation *Outback* you will see that except for **Men at Work** and possibly **the Bee Gees**, every one of them could easily have been Canadian. The point is that America put some fairly tight restrictions on immigration into the constellation *Outback*, keeping out the strange and admitting the most assimilated, just as it did with the constellation *Eurosomething*. But as morally indefensible as that barrier to entry might have been, it certainly ensured that only the truly strong Australian exports would survive in America. And that, in turn, explains why the constellation *Outback*, pound for pound and star for star, is one of the most popstrologically Massive groupings in all the pop universe.

RELATIONSHIP ISSUES

Like the children of the constellation *Oh...Canada*, those who are born under the influence of the stars in the constellation *Outback* tend to make intriguing partners because of their delicious mix of strangeness and familiarity. The only difference between the two—and it's a meaningful difference—is in the direction the balance tips between those two qualities. Get yourself a friend or lover who's a child of the *Outback*, and you'll tend to find that familiarity breeds wonderment—wonderment at the seemingly endless layers of oddity that he or she reveals to you over time.

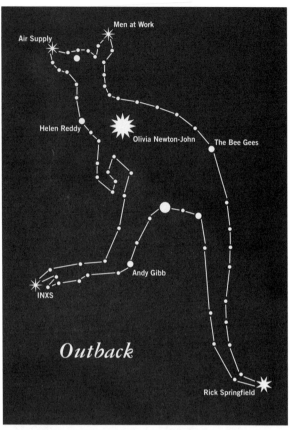

THE STARS
(*in order of appearance*):
1. The Bee Gees
2. Helen Reddy
3. Olivia Newton-John
4. Andy Gibb
5. Air Supply
6. Rick Springfield
7. Men at Work
8. INXS

Outerborough

There are five boroughs in the city of New York, but for popstrological purposes, there may as well be only four. And it's the first borough most people think of that would be the first borough to go. For if you were to rid the popstrological firmament of every star born and raised on the island of Manhattan, you might not even notice their absence, but rid the pop universe of every star from Brooklyn, Queens, the Bronx, and Staten Island, and you might not even recognize what was left behind. Yes, a world without **Barry Manilow** is a world some people think they'd be perfectly happy living in, but a world without **Barbra Streisand**, **Neil Diamond**, and **Carole King**, to name just three prominent Brooklynites, is a world too desolate for most of us even to contemplate. It is certainly interesting to note that every star in the constellation *Outerborough*, with the exception of **Cyndi Lauper** and **Lisa Lisa and Cult Jam**, came of age in the 1950s, and that even Ms. Lauper did her very best to sound as if she did. Was there something in the water or the U-Bet syrup that filled these future stars with a certain something extra? Who knows, but whatever the cause, it can be stated unequivocally that within the entire space-time continuum, no time and place was as densely packed with future popstrological stars as the public high schools of New York City's outer boroughs in the 1950s.

RELATIONSHIP ISSUES

Geographically, they were only a subway or ferry ride away, but the cultural distance that separated them from the center of the world is not to be underestimated. And perhaps that's why so few (if any) of the stars in the constellation *Outerborough* ever moved back to their home boroughs after making it to Manhattan, or L.A., or Vegas: they couldn't return to their roots for fear of being strangled by them. Make new friends, lovers, or colleagues of children of the constellation *Outerborough* and there's a chance they will stick around, but perhaps only after they feel they've reached their proper place in life.

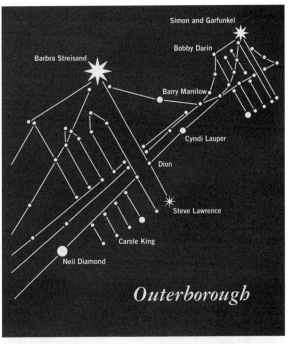

Outerborough

THE STARS
(*in order of appearance*):

1. The Elegants
2. Santo and Johnny
3. Bobby Darin
4. Dion
5. Brian Hyland
6. The Tokens
7. Neil Sedaka
8. The Crystals
9. Steve Lawrence
10. The Shangri-Las
11. Simon and Garfunkel
12. Neil Diamond
13. Carole King
14. Barbra Streisand
15. Barry Manilow
16. Paul Simon
17. Barbra Streisand and
    Neil Diamond
18. Cyndi Lauper
19. Lisa Lisa and Cult Jam

KEY: *Their boroughs of origin*
1. Staten Island 2. Brooklyn
3. Bronx 4. Bronx 5. Queens
6. Brooklyn 7. Brooklyn 8. Brooklyn 9. Brooklyn 10. Queens
11. Queens 12. Brooklyn
13. Brooklyn 14. Brooklyn
15. Brooklyn 16. Queens
17. Brooklyn and Brooklyn
18. Queens 19. Their membership is disputed by some popstrologists on the understandable grounds that Lisa "Lisa Lisa" Velez was from Hell's Kitchen, but the fact that she took the D train from Manhattan to achieve stardom with Brooklyn-based Cult Jam and Full Force, rather than the reverse, tilts the balance officially in favor of L.L. Cult J.'s *Outerborough* status.

Power Couple

It started with the pairing of Nancy and Frank Sinatra on *Somethin' Stupid*—the first instance in the popstrological era of freestanding pop stars reaching the top of the pop charts while joined in a short-lived entity known as a ***Power Couple***. But if you figured in 1966 that this new phenomenon was merely cute and clever, and that it would never lead to anything more disturbing or dysfunctional than a father-daughter duet about unrequited love, you were very wrong indeed. For in the decades that followed, and particularly in the 1980s, ad hoc conglomerations of prominent pop stars became a powerful force of evil as often as they became a powerful force of good. If popstrology had existed as a formal science back in 1982, perhaps the world could have been warned of the dangerous forces that can be unleashed when a star like **Paul McCartney** is allowed to collide with a star of roughly equal stature, but perhaps the world would not have listened. All popstrology can do now is point out that for every *Don't Go Breaking My Heart* that emanated from the constellation ***Power Couple***, there was also an *Ebony and Ivory*, and for every Minor star that emerged from a ***Power Couple*** none the worse for wear (**Kiki Dee**, **Jennifer Warnes**), there is a long list of Massive stars who were either damaged beyond recognition (**Stevie Wonder**, **Michael Jackson**) or who never emerged at all (**Neil Diamond**, **Donna Summer**, **Aretha Franklin**).

RELATIONSHIP ISSUES

Who could have predicted that Stevie Wonder's alliance with Paul McCartney would cost him his Soul, or that Paul McCartney's alliance with Michael Jackson would cost him his publishing rights? No one, perhaps, but that's sort of the whole point. Who can predict the outcome of any relationship, even those that seem like such brilliant ideas on paper? Certainly no one should try to predict the outcome of a relationship involving a child of the constellation ***Power Couple***, for while the alliances such a person forms are almost always, well, powerful, the consequences of that power are almost impossible to foresee.

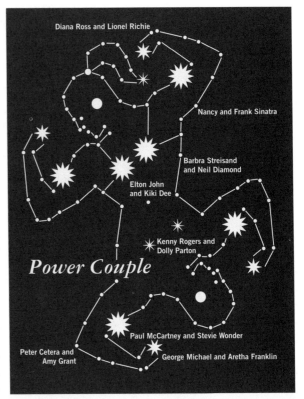

Power Couple

Diana Ross and Lionel Richie
Nancy and Frank Sinatra
Barbra Streisand and Neil Diamond
Elton John and Kiki Dee
Kenny Rogers and Dolly Parton
Paul McCartney and Stevie Wonder
Peter Cetera and Amy Grant
George Michael and Aretha Franklin

THE STARS
(*in order of appearance*):
1. Nancy and Frank Sinatra
2. Dionne Warwick and the Spinners
3. Elton John and Kiki Dee
4. Johnny Mathis and Deniece Williams
5. John Travolta and Olivia Newton-John
6. Barbra Streisand and Neil Diamond
7. Barbra Streisand and Donna Summer
8. Diana Ross and Lionel Richie
9. Paul McCartney and Stevie Wonder
10. Joe Cocker and Jennifer Warnes
11. Patti Austin and James Ingram
12. Kenny Rogers and Dolly Parton
13. Paul McCartney and Michael Jackson
14. USA For Africa
15. Phil Collins and Marilyn Martin
16. Dionne Warwick and Friends
17. Patti LaBelle and Michael McDonald
18. Peter Cetera and Amy Grant
19. George Michael and Aretha Franklin
20. Bill Medley and Jennifer Warnes

Reaganrock

When the constellation *Disco Ball* collapsed in 1980, the diametrically opposed forces of *Mustache Rock* and *Lite & White* were sucked into the resulting power vacuum to emerge as a strange, mutant form that would come to be called *Reaganrock*. It began when a group of nominal rockers called REO Speedwagon unveiled a weapon called the "power ballad" in 1981. Like a popstrological neutron bomb, the power ballad caused a massive loss of life, musically speaking, but left the surface of things undamaged. REO Speedwagon had once been rockers, and they still looked like rockers, but *Keep On Lovin' You* definitely didn't rock. Nor did it possess the gentle, Whitebread charm of an Air Supply or Christopher Cross song. It was as if this thing called *Reaganrock* had taken from its parent constellations their least essential elements—the hair and maleness of *Mustache Rock* and the blandness of *Lite & White*—while leaving their greatest charms behind. Step by step, *Reaganrock* consolidated its power until it was the dominant force of the 1980s, winning converts ready to disavow their more thrilling pasts (**Heart, Lionel Richie, Starship**) and giving birth to lifeless new stars fully steeped in its ideology from birth (**Mr. Mister, Richard Marx**). If synthy marimba solos in place of guitars are not your bag, then you will agree with those who say that there was little in the way of positive trickle-down from the *Reaganrock* revolution. The gulf that *Reaganrock* created between the popstrologically rich and poor, however, did eventually foster the grassroots growth of a force called hip-hop, which would help bring this mighty constellation to its knees after the popstrological era came to a close.

RELATIONSHIP ISSUES

What makes a relationship work over the long haul? Some would say sexual chemistry, shared interests, and mutual respect, but the most important quality that two lovers (or friends, or colleagues) can possess is a willingness to compromise. Nowhere in the pop universe will you find a grouping of stars more ready, willing, and able to compromise than the stars in the constellation *Reaganrock*, and nowhere will you find potential partners with the same quality as surely as you will among those born under that constellation's influence.

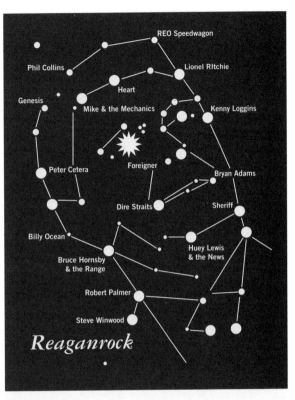

Reaganrock

THE STARS
(*in order of appearance*):
1. REO Speedwagon
2. Survivor
3. Lionel Richie
4. Toto
5. Kenny Loggins
6. Phil Collins
7. Billy Ocean
8. Foreigner
9. Simple Minds
10. Bryan Adams
11. Huey Lewis and the News
12. John Parr
13. Dire Straits
14. Starship
15. Mr. Mister
16. Heart
17. Robert Palmer
18. Patti LaBelle and Michael McDonald
19. Genesis
20. Peter Gabriel
21. Peter Cetera
22. Steve Winwood
23. Peter Cetera and Amy Grant
24. Bruce Hornsby and the Range
25. Gregory Abbott
26. Billy Vera and the Beaters
27. Aretha Franklin and George Michael
28. Cutting Crew
29. Bob Seger
30. Richard Marx
31. Sheriff
32. Mike and the Mechanics
33. Michael Damian

Regifted

The constellation *Invisible Hand* is made up of stars whose talent for supporting others was sometimes greater than their talent as performers. The constellation *Regifted*, on the other hand, is made up of stars whose talent as performers might never have come to light without the support of others. Sometimes they rose as a result of pure luck (**Bobby Vee**, **Tommy James and the Shondells**) and sometimes as a result of lucky connections (**Little Eva**, **Gary Lewis and the Playboys**), but always they rose because someone or something outside themselves took critical steps to grant them popstrological viability. This is not to say that the *only* gift these stars exhibited was for receiving the gift of stardom from others. Indeed, if **Ricky Nelson** owed his success *entirely* to the prime-time popularity of *The Adventures of Ozzie and Harriet*, then *Eight Is Enough* really should have been enough to make a pop star out of Grant Goodeve. And if **Simon and Garfunkel** owed their success exclusively to a producer's decision to reinvent *Sounds Of Silence* well after its initial release, then surely the transmogrified *Tom's Diner* should have been enough to usher Suzanne Vega into the popstrological elite. The talent and outright appeal of many stars in the constellation *Regifted* is undeniable, but equally undeniable is the fact that but for some combination of timing, luck, and receptiveness to assistance, you might never have heard their names.

RELATIONSHIP ISSUES

If everyone entered into their relationships as fully formed individuals who didn't need the support of a partner to make them whole, then how many relationships would people even enter into? Whether your relationship with a child of the constellation *Regifted* will lead to greatness depends on many factors outside of popstrology's reach, but popstrology can assure you of this: greatness in these relationships will almost certainly result from teamwork more than from individual achievement.

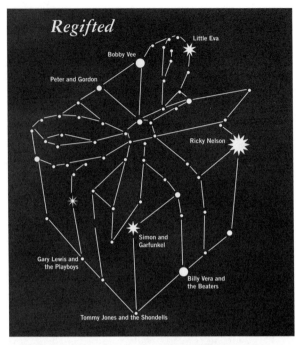

THE STARS
(*in order of appearance*):
1. Ricky Nelson
2. Tommy Edwards
3. Johnny Preston
4. Larry Verne
5. Ernie K-Doe
6. Bobby Vee
7. Shelly Fabares
8. Little Eva
9. The Chiffons
10. Jan and Dean
11. Peter and Gordon
12. The Supremes
13. Gary Lewis and the Playboys
14. The McCoys
15. Simon and Garfunkel
16. Tommy James and the Shondells
17. The Monkees
18. The Lemon Pipers
19. Bo Donaldson and the Heywoods
20. The Hues Corporation
21. George McCrae
22. Johnnie Taylor
23. Patti Austin and James Ingram
24. Simple Minds
25. Billy Vera and the Beaters
26. UB40

KEY: *Regifted by...*
1. NBC and *The Adventures of Ozzie and Harriet* 2. stereophonic recording 3. J. P. "the Big Bopper" Richardson 4. Fred Darian, Al de Lory, and Joe Van Winkle 5. Allen Toussaint 6. Buddy Holly 7. NBC and *The Donna Reed Show* 8. Gerry Goffin and Carole King 9. Ronnie Mack 10. Brian Wilson 11. John Lennon and Paul McCartney 12. Berry Gordy 13. Jerry Lewis, Snuff Garrett, and Ed Sullivan 14. Bert Berns of Bang Records 15. Tom Wilson 16. the city of Pittsburgh 17. Bert Schneider, Bob Rafelson, NBC, Don Kirshner, Neil Diamond, Carole King, Tommy Boyce and Bobby Hart, the Wrecking Crew... 18. Paul Leka 19. Mitch Murray and Peter Callandar via Paper Lace 20. the patrons of New York City discos circa 1974 21. Harry Wayne Casey and Richard Finch 22. disco madness circa 1976 23. *General Hospital* 24. John Hughes 25. *Family Ties* 26. KZZP-FM, Phoenix, AZ

Royal Court

In every year of the popstrological era but one (1974), a single Dominant Star arose from among the many stars active in the pop universe of that time, and the constellation *Royal Court* is the collection of those popstrological kings and queens. The first was **Elvis Presley**, of course, as were the second, third, and fifth, but while **the Beatles**, too, managed to rule across multiple years, the remainder of the *Royal Court* is made up of stars whose overall accomplishments were less grand, and were sometimes strictly limited to the year in which they ruled. **Bobby Darin**, **Bobby Lewis**, and **Jimmy Gilmer and the Fireballs** each became popstrological kings during the strange interregnum between Elvis and the Beatles on the strength of a single song—a feat that was to be achieved only four more times in the next twenty-five years. For the most part, the names in the constellation *Royal Court* are familiar ones, and their faces and songs come readily to mind. But Massive or Minor, Lasting or Forgotten, each and every star in the *Royal Court*, from **Gilbert O'Sullivan** to **Donna Summer**, did something that the other 423 stars in the popstrological firmament did not, which was place their stamp, for good or for ill, over an entire micro-generation of human beings born in the year of their popstrological reign.

RELATIONSHIP ISSUES

They say that everyone loves a winner, and certainly few of us can claim to be exceptions to that rule, but what about those who are simply the popstrological children of winners? Does everyone love them, too? Are the children of the *Royal Court*—the double Monkees and double Blondies of the world—more likely to win hearts and loyal friends than the rest of us? Perhaps, perhaps. But never forget that the label "winner" can be a burden for them as well as a blessing, for if you do find yourself involved somehow with a child of the *Royal Court* who is not living up to his or her own lofty expectations, he or she might turn out not to be the only disappointed one.

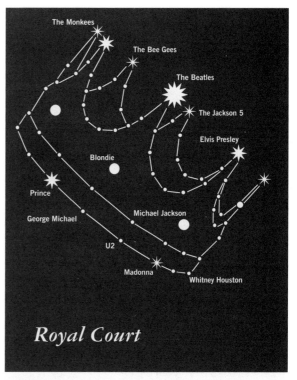

Royal Court

THE STARS
(*in order of appearance*):
1. Elvis Presley (1956, 1957, 1958, and 1960)
2. Bobby Darin (1959)
3. Bobby Lewis (1961)
4. The Four Seasons (1962)
5. Jimmy Gilmer and the Fireballs (1963)
6. The Beatles (1964, 1965, 1966, and 1968)
7. The Monkees (1967)
8. The Fifth Dimension (1969)
9. The Jackson 5 (1970)
10. Carole King (1971)
11. Gilbert O'Sullivan (1972)
12. Roberta Flack (1973)
13. Elton John (1975)
14. Rod Stewart (1976)
15. Debby Boone (1977)
16. The Bee Gees (1978)
17. Donna Summer (1979)
18. Blondie (1980)
19. Diana Ross and Lionel Richie (1981)
20. Paul McCartney and Stevie Wonder (1982)
21. Michael Jackson (1983)
22. Prince (1984)
23. Madonna (1985)
24. Whitney Houston (1986)
25. U2 (1987)
26. George Michael (1988)
27. Paula Abdul (1989)

Shaking Booty

For a combination of genetic, environmental, and sociological reasons, some people won't do it no matter what the music demands. But for everyone else, all it takes is a certain groove at a certain tempo to make them let loose with the moves that gave the constellation *Shaking Booty* its name. More funky than disco, and more groovy than straight soul, the music of **KC and the Sunshine Band** and **the Ohio Players** comes very close indeed to the platonic, booty-shaking ideal, which is easier to recognize than it is to define. Though the stars of *Shaking Booty* are sometimes difficult to distinguish from the stars of the constellations *Disco Ball* and *So-Soul* in rigorous, intellectual terms, perhaps the best way to define their essence is to say that intellectual rigor has no place in understanding their appeal. Stars like **the Jackson 5**, **Earth, Wind & Fire**, and **the Sylvers** are united by a power that acts on a level far deeper than the human intellect—a power capable of loosening the hips of the stiffest of stiffs and converting the tightest of tight-*sses into, well, *Shaking Booty*s.

RELATIONSHIP ISSUES

Why deny that the glue that holds all really great relationships together—whether romantic or platonic—has little to do with things we can enumerate and analyze, and very much to do with things that can only be understood on a purely gut level? Is it really shared interests and common goals that make you love your lover or love your best friend, or is it just that it feels groovy hanging out with him or her? Whether the children of the constellation *Shaking Booty* have more than this to offer in relationships varies from case to case, but the value of being able to make their partners feel good is not to be underestimated.

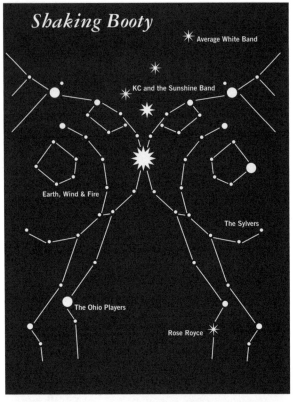

Shaking Booty

THE STARS
(in order of appearance):
1. The Jackson 5
2. MFSB
3. George McCrae
4. Carl Douglas
5. The Ohio Players
6. Average White Band
7. Earth, Wind & Fire
8. KC and the Sunshine Band
9. The Miracles
10. The Sylvers
11. Wild Cherry
12. Rose Royce

Shape-Shifter

As difficult as it is to achieve popstrological immortality, we should hardly be surprised that most stars who make it to the highest reaches of the pop universe are reluctant to deviate from the formula that got them there. And yet within the popstrological firmament there is one group of stars who embraced fundamental change— a group of stars for whom deviation from formula *was* a part of their formula. The constellation *Shape-Shifter* was established when **Conway Twitty** shed his well-developed and highly successful identity as an Elvis-like rock and roll star for an unknown future in country music, and many of the *Shape-Shifter*s who followed him (**the Beatles**, **Marvin Gaye**, **David Bowie**) took similar career risks with their own re-inventions. Did **Olivia Newton-John** take a similar risk by shedding her squeaky-clean image (and her clothing) for 1981's *Physical*? Probably not, but even if she and several other stars (**Exile**, **Sheena Easton**, **the Chipmunks**) shifted shapes only in the face of career oblivion, the fact still remains that they shifted shapes dramatically. And it is fair to say that it was the combined success of the artistically and pragmatically motivated *Shape-Shifter*s that paved the way for the most famous and rapid-fire *Shape-Shifter* of them all, **Madonna**.

RELATIONSHIP ISSUES

People change as they get older, and so do relationships. Adjusting to these changes is often painful, even if we know, on some level, that it's a necessary and unavoidable part of social existence. But while a certain degree of continuity is probably reasonable to expect from those we call our friends and lovers, it may not be as reasonable to expect it from friends and lovers born under the influence of the constellation *Shape-Shifter*. They'll never let things get stale—on that you can depend—but their distaste for unconditional commitment and comfortable ruts sometimes borders on the extreme.

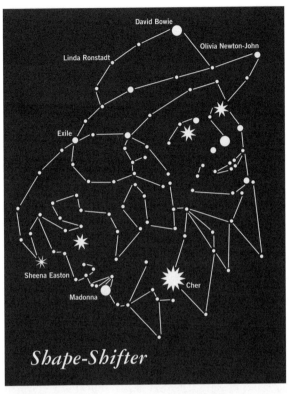

Shape-Shifter

THE STARS
(*in order of appearance*):
1. Conway Twitty
2. The Chipmunks
3. Bobby Darin
4. The Beatles
5. Marvin Gaye
6. Rod Stewart
7. Cher
8. Al Green
9. Charlie Rich
10. Olivia Newton-John
11. Linda Ronstadt
12. David Bowie
13. The Bellamy Brothers
14. Exile
15. Sheena Easton
16. Dexy's Midnight Runners
17. Madonna
18. Heart

KEY: *Their shifts in shape*
1. from rock and roller to country legend 2. from novelty singers to punk rockers 3. from teen idol to lounge singer to folk singer 4. from mop-top cutie pies to long-haired revolutionaries 5. from pop soulster to social crusader to sexual healer 6. from folk rocker to disco hedonist to LITE-FM balladeer to tuxedo-clad crooner 7. from Cher I to Cher II to Cher III, etc. 8. from saint to sinner to saint to sinner, ad infinitum 9. from rock and roller to country star 10. from country good girl to *Lite & White* icon to sweaty, sexy exerciser 11. from folk rocker to country rocker to operetta singer, etc. 12. from mime to androgyne to Ziggy Stardust to Thin White Duke, etc. 13. from gentle *Mustache Rockers* to country stars 14. from *Lite & White* to country stars 15. from Scottish sweetheart to Prince-influenced hussy 16. from jogging outfits to Irish rags to preppy sweaters 17. from Madonna I to Madonna II to Madonna III, etc. 18. from arena rockers to *Reaganrock*ers

So-Soul

opstrological Soul is one of those things that's easier to recognize than it is to define. It's a quality that transcends both skin color and musical style and is as present in a star like Roy Orbison as it is in **Gladys Knight**, and as absent in a star like Lionel Richie as it is in Olivia Newton-John. But one needn't get into that epistemological thicket to understand the quality that unites the stars of the constellation *So-Soul*, because that's a straightforward matter of music. Gospel music for the secular world—that's what soul music started out as, so it's only appropriate that the inaugural star in the constellation *So-Soul* was **Sam Cooke**, whose Massive pop career began when he abandoned a successful career in the world of gospel to write and perform worldly spirituals like *You Send Me* instead. Motown pushed soul music in a decidedly poppy direction in the 1960s, so it took fully ten years from the time of Cooke's arrival before this constellation began to reach critical mass with the addition of such legendary figures as **Marvin Gaye**, **Al Green**, **the Chi-Lites**, and **Barry White.** Fully two thirds of the stars in the constellation *So-Soul* joined during its late-sixties/early-seventies heyday, but it is well worth noting that three stars, including *So-Soul*'s token red-haired Englishman, managed to keep this Soulful constellation cooking even in the face of the Soul-sucking constellation *Reaganrock*.

RELATIONSHIP ISSUES

We don't really like to think about it going into a new relationship, but the fact is, no matter how much passion there is at the start, the passion will always fade eventually, even in platonic relationships. Indeed, the relationships that make it in the long haul aren't the relationships that are exceptions to this rule, but the relationships that include at least one person with the same gift as the children of the constellation *So-Soul*: an ability to stir up those old emotions in approximately three minutes or less when the situation demands it.

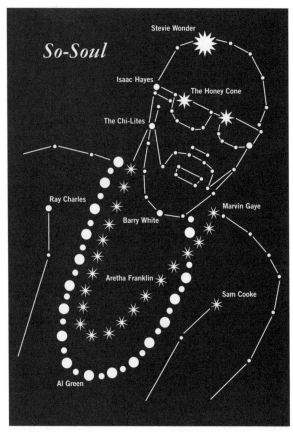

THE STARS
(*in order of appearance*):
 1. Sam Cooke
 2. Ray Charles
 3. Stevie Wonder
 4. Percy Sledge
 5. Aretha Franklin
 6. Archie Bell and the Drells
 7. The Temptations*
 8. Marvin Gaye
 9. Sly and the Family Stone
10. The Honey Cone
11. Isaac Hayes
12. Al Green
13. The Chi-Lites
14. The Staple Singers
15. Bill Withers
16. Billy Paul
17. The O'Jays
18. Billy Preston
19. Gladys Knight and the Pips
20. Eddie Kendricks
21. Al Wilson
22. Barry White
23. Johnnie Taylor
24. The Manhattans
25. The Commodores
26. Peaches and Herb
27. Prince
28. Simply Red
29. Terence Trent D'Arby

* If *My Girl* had been a true soul song, the Temptations would have been the fourth star to join the constellation *So-Soul*, but it was 1969 before they entered the *So-Soul*ful Whitfield-Strong phase of their Massive career and added *Can't Get Next To You* to the popstrological canon.

Speechless

They say that actions speak louder than words, but if there is one thing that speaks even louder than both, it is wordless music. A great lyric is a wonderful thing, and the popstrological canon is certainly filled with songs whose lyrics have etched themselves in our collective memory, but there's something special about a song that requires no assistance from the language centers of the cerebral cortex in order to make a powerful emotional impact. **The Champs** brought the constellation *Speechless* into existence with a song that may still be rousing barroom crowds a thousand years from now, even if those crowds do not understand the meaning of its shouted, one-word lyric, *Tequila*. Play a song like *Let's Get It On* for those crowds, and they may have no idea what to make of it, but play the instrumental hits of **Percy Faith** and **Barry White**, and you can be sure they'll know exactly what to do.

RELATIONSHIP ISSUES

We're all drawn to them, those strong-but-silent types, but what happens when that man (or woman) of few words turns out to be a man (or woman) of no words at all? It's perfectly fine to be fluent in an unspoken language, but the children of the constellation *Speechless* will often prove frustrating to their relationship partners during those times when nonverbal communication simply won't do.

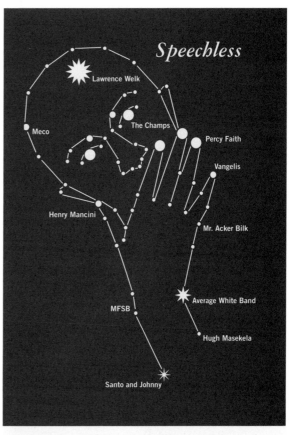

Speechless

THE STARS
(*in order of appearance*):

1. The Champs
2. Dave "Baby" Cortez
3. Santo and Johnny
4. Percy Faith
5. Bert Kaempfert
6. Lawrence Welk
7. Mr. Acker Bilk
8. David Rose
9. The Tornados
10. Paul Mauriat
11. Hugh Masekela
12. Henry Mancini
13. The Edgar Winter Group
14. Barry White
15. MFSB
16. Average White Band
17. Rhythm Heritage
18. Walter Murphy and His Big Apple Band
19. Bill Conti*
20. Meco
21. Herb Alpert **
22. Vangelis
23. Jan Hammer

* Technically, the song that launched Bill Conti into the popstrological firmament exceeded the traditional three-to-five-word limit on lyrics for a song to be considered an instrumental. But rules are made to be bent, and since *Gonna Fly Now*, the theme from *Rocky*, clearly needed none of its eight or nine words in order to make its emotional point, common sense dictates that the man who performed it be included among the stars of the constellation *Speechless*.
** Herb Alpert first entered the popstrological firmament in 1968, but as a singer. He did not join the constellation *Speechless* until *Rise* reached #1 in 1979.

Spin-Off

It took years before they started calling it the "me" decade, but Diana Ross gave the seventies that popstrological stamp in September of 1970 when she became the inaugural star in a group of ship-jumpers and breakup survivors known as the constellation *Spin-Off*. And it didn't take long for others to follow in her footsteps, for the Supremes were not the only stabilizing force in the pop universe of the sixties to come undone at the dawn of the seventies. **George Harrison**, **Paul McCartney**, **Ringo Starr**, and **John Lennon**, in that order, would all join the popstrological firmament as solo stars by mid-decade, as would **Paul Simon** and **Cher**. And soon enough, the constellation *Spin-Off* was filling up with stars like **Donny Osmond** and **Michael Jackson**, who left thriving popstrological entities behind them in pursuit of individual glory, with mixed results. Did the pop universe become a better place for this new-found spirit of self-actualization and rejection of the communal spirit? Reasonable people can disagree on the answer to that question, but at the very least, any answer must take into account the fact that for every **Neil Young** and **Eric Clapton** in the constellation *Spin-Off*, there is also a **Lionel Richie** and a **Phil Collins**.

RELATIONSHIP ISSUES

We all have histories, heaven knows, and all of our histories include an emotional shipwreck or two, but some of us go down with the ship while others always seem to find a lifeboat. Start a relationship of one kind or another with a child of the constellation *Spin-Off*, and on the one hand you know you're getting involved with a survivor. On the other hand, you should also know that you're getting involved with someone who left security behind once before and might easily do so again.

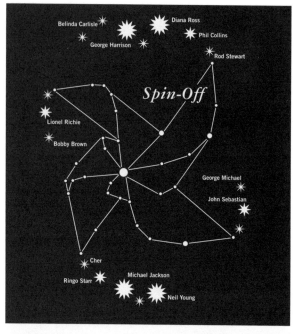

THE STARS
(*in order of appearance*):

1. Diana Ross
2. George Harrison
3. Paul McCartney (and Wings)
4. Donny Osmond
5. Rod Stewart
6. Cher
7. Neil Young
8. Michael Jackson
9. Eddie Kendricks
10. Ringo Starr
11. Eric Clapton
12. Bachman-Turner Overdrive
13. John Lennon
14. Frankie Valli
15. Paul Simon
16. The Miracles
17. John Sebastian
18. Marilyn McCoo and Billy Davis, Jr.
19. Lionel Richie
20. Diana Ross and Lionel Richie
21. Paul McCartney and Michael Jackson
22. Phil Collins
23. Tina Turner
24. Patti LaBelle and Michael McDonald
25. Peter Gabriel
26. Peter Cetera
27. Steve Winwood
28. George Michael
29. Belinda Carlisle
30. Bobby Brown
31. Mike and the Mechanics
32. Fine Young Cannibals

KEY: *The groups off which they spun*
1. the Supremes 2. the Beatles 3. the Beatles 4. the Osmonds 5. the Faces 6. Sonny and Cher 7. Buffalo Springfield 8. the Jackson 5 9. the Temptations 10. the Beatles 11. the Yardbirds, John Mayall's Bluesbreakers, Cream, Blind Faith, Derek and the Dominos 12. the Guess Who 13. the Beatles 14. the Four Seasons 15. Simon and Garfunkel 16. Smokey Robinson and the Miracles 17. the Lovin' Spoonful 18. the Fifth Dimension 19. the Commodores 20. the Supremes, the Commodores 21. the Beatles, the Jackson 5 22. Genesis 23. Ike and Tina Turner 24. Labelle, the Doobie Brothers 25. Genesis 26. Chicago 27. Spencer Davis Group, Traffic, Blind Faith 28. Wham! 29. the Go-Go's 30. New Edition 31. Genesis 32. the English Beat

Storyteller

I f all you want to do is write a hit song, then three chords, a good beat, and a handful of shouted lyrics may be enough to do the trick. But if you want to write a hit *story* song, you'll need a scenic backdrop, compelling characters, dramatic tension and, more often than not, a dead body. Run through the #1 hits from the stars in the constellation *Storyteller*, and you'll get all of the above and more: a history lesson (from **Johnny Horton**), an unsolved mystery (from **Bobbie Gentry**), and a shocking miscarriage of justice (from **Vicki Lawrence**). Six of the popstrological *Storyteller*s preferred subject matter of a nonlethal sort, giving the world an inverted version of *The Scarlet Letter* (from **Jeannie C. Riley**), an unsophisticated plea for racial harmony (from **Stories**), and a kindhearted tale of attempted adultery (from **Rupert Holmes**). For the most part, however, the stars in the constellation *Storyteller* focused on satisfying Americans' evident bloodlust, and listening to their songs is every bit as satisfying as watching an excellent western or police thriller. And even **Bobby Goldsboro**'s *Honey*, which is no more thrilling than watching *Love Story,* still ends in death.

RELATIONSHIP ISSUES

We all want friends, lovers, and colleagues we can trust and respect, whose inner strength can provide us with a sense of security as we face life's challenges. But perhaps more than that, we all want friends, lovers, and colleagues who can keep us entertained, and in this world there is no group of people more popstrologically gifted with the ability to do that than the children of the constellation *Storyteller*. Your ability to be happy in the long term with a romantic or platonic partner born under the constellation *Storyteller*, however, may depend entirely on your ability to remain entertained even when his or her material begins to get stale.

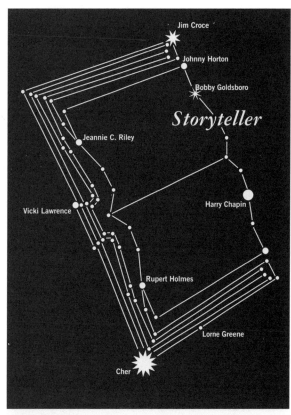

Storyteller

THE STARS
(*in order of appearance*):
1. The Kingston Trio
2. Lloyd Price
3. Johnny Horton
4. Marty Robbins
5. Johnny Preston
6. Mark Dinning
7. Jimmy Dean
8. Lorne Greene
9. Bobbie Gentry
10. Bobby Goldsboro
11. Jeannie C. Riley
12. Cher
13. Helen Reddy
14. Vicki Lawrence
15. Jim Croce
16. Stories
17. Terry Jacks
18. Bo Donaldson and the Heywoods
19. Paper Lace
20. Harry Chapin
21. Rupert Holmes
22. J. Geils Band

Key: *Body counts*
1. two 2. one 3. hundreds 4. two 5. two 6. one 7. one 8. one confirmed, dozens implied 9. one 10. one 11. none 12. two (in *Dark Lady*) 13. one, maybe (in *Angie Baby*) 14. two 15. none 16. none 17. one 18. one confirmed, dozens implied 19. "about a hundred" 20. none 21. none 22. none

Sui Generis

It may be tempting to say of all the stars in the popstrological firmament that, like snowflakes, no two are exactly alike, but there's uniqueness of the kind that only a microscope can reveal and there's uniqueness of the kind that jumps right out and smacks you in the face. It is uniqueness of the latter sort that unites the stars of the constellation *Sui Generis*—a collection of strange and marvelous popstrological entities the exact likes of which have never been seen and are unlikely ever to be seen again. Have dozens, if not hundreds, of pop stars made themselves in the image of **Elvis Presley** and **the Beatles**? Of course they have, but have they ever come close to duplicating the essence of the two most Massive stars in all the pop universe? Have numerous pop stars made themselves in the image of **the Singing Nun** or **Milli Vanilli**? No, but the fact that they haven't leads one to believe that they never will. The quality that can be found among all the stars of the constellation *Sui Generis* is not greatness, although there is plenty of that to be found here. It is broken-mold uniqueness that made these stars once and probably forever the only true examples of their kind.

RELATIONSHIP ISSUES

Do you have a consistent "type" that you historically gravitate toward in romance and friendships? If so, does this type tend to actually make you happy? If your answer to the first question is yes, then at first glance it may seem that the children of the constellation *Sue Generis* are not for you, but if your answer to the second question is no, then perhaps they might be worth a second look. For whatever else you might say about them, both good and bad, those born under this constellation of mold-breakers are unlikely to conform to any expectations you bring into a relationship with them. On the other hand, it is also likely that, should such a relationship end, you will look back on it and say to yourself, "Never again."

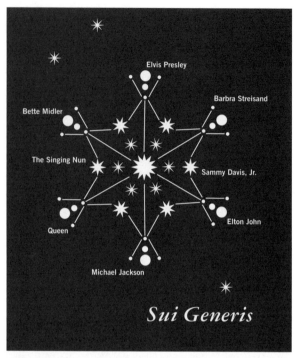

Sui Generis

THE STARS
(*in order of appearance*):
1. Elvis Presley
2. The Singing Nun
3. The Beatles
4. Janis Joplin
5. Sammy Davis, Jr.
6. Michael Jackson
7. Chuck Berry
8. Elton John
9. Barbra Streisand
10. John Denver
11. Queen
12. Billy Joel
13. Prince
14. Bette Midler
15. Milli Vanilli

Teen Idol

Teenagers are capable of making many choices for themselves, though the choices they make often surprise and confound the adults who seek to influence them. Yet there are some things teenagers down the generations can be depended on to choose, and one of those is to embrace their fellow teenagers (and those who can pass as teenagers) when put forth as pop stars. It is, in fact, one of the few transcendent, ironclad truths in popular music, and it is a truth upon which the stars of the constellation *Teen Idol* depended. Why are Elvis Presley and the Beatles not members of this constellation? Were they not idolized by millions of teens? Of course they were, but there was a bit more fueling the rise of those Massive stars than merely the fact of their being teen-dreamy. **Tab Hunter** was the first star whose popstrological existence can be understood only in terms of his appeal to the middle- and high-school set, and while stars like **Paul Anka** and **Ricky Nelson** were certainly more worthy than Tab of musical respect, the support of starry-eyed teenagers was as critical to their popstrological rise as it was to the rise of **Donny Osmond** and **Shaun Cassidy**. **Tiffany** and **Debbie Gibson** broke the gender barrier in the constellation *Teen Idol* near the end of the popstrological era, and while the arrival of **New Kids on the Block** to round out the list more accurately reflected this constellation's past, the rise of dueling girl *Teen Idol*s presaged major developments in the pop-musical future.

RELATIONSHIP ISSUES

It will forever be true that the quality of being dreamy is enough on its own to guarantee one a certain degree of relationship success, but if there is a glitch in the approach so many children of the constellation *Teen Idol* take toward their relationships, it is not just that they tend not to be as dreamy as their Birthstars. It is that they seem to believe that their only job in a relationship is to bedazzle, and this can cause them great stress as they struggle to conceal their many flaws and to adjust to the inevitable decline in starriness in the eyes that behold them.

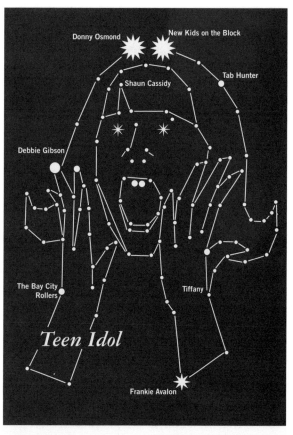

THE STARS
(*in order of appearance*):
1. Tab Hunter
2. Paul Anka
3. Ricky Nelson
4. Frankie Avalon
5. Brian Hyland
6. Bobby Vee
7. Dion
8. Donny Osmond
9. The Bay City Rollers
10. Shaun Cassidy
11. Tiffany
12. Debbie Gibson
13. New Kids on the Block

Texstyle

O f all the states in the Union, only New York has launched more of its native sons and daughters into the popstrological firmament than Texas. But don't tell that to the Texans, or they might start a movement to annex the popstrological riches of Louisiana. The Texas Invasion began with **Buddy Knox**, who wrote *Party Doll* while "relaxing" behind a haystack on his family's farm in the west Texas town of Happy, and within three years of his rise, the constellation *Texstyle* was even larger than the thriving constellation *Outerborough*. Ultimately, though, what makes the constellation *Texstyle* so fascinating is not its scale, but its striking diversity. As one might expect, Texas contributed a significant number of *Country Cousins* to the popstrological firmament, but for every **Marty Robbins** and **Kenny Rogers** in the constellation *Texstyle*, there is also a **Janis Joplin** and a **Johnny Nash**. Indeed, if one had to choose between a fantasy *Texstyle* reunion featuring **Debbie Reynolds** and **Steve Miller** and a *Jersey Pride* reunion featuring Frank Sinatra and Kool and the Gang, that choice might be too difficult to make.

RELATIONSHIP ISSUES

Does size really matter? It depends who you ask, but if you ask a child of the constellation *Texstyle* you're likely to get a surprising answer. The state from which their Birthstars hailed may pride itself on bigness, but let's not forget that their Birthstars made it out of Texas. It's not entirely unheard of for the children of this constellation to inhabit stereotypes and adhere to expectations, but in relationships and elsewhere, they're more likely to embrace values very different from the ones they were raised with.

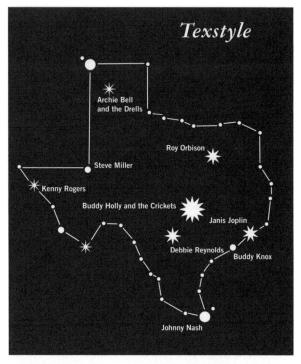

Texstyle

THE STARS
(*in order of appearance*):
1. Buddy Knox
2. Debbie Reynolds
3. Buddy Holly and the Crickets
4. Marty Robbins
5. Johnny Preston
6. Roy Orbison
7. Jimmy Dean
8. Bruce Channel
9. Paul and Paula
10. Archie Bell and the Drells
11. Jeannie C. Riley
12. B. J. Thomas
13. Janis Joplin
14. Mac Davis
15. Johnny Nash
16. Steve Miller
17. Freddy Fender
18. Kenny Rogers

Thanks, Dick

They call him America's Oldest Living Teenager, but if Dick Clark ever actually was a teenager, he was probably the type they call seventeen going on thirty-five. Behind his famously boyish, pleasingly vacuous demeanor has always lurked a razor-sharp businessman, and it is difficult for those who first encountered him in his TV Bloopers days to understand the godlike popstrological power he once wielded from his platform on *American Bandstand*. Indeed, Dick Clark's power in the late 1950s was not only great enough to make a star out of just about anyone he chose, but also great enough to attract the attention of the congressional subcommittee investigating the Payola scandal. By the time Mr. Clark launched **Connie Francis** as the third star in the constellation *Thanks, Dick* merely by playing *Everybody's Somebody's Fool* on the air and saying that it "sounds like it's headed to number one," he'd already been forced by his employer, ABC, to divest himself of his suspicious financial interest in the labels, distributors, and manufacturers who profited handsomely from the rise of Clark-anointed stars like **Danny and the Juniors** and **Frankie Avalon**. But all that did was lead to the formation of Dick Clark's TV-production empire, through which he preserved enough starmaking power to launch two stars into his namesake constellation in the 1970s and one, **Michael Damian**, in 1989, the very last year of the popstrological era.

RELATIONSHIP ISSUES

Everyone brings some kind of baggage into their relationships, but there's a big difference between the everyday baggage of, say, a trail of bitter romantic disappointment and the baggage of being almost completely beholden to someone else for everything you have. Parents, bosses, therapists—these and other kinds of power brokers are likely to have played a significant role in getting the children of the constellation *Thanks, Dick* where they are today, and while the presence of such figures hovering over a relationship need not necessarily become an obstacle to true togetherness, it's something you might want to be aware of before you dive in too deep.

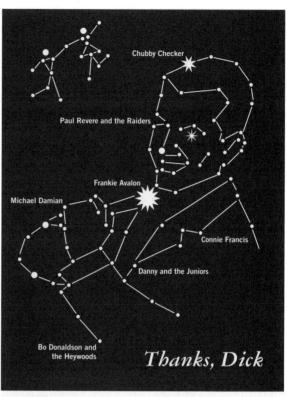

Thanks, Dick

THE STARS
(*in order of appearance*):
1. Danny and the Juniors
2. Frankie Avalon
3. Connie Francis
4. Chubby Checker
5. Paul Revere and the Raiders
6. Bo Donaldson and the Heywoods
7. Michael Damian

Theme Singer

When popstrologists speak of "the pop universe," they are referring to the infinitely large and ever-expanding cosmos of pop music, but the line separating the universe of pop from parallel dimensions in pop-cultural reality has been blurred repeatedly throughout the popstrological era. Indeed, there is no larger constellation in the popstrological firmament than the grouping of stars who breached that divide by reaching the top of the pop charts with songs from movie sound tracks and television programs. The stars in the constellation *Theme Singer* range from the truly Massive (**Barbra Streisand**, **Lionel Richie**) to the incredibly Minor (**Maureen McGovern**, **John Parr**), and the movies and TV shows with which their songs were associated range from timeless classics (*Butch Cassidy and the Sundance Kid*, *Rocky*) to mercifully forgotten clunkers (*Tammy and the Bachelor*, *You Light Up My Life*). It is interesting to note, however, that some of the dimmest stars in the entire pop universe were responsible for some of the biggest hits emanating from the constellation *Theme Singer*. The names **Rose Royce** and **Vangelis**, for instance, have largely been lost to our collective memory, but *Car Wash* and *Chariots Of Fire* most certainly have not.

RELATIONSHIP ISSUES

Movies are popular first-date destinations for a very good reason: they give humans who are just getting to know each other a chance to sit close together without the pressure of making conversation or having sex. Television serves essentially the same purpose for humans in long-term relationships, so perhaps it should not be surprising that the children of the constellation *Theme Singer* are ideal companions with whom to pass the time amiably, though perhaps at the expense of genuine, substantive interaction.

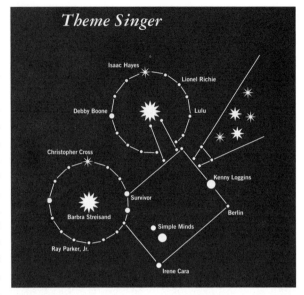

Theme Singer

Isaac Hayes
Lionel Richie
Debby Boone
Lulu
Christopher Cross
Kenny Loggins
Survivor
Berlin
Barbra Streisand
Simple Minds
Ray Parker, Jr.
Irene Cara

THE STARS
(in order of appearance):

1. Debbie Reynolds
2. Percy Faith
3. Louis Armstrong
4. Lulu
5. Henry Mancini
6. B. J. Thomas
7. Isaac Hayes
8. Maureen McGovern
9. Barbra Streisand
10. MFSB
11. Rhythm Heritage
12. John Sebastian
13. Rose Royce
14. Bill Conti
15. Meco
16. Debby Boone
17. John Travolta and Olivia Newton-John
18. Frankie Valli
19. Blondie
20. Dolly Parton
21. Diana Ross and Lionel Richie
22. Christopher Cross
23. Vangelis
24. Survivor
25. Joe Cocker and Jennifer Warnes
26. Lionel Richie
27. Irene Cara
28. Michael Sembello
29. Kenny Loggins
30. Phil Collins
31. Deniece Williams
32. Ray Parker, Jr.
33. Madonna
34. Simple Minds
35. Bryan Adams
36. Duran Duran
37. Huey Lewis and the News
38. John Parr
39. Jan Hammer
40. Phil Collins and Marilyn Martin
41. Peter Cetera
42. Berlin
43. Bill Medley and Jennifer Warnes
44. The Beach Boys
45. Fine Young Cannibals

KEY: *The movies and television shows*
1. *Tammy and the Bachelor* 2. *A Summer Place* 3. *Hello, Dolly!* 4. *To Sir With Love* 5. *Romeo and Juliet* 6. *Butch Cassidy and the Sundance Kid* (song: *Raindrops Keep Falling On My Head*) 7. *Shaft* 8. *The Poseidon Adventure* 9. *The Way We Were* and *A Star Is Born* 10. *Soul Train* (TV) 11. *S.W.A.T.* (TV) 12. *Welcome Back, Kotter* (TV) 13. *Car Wash* 14. *Rocky* 15. *Star Wars* 16. *You Light Up My Life* 17. *Grease* 18. *Grease* 19. *American Gigolo* (song: *Call Me*) 20. *9 to 5* 21. *Endless Love* 22. *Arthur* 23. *Chariots of Fire* 24. *Rocky III* 25. *An Officer and a Gentleman* 26. *White Nights* (song: *Say You, Say Me*) 27. *Flashdance* 28. *Flashdance* 29. *Footloose* 30. *Against All Odds* 31. *Footloose* 32. *Ghostbusters* 33. *Vision Quest* (song: *Crazy For You*) 34. *The Breakfast Club* 35. *A Night in Heaven* 36. *A View to a Kill* 37. *Back to the Future* (song: *Power Of Love*) 38. *St. Elmo's Fire* 39. *Miami Vice* (TV) 40. *White Nights* 41. *Karate Kid, Part II* 42. *Top Gun* 43. *Dirty Dancing* 44. *Cocktail* (song: *Kokomo*) 45. *Tin Men* (song: *Good Thing*)

Tip of the Iceberg

You know every one of them by name, and depending on your age, you could probably pick every one of them out of a lineup and sing along with several of their famous songs. They are the stars of the constellation *Tip of the Iceberg*—stars with only a single #1 hit to show for the incredibly Massive impact they made on the universe of pop. It is easy to imagine in some cases (**Buddy Holly, Sam Cooke, Janis Joplin**) that more time among the living might have led to more in the way of overt popstrological accomplishment, but how then to explain **ABBA, Chuck Berry,** and **Smokey Robinson and the Miracles** having just one #1 hit apiece despite ample time to try for more? And how to explain James Brown, Little Richard, Fats Domino, Bob Dylan, Creedence Clearwater Revival, and Bruce Springsteen having none at all? The fact is that the pop stars can only do so much on their own to attain the highest reaches of the pop universe. No matter how brilliant they may be, or may seem to have been in retrospect, each and every star that has ever shone its light in the universe of pop has risen only as far as we the mortal public have allowed it to rise. And while we may not like what it says about ourselves that we have thrown our support more readily behind the likes of Richard Marx and Tony Orlando than **Aretha Franklin** and **Chuck Berry**, that, alas, is simply who we are.

RELATIONSHIP ISSUES

It's entirely possible that the key to sustaining a long-term relationship is to possess far greater resources than at first meet the eye. And if this is true, then perhaps the children of the constellation *Tip of the Iceberg* are better suited than any of us to stick it out over the long haul. On the other hand, there is something to be said for finding a partner whose life accomplishments, whether great or small, have not left him or her feeling thwarted or undervalued—feelings that more than a few children of this powerful constellation bring to the relationship table.

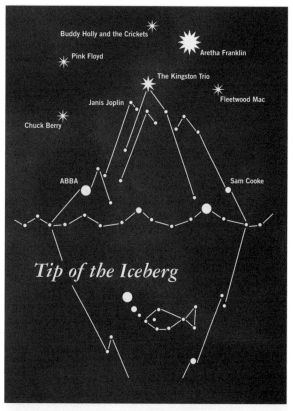

THE STARS
(*in order of appearance*):
1. Buddy Holly and the Crickets
2. The Kingston Trio
3. Sam Cooke
4. The Drifters
5. Frank Sinatra
6. Louis Armstrong
7. Aretha Franklin
8. Peter, Paul and Mary
9. Smokey Robinson and the Miracles
10. Janis Joplin
11. Chuck Berry
12. ABBA
13. Fleetwood Mac
14. Pink Floyd
15. Van Halen
16. Tina Turner
17. Janet Jackson*

*Only one of her many #1 hits came within the popstrological era.

Tip of the Ice Cube

Of the 450 stars in the popstrological firmament, fully 329 eked their way in with just a single #1 hit, so the term "one-hit wonder" has no practical meaning within the science of popstrology. Still, there are clear distinctions to be made among these stars, for while each of them ruled the pop universe but once, there is more to some than meets the hit-minded eye. On the one extreme, you have stars like Bobby Lewis and Dexy's Midnight Runners, whose impact on the universe of pop starts and stops with their one huge hit. On the other extreme, you have stars like Frank Sinatra and Chuck Berry, who reside in the constellation *Tip of the Iceberg* by virtue of the super-Massive careers that lie beneath the popstrological surface. And somewhere in between, you have forty-five stars who reached the top of the charts just once, but whose contribution to our popstrological reality was more Massive than that fact might indicate. Just not *that* much more Massive. From **Dion** to **New Kids on the Block**, with **the O'Jays**, **Linda Ronstadt**, and **Air Supply** in between, there is not a popstrological slouch to be found among the stars of the constellation *Tip of the Ice Cube*. Did any one of them make foundational contributions without which the universe of pop might be unrecognizable? No, not quite. And yet a pop universe without *any* of **the Crystals**, **Otis Redding**, **Culture Club**, **Def Leppard**, *et al.* is not a universe that many of us would wish to inhabit.

RELATIONSHIP ISSUES

Some people want one thing above all others from a romantic or platonic partner, and that's someone who's got nothing to hide. Others, whether consciously or not, are drawn to those who've got quite a bit to hide. But what most of us probably want over the long haul is someone right in between, and that's where the children of the constellation *Tip of the Ice Cube* come in. As a rule, they're not going to reveal themselves to be something utterly different from what first appearances would indicate ("Oh, I didn't mention my other wives?"), but neither will they fail to surprise you, on occasion, with just enough previously hidden information to keep things interesting ("You didn't know that I like piña coladas?").

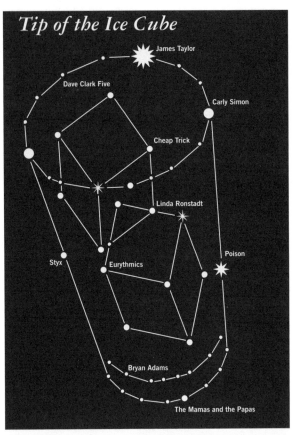

Tip of the Ice Cube

THE STARS
(*in order of appearance*):

1. Dion
2. The Crystals
3. Jan and Dean
4. The Dave Clark Five
5. The Mamas and the Papas
6. The Lovin' Spoonful
7. Donovan
8. Johnny Rivers
9. The Turtles
10. Otis Redding
11. Paul Revere and the Raiders
12. James Taylor
13. Al Green
14. Neil Young
15. Carly Simon
16. The O'Jays
17. Gladys Knight and the Pips
18. Eric Clapton
19. Linda Ronstadt
20. Earth, Wind & Fire
21. Paul Simon
22. Styx
23. Kool and the Gang
24. Air Supply
25. John Cougar
26. The Police
27. Eurythmics
28. Yes
29. Culture Club
30. Kenny Loggins
31. Foreigner
32. Bryan Adams
33. Genesis
34. Peter Gabriel
35. Boston
36. Bob Seger
37. Billy Idol
38. INXS
39. Gloria Estefan and the Miami Sound Machine
40. Cheap Trick
41. Guns n' Roses
42. Def Leppard
43. Poison
44. Bette Midler
45. New Kids on the Block

Tragic Demise

The death that gave rise to the constellation *Tragic Demise* was the first death of any popstrological star, but by the time Don McLean memorialized the tragic events of February 3, 1959, in *American Pie*, five more stars (**Sam Cooke, Joe Meek, Otis Redding, Janis Joplin**, and **Jim Morrison**) had joined **Buddy Holly** by dying well before their time. But of course they didn't die well, or they wouldn't belong to this collection of twenty-six stars whose deaths were, for the most part, tragically avoidable. Five stars (**Bobby Darin, Minnie Riperton, Van McCoy, Andy Gibb**, and **Mary Wells**) joined the constellation *Tragic Demise* by dying of wholly natural causes very prematurely, but it was guns, drugs, and charter flights that took nearly all the rest. Four suicides and three homicides, six airplanes and two cars, four probable overdoses, and one case of anorexia are to blame for the many days on which a little piece of music died, and, sadly, one or more of these will probably strike again in the coming years, adding even more popstrological mass to this constellation of fallen greats (and near-greats).

RELATIONSHIP ISSUES

Now is the time to be thankful that popstrology is not as grim a science as genetics, for if you find yourself involved in one way or another with a child of the constellation *Tragic Demise*, you can rest assured that his family medical history will have a greater impact on his health and longevity than his popstrological legacy will. The same cannot necessarily be said about the health and longevity of your relationship, though, for this is a constellation whose popstrological children are well known for disappearing emotionally from their relationships, sometimes after a long and visible decline in affection, but often quite suddenly and unpredictably.

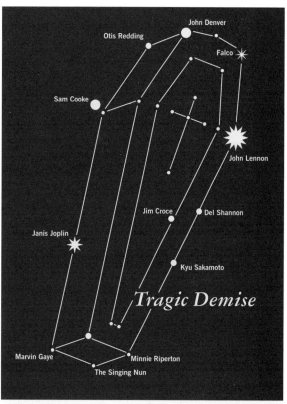

THE STARS
(*in order of disappearance*):
1. Buddy Holly and the Crickets (Buddy Holly)
2. Sam Cooke
3. The Tornados (Joe Meek)
4. Otis Redding
5. Janis Joplin
6. The Doors (Jim Morrison)
7. Jim Croce
8. Bobby Darin
9. Elvis Presley
10. Minnie Riperton
11. Van McCoy
12. John Lennon
13. Harry Chapin
14. The Carpenters (Karen Carpenter)
15. Marvin Gaye
16. The Singing Nun
17. Kyu Sakamoto
18. Ricky Nelson
19. Andy Gibb
20. Staff Sergeant Barry Sadler
21. Del Shannon
22. Mary Wells
23. Milli Vanilli (Rob Pilatus)
24. John Denver
25. Falco
26. INXS (Michael Hutchence)

KEY: *The tragic causes of their demise*

1. plane crash 2. gunshot 3. suicide 4. plane crash 5. overdose 6. "heart failure" 7. plane crash 8. heart surgery (lifelong condition) 9. polypharmacy/heart disease 10. cancer (age 31) 11. heart attack (age 35) 12. gunshot 13. auto accident 14. anorexia nervosa 15. gunshot 16. suicide 17. plane crash 18. plane crash 19. cocaine/heart infection 20. heart failure (while recovering from gunshot) 21. suicide (while on Prozac) 22. cancer (age 49, penniless, no health insurance) 23. drugs and alcohol (and maybe shame) 24. plane crash (ultralight) 25. auto accident 26. suicide

Underage

Brenda Lee may have sounded as if she were thirty-five, but she was only fifteen when *I'm Sorry* reached the top of the pop charts and she joined the popstrological firmament as the inaugural star in the constellation *Underage*. Stars like Ricky Nelson, Bobby Vee, and Shelly Fabares barely missed out on membership in this constellation by turning eighteen just slightly before their popstrological breakthroughs, but still Brenda was surrounded in relatively short order by a swinging group of her not-yet-legal peers. Run down the roster of this constellation and you will find a couple of names (besides Brenda Lee's) of stars whose careers continued well past their own teens. For the most part, though, the constellation *Underage* was a constellation not just *of* teens but also *for* teens, and so one finds within it fewer **Stevie Wonder**s and **Michael Jackson**s than **Lesley Gore**s and **Debbie Gibson**s— stars who exited the popstrological stage at essentially the same time as they and their fans exited their teens.

RELATIONSHIP ISSUES

It would have been illegal to sleep with any of their Birthstars at the moment of their popstrological debuts, but by 2007, there will be nothing illegal about sleeping with anyone born under the influence of the constellation *Underage*. Of course, many children of the constellation *Underage* stars are old enough now to have barely underage children of their own, yet even they are likely to have retained their natural capacity for youthful ardor. Which is great, if that's your thing, but if you expect your romantic partner's emotional and chronological ages to be in the same rough ballpark, you may want to think twice before diving in too deep with one born under the constellation of the immature.

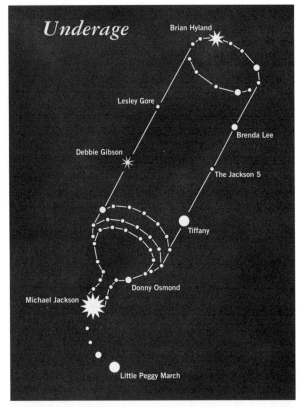

THE STARS
(*in order of appearance*):

1. Brenda Lee
2. Brian Hyland
3. The Marvelettes
4. Little Peggy March
5. Lesley Gore
6. Stevie Wonder
7. The Shangri-Las
8. The Box Tops*
9. The Jackson 5*
10. The Osmonds*
11. Donny Osmond
12. Michael Jackson
13. Tiffany
14. Debbie Gibson

* Not every member of these groups was personally underage, but their average age at the time of their popstrological debuts was less than eighteen, and all three groups were led by young men short of that age.

Neither/Nor

There are forty-five true and proper constellations in the popstrological firmament, organized around such widely varied characteristics as the way their stars wore their hair and the way their stars made their names. And yet, with forty-five different ways to join a cohesive group of popstrologically related fellow stars, there are nine stars who never did. They are the stars of the nonconstellation *Neither/Nor*. Go down the list from **Tommy Roe** to **Martika**, and you will find neither a Brit nor a family act, neither a *Novelty Merchant* nor a *Storyteller*. You will find neither a star whose demise was tragic, nor a star whose career was much bigger than it appears. You will find stars who were neither *Underage* nor members of the *Old Guard*, and stars who neither shifted their shapes nor shook their respective booties. You will find stars, in short, whose essences are to be found neither in their alignment with a popstrological constellation nor in their relationship to one another, for the only quality they share in common is their status as being neither this nor that. Not to be confused with the stars of the constellation *Sui Generis*, the stars of the nonconstellation *Neither/Nor* are not without musical and stylistic points of comparison—they are simply without popstrological affiliation.

RELATIONSHIP ISSUES

The quality of not quite fitting in is all that unites the stars of the nonconstellation *Neither/Nor*, and so it is naturally difficult for popstrologists to make broad generalizations about the relationship potential of those born under the influence of these stars. But if there is one thing that can safely be said, it is not the negative thing you might expect, for there may be no one more capable of displaying unshakable loyalty to his or her romantic or platonic companions than someone who finds in those relationships a kind of unquestioning acceptance that life has historically withheld.

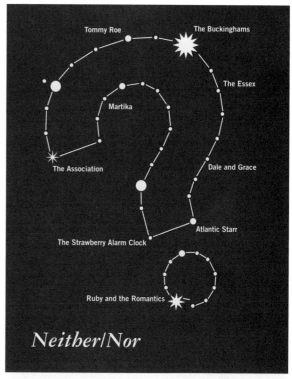

Neither/Nor

THE STARS
(*in order of appearance*):
1. Tommy Roe
2. Ruby and the Romantics
3. The Essex
4. Dale and Grace
5. The Association
6. The Buckinghams
7. The Strawberry Alarm Clock
8. Atlantic Starr
9. Martika

Acknowledgments

For making the discovery of popstrology possible, the author would like to thank radio stations KFRC, KMEL, KQAK, KSOL, KFJC, and KALX; everyone who ever gave him a record as a birthday gift; every cool older brother of a friend who took the time to talk him through their record collections; and most of all his mother, for keeping the car radio on throughout the 1970s.

For making the creation of this book possible, the author would like to thank Owen Grover, Daniel Greenberg, Colin Dickerman, Greg Villepique, Elizabeth Van Itallie, Fred Bronson, Marc Borkan, Diane Achaibar, Emma Rojas-Castro, Donna Bollers, Anne Joseph, and the Jewish Theological Seminary of America. And for making the creation of this book survivable (and necessary), the author would like to thank his wife, Valli, and children, Suria and Eamon, for their support, enthusiasm, and willingness to immerse themselves in the full popstrological canon.

A Note on the Author

The first pop single Ian Van Tuyl owned was a Jackson 5 giveaway pressed on thin, flexible plastic and painstakingly extracted from a full box of Honeycombs cereal. His first LP was Elton John's *Captain Fantastic and the Brown Dirt Cowboy*. At the age of eight, Ian recorded (through the air) every minute of an epic radio special playing every #1 song of the rock era to that date. He listened to the tapes of that broadcast obsessively for many years to follow, preparing his mind, unknowingly, for the eventual revelation that led to *Popstrology*. He is a Double Monkee, born under the influence of the song *I'm A Believer*.